Routledge Handbook of International Law

Routledge Handbook of International Law provides a definitive global survey of the interaction of international politics and international law. Each chapter is written by a leading expert and provides a state-of-the-art overview of the most significant areas within the field.

This highly topical collection of specially commissioned papers from both established authorities and rising stars is split into four key sections:

- **The Nature of International Law** including the interaction between the disciplines of international law and international relations
- **Evolution of International Law** progressing from the ancient world to present day
- **Law and Power in International Society** discussing topical issues such as the war in Iraq and the international criminal court
- **Key Issues in International Law** including international refugee law, indigenous rights, intellectual property, trade and the challenges presented by 'new terrorism'

A comprehensive survey of the state of the discipline, *Routledge Handbook of International Law* is an essential work of reference for scholars and practitioners of international law.

David Armstrong is Emeritus Professor of International Relations at the University of Exeter. His research interests include the historical evolution of international legal norms and institutions. He is the author and co-author of a number of books and was formerly editor of the *Review of International Studies*.

Contributors: David Armstrong, Mashood Baderin, Robert J. Beck, David J. Bederman, Andrea Bianchi, Allen Buchanan, Anthony Carty, Marie-Claire Cordonier Segger, Anthony D'Amato, Allison Danner, Karen Engle, Markus W. Gehring, Edward Keene, Martti Koskenniemi, Friedrich Kratochwil, Hélène Lambert, Ikechi Mgbeoji, John F. Murphy, Amrita Narkilar, Liliana Obregón, Obiora Chinedu Okafor, Andreas Paulus, Russell Powell, Wayne Sandholtz, William A. Schabas, Shirley V. Scott, Dinah Shelton, Beth Simmons, Gerry Simpson and Marc Weller.

Routledge Handbook of International Law

Edited by David Armstrong

EDITORIAL BOARD
Jutta Brunée
Michael Byers
John H. Jackson
David Kennedy

Routledge
Taylor & Francis Group

LONDON AND NEW YORK

First published 2009 by Routledge
2 Park Square, Milton Park, Abingdon, Oxon OX14 4RN

Simultaneously published in the USA and Canada
by Routledge
270 Madison Avenue, New York, NY 10016

Routledge is an imprint of the Taylor & Francis Group, an informa business

© 2009 Selection and editorial matter, David Armstrong; individual contributors,
their contributions

Typeset in Bembo by Graphicraft Limited, Hong Kong
Printed and bound in Great Britain by MPG Books Ltd, Bodmin

British Library Cataloguing in Publication Data
A catalogue record for this book is available from the British Library

Library of Congress Cataloging in Publication Data
Library of Congress Cataloging-in-Publication Data

Routledge handbook of international law / edited by David Armstrong.
   p. cm.
  ISBN 978-0-415-41876-8 – ISBN 978-0-203-88462-1   1. International law–Political aspects.
  2. International law.   I. Armstrong, J. D. (James David), 1945–

  KZ1250.R68 2008
  341–dc22
  2008027374

ISBN 13: 978-0-415-41876-8 (hbk)
ISBN 13: 978-0-203-88462-1 (ebk)

ISBN 10: 0-415-41876-3 (hbk)
ISBN 10: 0-203-88462-0 (ebk)

Contents

Author biographical sketches

David Armstrong is Emeritus Professor of International Relations at the University of Exeter. He has published numerous books and articles on many aspects of international relations, including Chinese foreign policy, international organization and revolutionary states. He is a former editor of the *Review of International Studies*. For the last 10 years he has focused on international law and his most recent book is *International Law and International Relations* (co-authored with Theo Farrell and Hélène Lambert: Cambridge University Press 2007).

Mashood Baderin is Professor of Law at the School of Law of the School of Oriental and African Studies (SOAS), University of London. He is also a barrister and solicitor of the Supreme Court of Nigeria. He is founding co-editor of the *Muslim World Journal of Human Rights*. He researches in the areas of Islamic law, international law, international and comparative human rights law, human rights and Islamic law, with particular interest in the interaction between international law, human rights law and Islamic law in Muslim states. His most recent book is *International Law and Islamic Law* (Ashgate 2008).

Robert J. Beck is Associate Professor of Political Science at the University of Wisconsin – Milwaukee where he teaches international law. He is author of *The Grenada Invasion* (1993), co-author of *International Law and the Use of Force* (1993) and co-editor of *International Rules* (1996) and *International Law and the Rise of Nations* (2002) and author of numerous articles in journals including *International Security*, *Review of International Studies*, *Virginia Journal of International Law* and the *International Journal of Refugee Law*.

David J. Bederman is the K.H. Gyr Professor of Private International Law in the Emory University School of Law, Atlanta, Georgia. He holds the Diploma of the Hague Academy of International Law and has also served as a legal advisor at the Iran–US Claims Tribunal in The Hague. After a stint in private practice, he accepted his current teaching appointment at Emory. He is a member of the board of editors of many international law journals, including the *American Journal of International Law*. His contribution is based on portions of the author's previous volume, *International Law in Antiquity* (Cambridge University Press 2001). He is also the author of *The Spirit of International Law* (University of Georgia Press 2002); *The Classical*

Foundations of the American Constitution (Cambridge University Press 2008) and *Globalization and International Law* (Palgrave-Macmillan 2008).

Andrea Bianchi is Professor of Public International Law at the Graduate Institute of International Studies in Geneva and the Catholic University in Milan. His publications range from international human rights law, international economic law, the law of jurisdiction and jurisdictional immunities to international environmental law, state responsibility and the law of treaties. He is currently working on international human rights before municipal courts, the status of the precautionary principle in international and European law and the enforcement of international law norms against terrorism. He edited *Enforcing International Law Norms against Terrorism* (Hart 2004).

Allen Buchanan is James B. Duke Professor of Philosophy and Investigator, Institute for Genome Sciences and Policy, Duke University. Apart from being the author of many books and articles he was official Staff Philosopher for the President's Commission for the Study of Ethical Problems in Medicine and Behavioral and Biomedical Research, 1982, Consultant to the Office of Technology Assessment of the US Congress, Staff Consultant to the President's Advisory Committee on Human Radiation Experiments, 1994, Consultant to the Transitional Government of Ethiopia, Consultant to the European High Commissioner on National Minorities in the Hague and was commissioned by Canadian Government, Office of the Privy Council, to write a commentary on the Canadian Supreme Court Reference Ruling on the Possible Secession of Quebec, 1997. He served on the Advisory Council for the National Human Genome Research Institute, 1997–2000.

Anthony Carty is Professor of Public Law at the University of Aberdeen. He has published various books such as *The Decay of International Law* (Manchester University Press 1986), *Post-Modern Law* (Edinburgh University Press 1990), *Was Ireland Conquered?* (Pluto Press 1996) and *Philosophy of International Law* (Edinburgh University Press 2007). His interests and articles span history, philosophy, politics, theology and law. He has been a Visiting Professor, inter alia, at the University of Tokyo, Paris I and II, the Free University of Berlin and the Autonomous University of Madrid.

Marie-Claire Cordonier Segger is Director of the Centre for International Sustainable Development Law (CISDL), a Fellow of the Lauterpacht Centre for International Law at Cambridge University and directs international affairs at the Canadian Ministry of Natural Resources. She serves on the World Future Council and other bodies working on sustainable development issues. She has authored or edited 12 volumes and numerous articles on sustainable development.

Anthony D'Amato is the Leighton Professor of Law at Northwestern University School of Law, where he teaches courses in international law, international human rights, analytic jurisprudence and justice. He is admitted to practice before the US Supreme Court, the US Tax Court and several US Circuit Courts of Appeal and is a member of the New York Bar. Professor D'Amato was the first American lawyer to argue (and win) a case before the European Court of Human Rights in Strasbourg and he has litigated a number of human rights cases around the world. He was lead counsel at the International Criminal Tribunal for the former Yugoslavia. He is the author of over 20 books and over 110 articles.

Allison Danner is Professor of Law at the Vanderbilt University Law School. She is the author of numerous articles and papers on international criminal law and is currently completing a major empirical study on the International Criminal Court with Beth Simmons. She has served on the Executive Council of the American Society of International Law.

Karen Engle is Cecil D. Redford Professor in Law and Director of the Bernard and Audre Rapoport Center for Human Rights and Justice at the University of Texas School of Law. Her primary areas of scholarship are women's human rights, humanitarian law and indigenous and Afro-descendant rights in Latin America, on all of which subjects she has published widely in major journals. She has been named a Fulbright Senior Specialist.

Markus W. Gehring is Lecturer in International and European Law at the University of Cambridge in the Centre of International Studies and Fellow in Law at Robinson College. He practised European competition and international trade law with Cleary Gottlieb in their Brussels office and is a member of the Frankfurt-am-Main Bar, lead Counsel for Sustainable International Trade, Investment and Competition Law with the Centre of International Sustainable Development Law (CISDL) and a member of the Sustainable Development Law Committee of the International Law Association (ILA). His recent books, with Marie-Claire Cordonier Segger, include *Sustainable Development in World Trade Law* (Kluwer Law International 2005) and *World Trade Law in Practice* (Globe Publishing 2007).

Edward Keene is Associate Professor at the Sam Nunn School of International Affairs at Georgia Tech. He is the author of *Beyond the Anarchical Society: Grotius, Colonialism and Order in World Politics* (Cambridge University Press 2002) and *International Political Thought: A Historical Introduction* (Polity Press 2005), as well as several articles and book chapters on international law and international relations theory.

Martti Koskenniemi is Professor of International Law at the University of Helsinki and Global Professor of Law at New York University. He is a former member of the International Law Commission. He served in the Finnish Diplomatic Service, lastly as Director of the Division of International Law. He was Finland's counsel in the International Court of Justice in the Passage through the Great Belt Case (Finland v. Denmark) (1991–2). He has also served as a judge in the administrative tribunal of the Asian Development Bank. His major books are *The Gentle Civilizer of Nations: The Rise and Fall of International Law 1870–1960* (Cambridge University Press 2001) and *From Apology to Utopia: The Structure of International Legal Argument* (Cambridge University Press 1989, reissued 2005).

Friedrich Kratochwil taught at Maryland, Princeton, Columbia, Delaware and Pennsylvania, before returning (in 1995) to Germany and taking the chair in international politics at the European University Institute in Florence (2002). He has published widely on international relations, social theory, international organization and international law in US and European journals. He is a former editor of the *European Journal of International Relations*. His latest book (edited with Ed Mansfield) is *International Organization and Global Governance* (Pearson 2005).

Hélène Lambert is Reader in Law in the Postgraduate Legal Studies Department at the University of Westminster. She is author of numerous articles on the protection of refugees in human rights and refugee law. Her recent books include *The Position of Aliens in relation to the European Convention on Human Rights* (Council of Europe 2006) and, co-authored with David

Armstrong and Theo Farrell, *International Law and International Relations* (Cambridge University Press 2007). She is currently completing an edited volume with Guy S. Goodwin-Gill on the *Limits of Transnational Law: Refugee Law, Policy Harmonization and Judicial Dialogue in the European Union*, based on a 2-year project funded by the Nuffield Foundation and the British Academy.

Ikechi Mgbeoji is Associate Professor at Osgoode Hall Law School of York University, Toronto, Canada. Educated in Nigeria, Canada and Germany, his main research and teaching interests are in the areas of international, comparative and transnational law, international intellectual property law and environmental law. His recent books include *Collective Insecurity* (University of British Columbia Press 2003) and *Global Biopiracy* (University of British Columbia Press 2006).

John F. Murphy is Professor of Law, Villanova University School of Law. His career has included a year in India on a Ford Foundation Fellowship, private practice in New York City and Washington, DC, and service as an attorney/adviser in the Office of the Assistant Legal Adviser in the US Department of State. He is the author of many publications on international law and relations, most recently *The United States and the Rule of Law in International Affairs* (Cambridge University Press 2004). His casebook (with Alan C. Swan) *The Regulation of International Business and Economic Relations* (2nd edn, Lexis Publishing 1999) was awarded a Certificate of Merit by the American Society of International Law in 1992. He is currently the American Bar Association's Alternate Observer at the US Mission to the United Nations.

Amrita Narlikar is University Lecturer in International Relations at the Centre of International Studies, University of Cambridge, and Official Fellow-Elect of Darwin College, Cambridge. She is also Senior Research Associate at the Centre for International Studies, University of Oxford, and Senior Adjunct Professor at the Delhi-based think-tank, Research and Information System for Developing countries. She is a member of the Warwick Commission on the Future of the Multilateral Trading System, and Editor-in-Chief of the book series, *Studies in International Institutional Dynamics*, with Martinus Nijhoff/Brill. Her single-authored books include *International Trade and Developing Countries: Bargaining coalitions in the GATT and WTO* (Routledge 2003, paperback 2005); and *The World Trade Organization: A Very Short Introduction* (Oxford University Press 2005). She is currently completing two new books, *New Powers: How to become one and how to manage them*, under contract with Hurst and Columbia University Press, and a collection of reprints and new powers, *Bargaining with the Strong*, to be published with World Scientific Publishers.

Liliana Obregón is Associate Professor and Director of the International Law Program at the University of Los Andes in Bogotá, Colombia. She holds a doctoral degree (SJD) from Harvard Law School, an MA from the School of Advanced International Studies of the Johns Hopkins University and a law degree from Los Andes and has published extensively on the work of Latin American writers of international law.

Obiora Chinedu Okafor is an Associate Professor at the Osgoode Hall Law School at York University, Toronto, Canada. He recently served as a Canada–US Fulbright Scholar at the Massachusetts Institute of Technology and has previously served as an SSRC–MacArthur Foundation Fellow at Harvard Law School's Human Rights Program. He was recently an expert panelist for the United Nations Human Rights Council's Working Group on People of African Descent.

Andreas Paulus is Professor of Public and International Law and director of the Institute of International and European Law at the Georg-August-University, Göttingen. His publications deal with international legal theory, the law of the United Nations, international adjudication, as well as international criminal law. He also served as counsel of the Federal Republic of Germany in the LaGrand case (Germany v. United States) and adviser to the German team in the Certain Property (Liechtenstein v. Germany) case before the International Court of Justice.

Russell Powell is Greenwall Postdoctoral Fellow and Senior Research Scholar at the Kennedy Institute of Ethics, Georgetown University.

Wayne Sandholtz is Professor of Political Science at the University of California, Irvine. He is the author, most recently, of *Prohibiting Plunder: How Norms Change* (Oxford University Press 2007) and co-author, with Kendall Stiles, of *International Norms and Cycles of Change* (Oxford University Press, forthcoming). Current research includes projects on the evolution of international norms, international courts and tribunals and the comparative study of corruption. His past work has focused on the politics of European integration, including work on integration theory, high-technology cooperation, telecommunications and monetary union.

William A. Schabas is director of the Irish Centre for Human Rights at the National University of Ireland, Galway, where he also holds the professorship in human rights law. He is also a Global Legal Scholar at the University of Warwick School of Law, a professor at Queen's University Belfast, *professeur associé* at the Université du Québec à Montréal and a "door tenant" at 9 Bedford Row, London. He is the author of 18 monographs and more than 200 articles dealing with international human rights law and international criminal law. He was a member of the Sierra Leone Truth and Reconciliation Commission. He serves as one of five trustees of the United Nations Voluntary Fund for Technical Cooperation in Human Rights. He is an Officer of the Order of Canada and a Member of the Royal Irish Academy and has an LLD *honoris causa* from Dalhousie University, Halifax.

Shirley V. Scott is Associate Professor at the School of Social Sciences, University of New South Wales. She has published numerous articles in leading journals on the place of international law in international relations. Recent books include *The Political Interpretation of Multilateral Treaties* (Martinus Nijhoff 2004) and *International Law in World Politics* (Lynne Rienner 2004).

Dinah Shelton holds the Manatt/Ahn Professorship in International Law at George Washington University. She is the author of three prize-winning books: *Protecting Human Rights in the Americas* (winner of the 1983 Inter-American Bar Association Book Prize, co-authored with Thomas Buergenthal) (Editorial Juricentro 1983), *Remedies in International Human Rights Law* (awarded the 2000 Certificate of Merit, American Society of International Law) (Oxford University Press 1999) and the three-volume *Encyclopedia of Genocide and Crimes against Humanity* (Best Reference Book 2006, as cited by the New York Public Library) (Macmillan 2005). She has also authored many other articles and books on international law, human rights law and international environmental law. She serves on the boards of many human rights and environmental organizations. From 1987 to 1989 she was the director of the Office of Staff Attorneys at the US Court of Appeals for the Ninth Circuit. She has also served as a legal consultant to the United Nations Environment Programme, UNITAR, World Health Organization, European Union, Council of Europe and Organization of American States. She was awarded the 2006 Elisabeth Haub Prize for Environmental Law.

Beth Simmons is Clarence Dillon Professor of International Affairs at Harvard University. Her book, *Who Adjusts? Domestic Sources of Foreign Economic Policy During the Interwar Years, 1924–1939* (Princeton University Press 1994), was recognized by the American Political Science Association in 1995 as the best book published in 1994 in government, politics or international relations. She has worked at the International Monetary Fund, has spent a year as a senior fellow at the United States Institute of Peace (1996–7), and a year in residence at the Center for Advanced Study in the Behavioral Sciences at Stanford. She currently serves as Director of the Weatherhead Center for International Affairs at Harvard and is finishing a book on the effects of international law on human rights practices.

Gerry Simpson is a Professor of International Law at the London School of Economics and holds a Chair in Law at the University of Melbourne Law School. Recent books include *Law, War and Crime: War Crimes Trials and the Reinvention of International Law* (Polity Press 2007) and *Great Powers and Outlaw States* (Cambridge University Press 2004). He has worked for several NGOs and was a member of the Australian Government Delegation to the Rome Diplomatic Conference for the Negotiation of the Statute for the International Criminal Court.

Marc Weller is Reader in International Law and Relations at the University of Cambridge, Director of the Centre for International Constitutional Studies at Hughes Hall, Cambridge, a Fellow of the Lauterpacht Centre for International Law and Director of the European Centre for Minority Issues. He has advised governments and international organizations on matters of international law and participated in a series of international peace processes. His latest publications include *Universal Minority Rights* (Open University Press 2007) and (with Barbara Metzger), *Settling Self-Determination Conflicts* (Nijhoff 2008).

Preface

The *Handbook of International Law* brings together contributions from authors from all five continents, including some of the most eminent international lawyers, as well as specialists in international relations, political science and philosophy. Our authors were invited to set out what they saw as the key issues involved in the many distinct aspects of international law that are considered here at what is a particularly fascinating point in the discipline's long evolution, with enormous challenges and opportunities coexisting in roughly equal amounts.

A great many people have assisted, inspired, enthused (and tolerated) our authors. We would particularly like to mention the generous support of the EU Network of Excellence on Globalisation and Regional Governance (GARNET) for the task of editing this work. Maggie Armstrong and Jocelyn Vaughan have provided absolutely invaluable research and editing assistance. We are also grateful to Craig Fowlie, Nicola Parkin and Antonia Edwards at Taylor & Francis for responding to our occasionally anxious queries.

Our authors would also like the following to receive special mention for their research assistance, comments, feedback and many other kinds of help: Annette Bazira-Okafor, Benjamin Bohris, Professor B.S. Chimni, the CISDL research group, William Currie, Kristina Davies, John S. Duffield, Theo Farrell, Richard Friman, Carlos Iván Fuentes, Evan Haas, J. Ryan Hall, Professor J.C. Hathaway, Mary Beth Hickcox-Howard, Katherine Nobbs, Mbabazi Okafor, Ojiako Okafor, Matthew Wooten and audiences at American University-Cairo, the Latin American Studies Association meeting in Montreal and law schools at the Universidad de Los Andes (Bogotá), the University of Texas and Harvard University.

List of abbreviations

AA	American anthropologist
ADCL	Anuario de Derecho Constitucional Latinoamericano
AHR	American Historical Review
AIPLAQJ	American Intellectual Property Law Association Quarterly Journal
AJCL	American Journal of Comparative Law
AJIA	Australian Journal of International Affairs
AJICL	Arizona Journal of International and Comparative Law
AJIL	American Journal of International Law
AJP	American Journal of Philology
ALR	Akron Law Review
AMR	Academy of Management Review
ANAAPSS	Annals of American Academy of Political and Social Science
APSR	American Political Science Review
ARIPO	African Regional Industrial Property Organization
ARLSS	Annual Review of Law and Social Science
ASIL	American Society of International Law
ASILP	American Society of International Law Proceedings
AUILR	American University International Law Review
AUJILP	American University Journal of International Law and Policy
AULR	American University Law Review
AV	Archiv des Völkerrecht
B	Boundary 2: An International Journal of Literature and Culture
BCEALR	British Columbia Environmental Affairs Law Review
BCICLR	Boston College International and Comparative Law Review
BELJ	Buffalo Environmental Law Journal
BJIL	Brooklyn Journal of International Law
BJPIR	British Journal of Politics and International Relations
BUILJ	Boston University International Law Journal
BYIL	British Yearbook of International Law
BYULR	Brigham Young University Law Review

CBD	Convention on Biological Diversity
CC	constitutional comment
CC	cultural critique
CERES	Coalition for Environmentally Responsive Economics
ChJIL	Chinese Journal of International Law
ChLR	Chicago Law Review
CHRY	Canadian Human Rights Yearbook
CIJCDT	Constellations: An International Journal for Critical and Democratic Theory
CISDL	Centre for International Sustainable Development Law
CILJ	Cornell International Law Journal
CILSA	Comparative and International Journal of Southern Africa
CITES	Convention on International Trade in Endangered Species of Wild Fauna and Flora
CJICL	Cardozo Journal of International and Comparative Law
CJIL	Chicago Journal of International Law
CJLJ	Canadian Journal of Law & Jurisprudence
CJTL	Columbia Journal of Transnational Law
CLP	current legal problems
CLR	Columbia Law Review
CLR	Connecticut Law Review
CLYIB	Comparative Law Yearbook of International Business
CMLR	Common Market Law Review
CQ	Classical Quarterly
CRIA	Cambridge Review of International Affairs
CSW	Christian Solidarity Worldwide
CTC	Counter-Terrorism Committee
CTE	Committee on Trade and Environment
CWILJ	California Western International Law Journal
CWRJIL	Case Western Reserve Journal of International Law
CYIL	Canadian Yearbook of International Law
D	Daedalus
DDA	Doha Development Agenda
DJIL	Dickinson Journal of International Law
DJILP	Denver Journal of International Law and Policy
DLJ	Duke Law Journal
DLR	DePaul Law Review
Dm	democratization
Documents	Documents on British Policy Overseas: Britain and China 1945–1950
DS	Der Staat
DSA	development Southern Africa
DSB	dispute settlement body
DSM	Dispute Settlement Mechanism
DSU	dispute settlement understanding
E	ethics
EC	European Commission
EIA	Ethics & International Affairs
EILR	Emory International Law Review
EJIL	European Journal of International Law

EJIR	European Journal of International Relations
EJLS	European Journal of Legal Studies
EJML	European Journal of Migration and Law
ELJ	Emory Law Journal
ELR	Environmental Law Review
ER	European Review
ESR	European Studies Review
EU	European Union
EuLJ	European Law Journal
FA	foreign affairs
FAO	Food and Agriculture Organization
FdR	federal register
FILJ	Fordham International Law Journal
FIPMELJ	Fordham Intellectual Property Media and Ent. L. J.
FJIL	Florida Journal of International Law
FLR	Florida Law Review
FM	forced migration
FMR	Forced Migration Review
FR	federal regulation
FYIL	Finnish Yearbook of International Law
G	Governance
GATT	General Agreement of Tariffs and Trade
GEF	global environment facility
GG	global governance
GJIL	Georgetown Journal of International Law
GLJ	Georgetown Law Journal
GLR	Georgia Law Review
GNS	Grotiana New Series
GRBS	Greek, Roman and Byzantine studies
GrLJ	German Law Journal
GSP	generalized system of tariff preferences
GYIL	German Yearbook of International Law
HAHR	Hispanic American Historical Review
HHRJ	Harvard Human Rights Journal
HICJ	Harvard International Club Journal
HICLR	Hastings International and Comparative Law Review
HILJ	Harvard International Law Journal
HJLPP	Harvard Journal of Law and Public Policy
HJLT	Harvard Journal of Law and Technology
HLJ	Hastings Law Journal
HLR	Harvard Law Review
HLR	Houston Law Review
HRLR	Human Rights Law Review
HRQ	Human Rights Quarterly
HWLJ	Harvard Women's Law Journal
IA	international affairs
IAEA	International Atomic Energy Agency
IARLJ	International Association of Refugee Law Judges

ICC	International Criminal Court
ICCPR	International Covenant on Civil and Political Rights
ICJ	International Court of Justice
ICLQ	International and Comparative Law Quarterly
ICTY	Appeals Chamber of the International Tribunal on former Yugoslavia
IELR	international enforcement law reporter
IGOs	International Governmental Organizations
IICLR	Indiana International & Comparative Law Review
IJGLS	Indiana Journal of Global Legal Studies
IJIL	Indian Journal of International Law
IJMGR	International Journal on Minority and Group Rights
IJRL	International Journal of Refugee Law
IJWP	International Journal of World Peace
IL	international law
ILC	International Law Commission
ILJ	Indiana Law Journal
ILO	international law opinions
ILO	International Labour Organization
ILR	Iowa Law Review
ILS	international legal system
ILSA	International Law Students Association
ILSAJICL	ILSA Journal of International and Comparative Law
IMF	International Monetary Fund
IMR	International Migration Review
IMT	International Military Tribunal
INPI	French National Patent Rights Institute
IntLR	international law reporter
IO	international organization
IOLR	International Organizations Law Review
IP	intellectual property
IPHR	intellectual property and human rights
IPJ	Intellectual Property Journal
IPR	intellectual property rights
IRIPCL	International Review Industrial Property and Copyright Law
IRRC	International Review of the Red Cross
IS	international security
ISQ	International Studies Quarterly
ISR	International Studies Review
ITFY	International Tribunal on former Yugoslavia
IYHR	Israel Yearbook on Human Rights
JAH	Journal of American History
JCL	Journal of Civil Liberties
JCMS	Journal of Common Market Studies
JCR	Journal of Conflict Resolution
JCS	Journal of Church and State
JCSL	Journal of Conflict and Security Law
JDS	Journal of Development Studies
JEA	Journal of Egyptian Archaeology

JELPLAC	Journal of Environmental Law and Policy in Latin America and the Caribbean
JHIL	Journal of the History of International Law
JIEL	Journal of International Economic Law
JILIR	Journal of International Law and International Relations
JLR	Journal of Law and Religion
JLS	Journal of Legal Studies
JPOI	Johannesburg Plan of Implementation
JPP	Journal of Political Philosophy
JR	juridical review
JRE	Jahrbuch für Recht und Ethik
JRS	Journal of Refugee Studies
JWIP	Journal of World Intellectual Property
JWT	Journal of World Trade
KJ	Kritische Justiz
KJLPP	Kansas Journal of Law & Public Policy
LAIL	Latin American International Law
LCP	law and contemporary problems
LJIL	Leiden Journal of International Law
LJPIL	Loyola Journal of Public Interest Law
LPBR	Law and Politics Book Review
LPIB	law and policy in international business
LQR	Law Quarterly Review
LRLJ	La Raza Law Journal
M	millennium
McLR	Michigan Law Review
MEA	multilateral environmental agreement
MJIL	Melbourne Journal of International Law
MJIL	Michigan Journal of International Law
MLR	Modern Law Review
MnLR	Minnesota Law Review
MPYUNL	Max Planck Yearbook of United Nations Law
MULR	Melbourne University Law Review
MWJHR	Muslim World Journal of Human Rights
NCJILCR	North Carolina Journal of International Law and Commercial Regulation
ND	No date
NGO	non-governmental organization
NI	national interest
NILR	Netherlands International Law Review
NJIL	Nordic Journal of International law
NJILB	Northwestern Journal of International Law and Business
NLR	Nebraska Law Review
NR	Nueva Revista
NRBA	Nueva Revista de Buenos Aires
NSAHR	Non-state Actors and Human Rights
NUJIHR	Northwestern University Journal of International Human Rights
NULR	Northwestern University Law Review
NYBIL	Netherlands YB Int'l L

NYIL	Netherlands Yearbook of International Law
NYUJILP	New York University Journal of International Law and Politics
OAMPI	African Malagasy Patent Rights Authority
OAPI	African Intellectual Property Organization
OAS	Organization of American States
OECD	Organization for Economic Cooperation and Development
OEJIPR	Oxford Electronic Journal of Intellectual Property Rights
OIC	Organization of Islamic Conference
OLR	Oklahoma Law Review
OREP	Oxford Review of Economic Policy
PASIL	Proceedings of the American Society of International Law
PB	philosophical books
PKPF	Phi Kappa Phi Forum
PPA	Philosophy & Public Affairs
PR	Policy Review
RBDI	Revue Belge de Droit International
RC	Recueil des Cours
RCADIH	Recueils des Cours de l'Academie de Droit International de la Haye
RCDI	Revista Colombiana de Derecho Internacional
RDI	Revista de Derecho Internacional
RDILC	Revue de Droit International et de Législation Comparée
RECIEL	Review of European Community and International Environmental Law
RFIC	Rivista di Filologia et di Istruzione Classica
RGDIP	Revue Générale de Droit International Public
RHDFE	Revue Historique du Droit Français et Étranger
RHDI	Revue d'Histoire du Droit International
RIDA	Revue Internationale des Droits de l'Antiquité
RIE	Review of International Economics
RIGO	regional inter-governmental organization
RIL	robust international law
RIS	Review of International Studies
RLS	Research in Law and Sociology
RP	Review of Politics
RRLR	Rutgers Race and the Law Review
RSQ	Refugee Survey Quarterly
SCLR	Southern California Law Review
SDILJ	San Diego International Law Journal
SGOTILC	Study Group of the International Law Commission
SIDS	small island developing states
SLLR	St Louis Law Review
SLR	Stanford Law Review
SLS	social legal studies
SsLR	Saskatchewan Law Review
SULR	Seattle University Law Review
SYBIL	Singapore Year Book of International Law
SZIER	Schweizerische Zeitschrift für internationales und europäisches Recht
T	telos
TED	turtle excluder device

TJIL	Texas Journal of International Law
TLR	Texas Law Review
TRIPs	trade-related aspects of intellectual property rights
TWLS	third world legal studies
UCLAJIFA	UCLA Journal of International Law and Foreign Affairs
UCLR	University of Chicago Law Review
UDHR	Universal Declaration of Human Rights
ULR	Utah Law Review
UN	United Nations
UNCBD	United Nations Convention on Biological Diversity
UNCCD	United Nations Convention to Combat Desertification and Drought
UNCED	United Nations Conference on Environment and Development
UNCHE	United Nations Conference on the Human Environment
UNCSD	United Nations Commission for Sustainable Development
UNCTAD	United Nations Conference on Trade and Development
UNDP	United Nations Development Program
UNEP	United Nations Environment Program
UNFCCC	United Nations Framework Convention on Climate Change
UNGA	United Nations General Assembly
UNSC	United Nations Security Council
UNTS	United Nations Treaty Series
UPLR	University of Pennsylvania Law Review
URLR	University of Richmond Law Review
UTLR	University of Toledo Law Review
VJIL	Virginia Journal of International Law
VJTL	Vanderbilt Journal Transnational Law
VLR	Virginia Law Review
VLR	Vanderbilt Law Review
WB	World Bank
WCED	World Commission on the Environment and Development
WD	world development
WECD	World Commission on Environment and Development
WGSLR	Washington Global Studies Law Review
WILJ	Wisconsin International Law Journal
WIN	World Indigenous News
WIPO	World Intellectual Property Organization
WLLR	Washington and Lee Law Review
WOLR	Western Ontario Law Review
WP	world politics
WSSD	World Summit for Sustainable Development
WTO	World Trade Organization
WULQ	Washington University Law Quarterly
YHRDLJ	Yale Human Rights and Development Law Journal
YIEL	Yearbook of International Environmental Law
YJIL	Yale Journal of International Law
YLJ	Yale Law Journal
ZAORV	Zeitschrift für ausländisches öffentliches Recht und Völkerrecht

Legal cases

African Commission on Human and Peoples' Rights, *Case of the Social and Economic Rights Action Center and the Center for Economic and Social Rights v. Nigeria* (2002) 96 AJIL 937, 47 J African L 126 [52]

AG Israel v. Eichmann (1968) 36 ILR 5 (District Court, Jerusalem)

AG Israel v. Eichmann (1968) 36 ILR 277 (Supreme Court of Israel)

Akkoç v. Turkey, 10 October 2000. Available at http://www.echr.coe.int/Eng/Press/2000/Oct/akkoc%20jud%20epress.htm

Almog v. Arab Bank, PLC (2007) 471 F. Supp. 2d 257 (E.D.N.Y. 2007)

Argentina v. Uruguay, Case Concerning Pulp Mills on the River Uruguay (2006), Request for the Indication of Provisional Measures: Order of 13 July 2006, General List No. 135, 45 ILM 1025 [67]

Attorney-General v. Adelaide Steamship Co. (1913) Appeal Cases 781

Balankulama v. The Secretary, Ministry of Industrial Development, SAER (2000) Vol. 7(2) June 2000 (Supreme Court, Sri Lanka – Supreme Court of the Democratic Socialist Republic of Sri Lanka)

Bautista de Arellana v. Colombia (1993) No. 563/1993, UN Doc. CCPR/C/55/D/563/1993

Behrami v. France, Application No. 71412/01

Belgium v. Spain, Case Concerning the Barcelona Traction, Light and Power Company, Limited (New Application: 1962) (1970) (Second Phase, Separate Opinion of Judge Jessup) General List No. 50, [1970] ICJ 3

Berić and Others v. Bosnia and Herzegovina (2007) Application No. 36357/04, Admissibility decision, 16 October 2007

Bosnia and Herzegovina v. Serbia and Montenegro, Case Concerning the Application of the Convention on the Prevention and Punishment of the Crime of Genocide (2007) Judgment of 26 February 2007

Boumediene [and Al Odah] v. Bush (2007) 476 F.3d 981 (DC Cir. 2007), cert. denied 4/2/07

Bulankulame v. Secretary, Ministry of Industrial Development and Others (2000) 3 SriLR 243 (the Eppawela Case 2000, Supreme Court of Sri Lanka)

Caroline Case (1841) BFSP, Case No. 29: 1137-38

Case Concerning Armed Activities on the Territory of the Congo, Merits (Democratic Republic of the Congo v. Uganda) ICJ Reports (2005)

Case Concerning the Gabčíkovo-Nagymaros Project (Hungary/Slovakia) (Judgment) General List No. 92 [1997] ICJ 7, (1998) 37 ILM 162

Case Concerning the Gabčíkovo-Nagymaros Project (Hungary/Slovakia) (1994) Memorial submitted by the Slovak Republic, Vol. 1, 2 May 1994, 294. Available at http://www.icj-cij.org/docket/files/92/10939.pdf

Case Concerning the Gabčíkovo-Nagymaros, Separate Opinion of Vice-President Weeramantry

Case Concerning Sovereignty over Pulau Ligitan and Pulau Sipadan (Indonesia v. Malaysia) (2002) Judgment, General List No. 102 [2002] ICJ 625

Case Concerning the Territorial Dispute, Libyan Arab Jamahiriya v. Chad (1994) Judgment, General List No. 83 [1994] ICJ 6, (1994) 33 ILM 571 [41]

Laureano v. Peru (1993) No. 540/1993, UN Doc. CCPR/C/56/D/540/1993

Layla Sahin v. Turkey (2005) ECHR 44774/98

Leatch v. National Parks and Wildlife Service and Shoalhaven City Council (1993) 81 LGERA 270 (1993) (NSW Land and Environment Court, Australia)

Legal Consequences of the Construction of a Wall in the Occupied Palestinian Territory (2004) ICJ Advisory Opinion, 9 July 2004, ICJ Reports 2004

Legality of the Threat or Use of Nuclear Weapons (1996) 35 ILM. Online. Available at http://www.icj-cij.org/docket/files/95/7495.pdf

Libya v. US, Case concerning Questions of Interpretation and Application of the 1971 Montreal Convention arising from the Aerial Incident at Lockerbie, Jurisdiction and Admissibility (1998) ICJ Reports, 37 ILM 187

Libyan Arab Jamahiriya v. United States of America, Questions of Interpretation and Application of the 1971 Montreal Convention arising from the Aerial Incident at Lockerbie, Dissenting opinion by Judge Weeramantry (1992) International Court of Justice

LICRA et UEJF v. Yahoo! Inc. (2000) Ordonnance Référé, TGI. Paris, Nov. 20, 2000. Available in English at http://www.lapres.net/yahen11.html (Daniel Lapres trans.)

MC v. Bulgaria (Application No. 39272/98), Judgment, 4 December 2003

Military Commissions Act (2006) Public Law No. 109-366, 120 Stat. 2600

Military Order, Detention, Treatment, and Trial of Certain Non-Citizens in the War Against Terrorism (2001) 66 Fed. Reg. 57, 833, 16 November 2001

Milpurrurru v. Indofurn (Pty) Ltd (1995) 30 IPR 209

Minors Oposa v. Secretary of the Department of Environment and Natural Resources, DENR (1994) 33 I.L.M. 173 (Philippines)

Nicaragua v. USA, Case concerning Military and Paramilitary Activities in and against Nicaragua (1986) ICJ Reports 1986, 76 ILR 1

North Sea Continental Shelf Case (Federal Republic of Germany vs. Denmark/Netherlands) ICJ Reports (1968)

Nuclear Tests Case (New Zealand v. France) (1995) Request for an Examination of Situation in Accordance with Paragraph 63 of Court's Judgment of 20 December 1974: Order, Dissenting opinion by Judge Weeramantry, General List No. 97, ICJ 288

Oil Platforms Case (Islamic Republic of Iran v. United States), ICJ Reports (2003) Available at http://212.153.43.18/icjwww/idocket/iop/iopjudgment/iop_ijudgment_20031106.PDF

Portugal v. Australia, Case concerning East Timor (1995) Judgment, Dissenting opinion of Judge Weeramantry, General List No. 84, [1995] ICJ 90, 34 ILM 1581

Prosecutor v. Dusko Tadic (1999) ICTY, No. IT-94-1-A, Appeals Chamber, 15 July 1999

Prosecutor v. Erdemović (1997a) Case No. IT-96-22-A, Joint Separate Opinion of Judge McDonald and Judge Vohrah, 7 October 1997

Prosecutor v. Erdemović (1997b) Case No. IT-96-22-A, Separate and Dissenting Opinion of Judge Li, 7 October 1997

Prosecutor v. Milošević (2001) Case No. IT-02-54-PT, Decision on Preliminary Motions, 8 November 2001

Prosecutor v. Nikolić, Decision on Interlocutory Appeal Concerning Legality of Arrest (2003) Case No. IT-94-2-AR73, 5 June 2003

Prosecutor v. Stanislav Galić (2003) Case No. IT-98-29-A, Judgment, Trial Chamber 3 December 2003, and Appeals Chamber, 30 November 2006

Prosecutor v. Tadić, Decision on Defence Motion for Interlocutory Appeal on Jurisdiction (1995) ICTY, Case No. IT-94-1-AR72. Available at http://www.un.org/icty/tadic/appeal/decision-e/51002.htm

Prosecutor v. Taylor (2004) Case No. SCSL-2003-01-I, Decision on Immunity from Jurisdiction, 31 May 2004

R. v. Bartle and the Commissioner of Police for the Metropolis and Others, ex parte Pinochet Ugarte (1999) 2 All ER 97 (HL)

Rajendra Parajuli and Others v. Shree Distillery Pvt Ltd and Others, Supreme Court of Nepal (Writ No. 3259, 1996)

Reid v. Covert (1957) 354 US 1

Republic of the Congo v. France, Case Concerning Certain Criminal Proceedings in France (2002) Application, 9 December 2002

Republic of the Congo v. France, Case Concerning Certain Criminal Proceedings in France, Request Provisional Measure, Order of 17 June 2003 (2003) ICJ Reports 102

Reports, legislation and treaties

Administration of George W. Bush (2001) Military Order, Detention, Treatment, and Trial of Certain Non-Citizens in the War against Terrorism, FR, 66: 1665. Available at http://www.law.cornell.edu/background/warpower/fr1665.pdf

African Union (2007) Decision on the United Nations Declaration on the Rights of Indigenous Peoples, Addis Ababa, Ethopia: African Union. Available at http://www.africa-union.org/root/UA/Conferences/2007/janvier/SUMMIT/Doc/Decisions/Decisions%20and%20Declarations%20-%208th%20Ordinary%20Session%20of%20the%20Assembly.doc

Agenda 21 (Annex 2), in Report of the UN Conference on Environment and Development Vol. I (13 June 1992) UN Doc. A/CONF.151/26 (Vol. I); 31 ILM 874

Agreement Establishing the World Trade Organization (1994) 33 ILM 81, 15 April 1994. Available at http://www.wto.org/english/docs_e/legal_e/04-wto.pdf

Agreement for the Prosecution and Punishment of Major War Criminals of the European Axis, and Establishing the Charter of the International Military Tribunal (IMT), annex, (1951) 82 UNTS 279

Amnesty International (2003) *Iraq: Memorandum on concerns relating to law and order*, 23 July 2003. MDE 14/157/2003. Available at http://web.amnesty.org/library/Index/ENGMDE141572003?open&of=ENG-IRQ

Antarctic Treaty (1959) 402 UNTS 71

Assemblée Nationale (1999) *Rapport d'Information déposé en Application de l'Article 145 du Règlement par la Mission d'Information de la Commission de la Défense nationale et des Forces armées et de la Commission des Affaires étrangères, sur les Opérations militaires menées par la France, d'autres pays et l'ONU au Rwanda entre 1990 et 1994*, Assemblée Nationale, No. 1271. Available at http://www.assemblee-nationale.fr/11/dossiers/rwanda/r1271.asp

Association of the Bar of the City of New York and Center for Human Rights and Global Justice (2004) *Torture by Proxy: International and Domestic Law Applicable to "Extraordinary Renditions"*, revised June 2006. Available at http://www.chrgj.org/docs/TortureByProxy.pdf

Australia, A.G. (2003) *The Memorandum of Advice on the Use of Force Against Iraq, provided by the Attorney General's Department and the Department of Foreign Affairs and Trade, March 18, 2003*, 19 March 2003

Banks, R. (2006) UNGA Third Committee 61st Session, Monday 16 October, Item 64(a) Declaration on the Rights of Indigenous Peoples, Statement by H.E. Ms. Rosemary Banks, Ambassador and Permanent Representative of New Zealand, on behalf of Australia, New Zealand and the United States, New York: Australian Permanent Mission to the United Nations. Available at http://www.australiaun.org/unny/Soc%5f161006.html

Basis for Relations between Finland and the Russian Federation (signed 20 January 1992, entered into force 11 July 1992) 1691 UNTS 255

Bellinger, J.B. (2003) *Authority for Use of Force by The United States against Iraq under International Law*, 10 April 2003. Council on Foreign Relations

Breton-Le Goff, G. (2001) Mondialisation et Démocratie: Evaluation de la Participation normative des OING à la Gouvernance globale, Montreal: Chaire UNESCO d'Études des Fondements philosophiques de la Justice et de la Société démocratique. Available at http:www.humansecuritygateway. info/data/item761840995/view

Brownlie, Chinkin, Greenwood and Lowe (2000) Memoranda on Kosovo to House of Commons Foreign Affairs Committee, 49 *International Comparative Law and Quarterly*, 876–943

Bush, G.W. (2003) *State of the Union*, 28 January 2003. Available at http://www.whitehouse.gov/ news/releases/2003/01/20030128-19.html

Carnegie Endowment for International Peace. Division of International Law (1938) Conferencias internacionales americanas, 1889–1936; recopilación de los tratados, convenciones, recomendaciones, resoluciones y mociones adoptadas por las siete primeras conferencias internacionales americanas, la Conferencia internacional americana de conciliación y arbitraje y la Conferencia interamericana de consolidación de la paz; con varios documentos relativos a la organización de las deferidas conferencias, Washington: Dotación Carnegie Para la Paz Internacional

—— (1943) Conferencias internationales americanas, primer-suplemento, Washington: Dotación Carnegie Para la paz internacional

Charter of the International Military Tribunal Agreement for the Prosecution and Punishment of Major War Criminals of the European Axis, and Establishing the Charter of the International Military Tribunal (IMT), Annex, (1951) 82 UNTS 279

Charter of the Organization of Islamic Conference. Available at http://www.oic-un.org/about/Charter.htm

Chatham House (2005) High-level Expert Group, Principles of International Law on the Use of Force by States in Self-Defence, *International & Comparative Law Quarterly*, 2006, 55: 963–972

Coalition Provisional Authority (2003) *Coalition Provisional Authority Regulation Number 1*, 16 May 2003. CPA/REG/16 May 2003/01

Coalition Provisional Authority (2004) *Law of Administration for the State of Iraq for the Transitional Period*, 8 March 2004

Commission of the European Communities (2002) Action Plan "Simplifying and Improving the Regulatory Environment", Brussels, COM(2002)278 final, 5 June 2002

—— (2003) Communication from the Commission to the Council, the European Parliament, the European Economic and Social Committee and the Committee of the Regions: Updating and simplifying the Community acquis, Brussels, COM(2003)261 final, 11 February 2003

Committee on Trade and Environment, *Report of the Meeting held on 6 July 2005* (2 September 2005) WT/CTE/M/40

Committee on Trade and Environment, *Trade in Used and Retreated Tyres, Submission by Brazil* (12 July 2005) WT/CTE/W/241

Consistency of Certain Danzig Legislative Decrees with the Constitution of the Free City, Advisory Opinion (1935) PCIJ 2, Series A/B, No. 65, 4 December 1935

Consolidated Versions of the Treaty on European Union (signed 17 February 1992) OJ C 321E of 29 December 2006. Available at http://eur-lex.europa.eu/en/treaties/index.htm

Convention on Biological Diversity (1992) Rio Earth Summit

Convention on the Conservation of Migratory Species of Wild Animals (1980) 19 ILM 15

Convention for Cooperation in the Protection and Sustainable Development of the Marine and Coastal Environment of the Northeast Pacific (18 February 2002). Available at http://dinrac.nowpap.org/3-sea-north-west-pacific-convt.htm

Convention on International Trade in Endangered Species of Wild Fauna and Flora (1973) (adopted 3 March 1973, entered into force 1 July 1975) 993 UNTS 243, 12 ILM 1085

Convention on the Non-Applicability of Statutory Limitations to War Crimes and Crimes against Humanity (1968) 754 UNTS 73

Convention on the Prevention and Punishment of the Crime of Genocide (1951) 78 UNTS 277

Convention on the Prior Informed Consent Procedure for Certain Hazardous Chemicals and Pesticides in International Trade (1999) 30 ILM 1

Convention against Torture and Other Cruel, Inhuman or Degrading Treatment or Punishment, GA Res. 39/46

Daes, E. (2001) Report to the United Nations Economic and Social Council. Prevention of Discrimination and Protection of Indigenous Peoples and Minorities: Indigenous Peoples and their Relationship to Land, Geneva: United Nations. Available at http://www.unhchr.ch/Huridocda/Huridoca.nsf/ e06a5300f90fa0238025668700518ca4/78d418c307faa00bc1256a9900496f2b/$FILE/G0114179.pdf

Department of Foreign Affairs and International Trade Canada, Framework for Conducting Environmental Assessments of Trade Negotiations. Available at http://www.international.gc.ca/trade-agreements-accords-commerciaux/ds/Environment.aspx

Differential and More Favourable Treatment Reciprocity and Fuller Participation of Developing Countries (28 November 1979) L/4903, BISD 26S/203

Dissenting Opinion of Judge Weeramantry. Available at http://www.cornnet.nl/~akmalten/uweerama.html

Documents on British Policy Overseas: Britain and China 1945–1950 (2002) Series 1, Vol. VIII, S. R. Ashton (ed.) Whitehall History Publishing, Frank Cass

Doha Ministerial Declaration (14 November 2001) WT/MIN(01)/DEC/1. Available at http://www.wto.org/english/thewto_e/minist_e/min96_e/singapore_declaration96_e.pdf

Elsea, J.K. (2006) *US Policy Regarding the International Criminal Court*, CRS Report for Congress, Order Code RL31495. Available at http://vienna.usembassy.gov/en/download/pdf/crs_icc.pdf

European Commission, *Sustainability Impact Assessment*. Available at http://ec.europa.eu/comm/trade/issues/global/sia/index_en.htm

European Convention on the Non Applicability of Statutory Limitation to Crimes against Humanity and War Crimes of January 25, 1974, ETS 82

Final Act Embodying the Results of the Uruguay Round of Multilateral Trade Negotiations, 33 ILM 1143. Available at http://www.wto.org/english/docs_e/legal_e/03-fa.pdf

Final Report of the Independent Panel to Review DoD Detention Operations (August 2004) (2005) in K.J. Greenberg and J.L. Dratel (eds), *The Torture Papers: The Road to Abu Ghraib*, Cambridge: Cambridge University Press, pp. 908–75

Gaja, G. (ILC Special Rapporteur) (2007) Fifth Report on Responsibility of International Organizations, International Law Commission, 59th Session, 2 May 2007, A/CN 4/583

General Treaty for the Renunciation of War (1928) 94 LNTS 57

Geneva Convention for the Amelioration of the Condition of the Wounded and Sick in Armed Forces in the Field (1949) 75 UNTS 31

Geneva Convention for the Amelioration of the Condition of the Wounded, Sick and Shipwrecked Members of the Armed Forces at Sea (1949) 75 UNTS 85

Geneva Convention Relative to the Protection of Civilians (1949) 75 UNTS 135

Geneva Convention Relative to the Treatment of Prisoners of War (1949) 75 UNTS 135

Geneva Ministerial Declaration (20 May 1998) WT/MIN(98)/DEC/1. Available at http://docsonline.wto.org

German War Trials, Report of Proceedings before the Supreme Court in Leipzig, Cmd. 1450, London: HMSO, 1921

Goldsmith, J. (2004) *Memorandum for Alberto R. Gonzales, Counsel to the President*, 19 March 2004. Available at http://www.washingtonpost.com/wp-srv/nation/documents/doj_memo031904.pdf

Goldsmith, P. (2003a) *Legal basis for use of force against Iraq*, 17 March 2003. Available at http://www.number-10.gov.uk/output/Page3287.asp

Goldsmith, P. (2003b) *Memorandum to the Prime Minister: Iraq: Resolution 1441*, 7 March 2003. Available at http://www.ico.gov.uk/upload/documents/library/freedom_of_information/notices/annex_a_-_attorney_general's_advice_070303.pdf

Grundgesetz für die Bundesrepublik Deutschland (German Constitution)

Hagen, R. (2007) Explanation of vote by Robert Hagen, U.S. Advisor, on the Declaration on the Rights of Indigenous Peoples, to the UN General Assembly, New York: United States Mission to the United Nations. Available at http://www/usunnewyork.usmission.gov/press_release/20070913_204.html

Hague Convention respecting the Limitation of the Employment of Force for the Recovery of Contract Debts, 18 October (1907). Available at http://www.yale.edu/lawweb/avalon/lawofwar/hague072.htm

Hague Convention (IV), Convention Respecting the Laws and Customs of War on Land, 18 October 1907. The Avalon Project at Yale Law School

Havana Charter for an International Trade Organization, UN Conference on Trade & Development, Final Act and Related Documents (24 March 1948) UN Doc. E/Conf 2/78 (1948)

Human Rights Watch (2002) Fast Track Land Reform in Zimbabwe, Human Rights Watch, March 2002, Vol. 14, No. 1 (A)

ICJ Reports 1969, 3 at 77

ICJ (1980) United States Diplomatic and Consular Staff in Tehran, ICJ Report 3

International Committee of the Red Cross (1958) *Commentary on the Geneva Convention (IV) Relative to the Protection of Civilian Persons in Time of War*, Available http://www.icrc.org/ihl.nsf/WebList? ReadForm&id=380&t=com> (accessed 2 October 2007)

ILA New Delhi Declaration of Principles of International Law Relating to Sustainable Development (2002) 2 Intl Environmental Agreements 209

Independent International Commission on Kosovo (2000) *The Kosovo Report: Conflict, International Responses, Lessons Learned*. Oxford: Oxford University Press

Indigenous Peoples of Africa Co-ordinating Committee (2006) Press Release 5 December 2006: IPACC Statement on the UN General Assembly decision to postpone the vote on the UN Declaration on the Rights of Indigenous Peoples, Indigenous Peoples of Africa Co-ordinating Committee. Available at http://www.unep.org/indigenous/pdfs/IPACCDeclarationStatement2006EFS.pdf

International Atomic Energy Agency (1971) *The Structure and Content of Agreements Between the Agency and State Required in Connection with the Treaty on the Non-Proliferation of Nuclear Weapons*, IAEA Doc. INFCIRC/153, May 1971

International Commission on Intervention and State Sovereignty (2001) *The Responsibility to Protect*, Ottawa: International Development Research Centre, December 2001. Available at http://www.iciss.ca

International Convention of American States (1933) Montevideo Convention on the Rights and Duties of States, Montevideo: International Convention of American States. Available at http://www.yale.edu/lawweb/avalon/intdip/interam/intam03.htm

International Convention for the Protection of All Persons from Enforced Disappearance, UN Doc. A/RES/47/133, 18 December 1992. Available at http://untreaty.un.org/English/notpubl/IV_16_english.pdf

International Convention on the Suppression and Punishment of the Crime of Apartheid (1976) 1015 UNTS 244

International Covenant on Civil and Political Rights (1966) Adopted and opened for signature, ratification and accession by General Assembly resolution 2200A (XXI) of 16 December 1966, entered into force 23 March 1976, in accordance with Article 49. Available at http://www.unhchr.ch/html/menu3/b/a_ccpr.htm

International Covenant on Civil and Political Rights (1966) 999 UNTS 171

International Covenant on Economic, Social and Cultural Rights (1966) Adopted and opened for signature, ratification and accession by General Assembly resolution 2200A (XXI) of 16 December 1966. Available at http://www.unhchr.ch/html/menu3/b/a_cescr.htm

International Labour Organization (1957) Indigenous and Tribal Populations Convention (Convention No. 107), Geneva: International Labour Organization. Available at http://www.ilo.org/ilolex/english/convdisp1.htm

—— (1989) Indigenous and Tribal Peoples Convention (Convention No. 169), Geneva: International Labour Organization. Available at http://www.ilo.org/ilolex/english/convdisp1.htm

International Law Commission, Principles International Law Recognizing in the Charter of the Nuremberg Tribunal and in the Judgment of the Tribunal (1950) *Yearbook of the International Law Commission*, 1950 II, (5 June–29 July 1950) UN Doc. A/CN.4/SER.A/1950 368-72

International Law Commission and Koskenniemi, M. (2006) Fragmentation of International Law, UN Doc. A/CN.4/L.686

Johannesburg Declaration on Sustainable Development and Johannesburg Plan of Implementation, in Report of the World Summit on Sustainable Development (4 September 2002) UN Doc. A/CONF.199/L20

Jones-Fay Report (2004) *Investigation of Intelligence Activities at Abu Ghraib*, August 2004

Law No. 03-18 on Trademarks (9 Ramadhan 1424 corresponding to 4 November 2003) approving Ordinance No. 03-06 (19 Joumada El Oula 1424 corresponding to 19 July 2003). Available at http://www.wipo.int/clea/en/fiche.jsp?uid=dz003

Law No. 03-19 on Patents (of 9 Ramadhan 1424 corresponding to 4 November 2003) approving Ordinance No. 03-07 (of 19 Joumada El Oula 1424 corresponding to 19 July 2003). Available at http://www.wipo.int/clea/en/fiche.jsp?uid=dz005

Lexikon der Nachhaltigkeit. Available at http://www.nachhaltigkeit.info/

Lincoln, A. (1838) The Perpetuation of our Political Institutions, Address to the Young Men's Lyceum of Springfield, Illinois, 27 January 1838. Available at http://teachingamericanhistory.org/library/index.asp?document=157

Marrakesh Agreement Establishing the World Trade Organization (signed 15 April 1994, entered into force 1 January 1995) 1867 UNTS 4, 33 ILM 1144

Memorandum of the Office of Legal Affairs, UN Secretariat, 34 UN ESCOR, Supp. (No. 8), 15, UN Doc. E/CN.4/1/610 (1962)

Military Order of 13 November 2001, Detention, Treatment, and Trial of Certain Non-Citizens in the War Against Terrorism, 66 FdR 57833

Ministerial Decision on Trade and Environment (15 April 1994) LT/UR/D-5/8, 33 ILM 1267. Available at http://docsonline.wto.org

Monty, M. and Gurr, T.R. (2005) Peace and Conflict 2005: A Global Survey of Armed Conflicts, Self-Determination Movements, and Democracy, Center for International Development and Conflict Management, College Park, MD: University of Maryland. Available at http://www.cidcm.umd. edu/publications/publication.asp?pubType=paper&id=15

National Commission on Terrorist Attacks upon the United States (2004) *9/11 Commission Report Final Report of the National Commission on Terrorist Attacks Upon the United States* (2004). Available at http://www.9-11commission.gov/report/911Report.pdf

Nieuwkoop, M. and Uquillas, J.E. (2000) Defining Ethnodevelopment in Operational Terms: Lessons from the Ecuador Indigenous and Afro-Ecuadorian Peoples Development Project, Latin America and Caribbean Region Sustainable Development Working Paper No. 6, Ecuador: The World Bank. Available at http://go.worldbank.org/7WPIEYMOP0

Office of the United States Trade Representative, Environmental Reviews in FTAs. Available at www.ustr.gov/Trade_Sectors/Environment/Environmental_Reviews/Section_Index.html

Peace Treaty of Westphalia of 24 October 1648. Available at http://www.yale.edu/lawweb/avalon/westphal.htm

Pella, V. (1957) Memorandum présenté par le Secrétariat, Report to United Nations International Law Commission, UN Doc. A/CN.4/39

Permanent Sovereignty over Natural Resources, UNGA Res 1803 (XVII) (14 December 1962) UN Doc. A/Res/1803 (XVII)

Peru's State Policies on Sustainable Development and Environment. Available at http://www.conam.gob.pe/modulos/home/PolicitaDeEstado.asp

Protocol on Environmental Protection to the Antarctic Treaty (opened for signature 4 October 1991, entered into force 14 January 1998) 30 ILM 1461

Report of the Convening Group of the Conference on Interfaith Cooperation for Peace: Enhancing Interfaith Dialogue and Cooperation towards Peace in the 21st Century (22 June 2005), United Nations Headquarters, New York

Report of the Study Group of the International Law Commission, A/CN.4/L.682, 13 April 2006, in M. Koskenniemi (ed.) *Research Reports by the Erik Castren Institute of International Law and Human Rights*. Helsinki, Erik Castren Institute of International Law and Human Rights

Reservations to the Convention on the Prevention and Punishment of the Crime of Genocide (Advisory Opinion) (1951) ICJ Reports 16

Rio Declaration on Environment and Development, adopted by the UN Conference on Environment and Development (UNCED) at Rio de Janeiro, 13 June 1992, UN Doc. A/CONF.151/26 (vol. I) (1992)

Rome Statute of the International Criminal Court (17 July 1998) 2187 UNTS 90, 37 ILM (1998) 999

Rome Statute of the International Criminal Court (2002) 2187 UNTS 90

Schlesinger Report (2004) *Final Report of the Independent Panel to Review DoD Detention Operations*, August 2004

Singapore Ministerial Declaration (18 December 1996) WT/MIN(96)/DEC, 36 ILM 218. Available at http://www.wto.org/english/thewto_e/minist_e/min96_e/singapore_declaration96_e.pdf

Statement of Principles Applicable to the Formation of General Customary International Law, ILA London Conference 2992, Final Report of the Committee on Formation of Customary (General) International Law

Statute of the Special Court for Sierra Leone (2002) 2178 UNTS 138

Statute of the Special Tribunal for Lebanon (2007) UN Doc. S/RES/1757

Stockholm Declaration of the United Nations Conference on the Human Environment (1972) 5–16 June 1972, UN Doc. A/CONF.48/14

Summit of the Americas on Sustainable Development, *Declaration of Santa Cruz de la Sierra* (adopted 7 December 1996). Available at http://www.summit-americas.org/Boliviadec.htm

Taguba Report (2004) *Article 15-6 Investigation of the 800th Military Police Brigade*, March 2004

Trademark Registration Treaty (1975) Vienna, Austria

Treaty of Amsterdam Amending the Treaty on European Union (signed 2 October 1997, entered into force 1 May 1999) [1997] OJ C 340/1. Available at http://www.europarl.europa.eu/topics/treaty/pdf/amst-en.pdf

UK Attorney-General's (Secret) Advice to Prime Minster on the Legality of the War (March 7, 2003). Available at http://news.bbc.co.uk/1/shared/bsp/hi/pdfs/28_04_05_attorney_general.pdf

UK Attorney-General's Opinion, Written Answer to Baroness Ramsay, H.L. Debates, 17 March, 2003 cWA1. Available at http://news.bbc.co.uk/1/hi/uk_politics/2857347.stm

UK Attorney-General's Statement to House of Lords (2004) Hansard, Col. 371, 21 April 2004

United Kingdom, Foreign Office (ND) FO/371/126877/EA1015/89

—— (ND) FO/371/126887/EA1015/365

—— (ND) FO/371/126878/EA1015

—— (ND) FO/371/126887/EA1015/371

—— (ND) FO/371/26882/EA1015/235

—— (ND) *FO Confidential Print on the Buraimi*

—— (1949a) FO 371/75815, F14109

—— (1949b) FO 371/75826, F18535: 49, 5 December, 1949

—— (1949c) FO 371/75826, F 18695/1023/10, 5 December 1949

—— (1949d) FO 800/462, 17 December 1949

—— (1949e) FO 371/75818, F6028, 20 and 22 October 1949

—— (1950) Recognition of States and Governments, circular produced by Foreign Secretary June 1950, L 280/1 Circular No. 059, found at FCO 25/046

—— (1957a) FO/371/126884/EA1015/282(A), 20 August 1957

—— (1957b) FO/371/126884/EA1015/283, 20 August 1957

—— (1957c) *FO Confidential Note on the Agreement of Sib, and Sir Pierson Dixon's Speech in the Security Council of 20/8/1957*, prepared by Sir Ronald Wingate FO/371/126829

United Kingdom Parliament (2003) *House of Commons Liaison Committee, 21 January 2003*, Available at http://www.parliament.the-stationery-office.co.uk/pa/cm200203/cmselect/cmliaisn/uc334-i/uc33402.htm

United Nations (ND) Draft Code of Offences Against the Peace and Security of Mankind, Report by J. Spiropoulos, Special Rapporteur, UN Doc. A/CN.4/25

—— (1945) Charter of the United Nations, San Francisco: United Nations. Available at http://www.un.org/aboutun/charter/index.html

—— (1946) Draft Resolution, UN Doc. A/BUR/50

—— (1947) General Assembly Resolution 177 (II), GA RES. 177 (II)

—— (1948a) Report of the Drafting Committee to the Commission on Human Rights. Lake Success, New York: United Nations Commission on Human Rights

—— (1948b) Universal Declaration on Human Rights, GA Res. 217 A (III), UN Doc. A/810, Geneva: United Nations. Available at http://www.unhchr.ch/udhr/lang/eng.htm

—— (1948c) United Nations General Assembly Resolution, UN Doc. A/C.6/SR.100

—— (1950) Question of International Criminal Jurisdiction, Report by Ricardo J. Alfaro, Special Rapporteur, UN Doc. A/CN.4/15

—— (1951) Report of the International Law Commission covering the Work of its Third Session, 16 May–27 July 1951, UN Doc. A/1858

—— (1954) Report of the International Law Commission covering the Work of its Sixth Session, 3 June–28 July 1954, UN Doc. A/2693

—— (1966) International Covenant on Civil and Political Rights, Geneva: United Nations. Available at http://www.unhchr.ch/html/menu3/b/a_ccpr.htm

—— (1966) International Covenant on Economic, Social and Cultural Rights, Geneva: Untied Nations. Available at http://www.unhchr.ch/html/menu3/b/a_cescr.htm

—— (1972a) Permanent Sovereignty over Natural Resources of Developing Countries, UNGA Res. 3016 (XXVII) (18 December 1972) UN Doc. A/Res/3016 (XXVII) [1]

—— (1972b) Stockholm Declaration: Declaration of the United Nations Conference on the Human Environment, Adopted (16 June 1972) UN Doc. A/Conf 48/14/Rev.1, 11 ILM 1461

—— (1974) Declaration on the Establishment of a New International Economic Order, Adopted by General Assembly resolution 3201 (S-VI) (1 May 1974), UN Doc. A/Res/3201(S-VI)

—— (1983) Process of Preparation of the Environmental Perspective to the Year 2000 and Beyond, Meeting No. 102, Adopted by General Assembly resolution 38/161 (19 December 1983), UN Doc. A/RES/38/161

—— (1984) Report of the International Law Commission on the Work of its Thirty-sixth Session (7 May–27 July 1984), UN Doc. A/39/10

—— (1985) Report of the International Law Commission on the Work of its Thirty-seventh Session (6 May–26 July 1985), UN Doc. A/40/10

—— (1986a) Declaration on the Right to Development, Adopted by General Assembly Res. 41/128 (4 December 1986), UN Doc. A/Res/41/128

—— (1986b) Report of the International Law Commission on the Work of its Thirty-eighth Session (5 May–11 July 1986), UN Doc. A/41/10

—— (1987) Report of the World Commission on Environment and Development, Adopted by General Assembly resolution 42/187 (11 December 1987) UN Doc. A/Res/42/187

—— (1988) Report of the International Law Commission on the Work of its Fortieth Session (9 May–29 July 1988), UN Doc. A/43/10

—— (1989a) Report of the International Law Commission on the Work of its Forty-first Session (2 May–21 July 1989), UN Doc. A/41/10

—— (1989b) UN Convention on the Rights of the Child, 1577 UNTS 3

—— (1991) Report of the International Law Commission on the Work of its Forty-third Session (29 April–19 July 1991), UN Doc. A/46/10

—— (1992a) Agenda 21 (Annex 2), in Report of the UN Conference on Environment and Development Vol. I (13 June 1992) UN Doc. A/CONF.151/26 (Vol. I)

—— (1992b) Rio Declaration on Environment and Development (Annex 2), Report of the UN Conference on Environment and Development Vol. I (13 June 1992) UN Doc. A/CONF.151/26 (Vol. I), 31 ILM 874

—— (1992c) United Nations Convention on Biological Diversity, (opened for signature 5 June 1992, entered into force 29 December 1) 1760 UNTS 79, 143; 31 ILM 1004

—— (1992d) United Nations Framework Convention on Climate Change (opened for signature 4 June 1992, entered into force 21 March 1994) 1771 UNTS 107, 31 ILM 849

—— (1993a) Establishment of the Commission on Sustainable Development, UNESC Res. 1993/207 (12 February 1993) UN Doc. E/1993/207; Institutional arrangements to follow up the United Nations Conference on Environment and Development, UNGA Res. 47/191 (29 January 1993) UN Doc. A/RES/47/191 [3]–[5]

—— (1993b) Report of the Secretary-General Pursuant to Paragraph 2 of Security Council Resolution 808 (1993), UN Doc. S/25704

—— (1994) United Nations Convention to Combat Desertification in those Countries Experiencing Serious Drought and/or Desertification, Particularly in Africa (opened for signature 14 October 1994, entered into force 16 December 1996) 1954 UNTS 3, 33 ILM 1328

—— (1996) Report of the International Law Commission on the Work of its Forty-eighth Session (6 May–26 July 1996), UN Doc. A/51/10

—— (1997a) International Convention for the Suppression of Terrorist Bombing. Available at http://cns.miis.edu/pubs/inven/pdfs/bomb.pdf

—— (1997b) Program for the Further Implementation of Agenda 21, UNGA Res. S-19/2 (19 September 1997) UN Doc. A/Res/S-19/2

—— (1998) UN Guiding Principles on Internal Displacement, UN Doc. E/CN.4/1998/53/Add.2

—— (2000a) Report of the Secretary-General on the Establishment of a Special Court for Sierra Leone, UN Doc., S/2000/915

—— (2000b) Ten-year Review of Progress achieved in the Implementation of the Outcome of the United Nations Conference on Environment and Development, Adopted by General Assembly Resolution 55/199 (20 December 2000) UN Doc. A/RES/55/199

—— (2001a) International Instruments Related to the Prevention and Suppression of International Terrorism, 2–131

—— (2001b) General Assembly, Resolution 56/83, of 12 December 2001

—— (2001c) Note on International Protection, A/AC.96/951, 13 September 2001. Available at http://www.unhcr.org/excom/EXCOM/3bb1c6cc4.pdf

—— (2002) Note on International Protection, A/AC.96/965, 11 September 2002. Available at http://www.unhcr.org/excom/EXCOM/3d8857cb7.pdf

—— (2003a) Convention for the Safeguarding of Intangible Cultural Heritage, Paris: United Nations. Available at http://unesdoc.unesco.org/images/0013/001325/132540e.pdf

—— (2003b) Letter Dated 20 March 2003 from the Permanent Representative of the United States of America to the United Nations Addressed to the President of the Security Council, UN Doc. S/2003/351

—— (2003c) Letter Dated 20 March 2003 from the Permanent Representative of the United Kingdom of Great Britain and Northern Ireland to the United Nations Addressed to the President of the Security Council, UN Doc. S/2003/350

—— (2003d) *Report of the Secretary-General pursuant to paragraph 24 of Security Council resolution 1483 (2003)*, 17 July 2003. S/2003/715

—— (2004) Secretary-General's High-Level Panel on Threats, Challenges and Change, A More Secure World: Our Shared Responsibility

—— (2005a) In Larger Freedom: Towards Development, Security, and Human Rights for All, UN Doc. A/59/2005, 21 March 2005. Available at http://www.un.org/largerfreedom

—— (2005b) International Convention on the Suppression of Acts of Nuclear Terrorism, UN General Assembly Resolution 59/290, 13 Apr. 2005

—— (2005c) World Summit Outcome of the Heads of State and Government of the UN Member States, UN Doc. A/RES/60/1

—— (2007) Declaration on the Rights of Indigenous Peoples, New York: United Nations. Available at http://daccessdds.un.org/doc/UNDOC/LTD/N07/498/30/PDF/N0749830.pdf?OpenElement

United Nations Commission on Human Rights, Working Group on the Declaration on the Rights of Indigenous Peoples (2005) Report of the Working Group. New York: United Nations, E/CN.4/2005/89, 28 February 2005. Available at http://daccessdds.un.org/doc/UNDOC/GEN/G05/113/65/PDF/G0511365.pdf?OpenElement

UNCTAD (1996) The TRIPS Agreement and Developing Countries, Geneva: UNCTAD

United Nations Convention on the Law of the Sea (signed 10 December 1982, entered into force 16 November 1994) 1833 UNTS 396, 21 ILM 1245

United Nations Development Programme (2008a) *Human Development Reports*. Available at http://hdr.undp.org/

United Nations Development Programme (2008b) *Making Global Trade Work for People*, 2nd edn. London: Earthscan Publications. Available at http://www.boell.org/docs/UNDPTradeBook2003NEW.pdf

United Nations Diplomatic Conference of Plenipotentiaries on the Establishment of an International Criminal Court (1998) Final Act of the United Nations Diplomatic Conference of Plenipotentiaries on the Establishment of an International Criminal Court, Rome, Italy, 15 June–17 July 1998, A/CONF.183/10★. Available at http://daccessdds.un.org/doc/UNDOC/GEN/N98/241/85/PDF/N9824185.pdf?OpenElement

UNHCR (2001) Note on International Protection (13 September 2001). Available at http://www.unhcr.org/excom/EXCOM/3bb1c6cc4.pdf

—— (2002) Note on International Protection (11 September 2002). Available at http://www.unhcr.org/excom/EXCOM/3d8857cb7.pdf

—— (2005) A Thematic Compilation of Executive Committee Conclusions, 2nd edn, June 2005. Available at http://www.unhcr.org/protect/

United Nations International Conference on Human Rights (1968) UN Doc. A/CONF/32/41 at 3 (13 May 1968)

UN Security Council (1990) *Resolution 678*, 29 November 1990. Available at http://daccessdds.un.org/doc/RESOLUTION/GEN/NR0/575/28/IMG/NR057528.pdf?OpenElement

—— (1991a) *Resolution 686*, 2 March 1991. Available at http://daccessdds.un.org/doc/RESOLUTION/GEN/NR0/596/22/IMG/NR059622.pdf?OpenElement

—— (1991b) *Resolution 687*, 3 April 1991. Available at http://daccessdds.un.org/doc/RESOLUTION/GEN/NR0/596/23/IMG/NR059623.pdf?OpenElement

—— (1993a) Resolution 808 (1993), Adopted by the Security Council at its Sess. 3175th mtg, on 22 February 1993

—— (1993b) *Statute of the International Criminal Tribunal for the former Yugoslavia*, UN Doc. S/RES/827

—— (1994) *Statute of the International Criminal Tribunal for Rwanda*, UN Doc. S/RES/955

—— (2001a) United Nations Security Council Resolution 1368

—— (2001b) United Nations Security Council Resolution 1373, UN SCOR, 56th Sess., 4385th mtg., UN Doc. S/Res/1373

—— (2002) United Nations Security Council Resolution 1390, UN SCOR, 57th Sess., 4452d mtg., UN Doc. S/Res/4452

—— (2002a) *4644th Meeting*, 8 November 2002. S/PV.4644. Available at http://daccessdds.un.org/doc/UNDOC/PRO/N02/680/99/PDF/N0268099.pdf?OpenElement

—— (2002b) *Resolution 1441*, 8 November 2002. Available at http://daccessdds.un.org/doc/UNDOC/GEN/N02/682/26/PDF/N0268226.pdf?OpenElement

—— (2003a) *4701st Meeting*, 5 February 2003. S/PV.4701. Available at http://daccessdds.un.org/doc/UNDOC/PRO/N03/236/00/PDF/N0323600.pdf?OpenElement

—— (2003b) United Nations Security Council Resolution 1483, UN GAOR, 58th Sess., UN Doc. S/RES/1483

—— (2003c) United Nations Security Council Resolution 1511, UN SCOR, 58th Sess., 4844th mtg., at 3, UN Doc. SC/RES/1511

—— (2003d) *Letter Dated 8 May 2003 from the Permanent Representatives of the United Kingdom of Great Britain and Northern Ireland and the United States of America to the United Nations Addressed to the President of the Security Council*, 8 May 2003. S/2003/538. Available at http://documents-dds-ny.un.org/doc/UNDOC/GEN/N03/353/19/pdf/N0335319.pdf?OpenElement

—— (2004a) United Nations Security Council Resolution 1546, 8 June 2004, UN Doc. S/RES/1546

—— (2004b) United Nations Security Council Resolution 1540, UN SCOR, 59th Sess., 4956th mtg., UN Doc. S/1540 (2004)

—— (2007) United Nations Security Council, 62nd year: 5796th meeting, Monday, 10 December 2007, New York, S/PV.5796. Available at http://daccessdds.un.org/doc/UNDOC/PRO/N07/633/72/PDF/N0763372.pdf?OpenElement

United Nations War Crimes Commission (1948) *History of the United Nations War Crimes Commission and the Development of the Laws of War*. London: His Majesty's Stationery Office

United States (1787) *The Constitution of the United States of America*. Philadelphia, 14 May 1787. Available at http://www.gpoaccess.gov/constitution/index.html

—— (1996) Information Security: Computer Attacks at Department of Defense Pose Increasing Risks, Abstracts of GAO Reports and Testimony, GAO/T-AIMD-96-92 Available at http://www.gao.gov/archive/1996/ai96092t.pdf

—— (2002) *National Security Strategy of the United States of America*. Available at http://www.whitehouse.gov/nsc/nss.pdf

—— (2005) *The National Defense Strategy of the United States of America*. Available at http://www.defenselink.mil/news/Mar2005/d20050318nds2.pdf

—— (2006a) *National Space Policy*, 6 October 2006. Available at http://www.globalsecurity.org/space/library/policy/national/us-space-policy_060831.pdf

—— (2006b) *Military Commissions Act of 2006*, Pub. L. No. 109-366, 120 Stat. 2600

—— (2006c) *Department of Defense Appropriations Act of 2006* (incorporating Detainee Treatment Act of 2005). 10 USC 801

United States Department of State (2003) *Bush Has Legal Authority to Use Force in Iraq, Adviser Says*, 21 March 2003. Available at http://usinfo.state.gov/dhr/Archive/2003/Oct/09-215033.html

United States Federal Crime Code 18 USC Section 2331 (1)

United States Foreign Intelligence Surveillance Act (1978) 50 USC Sections 1801–1863

United States Protect America Act of 2007 (2007) Pub. No. 110-55, 121 Stat. 552

US Department of State (2007) *Briefing on Release of 2006 Country Reports on Terrorism*, 30 April 2007

Vienna Convention on the Law of Treaties (Vienna, 23 May 1969, entered into force 27 January 1980) 1155 United Nations, Treaty Series (UNTS) 331, 8 ILM 679

Warwick Commission, First Report (2007) The Multilateral Trade Regime: Which Way Forward?, Coventry: University of Warwick, December 2007. Available at http://www2.warwick.ac.uk/research/warwickcommission/report

World Commission on Environment and Development (WCED) (1987) *Our Common Future*. Oxford: Oxford University Press

World Commission on Environment and Development (WCED) (1987) Our Common Future, UN World Commission on Environment and Development Rep (4 August 1987) UN Doc. A/42/427

World Intellectual Property Organization (2007) *WIPO Patant Report: Statistics on Worldwide Patent Activities*. Available at http://www.wipo.int/export/sites/www/freepublications/en/patents/931/wipo_pub_931.pdf

World Summit (2005) World Summit Outcome Document (Follow-up to the Outcome of the Millennium Summit), UN Doc. A/60/L.1, 20 September 2005. Available at http://www.un.org/summit2005

Introduction

David Armstrong

This handbook represents an attempt to convey the extraordinarily exciting point that international law (IL) has reached today, both as an academic discipline and as a working system of law. In disciplinary terms, legal theorists have engaged with international relations (IR) and other academic fields to offer new, sophisticated ways of tackling – and going well beyond – old questions about the authentic "legality" or otherwise of international law and its essential nature, effectiveness, content and sources, the community it serves as well as its future potential. In so doing they have reinvestigated the history of international law, questioning, among other things, old certainties about its emergence as a by-product of European modernity, its emphasis on state sovereignty, its embodiment of a "standard of civilization" as determined by its European members, its relation to natural law and other moral, religious and ideological doctrines and the degree to which it helped to legitimate oppression of indigenous peoples and was complicit in other acts of imperial exploitation. As far as the practice of IL is concerned, the twenty-first century has already presented not only extensive and complex challenges that have sometimes seemed to indicate the fragility of IL but also responses to those challenges alongside other developments that seem to point to its robustness and indeed its growing significance. The seeming powerlessness of the law of force in the face of multifaceted assaults on it from various quarters coexists with far reaching extensions of the law of force since the end of the cold war. The same picture of an underlying vitality apparent in the constant dialectic of challenge and response can be seen in developments in the IL of the environment, trade, criminality, human rights and other areas, while its centrality to some of the key issues of the day is apparent in its role in serious international problems such as terrorism, refugees and the many difficult issues relating to international distributive justice.

None of this is to argue that one can point unreservedly to a picture of constant, unambiguous progress and academic consensus. It is perhaps appropriate in a subfield of law that any proposition is likely to be immediately countered by an equally forceful counter-proposition. The glass is half full for some, half empty for others. The United States has become the greatest threat to IL or its greatest hope. Violence is out of control, evidenced by death rates in Iraq, the Congo, Somalia and elsewhere or it is increasingly coming under law's remit, as evidenced by the first true UN collective security operation against Kuwait in 1991 and the various humanitarian interventions since then. Indeed, humanitarian interventions are a violation of the core international legal principles of sovereignty and non-intervention or they represent enormously important advances on that doctrine. Human rights are subject to more systematic and widespread abuses than ever before and are even threatened in their western homeland by anti-terror legislation or, with the International Criminal Court (ICC) and other developments, especially in the European Union, they are increasingly coming under international protection and are sustained by effective international institutions. Environmental law is unlikely to be able to overcome the self-interested short-termism of powerful national, sub-national and transnational lobbies or the increasingly strong scientific consensus about climate change is leading inevitably to an extensive and effective legal regime. The rules and disputes settlement system of the WTO represent a significant and more institutionalized advance on its General Agreement on Tariffs and Trade (GATT) predecessor or they merely reflect the interests of the powerful against the weak and are in any case imperilled by deep divisions between the EU and the USA or between the richest and poorest states. Even in the area of theoretical development there are deep divisions between positivist, critical, constructivist, postmodern and other theorists and also over the broader issue of whether IL gains from its interaction with IR and other disciplines or loses by diluting its claim to be a true form of law and hence to be assessed by the kinds of criteria that apply to law generally, namely the existence of rules that are set out in precise linguistic forms, that are administered and enforced through well-understood and universally applicable procedures by independent institutions specifically established for that purpose and by professionally trained individuals employing legal reasoning rather than moral arguments, with outcomes determined by purely legal, rather than political, moral or other considerations.

This discourse forms the context within which the handbook has been written. We have invited a group of leading academic writers, together with some of the younger "rising stars" of the profession to discuss important aspects of international law today: both disciplinary and practical. Perspectives from all five continents are represented here. While all authors were asked to set out the key issues involved in each subject area, they were also invited to range as freely as they wished over any facets they considered to be particularly significant or exciting. Although most of our contributors are international lawyers, several (including the editor) are IR specialists since (notwithstanding reservations a few of our contributors have expressed on other occasions) some of the more interesting intellectual speculation in recent years has sprung from IR–IL interaction. The handbook is broadly organized into four sections, as outlined next, although some topics have been addressed from very different perspectives by authors in two or more sections.

The first section, entitled "The nature of international law" investigates six crucial aspects of contemporary international law, with the aim of both providing readers with an up-to-date introduction to them and exploring some more cutting-edge facets. In their different ways, all six chapters illustrate the practical and intellectual linkages between IR and IL. This is most explicitly the case of Robert Beck's chapter on IL and IR scholarship, which offers the most comprehensive appraisal yet to have appeared anywhere of the interdisciplinary engagement between scholars in both fields of study. Interestingly, Beck's conclusions in his definitive study are to be found in some of the handbook's recurring themes: that interdisciplinary scholarship will pay increasing attention to the "vital roles of non-state actors and processes," that the relationship between domestic and international relations will incur "sustained, if not increased, interdisciplinary attention" and that interdisciplinary scholarship, like much of social science generally, is likely to remain separated into rational choice and sociological (especially social constructivist) camps.

The interdisciplinary engagement is also apparent in what, on the face of it, is the most obviously "legal" chapter in this section, Dinah Shelton's "Soft law," which emphasizes the limitations imposed by the political context within which states and other actors construct international law, while concluding that strong expectations of compliance with non-binding norms may still be possible. The "soft law" concept, which obviously relates closely to IR's "soft power," thus conceives of a structure of normative constraints on non-state as well as state actors that is not dependent on the coercive accoutrements that some require of "true law." Similarly, Tony Carty's chapter on "The practice of IL," in seeking to unravel what the core IL concept of custom and its requirement of *opinio juris* really mean, points to the need for the international lawyer "to understand state conduct and this means having reliable access to state intentions." This in turn requires "a framework of analysis of state activity that allows a legal analyst to engage in effective analysis of the conduct of states as actors in international society." He uses archival sources to consider specific case studies of British foreign policy but the larger implication of his argument is that, while it is eminently possible for lawyers to retain a perspective that remains distinctively "legal," we also need to develop ways of understanding state practice that take fuller account of how decision making actually works in a society of competing states pursuing their own interests.

The three remaining chapters also reflect the interplay between the two disciplines. Friedrich Kratochwil – the only IR professor in this section – argues that "while the self-description of law as the application of relevant norms to a case is susceptible to traditional 'jurisprudential' modes of reflection, the task of legal theory is wider as it brings into focus the background conditions that are not necessarily part of law but that are crucial for its acceptance and legitimacy." The theorist attempting to distinguish legal from non-legal norms, for instance, needs to understand various extra-legal and historically contingent factors and the impact of the many wide-ranging socioeconomic processes encapsulated in the term "globalization." Andreas Paulus addresses a key question for both IL and IR: is there such a thing as an international "community" and, if so, what do we mean by the term? On the one hand, references to the "emergence of a new global home, a worldwide village of human commonality emphasizing interpersonal bonds rather than territorial borders" have proliferated in the era of globalization. On the other, some have argued that the post-9/11 world has made the notion of globally shared values and a sense of community harder to sustain. He tackles this conundrum from three theoretical perspectives that are common to IR and IL: institutionalist, neoliberal and postmodernist as well as from the new concept of "global administrative law." The notion of an international community was first put forward by such early IL theorists as Suarez, Grotius, Wolff and Vattel and has become the central concept of the so-called "English school" of IR, so it is one of the clearest instances of the way in which the two disciplines intermesh. Anthony D'Amato's chapter, "International law as a unitary system," starting with the same difficulty about the *opinio juris* requirement also addressed by Carty, asserts "no one in the 4000-year history of international law has ever been able to determine, even once, whether any state was acting under the belief that its action was compulsory under international law." He goes on to suggest that international lawyers should draw on the political science concept of a "system" to develop an understanding of the context within which IL operates not just as a neutral background, but in effect as an active player taking "an active role in avoiding, reducing, or resolving conflicts" and promoting "international cooperation by fostering rules that maximize the interconnections among states." The notion of an international legal system (ILS) thus becomes the "long-awaited interdisciplinary bridge to political science."

Our second section, "Evolution of international law," considers from a historical perspective some of the interesting developments in IL from ancient times to today. The history of IL is a field that has attracted growing interest in recent years, as evidenced particularly by the appearance of the *Journal of the History of International Law* in 1999. This interest was not merely a reflection of the need for greater scholarship in a hitherto neglected area but also grew out of an increasing discontent in Asia, Latin America, Africa and elsewhere about what were seen as the Eurocentric and US-dominated study of IL generally. The assumption that international law does not really commence until sixteenth-century Europe has also been one of the reasons behind a neglect of ancient international law. Here the leading specialist on ancient international law, David Bederman, points to the "double blight" faced by students of ancient international law, namely the "perception that *all* law in ancient times was primitive. Ancient law was formalistic, dominated by fictions, had a limited range of legal norms, and was based solely on religious sanction" and also the belief that international law as such, is a "primitive legal order." He examines three fundamental areas of states' relations that appeared to be influenced by consistent rules or norms of international behavior, concluding "that there did exist in the ancient world a set of sources, processes and doctrines that constitute the beginnings of an international legal consciousness."

Edward Keene focuses on two related questions: the evolution of the underlying doctrines of IL from the sixteenth to the eighteenth centuries and the changes in legal training during the same period that filtered through into the practice of IL. These are both areas that have attracted increasing attention in recent years, with easy assumptions about how developments during this period mainly reflected the transition from late medieval Christendom to the Westphalian era of sovereign states now challenged by more complex and sophisticated analyses such as Keene's. Martti Koskenniemi takes us to the nineteenth century, where, drawing on some of his own recent work in this area, he presents a magisterial overview of the "vocabularies of legitimacy that accompanied the consolidation of the (European) states system." Using his famous distinction between IL as "apology" (searching for effectiveness by associating itself with state power) and "utopia" (trying to emphasize its autonomy from the policies and diplomacy of states with a view to grounding itself in universal moral and political values) he concludes that IL has severely weakened its capacity to act as "a platform over which the struggles for the distribution of the world's economic and spiritual resources are being waged." By way of contrast, Liliana Obregón points to the importance of sovereignty as a principle that helped to underwrite the international legal system that developed among the newly independent Latin American states in the nineteenth century. She shows how a distinctive Latin American international law (LAIL) emerged that drew on the experience of the "creole" elites both during and after Spanish rule. The transnational legal consciousness that underpinned this continued to be influential with attempts to articulate a regional IL in the twentieth century: albeit one that still reflected the outlook of the (male) elites.

Mashood Baderin's starting point in his study of the relation between religion and IL is that both are important social phenomena that relate to fundamental social issues. He then proceeds to consider their interaction from historical, theoretical, empirical and legal perspectives. He indicates how recent research has provided a much subtler and richer picture of the origins of IL than the Westphalian Euro- and Christian-centric analyses, especially with regard to Islam but also other religions such as Hinduism and Buddhism. Although IL became increasingly secular and positivist, the post-9/11 world was increasingly to reflect the divisions between secular and non-secular states. Theorists have responded to this and other challenges by elaborating "separationist," "accommodationist" and "double-edged" perspectives while in the world of legal practice he points to four main ways in which religion and law interact, concluding that, if IL is to go beyond a narrow positivism and instrumentalism, it cannot continue to ignore religion. Finally, Marc Weller, looking to the near future, disintegrative tendencies such as the fragmentation of the legal order and unilateralism by the USA notwithstanding, sees a move towards a universal constitutional system emerging from the need for genuinely global responses to global problems. Pointing to the increasing empowerment of nonstate actors, including international institutions, he goes so far as to speculate that the modern state system may actually be "melting away."

Section III, on law and power, confronts what many would see as the most crucial question facing contemporary IL: whether its foundational principle of sovereignty, taken to its logical conclusion, produces a world in which the most powerful states disregard IL whenever it does not suit them, which many see as having been characteristic of the post-9/11 American administration. Gerry Simpson looks at the interplay and debate between this perspective and two other viewpoints about the law of force and international order: an "absolutist" view that "seeks to approach war and peace through non-negotiable, universalizeable and unqualified moral truths" and a legal pacifism attempting to use law to abolish war. After presenting a brief historical account of the law of force, he analyzes in depth the legal complexities raised by the – theoretically uncontroversial – notion of self-defense and by the way in which the UN and NATO, following the success of the collective security operation of the first Iraq war, embarked on various "humanitarian interventions." Shirley Scott concentrates more directly on

the specifically American dimension of the question of law and power. Where many observers focus on what they see as an increasing American disregard for IL she offers a more nuanced view which does not seek to condemn *or* excuse the US but to try to understand apparent anomalies in US behavior and to highlight elements of both continuity and change in the US approach. Rejecting simplistic explanations of US actions in terms of its "unilateralism," she identifies recurring trends: the US use of IL to disseminate its policy preferences, its guarding against the use of IL to influence its own law and policy where important national interests are involved and the fact that – with certain provisos – it takes IL seriously.

Wayne Sandholtz examines the most controversial aspect of recent American (and British and other coalition partners') behavior: the Iraq war. In a careful and thoroughgoing analysis of all of the major legal arguments that this war has thrown up – whether certain UN Security Council resolutions gave it direct or implied authorization, whether it could be justified by other legal arguments such as self-defense or humanitarian intervention, whether the coalition observed IL relating to occupation and detainees – he concludes that, while the picture with regard to occupation contain some complexities, the various legal justifications of the war and the treatment of detainees are fundamentally flawed.

Beth Simmons and Allison Danner examine the International Criminal Court: another case where some have criticized US intransigence as evidence of its hostility towards international law. Although Russia, China, India, Pakistan and Israel have also refused to join, the US was seen as the most hostile inasmuch as it actively worked against the ICC in various ways until recently when it did not veto a referral of Darfur to the ICC by the UN Security Council. Simmons and Danner outline the history of the ICC's formation including the tussles between advocates and opponents of a much stronger regime. They point to some of its key weaknesses, especially its dependence on state cooperation and the fact that it has so far tended to focus on incidents in defeated and weak countries. They also refer to their earlier empirical research on reasons for ratification of the ICC. They see the Court – still in its infancy – as, various problems notwithstanding, a significant innovation in international law.

Our remaining contributions examine in much greater detail some of the key issues in IL. All of them are concerned, in different ways with what Allen Buchanan and Russell Powell term "robust international law": rules that do not simply concern themselves with IL's traditional remit of relations *between* states but which aspire to regulate matters *within* states. Buchanan and Powell's carefully structured argument in their "Fidelity to constitutional democracy and to the rule of international law" considers an assertion advanced by "new sovereigntists," especially in the US, namely that robust IL is incompatible with democracy. They suggest that this rests on implausible assumptions but accept that there are genuine problems relating to how much self-government a democratic people should relinquish to international institutions and the kinds of democratic process required when democracies accept such limitations. While arguing that American writers should pay more attention than they do to the EU experience, they reject the EU principle of subsidiarity, arguing instead for a process of authorization of the transfer of significant powers to external bodies that is clearly consonant with the core ideas of constitutional democracy.

The next two chapters are concerned with different aspects of international crime. William Schabas looks at the legal implications of attempts since 1945 to expand what is encompassed under the term "international crime." These have included arguments put before the UN's International Law Commission and elsewhere to add piracy, the slave trade, traffic in women and children, apartheid, colonialism, counterfeiting,

terrorism, injury to submarine cables, the use of nuclear weapons, environmental issues, hostage taking and economic aggression to the list of crimes against the "peace and security of mankind." Schabas outlines the legal consequences of increasing international criminalization and argues for the development of a theoretical construct that enables us more clearly to define international crimes and distinguish them from other kinds of offence. John Murphy's chapter on terrorism begins robustly with the assertion that the term "terrorism" is "imprecise, it is ambiguous, and it serves no operative legal purpose." But "the hard school of experience" shows that the term has constituted, and continues to constitute, a major barrier to efforts to combat the criminal acts often loosely described as "terrorism". He stresses that the more recent versions of Islamist terrorism have posed particular problems because their practitioners appear much less constrained than previous terrorist groups by the need not to lose popular support. He reviews the debate between those advocating a criminal law approach to terrorists and those emphasizing a military response, although he notes that there has been a greater convergence recently between these two perspectives. He concludes by looking at the various issues, both legal and operational, involved in the "war on terror."

The following five chapters address – albeit in very different ways – problems stemming in part from the marginalization or exclusion of some of those most affected by particular areas of RIL. For Amrita Narlikar, the WTO's diminished legitimacy compared with its predecessor, the GATT, suggests that the increased legalization that accompanied the creation of the WTO can "trigger processes of delegitimation if a legal system upholds rules that are perceived to be poorly negotiated." Her careful analysis identifies several distinct reasons for this, including perceptions of lack of transparency and unfairness by developing countries which the Doha Round – supposedly focusing on development issues – has tended to highlight rather than resolve. She argues that there is a need to ask fundamental questions about whether the WTO is truly fit for purpose and to engage in a process of rethinking and renegotiation with that in mind. Obiora Okafor presents a far reaching critical review of the international human rights discipline, in particular its *attainments*, but also the "*eclipses* that trouble it and the bouts of disciplinary *renewal* that it has experienced from time to time." He is especially concerned to identify deficiencies arising from the tendency to see western states as the sole originators of human rights as well as their chief practitioners, with Third World countries mainly regarded as part of the problem rather than solution. Like Narlikar, he calls for a wide-ranging cross-cultural dialogue with a view to engaging in a new process of renewal but he remains pessimistic about the prospects for the kind of "adequate and sustained *transformation*" that he seeks. Ikechi Mgbeoji adopts a similar starting point in his discussion of the "inability of contemporary African states to internalize some of the key doctrines of intellectual property rights (IPRs) regimes," which he attributes to the colonial roots of IPRs regimes in African states and the Eurocentric philosophies underpinning IPRs regimes. After briefly reviewing the history of patent law from its origins in medieval Italy, he develops a series of carefully argued points about the inappropriateness of IPRs regimes for contemporary Africa. For example, many biological resources such as varieties of rice and other plants are the result of incremental and collective inventiveness over many years in rural economies in Africa and elsewhere but cannot be accommodated by patent laws that cater for the individualistic assumptions of western capitalism. African states he sees as passive recipients of laws and norms, which in his view need reappraising to assess their relative costs and benefits.

Indigenous peoples were early victims both of colonialism and of attempts to rationalize their deprivation of rights through various international legal formulations. Karen Engle considers the way in which the right to culture has emerged in recent discourse as the primary legal and political strategy for making rights claims on behalf of indigenous peoples. She examines the different ways in which the right to culture has been invoked, many of which she sees as relying on "overly stereotyped and essentialized ideas of indigenous culture." While acknowledging the power of a rights package that, in its most radical form, combines heritage, land and economic development, she argues that there are also weaknesses arising from the tendency to use such claims as a defense mechanism, and she calls for greater reflexivity among activists.

Modern international refugee law commenced with the need to respond to mass population displacement in Europe at the end of the Second World War and the beginning of the cold war. The underlying perspectives of the post-war legal regime continued to prevail, including their emphasis on states and international governmental organizations. As Hélène Lambert argues here, this structure has long ceased to be appropriate to a world where most refugees come from developing countries involved in internal or interstate conflict. She calls for a focus on two emerging approaches: transnational and participatory, each of which originates in liberal theories of international law and stresses the need for greater involvement of refugees themselves and non-western countries in discussions based on deliberative democracy rather than competitive self-interest: in essence the same call for greater empowerment of victims that others in this section have also made.

The issue that, more than any other, encapsulates all the difficulties and opportunities raised in the handbook may be summarized by the term "sustainable development." The simplest definition of this is that it consists of "development that meets the needs of the present without compromising the ability of future generations to meet their own needs" – but inevitably this raises many more questions than it answers, especially in the context of the dilemmas posed by the growing concern with climate change. If global warming has been caused to a significant extent by the industrialization and consequent consumption patterns of the wealthy west, how can it be possible for the two billion peoples of the rapidly developing India and China to aspire to anything like those levels – let alone the rest of the Third World? But how, in fairness, can such prosperity be denied them? And how, in an anarchical international society of sovereign states can an effective and powerful legal regime be established to implement the changes necessary to prevent global catastrophe while also ensuring a more equitable distribution of the world's wealth?

Marie-Claire Cordonier Segger and Markus Gehring investigate two crucial aspects of these questions. Cordonier Segger analyzes the normative status of sustainable development. She considers the emergence of the concept from the 1960s and attempts to give it legal form. She uses ICJ cases and other evidence to argue that there are three broad views of the legal status of sustainable development: the first seeing it as a new customary principle, the second as a policy objective of treaties, the third as a kind of "meta-principle," exerting "a certain pull between conflicting international norms relating to environmental protection, social development and economic growth." Gehring looks at the key case of trade law, where advocates of free trade as an aspect of more general economic liberalization are involved in an ongoing debate with those arguing that unrestrained free trade has serious environmental consequences and those wishing to prioritize the needs of developing countries. He explores the issues that have emerged in the recent Doha development agenda of trade negotiations, as well as the way the concept of sustainable development was interpreted and applied in three specific WTO disputes.

Andrea Bianchi's concluding chapter looks at the challenges ahead for international law arising from the issues raised in this handbook. Many of these stem from what Bianchi refers to as the "inferiority complex"

many international lawyers feel vis-à-vis their domestic counterparts because of IL's lack of an effective system of enforcement of its rules. A more recent concern is whether the fragmentation of IL into distinct but separate regimes raises the related issue of whether there is a unitary system of IL: another requirement that some would have for "true law." As Bianchi points out, theoretical discourse has also become fragmented and while this has some strengths in terms of intellectual richness, it does not meet the need for an agreed theoretical response to such fundamental uncertainties about IL.

While the contributions to the handbook represent several distinct perspectives on such issues, it is, nonetheless, possible to draw from them at least the basis of a coherent intellectual framework to inform future research and perhaps form the foundation of future theoretical development. Four key aspects of such a framework may be identified:

1   The *nature of the international community*. The aphorism *ubi societas ibi lex* is the most appropriate starting point. The state is simply one form of society or community, one characterized by a central authority possessing the means to enforce compliance with its rules. But any social interaction requires rules and the more complex the interaction the more sophisticated the system of rules must be. The international community – which contains many non-state as well as state actors, as several of our contributors have pointed out – may, literally, be an anarchy in one sense of the word by virtue of its absence of government but it has never been an anarchy in the other sense of the word: chaos. Like any community it is rule bound – increasingly so as its interaction becomes more complex.

2   The *relationship between laws and norms*. Laws derive ultimately from a prevailing normative consensus in the society to which they apply. As has been very

apparent in all of the contributions to the handbook, international society has an increasingly powerful normative basis that goes well beyond the traditional norms of sovereignty and non-intervention that lie at the root of much earlier IL. Some would see in this process the building blocks of an emerging constitutional order but even without some such state-like structure emerging, it is possible to conceive of many other ways in which international norms can become institutionalized into well-understood and accepted legal regimes.

3 *Effectiveness*. A coercive enforcement structure is not an absolute essential for a legal regime to be effective. Indeed, even in societies where a regime has the power to enforce its will, true effectiveness may depend as much on acceptance by the members of the society of the legitimacy and value of the laws in question. There are also many sanctions – such as incurring shame, dishonor or a reputation as dishonest or unreliable – that may be brought to bear against lawbreakers apart from punishments imposed by courts of law.

4 *Participation*. Effectiveness of this broader social kind also depends on the degree to which those to whom the rules apply feel a sense of ownership of and involvement in the processes of rule creation and implementation. As several contributors have pointed out, this is a major problem with many key areas of IL that can best be met by developing new and far reaching forms of dialogue embracing many actors, state and non-state, rich and poor.

Section I

The nature of international law

International law and international relations scholarship

Robert J. Beck

This chapter addresses four crucial and related questions. First, how far have the disciplines of international law (IL) and international relations (IR) progressed along the path of cooperation charted nearly two decades ago by such celebrated scholars as Kenneth Abbott and Anne-Marie Slaughter? Second, what theoretical approaches from IL and IR have been most effectively exploited by interdisciplinarians? Third, what substantive questions seem to have been most productively addressed in an interdisciplinary context? Finally, what lies ahead for IL/IR interdisciplinarity?

To help answer these questions, the chapter briefly highlights major developments in the interdisciplinary literature, identifying key books, edited volumes, articles, and special issues of journals. In addition, it reviews how scholars of IL and IR have themselves characterized the current state of affairs. It also offers important insights into the nature and challenges of the interdisciplinary enterprise.

Perhaps not coincidentally, with the end of the cold war came increasing calls by scholars for collaboration between the disciplines of international law (IL) and international relations (IR).[1] "Law" should once again be taken seriously by political scientists, it was contended, while political science methods might effectively be employed by lawyers. In his seminal 1989 essay,[2] for example,

Kenneth Abbott argued that the "analytical approaches, insights and techniques of modern IR theory" presented an "opportunity to integrate IL and IR" (1989: 340). Four years later, Anne-Marie Slaughter averred in an award-winning essay:[3] "Just as constitutional lawyers study political theory, and political theorists inquire into the nature and substance of constitutions, so too should disciplines that study the laws of state behavior [IL and IR] seek to learn from one another" (Slaughter Burley 1993: 205). But just how far have the two disciplines progressed along the path of cooperation charted nearly two decades ago[4] by these celebrated scholars? What theoretical approaches from IL and IR have been most effectively exploited by interdisciplinarians? What substantive questions seem to have been most productively addressed in an interdisciplinary context? And what lies ahead for IL/IR interdisciplinarity? This chapter will address these four crucial and related questions in turn.[5]

Before proceeding, however, five preliminary observations may be offered. A 1996 essay posited that the borders between the disciplines of international law and international relations were not readily demarcatable and therefore contestable (Beck 1996: 4). This characterization remains accurate today.

It should be added, however, that the discipline with which a given *scholar* may be associated is also contestable, or at least, not always self-evident.[6] For how does one decide who constitutes an "international relations" or an "international law" scholar? By the highest academic degree that the scholar has earned? This approach works reasonably well except for scholars such as Craig Barker, Michael Byers, Christine Chinkin, Robyn Eckersley, Vaughan Lowe, Kal Raustiala, Anne-Marie Slaughter, Chandra Lekha Sriram, Richard Steinberg, Stephen Toope, and Edith Brown Weiss, who hold law degrees[7] *and* doctoral degrees in international relations. Or for those including Charlotte Ku[8] who have received their degrees from policy-oriented graduate institutions such as Tufts University's Fletcher School or Princeton's Woodrow Wilson School where "law" figures in the curriculum but which have not historically granted law degrees.[9] Alternatively, should one simply use the scholar's current academic home as the indicator of disciplinary affiliation? This approach, too, works reasonably well when a scholar serves exclusively in a "political science" department or "school of law." But some scholars, including Kenneth Abbott, Anthony Clark Arend, Kathryn Sikkink, and Richard Steinberg hold joint appointments. And how does one characterize scholars serving in policy-oriented graduate institutions like the Woodrow Wilson School? To be sure, the *quality* of interdisciplinary scholarship – and not its authors' labels – should be our ultimate concern. Even so, for any accurate assessment of the nature, current status, and trajectory of IL/IR interdisciplinary efforts, the disciplinary affiliations of authors should be characterized with as much precision as possible. Moreover, it is instructive to note – although, on reflection, perhaps to be expected – that some of the most well-regarded interdisciplinary scholars hold multiple advanced degrees and/or serve in multiple departments or in practice-oriented professional schools, thereby eluding straightforward disciplinary identification.[10]

Just as scholars' disciplinary affiliations may be contested, so too one may debate what constitutes genuine "*interdisciplinary*" scholarship. In a 2005 essay, for example, Jan Klabbers questioned whether the work of Martti Koskenniemi, David Kennedy, Gerry Simpson and others writing in the "counter-hegemonic" tradition represented "interdisciplinary" or simply international "legal" scholarship. "Why this need to somehow elevate their work beyond the legal? Why this urge to have it represent something else than good legal work?" asked Klabbers (2005: 47). Ultimately, to label another's scholarship – whether as "interdisciplinary," as representative of the IR or IL discipline, or in some other fashion – is to some extent intellectually presumptuous. Accordingly, the identification of works here as "interdisciplinary" is based primarily on their authors' *own* characterizations. Where scholars have not personally described their works as "interdisciplinary," any judgment of a given work's interdisciplinary character must inevitably be only provisional.

One should also appreciate that the scholarly division in the cold war period between IR and IL was probably never as stark as was sometimes portrayed then and thereafter. At least some international relations scholars continued to take "law" seriously,[11] while some international lawyers – perhaps most famously, Louis Henkin[12] – called for dialogue with political scientists. Moreover, within the "English school" of IR,[13] there was arguably never an estrangement between IR and IL, the school's scholars "embrac[ing] the role of law, rules and norms in international society, often proclaiming themselves to be working in a 'Grotian tradition'."[14] Furthermore, the IL/IR divide was, generally speaking, less pronounced in the United Kingdom than it was in the United States,[15] and, arguably, remains so today.[16]

In any discussion of scholarly collaboration across the "two cultures" of IL and IR (Beck

1996: 17–19; Keohane 1997), one must also continue to bear in mind the crucial importance of language. Although many examples can certainly be adduced, perhaps nowhere is the difference between the two discourse communities better evinced than in their strikingly different understandings of the word "theory."[17] For IR scholars, at least those working in the positivist tradition, a "theory" explains or predicts; for IL scholars, by contrast, a "theory" can connote a social science theory per se, a scholarly "approach" like the New Haven school that is not strictly predictive,[18] or even merely a novel legal argument.[19]

The majority of work on interdisciplinarity is written, naturally, from an advocacy standpoint. This scholarly inclination should not obscure our appreciation, however, that for all its manifold virtues, interdisciplinarity should not be viewed as an end in itself, or as inherently preferable to work conducted within a single discipline per se. High-quality interdisciplinary work requires that the scholar know well the literature, language, tools, and methods of the scholar's own *and* another discipline: an impressive background and skill set with which not all researchers are adequately endowed. Furthermore, there remains a danger that interdisciplinarity may be embraced merely as a fad or as an attempt to gain the respect of one's peers. David Bederman has decried, for example, the "aggressive tendency" on the part of his fellow international lawyers "to borrow things from other disciplines and to apply them to their own work . . . part of a larger phenomenon in legal academe to boost the legitimacy and self-esteem of law professors in academic settings by constantly and courageously asserting their interdisciplinary credentials."[20] For Bederman, there is "a profound danger that unbridled interdisciplinarity will result in law losing any status it might aspire to as neutral and objective, autonomous, and scientific."[21] While Bederman may be unduly pessimistic,[22] his admonition is nevertheless worthy of international lawyers' attention. IR scholars, too,

might reflect at least briefly on the potential effects of interdisciplinarity on their own discipline's standing and distinctive character.[23]

Progress?

How far have interdisciplinary efforts advanced in the years since the first calls for collaboration by Professors Abbott and Slaughter? What theoretical approaches from IL and IR have been profitably employed by interdisciplinarians? To help answer these questions, this chapter will take two approaches. First, it will briefly highlight major developments in the interdisciplinary literature, identifying key books, edited volumes, articles, and special issues of journals. Next, it will review how scholars of IL and IR have themselves characterized the current state of affairs.

Major works

Perhaps the first comprehensive interdisciplinary edited volume, *International Rules*, was published by Oxford University Press in 1996 (Beck, Arend, and Vander Lugt 1996). *Rules* was arguably most distinctive for its inclusion of full-length archetypal works of IL and IR: from Hugo Grotius to David Kennedy of IL,[24] from George Kennan to Robert Keohane of IR.[25] Robert Beck's introductory chapter proposed a novel two-by-two matrix (empiricist/critical; explanatory/prescriptive) for classification of the disciplines' various approaches and assessed the prospects for interdisciplinary collaboration (Beck 1996). Anthony Clark Arend's concluding chapter, on which he would subsequently build, sought to "formulate an analytical approach to international legal rules" (Arend 1996: 290).

In 1998 Anne-Marie Slaughter, Andrew Tulumello, and Stepan Wood published "International law and international relations theory: a new generation of interdisciplinary scholarship" in the *American Journal of*

International Law. After reviewing recent use of IR theory by international law scholars and vice versa, the essay "explore[d] how IR and IL scholars might collaborate most profitably in the future," suggesting a "collaborative research program" and then offering an extensive bibliography of nearly 100 works (1998: 383, 385, 393–7). Slaughter and her collaborators submitted that international lawyers had been able to contribute to IR theory by analyses of the legal process as a causal mechanism, by demonstrating how legal norms "constructed" the international conceptual system, and by highlighting the effects of transnational and domestic law. The "joint discipline" they proposed would study the design of international processes and regimes, analyze law's constructive effects, describe transformations of structure, and investigate state disaggregation and the embeddedness in domestic societies of international institutions (369).

Also in 1998, Arend published the subsequently much cited "Do legal rules matter?" in the *Virginia Journal of International Law,* extending that analysis in his *Legal Rules and International Society* (Arend 1999).[26] Arend's 1999 book was hailed as "the fullest attempt made at interdisciplinary communication between international law doctrine and international relations theory in some time" (Bederman 2001a: 498) and as a "landmark of constructivist political thought" (Schoenbaum 2006: 94). The book addressed four questions: How are international legal rules distinctive? How does one know when an international legal rule exists? Does international law really matter? And what effect could international politics' changing nature exert on international law? Perhaps the two most significant contributions of Arend's work were his most elaborate articulation thus far[27] of an "authority control test" for determining the existence of an international legal rule (1999: 67–110) and his use of "constructivist" theory to explain international law's effect on state identity and behavior (124–48).

Another 1999 work of self-conscious interdisciplinarity was Michael Byers' *Custom, Power, and the Power of Rules.*[28] Here, Byers submitted that the "*process*" of customary international law was a "power-transforming, and thus power-qualifying, *institution*" (1999: 33, emphasis added). Sharing with Arend's *Legal Rules* an interest in *opinio juris,* the work sought to analyze "the effects that four principles of international law [jurisdiction, personality, reciprocity, and legitimate expectation] have had on applications of power by states as those states have sought to develop, maintain and change a variety of different customary rules" (1999: 50). Byers' treatment of "legitimate expectation" was arguably a "cornerstone principle" for his understanding of the international legal system, one reminiscent of Kelsen's analysis of international law's *Grundnorm* (Barker 2000: 87). Although *Custom* has been criticized for failing systematically to test alternative explanations and for selecting cases that lacked substantial variation, the work has nevertheless been hailed for providing "a laudable example of the synergies and challenges of conducting research across the disciplinary divide."[29]

The year 1999 also saw the publication of a special issue in the *American Journal of International Law:* "Symposium on method in international law." The issue featured some of the most prominent IL scholars whose work drew on or spoke to questions of IR theory, including Kenneth Abbott, Hilary Charlesworth, Jeffrey Dunoff, Martti Koskenniemi, Mary Ellen O'Connell, Steven Ratner, Anne-Marie Slaughter, and Joel Trachtman.[30] The volume's focus was on *practical* theories relevant "for lawyers and legal scholars facing contemporary issues," not "abstract" ones "that explain[ed] the nature of international law" (Ratner and Slaughter 1999: 292). The symposium sought to appraise seven "methods": legal positivism, the New Haven school, international legal process, critical legal studies, international law and international relations, feminist jurisprudence, and law and economics.[31] Perhaps somewhat strangely for IR readers, "international law and international relations" was treated in this *AJIL* issue as a single "method."[32] All contributors to the volume approached the same contemporary issue, "the question of individual accountability for violations of human dignity committed in internal conflict" (Ratner and Slaughter 1999: 294), addressing explicitly or implicitly the same core questions.[33] Most interesting of the issue's collection of essays for interdisciplinarians was probably Kenneth Abbott's essay, "International relations theory, international law, and the regime governing atrocities in internal conflicts." Here, after emphasizing that IR comprised "several distinct theoretical approaches or 'methods'," Abbott applied each approach – realist, institutionalist, liberal and constructivist – to the "norms and institutions governing serious violations of human dignity during internal conflicts (the 'atrocities regime')" (Abbott K. 1999: 361).

If the 1999 *AJIL* symposium issue featured a veritable "who's who" of interdisciplinary-minded international lawyers, the 2000 issue of *International Organization* on "Legalization and world politics" returned the favor for IR scholars, featuring (in addition to Anne-Marie Slaughter and Kenneth W. Abbott) such luminaries as: Judith Goldstein, Miles Kahler, Robert O. Keohane, Lisa L. Martin, Andrew Moravcsik, Kathryn Sikkink, Beth A. Simmons, and Duncan Snidal.[34] This issue of one of IR's pre-eminent journals offered sections on legalization and world politics,[35] legalization and dispute resolution,[36] law and economic integration,[37] legalization in three issue areas (international monetary affairs,[38] trade,[39] and international human rights law),[40] and concluding remarks.[41] The *IO* special issue defined "legalization" as a "particular form of institutionalization," representing "the decision in different issue areas to impose international legal constraints on governments" (Goldstein, Kahler, Keohane, and Slaughter 2000: 386). "Legalization" was

further characterized as varying across three dimensions: "the degree to which rules are *obligatory*, the *precision* of those rules, and the *delegation* of some functions of interpretation, monitoring, and implementing to a third party" (Goldstein, et al. 2000: 387, emphasis added). IL scholars had described and categorized "this 'move to law,'" the volume's editors contended, but had largely failed to evaluate or challenge it" (Goldstein, et al. 2000: 388). Cynical IL scholars, by way of contrast, might have been tempted to view the 2000 *IO* issues as merely IR's rediscovery of "law" per se or as a slightly revised take on institutionalism. To be sure, as a "collaborative investigation by neoliberal international relations scholars and like-minded international legal theorists" (Reus-Smit 2004b: 11), the volume was criticized by some for its formalistic rationalism.[42]

The second especially noteworthy work of interdisciplinarity published in 2000 was *The Role of Law in International Politics*, a volume edited by Michael Byers. The result of the British Branch of the International Law Association's 1998 conference at Oxford, *Role of Law* evinced the "maturity of academic thinking" that had developed on the volume's subject, providing also a "rare window" into the "self-perception of international lawyers" (Byers 2000: 2–3). Especially notable was the book's inclusion of scholars from Canada, Finland, France, Germany, Israel, and Switzerland, in addition to those from Britain and the United States.[43] Indeed, the volume and the conference that preceded it constituted a challenge to the assertion of Martti Koskenniemi, one of the volume's own contributors, that "academic calls to integrate international law and international relations theory" were "an American crusade."[44] Drawing critical attention to IR's "overwhelmingly rationalist style of analysis" (Hurrell 2000: 329), Byers' volume added "new voices and ideas to an already lively discussion" (Byers 2000: 3). Three especially insightful essays featured in this excellent collection – all of which represented work

17

outside the traditional rationalist idiom – were: "How do norms matter?" (Kratochwil 2000), "Emerging patterns of governance and international law" (Toope 2000), and "Carl Schmitt, Hans Morgenthau, and the image of law in international relations" (Koskenniemi 2000).[45]

Interdisciplinary scholar[46] J. Craig Barker published *International Law and International Relations* in 2000. Barker's introductory text was arguably the first work suitable for undergraduates that squarely, and at some length, addressed interdisciplinarity matters, taking into account the scholarship of the 1990s.[47] Of special note was Chapter 3, "International relations perspectives on international law," which reviewed the recent work of Michael Byers (85–9), "transnational legal process" scholar Harold Hongju Koh[48] (89–92), and Anthony Clark Arend (92–4).

In 2003 Michael Byers and Georg Nolte published their co-edited *United States Hegemony and the Foundations of International Law*, a collection of essays by international law[49] and international relations scholars[50] deliberately drawn from "a range of cultural, linguistic, and academic backgrounds" (xv). The volume was informed by a succession of workshop and conference meetings in 2001 at Duke University and the University of Göttingen. With an introduction by Byers and conclusion by Nolte, the explicitly interdisciplinary collection featured six substantive sections on international community (Kwakwa 2003; Paulus 2003), sovereign equality (Cosnard 2003; Krisch 2003), the use of force (Kohen 2003; Roth 2003), customary international law (Skordas 2003; Toope 2003), the law of treaties (Klein 2003; Redgwell 2003), and compliance (Scott 2003; Stoll 2003), with associated commentaries offered by highly distinguished scholars. Exploring whether, and how, current U.S. predominance might be leading to "foundational change" in the international legal system, the work substantiated American hegemonic influence, characterizing it as

intensely complex. IL and IR contributors portrayed hegemony as constrained by the international legal system and variably influenced by an array of actors.

One indicator of scholarly trajectory has been the emergence of new journals. In 2004 the *Journal of International Law and International Relations* was introduced.[51] Administered by students from the Faculty of Law and the Munk Centre for International Studies at the University of Toronto, the journal features in its advisory board a lengthy list of "A list" interdisciplinarians.[52] Over time, the *JILIR* may establish itself as a prominent venue for interdisciplinary scholarship.[53] Nevertheless, it will almost inevitably confront the general reluctance by IR scholars to submit their work to student-edited publications (Beck 1996: 18).

Further compelling evidence that IL/IR interdisciplinarity was not solely an *American* project, or solely a *rationalist* project,[54] was offered by the *Politics of International Law*, a 2004 volume published in the Cambridge Series in International Relations and edited by Christian Reus-Smit.[55] Inspired by a small research workshop in November 2000 organized at the Australian National University by Reus-Smit and Paul Keal, the volume advanced a new constructivist perspective on the politics of international law.[56] It reconceived "politics" as "interstitial," a field of human action standing at the intersection of issues of identity, purpose, ethics, and strategy. It defined "law" as a "historically contingent institutional practice and process," characterizing the relationship between politics and law as "reciprocally implicated" (Reus-Smit 2004c: 290). The work featured case studies by both IR[57] and IL[58] scholars on the use of force (Kritsiotis 2004), climate change (Eckersley 2004), landmines (Price 2004), migrant rights (Gurowitz 2004), the International Criminal Court (Wippman 2004), the Kosovo bombing campaign (Wheeler 2004), international financial institutions (Anghie 2004), and global governance (Sandholtz and Sweet 2004).

A second noteworthy 2004 volume was edited by Israel-based professors Eyal Benvenisti and Moshe Hirsch, *The Impact of International Law on International Cooperation: Theoretical Perspectives.*[59] A compilation of papers presented at a June 2001 conference convened at the Hebrew University of Jerusalem Faculty of Law,[60] the volume included works by prominent IR[61] and IL[62] scholars from schools in the United States and Israel, including interdisciplinarians Kenneth Abbott and Anne-Marie Slaughter. *Impact* sought to enhance understandings of the influences of norms and international institutions on states' incentives to cooperate on such issues as trade and the environment. The volume's contributions adopted two different approaches. One focused on "the constitutive elements of the international legal order, including customary international law, soft law, and framework conventions" (Benvenisti and Hirsch 2004b: 1) and on other state incentives. The second approach closely examined the international trade and environmental protection areas.

Attracting significant attention in 2005 was *The Limits of International Law* by Jack L. Goldsmith and Eric A. Posner.[63] A rationalist, statist account of law, this "rational choice" work[64] evinced a relatively strong skepticism about international law's efficacy. In their integration and extension of a succession of seven prior law review articles,[65] the authors advanced an "instrumentalist" argument reminiscent of realist IR thinking: rational states pursue their own interests, with legal rhetoric often masking the underlying motives of states and their leaders.[66] Goldsmith and Posner parted company somewhat with realists, however, refusing to make "strong assumptions about the content of state interests" and assuming that such interests "could vary by context" (2005: 6). While conceding that international law was "a real phenomenon," Goldsmith and Posner nevertheless submitted that international law scholars had "exaggerated its power and significance" and that there were

"limits to what treaties can achieve" (225). Rejecting the arguments, respectively, of Harold Koh,[67] Louis Henkin,[68] and Thomas Franck,[69] Goldsmith and Posner concluded that "the best explanation for when and why states comply with international law is not that states have internalized international law, or have a habit of complying with it, or are drawn by its moral pull, but simply that states act out of self-interest" (225). Controversial to some would be Goldsmith and Posner's flexible conception of state "interest" and their a priori rejection of international legal compliance as a state preference in interest calculations (2005: 9).

In 2005, Yale Law School's Oona Anne Hathaway and Harold Koh published *Foundations of International Law and Politics.* Featuring excerpts from much of the most prominent classic and more recent scholarship,[70] with supplemental "Notes" and "Comments" sections, the compilation seems likely to become a standard text for law school courses addressing the politics of international law. The editors sought to "lay out several of the most central and current theoretical approaches found in international law and international relations scholarship, with an eye toward creating a common framework upon which both sets of scholars can build" and to "offer a series of practical applications to spark discussion and debate" (2005: iii). The book's first seven sections presented "interest-based" approaches (realism, institutionalism, liberal theory) and "norms-based" ones (constructivism, fairness/legitimacy, legal process); the final six highlighted applications of the theories (human rights, the environment, trade, humanitarian intervention, international criminal law, and war).

International Law and International Relations by Beth A. Simmons and Richard A. Steinberg was published in 2006. This work – edited, respectively, by a Harvard Professor of Government and a UCLA professor of law – featured what essentially constituted a "greatest hits" collection of 26 excerpted articles on regimes, institutions, norms, and law from the venerable international relations journal, *International Organization*. The work included dedicated sections on international regimes theory (Keohane 1982; Krasner 1982), commitment and compliance (Chayes and Chayes 1993; Downs, Rocke, and Barsoom 1996; Gaubatz 1996), legalization and its limits,[71] international law and international norms (Jackson 1987; Legro 1997; Zacher 2001), treaty design and dynamics (Diehl, Ku, and Zamora 2003; Koremenos 2001; Lipson 1991; Smith 2000; Wendt 2001), law and legal institutions (Garrett, Kelemen, and Schultz 1998; Slaughter Burley and Mattli 1993), and other substantive areas of international law: security,[72] trade,[73] money,[74] war crimes,[75] human rights,[76] the environment,[77] and intellectual property.[78] If Hathaway and Koh's seems likely to become a standard text for law schools, so Simmons and Steinberg's seems likely for graduate programs in IR.

A second IL/IR Cambridge University Press publication from 2006 was Thomas J. Schoenbaum's *International Relations – The Path Not Taken: Using International Law to Promote World Peace and Security*.[79] Arguing that "international law and international institutions must be the focal points of foreign policy" (vii), Schoenbaum sought to move U.S. policymakers away from unilateralism and toward a reassertion of constructive leadership in the international legal and institutional realms (xiv, 33, 276). *The Path Not Taken* reviewed and modestly engaged the theoretical literatures of the international law and the contemporary international relations (IR) disciplines: realism, neorealism, game theory, functionalism, neofunctionalism, complex interdependence, regime theory, constructivism, and the English school (46–9, 56–9). It did not, however, offer a sustained, self-consciously "theoretical" argument, in the strictest social scientific sense of the term.[80]

Published in 2007 was *International Law and International Relations: Bridging Theory and Practice*. Edited by Thomas J. Biersteker, Peter J. Spiro, Chandra Lekha Sriram, and Veronica Raffo, this excellent volume was inspired by a series of four Social Science Research Council-sponsored workshops in 2002 and 2003 of IL scholars,[81] IR scholars,[82] and practitioners.[83] The work focused on four clusters of policy challenges: small arms and light weapons (Koh 2007; Muggah 2007; Reno 2007), terrorism (Adamson 2007; O'Connell 2007; Simpson and Wheeler 2007; Ward 2007), internally displaced persons (Abbott 2007; Deng 2007), and international criminal accountability (Lutz 2007b; Morris 2007; Orentlicher 2007; Sadat 2007; Sriram and Mahmoud 2007). Offering four broad, synthetic essays on the IL/IR relationship (Dias 2007; Finnemore 2007; Raffo, Sriram, Spiro and Biersteker 2007; Spiro 2007), the collection was especially notable in its concern for international "practice," and its juxtaposition of theoretical and practice-oriented essays.

How have scholars of IL and IR characterized the current state of affairs?

The self-consciously interdisciplinary scholarship of the past decade or so has thus far generated *at least*: four prominent monographs (Arend 1999; Byers 1999; Goldsmith and Posner 2005; Schoenbaum 2006); five edited collections of scholarly conference papers (Benvenisti and Hirsch 2004a; Biersteker, Spiro, Sriram, and Raffo 2007; Byers 2000; Byers and Nolte 2003; Reus-Smit 2004a); three compendium volumes (Beck, Arend, and Vander Lugt 1996; Hathaway and Koh 2005; Simmons and Steinberg 2006); one undergraduate textbook (Barker 2000); one special symposium issue of the *American Journal of International Law* (1999); one special issue of *International Organization* (2000); scores of journal articles,[84] and one new dedicated interdisciplinary journal (*Journal of International Law and International Relations*). Over 100 scholars and practitioners based in at least 10 different countries have been engaged in this interdisciplinary enterprise. But how have the interdisciplinarians viewed the statuses of the IL and IR disciplines? And how have they characterized the interrelationship between the two disciplines? Given the number and variety of scholars engaged in IL/IR dialogue, it is perhaps not surprising that opinions have differed, sometimes markedly, on these important questions.

In his provocative 2005 essay, "The relative autonomy of international law or the forgotten politics of interdisciplinarity," published in the inaugural edition of the *Journal of International Law and International Relations*, Jan Klabbers "deliberately refrain[ed] from using the capitals IR, if only to prevent the unwarranted reification" of what he contended was "in reality, a rather incoherent, heterogenous body of scholarship" (Klabbers 2005: 36). Indeed, Klabbers submitted that "international relations, as a discipline, does not exist and cannot exist, and . . . its most enlightened practitioners are fully aware of this (without of course, understandably, telling anyone)" (2005: 42). While this particular conclusion was surely controversial, Klabbers' general line of argument nevertheless illuminated a crucial point: Like that of IL, the scholarship of "international relations" (capitalized or otherwise) encompasses a broad spectrum of scholarly approaches, the dividing lines between which may often become obscured (Beck 1996: 4). Furthermore, "scholars from both IR and IL either may personally reject efforts to categorize them by approach or may effectively elude such categorization because of the unique natures of their works. To be sure, whenever labels are used, the danger exists that they will obscure more than they illuminate."[85] Moreover, as Clarence Dias has noted, "though we talk of IR and IL as being 'fields,' there are many actors involved in each, and no one set of actors can lay claim to being the sole/authoritative spokesperson for their field" (Dias 2007: 279).

Most interdisciplinarians have supported the notion that IR and IL do in fact constitute authentic disciplines, however much the literature within each of those two disciplines may be heterogeneous or challenging to characterize. Even so, they have agreed far less on the actual *relationship* between the disci-

plines. Some have described the relationship as inevitably intimate, with IR and IL linked "inextricably" (Barker 2000) or "inexorably" (Benvenisti and Hirsch 2004a: 1). Others have suggested that scholarly collaboration may have fostered the emergence of a "joint discipline."[86] Still others, meanwhile, have noted the general ascendance of IL,[87] with some like Peter Spiro having seen international law as elevating in status relative to international relations: "IR and IL are on intersecting rather than parallel trajectories: IR on the decline, IL on the rise."[88]

Whether or not they have accepted the characterization of IR and IL as bona fide disciplines, some scholars have found the *interdisciplinary enterprise in some way troubled* or problematic. In 2001, for example, David Bederman compared international law and international relations to "bickering spouses in a paradigmatic dysfunctional family" (Bederman 2001a: 469). Jan Klabbers subsequently dubbed the "call for interdisciplinarity . . . curious" and one-sided (Klabbers 2005: 44). In his "Introduction" to *The Politics of International Law*, moreover, Christian Reus-Smit criticized typical interdisciplinary efforts as insufficiently ambitious, failing generally to question basic assumptions: "[F]ew of these bridge-building exercises start by critically reconsidering the foundational concepts on which these bridges will be constructed" (Reus-Smit 2004b: 2). Perhaps the harshest criticism of appeals for IL/IR collaboration was leveled by Martti Koskiennemi in his 2000 essay, "Carl Schmitt, Hans Morgenthau, and the image of law in international relations." For Koskenniemi, the call to collaborate constituted an "American crusade . . . an academic project that [could not] but buttress the justification of American hegemony in the world" (Koskenniemi 2000: 29–30). Certainly, scholars from the United States have played very prominent roles in the post-cold war interdisciplinarity enterprise. Notably, however, researchers from Australia, Belgium, Canada, Finland, France,

Germany, Israel, Switzerland, and the United Kingdom have also proven regular and enthusiastic participants.[89]

Trends in scholarship?

Self-consciously interdisciplinary scholars have focused their attentions on a full range of substantive issue areas. Notable works[90] since *AJIL*'s 1998 publication of the comprehensive bibliography by Slaughter, et al. include those on: the *environment, global resources, and science* (Benvenisti 2000; Eckersley 2004; Raustiala and Victor 2004; Toope 2000); *the global economy*, including financial and monetary matters (Anghie 2004; Kwakwa 2000; Simmons 2000; Slaughter 2000a); *human rights and international humanitarian law* (Abbott K. 1999; Chinkin 2000; Dunoff and Trachtman 1999; Goldsmith and Posner 2005; Koh 1999; Lutz and Sikkink 2000; Moravcsik 2000; Morris 2007; Mutua 2000; Price 2004; Redgwell 2003; Simma and Paulus 1999); *trade and development* (F. Abbott 2000; Downs and Jones 2004; Goldsmith and Posner 2005; Goldstein and Martin 2000; Howse 2004; Mavroidis 2004; Milner, Rosendorff, and Mansfield 2004; J.M. Smith 2000; Steinberg 2002); *security*, including terrorism, small arms, post-atrocity justice, and the U.N. Security Council (Adamson 2007; Gowlland-Debbas 2000; Koh 2007; Kohen 2003; Kritsiotis 2004; Muggah 2007; Nolte 2000; O'Connell 2007; Perrin de Brichambaut 2000; Reno 2007; Roth 2003; Simpson and Wheeler 2007; Sriram 2006; Sriram and Mahmoud 2007; Ward 2007; Wheeler 2004); *internal displacement, migration, and immigration* (Bank and Lehmkuhl 2005; Deng 2007; Gurowitz 2004); *territorial disputes* (Kacowicz 2004; Zacher 2001); and *international criminality and universality jurisdiction* (Lutz 2007b; Orentlicher 2007; Rudolph 2001; Sadat 2007; Wippman 2004).

Exactly what research questions[91] *have* inspired IL/IR interdisciplinarians of the last decade or so? Perhaps the broadest focus

of inquiry has been into international "governance" and the related, though slightly narrower question of international law's creation/constitution, evolution, and dissemination. Stephen Toope (2000) and Wayne Sandholtz and Alec Stone Sweet (2004), for example, have explored the phenomenon of international "governance," including its modes and mechanisms. Paul F. Diehl, Charlotte Ku, and Daniel Zamora have introduced the notions of international law's "operating" and "normative" systems as core elements of a conceptual framework that permits analysis and understanding of international legal change (Diehl, Ku, and Zamora 2003; Ku and Diehl 2006). Finally, with Sandholtz and Sweet (2004), other interdisciplinarians – including Richard Price (2004) and Eyal Benvenisti and Moshe Hirsch (2004a) – have considered the general process by which international rules are produced and modified over time.[92]

Many scholars have sought to identify key actors and elements in the international law-creating process. Harold Koh, for example, has depicted a "transnational legal process" comprised of "horizontal" and "vertical" dimensions, with roles played by NGOs and civil society networks, committed individuals, intergovernmental deliberation, and state governments (Koh 1997a, 2007). In work reminiscent of this, Diane Orentlicher has considered the relationship between the "transnational lawmaking process" and international law (2007). Christine Chinkin (2000), moreover, has explored the role of NGO social movements in shaping the development of rules, while Robert Muggah (2007) has traced the effects of "epistemic communities"[93] on international legal and regulatory efforts. Anne-Marie Slaughter, meanwhile, has considered the significance for international law of regulatory transgovernmental networks (2000a).

The nature and mechanisms associated with customary international law's emergence have proven areas of particular interest. How do "behavioral regularities" associated with customary law arise? (Goldsmith and Posner 1999, 2005: 23–78). How does one know when a rule has acquired the status of customary international law? (Arend 1999; Bederman 2001a: 487–8; Byers 1999; Finnemore and Toope 2001a; Price 2004). What role can/do international judges and arbitrators play in advancing international law by "finding" customary international law? (Benvenisti 2004). What role does the United States play in the evolution of customary international law (Toope 2003), and does "hegemonic custom" exist? (Skordas 2003). Scholars have wondered, too, about "soft law." In what ways and by what actors is soft law created?[94]

The treaty creation process has also attracted notable interdisciplinary intention, with important works published by rationalists John Setear (1996) and Jack Goldsmith and Eric Posner (2003, 2005: 83–162) and by critical constructivist Robyn Eckersley (2004). Pierre Klein (2003) has specifically considered the effects of U.S. predominance on the elaboration of treaty regimes and the evolution of the law of treaties.

As has already been noted, a large number of scholars have viewed the law creation process through the particular optic of "legalization." How should "legalization" be understood? What is its nature and significance? Whence and why does it vary (1999 IO volume; Abbott and Snidal 2004)? How do domestic actors and domestic politics generate demand for legalization (Abbott and Snidal 2000; Kahler 2000b)? Others not working in the "legalization" idiom per se including Anthony Clark Arend (1996, 1998, 1999) and Michael Byers (1997) have nevertheless explored whether a given international rule's status of "law" actually matters. Antony Anghie (2004) and Christian Reus-Smit (2003), moreover, have asked how formal international institutions seek to legitimize themselves and why states view particular international institutions as legitimate.[95] Anghie's work was a response in part to that of constructivists Michael Barnett and

Martha Finnemore on the "dysfunctional, even pathological, behavior of international organizations" (1999: 699).

Still another significant area of interdisciplinary scholarly inquiry has been into putative or potential changes of international law's sources, subjects, and substance, especially vis-à-vis the state. Amy Gurowitz (2004) and David Wippman (2004), for example, have traced international law's progressive "cosmopolitanization." An entire AJIL symposium issue (1999), meanwhile, has addressed how individuals are becoming accountable for violations of human dignity committed in internal conflict. Michel Cosnard (2003) and Nico Krisch (2003), moreover, have addressed the nature and implications of "sovereignty equality" in a period of U.S. hegemony. Ellen Lutz (2007b), Madeline Morris (2007), Leila Sadat (2007), and Diane Orentlicher (2007), furthermore, have considered what entities possess lawful jurisdiction over international criminals, and the basis of that jurisdiction.

Interdisciplinarians have scrutinized international law not only as an "object" that is created and influenced by external factors, but also as a "subject" that exerts effects (as an "independent" variable, for those working in a positive social science idiom). In rather different ways, for example, both Christian Reus-Smit (2004c) and Anne-Marie Slaughter (2004a) have considered how law has structured or shaped politics. Leila Sadat (2007), among others, has looked at the narrower question of international law's role in constituting states. In addition, a number of scholars (Benvenisti 2000; Gurowitz 2004; Koh 1999), have explored the relationship between international human rights law and domestic politics, including political change. Benvenisti (2004) has sought to demonstrate how customary international law can promote efficiency. Meanwhile, Kenneth Abbott, Duncan Snidal, and Robyn Eckersley have attempted to ascertain the various roles that soft law can play (Abbott 2007; Abbott and Snidal 2000, 2004; Eckersley 2004).

Law's effects on cooperation and compliance, of course, have provided perennial questions for IL and IR scholars, interdisciplinary and otherwise.[96] The entire interdisciplinary volume edited by Benvenisti and Hirsch (2004a), for example, considered how international law and institutions affected state cooperation – with a special emphasis on the environment and trade. Within that work, George Downs and Michael Jones (2004), Edith Brown Weiss (2004), and Arie Kacowicz (2004) each addressed the general matter of state compliance. Downs and Jones (2004) asked: What influence does state "reputation" have on compliance? Can states have multiple reputations? Finally, Moshe Hirsch (2004) reflected on whether compliance could be enhanced or lessened by globalization. In the volume edited by Byers and Nolte, moreover, both Scott (2003) and Stoll (2003) explored legal compliance within an international setting of predominant power(s).

As a discipline, international law has traditionally taken words very seriously, with the texts of treaties, judicial decisions, and formal negotiating records often assiduously parsed. Interdisciplinary scholars, particularly those of a constructivist or otherwise critical orientation, have often shared this special appreciation of language. In their separate contributions to *The Politics of International Law*, for example, Robyn Eckersley (2004), Dino Kritsiotis (2004), Richard Price (2004), and Nicholas Wheeler (2004) have traced how rhetorical/discursive practices constitute legal (and political) practice. Similarly, in their contributions to the *International Law and International Relations* edited volume, Gerry Simpson and Nicholas Wheeler (2007) and Mary Ellen O'Connell (2007) have explored how legal discourse has been used as a tool by state governments.

The relationship to international law of a particular state – the United States – has drawn special scholarly scrutiny. As already noted, Michael Byers and Georg Nolte published an excellent collection of essays and expert commentary[97] that specifically addressed various implications of United States hegemony for the "foundations" of international law (2003). Robyn Eckersley, moreover, has viewed U.S. behavior associated with the Climate Change Treaty through a critical constructivist lens (2004). Contending that "international law and international institutions must be the focal points of foreign policy" (2006: vii), meanwhile, Thomas Schoenbaum has sought to return U.S. leaders to multilateralism and constructive engagement in the international legal and institutional realms (2006: xiv, 33, 276). Gerry Simpson and Nicholas Wheeler, furthermore, have asked whether the Bush administration was seeking to create a new legal basis for the use of force (2007). Finally, Peter Spiro has proposed a new "theory of liberal transnationalism" to help explain how international law might be incorporated into U.S. law (2007).

Aside from a general scholarly willingness to address a wide array of subjects and research questions, what patterns may be discerned in the recent efforts of interdisciplinarians? Let us consider here four noteworthy trends in turn.

First, irrespective of method, a significant number of interdisciplinary scholars have begun recently to evince explicit concern for the *practical, "real world"*[98] dimensions and *relevance* of their work. This development is striking given the marked preference historically of scholars, especially those in IR, for theory over praxis. Martha Finnemore lamented in 2007 that: "[U]nderstanding what . . . practitioners do and how their efforts succeed or fail should be central for IR and IL as academic disciplines, but in fact has not been so" (268). While a practical policy/practitioner orientation surely has not been manifested regularly, it nevertheless conspicuously informed the high-profile "Appraising the methods" *AJIL* review essay of Ratner and Slaughter (1999) and the entire symposium volume in which it appeared, the conference-based volume of Benvenisti and Hirsch

(2004), and also the workshop series-based volume of Biersteker, Spiro, Sriram, and Raffo (2007).[99] An associated development has been the "growing and significant genre of 'participant–observer' analyses of international governance" (Abbott 2007: 166). Possibly the best example of that genre was the provocative account of the U.N.'s profoundly deficient response to the 1994 Rwanda tragedy, *Eyewitness to a Genocide* (2002), by constructivist scholar Michael Barnett.[100]

Second, and in a perhaps related development, interdisciplinary scholars have started to *step away somewhat from abstract theory and from foundational questions* such as whether law genuinely "matters."[101] In the introduction to their 2006 compendium volume, for example, Beth Simmons and Richard Steinberg noted that: "[I]ncreasingly contemporary IL/IR research organizes less around abstract theoretical debates and more around particular methods and concepts that may be seen as hybrids of the main approaches." Simmons and Steinberg found an increasingly "conscious engagement across meta-theories, with a focus on mid-level analysis of international legal and political developments using hybrid theories and powerful methods to test those theories" (2006: xxxiv). Meanwhile, Veronica Raffo and her colleagues observed in 2007 how some scholars had "begun to move past debates about the relevance or status of international law, to queries or arguments about *how* it functions in international life."[102] The "emergent work devoted to the so-called legalization of international politics," for example, "focuses less on debates about whether or not international law is important in international politics and more on explaining how legalized institutional arrangements come to be" (Raffo, et al. 2007: 5–6).

Third, despite much prominent international law-oriented work that has been done in the traditional statist, rationalist idiom (often explicitly neoliberal – e.g. Abbott 1989; Goldsmith and Posner 2005; Keohane 1997;

Slaughter, et al. 1998; Slaughter Burley 1993; 2000 *IO* special issue on legalization), a significant number of scholars – interdisciplinary and otherwise – have moved in new theoretical directions.[103] Some, for example, have come to embrace what A. Claire Cutler dubbed "*unconventional*" *approaches* to international law (2002). Albeit of many varieties, these approaches nevertheless generally reject formalistic conceptions of law, a preoccupation with the "state" as unitary, monolithic source and subject of law,[104] and a view of law as autonomous, neutral, and objective.[105] While not responding directly to Cutler per se, the constructivist scholar Martha Finnemore nevertheless highlighted in a 2007 essay numerous "grounds for collaboration" between IL and IR that were reminiscent of, and to a large extent consistent with, such unconventional approaches. Here, Finnemore endorsed research into: the nature and dynamics of state, individual, and group identities (268–9); the impact of "world culture" on law and politics (269); law's contestation and creation "by people working outside government and formal legal structures" (270); the social context of law (270–72); and non-state actors (272–5). Surely, international law-oriented work in both "conventional" and "critical" constructivist (Hopf 1998) theory would seem most promising.[106]

Fourth, lamentably, interdisciplinary scholarship thus far has too often proved to be *insufficiently* "*dialogic*" in character.[107] Instead, scholars commonly have failed to exploit the literature of both disciplines, have simply imported a theory or approach from another discipline (typically IR) into their own, or have merely juxtaposed their own discipline's theories with those of the other discipline.[108] In 1999, for example, Kenneth Abbott noted how "relatively little IR literature" had analyzed the "atrocities regime," insisting that "interdisciplinary cross-fertilization must flow both ways" (364). Jan Klabbers averred in 2005 that "lawyers [had been] asked to take international relations seriously, while the international relations people [had] refuse[d], more often than not, to dig into legal thought" (2005: 44). Similarly, in 2006 Chandra Lekha Sriram observed that "attempts to link the disciplines have often involved transferring theories of IR whole-sale to apply to 'problems' of international law. This results less in serious dialogue than in a largely unidirectional application" (467). Sriram regretted that there had been "precious few attempts to apply international legal theories or methods to contemporary prob-lems in IR journals; such discussions remain confined to IL journals" (2006: 470–71). Meanwhile, Hathaway and Koh reported the tendency of "most existing efforts to examine international law and international relations literature [by] plac[ing] the two side-by-side, thus emphasizing the discip-linary divide" (2005: 2).

The lack thus far of routine, sustained, and robust dialogue arguably reflects the stubborn persistence of "two cultures" in the scholarly realm and other inherent barriers confronted by prospective interdisciplinarians (Beck 1996: 17–18; Bank and Lehmkuhl 2005: 166–71).

What lies ahead?

Many of interdisciplinarity's advocates have observed with satisfaction the developments of the past two decades, while remaining guarded about the long-term prospects – conceding that challenges remain, progress is not inevitable, and a return to disciplinary insu-larity is still possible. As Veronica Raffo and her colleagues noted in the introduction to their 2007 volume: "[T]he fields of interna-tional law and international relations have become increasingly intertwined in recent years, beginning to reverse a long tradition of viewing them as separate areas . . . Myriad books and articles have been devoted to the subject, seeking to identify the gap between international law and international relations . . . [b]ut more remains to be done."[109] Similarly, in their co-edited compendium,

Oona Hathaway and Harold Koh submitted: "Progress in generating interdisciplinary dialogue between law and political science has been slow but steady on both sides . . . Today, international law and international relations are increasingly viewed as a single discipline. Yet significant differences re-main."[110] In their essay in the 1999 *American Journal of International Law* special issue, moreover, Stephen Ratner and Anne-Marie Slaughter cautioned: "[W]e do not wish to suggest that international law has witnessed an inevitable march of progress in the devel-opment of new theories and methods."[111] Almost a decade later, Gerry Simpson and Nicholas Wheeler sketched "two possible futures for the IR-IL conversation." Under their pessimistic scenario, in the wake of the Bush doctrine and American exception-alism, "we might be looking at a freezing of relations . . . after a decade or so of multi-lateralism, of institutional proliferation, of leg-alization, and of cross-disciplinary ardor."[112] Under their preferred scenario, international lawyers might "finally recognize the ways in which inequality and 'the exception' are found in the very origins of their field, while IR scholars [might] begin (and in some cases continue) to acknowledge the distinctiveness (not just another regime), power (not just material), and constituting power (circum-scribing how we speak and understand) of law" (Simpson and Wheeler 2007: 124).

What, then, lies ahead? Prediction, whe-ther of political, legal, or scholarly trends, is an intrinsically perilous exercise. Even so, assuming – as many observers do – that the IL/IR collaborative enterprise will endure in some form, at least three conclusions about its future seem reasonably safe.[113]

First, it appears highly likely that interdis-ciplinary scholars will continue to appreciate the *vital roles of non-state actors and processes*, per-haps increasingly so.[114] In a globalized world characterized by terrorism, transborder flows of small arms, massive internal displacements of populations, international criminality, large-scale human rights abuses, and other maladies, "a growing number of actors and analysts are beginning to see the state as a problem, not as the sole source of effective solutions."[115] Furthermore, as Chandra Lekha Sriram has observed, "overreliance upon state-centric modes of analysis common to many sets of IR theories and to some traditional approaches to international law" obscures "the range of actors in contemporary law and politics" (2006: 467–8). It may well be, moreover, that the global system will increasingly evince a "cosmopolitanisation" of international law – "the movement away from a legal system in which states are the sole subjects, and in which the domestic is tightly quarantined from the international, toward a transnational legal order that grants legal rights and agency to individuals and erodes the traditional boundary between inside and outside."[116] In an environment where non-state actors and processes have already proven manifestly consequential, constructivist,[117] liberal,[118] and "transnational legal process"[119] approaches should be particularly attractive to interdisciplinarians. Surely, the recent attention paid to "transnational advocacy networks" (Keck and Sikkink 1998), "transnational moral entrepreneurs" (Andreas and Nadelmann 2006; cf. Finnemore and Sikkink 1998; Nadelmann 1990), "epistemic communities" (Adler and Haas 1992; Eyre and Suchman 1996; Haas 1992; Muggah 2007), and "transnational judicial dialogue" (Orentlicher 2007; Slaughter 2000c) has already yielded important insights.[120] Even so, as Martha Finnemore has noted, scholars will ultimately "need better theoretical tools for understanding and prescribing action" for non-state actors (2007: 273).

Second, reflecting an increased scholarly appreciation for non-state actors and processes, the *relationship between the domestic and international realms* – including their legal and political dimensions – seems apt to garner sustained, if not increased, interdisciplinary attention.[121] Globalization has challenged "borders" of all types, material and ideational. Moreover, as we have seen, inter-

disciplinarians of various stripes have already begun to explore globalization's manifold implications. Harold Koh, for example, has sketched a "transnational legal process" under which "those seeking to create and embed certain ... [legal] principles into international and domestic law ... promote transnational *interactions*, that generate legal *interpretations*, that can in turn be *internalized* into the domestic law of even skeptical nation-states" (Koh 2007: 62, emphasis in original). Various scholars working in the rationalist "legalization" idiom (e.g. Abbott and Snidal 2000; Kahler 2000b), meanwhile, have sought to understand how domestic actors and domestic politics generate demand for international rules that are *obligatory* (legally binding), *precise*, and admitting of *delegation* (i.e. that feature authorized third-party mechanisms for interpretation and application). Constructivists, too, have studied internationally relevant phenomena and actors operating within the domestic realm, including the formation of group and state "identity" and the operation of activists and norm entrepreneurs, people often "working outside government and formal legal structures," domestic or otherwise (Finnemore 2007: 271–72, 270). Liberal IR theorists, of course, have been *especially* mindful of the domestic space: advocating a "bottom up" view, emphasizing interactions between individuals operating in the society and the state, and contending that "domestic regime type" affects state behavior (Slaughter 2000b, 2004a). Ultimately, given the significant illumination it has already provided, this domestic/international orientation of many interdisciplinary scholars appears unlikely soon to end.

Third, although complementarities between the two surely exist,[122] *interdisciplinary scholarship nevertheless seems liable to remain separated into rationalist and sociological/constructivist camps.* Eyal Benvenisti and Moshe Hirsch have observed that the "distinction between rational choice and sociological analyses constitutes one of the major dividing lines in social sciences scholarship" in general (Benvenisti and Hirsch 2004b: 4). So, too, does a rationalist–sociological division specifically mark IL/IR scholarship, with constructivism currently representing the most prominent sociological approach. The divide reflects primarily a fundamental difference of opinion among scholars regarding the most effective "lens" through which to view behavior and other law-associated phenomena: a "logic of consequences"/instrumental optic or a "logic of appropriateness"/norms one.[123]

A second significant rationalist–sociological/constructivist division exists, too, separating rationalist scholars who reject critical theory from those constructivists who embrace it.[124] Because disagreements on foundational methodological, ontological, and epistemological issues separate rationalists and constructivists, their scholarly divide exhibits an almost "religious war" or "Mac vs. PC" quality that makes the breach seem unlikely ever to be effectively bridged. "These are differences that make a difference."[125] Even so, the persistence of multiple IL/IR perspectives and of the rationalist–sociological divide should not ultimately be viewed as problematic – for genuine interdisciplinarity should embrace diversity.

It is perhaps fitting now to close this account of the IL/IR scholarly trajectory in the same way in which it commenced – with an invocation of the words of Anne-Marie Slaughter. One of the interdisciplinarity movement's most indefatigable and compelling advocates, Slaughter reminds researchers always to bear in mind the crucial human dimensions and practical implications of the enterprise: "As a scholar, it is relatively easy to survey the literature, the conferences, and the collaborations and to evaluate the academic value of such cross-fertilization. The real test, however, is the world. Both international lawyers and international relations scholars confront pressing global problems, issues of such urgency and import that lives and lands hang in the balance" (Slaughter 2004a: 49).

[Author note: An early version of this chapter was presented at "America, human rights and the world," an interdisciplinary conference convened by Marquette University's Human Rights Initiative in Milwaukee, Wisconsin, September 27–29, 2007.]

Notes

1 As Martha Finnemore has noted, "[r]eal-world political changes have reinforced, perhaps even caused, these intellectual shifts" in the IR and IL disciplines (2007: 266). Similarly, Toope observes: "[W]ith the failure of international relations to predict, or even explain, the end of the Cold War, new questions gained currency, questions more closely allied with the historical preoccupations of international law" (2000: 91). See also Raffo, et al. 2007: 6.

2 Suggestive of its influence, Abbott's essay was tied for first as the "most-cited" article in the *Yale Journal of International Law* over a 25-year period (Abbott 2000: 273–6). Another early articulation of Abbott's perspective was provided in the *American Society of International Law Proceedings* (1992).

3 The essay won the Francis Deák Prize for 1994, bestowed by the Board of Editors of the *American Journal of International Law*.

4 When IL began again seriously to be of interest to IR is debatable, with Simmons and Steinberg suggesting the early 1980s (2006: xxx). Even so, IR work tended to focus more then on "regimes" or "institutions" and not on "law" per se. Arguably, the resurgence of a focus on law began in the late 1980s and early 1990s.

5 For other recent accounts of the nature and status of IL/IR interdisciplinary efforts, see Barker (2000: 70–96); Benvenisti and Hirsch (2004b: 1–4); Cutler (2002); Finnemore (2007); Goldsmith and Posner (2005: 14–17); Hathaway and Koh (2005: 1–3, 19–25); Kacowicz (2001); Klabbers (2005); Schoenbaum (2006: 54–95); Slaughter (2004a: 16–49); Spiro (2000a: 576–590); and Sriram (2006). In "How do norms matter?" Kratochwil traces how the development of the IR and IL disciplines reinforced the division between international politics and international law (Kratochwil 2000). Also noteworthy is Hurrell 2000.

6 Sriram counts Kenneth Abbott among "scholars of IR" (2006: 467) though Abbott

holds a J.D. and until fairly recently taught exclusively at a law school. Peter Haas is included as a "legal scholar" by Bederman (2001a: 475), although Haas holds a Ph.D. and teaches in a political science department. Anthony Clark Arend has also been called an IL scholar, despite his Ph.D. and teaching position in a government department.

7 "Law degrees" include: (1) doctor of law (J.D., Juris Doctor), the professional practice of law degree in the United States; (2) bachelor of civil law (B.C.L.); (3) bachelor of laws (LL.B., Legum Baccalaureus), the principal academic degree in law in the majority of common law countries other than the United States – akin to the U.S. J.D.; (4) bachelor of jurisprudence (B. Juris), not a qualification for the professional practice of law; (5) the master of laws (LL.M., Legum Magister), an advanced law degree; (6) doctor of laws (LL.D., Legum Doctor; or Dr. iur., in Germany), a doctorate-level academic degree in law; and (7) doctor of juridical science (S.J.D.), U.S. degree designed for aspiring legal academics, comparable to the LL.D.

8 See Ku, et al. 2001; Diehl, Ku, and Zamora 2003; Ku and Diehl 2006.

9 The Fletcher School began to offer an LL.M. Program in September of 2008. See http://fletcher.tufts.edu/llm/default.shtml, retrieved from the World Wide Web October 16, 2007.

10 Another permutation: Alec Stone Sweet, Leitner Professor of Law, Politics and International Studies at Yale Law School, received a Ph.D. in Political Science from the University of Washington, but does not hold a J.D. per se.

For a comprehensive compilation of IL/IR interdisciplinarians, see Appendix.

11 A few prominent examples would include: Claude (1966), Claude (1988), Forsythe (1972), Joyner (1984), Kratochwil (1989), LeBlanc (1977), LeBlanc (1984), Onuf (1985), Onuf (1989), Young (1972), and Young (1986–7).

12 "[T]he student of law and the student of politics . . . purport to be looking at the same world from the vantage point of important disciplines. It seems unfortunate, indeed destructive, that they should not, at the least, hear each other" (Henkin 1968: 6). The "New Haven school" of "configurative jurisprudence" introduced by Harold Lasswell and Myres McDougal in the mid-1940s was arguably the most interdisciplinary of the cold

war period. For more on the approach, see Arend 1999: 76–86; Beck, Arend, and Vander Lugt 1996: 110–143; and McDougal and Lasswell 1959. One arguable member of the New Haven school was Richard Falk, who served as a member of the Princeton faculty, with a joint appointment in the Woodrow Wilson School of Public International Affairs and the Department of Politics between 1961 and 2001. Falk holds J.S.D. and LL.B. degrees. For some of his cold war era work, see Falk 1983, 1984, and 1987.

13 A comprehensive online bibliography of the English school is maintained at http://www. leeds.ac.uk/polis/englishschool/documents. htm, retrieved from the World Wide Web, September 13, 2007. Prominent English school works published during the cold war period include: Bull 1966, Bull 1977, Bull and Watson (eds) 1984, Butterfield and Wight (eds) 1966, Wight 1977, and Wight 1978. The English school's relationship to international law was also noted in Slaughter, et al. 1998: 372.

14 Sriram 2006: 468. See also Hathaway and Koh 2005: 22; Raffo, et al. 2007: 5.

15 Raffo, et al. 2007: 4; Sriram 2006: 468.

16 For discussions of the American (i.e. "U.S.") role in the IR discipline, see Crawford and Jarvis (2001); Hoffmann 1977; Smith 2000. Dias argued that "the divide between international relations and international law is both tenuous and tendentious. Without international law, international relations theory would amount to little more than a constant affirmation that *might is right*. Without international relations, we would not be able to expose instances when international law is an instrument of might or to advocate what needs to be done to reaffirm the principle *right not might*. Without international relations, our ability to succeed strategically in developing new international law, founded on the principle *right not might*, would be considerably limited" (Dias 2007: 278, emphasis in original).

17 For a discussion of "theory" in the context of IL/IR interdisciplinarity, see Slaughter 2004a: 17–19. For a similar discussion, addressing also the related notion of "method," see Ratner and Slaughter 1999: 291–93. See also Abbott K.W. 1999: 362–3.

18 See, e.g. Sriram's recent treatment of legal positivism, policy-oriented jurisprudence and transnational legal process (2006: 471–72).

19 Slaughter, et al. 1998 identified three ways in which international lawyers "used" international relations theory: "(1) to diagnose

international policy problems and to formulate solutions to them; (2) to explain the function of particular international legal institutions; and (3) to examine and reconceptualize particular institutions of international law generally" (Slaughter, et al. 1998: 373).

20 Bederman 2000: 81. Similarly, Spiro argued that IL's "rush to transplant refined approaches [e.g. economic, critical, feminist] also evidences a persistent inferiority complex on the part of international law scholars, a sort of 'model envy'" (Spiro 2000a: 580).

21 Bederman 2000: 81. Jan Klabbers argues, too, that "while the best international lawyers will have a working knowledge of neighbouring disciplines including international relations theory, they should guard against the risk of doing merely history, or economics, or ethics, or international relations, under a thin veneer of international law." In his view, "international lawyers should not immediately heed to the siren song of interdisciplinarity, for the simple reason that it will not always and automatically enable them to come to a better understanding of international law" (Klabbers 2005: 36). He concludes that "the main challenge for the lawyer is . . . to cherish and preserve the relative autonomy of the law, for a law that has lost its autonomy ceases to be law" (2005: 42).

22 On the "distinctiveness and independence of international law as a discipline for approaching questions of international relations," see Ratner and Slaughter 1999: 298–99. See also Slaughter, et al. 1998: 379.

23 As Reus-Smit has observed, "the disciplines of International Relations and International Law have evolved as parallel yet carefully quarantined fields of inquiry, each with its own account of distinctiveness and autonomy" (2004b: 1). A call for "disciplined interdisciplinarity" is made in Bank and Lehmkuhl 2005: 171–72.

24 IL works featured: Acheson (1963a); Charlesworth, Chinkin, and Wright (1991); Grotius (1925); Hart (1994); Kelsen (1942); Kennedy (1988); and McDougal and Lasswell (1959).

25 IR works featured: Grieco (1988); Hurrell (1993); Kennan (1984); Keohane (1988); and Krasner (1982).

26 Addressing the same question was Finnemore (2000).

27 Arend employed this test for "law" in earlier works, including Arend and Beck (1993).

28 The book built on Byers' Cambridge Ph.D. thesis and his earlier essay, Byers (1995).

29 Cardenas 2000: 148, 149. See also Barker 2000: 85–9. Klabbers judged Byer's "(understandable) reluctance to make a choice" among specific versions of international relations thought one of the reasons Byers' work was "less than fully satisfactory" (Klabbers 2005: 37–8). See also Klabbers 1999.

30 The featured articles in the symposium: Abbott K. (1999); Charlesworth (1999); Dunoff and Trachtman (1999); O'Connell (1999); Ratner and Slaughter (1999); Simma and Paulus (1999); Slaughter and Ratner (1999); and Wiessner and Willard (1999). Koskenniemi (1999) submitted a lengthy "letter." The positivist analysis offered by Simma and Paulus, and the New Haven analysis offered by Wiessner and Willard, would likely be of somewhat less interest to IR scholars.

Arguably "IL" scholars: Stephen Ratner, J.D. (Professor of Law, University of Michigan Law School); Bruno Simma (currently a judge on the International Court of Justice and former Dean of the University of Munich Faculty of Law), Andreas Paulus (Professor of International and Public Law at the University of Göttingen); Siegfried Wiessner, Dr. iur., LL.M. (Professor of Law; Founder and Director, LL.M./J.S.D. Program in Intercultural Human Rights at St. Thomas University School of Law), Andrew Willard (Senior Research Scholar at Yale Law School and President of the Policy Sciences Center), Mary Ellen O'Connell, LL.B., J.D. (Robert and Marion Short Professor of Law, University of Notre Dame); Kenneth Abbott, J.D. (Professor of Law, Willard H. Pedrick Distinguished Research Scholar, College of Law, but also Professor of Global Studies, School of Global Studies, Arizona State University); Hilary Charlesworth, LL.B., S.J.D. (Professor in RegNet and Director of the Centre for International Governance and Justice, Australian National University); Jeffrey L. Dunoff, J.D., LL.M. (Charles Klein Professor of Law and Government and Director, Institute for International Law and Public Policy at Temple University Beasley School of Law), Joel P. Trachtman, J.D. (Professor of International Law, The Fletcher School); Martti Koskenniemi, LL.B., LL.M., LL.D. (Professor of International Law in the University of Helsinki).

Holding both J.D. and D.Phil. degrees and having served both schools of law and policy, Anne-Marie Slaughter eludes ready categorization.

31 The volume explicitly excluded Roman law, canon law, socialist/Soviet law, natural law, the comparative method, and functionalism (Ratner and Slaughter 1999: 293).

32 This treatment of IR arguably reflected a trend described by Klabbers: "Interdisciplinarity often . . . presumes a flat, one-dimensional vision of the discipline-to-relate-with." He warned that "such a one-dimensional view [would] rarely, if ever, be persuasive" (Klabbers 2005: 37).

33 "1. What assumptions does your method make about the nature of international law? 2. Who are the decision makers under your method? 3. How does your approach address the distinction between *lax lata* and *lex ferenda*? Is it concerned with only one, both, or neither? 4. How does it factor in the traditional 'sources' of law, i.e. prescriptive processes? 5. Is your method better at tackling some subject areas than others, both as regards the issue noted above and as compared to other subjects? 6. Why is your method better than others?" (Ratner and Slaughter 1999: 298).

34 Arguably "IR" scholars: Judith Goldstein, Ph.D. (Professor of Political Science, Stanford University); Miles Kahler, Ph.D. (Rohr Professor of Pacific International Relations at the Graduate School of International Relations and Pacific Studies); Robert O. Keohane, Ph.D. (Professor of International Affairs, Woodrow Wilson School, Princeton University); Andrew Moravcsik, Ph.D. (Professor of Politics and Director of the European Union Program at Princeton University); Duncan Snidal, Ph.D. (Associate Professor, Department of Political Science, University of Chicago); Karen J. Alter, Ph.D. (Associate Professor, Department of Political Science, Northwestern University); Beth A. Simmons, Ph.D. (Professor of Government at Harvard University); Lisa L. Martin, Ph.D. (Professor of Government at Harvard University).

Kathryn Sikkink, Ph.D., Arleen C. Carlson Professor of Political Science at the University of Minnesota, is also a Professor of Law at the University of Minnesota's Law School.

Arguably "IL" scholars: Ellen L. Lutz, M.A., J.D. (Executive Director of Cultural Survival and former Executive Director of the Center for Human Rights and Conflict Resolution at Tufts University's Fletcher School of Law and Diplomacy); and Frederick M. Abbott, J.D., LL.M. (Edward Ball Eminent Scholar, Florida State University, College of Law).

35 Abbott, Keohane, Moravcsik, Slaughter, and Snidal 2000; Goldstein, et al. 2000.

36 Abbott and Snidal 2000; Keohane, Moravcsik, and Slaughter 2000.

37 F. Abbott 2000; Alter 2000; Kahler 2000a.

38 Simmons 2000.

39 Goldstein and Martin 2000.

40 Lutz and Sikkink 2000.

41 Kahler 2000b.

42 A critique of this high-profile volume was offered by Martha Finnemore and Stephen Toope in their *IO* essay, "Alternatives to 'legalization': richer views of law and politics" (Finnemore and Toope 2001a). "Narrow and stylized frameworks like this one may be useful if they provide conceptual clarity and facilitate operationalization of concepts," they submitted. Even so, "the empirical applications of legalization . . . suggest the opposite" (2001: 743–4). Finnemore and Toope contended that law "in this [legalization] view is constraint only: it has no creative or generative powers in social life. Yet law working in the world constitutes relationships as much as it delimits acceptable behavior" (2001a: 745).

In 2007 Routledge published *Law and Legalization in Transnational Relations*, a *multidisciplinary* volume (i.e. not strictly a work of IL/IR interdisciplinarity per se) edited by Christian Brütsch and Dirk Lehmkuhl (2007a). Based on a 2002 workshop on "Legalization" convened in Zurich, the volume also challenged the rationalist–institutionalist conception of "legalization" advanced in the 2000 *International Organization* symposium issue. The editors contended that "legalization" should be thought of as "a series of complex transformations of the structures, institutions and actors that shape international and transnational politics" (226). They rejected as "misleading" the depiction of legalization as "a linear development or a general trend," proposing instead that "research should focus on the elusive and often contradictory conditions, patterns and dynamics that determine the success, scope and reach of emerging legal and law-like arrangements" (226). Proposing a common, broad, interpretative framework that included "the increase in international law-making, the variation among legalized and legalizing regimes, and the differentiation of legal and law-like arrangements," Brütsch and Lehmkuhl sought to test the "usefulness and integrative potential" of their framework by inviting scholars with different disciplinary backgrounds – including political science, forest and nature conservation, accounting and auditing, criminal law and criminology, and business administration (but notably, not international law) – to address different aspects of legalization in their respective fields of expertise (xii–xiii, 226). The collection included essays on "complex legalization" (Brütsch and Lehmkuhl 2007b); "transnational legalization of accounting" (Wüstemann and Kierzek 2007); "harmonization of private commercial law" (Cohen 2007); "money laundering and bribery" (Pieth 2007); "organic agriculture" (Coleman and Reed 2007); "emerging transnational regulatory systems" (Meidinger 2007); the function of "global standards" (Arts and Kerwer 2007; Schanze 2007); "legalization and world society theory" (Albert 2007); and "the role of the transnational corporation in legalization" (Scherer and Baumann 2007).

43 Conference participant/volume contributors included these professors: Stephen Toope (Canada), Martti Koskenniemi (Finland), Brigitte Stern (France), Friedrich Kratochwil, Georg Nolte (Germany), Eyal Benvenisti (Israel), Vera Gowlland-Debbas (Switzerland), Philip Allott, Christine Chinkin, Andrew Hurrell, Vaughan Lowe (United Kingdom) and Anne-Marie Slaughter (United States).
Arguably "IR" scholars: Friedrich Kratochwil, Ph.D. (Chair of International Relations, European University Institute, Political and Social Sciences), Vera Gowlland-Debbas, Ph.D. (Professor in the International Law section of the Graduate Institute of International Studies, Geneva), and Andrew Hurrell, D.Phil. (University Lecturer in International Relations, Director of the Centre of International Studies, Faculty Fellow, Nuffield College, Oxford).
Arguably "IL" scholars: Philip Allott (Reader in International Public Law and a Fellow of Trinity College, University of Cambridge; formerly a legal counselor in the British Foreign and Commonwealth Office), Eyal Benvenisti, J.S.D. (Professor of Law at Tel Aviv University Faculty of Law), Martti Koskenniemi, LL.B., LL.M., LL.D. (Professor of International Law in the University of Helsinki), Dr. Georg Nolte (Professor of Law at the University of Munich), Brigitte Stern (Professor at the University of Paris 1 – Panthéon-Sorbonne).

Holding both J.D. and Ph.D. degrees and having served both schools of law and policy, Anne-Marie Slaughter eludes ready categorization. Similarly, Michael Byers serves on the Duke Law School Faculty, but holds both Ph.D. and B.C.L. (Bachelor of Civil Law) degrees. Christine Chinkin of the London School of Economics and Political Science holds LL.B., two LL.M., and Ph.D. degrees. Vaughan Lowe, LL.B., LL.M., Ph.D. is Chichele Professor of Public International Law and a Fellow of All Souls' College in the University of Oxford. Stephen Toope holds LL.B., B.C.L., and Ph.D. degrees and since 2006 has served as President of the University of British Columbia. He had served as Professor of Law, McGill University.

44 Koskenniemi 2000: 29. "[T]he particular combination of a call to increase 'collaboration' between international lawyers and international relations theorists, together with the sociology of the end-of-State (as we know it) and the political enthusiasm about the spread of 'liberalism,' constitutes an academic project that cannot but buttress the justification of American hegemony in the world. This is not because of bad faith or conspiracy on anybody's part. It is the logic of an argument . . . that creates the image of law as an instrument for the values (or better, 'decisions') of the powerful that compels the conclusion" (Koskenniemi 2000: 30).

45 Other essays included: Allott (2000: 69–89); Benvenisti (2000: 109–29); Chinkin (2000: 131–47); Gowlland-Debbas (2000: 277–313); Hurrell (2000: 327–47); Kwakwa (2000: 227–46); Lowe (2000a: 207–26); Mutua (2000: 149–75); Nolte (2000: 315–26); Perrin de Brichambaut (2000: 269–313); Slaughter (2000a: 177–205); Stern (2000: 247–68); and Watts (2000: 5–16). Hurrell (2000: 327–47).

46 Professor of Law at the University of Sussex, Barker holds both LL.B. and Ph.D. degrees. Accordingly, he might be considered an "IL" (or perhaps) "IR" scholar.

47 Scott (2004a) is another textbook that addresses issues of interdisciplinarity, albeit relatively briefly so.

48 For brief synopses of the "transnational legal process" approach, see Hathaway and Koh 2005: 190–91, 195–204; Koh 2007: 62; and Sriram 2006: 472.

49 Arguably "IL" scholars: Georg Nolte; Andreas Paulus (Professor of International and Public Law at the University of Göttingen), Michel Cosnard (Professor of International

Law, University of Maine – Le Mans, France), Nico Krisch, Dr. iur. (Lecturer in Law in the Department of Law of the London School of Economics), Marcelo Kohen, Ph.D. in Political Science – International Law (Professor of International Law at the Graduate Institute of International Studies, Geneva), Achilles Skordas, Ph.D. in Law (Reader in Law at the University of Bristol School of Law), Pierre Klein (Professor of International Law and Director of the Centre for International Law, Université Libre de Bruxelles), Catherine Redgwell, LL.B., M.Sc. (Professor of International Law at University College London), and Peter-Tobias Stoll (Professor of Law and Managing Director, Institute of International Law at Georg-August-Universität Göttingen).

50 Arguably IR scholars were: Brad R. Roth, Ph.D. (Associate Professor in the Department of Political Science at Wayne State University), and Shirley Scott, Ph.D. (Associate Professor in International Relations, University of New South Wales).

Arguably a "practitioner": Edward Kwakwa, LL.M., J.S.D. (Deputy Legal Counsel and Head of the Legal and Constitutional Affairs Section, WIPO).

Arguably "hybrid" scholars: Michael Byers and Stephen Toope.

51 http://www.jilir.org/, retrieved from the World Wide Web, September 16, 2007.

52 As of September 2007, the Board included Kenneth Abbott (Arizona State University); Jose Alvarez (Columbia University); Upendra Baxi (American Unversity); Laurence Boisson de Chazournes (University of Geneva); Jutta Brunnée (University of Toronto); Michael Byers (University of British Columbia); Martha Finnemore (George Washington University); Thomas Franck (NYU); Robert Keohane (Duke University); Benedict Kingsbury (New York University); Karen Knop (University of Toronto); Martti Koskenniemi (University of Helsinki); Stephen Krasner (Stanford University); Friedrich Kratochwil (European University Institute); Oona Hathaway (Yale University); Réné Provost (McGill University); Philippe Sands (University College London); Shirley Scott (University of New South Wales); Gerry Simpson (London School of Economics); Janice Stein (University of Toronto); Stephen Toope (Trudeau Foundation and University of British Columbia); and Rob Walker (Keele University).

53 Two especially noteworthy essays from the new journal: Klabbers 2005; Simpson 2005.

54 Reus-Smit (2004b: 11).

55 For a comparative review of the book, see Sriram 2005.

56 The contributors to the volume include both "critical" and "conventional" constructivists. Reus-Smit (2004b: 12). For his constructivist argument, Reus-Smit built on his earlier "The strange death of liberal international theory" (2001) and "Politics and international legal obligation" (2003).

57 Arguably "IR" scholars: Dr. Robyn Eckersley (Senior Lecturer in the Department of Political Science at the University of Melbourne, although she has previously served as a public lawyer), Amy Gurowitz, Ph.D. (Lecturer in Political Science at the University of California at Berkeley), Richard Price, Ph.D. (Associate Professor of Political Science at the University of British Columbia), Christian Reus-Smit, Ph.D. (Professor and Head of the Department of International Relations in the Research School of Pacific and Asian Studies at the Australian National University), and Wayne Sandholtz, Ph.D. (Professor in the Department of Political Science at the University of California, Irvine).

Based on his degree (but not institutional affiliation), Alec Stone Sweet might also be considered an "IR" scholar: Ph.D. (Leitner Professor of Law, Politics and International Studies at Yale Law School but formerly Official Fellow, Chair of Comparative Politics, at Nuffield College, Oxford).

Notably, Gurowitz, Price, and Reus-Smith all received their doctoral degrees from Cornell University.

58 Arguably "IL" scholars: Antony Anghie, S.J.D. (Professor at the S. J. Quinnery School of Law at the University of Utah); Dino Kritsiotis, LL.M. (Reader in Public International Law at the University of Nottingham); David Wippman, J.D. (Professor of Law at Cornell University).

59 For a review, see Silverburg 2006.

60 Abbott and Snidal (2004), Benvenisti (2004), Brown Weiss (2004), Downs and Jones (2004), Hirsch (2004), Howse (2004), Kacowicz (2004), Milner, Rosendorff, and Mansfield (2004), Mavroidis (2004), and Slaughter (2004a). Abbott and Snidal 2004 extends the analysis offered in Abbott and Snidal 2000.

61 Arguably "IR" scholars: George W. Downs, Ph.D. (Professor in the Department of

Politics at New York University); Arie M. Kacowicz, Ph.D. (Senior Lecturer in International Relations at Hebrew University of Jerusalem); Edward D. Mansfield, Ph.D. (Hum Rosen Professor of Political Science at the University of Pennsylvania); Helen V. Milner, Ph.D. (B. C. Forbes Professor of Politics and International Affairs at Princeton University); Peter Rosendorff, Ph.D. (Economics) (Associate Professor of International Relations and Economics at the University of Southern California); and Duncan Snidal, Ph.D. (Associate Professor in the Department of Political Science at the University of Chicago).

Collaborating with Downs was Michael A. Jones, an Associate Professor in the Department of Mathematics at Montclaire State University.

62 Arguably "IL" scholars: Eyal Benvenisti, LL.B., LL.M., J.S.D. (Professor of Law, Tel Aviv University Faculty of Law); Moshe Hirsch, L.B., LL.M., Ph.D. (Faculty of Law); Arnold Brecht (Chair in European Law, Vice Dean of the Faculty of Law, and Senior Lecturer, Faculty of Law and Department of International Relations, Hebrew University of Jerusalem); Robert Howse, LL.B., LL.M. (Professor of Law, University of Michigan Law School); and Petros C. Mavroidis, LL.B., LL.M., Ph.D. (Law) (Professor of Law, Columbia Law School).

63 For reviews of this work, see Silverburg 2005 and Sriram 2005. The work, and "rational choice" approaches to law more generally, were also critiqued by Schoenbaum (2006: 87–90).

64 Other rational choice works of interdisciplinary scholarship are Setear 1996 and 1997. John Setear, J.D., teaches at the University of Virginia's Law School and is arguably an "IL" scholar. A response to an early articulation of the game theoretical approach of Goldsmith and Posner was offered by Chinen 2001.

65 Goldsmith 2000, 2003; Goldsmith and Posner 1999, 2000a, 2002, 2003a; Posner 2003.

66 "We identify *state interests* in connection with particular legal regimes by looking, based on many types of evidence, to the preferences of the state's *political leadership*" (Goldsmith and Posner 2005: 6, emphasis added).

67 For example, see Koh 1997a.

68 Henkin 1968.

69 Franck 1990.

70 Among the featured works in Hathaway and Koh 2005 that are also featured in other IL/IR compendium volumes: Abbott K.W. (1999); Downs, Rocke, and Barsoom (1996); Koh (1997a); Moravcsik (2000); and O'Connell (1999).

71 From the "Legalization" special issue of *IO*: Abbott, et al. 2000; Goldstein and Martin 2000; Keohane, et al. 2000. "The rejoinder" Finnemore and Toope 2001a.

72 Fortna 2003.

73 Steinberg 2002.

74 Simmons 2000.

75 Rudolph 2001.

76 Moravcsik 2000.

77 Mitchell 1994.

78 Raustiala and Victor 2004.

79 For a review, see Beck 2006. Schoenbaum is an "IL" scholar, with J.D. and Ph.D. (Law) degrees. Even so, he serves as both Dean and Virginia Rusk Professor of International Law and Professor of Political Science at the University of Georgia.

80 Schoenbaum submitted that "state interests" in the twenty-first century had broadened, with those interests "rooted in cooperation" and also those "held in common with all of international society" predominating (2006: viii). The world was small and interconnected, as never before. Security, traditionally viewed exclusively through a "state" lens, now had vital "human" and "environmental" aspects (2006: viii). In the globalized realm, international rules were "indispensable to furthering state interests," creating legitimacy, order, and predictability (2006: ix). International institutions, meanwhile, might exert a "multiplier effect" that was "indispensable to the solution of world problems" (2006: ix). While reform would be difficult, Schoenbaum insisted, his liberal internationalist approach offered the best, if inevitably imperfect, "path" to world peace and security (2006: xiv). Elaborating this argument, *The Path Not Taken* addressed such crucial areas as peace and security (2006: 96–147), international political economy (2006: 148–95), international environmental protection (2006: 196–249), international human rights (2006: 250–84), and international crimes (2006: 285–301).

81 Arguably "IL" scholars: Kenneth Abbott; Harold Hongju Koh; Madeline Morris, J.D. (Professor of Law, Duke University); Mary Ellen O'Connell; Diane Orentlicher, J.D. (Professor of Law, American University, Washington College of Law); Leila Nadya Sadat, J.D., LL.M. (Henry H. Oberschelp Professor of Law, Washington University –

St. Louis Law); Gerry Simpson, LL.B., LL.M., S.J.D. (Professor in Public International Law, Department of Law, London School of Economics); and Peter J. Spiro, J.D. (Charles R. Weiner Professorship in International Law, Temple University, Beasley School of Law).

82 Arguably "IR" scholars: Fiona Adamson, Ph.D. (Assistant Professor, School of Public Policy, University College London); Thomas J. Biersteker, Ph.D. (Luce Professor of Transnational Organizations, Brown University); Martha Finnemore, Ph.D. (Professor of Political Science and International Affairs, George Washington University); William Reno, Ph.D. (Associate Professor, Northwestern University); Nicholas J. Wheeler, Ph.D. (Professor, Department of International Politics University of Wales, Aberystwyth).

Arguably a "hybrid" scholar: Chandra Lekha Sriram, J.D., Ph.D. (Politics), Professor, Chair in Human Rights and Director, Centre on Human Rights in Conflict University of East London, School of Law.

83 "Practitioners": Dr. Clarence J. Dias, President of the International Center for Law in Development, a Third World NGO concerned about human rights in the development process, Ph.D. degree in law from Bombay University and S.J.D. degree from Cornell Law School; Francis M. Deng is a senior fellow in the Foreign Policy Studies Program at the Brookings Institution; Youssef Mahmoud, U.N. Secretary-General's Deputy Special Representative for Burundi, Ph.D. in Linguistics from Georgetown University and an M.A. in American and British studies from the University of Tunis; Ellen L. Lutz, M.A. J.D., Executive Director of Cultural Survival, Former Executive Director of the Center for Human Rights and Conflict Resolution, Tufts University's Fletcher School of Law and Diplomacy; Robert Muggah, a doctoral candidate at Oxford University and a project manager at the Small Arms Survey, an independent research project located at the Graduate Institute of International Studies in Geneva, Switzerland; Veronica Raffo, Consultant, World Bank, Poverty Reduction and Economic Management Network; and Curtis Anthony Ward, J.D., LL.M. – an independent expert and advisor on technical assistance to the United Nations Security Council Counter-Terrorism Committee (CTC), and CTC liaison with regional and international organizations.

84 For examples of interdisciplinary articles written before 1998, see the bibliography of Slaughter, et al. 1998: 394–7).

85 Beck 1996: 4. Stephen Toope found "the incessant self-labeling of international relations scholars somewhat precious" (Toope 2000: 93). Martti Koskenniemi, meanwhile, noted that "like many others, [he] dislike[d] being labeled and marketed in accordance with the logic of consumer capitalism" (1999: 352).

86 Abbott 1992: 167; Spiro 2000a: 581. According to Hathaway and Koh, "Today, international law and international relations are increasingly viewed as a single discipline" (2005: 2).

87 "[T]he study of international law has enjoyed something of a renaissance in the last two decades" (Simmons and Steinberg 2006: xxix).

88 Spiro 2000a: 585. "The risk for international law scholarship in over-committing to IR is that the latter's models prove unable to fully explain globalization as it becomes further embedded."

89 As a convention, scholars' associations with given states have been based on the locations of their institutions, not on their nationalities. Even so, as one might expect, a number of scholars teach in states other than those of their birth or nationality. Argentine native Marcelo G. Kohen teaches in Switzerland, for example, while Greek native Achilles Skordas teaches in the United Kingdom.

90 The following treatment of subject areas and representative interdisciplinary scholarship is only illustrative, not exhaustive.

91 The following treatment of research questions and representative interdisciplinary scholarship is only illustrative, not exhaustive. Important questions not treated in detail here are: What are the relationships between international law, norms, and "practical reason?" (Reus-Smit 2001; Toope 2000: 101–104). What is the relationship between constructivism and the English school? (Abbott 1999: 367; Beck 1996: 21, n. 10; Bederman 2001a: 476; Hathaway and Koh 2005: 18–19, 132; Reus-Smit 2002; Ruggie 1998.

92 On the role of U.S. hegemony in international legal change, see Byers and Nolte 2003.

93 Eyre and Suchman 1996; Haas 1992.

94 Abbott 2007; Deng 2007. For an account of the interwar creation of soft law related to international refugee protection, see Beck 1999.

95 A seminal work on legitimacy is by IR scholar, Inis L. Claude, Jr. (1966). A more recent high-profile work on the "power of legitimacy" by an IL scholar is Franck 1990. Also noteworthy are Franck 1995 and Hurd 1999. For an overview of "theories of fairness and legitimacy," see Hathaway and Koh 2005: 135–73). For a prominent critique of Franck's "legitimacy" perspective, see Keohane 1997.

96 For a review essay, "Why do nations obey international law?", see Koh 1997a.

97 Cosnard 2003; Klein 2003; Kohen 2003; Krisch 2003; Kwakwa 2003; Paulus 2003; Redgwell 2003; Roth 2003; Scott 2003; Skordas 2003; Stoll 2003; and Toope 2003.

98 Raffo, et al. 2007: 2.

99 To a somewhat lesser extent, a practitioner orientation also informed the Byers and Nolte (2003) edited volume.

100 Barnett is an eminent constructivist who holds a Ph.D. and serves the University of Minnesota as Harold Stassen Chair of International Affairs in Hubert Humphrey Institute of Public Policy and as Professor of Political Science.

101 Hirsch noted: "Less preoccupied with the question of how much compliance, scholars now pose the more intriguing question of why compliance is prevalent in the international community" (2004: 166). Still, a volume on law's role in international politics included essays that addressed fundamental questions on international law's salience: Allott 2000; Lowe 2000a; and Watts 2000. Moreover, a key question addressed by Goldsmith and Posner's prominent book (2005) was whether international law mattered.

102 Raffo, et al. 2007: 4, emphasis added. Even so, Thomas Schoenbaum contends: "International relations experts now readily admit the relevance of legal rules and processes in the construction and operation of international regimes and international problem solving. International law also offers IR new and useful models of cooperation. . . . But not everyone is convinced; in fact, doubters are probably in the majority" (Schoenbaum 2006: 61–62).

103 See, for example, all the contributors to Reus-Smit 2004a and some of the contributors – e.g. Kratochwil – to Byers 2000.

104 Cutler noted, however, that IR scholars tended to "refer to agents or actors, conflating the analytical concepts of source and subject" (2002: 65).

105 Cutler (2002, 61–62). This relatively novel development constitutes a departure from more traditional "calls for interdisciplinarity . . . premised on singling out a more or less realist version of international relations scholarship as the ideal companion, probably on the basis of the unarticulated thought that at least the realists know how the world works, how power politics operate, and how statesmen think" (Klabbers 2005: 38).

106 For treatments of constructivism in the context of international law, see, for example: Arend 1999; Finnemore 1996: 139–49, 2007; Hathaway and Koh 2005: 112–35; Kacowicz 2001; Price 2004: 107–109; Reus-Smit 2004a; Slaughter 2004a: 32–9; and Toope 2000: 93–9.

107 Slaughter was more sanguine in a recent assessment: "International lawyers . . . have learned to deploy political science techniques and draw on empirical data to make positive claims about how law works. Political scientists, on the other hand . . . have learned to listen to international lawyers' insights about how phenomena such as compliance actually work, and to build those insights into their theories and models" (2004a: 48–9).

108 Discussing interdisciplinarity per se, Bank and Lehmkuhl warned of other perils: "[A]ll too often the promise of interdisciplinarity is not kept. Rather, interdisciplinarity is confused with either crude instrumentalization of other disciplines' knowledge while ignoring the underlying methodological assumptions or an oversimplified dissolution of disciplinary distinctions" (2005: 155).

109 Raffo, et al. 2007: 6. Sriram noted in an earlier essay, too, that "great strides [had] been made" but "more remain[ed] to be done" (Sriram 2006: 467).

110 Hathaway and Koh 2005: 20. Barker noted in 2000: "[T]he prospects for interdisciplinary scholarship between international relations and international law have improved greatly in recent years" (96).

111 Ratner and Slaughter 1999: 302.

112 Simpson and Wheeler 2007: 124. Dias offered an even starker admonition: "Now is the time for the IL and IR communities to bridge their divide and address the multiple crises facing international law. Otherwise, not only will international law become redundant, but the IR and IL communities will face the threat of extinction as well" (Dias 2007: 286).

113 Three recent detailed expositions of promising areas for interdisciplinary research were offered by Slaughter ("The road ahead") (2004a: 39–49), Sriram ("Beyond responses from IR theory") (2006: 470–72), and Finnemore (2007).

114 In a 1996 reflection on "The prospects for interdisciplinary collaboration," it was already observed that "both International Relations and International Law began as largely state-centered disciplines," but that each had "come increasingly to appreciate the significance of non-state actors and phenomena. Indeed, some . . . scholars now even [found] the very notions of state-centric analysis and state sovereignty problematic" (Beck 1996: 5). For the view that IR remains fundamentally state-centric, to the discipline's detriment, and perhaps leading to its ultimate irrelevance and hence demise, see Spiro 2000a: 582–5.

115 Raffo, et al. 2007: 7. See also Finnemore 2007: 267.

116 Reus-Smit 2004b: 7. See also Gurowitz 2004; Spiro 2000a: 569; and Wippman 2004. For another view of the international legal system's future, see Arend 1999: 165–88.

117 See, for example, Finnemore 2007: 272–5. For a discussion of constructivism's special appeal for international lawyers, see Slaughter 2004a: 37. Here, she conceded that "most standard overviews of IR theory privilege the Rationalist versions of each of the paradigms. Constructivist variants are thus often found in the role of critique" (37).

The "liberal transnationalist" approach might also have some appeal for interdisciplinarians (e.g. Spiro 2007).

118 For useful overviews, see Hathaway and Koh 2005: 78–110; Slaughter 2000b, 2004a: 29–32.

119 See especially Koh 1996a, 1997a, 1997b, 1999.

120 For example, *Activists Beyond Borders* (Keck and Sikkink 1998), an analysis of transnational advocacy networks, won the 2000 University of Louisville Grawemeyer Award for ideas that improve world order: http://www.grawemeyer.org/winners/index.html.

121 As Slaughter recently averred in her "Prospectus" on IL and IR theory: "Domestic politics are as important for international lawyers as international politics" (2004a: 46).

Interdisciplinary interest in the domestic realm seems likely to continue in the near term, even as the prospect looms of further "cosmopolitanisation" in the global realm – with its potential blurring of the domestic and the international.

122 See Price and Reus-Smit 1998 and Slaughter 2004a: 37–9.

123 On the "logic of consequences" and "logic of appropriateness," concepts drawn from cognitive psychology, see March and Olsen (1999: 309–12). Hathaway and Koh depict "a conceptual divide [that] . . . interweaves the work of legal scholars and political scientists. The divide stands between those theories that tend to portray states primarily as unitary actors that engage in instrumental behavior designed to promote exogenously given national interests – which we term 'interest-based' theories – and those that tend to view states instead as motivated as much by ideas (or 'norms') that help to construct their perceived self-interest – grouped here together under the general heading of 'norm-based' theories" (Hathaway and Koh 2005: 2).

Of course, constructivists care also about the "logic of argumentation" (Reus-Smit 2004b: 23). (See also, e.g. Kratochwil 1989: 12.)

124 For a recent example of "critical constructivism," see Eckersley 2004. For an analysis of the affinities between critical theory and constructivism, see Price and Reus-Smit 1998.

125 Slaughter 2004a: 33. Although Slaughter was speaking largely to differences between instrumental and normative outlooks, her words may also be applied to broader distinctions between rationalist and sociological/constructivist perspectives (e.g. critical vs. otherwise).

Appendix

IL/IR interdisciplinary scholars

**** indicates *Journal of International Law and International Relations* board members

		IL scholars	
Name	*Degree*	*Title*	*Institutional affiliation(s)*
Abbott, Frederick M.	J.D., LL.M.	Edward Ball Eminent Scholar	Florida State University College of Law
Abbott, Kenneth	J.D.	Professor of Law Willard H. Pedrick Distinguished Research Scholar College of Law Also Professor of Global Studies, School of Global Studies	Arizona State University
**Allott, Philip	M.A., LL.M., LL.D.	Reader in International Public Law and a Fellow Formerly a legal counselor in the British Foreign and Commonwealth Office	Trinity College, University of Cambridge
** Alvarez, José	J.D.	Hamilton Fish Professor of International Law and Diplomacy Director of the Center on Global Legal Problems	Columbia University
Anghie, Antony	S.J.D.	Professor at the S. J. Quinney School of Law	University of Utah
** Baxi, Upendra	LL.B., LL.M., J.S.D.	Professor of Law in Development	University of Warwick
Bederman, David	J.D., M.Sc., Ph.D. in Law	Professor of Law	Emory University School of Law
Benvenisti, Eyal	LL.B., LL.M., J.S.D.	Professor of Law	Tel Aviv University, Faculty of Law, Israel
** Boisson de Chazournes, Laurence	Ph.D. (international law)	Professor and Director of the Department of Public International Law and International Organization	Faculty of Law, University of Geneva

IL scholars

Name	Degree	Title	Institutional affiliation(s)
** Brunnée, Jutta	LL.M., Dr. iur.	Metcalf Chair in Environmental Law	Faculty of Law, University of Toronto
Charlesworth, Hilary	LL.B., S.J.D.	Professor in RegNet and Director of the Centre for International Governance and Justice	Australian National University, Canberra
**Cosnard, Michel	B.Sc., M.Sc., Ph.D.	Professor of International Law	University of Maine (Le Mans, France)
Dunoff, Jeffrey L.	J.D., LL.M.	Charles Klein Professor of Law and Government and Director of the Institute for International Law and Public Policy at	Temple University Beasley School of Law
** Franck, Thomas	LL.B., LL.M., S.J.D.	Murry and Ida Becker Professor of Law Emeritus	New York University School of Law
** Hathaway, Oona A.	J.D.	Associate Professor of Law	Yale Law School
Hirsch, Moshe	LL.B., LL.M., Ph.D.	Arnold Brecht Chair in European Law, Vice Dean of the Faculty of Law, Senior Lecturer	Faculty of Law and Department of International Relations, Hebrew University of Jerusalem
Howse, Robert	LL.B., LL.M.	Professor of Law	University of Michigan Law School
** Kingsbury, Benedict W.	LL.B., M.Phil., D.Phil. (law)	Murry and Ida Becker Professor of Law Director, Institute for International Law and Justice	New York University School of Law
Klabbers, Jan	LL.D.	Professor	University of Helsinki, Faculty of Law
**Klein, Pierre	Licence en droit; licence spéciale en Droit International; PhD (Law)	Professor of International Law and Director of the Centre for International Law	Université Libre de Bruxelles (Belgium)
**Knop, Karen	LL.B., LL.M., S.J.D.	Professor	University of Toronto Faculty of Law
Koh, Harold Hongju	M.A. (Oxford), J.D.	Latrobe Smith Professor of International Law	Yale Law School
Kohen, Marcelo	Ph.D. (international law)	Professor of International Law	Graduate Institute of International Studies, Geneva, Switzerland
** Koskenniemi, Martti	LL.B., LL.M., LL.D.	Professor of International Law	University of Helsinki Finland
Krisch, Nico	Dr. iur.	Lecturer in Law	London School of Economics, Department of Law
Kritsiotis, Dino	LL.M.	Reader in Public International Law	University of Nottingham
Mavroidis, Petros C.	LL.B., LL.M., LL.M., Ph.D. (law)	Professor of Law	Columbia Law School
Morris, Madeline	J.D.	Professor of Law	Duke University
Nolte, Georg	Dr. iur.	Professor of Law	University of Munich, Germany
O'Connell, Mary Ellen	LL.B., J.D.	Robert and Marion Short Professor of Law	University of Notre Dame

		IL scholars	
Name	*Degree*	*Title*	*Institutional affiliation(s)*
Orentlicher, Diane	J.D.	Professor of Law	American University, Washington College of Law
**Paulus, Andreas	Ph.D.	Professor of International and Public Law	University of Göttingen
** Provost, René	LL.B., LL.M., D.Phil. (international law)	Director, CHRLP (Law)	McGill University Faculty of Law
Ratner, Steven	J.D.	Professor of Law	University of Michigan Law School
Redgwell, Catherine	LL.B., M.Sc.	Professor of International Law	University College London
Sadat, Leila Nadya	J.D., LL.M.	Henry H. Oberschelp Professor of Law	Washington University – St. Louis Law
**Sands, Philippe	LL.M.	Professor of Law and Director of the Centre on International Courts and Tribunals in the Faculty	Faculty of Laws – University College London
Schoenbaum, Thomas J.	J.D., Ph.D. (law)	Dean and Virginia Rusk Professor of International Law	University of Georgia School of Law
		Professor of Political Science	University of Georgia
Setear, John	J.D.	Thomas F. Bergin Professor	University of Virginia
Simma, Bruno	Dr. iur.	Judge	International Court of Justice
		Former Dean	University of Munich Faculty of Law
**Simpson, Gerry	LL.B., LL.M., S.J.D.	Professor in Public International Law, Department of Law	London School of Economics
Skordas, Achilles	Dr. iur.	Reader in Law	University of Bristol School of Law
Spiro, Peter J.	J.D.	Charles R. Weiner Professorship in International Law	Temple University Beasley School of Law
Stern, Brigitte	LL.M., M.C.J.	Professeur à l'Université	Paris 1 – Panthéon-Sorbonne France
Stoll, Peter-Tobias	Dr. iur.	Professor	Georg-August-Universität Göttingen – Law
		Managing Director, Institute of International Law	
Trachtman, Joel P.	J.D.	Professor of International Law	The Fletcher School
Wiessner, Siegfried	Dr. iur. LL.M.	Professor of Law; Founder and Director LL.M./J.S.D. Program in Intercultural Human Rights at	St. Thomas University School of Law
**Willard, Andrew	B.A.	Senior Research Scholar	Yale Law School
		President of the Policy Sciences Center	
Wippman, David	J.D.	Professor of Law	Cornell University

IR scholars

Name	Degree	Title	Institutional affiliation(s)
Adamson, Fiona	Ph.D.	Assistant Professor, School of Public Policy	University College London
Alter, Karen J.	Ph.D.	Associate Professor, Department of Political Science	Northwestern University
Arend, Anthony Clark	Ph.D.	Professor of Government / Adjunct Professor of Law	Georgetown University Department of Government / Georgetown University Law Center
Barnett, Michael N.	Ph.D.	Harold Stassen Chair of International Affairs / Professor of Political Science	University of Minnesota, Hubert Humphrey Institute of Public Policy
Beck, Robert J.	Ph.D.	Associate Professor, Department of Political Science	University of Wisconsin – Milwaukee
Biersteker, Thomas J.	Ph.D.	Luce Professor of Transnational Organizations	Brown University
Diehl, Paul F.	Ph.D.	Henning Larsen Professor of Political Science	University of Illinois at Urbana-Champaign
Downs, George W.	Ph.D.	Professor, Department of Politics	New York University
★★Finnemore, Martha	Ph.D.	Professor of Political Science and International Affairs	George Washington University
Goldstein, Judith	Ph.D.	Professor of Political Science	Stanford University
Gowlland-Debbas, Vera	Ph.D.	Professor in the International Law section	Graduate Institute of International Studies, Geneva Switzerland
Gurowitz, Amy	Ph.D.	Lecturer in Political Science	University of California at Berkeley
Hurrell, Andrew	D.Phil.	University Lecturer in International Relations, Director of the Centre of International Studies, Faculty Fellow	Nuffield College, Oxford
Kacowicz, Arie M.	Ph.D.	Senior Lecturer in International Relations	Hebrew University of Jerusalem
Kahler, Miles	Ph.D.	Rohr Professor of Pacific International Relations	Graduate School of International Relations and Pacific Studies
★★Keohane, Robert O.	Ph.D.	Professor of International Affairs	Woodrow Wilson School, Princeton University
★★Krasner, Stephen D.	Ph.D.	Graham H. Stuart Professor, Department of Political Science	Stanford University
★★Kratochwil, Friedrich	Ph.D.	Chair of International Relations	European University Institute, Political and Social Sciences
Mansfield, Edward D.	Ph.D.	Hum Rosen Professor of Political Science	University of Pennsylvania
Martin, Lisa L.	Ph.D.	Professor of Government	Harvard University
Milner, Helen V.	Ph.D.	B. C. Forbes Professor of Politics and International Affairs	Princeton University
Moravcsik, Andrew	Ph.D.	Professor of Politics and Director of the European Union Program	Princeton University
Price, Richard	Ph.D.	Associate Professor of Political Science	University of British Columbia Canada

IR scholars

Name	Degree	Title	Institutional affiliation(s)
Reno, William	Ph.D.	Associate Professor	Northwestern University
Reus-Smit, Christian	Ph.D.	Professor and Head of the Department of International Relations	Research School of Pacific and Asian Studies at the Australian National University, Canberra
Rosendorff, Peter	Ph.D. (economics)	Associate Professor of International Relations and Economics	University of Southern California
Roth, Brad R.	Ph.D.	Associate Professor, Department of Political Science	Wayne State University
Sandholtz, Wayne	Ph.D.	Professor, Department of Political Science	University of California, Irvine
**Scott, Shirley V.	Ph.D.	Associate Professor in International Relations	University of New South Wales, Australia
Sikkink, Kathryn	Ph.D.	Arleen C. Carlson Professor of Political Science: Professor of Law	University of Minnesota University of Minnesota Law School
Simmons, Beth A.	Ph.D.	Professor of Government	Harvard University
Snidal, Duncan	Ph.D.	Associate Professor, Department of Political Science	University of Chicago
**Stein, Janice	Ph.D.	Harrowston Professor of Conflict Management and Negotiation	University of Toronto Department of Political Science
**Walker, R. B. J. (Rob)	Ph.D.	Professor of International Relations	Keele University
Wheeler, Nicholas J.	Ph.D.	Professor, Department of International Politics	University of Wales Aberystwyth

Hybrid scholars

Name	Degree	Title	Institutional affiliation(s)
**Byers, Michael	D.Phil., Ph.D., LL.B., B.C.L.	Canadian Research Chair in International Law and Politics	University of British Columbia
Chinkin, Christine	LL.B., LL.M., LL.M., Ph.D.	Professor of International Law	London School of Economics and Political Science
Eckersley, Robyn	B.Juris, LL.B., M.Phil., Ph.D.	Professor, School of Political Science, Sociology and Criminology Previously served as a public lawyer	University of Melbourne
Ku, Charlotte	M.A.L.D., Ph.D.	Assistant Dean for Graduate and International Legal Studies Formerly Executive Director of the American Society of International Law	University of Illinois College of Law
Lowe, Vaughan	LL.B., LL.M., Ph.D.	Chichele Professor of Public International Law and a Fellow of All Souls' College	University of Oxford
Slaughter, Anne-Marie	J.D., D.Phil. (international relations)	Dean	Princeton University Woodrow Wilson School

Hybrid scholars

Name	Degree	Title	Institutional affiliation(s)
Sriram, Chandra Lekha	J.D., Ph.D. (politics)	Professor; Chair in Human Rights; Director Centre on Human Rights in Conflict	University of East London School of Law
Steinberg, Richard H.	J.D., Ph.D.	Professor of Law Senior Scholar, Division of International, Comparative, and Area Studies	UCLA Stanford University
Sweet, Alec Stone	Ph.D.	Leitner Professor of Law, Politics and International Studies	Yale Law School
**Toope, Stephen	LL.B., B.C.L., Ph.D.	President (2006–) Professor of Law	University of British Columbia McGill University
Weiss, Edith Brown	J.D., Ph.D.	Francis Cabell Brown Professor of International Law Co-director of the Joint Degree in Law and Government	Georgetown University Law Center

Practitioners

Name	Degree	Title	Institutional affiliation(s)
Deng, Francis M.	LL.B., LL.M., J.S.D.	Senior Fellow United Nations Secretary-General's representative on internally displaced persons	Brookings Institution Foreign Policy Studies Program
Dias, Clarence J.	Ph.D., S.J.D.	President	International Center for Law in Development
Kwakwa, Edward	LL.M., J.S.D.	Deputy Legal Counsel and Head of the Legal and Constitutional Affairs Section	WIPO
Lutz, Ellen L.	M.A., J.D.	Executive Director Former Executive Director	Cultural Survival Tufts University Fletcher School's Center for Human Rights and Conflict Resolution
Mahmoud, Youssef	Ph.D. (linguistics)	U.N. Secretary-General's Deputy Special Representative for Burundi	
Muggah, Robert		Doctoral candidate Project manager	Oxford University Small Arms Survey, an independent research project located at the Graduate Institute of International Studies, Geneva
Raffo, Veronica		Consultant	World Bank, Poverty Reduction and Economic Management Network
Ward, Curtis Anthony	B.A., J.D., LL.M.	Independent expert and advisor on technical assistance CTC liaison with regional and international organizations	United Nations Security Council Counter-Terrorism Committee (CTC)

2

International law and international community

Andreas Paulus

The term "international community" adds a normative element of common values to the more factual notion of an interconnected international society composed of states and other international actors. The chapter analyzes institutionalist, liberal and postmodern views of the international community. It also looks at more recent claims that international law is fragmenting rather than developing into a community. The chapter concludes that a common ground of values is needed for international law to function. The international community does not constitute a system superior to all others, but is a shortcut for the dealings of states and non-state actors beyond state boundaries, and for a collective endeavor to tackle problems such as the protection of the environment and the prevention of genocide and famine.

> But do the nations constitute a community?
> . . . The history of International Law is, largely, the history of the formation of this community, so far as it may be said to have been formed – the building up of common opinions upon common practices and the writings of commonly accepted commentators.
>
> (Wilson 1969: 455; emphasis in original)

Introduction

In the age of globalization, the "international community" appears omnipresent: it acts and intervenes, as in the case of Kosovo (Klein 2000), it helps the victims of natural disasters, is called on to redouble its efforts to prevent and suppress terrorist acts, as after the attacks against the United States on September 11 (UN Security Council 2001a), or seems helpless and inactive in spite of the best of its intentions, as in Darfur (Paulus 2008a). Resolutions of international organizations and NGO conferences alike use the term in an almost inflationary way. It is invoked by statespersons around the world. Even the Bush administration, which came into office reluctant to use a concept so much tied to a more egalitarian view of international relations than its own (Rice 2000), is now using the term regularly in its press releases (White House 2008).

It is perhaps no coincidence that the popularity of the concept has grown along with the awareness of the consequences of globalization. Whereas the latter stands for the sometimes harsh economic realities of an age which seems no longer to allow for the territorial protection of local habits and mores, the "international community" connotes the emergence of a new global home, a worldwide village of human commonality emphasizing interpersonal bonds rather than territorial borders. And yet, it may also be used for the exclusion of others, such as rogue states, terrorists, and, at times, anti-globalization activists.

The term "international community" is sometimes used interchangeably with the term "international society" (Henkin 1995a).[1] As a more extensive inquiry has shown, the usage is far from uniform (Paulus 2001b: 9, 439). Nevertheless, one may say – with the necessary caution – that a community adds a normative element, a minimum of subjective cohesion to the social bond between its members. Whereas society emphasizes factual interconnections and interrelations, community looks to values, beliefs and subjective feelings. The differentiation between society and community thus echoes the German sociologist Ferdinand Tönnies' distinction between *Gemeinschaft* and *Gesellschaft* (Tönnies 1935). But despite the inclusiveness of the term, even a universal community knows an outside, an environment against which it defines and delineates its identity (Simma and Paulus 1998: 268). Hence the debate on "rogue states" and an "axis of evil" composed of states that do not seem to share the alleged consensus (Bush 2002a).

Recent developments, from September 11 to the war in Iraq, have pushed the idea of an international community based on common values and international law farer away than ever. The counter-image of international community, the "clash of civilizations" (Huntington 1996), appears nearer to reality. It is however precisely the multiplicity of religious and ethical approaches to the world that make the agreement on a minimum of common values so important. It is one of the main tasks of international law to provide rules of coexistence and, increasingly, to find avenues to solutions to global problems not in spite, but because of the global pluralism of value and belief systems.

Analyzing the international community requires more than the development of abstract concepts, however. It requires the analysis of the impact of the concept on legal, social, and political practice, including an analysis of its effects on the persons at the receiving end, so to speak. Which purposes does the term serve? Is the invocation of the "international community" a move to hide one's own lust for power behind a smoke-screen of high-mindedness – or, in Martti Koskenniemi's provocative words, "kitsch" (Koskenniemi 2005b: 121–23)?[2] Or does it serve the useful purpose of pointing to a claim of authority rooted not in a domestic source, but in some internationally agreed basic values of global import? Obviously, to answer these questions in any comprehensive way is impossible.[3] But this chapter intends to show that most concepts of international law are based on a particular view of the international community.

We will look at three different understandings of the international community, institutionalist, (neo)liberal, and postmodernist. Whereas an institutional view couples the development of an international community to the establishment of successful international institutions (Abi-Saab 1987; Dupuy 2002; Simma 1994; Tomuschat 1999; cf. Miller and Bratspies 2008), liberal views are increasingly skeptical of public international institutions and base the international legal order on individual preferences and human rights instead (Buchanan and Keohane 2006; Reisman 1990; Slaughter 1995). Finally, postmodernist writers reject the universality of liberal principles and demand a regard for the other, for difference rather than unity, for unintended consequences rather than good intentions (Kennedy 1999).

We will proceed to conceptualize the emerging pluralism of legal orders and ask ourselves whether the increasing perception of the "fragmentation" of the international legal order will render any attempt at a holistic, communitarian view of the international legal realm impossible (Teubner and Fischer-Lescano 2004). We will also look at the emerging discipline of "global administrative law" that develops a view of the role of international law "from the bottom" rather than starting at the "constitutional" level of the ordering of the global international society (Krisch and Kingsbury 2006a; Kingsbury et al. 2005).

This contribution concludes that contemporary international law embraces parts of all the conceptions developed earlier. However, the different attempts to establish an international legal order are evidence of the need to develop a comprehensive vision, even if such conception will always remain partial and incomplete. Laying out one's view of the whole appears preferable to the holding of implicit assumptions without admitting much criticism or debate. *Ubi societas, ibi jus*, a Roman proverb says: No society without law. But the reverse is also true: *Ubi jus, ibi societas*. While law cannot create a community alone, it needs a minimum of common values and procedures to function. Thus, the debate on the legal character of international law is also a debate on whether a minimum of international community can be established to allow for international law to develop.

Conceptions of the "international community"

Every concept of international law is based on an understanding of the social structure international law applies to. Accordingly, every theory of international law involves, explicitly or implicitly, a concept of international community or society. At the same time, these background understandings are not of an exclusively legal character. Thus, international law does not require the acceptance of one, or any, of the following conceptualizations. And yet, conceptions of "international community" shed light on the way international law is understood and interpreted.

Concepts of international law and order do not exist somewhere in a vacuum. Rather, they are related to perceptions of political and legal events. Both the terrorist attacks on the United States of September 11, and the latest war against Iraq by the United States and a "coalition of the willing" (Benvenisti

2006), a war that was, according to most accounts, contrary to international law (Fisler Damrosch and Oxman 2003: 553–642; Paulus 2004b), challenge traditional concepts of an international community based on the "sovereign equality" of states, as Article 2, para. 1, of the Charter of the United Nations has it. September 11 puts into question the conceptualization of the international community as a "community of states" with little, if any, direct participation of individuals in global governance. When the main security threat does not emanate from states but from terrorist groups of individuals, states appear to have lost some of their monopoly of the use of force. When the remaining superpower feels free to ignore the most basic rules of international law regarding the prohibition on the use of force, but demands strict adherence from other states, sovereign equality cannot be taken for granted, not even as a normative ideal.

Do September 11 and Iraq uncover permanent flaws in the idea of an international community based on a global political "overlapping consensus" (Franck 1995: 14; Rawls 1996: 147; Roth 1999: 6) and the rule of law, or do they merely reflect the broadening of globalization from the economic to the political realm? International law can serve both as a constraint on power – for instance prohibiting the use of force – and as a translation of power into concrete orders and prohibitions. If the international community threatened the "right to survival" of societies by rendering the state incapable of countering new threats from non-governmental actors such as al-Qaeda by legal means, states might choose to protect themselves as they see fit and look for international justification later. Democratic constitutions may question the legitimacy of a legal order that emanates from the consensus of states independently of their democratic legitimacy. If, contrariwise, the so-called "global war on terror"[4] resulted in an international law embodying the writ of a superpower rather than sovereign equality, its worldwide acceptance would suffer. However, the United States does not seem to lay out a coherent vision of such a hegemonic international order (Alvarez 2003; Krisch 2005; Vagts 2001).

Let us have a look at some conceptualizations of the international community to see whether and how they accommodate the situation after "September 11" and "Iraq." This chapter will single out three strands of responses to these questions – institutionalist–communitarian, (neo)liberal, and postmodernist. We will use recent developments as a kind of "hard case" to test some of the conceptualizations of the international community.

Institutionalist theory and globalization

Many international lawyers base the development of a true international community or society on a societal consciousness encompassing the whole of humanity (Allott 1990; Dupuy 1986). Wolfgang Friedmann established the distinction between the law of coexistence and the law of cooperation (Friedmann 1964). Taking up that distinction, some contemporary scholars, especially in the German constitutional tradition, developed concepts of a more institutionalized international community. In that view, international law moves – or should move – "from bilateralism to community interest" (Simma 1994), is about to establish "world interior politics" (Delbrück 1993/4), or shall ensure "the survival of mankind on the eve of a new century" (Tomuschat 1999). Instances of such an order in contemporary international law can be seen, e.g. in *jus cogens* (Paulus 2005), obligations *erga omnes* (Tomuschat and Thouvenin 2006), in the concept of the common heritage of mankind (Dupuy 1986: 159–68), in the alleged "constitutionalization" of the UN security system (Fassbender 1998b) and of the WTO trading system (Petersmann 1997: 421), and in the establishment of the International Criminal Court.[5] Those who believe in a parallelism between legal norms and institutions – what Georges Abi-Saab

has called the "law or fundamental hypothesis of 'legal physics'" (Abi-Saab 1998: 256) – demand the strengthening of global institutions to respond to the challenge of globalization.

However, institutionalism faces increasing difficulty with the current political mood after September 11 and Iraq. The terrorist attacks on the United States have confirmed the critical attitude of the United States towards European institutionalism. The U.S. government, at the time by-and-large supported by the American public, concluded that America needed to protect itself, and would not depend on the support of others.[6] Indeed, in the writings of Robert Kagan (Kagan 2002, 2003), which have been widely cited, European institutionalism is presented as a system for good times only. In the European paradise, slow and bureaucratic institutions may be useful, but the world writ large is a dangerous place, in which an America untied by international institutions needs to provide order – in the best interests of the world in general, and of Europe in particular.

Since the Iraq adventure has turned into a quagmire, such self-assuredness appears increasingly unwarranted. In a postscript to his book, Kagan admits that the exercise of power needs legitimacy to be successful, and that international institutions in general, and Europe in particular, can provide it (Kagan 2004: 65). However, he charges Europe with not fulfilling that role properly when it withholds legitimacy from American unilateral actions that the United States deems necessary for the maintenance of international peace and security. Thus, the display of military power needs to be grounded in legitimacy to provide for order. However, what power can legitimacy have if it has no other option than to approve the use of force? Nevertheless, there seems to be agreement that international institutions may indeed serve a useful function even for the single superpower.

Thus, the aftermath of September 11 has not led to a diminishing of the role of international institutions, and has not stopped the institutionalization of international or rather global relations. Indeed, one could make the point that the role of the Security Council has been enhanced rather than diminished: Its lack of approval made the attack on Iraq even more risky, and the result so far certainly does not invite repetition. Both the United States and the United Kingdom brought forward legal arguments that presented their action as an implementation of, rather than derogation from, existing Security Council mandates (Taft and Buchwald 2003).[7] Indeed, although they did not receive backing from the Security Council for the attack itself, the United States and the United Kingdom returned to the Council to legitimize the occupation and the establishment of a new democratic order in Iraq.[8]

In areas beyond security, from trade to health and human rights, it is even more difficult to question the idea of an unstoppable march of globalization towards the construction of global institutions. The German sociologist Niklas Luhmann has described this development as a move from territoriality to functionality (Luhmann 1997: 158–60, 1995b: 571), from a world of sovereign territorial states to a world of functional institutions. The main characteristic of international institutionalism consists in the multiplicity of institutions in the international realm without an overarching hierarchy (Teubner and Fischer-Lescano 2004; Paulus 2004a).[9] Thus, international institutionalism will not end in a world state, but will have to deal with pluralism and multiplicity of institutional designs, from governmental to non-governmental actors. Teubner and Fischer-Lescano regard collisions of different regimes as collisions between the diverse rationalities within global society. Their cure lies in a constitutionalization of the particular rather than in the search for a representation of the general.

Discourse ethics and democracy theory emphasize the need of embedding global democracy into institutional designs (Habermas 1996: 132, 672; Held 1995). Some suggest the development of global

democracy – a people's chamber of the U.N. General Assembly might constitute a beginning (Franck 1995: 483). Others have insisted on the nation state as the primary place of democratic legitimation, control, and accountability (Habermas 1996: 225, 672). Further means of legitimation seem necessary, in particular for the more informal exercise of power by international bodies not subject to state control. But the pluralism of the international community seems not to fulfill a basic condition for a democracy based on simple majority voting. Rather, considerable modifications of domestic notions of democratic legitimacy are required to apply them to the international community (Besson 2007; Paulus 2008b).

Liberalism after September 11

The interstate model of international community, in which individual human beings acquire rights and duties only via their national states, appears to be in trouble when not only goods and services, but also individuals are increasingly moving internationally, and where their ideas cross borders via the internet or other means of global communication. A liberal concept of international community draws the consequences of these developments by focusing on individual rights and duties. Liberals and neoliberals demand a reconstruction of international law on an interindividual basis. Informal "government networks" may become effective regulators, balanced by a minimum of effective domestic control (Slaughter 2004b).

Anne-Marie Slaughter has concluded that the state as unitary actor has largely become an abstraction far from reality. Rather, the liberal state is "disaggregated" into its component parts, in particular in the three branches of government: legislative, executive, judicial (Slaughter 1995, 2004b: 131–65).[10] Accordingly, these branches of government are becoming separate, if not independent, actors at the international level, building "transgovernmental" networks with their counterparts from other liberal states. "Transjudicial networks" of judges and lawyers play an increasing role in the self-awareness of courts and tribunals all over the world: "The system these judges are creating is better described as a community of courts than as a centralized hierarchy" (Slaughter 2004b: 68; see also Slaughter 2003). Of course, this community also includes "legitimate differences." Nevertheless, lawyers from liberal states are considered to have as much, if not more, in common with each other than with their domestic counterparts in the other branches of government.

Whereas more moderate representatives of liberal ethics justified classical international law as allowing for multiple, diverse societies (Rawls 1999), more radical philosophers demand the establishment of a "world social order" fulfilling the promises of human rights at the international level (Beitz 1979; Pogge 1989). The international community is not based on formal legitimacy alone, but also incorporates material fairness, with "shared moral imperatives and values" (Rawls 1999: 10–11). The institutional expression of liberal values is less important than the protection of individual rights. In a liberal community of individuals, the justification of state sovereignty is removed when the state fails to protect the rights of its citizens. In the case of some writers, this position translates into a justification of unilateral intervention for the protection of human rights – from Kosovo to Iraq (Tesón 2005).

September 11 has bolstered the views of those who share both the belief in the superiority of western values and the disdain for strong international institutions beyond the (democratic) nation state (White House 2002). Control of the superpower seems less important than the confidence in its values and ability to act for the common good – or, rather, for the safeguard of individual rights of people everywhere. Islamic fundamentalists have literally declared war against liberal democracy, and the only recipe against these enemies of liberty is accepting the challenge.

Mechanisms of negotiation, accommodation and consensus seem inapt to counter the threat. "Either you are with us, or you are with the terrorists" (Bush 2001). Thus, liberalism is (ab)used by neoconservatives for the benefit of a hegemonic project. As the Iraq war shows, this odd combination of liberalism with Schmittian concepts of friend and foe may become a self-fulfilling prophecy.

While the Iraq war separated a legalist and an imperialist wing of liberalism, these models share a potentially revolutionary individualist view of international law, in which statist models and ideas are discarded for the benefit of individuals (Buchanan 2004; Buchanan and Keohane 2006; Tesón 1992). Human rights are the new paradigm, also at the cost of delegitimizing interstate institutions. However, this raises not only the question of how to stabilize international law without institutions, but also the question of how the international community can cope with pluralism and difference. This question is at the core of the postmodern challenge.

Postmodern critique of international community

In a postmodern understanding, community is not possible without exclusion and suppression of "the other." And indeed, the exclusion of others is as much part of any community concept as their inclusion. Thus, community may be used as an ideological construct for the maintenance of structures of power, excluding the "other," the marginal, the different. Postmodernists criticize both the social–democratic enthusiasm for new international bureaucracies and the neoliberal reliance on unquestioned liberal values.

The liberal concept of community is rejected because it does not take account of the multiplicity of ethical approaches and marginalizes those opposed to the dominant model (Kennedy 1999: 123). Accordingly, in the last resort, liberal models of the international community stabilize – voluntarily or involuntarily – American hegemony. The reliance on the market hides the political nature of this choice and ultimately strives in vain to protect neoliberalism from critique.

The postmodern critique of institutionalism is no less acerbic than the neoliberal one: Accordingly, the vision of communitarian unity shares the vice of the ideal of a liberal community: it excludes and marginalizes the outsider. In addition, an international institutionalism cannot cure the lack of legitimacy of its universalism. In the eyes of some postmodernists, international community is thus nothing but a "reification"[11] of a theoretical construct for ideological purposes. In the words of David Kennedy: "[I]nternational law [is] not as a set of rules or institutions, but . . . a group of professional disciplines in which people pursue projects in various quite different institutional, political, and national settings" (Kennedy 1999: 83).

The reactions to September 11 by the Bush administration and many other governments have demonstrated how the language of community may be used for curtailing civil liberties. The language of "either you are with us or with the terrorists" shows the utility of community for the exclusion of critique. Nevertheless, the ideological (ab)use of international law in general, and the community concept in particular, should not obscure the need for finding a more than subjective basis for grounding an international legal order which appears under increasing strain, even existential threat. Maybe this is indeed the time for the defense of an international legal community of some sort, based on imperfect, but consensual legal rules as the expression of, in Martti Koskenniemi's term, a "culture of formalism" (Koskenniemi 2001: 494). In this vein, the true test for the emergence of an international community does not consist in the justificatory value of the community concept, but in the inclusiveness of its results.

More liberal mainstreamers – institutionalists and neoliberals alike – point to the postmodernist lack of a normative vision as either resulting in an unfettered political realism (Paulus 2001a),[12] or in a complete lack of defense against the fundamentalist challenge (Franck 2002). If any normative international legal project is rejected, no yardstick exists to evaluate international behavior of states, or terrorists, or anybody else. But such critique needs to differentiate between legitimate ideology critique and an extreme moral relativism – which many, if not all postmodernists reject.

The international community between fragmentation and unity

Any comprehensive vision of the international community will have to respond to the objection that the diversity of international society cannot be captured by one single concept. Indeed, it appears that in view of the diversity of contemporary international law, fragmentation rather than community has become the key term to describe contemporary international society (Koskenniemi 2006b; Koskenniemi and Leino 2002). Whereas some lament – or try to re-establish (Dupuy 2002) – the lost unity, others embrace the shift "from territoriality to functionality," from a world of sovereign territorial states to a world of functional institutions limited to specific issue areas (Luhmann 1995b: 571, 1997: 158–60). More radical representatives of this view claim that the different systems lack minimal commonality to maintain any coherent overarching system of general international law (Fischer-Lescano and Teubner 2004: 1004–16). This chapter argues that the perception of an increasing autonomy of the subsystems does not lead to a complete substitution of general international law. On the contrary, in a fragmented international legal order, some sort of bond between the different parts is necessary. The use of the concept of the international community is an expression of the need for such an overarching conception of the "whole" of international law, even if it appears, for obvious reasons, impossible to identify one single all-encompassing model.

According to the fragmentation critique, the increasing compartmentalization of international society requires specifically tailored solutions to common and indeed collective action problems of states. Legal regimes need to be specific, not general. The lofty abstractness of classical international law leads it to oblivion. Rather, international law ought to become divided up into different issue areas: criminal law, trade law, human rights law, etc. "General" international law has all but ceased to exist, or matter (Teubner 1997; Zumbansen 2001). Following the German sociologist Niklas Luhmann, Gunther Teubner and Andreas Fischer-Lescano have argued that legal systems can establish themselves in acts of "autopoiesis" (self-creation) without the need of a centralizing and over-arching system of law (Fischer-Lescano and Teubner 2004: 1009, 1014, 1032; Teubner 1989). Accordingly, international law cannot constitute an overarching system of universal law because it lacks a subject in need of regulation. An international society or community is an abstraction that does not reflect social reality.

According to the proponents of auto-poiesis, each subsystem of international law is itself capable of developing the relevant decision-making processes in a transparent and democratic fashion. But this proposition presupposes an analysis of the proper identification of those affected by the decisions within a given issue area. Due to the uncertainty and fallibility of all consequential analysis, however, the effects of decisions in one subsystem on others will also be indeterminate and uncertain. Therefore, the presumption underlying the general competence of states – namely that most decisions in the public sphere affect all citizens and must therefore be legitimized, directly or indirectly, by all of them – is also valid internationally, whether one deals with human rights, the environment, or trade and development. In turn, this demonstrates that the compart-

mentalization of political decisions into issue areas carries considerable political and democratic costs. As soon as public interests are at stake, only public decision making can claim to be representative of the whole of society independent of a specific issue area (von der Pfordten 2001: 128, 218).

Furthermore, general international law still provides the basic rules on international lawmaking and, at least subsidiarily, on their enforcement (Simma and Pulkowski 2006: 529). The subsystems often refer back to general international law on these matters (Koskenniemi 2006b). The legal regulations applied in the different issue areas, from internet regulation to the WTO, from environmental treaties to the International Criminal Tribunal for the former Yugoslavia, stem from the very state or interstate bodies that proponents of fragmentation have dismissed before as increasingly irrelevant. Thus, a trend from territorial to functional tasks will be followed by functional rather than territorial conflicts of norms. These conflicts, however, cannot be decided at the national level, but require international regulation. Hence the perceived need of some sort of international constitution as repository of conflict rules between different issue areas (Trachtman 2006: 627; but see Dunoff 2006: 674).

The parsimonious character of international law makes it quite malleable for the self-ordering of regimes, within certain limits. International law grounds its obligations either in consent or in custom and recognizes certain general principles, either internationally or as derived from domestic legal systems (Article 38 of the ICJ Statute). One may dispute whether such an order fulfills Hart's requirements for a legal system (Hart 1994: 213), but it certainly provides enough leeway for the *leges speciales* of functionally differentiated regimes. The main problem does not lie in the international legal requirements for binding norms, but in the limitation of its law-making subjects to states. Yet this problem is not impossible to overcome if one

51

contemplates applying the same criteria – namely, the legally binding nature of formal commitments and of custom accompanied by a joint conviction regarding their legally binding nature – to the pronouncements of non-state actors. Moreover, different from political communities, non-state actors can only bind themselves, not others.

It is thus not surprising that the need for legitimation beyond one single subsystem leads to the acceptance of rules for the common ordering of the international realm, such as human rights or the protection of the global commons. Some of these rules will be more of a formal nature – how rules are to be made and to be interpreted – others will be substantive, setting material limits to the self-ordering of subsystems. Ultimately, of course, it is a matter of perspective whether one interprets the use of norms from other systems as an autonomous incorporation or as evidence for the existence of one common system. By the same token, however, recognition of the same body of non-derogable norms beyond the fallback rules of international law demonstrates the "staying power" of an international *jus cogens* over and above the ordinary norms of specific legal regimes (Paulus 2005; Tomuschat and Thouvenin 2006). The main problem with the theory of the autopoietic character of the law of new legal regimes most likely relates to its lack of attention for questions of legitimacy – a legitimacy that each subsystem alone cannot provide.

To give an example: In the Yahoo! case (Reimann 2003),[13] a French court decided that Yahoo! had to block a racist memorabilia-auctioning webpage as far as it can be accessed in France because its display there violates section R.645-2 of the French Criminal Code. In this case, a solution on the basis of internet self-ordering appears illegitimate. The 80-year-old Holocaust victim is affected (and offended) by neo-Nazi propaganda on right-wing websites even if she does not use the internet, but learns of the contents of the sites

in her local newspaper. She is not represented, however, when the internet community is allowed to regulate itself. Likewise, everybody, not only the potential internet users, will be affected by the success of strategies to improve access to the internet. This would require, in turn, that legitimate decisions need to include representatives of society as a whole – and leads, in the absence of representative international fora, to a preference for local or national decisions based on democratic legitimacy rather than for international decisions of unaccountable expert bodies. The best solution, however, would consist in a truly international regulation that takes account of the non-systemic concerns – i.e. the integration of internet regulation in the general international legal regime – which may include the delegation of competences to the most subsidiary and most special level (Grewlich 2006; Mayer 2004; but see also Caral 2004).

Because decisions made within many systems profoundly influence the fate of those not within the system, some general system of accountability and legitimacy appears necessary. At the very least, functional systems should be built by processes of a general nature – such as public international law treaties – and not by custom-designed special procedures. In other words, the move from territoriality to functionality should not be accompanied by a move from democracy to technocracy. Subsystems must include a minimum degree of public control over the private exercise of power.

In the end, decision makers do not represent functional systems, but human beings, human beings who are not – or at least should not be – the objects, but the subjects of the system. Although each human being belongs to several functional associations, she is a whole, not a functionally disaggregated entity (von der Pfordten 2001: 125). As such, she needs not only functional systems that serve her specific needs, but also a comprehensive system of representation which is able to weigh different interests against each other. Thus, states as representatives of the public appear to be not at all redundant.

Attempts to reduce quasi-"constitutional" questions of the ordering of international society to an analysis of "global administrative law," have demonstrated the broad range of tasks international law has been fulfilling in different administrative settings, from administrating territory to the (de)regulation of global markets (Kingsbury et al. 2005; Krisch and Kingsbury 2006a). But for its valuable insights, this approach has not been successful in showing that the idea of an international public order should be discarded. Rather, it appears that, in reverse, the development of an international administrative law depends on the understanding of the "constitutional" grounding of such law (but see Krisch 2006).

Thus, fragmentation, whether cultural, ideological, or functional, does not do away with the need for the intervention by the general body politic. However, it makes the absence of a global public opinion, let alone a global democracy of a representative nature, even more glaring. If many global problems can only be solved at the world level, decisions should not be left to bureaucratic functionalists, but to representatives of broader constituencies.

Conclusion

This chapter has tried to identify the basic idea of international communitarianism, namely that international legal theory should not shy away from comprehensive views of the international society or from normative concepts of international community. Not as an imperialist idea of prescribing one single model of international community, but as a forum for debate, even contestation, of the differing views on the social fabric of international law and of the road ahead towards greater inclusivity of international law.

Such a result is compatible with each of our community models, but requires important qualifications. For an institutionalist, it entails a less hierarchical, pluralist understanding of community. There may be common values as expressed, in particular, in *jus cogens* norms. However, the profound pluralism of the contemporary international community prevents the emergence of a Kelsenian, monist structure. A (neo)liberal understanding of community correctly identifies the addressee of the decisions in question, namely the individual. But it may underestimate law's enmeshment into a particular social fabric or national community that may prevent the application of one solution to all. Indeed, postmodernists are right to insist on the contested nature of all values, local or global, and on the open, and at times compromising or even complicit, nature of each and every legal decision. However, the legal community beyond borders provides more guidance to local authorities and courts than a strong postmodern relativism would be prepared to admit.

The international community appears thus not as a superior system encompassing all other, lesser, domestic ones. Rather, it is a shortcut for the direct and indirect dealings of state authorities, non-state organizations and businesses, as well as individual citizens, beyond state boundaries, and for the endeavor to tackle common problems, from the protection of the environment to the prevention of genocide and famine, for which states alone are unwilling, incapable, or illegitimate to act unilaterally. While it may be still too early to call it a success, the endorsement by the heads of state and government at the 2005 UN anniversary summit[14] of the "responsibility to protect" of states towards their societies and individual human beings, and the need for collective action in case it is not met, constitutes the most recent harbinger for the advent of the international community in contemporary international relations.

53

Notes

1 The term "international society" is preferred by the "English school" of international relations (see Bull 1977).

2 Koskenniemi has used the word "kitsch" for general concepts of international law such as *jus cogens* and obligations *erga omnes*. His critics (see Dupuy 2005; Gerstenberg 2005) have largely failed to see that Koskenniemi distinguishes between the slide of the use of these concepts into "kitsch" and, following Milan Kundera, the possibility of averting this danger by recognizing it (Koskenniemi 2005b: 123).

3 For pre-September 11-analysis, see, e.g. Abi-Saab 1998: 248–65; Dupuy 1986; Paulus 2001b; Simma 1994; Tomuschat 1999: 72–90; see also Allott 1990.

4 "Global war on terror" is the label attached by the Bush Jr. administration to the struggle against al-Qaeda and other terrorist groups. Attempts by the Pentagon to relabel the term to "global struggle against violent extremism" (see Packer 2005) appear to have failed to convince the President (see Stevenson 2005: 12).

5 Rome Statute of the International Criminal Court, July 17, 1998, 2187 UNTS 90, 37 ILM (1998) 999. The Preamble speaks several times of the "most serious crimes of concern to the international community as a whole."

6 See also Bush 2003 (George Bush, State of the Union Address. 39, Weekly Compilation of Presidential Documents, 109): "Yet the course of this nation does not depend on the decisions of others."

7 Letter dated 20 March 2003 from the Permanent Representative of the United States of America to the United Nations addressed to the President of the Security Council, UN Doc. S/2003/351 (2003); Letter dated 20 March 2003 from the Permanent Representative of the United Kingdom of Great Britain and Northern Ireland to the United Nations addressed to the President of the Security Council, UN Doc. S/2003/350 (2003). See also Lord Goldsmith 2003.

8 See UN Security Council (2003a, 2003b: 3). Finally, it was the UN who legitimized the end of the formal occupation (see UN Security Council 2004a: para. 2 and *passim*).

9 The disagreements between Teubner and Fischer-Lescano and the present author relate to the question of whether international law provides for a minimum of value glue between different legal regimes.

10 For a criticism from a "sovereignist" standpoint, see Anderson 2005. For a more institutionalist view, see Alston 1997.

11 For the meaning of this term, see Carty 1991: 67.

12 Cf. Habermas 1985: 11–12 et passim. Similarly Brown 1992: 218, 237.

13 In France see *LICRA et UEJF vs. Yahoo! Inc.* (2000). For the quite fragmented U.S. litigation drawing on questions of competence rather than substance, see *Yahoo! Inc. vs. La Ligue Contre Le Racisme et l'Antisémitisme* (2006).

14 See United Nations (2005c: para. 139): "[W]e are prepared to take collective action, in a timely and decisive manner, through the Security Council, in accordance with the Charter, including Chapter VII, on a case-by-case basis and in cooperation with relevant regional organizations as appropriate, should peaceful means be inadequate and national authorities are manifestly failing to protect their populations from genocide, war crimes, ethnic cleansing and crimes against humanity."

3

Legal theory and international law

Friedrich Kratochwil[1]

This chapter reviews the contribution of legal theory to an understanding of international law and its role in shaping international relations. It first considers some of the challenges facing such an enterprise. While the self-description of law as the application of relevant norms to a case is susceptible to traditional "jurisprudential" modes of reflection, the task of legal theory is wider as it brings into focus the background conditions that are not necessarily part of law but that are crucial for its acceptance and "legitimacy." The theorist attempting to distinguish legal from non-legal norms needs to understand various extra-legal and historically contingent factors and the impact of the many wide-ranging socioeconomic processes encapsulated in the term "globalization." The chapter then proceeds to examine the concept of law both in terms of social theory and in touching on some of the fundamental discussions within the discipline. The third section takes up the issue of the international "constitution" and the "fragmentation" of the international legal order. Lastly, the fourth section examines the issues of "style" and narratives of progress.

Introduction

Assessing the contribution of legal theory to an understanding of international law and its role of shaping international relations faces several challenges. One is, of course, that the concept of "law" will have to be defined in "system-neutral" terms as otherwise the identification of law with the "command of the sovereign" (Austin 1954) disposes of the problem by a simple definition (since there is no sovereign in international relations, there is no law, q.e.d.). While disposing of a problem by "precise" definitions might score debating points, it is hardly illuminating. It impoverishes analysis by identifying a specific historical configuration, i.e. that of the state, with law in general – even though we had law long before the state – and by surreptitiously collapsing the issue of law and that of its "effectiveness."

Similarly dangerous is to begin with a preconceived notion of "theory" imposing on the subject matter an inappropriate model, derived either from the highly stylized, problematic model of logical positivism (Popper 1968), or a "rigorous" but limited conception of "rationality" (Searle 2003). When we try to avoid these pitfalls and turn to one of "law's" most influential self-descriptions, conceiving of it as "*ars aequi et boni*" (of the equitable and the good), this definition places it clearly within *praxis* rather than "theory." Unless however, we believe that the good and equitable can be grasped intuitively, the terms seem to be empty place-holders rather than clear indicators. Besides, the addition of the term "*ars*" (art) seems not accidental. Law is seen as an *activity* rather than an "object" or agglomeration of items that can be treated like natural kinds. Rather, the "equitable" and the "good" are the result of some "artful" process of determination. Thus, even at the time when ontology and values were not yet strictly separated – as after the onslaught of Humean skepticism – the collision of duties and the indeterminacy of the principles all show that the decisive factors for arriving at a decision and of having it accepted by the "audience" might lie beyond the "law," i.e. its historical and sociological background conditions.

These initial remarks have several corollaries. First, while the self-description of law as the application of relevant norms to a case is susceptible to traditional "jurisprudential" modes of reflection, the task of legal theory is wider as it brings into focus the background conditions that are not necessarily part of law but that are crucial for its acceptance and legitimacy.

Second, while this distinction serves as a "first cut" for separating traditional jurisprudence from a wider "theory" of law, it should also be clear that the distinction cannot be categorical, living up to the ideal of taxonomic exclusiveness. As soon as "jurisprudence" has to reflect on the "sources" of law, it has to transcend the "art aspect" of norm application. Similarly, any "theory" of law focusing narrowly on legal norms and their creation – in order to distinguish legal from other norms (morals, simple courtesy, or "comity") – has to address "extra legal" matters, such as the *Grundnorm* (Kelsen 1966).

Third, given that these important elements of law are historically contingent and not a set of simple "functional" needs, any theory of law has to move both on the analytical and on the historical level. Only thus the changing structure of law and of the institutions it engenders become understandable.

This does not mean that a theory of law exhausts itself in telling a story of how things came to pass, but it suggests that some historical reflection is crucial for the understanding of law. Law is always more than simply an instrument of regulating present interferences and the inevitable conflicts among self-interested actors; it is also always part of a political project that connects the present via the past to a future "utopia." In short, it is one of the primary means of making sense in individual and collective life. The individual who "subjects" himself to the law in the social contract, and thus attains "property" and "freedom" (Rousseau 1967), is as significant as the contract by which a people becomes "one" out of different "tribes" as the biblical covenant shows, or where a "recessed" people becomes in the "theory" of popular sovereignty the main source of law. In the international sphere issues of self-determination as well as proposals to limit "sovereignty" when a government fails to "protect" the people are part and parcel of this problem (International Commission on Intervention and State Sovereignty 2001).

A fourth area for critical reflection is therefore the analogies and narratives within which doctrinal legal arguments are embedded. This is particularly important in international law where the link between law and the state project has come under severe pressure from "globalization." The latter seems to dissolve the most basic boundaries between the internal and the external, and between the public and the private. The issue, then, is less how these changes from the "billiard ball" model of the international system via regimes and institutions led to the present transnational networks, but rather how these changes are assessed by embedding them in a narrative of "progress" whereby international law's "primitiveness" is overcome.

From these remarks follow the steps in my argument. In the next section, I shall examine the concept of law both in terms of social theory and in touching on some of the fundamental discussions within the discipline.

The third section takes up the issue of the international "constitution" and the "fragmentation" of the international legal order, while the fourth section examines the issues of "style" and narratives of progress.

The concept of law and its "validity"

Since the human world is not "natural," as is the case with "gregarious" animals such as bees, but one of artifice, the importance of language and of "common understandings" for its creation and reproduction has been stressed (Aristotle 1972; Searle 1995). These common understandings might be ontologically compact not distinguishing between the "is" and the "ought" or between further differentiations such as morals, customs, or religion. It seems that for law to emerge as a distinct symbolic order two interconnected innovations have to occur. One is that the reproductive process of social order has to be revolutionized. In archaic understanding the taboo and the "damage" caused by a delict, required exact restitution (*lex talionis*). Later the notion of an abstract normative order arises that transcends not only the concrete violation but allows for a resolution of conflicts in terms of "new" solutions. Instead of trying to rend the social fabric whole through magic or ritual activity (which might include "casting out" the violator), new notions of retribution, accountability, intention, or negligence develop, even if the common normative order is still thoroughly conventional, i.e. based on unreflected custom (*mos maiorum*).

These developments are helped by a second innovation, i.e. the development of a specialized cadre which handles "violations" and settles conflicts in terms of the common normative understandings. "Law" becomes an order where a cadre of rule-handlers reinterprets, e.g. the *lex talionis* so that not the identical but "equivalent" restitution has to be provided. Law receives its aura from the notion that it is not "made" but that both

arbiter and transgressor or contesting parties are "bound" by it. Symmetry, the ordering principle that covered both nature and society in acephalic, segmented societies is increasingly challenged by notions of "hierarchy," i.e. by claiming to rule on the basis of "law" emanating from a transcendent source. Not accidentally, "law" emerges together with "higher" religions which legitimate hierarchies and substitute for the egalitarian principles of segmented societies. The pharaonic empire and the genesis of a "people" accepting the "law" of god are examples, as is the Athenian *synoikismos* (the living together of different tribes) where through the creation of a new law (*dike*) "the people" appear as a potential source of law substituting the old *nomos* (Meier 1990).

The close connection of law and politics, on the one hand, and of law and "universal" or "natural" principles, on the other, raises several important issues. If law is to stabilize the expectations of its "subjects" via norms, this ordering can only occur if it is generally accepted as "valid." But this means that the actors have to trust in a system of expectations rather than rely on their own experiences with others. To that extent "law" requires that we do not "learn," as Luhmann (1983) suggested, and do not adjust our strategies accordingly. Instead, we hold on to our decision premises, based on counterfactually valid norms, even in the face of disappointments. Thus, attempts to explain the emergence of norms in terms of "long-term utility" calculations of non-myopic rational actors in iterative bilateral bargains is often used for "explaining" the emergence of norms in international society. However, this approach is highly problematic (Axelrod 1981) due to its restrictive assumptions (no ambiguous moves, same actors, clear payoffs in iterative, non-decisive rounds) and the acceptance of a "niceness-rule" in the initial round.

The validity of the norms has little to do with the actual agreement among the actors but rather with the establishment of a largely fictive presumption among them so that the lawbreaker should be isolated in order to separate his actions from the ongoing interactions. Instead of consensus built on coalitions and the packaging of "interests," the "case" *sub judice* is "depoliticized" by transferring it to another "forum" where the violator has to face alone the consequences of his actions. Law "works" because we have expectations about expectations (i.e. distinguish "legitimate" from "other" ones) and have, in cases of conflict, expectations about what the "rule-handlers" can "legitimately" do in deciding which expectation about expectations is the "law." In short, law cannot be identified with the "stability" of expectations since a Hobbesian world where one is fighting everybody else is also characterized by "stability." This equilibrium is so stable that reaching the Pareto superior solution in a classical Prisoner's Dilemma is impossible, contrary to Hobbes's argument of solving the dilemma "by contract" (Hobbes 1968).

Finally, given that the emergence of law opens up the space for creative adjustment, it has to be exempted from the suspicion of manipulability in both application and legislation. The semantics developed in the European context ranges from the idea of a "mixed constitution" (preventing a capricious change of law according to shifting majorities) to the invocation of a "higher law," be it "nature" or the "ancient" constitution (Pocock 1987) and to the lawmaker's subjection to "god's" law (or customary rules that could not be changed). Even Bodin (1962), who emphasizes the legislative power of a sovereign "absolved" from all particular laws, limits the legislative capacity of the sovereign. He cannot change customary law (such as the *lex salica* regulating succession) or tax the subjects without their consent. The sovereign's "rule" remains firmly anchored in both tradition and natural law. Whenever these limits are undermined by "internalizing" law's legitimacy and viewing it as the "will" of the sovereign, countertendencies can be noticed. By advocating some form of judicial review, or an inquiry into the inner moral-

ity of law (Fuller 1964), issues of legitimacy can be reopened instead of being simply reduced to "legality" (Habermas 1993). Sometimes the result seems contorted such as when the International Commission on Kosovo concluded that NATO's response was "illegal" but "legitimate" (Independent International Commission on Kosovo 2000).

These considerations are relevant for deciding whether international law is "proper law." As suggested, what counts as law cannot simply to be read off from the type of norms (such as sanction), or from the origin or pedigree of a rule (Hart 1994). Such criteria are too narrow, leaving out "constitutive rules" that only indirectly sanction acts as "invalid," if not done in accordance with the stipulated provisions. Rather, what makes rules "legal" is their *principled use* in application (Kratochwil 1989). It is here that the weakness of international law appears. Since there is no general jurisdiction of the International Court of Justice or any court – except when some freestanding regimes include compulsory jurisdictional clauses – and the decisions of the world court have strictly speaking not precedential value, what *the law is* remains often unclear. Legal arguments frequently remain entirely on the level of *ex parte* arguments without an authoritative resolution of the issues. Thus, the "closure" of the legal systems occurs not through adjudication or legislation but largely through doctrinal elaboration in which notions of "coherence" (Franck 1990), of justice, or of some "transcendental" conditions (both in a naturalist or in a Kantian sense) are invoked to fill the gaps. Such moves, however, transfer the difficulties only to another level without ending the arguments. Here formal distinctions such as *lex lata* and *lex ferenda*, *lex specialis*, *lex posterior*, or more substantive considerations, such as the nature and hierarchy of the "sources," *ius cogens*, obligations *erga omnes* (Paulus 2005; Tomuschat and Thouvenin 2006), "community expectations," and "*policies*" provide the appropriate *topoi*. In short, the set of issues is far more extensive than the truncated debate between "realists" and "idealists" suggest. Neither position is, however, consistently sustainable. Politics always has as an intrinsic part a "vision" which contains normative elements, as the "original" realist Carr (1964a) noticed, and neither norms nor "interest" can determine choices in a causally efficient way. Are we then condemned to move endlessly between apology and utopia (Koskenniemi 1989), or do we have to submit to a more or less blind decisionism à la Hobbes or Carl Schmitt (1996)?

This argument points to a genuine dilemma that runs from the free will/determinism to the theoretical/practical reason controversy and pits conception of scientific explanation against methods of "*verstehen*" (Hollis and Smith 1990). Unpacking some of these controversies, therefore, seems necessary.

While dilemmas cannot be "solved," they can be circumvented when we recognize how they arise and on which conceptual presuppositions they rest. Thus, the failure to see how law molds decisions might be due more to some problematic theory of action that (mistakenly) holds that only efficient cause explanations shall count as an explanation rather than to the "failure" of law *per se* (indeterminacy of rules and principles, and contestability of the deontic status of norms or principles when applied to a "case"). But as the discussions about "constitutive explanations" have shown (Wendt 1999: ch. 2) not all explanations are "causally efficient" even in the natural sciences. Besides, rule-following is not simply a function of "sanctions" but is frequently informed by institutions (making X count for a Y e.g. by designation something as "money") that enable actors to pursue their goals. Furthermore, given that in the social world often "multiple equilibria" exist, "interests" are insufficient as explanations since even a rational choice approach needs interest plus coordination norms for explaining a particular outcome.

Seen from this perspective the narrowness of the vision just elucidated becomes clear. It is a particularly problematic version of the "Humean fork" problem. Since I cannot get by logical inference from an "is" to an "ought," am I – like Burrian's ass – condemned to oscillate between apology and utopia? As we have seen, this dilemma is the result of a conception of reason that is badly adapted to practical questions. After all, we do make choices and the Humean "desire plus belief model," where only "passion" can motivate while reason remains eternally its "slave" (Hume 1948), is on all fours with our practical experience as well as with the concept of "expected utility." Here the introduction of "sentiments," of "imagination" which counteracts the immediacy of passions by conjuring up "future delights," and of "secondary preferences" are to provide the necessary (but problematic) bridging principles.

All of this is hardly news and neither is the fact that law has always to move between "facticity" and "validity" (Habermas 1993). Ultimately, no rule can "decide" a case, and a "fact" by itself cannot determine its normative force. Nonetheless, decisions must be buttressed by arguments and these arguments are guided and constrained by a "style" or rhetoric (Kennedy 1994b; Koskenniemi 2000). In a way, we thereby return to a tradition where rhetoric is simply not a term for elocutionary flourish or "cheap talk" but for finding non-idiosyncratic reasons for deciding issues of *praxis* (Aristotle 1980).

Constitutive moments and their projects

According to traditional wisdom "Westphalia" and "sovereignty" mark the transition from medieval universalism to a territorial form of rule with internal hierarchy and "horizontal" equality among all members, a conception against which all change can be assessed (Black and Falk 1969–1972). Modern scholarship traced this near mythical rendition of the historical events to a particularly successful act of persuasion by Leo Gross (Gross 1948). It also has significantly corrected the historical and analytical claims of the Westphalia syndrome (Osiander 1994, 2001). To that extent Westphalia represents a "mid-point" in a longer transformative process rather than a radical new beginning.

That these criticisms do not concern minor corrections of historical facts but go to the very heart of international law's problematique can be seen from the examination of sovereignty, usually considered the cornerstone of the Westphalian order. Its significant "innovation" – i.e. the right to "make alliances" (*ius armorum*) – was, however, part of the old system of self-help exercised by the imperial "*estates.*" It is, therefore, not as Krasner (1993a) implied a new right of emerging "states." To read back the meanings of the late eighteenth and early nineteenth century is not only problematic, it also suggests that "sovereignty" is like a thing that once "invented" remains rather stable as an a-historical "systemic structure." Similarly, as Grewe (2000) has shown, the roots of international law as "law" lie in the feudal practices (infeodation of the pope as exemplified in the "division" of the New World at Tordesillas 1494) and in the encounters of the Europeans with the New World and its inhabitants. The latter sparked the debate of de Vitoria and Sepulveda, and the subsequent elaborations of Suarez. Both practices set the stage for discussing the "rights" of infidels and for marking off Europe as a different zone (with different rules) from the "colonial" territories.

It might therefore be useful to deal with issues of the constitutional order, its fragmentation and new articulation, by visiting various sites where these issues are debated. This glimpse at developments stretching across the disciplines of international relations, political theory, international law, and sociology has to be rather sketchy. Furthermore, there exist many overlaps, and one or several authors could fit in more than one category. Thus, no neat taxonomy is possible, but

people do emphasize different elements of the constitutional problem, use different vocabularies, and exhibit different sensibilities.

Beginning with the IR debates, there are two schools which develop out of opposition to the dominant theme of an international "anarchy:" one realist and one more sociologically/historically oriented. The "realist" version focuses on the role of hegemonic powers and their role in providing at least a rudimentary order. International systems are therefore (weakly) hierarchical in which uneven growth of power and the ability of the hegemon to make some rules and enforce them provide the dynamics. Derived from a particular interpretation of Thucydides, Gilpin (1981) developed an elaborate "theory" of hegemonic stability.

In this sense, Ikenberry (2001) who deals more recently with "constitutional moments" at the end of great wars is picking up on this challenge. He investigates the particular "constitutional" bargains underlying the orders after 1815, 1919, and 1945. The common theme is that leading power(s) lock in other states in a favorable set of relations that mitigate the latter's fears of abandonment and of domination by imposing some self-restraint on the preponderant power(s) through institutionalizing certain "rules of the game." Some work (Keohane 1984) addressed the puzzle why the post-war order remained relatively stable even when the lead position of the U.S. "weakened." In particular in the international political economy, states, despite increasing divergences in goals, did not escalate the conflicts or take unilateral action so familiar from the beggar thy neighbor policies of the interwar period. The answer was that a privileged group of industrialized nations could provide the collective goods and that robust "regimes" (Krasner 1983) had developed in the meantime.

The focus on regimes could have provided a new integrating "puzzle" for multidisciplinary work across law, sociology, and political science. But the mostly positivist orientation of political "science" prevented the lively debate to cash out in a new research program. The old Humean fork separating strictly the "is" and the "ought" and claiming that only "causal" explanations counted prevented an appreciation of how norms and rules "mold" (but do not determine) decisions and how institutions mediate between the "is" and the "ought." Thus, with the exception of "compliance" in which bridges between the "process" school of law and international relations analysis were built in arms control, in some areas of the political economy, and in environmental issues, the main sites concerning constitutional (system) questions remained within their separate disciplines.

The English school (Dunne 1998; Linklater and Suganami 2006), our second site, mounted perhaps the most spirited attack on the anarchy *problematique*. The existence of, for example, a balance of power required both a historical/comparative and an analytical examination. Thus, as Hume had remarked before, the existence of a balance of power was far from universal, and systems differed widely according to the institutional structures they had developed historically. Neither messengers nor spies functioned like diplomats, even though all of them served certain information functions (Wight 1977). It was perhaps a pity that the analytic discussion was not as lively as the one of the systems of states, which ironically reached its crescendo at a time when the state project was already under siege. Growing interdependencies had made it increasingly difficult to "cage" economic forces through the fetters of a "national economy" and to shield oneself from the forces which impacted at home although they were created elsewhere. Already in the interwar period states tried through the extension of jurisdictional claims to "protect" themselves (vide *Alcoa*), but these infringements had to be "balanced" by comity. Now, new designs were required. The dense network of "multilateral" international organizations (Ruggie and Kratochwil 1986) made assertions of exclusive "domestic jurisdiction" difficult to maintain.

A third site for vetting constitutional issues is the intersection between political theory and international relations. Here purposes of the state, on the one hand, and issues of distributive justice in the international arena, on the other, provided the foci. For those emphasizing the moral purposes of states (Reus-Smit 1999), notions of an international community had also to be different from those who saw the state as an Oakshottian "practical association" (Nardin 1983) designed simply to enable individuals to pursue their goals with minimal agreement on more substantive notions. Rather than a fundamental conception of the good life, the primacy of the "right" over the "good" and a basic notion of liberty as negative freedom is the key. The similarity to Rawls and the liberal tradition is obvious, although Rawls (1971) did enlarge the set of issues by including the "difference" principle. This in turn spawned a debate whether the principles of justice could be applied to international arrangements. A lively debate, largely unnoticed by international lawyers, ensued about different redistributive schemes and the limits of state autonomy for which the journals *Philosophy and Public Affairs* and *Ethics and International Affairs* became the main outlets. Among lawyers, who eschewed such *de lege ferenda* proposals, the debate focused instead more on the limits to state action and the emergence of a *ius cogens* (Verdross and Simma 1984) and the obligations *erga omnes* (Tomuschat and Thouvenin 2006).

This leads us to a fourth site, i.e. the "move to institutions." Starting with the recognized need of further development of international law, the focus on codification and the "peaceful settlement of issues" had been characteristic of the Hague system. It had been powerfully shaped by a general cultural belief in technical solutions to international problems and by the recognition to attend to problems resulting from technological change. It counteracted the traditional positivist preoccupation with the "will problematic" of law that had been part of the state project and of "sovereignty." It had led to the quandary that from this perspective no "higher law" could be conceived and only the self-limitation of the sovereign could explain and justify the existence of an international legal order (Jellinek 1882).

The technocratic vision of "functionalism" attempted to replace politics by tying claims to rule to particular forms of knowledge and social strata. The claim that modernity needed technical intelligence, instead of theology or philosophy, becomes oddly reconfigured in the "move to institutions" in the aftermath of the Second World War (Kennedy 1987). Thus the League was not only to mark a decisive break with the "non-institutionalized" past but it insisted that a peaceful order required a new organizational design, a theme that became even more important after the Second World War. It was one of the lessons of the interwar years that both "high politics" and "low politics" had to be institutionalized since the neglect of the "low politics" of welfare had been the reason for the rise of fascism and the collapse of the League. The bitter truth was that the old recipes of *laissez faire* were no longer adequate, and that the changes in the configuration of politics required the simultaneous solution to both welfare and security issues (Kratochwil 1998). Similarly, old hopes that the progressive development of international law in conjunction with public opinion would suffice, and that by "outlawing" war or threatening sanctions a new world order could be forged, had been thoroughly disappointed. Besides, the rise of socialism and communism introduced new welfare goals as proper domains for state action. It required regulatory rather than simple *laissez faire* regimes at both domestic and international levels as well as their *mutual compatibility*.

The functioning of a "collective security" system presupposed the continuation of the Alliance against the axis powers (the original United Nations), not only as an insurance against revanchism but simply because peace could not be secured against any "great power" without another world war. But no challenge to the "universal" order could be managed unless the great powers themselves were institutionally bound to uphold that order and to overcome their collective action problems. The design solutions consisted in the adoption of the veto, the institutionalization of the great powers in the Security Council, and a variety of "multilateral" regulatory organizations linked to the U.N. framework. Even if with the onset of the cold war the hopes for a "global" order were disappointed, the organizational blueprint provided the framework for the "free world" (nobly ignoring the developing world).

These developments were in the U.S. accompanied by a significant shift from the "settlement" of disputes (adjudicative perspective) to one emphasizing the problem-solving capacities of law. In Europe, on the other hand, the "unity" of the legal system – as in the case of international law without the existence of a rule of recognition as a capstone – continued to dominate the discussion. Arguments in favor of a unitary conception of law were opposed by a dualistic conception along the internal/external divide. American postwar legal scholarship emphasized *process* and was united in its criticism of formalism as practiced both by naturalists and positivists. This can be seen most clearly in legal scholarship that developed out of the application of the Ehrlich and Sacks process approach (O'Connell 1999) to international problems by Chayes (Chayes and Chayes 1995). But, an anti-formalist stance paired with an emphasis on problem solving went farther. Here the New Haven school of McDougal and his associates represented one side of the spectrum with the Columbia school at the other end. The Yale school focused on "policy" and the processes of claims and counter claims by which decision-makers pursue their goals, whereby the goal of *human dignity* allows for the appraisal of the normative status of an advanced claim. The Columbia school around Friedmann (1964), Henkin (1979), and Schachter (1985) emphasized more the centrality of rules in enhancing cooperation in an ideologically divided world while at the same time arguing against the resurgence of positivism and the shibboleth of "sovereignty." Thus, while the Columbia school wanted to create a normative order transcending the policy differences among the antagonistic "blocs," the Yale school was much more influenced by the tradition of American legal realism and much more favorable towards sovereign autonomy, notwithstanding its universalist rhetoric (McDougal 1955). Here only the new approaches of Koh (1996b) and Higgins (1994) provided an alternative.

The last site for constitutional discussions is the intersection of legal practice and sociological theory. Here three main themes can be identified, all of which are loosely connected with the problem of globalization. The emergence of global networks among "disaggregated" states (Slaughter 2004b) or new patterns of cooperation between public and private actors become respective foci (Cutler 2003; Hall and Biersteker 2002). While the new organizational form of networks gives these inquiries an unifying theme, the "disaggregated" state version emphasizes still "public" power for the solution of problems created by a quantum leap in interdependencies. This approach adds to the familiar argument of the "internationalization of the state" (Cox 1981) and of multilateralism as its organizational form. They engage in boundary spanning exercises of information sharing and regulatory activities after the disappearance of the unified state. Such an activity remains, however, a "technocratic model" of cooperation rather than one in which "the people" can more effectively exercise their voice. Whether such defects can be remedied by the inclusion of private actors or elements of civil society (as e.g. in World Bank projects) remains also doubtful, given the difficulties in identifying the relevant stakeholders and the vast asymmetry in information between outsiders and insiders.

In addition, two other topics have been: the judicialization of international politics and the "fragmentation" of the international legal order given the 125 existing international tribunals. In a sense, both topics rehearse in a new way the old Weimar agenda (Koskenniemi 2000: 29f.) that pitted Morgenthau and Schmitt, on the one side, against the formalism of Kelsen, on the other side. The former accorded primacy to political decisions and claimed that political decisions ought to be "non-justiciable" (Morgenthau 1929). In international law, this thesis led to Sir Hersch Lauterpacht's (1933) argument "establishing" the justiciability of all legal disputes. Nonetheless, in both theory and practice Morgenthau's victory can be gathered not only from the dominance of "realism" and instrumentalization of law by political projects, but also in the sluggish adherence to the "optional protocol" of the ICJ and to the inclusion of self-defining "reservations" (see the Connolly reservation for the U.S.).

In the legalization debate for which the special *International Organization* issue is perhaps the most prominent example, the seemingly neutral specification of three key concepts (precision, delegation, and obligation) was to guide an interdisciplinary debate among international lawyers and political scientists. While perhaps the concept of "obligation" linked directly to the debates of "hard" and "soft law," the reasons for choosing the other two concepts remained unclear, as they were not systematically related to legal theory (Finnemore and Toope 2001a). Nevertheless, the choice of the vocabulary was far from innocent. The term "delegation" immediately suggests the contractarian basis of a "liberal" conception of law, i.e. free and independent actors consenting to be subject to adjudication. As if much of international law were not customary or applied by national courts which "double up" as institutions of the international legal order (Scelle 1932–1934)! Here courts have both fact and rule discretion. To that extent the remarks of one of the authors seems rather strange: "to

63

paraphrase Clausewitz, law is a continuation of political intercourse with the addition of other means" (Abbott, et al. 2000: 419).

Similarly problematic is the emphasis on "precision." It is obviously derived from a misleading conception of "science" in which terms have meaning by their reference. "Precision" then actually "measures" the match between the concept and the "world out there." While this is already a highly misleading conception of scientific procedures – many key theoretical terms have no match at all – it is totally inappropriate for law. Even the clearest statement of a rule cannot decide its own application! Both the open texture of rules – forget that in most decisions indeterminate (imprecise) principles rather than rules do most of the justifying and explaining – and the difficulties of interpretation have been amply discussed in legal theory. Does the "clear" injunction "No dogs on the escalator" apply only to *dogs*, but not to "Ulysses," my (single) dog accompanying me? Does it apply also to a cat or a pet puma, or to a boa constrictor which lazily hangs around my neck and is arguably not "on" the escalator? In short, the idea that norms can be treated in a context-free fashion, and that interpretations need not constantly move from facts to norms and higher order principles and back, is a myopia of social "scientists" who think that their methods apply in a "one size fits all" fashion.

Within the internal debate among international lawyers on "fragmentation," the ICJ decision in the Teheran hostage case played a significant role as here the notion of a freestanding or self-contained regime was raised (ICJ, United States of America vs. Iran, 1979). Similarly, the remarks of the ICJ president on the danger of a fragmentation of the legal order, and finally the charge to the International Law Commission to study the issue (International Law Commission and Koskenniemi 2006) represent some of the main markers of this controversy.

In the hostage case the court had largely to decide whether the existence of a special regime (Vienna Convention of Diplomatic Relations) exhaustively regulated the issue area (ICJ 1979: 40). Similarly, the ICTY *Tadic* decision highlighted the problem of contradictory judgments for the international rule of law. While, of course, no regime can be entirely freestanding since any interpretation of the applicable rules will always have to refer to the general principles of international law (Simma and Pulkowski 2006) such as the law of treaties etc., different regimes often develop their own "imperialist" reading of a controversy, especially if they possess appropriate dispute-settling mechanisms, such as the WTO. Could the WTO invalidate sanctions taken by a state which is a member of the Kimberly diamond agreement while the complaining (sanctioned) state is not?

The traditional notion of dealing with self-contained regimes in terms of the *lex specialis* supervening general legal principles suddenly appeared problematic (see also Act 55 of the ICL articles on state responsibility). Given that the *lex specialis* argument depends also on the construal of a single legislative will but that under modern conditions treaties and custom increasingly are the result of particular bargains and package deals, the presumption of a unified will of a state across various issue areas is hardly convincing. Judges have therefore to decide on the basis of extraneous factors rather than on ascertaining the will of the parties. After all, the *law of presumption* belongs clearly to municipal law.

When faced with inconsistencies of decisions, norm collisions, or doctrinal disagreements, the tendency of "law" is to fall back on a *leges* hierarchy and thus on a domestic ordering scheme. The question remains, however, whether such a visceral response does justice to complexities of legal ordering in a post national world. Strangely enough, efforts to counteract fragmentation by domestic legal instruments might be a bit too optimistic (of what can be achieved) and too pessimistic (because of being too restrictive) at the same time. Especially if we no longer simply focus on law via "compliance and sanction" but understand it as a system of communication possessing a logic of its own, we understand this paradox.

Since the law creation process no longer is limited to states and their internal and external law-making capacity (legislation or contractual undertakings, declarations) it has been opened up to communicative processes of all kinds. Normative expectations do not solely emerge from state practice but result increasingly from the activities of other social systems (Luhmann 1995b; Teubner 1997). The role of the media and of social movements using spectacular events to "scandalize" the public and initiate a process of normative change comes here to mind, counteracting strict pessimism. Whether these influences of civil society on the process of law-making provide a viable alternative to the traditional legal order remains, of course, to be seen. In other words, the fragmentation of law is more radical than often suggested since it reflects the multidimensional fragmentation of global society. The functional differentiation remains, however, overlaid by territorial segmentation. To that extent the optimism of "domestic" solutions seems unwarranted. Consequently, fragmentation cannot be combated directly by some ordering of "public" international law, since public law itself has lost much of its ordering function. Perhaps the best we can hope for is the compatibility of the fragments through constant "translation" and adjustment (Fischer-Lescano and Teubner 2004).

Theoretical reprise: elements of style, narratives, and the role of the "professional"

For someone looking at these debates from the outside there is an odd disconnection between law and politics. Thus, the vision of a world constitutional moment or the efficacy of a constitutional discourse might be far too optimistic. The subtext here is that quite different from politics the international legal order is still "primitive" (see even Kelsen 1960) and needs to be remedied through decisive judicial and legislative action. Actually, nothing could be farther from the truth. The international legal system is quite a sophisticated assembly of practices (institutional rules), and primary and secondary rules (sources) that relies on conceptual distinctions unknown to systems of primitive law (distinction between ethics, customs, public and private etc.). When compared to this, *the international political system* is truly "primitive" in relying on both bargaining and force with no mediating representative institutions that can both claim effectiveness and legitimacy. It seems that the hope of improving the legal system by imitating the experiences of the state – by creating courts or new legislative initiatives – while being blind to all the enabling background conditions that determine the fate of the rule of law – betokens a professional myopia of considerable proportions.

It is here that the constitutional metaphor becomes strained in the international legal discourse. While the ICJ in the Lockerbie case (1992: 160ff.) speaks of any action taken by a U.N. organ as being subject to assessment in terms of a "co-ordinate exercise of powers" analogous to a constitution, it is hardly surprising that in the absence of a legislative body – not to speak of the enforcement problem – everything in the international arena falls to the judiciary. But it is also hard to see how outside "the profession" such arguments will resonate and lead to acquiescence. This is not only because many of the institutions familiar from domestic political process, such as parties aggregating and vetting interest, are missing. The problem is that "constitutional" politics by attempting to place an issue "above" normal politics and thus induce societal acquiescence, hardly ever works that way even in the domestic arena (Michelman 2003).

Thus, there is an inherent paradox in that "constitutional politics" cannot achieve what it pretends, i.e. provide "the legitimacy of higher law – irreversible, irresistible and comprehensive" (Howse and Nicolaïdis

65

2003: 74). The idea that constitutionalism can lift mankind into an apolitical space ending all disagreements because "ultimate values" demand respect and are able to silence objections is utterly mistaken, as it fails to notice that any reference to those "values is itself immensely and intensely political" (Klabbers 2004: 54). Nevertheless, two common themes among international lawyers are the fear of political interference with law and that of a constitutional remedy. It ranges from Petersmann (2002) who wants to protect against overarching and short-sighted decisions of governments which could ruin the world trading system to Cass's (2005) argument that the WTO's appellate body could become a "constitutional order." By "doctrine amalgamation," a new style of justifications reflecting deeper "constitutional" values is emerging. There is also Franck's attempt to replace politics with law, but not a law of codes but with a practice of "balancing between the imperatives of constitutionalism and flexibility" (Franck 1992: 128). In the latter case, we nearly encounter the Aristotelian *spoudaios*, characterized by a particular style of reflection and attitude (*hexis*).

This leads to two further questions: one paradoxical, one more speculative. The paradoxical question concerns the issue why in the face of the experiences in the constitutional law discourse, this project enjoys such prestige in international legal thought. Might it be that after the hopes placed in expertise (functionalism and multilateral management) the self-confidence of the international "professionals" has suffered? Both policy failures (poverty reduction, financial crises) and de-legitimization attempts by social movements have damaged the aura of a self-justifying "special knowledge" (Kratochwil 2006). Is it the dialectics between legality and legitimacy which explains this phenomenon?

The more speculative question concerns the following: how is a "*spoudaios*" possible in the absence of an ontological order or some "ultimate" source that declares what is the case

and what is to be done? Perhaps indeed only "translations" remain and the international lawyer can no longer serve as "rector" à la Wolff (Onuf 1998) to shape discourse and projects. Furthermore, given that with the death of god, the "people" became the main source of legitimacy, how can any legal ontology – after the "deconstruction" of historical and concrete people, and the subsequent efforts to deny moral (and often even legal) significance to particular institutions – still mediate the tension between the particular and the universal? Strangely enough, the "rights of man" have become more recessed – and not for chauvinistic reasons I suspect – so that the concept of man or woman as moral agents no longer dominates the discourse. The actor no longer claims rights in virtue of his or her personhood but s/he becomes the place-holder for ascribing rights. Given also the official agnosticism about "the good," anything desirable, or considered valuable, becomes in this procedural world a subjective human right. Thus, we have a "right to democracy" (Franck 1992) or a "clean environment" (Tomuschat 2003).

The popularity of these slogans notwithstanding, arguing for a "right to democracy" is simply committing a category mistake. Democracy is a way of organizing a particular polity; it does not constitute a "right" that accrues to a person *qua* human being. Similarly, the right to a clean environment – aside from containing the last flickers of the religious idea of man as the "crown of creation" (species chauvinism) – is misleading since the inviolability of nature is not at issue, but a specific use of natural resources within a particular social and political project (Haas 1975).

Another gambit is to utilize the narrative of progress. It creates through the division of a "before" and "after" two points through which we can lay a straight line leading to an all encompassing end state. All the differences of politics can then be discounted since they are just "reactionary" or not yet fulfilled aspirations. What is important and what gives legitimacy to a decision is whether it "serves" this ultimate goal. We know what to do when we know whether or not we are on the side of "progress!" That such a "theory" is likely to end up in imperial pretensions (Goldsmith and Posner 2005) or in coalitions of the willing is hardly news. The problem lies, however, far deeper.

As we see from Locke's famous narrative: "[I]n the beginning the whole world was America" (Locke 1689: para. 49), such a gambit is not at all innocent. It is not only dividing the world in a before and after, but it valorizes the "after" by telling how the "primitive stage" was soon overcome. As such it served to silence not only the resistance of the "primitives" and justified their dispossession. It also reduces law from an effort to create meaning by an open-ended historical process in which the pluri-vocality of pol-

itics gets sedimented in specific historical institutional structures to one of instrumental reason. Here the virtually exclusive focus on "dispute settlement" among "rational actors" and a rather disconnected "universal" goal towards which everything is evolving provide the parameters. It would be a lamentable outcome indeed, if the strange combination of "universalism" and "instrumental reason" which one notices lately in the international legal discourse would not only discount the "local" (where most of us still live) but also deprive us from finding meaning in acting together politically in order to shape our destinies.

Note

1 I gratefully acknowledge the research help of Hannes Peltonen.

4

Soft law

Dinah Shelton

The conventional understanding of international law sees its "legal" nature as deriving from the consent of states to binding obligations. However, states have engaged in a host of other normative commitments through means such as declarations and General Assembly resolutions that, while not having the binding force of formal treaties, may still have law-like consequences of the kind that the term "soft law" has been coined to describe. In practice, the distinction between "hard" and "soft" law may become increasingly blurred over time.

International law is a largely consensual system, consisting of norms that states in sovereign equality freely accept to govern themselves and other subjects of law. International law is thus created by states, using procedures that they have agreed are "legislative," that is, through procedures identified by them as the appropriate means to create legally binding obligations. These sources of law, at least for the purpose of resolving interstate disputes, are identified in the Statute of the International Court of Justice (ICJ). Article 38 of the ICJ Statute directs the Court to decide cases submitted to it primarily through applying treaties and international custom.[1] The ICJ Statute governs the Court, but it is the only text in which states have

expressly recognized general international law-making procedures.

In contrast to the agreed sources listed in the ICJ Statute, state practice in recent years, inside and outside international organizations, increasingly has placed normative statements in non-binding political instruments such as declarations, resolutions, and programs of action, and has signaled that compliance is expected with the norms that these texts contain. Commentators refer to these instruments as "soft law" and debate whether the practice of adopting them constitutes evidence of new modes of international law making. States, however, appear clearly to understand that such "soft law" texts are political commitments that can lead to law, but they are not law, and thus give rise only to political consequences (Raustiala 2005: 587). The distinction may not be as significant as expected, however, because such commitments have proved sometimes to be as effective as law to address international problems. Moreover, soft law norms may harden, being frequently incorporated into subsequent treaties or becoming customary international law as a consequence of state practice. Within states, the norms contained in non-binding instruments may provide a model for domestic legislation and thus become legally binding internally, while remaining non-binding internationally.

What is "soft law?"

In any community, efforts to resolve social problems do not invariably take the form of law. Societies strive to maintain order, prevent and resolve conflicts, and assure justice in the distribution and use of resources not only through law, but through other means of action. Issues of justice may be addressed through market mechanisms and private charity, while conflict resolution can be promoted through education and information, as well as negotiations outside legal institutions. Maintenance of order and societal values can occur through moral sanctions, exclusions, and granting or withholding of benefits, as well as by use of legal penalties and incentives. In the international arena, just as at other levels of governance, law is one form of social control or normative claim, but basic requirements of behavior also emerge from morality, courtesy, and social custom reflecting the values of society. They form part of the expectations of social discourse and compliance with such norms may be expected and violations sanctioned.

Legal regulation, however, has become perhaps the most prevalent response to social problems during the last century. Laws reflect the current needs and recognize the present values of society. Law is often deemed a necessary, if usually insufficient, basis for ordering behavior. The language of law, especially written language, most precisely communicates expectations and produces reliance, despite inevitable ambiguities and gaps. It exercises a pull toward compliance by its very nature. Its enhanced value and the more serious consequences of non-conformity lead to the generally accepted notion that fundamental fairness requires some identification of what is meant by "law," some degree of transparency and understanding of the authoritative means of creating binding

norms and the relative importance among them. A law perceived as legitimate and fair is more likely to be observed.

Soft law is a type of social rather than legal norm. While there is no accepted definition of "soft law," it usually refers to any written international instrument, other than a treaty, containing principles, norms, standards, or other statements of expected behavior. Soft law "expresses a preference and not an obligation that states should act, or should refrain from acting, in a specified manner" (Gold 1996: 301). This "expressed preference" for certain behavior aims to achieve functional cooperation among states to reach international goals (Lichtenstein 2001: 1433).

Some scholars alternatively or also use the term "soft law" to refer to weak or indeterminate provisions in a binding treaty.[2] The practice of states indicates that this use of the term "soft law," referring to the more hortatory or promotional language of certain treaty provisions, is the more appropriate usage. Treaties are binding and contain legal obligations, even if specific commitments are drafted in general or weak terms. It is a misnomer to refer to non-binding instruments as "law," soft or hard, although many scholars commonly do so and, for reasons of convenience and simplicity, the term is used herein as a synonym for normative statements contained in instruments that are not legally binding.

Soft law comes in an almost infinite variety. Many non-binding normative instruments emerge from the work of international organizations, which in most instances lack the power to adopt binding measures. The Security Council, under Article 25, is one of the few international bodies conferred the power to bind states and demand compliance with the measures it adopts.[3] The General Assembly, in contrast, is granted authority in the UN Charter to initiate studies, discuss matters, and make recommendations.[4] Thus, whether the General Assembly denominates a text a declaration, set of guidelines, or charter, the text remains a recommendation.

Nonetheless, the choice of titles is significant. A 1962 memorandum of the UN Office of Legal Affairs called a declaration "a formal and solemn instrument, suitable for rare occasions when principles of great and lasting importance are being enunciated."[5] The practice of the General Assembly confirms that states call a text a "declaration" in accordance with this interpretation.

Common forms of soft law include normative resolutions of international organizations, concluding texts of summit meetings or international conferences, recommendations of treaty bodies overseeing compliance with treaty obligations, bilateral or multilateral memoranda of understanding, executive political agreements, and guidelines or codes of conduct adopted in a variety of contexts. In some instances, a given text may be hard law for some states and soft law for others. A decision of the European Court of Human Rights or the Inter-American Court of Human Rights, for instance, is legally binding on the state or states participating in the proceedings but not on other states parties to the relevant human rights treaty. The jurisprudence of both courts is authoritative and may be preclusive or persuasive in domestic courts of all member states, but it is not legally binding on them. It is also a feature of soft law that it may address non-state actors, including business entities, international organizations, non-governmental organizations and individuals, while treaties rarely impose direct obligations on any entities other than states.

As a general matter, soft law may be categorized as primary and secondary. Primary soft law consists of those normative texts not adopted in treaty form that are addressed to the international community as a whole or to the entire membership of the adopting institution or organization. Such an instrument may declare new norms, often as an intended precursor to adoption of a later treaty, or it may reaffirm or further elaborate norms previously set forth in binding or non-binding texts. The UN Standard Minimum Rules for the Treatment of Prisoners, adopted by the First United Nations Congress on the Prevention of Crime and Treatment of Offenders, 1955, and approved by the UN Economic and Social Council in 1957, is an example of a primary declarative text.

Secondary soft law includes the recommendations and general comments of international supervisory organs, the jurisprudence of courts and commissions, decisions of special rapporteurs and other ad hoc bodies, and the resolutions of political organs of international organizations applying primary norms. Most of this secondary soft law is pronounced by institutions whose existence and jurisdiction is derived from a treaty and who apply norms contained in the same treaty. Secondary soft law has expanded in large part as a consequence of the proliferation of primary treaty standards and monitoring institutions created to supervise state compliance with treaty obligations. Sometimes the underlying treaty is quite general in nature. The Charter of the Organization of American States provided the framework for the OAS General Assembly to constitute the Inter-American Commission on Human Rights and confer on it the authority to supervise compliance with the rights and duties contained in the American Declaration of the Rights and Duties of Man, including the power to make recommendations to specific states. Thus, an institution established by soft law received a mandate to apply primary soft law to create secondary soft law, despite scant mention of human rights in the Charter.

Treaties may be distinguished from non-binding instruments by specific language, especially when the former contain clauses concerning ratification or entry into force. Nonetheless, the characteristics of each type of instrument are increasingly difficult to identify. In some instances, states may express "reservations" to parts of a declaration, as the US did with respect to the right to development in the Rio Declaration on Environment and Development.[6] The UN

Guiding Principles on Internal Displacement[7] has a title that suggests the contents of the instrument are non-binding, but the introduction to the principles says that they "reflect and are consistent with" international human rights and humanitarian law and they "identify rights and guarantees" (Abbott 2007: 166). The quoted introductory language appears to refer to treaty and customary law, but it has also been suggested that the Guiding Principles actually contain three different types of norm:

1 those restating legal rules binding as treaty or customary international law
2 new applications of existing general legal rules, adding substantive content
3 wholly new principles created by analogy to existing norms (Abbott 2007: 169).

Similar differentiation may be made among the norms contained in other non-binding instruments.

In another blurring of the distinction between law and non-binding norms, supervisory organs have been created recently to oversee compliance with some non-binding instruments. The UN Commission on Sustainable Development, for example, supervises implementation of Agenda 21, the plan of action adopted in 1992 at the Rio Conference on Environment and Development. In other instances, states have been asked to submit reports on compliance with declarations and action programs, in a manner that mimics if it does not duplicate the compliance mechanisms utilized in treaties.

Some scholars distinguish hard law and soft law by affirming that a breach of law gives rise to legal consequences while breach of a political norm gives rise to political consequences. Identifying the difference in practice is not always easy, however, because breaches of law may give rise to politically motivated consequences and failure to implement non-binding norms may result in retaliatory sanctions indistinguishable from countermeasures in the law of state responsibility. A government that recalls its ambassador can either be expressing political disapproval of another state's policy on an issue, or sanctioning non-compliance with a legal norm. Terminating foreign assistance also may be characterized either way. Even binding UN Security Council resolutions based on a threat to the peace do not necessarily depend on a violation of international law.

The most heated debate surrounding soft law concerns whether binding instruments and non-binding ones are strictly alternative or whether they are two ends on a continuum from legal obligation to complete freedom of action, making some such instruments more binding than others. If and when the term "soft law" should be used depends in large part on whether one adopts the binary or continuum view of international law. To many, the line between law and not-law may appear blurred, especially as treaties on new topics of regulation are including more "soft" obligations, such as undertakings to endeavor to strive to cooperate. In addition, both types of instrument may have compliance procedures that range from soft to hard.

Some international judicial and arbitral decisions have contributed to the debate. One decision referred to UN resolutions as having "a certain legal value" but one that "differs considerably" from one resolution to another.[8] Various factors, including the language, the vote, the drafting history, and subsequent state practice come into play in deciding on the value of a particular normative instrument.[9]

The relationship between soft law, treaties and custom

Despite their limited juridical effect, non-binding instruments have an essential and growing role in international relations and in the development of international law. In practice, non-binding norms are often the precursor to treaty negotiations and sometimes stimulate state practice leading to the formation of customary international law. In fact, soft law has many roles to play in relation to hard law. A non-binding normative instrument may do one or more of the following:

1 codify pre-existing customary international law, helping to provide greater precision through the written text
2 crystallize a trend towards a particular norm, overriding the views of dissenters and persuading those who have little or no relevant state practice to acquiesce in the development of the norm
3 precede and help form new customary international law
4 consolidate political opinion around the need for action on a new problem, fostering consensus that may lead to treaty negotiations or further soft law
5 fill in gaps in existing treaties in force
6 form part of the subsequent state practice that can be utilized to interpret treaties
7 provide guidance or a model for domestic laws, without international obligation
8 substitute for legal obligation when ongoing relations make formal treaties too costly and time consuming or otherwise unnecessary or politically unacceptable.

Binding norms have a potentially large impact on the development of international law. Customary law, for example, one of the two main sources of international legal obligation, requires compliance (state practice) not only as a result of the obligation, but as a constitutive, essential part of the process by which the law is formed. In recent years, non-binding instruments sometimes have provided evidence of the emergent custom and have assisted to establish the content of the norm. The process of drafting and voting

for non-binding normative instruments also or alternatively may be considered a form of state practice.

The interplay between soft law and custom is identified in the first three enumerations just given. Some soft law texts purport to do no more than set down in written form pre-existing legal rights and duties. The commentary to the UN "Basic principles and guidelines on the right to remedy and reparation for victims of gross violations of international human rights law and serious violations of international humanitarian law," approved by the Commission on Human Rights[10] and endorsed by the General Assembly in 2005,[11] claims that the principles and guidelines contain no new norms, but instead reflect existing law scattered among a large number of treaties and widespread state practice. Other instruments may contain a combination of pre-existing law and new developments. It is rare that a non-binding instrument is entirely codification or new norms.

Soft law texts also may be drafted to consolidate a trend towards changes in customary law or stamp with approval one among conflicting positions on a legal issue. Efforts in the economic arena to make such changes, from the Declaration on Permanent Sovereignty over Natural Resources,[12] to the General Assembly Declaration on the Establishment of a New International Economic Order[13] and the Charter of Economic Rights and Duties,[14] demonstrate that these efforts can be highly contentious and not always entirely successful. For the soft law texts to become hard law, conforming state practice is needed among states representing different regions and the major legal, economic and political systems.

Compliance with entirely new non-binding norms also can lead to the formation of customary international law. In recent years, non-binding instruments sometimes have provided the necessary statement of legal obligation (*opinio juris*) to precede or accompany state practice, assisting in establishing the content of the norm.[15] A declaration may reflect an ideal, moving away from emphasizing state practice to greater reliance on *opinio juris* (Roberts 2001: 765). Whether a declaration provides a statement of what customary law is or should be cannot be determined by reference to mandatory or permissive words alone, although language is important as a reflection of the drafters' intent. Declarations, however, often reflect a deliberate ambiguity between actual and desired practice and are designed to develop the law. Notably, the recent practice that seems to rely on statements of obligation rather than conduct allows more states to participate in the formation of the law than would be the case if conduct alone were relevant. An example of this can be seen in the development of the law of outer space, which occurred when few states engaged in space activities, but many more participated in the drafting and adoption of the Declaration of Legal Principles Governing the Activities of States in the Exploration and Use of Outer Space.[16] This process "democratized" the law-making process and precluded the rules being made solely by the only two powers active in space at the time.

The relationship between soft law and treaties is also complex. In probably the large majority of instances, soft law texts are linked in one way or another to binding instruments. First, as the fourth category enumerated earlier summarizes, soft law can initiate a process of building consensus towards binding obligations needed to resolve a new problem. Examples of this are seen in the preambles to numerous multilateral agreements concluded in recent years, which refer to relevant non-binding normative instruments as precedents. In the field of human rights, for example, regional and global treaties almost without exception invoke the Universal Declaration of Human Rights as a normative precursor. The Declaration itself states by its own terms that it was intended

as "a common standard of achievement" that could lead to binding agreement. In fact, in the human rights field, nearly all recent multilateral conventions at the global level have been preceded by adoption of a non-binding declaration.

In environmental law, Principle 21 of the Stockholm Declaration on the Human Environment,[17] which is repeated almost verbatim in the Rio Declaration on Environment and Development, is included not only in the preambles to many multilateral treaties, but also appears in Article 3 of the Convention on Biological Diversity.[18] Thus, the adoption of non-binding norms can and often does lead to similar or virtually identical norms being codified in subsequent binding agreements. Indeed, the process of negotiating and drafting non-binding instruments can greatly facilitate the achievement of the consensus necessary to produce a binding multilateral agreement. This was the case in the last decade with the Rotterdam Convention on Prior Informed Consent (1998).[19]

The next category considers that non-binding instruments act interstitially to complete or supplement binding agreements. Sometimes this is foreseen in the agreement itself, e.g. the Bonn Convention on Migratory Species of Wild Animals (1979),[20] the Antarctic Treaty (1959)[21] regime, and agreements of the IAEA concerning non-proliferation of nuclear weapons.[22] In other instances, the non-binding accords may appear relatively independent and freestanding, but, on examination, make reference to existing treaty obligations, as is the case, for example, with the Helsinki Accords that led to the Organization for Security and Cooperation in Europe (still lacking a treaty basis) and the Zangger Committee for multilateral weapons control.

Using non-binding texts to give authoritative interpretation to treaty terms is particularly useful when the issues are contentious and left unresolved in the treaty itself. Article 8(j) of the Convention on Biological

Diversity, which concerns respect for traditional knowledge as well as access to it and the sharing of benefits from its use, is one example where fundamental disagreements resulted in a provision that is complex, ambiguous and close to contradictory in its terms. Later negotiations during the Conferences of the Parties led to drafting the Bonn Guidelines on Access to Genetic Resources and Fair and Equitable Sharing of the Benefits Arising out of their Utilization (COP Dec. VI/24, April 2002), a detailed attempt to resolve some of the outstanding issues through the use of soft law.

Other non-binding instruments adopted by state parties similarly "authoritatively interpret" the obligations contained in pre-existing treaty provisions. The World Bank Operational Standards seem intended to give guidance to employees in furthering the mandate of the World Bank as set forth in its constituting treaty. The examples of the Inter-American and Universal Declarations of Human Rights, as they relate to the OAS and UN Charters, and the more recent ILO Declaration on Fundamental Principles and Rights at Work also can be cited as examples. In the case of the UDHR, the final declaration of the UN's International Conference on Human Rights (1968) proclaimed that "[t]he Universal Declaration of Human Rights . . . constitutes an obligation for members of the international community."[23] This proclamation can be seen as simply another resolution unsuccessfully trying to make law out of a prior resolution (non-law plus non-law can never equal law), or as support for the view that the Universal Declaration constitutes an authoritative interpretation of the human rights obligations in the UN Charter, or as a statement of *opinio juris*, which, together with state practice, demonstrates that the UDHR or at least some parts of it, have become customary international law. The consequences flowing from each of the three positions are radically different. If the UDHR is not law, it creates no binding obligations for any state; if it is

an authoritative interpretation of the UN Charter's human rights provisions it is binding on all UN member states; if it is customary international law, it binds even those states that are not members of the UN.

Soft law norms also may become "hard" law through adoption by states in their domestic law, or by the incorporation into private binding agreements. The latter occurs most frequently with standards governing contracts or other business activities. UNIDROIT (the Institute for the Harmonization of International Private Law) is an independent intergovernmental organization that prepares draft conventions, model laws, and principles based on comparative legal analysis. Its texts help fill the need for harmonization in transnational business interactions, providing reliable contractual terms and obligations and minimizing legal uncertainties and linguistic misunderstandings. National laws that vary considerably can raise transaction costs to the point where the inconsistencies can actually become considered as a non-tariff barrier to trade (Meyer 2006: 122). The UNIDROIT contract principles provide a catalogue of rules found in national and international contract law. This particular soft law may be used in a number of ways:

1 expressly incorporated in binding contract
2 as a supplement to domestic contract law
3 as model code for the development of further national and international law
4 as the basis for further harmonization
5 part of formation of lex mercatoria (customary international commercial law) (Meyer 2006: 134–5).

The last category just listed is perhaps the most interesting, because the extent to which members of the international community are willing to accept informal commitments and non-binding expressions of expected behavior in their relations with others may reflect a maturing of the legal system and international society. In ongoing cooperative relationships not all commitments need to be expressed as legally binding obligations. Clearly, there are instances of freestanding normative instruments that are neither related to nor intended to develop into binding agreements. The proliferating Memoranda of Understanding generally can be included here, along with non-binding export control guidelines developed by international weapons suppliers and the guidelines concerning money laundering adopted by the Financial Action Task Force (FATF). Such agreements often reflect an incremental approach to addressing problems, allowing consensus to be built ultimately to achieve hard law. In other instances, however, a freestanding non-binding instrument can be indicative of ongoing disagreement about the substantive norms. The 1981 General Assembly Declaration on the Elimination of All Forms of Intolerance and of Discrimination based on Religion or Belief, for example, took 20 years to negotiate and has never been followed by a treaty, largely due to objections from some states to a few provisions in the Declaration.

Once adopted, then, the soft law can be cited as a reflection of pre-existing customary law, in which case the normative contents, but not the text itself, may be taken as legally binding. The norms also may begin the process of creating new custom, or be relied on in subsequent treaty negotiations. They may also have an impact on the resolution of disputes, without constituting either treaty or custom, especially in new subject areas of international concern:

> Most international environmental issues are resolved through mechanisms such as negotiations, rather than through third-party dispute settlement or unilateral changes of behavior. In this second-party control process, international environmental norms can play a significant role by setting the terms of the debate, providing evaluative standards, serving as a basis to criticize other states' actions, and establishing a framework of principles within which

negotiations may take place to develop more specific norms, usually in treaties.
(Bodansky 2005: 118–19)

Why are states adopting soft law texts?

The increasing use of non-binding normative instruments in several fields of international law is evident (Shelton 2000). There are several reasons why states may choose to use soft law over a treaty or doing nothing. First, the emergence of global resource crises such as anthropogenic climate change and crashing fisheries, require rapid response, something difficult to achieve by treaty, given the long process required to negotiate and achieve wide acceptance of binding instruments. Non-binding instruments are faster to adopt, easier to change, and more useful for technical matters that may need rapid or repeated revision. This is particularly important when the subject matter may not be ripe for treaty action because of scientific uncertainty or lack of political consensus (Raustiala 2005: 582). In such instances, the choice may not be between a treaty and a soft law text, but between a soft law text and no action at all. Soft law may help mask disagreements over substance, overcome competing visions of organizations' purposes and resolve institutional crises (Schäfer 2006: 194).

Another reason for recourse to soft law is growing concern about the "free rider," the holdout state that benefits from legal regulation accepted by others while enhancing its own state interests, especially economic, through continued utilization of a restricted resource, such as depleted fish stocks, or by ongoing production and sale of banned substances, such as those that deplete stratospheric ozone. The traditional consent-based international legal regime lacks a legislature to override the will of dissenting states,[24] but efforts to affect their behavior can be made through the use of "soft law." International law permits states to use political pressure to induce

75

others to change their practices, although, in general, states cannot demand that others conform to legal norms the latter have not accepted. Non-binding commitments may be entered into precisely to reflect the will of the international community to resolve a pressing global problem over the objections of one or few states identified as among those responsible for the problem, while avoiding the doctrinal barrier of their lack of consent to be bound by the norm. The actions of the United Nations General Assembly banning driftnet fishing, for example, were directed at members and non-members of the United Nations whose fishing fleets decimated dwindling fish resources through use of the driftnet "walls of death." The international community made clear its resolve to outlaw driftnet fishing and enforce the ban, even though it was not contained in a legally binding instrument. The same approach may be taken with respect to norms that reflect widely and deeply held values, such as human rights or humanitarian law (Olivier 2002).

Non-binding instruments are also useful in addressing new topics of regulation that require innovative means of rule making with respect to non-states actors, which generally are not parties to treaties or involved in the creation of customary international law. The emergence of codes of conduct and other "soft law" reflects this development. The 2003 Norms on the Responsibilities of Transnational Corporations and Other Business Enterprises with Regard to Human Rights, adopted by the UN Sub-Commission on the Promotion and Protection of Human Rights, exemplifies such texts; the Sub-Commission asserted that the norms are not entirely voluntary, but instead provide corporations with an authoritative code of conduct.

In other instances, soft law texts allow non-state actors to sign the instrument and participate in compliance mechanisms, both of which are far more difficult to do with treaties. The Voluntary Principles for Security and Human Rights in the Extractive Industries, for example, was negotiated between the US and UK governments, major human rights NGOs such as Amnesty and Human Rights Watch, and oil and gas companies, including BP, Chevron/Texaco, and Royal Dutch/Shell (Williams 2004: 477–8).

Moving furthest away from traditional international law, some soft law is negotiated and adopted exclusively by non-state actors, establishing a type of private governance. Private soft law has the same advantages as state-generated norms of cost reduction and speed in reaching agreement, reduced sovereignty costs, opportunities for compromise, but also adds the possibility of muting or delaying states' opposition. The Global Reporting Initiative, for example, is a disclosure initiative of CERES (Coalition for Environmentally Responsive Economics). It uses shareholder activism to get companies to produce environmental reports and implement environmental management systems. The reporting format was developed by companies around the world, NGOs, accounting firms, institutional investors and labor. By March 2004, 416 companies had published reports based in part or totally on the Guidelines, although only 18 reported themselves fully in accordance with the principles (Williams 2004: 461). Some critics charge that such voluntary, non-binding initiatives do not change behavior, but merely put off necessary government regulation. Effective measures and compliance seem to come from integrated systems in which governments, international organizations and non-state actors are involved. An example is the Financial Stability Forum, created in 1999, which is composed of central bank regulators, securities regulators and insurance supervisors, as well as representatives of international financial institutions (the World Bank and the IMF) and OECD, an intergovernmental organization. The information produced by the network includes performance standards, codes of conduct and other models, through which best practices may be identified, which then become the basis for domestic legislation.

Soft law instruments adopted subsequent to a treaty are useful in allowing treaty parties to resolve authoritatively ambiguities in the binding text or fill in gaps, without the cumbersome and lengthy process of treaty amendment. This is part of an increasingly complex international system with variations in forms of instruments, means, and standards of measurement that interact intensely and frequently, with the common purpose of regulating behavior within a rule of law framework. The development of complex regimes is particularly evident in international management of commons areas, such as the high seas and Antarctica, and in ongoing intergovernmental cooperative arrangements. For the latter, the memorandum of understanding has become a common form of undertaking, perhaps "motivated by the need to circumvent the political constraints, economic costs, and legal rigidities that often are associated with formal and legally binding treaties" (Johnston 1997: xxiv).

The European Union has turned to soft law to introduce some flexibility into its regulatory system in the face of adhesion by new member states with weaker economies and political institutions. The EC has thus moved to deregulate and "simplify," ostensibly to remove "outdated" and "unnecessary" regulation, in the process advocating "soft law" as an alternative to traditional regulatory instruments such as directives (Commission 2002, 2003). The result has been controversial, especially as a means to improve the deteriorating working environment in central and eastern Europe. Critics say the non-legal alternative fails to take into account the significant imbalance in power between employers and employees and "[a]s such the necessary supports for various forms of soft law initiative and self-regulations within an enterprise are absent" (Woofson 2006: 196). If true, this could be an example of moving from hard law to soft law in order to weaken pre-existing standards.

Others note that non-binding rules of conduct have in fact had operational effects in European law (Snyder 1994: 198). In the social field, formally non-binding rules emerged through the open method of coordination. Although EU soft law has no formal sanctions and is not justiciable, it employs non-binding objectives and guidelines to bring about changes in social policy, relying on shaming, diffusion of the norms through discourse, deliberation, learning and networks to induce compliance (Trubek and Trubek 2005: 350, 356). Soft law is used because social policy and welfare standards are particularly critical to governments and traditionally the exclusive domain of national legislatures. States are very reluctant to turn over competence in these matters, especially where there is no pre-existing formula or agreed standards. The EU cannot insist on uniform measures but must ensure easy and rapid revisability of norms and objectives. The first 5 years of the program showed a convergence towards the common EU objectives in the policy guidelines.

Three further reasons may explain the increasing use of soft law. First, soft law is all that states can do in some settings. International organizations in which much of the modern standard setting takes place generally do not have the power to adopt binding texts. Second, non-binding texts serve to avoid domestic political battles because they do not need ratification as treaties do. Third, soft law can give the appearance that states are responding to a problem where public pressure has been exerted, while in fact the form and contents of the instrument adopted are designed to create little in the way of obligation (Graubart 2001–2: 425).

Compliance with soft law

Assertions that states are bound by law require identifying the process by which legal rules and principles are authoritatively created. If states expect compliance and, in fact, comply with rules and principles contained in soft law instruments as well as they do with norms contained in treaties and custom, then perhaps the concept of international law, or the list of sources of international law, requires expansion. Alternatively, it may have to be conceded that legal obligation is not as significant a factor in state behavior as some would think. A further possibility is that law remains important and states choose a soft law form for specific reasons related to the requirements of the problem being addressed, as noted earlier, and unrelated to the expectation of compliance.

Using data from 107 countries, one study sought to explain why countries comply with soft law standards. The results showed reputational considerations were significant, but also found a consistent positive effect of democratic systems on implementation: "Countries implementing the Basle Accord are wealthier, have higher savings, are more likely to have a current account surplus, are more democratic, less corrupt, and have less divided government" (Ho 2002: 672), with democracy consistently outperforming all other explanatory variables (Ho 2002: 676). Domestic institution building is thus of paramount importance to ensure compliance with political as well as legal agreements. Transnational NGO coalitions can assist to mobilize and empower affected groups, with the possibility of enmeshing governments in a web of norms and pressures from above and below to implement instruments such as the Helsinki Final Act.

In some instances, compliance with non-binding norms and instruments is extremely high and probably would not have been better if the norms were contained in a binding text. In fact, in many cases the choice would not have been between a binding and a non-binding text, but between a non-binding text and no text at all. In instances where the choice is presented, there is some evidence that there may be less compliance with non-binding norms, but that the content of the instrument is likely to be more ambitious and far reaching than would be the product of treaty negotiations, so the overall impact may still be more positive with a non-binding than a binding instrument.

Conclusion

From the perspective of state practice, it seems clear that resolutions, codes of conduct, conference declarations, and similar instruments are not law, soft or hard, even if they are usually related to or lead to law in one manner or another.[25] State and other actors generally draft and agree to legally non-binding instruments advertently, knowingly. They make a conscious decision to have a text that is legally binding or not. In other words, for practitioners, governments, and inter-governmental organizations, there is not a continuum of instruments from soft to hard, but a binary system in which an instrument is entered into as law or as not-law. The not-law can be politically binding, morally binding, and expectations can be extremely strong of compliance with the norms contained in the instrument, but the difference between a legally binding instrument and one that is not appears well understood and acted on by government negotiators. Although a vast amount of resolutions and other non-binding texts includes normative declarations, so-called soft law is not law or a formal source of norms. Such instruments may express trends or a stage in the formulation of treaty or custom, but law does not have a sliding scale of bindingness; neither does desired law become law by stating its desirability, even repeatedly.

The considerable recourse to and compliance with non-binding norms may represent an advance in international relations. The ongoing relationships among states and other actors, deepening and changing with globalization, create a climate that may diminish the felt need to include all expectations between states in formal legal instruments. Not all arrangements in business, neighborhoods, or in families are formalized, but are often governed by informal social norms and voluntary, non-contractual arrangements. Nonbinding norms or informal social norms can be effective and offer a flexible and efficient way to order responses to common problems. They are not law and they do not need to be in order to influence conduct in the desired manner.

The growing complexity of the international legal system is reflected in the increasing variety of forms of commitment adopted to regulate state and non-state behavior in regard to an ever growing number of transnational problems. The various international actors create and implement a range of international commitments, some of which are in legal form, others of which are contained in non-binding instruments. The lack of a binding form may reduce the options for enforcement in the short term (i.e. no litigation), but this does not deny that there can exist sincere and deeply held expectations of compliance with the norms contained in the non-binding form.

There is no "recipe" for success that will ensure the effective resolution of international problems and conflicts. While there may be particular factors that appear to influence state and non-state behavior, determinants of implementation, compliance, and effectiveness vary in a single subject area and for a single legal instrument. Ultimately, the issue centers on how to prevent and resolve conflict and promote international justice. In the end, the international legal system appears to be a complex, dynamic web of interrelationships between hard and soft law, legal norms given greater or lesser priority, national and international regulation, and various institutions that seek to promote the rule of law.

Notes

1 General principles of law are a third, more rarely used, source of international law, with judicial decisions and teachings of highly qualified publicists providing evidence of the existence of a norm. See ICJ Statute, Article 38.

2 See, for example, *International Covenant on Economic, Social and Cultural Rights* (1966), Article 2(1): Each state party "undertakes to take steps, individually and through international assistance and co-operation, especially economic and technical, to the maximum of its available resources, with a view to achieving progressively the full realization of the rights recognized . . . by all appropriate means, including particularly the adoption of legislative measures."

3 Article 25 provides that: "The members of the United Nations agree to accept and carry out the decisions of the Security Council in accordance with the present Charter."

4 UN Charter, Art. 13.

5 Memorandum of the Office of Legal Affairs, UN Secretariat, 34 UN ESCOR, Supp. (No. 8), 15, UN Doc. E/CN.4/1/610 (1962).

6 Rio Declaration on Environment and Development, adopted by the UN Conference on Environment and Development (UNCED) at Rio de Janeiro, 13 June 1992, UN Doc. A/CONF.151/26 (vol. I) (1992).

7 United Nations (1998), UN Guiding Principles on Internal Displacement, UN Doc. E/CN.4/1998/53/Add.2 (1998).

8 *Texaco/Calasiatic vs. Libya*, Arbitral Award (1978), 17 ILM 28–29.

9 See Principle 35 of Statement of Principles Applicable to the Formation of General Customary International Law, ILA London Conference 2992, Final Report of the Committee on Formation of Customary (general) International Law. In this text, the ILA claimed that resolutions accepted unanimously or almost unanimously and "which evince a clear intention on the part of their supporters to lay down a rule of international law are capable, very exceptionally, of creating general customary law by the mere fact of their adoption."

10 The Principles and Guidelines were first approved by the Commission on Human Rights, Res. 2005/35 of 19 April 2005 (adopted 40–0 with 13 abstentions).

11 UNGA Res. A/Res/60/147 of Dec. 16, 2005.

12 UNGA Res. 1803 (XVII) of 14 Dec. 1962, Permanent Sovereignty over Natural Resources, UN GAOR. Supp. (No. 17) 15, UN Doc. A/5217 (1963).

13 UNGA Res. 3201(S-VI), 6 (Special) of 1 May 1974, UN GAOR, Supp. (No. 1) 3, UN Doc. A/9559 (1974).

14 UNGA Res. 3281 (XXIX) of 12 December 1974, Charter of Economic Rights and Duties of States, UN GAOR, 29th Sess., Supp. No. 31, at 50, UN Doc. A/9631 (1975).

15 E.g. the UN General Assembly ban on Drift-net Fishing in UNGA Res 46/215 (2001).

16 GA Res. 1962 (XVII).

17 Stockholm Declaration of the United Nations Conference on the Human Environment, June 5–16, 1972, UN Doc. A/CONF.48/14 (1972).

18 *Convention on Biological Diversity*, 5 June 1992, 31 ILM 818 (1992).

19 *Convention on the Prior Informed Consent Procedure for Certain Hazardous Chemicals and Pesticides in International Trade*, 30 ILM 1 (1999).

20 *Convention on the Conservation of Migratory Species of Wild Animals*, 19 ILM 15 (1980).

21 *Antarctic Treaty*, 402 UNTS 71.

22 IAEA, *The Structure and Content of Agreements Between the Agency and State Required in Connection with the Treaty on the Non-Proliferation of Nuclear Weapons*, IAEA Doc INFCIRC/153 (May 1971).

23 UN International Conference on Human Rights (1968) UN Doc. A/CONF/32/41 at 3 (13 May 1968).

24 Thus Teubner argues that: "In principle . . . most rules of international law are only authoritative for those subjects that have accepted them" (Teubner 1997: 584).

25 See, e.g. the Decision adopted by the General Council of the WTO on 1 August 2004 containing frameworks and other agreements designed to focus the Doha round of negotiations, para 2: "The General Council agrees that this Decision and its Annexes shall not be used in any dispute settlement proceeding under the DSU and shall not be used for interpreting the existing WTO Agreements," http://www.wto.org/english/tratop_e/dda_e/draft_text_gc_dg_31july04_e.htm.

5

The practice of international law

Anthony Carty

Introduction: the state of the academic discussion

This chapter designates the analytical frame-work within which one can assess whether states, through their practice, recognize a rule, principle or practice as binding on them as law. Academic international lawyers do not usually go further in defining the practice of states than to look at the jurisprudence of the International Court of Justice on the issue of definition of customary international law, and, additionally, compiling official state communiqués in semi-official national yearbooks. We offer, instead, an explanation of how the archival tools of diplomatic history can reveal how far it is possible to construct an historical narrative that determines precisely whether law has formed part of the motivational structure of a state, when the question is whether it is observing or creating international law. At the same time, it is necessary, in expositions of state practice, to be aware, at the systematic, theoretical level, of the impact which the nature of international society will have on the willingness of states to give a place to international law alongside their anxieties about national interests and security. It is also valuable to consider not only the extent to which diplomatic history can make transparent the role of international law in state practice, but also the extent to which this practice does or does not confirm or deny the skepticism of realist theory about the place of international law in international society.

It is possible to give the concept "practice" several meanings. Perhaps the most obvious is to trace the practical activities of lawyers as international lawyers. In *The International lawyer as Practitioner* Wickremasinghe identifies 10 different roles for the international lawyer. As a U.K. Foreign Office legal adviser he has numerous functions: advising on the place of international law in making foreign policy; negotiating treaties; codification of the law; advising at the U.K. Permanent Mission at the United Nations or the European Union. The international lawyer also has a role as an advocate at a domestic or international court level. He serves as international judge or as arbitrator and he also advises both non-governmental and international organizations (Wickremasinghe 2000).

Another meaning, the one preferred here, is to designate an analytical framework within which one can assess whether states, *through their practice*, recognize a rule, principle or practice, as binding on them as law. In other words, we mean to address quite simply the practice of international law by states.

The first problem to consider is that orthodox international lawyers do not

81

usually go further in defining the practice of states than to look at the jurisprudence of the international court of justice and then, sometimes, in addition, to compile official communiqués with respect to a country's state practice in semi-official national yearbooks of international law. There are huge problems with respect to both these undertakings. The first approach generally does not even directly address the means to gather state practice but instead confines itself to considering the judgments of the I.C.J. (and its predecessor the Permanent Court of International Justice) on the meaning of state practice, in particular the concept of general customary law.[1] So, no student of international law will be invited actually to explore the practice of states, if he/she follows the guidance of the standard textbooks. Instead they will be invited to comment on the more or less pragmatic deliberations of the International Court.

According to the view of the I.C.J., one is to find that states have, in some sense, a legal conscience or sense of conviction. In the *North Sea Continental Shelf* cases, which are most usually cited, the Court said that the "practice of states" relevant to the assertion that a rule of customary international law exists must:

> [B]e such, or be carried out in such a way, as to be evidence of a belief that this practice is rendered obligatory by the existence of a rule of law requiring it (*opinio juris sive necessitatis*) . . . The States concerned must therefore feel that they are conforming to what amounts to a legal obligation.
>
> (I.C.J. Reports 1969: 77)

The basic problems with this formulation have been put squarely by both Sorensen and D'Amato. Sorensen (1946: esp.109) points out how the very nature of relations among states makes ascertainment of an evolving customary law virtually impossible. Diplomatic negotiations remain so closed and secret that not even the representatives of one state will know what are the underlying motives of their opposite numbers. Yet such motivation is

essential to the psychological element of custom. D'Amato (1971: 82–4) has been equally direct in questioning any possible legal method of observing customary law evolving out of the consciousness of a modern bureaucratic State.

It appears impossible to speak of states having an identity that allows one to suppose that, as centers of subjectivity, they have acquired a sense of obligation with respect to a particular matter. If the state is viewed as a corporate entity, the legal order that supports it should define the organs of the state competent for the purpose of creating general custom, and, furthermore, specify when in fact the organs are acting to this end. Yet the international legal order does not do this. Jurists are left fumbling with the idea that the state is itself, as a totality, in some undefined way, capable of having a "legal sense" that it is bound by a general custom that may even be supposed to be already existing. The reaction of some jurists has been to try to dispense with the psychological element of general custom altogether, yet without abandoning the concept of general custom itself (D'Amato 1971: 52; Sorensen 1946: 52).

Pierre-Marie Dupuy (2003a: 160, my translation) provides a most recent exhaustive and authoritative account of the formal problems for the mainstream. Dupuy draws attention to the fact that the profession must face a deficiency: "[T]hat, precisely, of the existence of *procedures*, duly formalized by the law itself, for the creation of customary norms." Dupuy (2003a: 160–61) remarks how there are very detailed rules for the conclusion of treaties, "but, there are not, to the contrary, to borrow the terminology of Hart, secondary rules governing the conditions of formation of custom . . . One contents oneself to affirm unilaterally that the rules of custom exist or one awaits a judge to say so himself, in place of the States." Until there is some form of "revelatory proof of its existence, generally judicial, a rule of custom remains a virtual rule. The paradox is that, trapped in its theoretical premises, the most classical positivist doctrine, says Dupuy, nonetheless persists in seeing in custom, despite this absence of forms, a formal source of law with respect to the conditions of its creation, and not merely with respect to its content.[2]

There is a clear residual confidence among international lawyers that the international judiciary can "reveal," to use Dupuy's language, the presence of custom, and turn it from virtual to real law. Yet, it is almost a commonplace of legal doctrine that the I.C.J. has reached decisions in such cases as the *Fisheries Jurisdiction* (1974) or the *Advisory Opinion on Namibia* (1971) in the face of so much conflicting state interest and interplay of power, as to leave one at a loss as to how general custom is supposed to arise out of state practice (see, e.g. Churchill 1975; Hevener 1978: 793–4).

Some doctrinal consideration of what would be involved in actual, direct analysis of state practice does directly address the difficulties of assembling practice and then presenting it systematically. An authoritative recent representation of the debates about the two elements that make up customary law, material practice and the subjective element, is Mendelson's (1995) article, in which he raises the important question of whether, in order to assess the subjective element of custom, it is necessary to know the inner workings of a state bureaucracy. States do not have minds of their own:

[A]nd in any case, since much of the decision making within government bureaucracies takes place in secret, we cannot know what States (or those who direct or speak for them) really think, but only what they say they think. There may be something of an exaggeration here. In some instances we can discover their views because the opinions of their legal advisers or governments are published. [fn. Though admittedly this is done only on a partial and selective basis and often only long after the event; and though it must also be conceded that the opinion of a government legal adviser does not invariably become that of the government.]

After these important deliberations, Mendelson (1995: 195–6) writes that it is better to speak of the subjective rather than the psychological element of custom:

[F]or it is more a question of the positions taken by the organs of States about international law, in their internal processes. [fn. Including the communications of governments to national legislatures and courts, and the express or implicit prise de position about rules of international law by national courts and legislatures in the exercise of their functions] and in their interaction with other States, than of their beliefs.

The United Kingdom *Materials on International Law* (until recently, edited by the late Geoffrey Marston) have been available in the British Yearbook annually since 1978. Marston has followed what is called the model plan for the classification of documents concerning state practice in the field of public international law, adopted by the Committee of Ministers of the Council of Europe in its Resolution (68)17 of June 28, 1968. This was amended by Recommendation (97)11 of June 12, 1997, following General Assembly Resolution 2099(XX) on technical assistance to promote the teaching, study, dissemination, etc. of international law. The changes are not significant, and the essence of Marston's approach is that he sets out, as Mendelson (1995) has put it "positions taken by organs of States about international law, in their internal processes and in their interaction with other States."[3]

Towards a phenomenology of the actual problem

In philosophical discourse the word *phenomenology* is used to describe the attempt to reach directly to the object one wishes to understand, through some scheme of full perception and digestion of the object. In this case, some general remarks have to be made about the significance of penetrating the bowels of the state to find out whether and how it is observing or contributing to the creation of international law. In strict legal terms, the issue can arise in distinct ways. It may be a matter of determining whether a country is observing or violating a rule of law. Alternatively this may be a matter of assessing what contribution the country is making to the development or clarification of the law, where it is taken to be uncertain. In either case, it is not enough simply to know what verbal positions state organs take up. It is necessary to know what the country has actually done. The discrepancy will arise where the official positions are either not true or not the whole truth. But it need not even be so black and white morally. It may simply be that without the full picture, the actions of a state, such as the U.K., may be unintelligible.

In an article published in 1986, a Foreign and Commonwealth Office (F.C.O.) legal adviser drew attention to the fact that "informal agreements" played a large part in British foreign relations (Aust 1986: 787). The basic principle is that a state is free to deny itself the advantages of concluding a legally binding treaty in order to benefit from the advantages of concluding informal instruments. Security and defence issues are not the only issues covered, but it is clear that the advantage here is the flexibility which comes from secrecy. This background will usually be relevant to cases involving the use of force, as there will be agreements between the U.K. and its allies that are not public knowledge, or there may be relevant agreements even if the U.K. is not itself formally a party to them.

To present the issue in a wider context, one might take a well-known and still uncertain case, the U.S. bombing of Libya in 1986 from bases within the U.K. The terms under which the U.S. enjoys the use of military bases within the U.K. are known only to be the subject of informal agreements or even understandings. With the U.S. bombing of Libya from British territory, one question was whether the U.K. had the full legal power to permit the U.S. action. The U.K. did not try to claim that the U.S. had acted independently of it, but supported U.S. action, again relying on intelligence information – which could not be disclosed for security reasons – that there were very specific Libyan targets engaged in terrorist activity. The information could not be disclosed for fear of jeopardizing sources. Prime Minister Thatcher, in the House of Commons on 16 April 1986, affirmed that her legal advice was that the bombing targets chosen were permitted by Article 51 of the U.N. Charter, as a matter of an inherent right of self-defence against armed attack (see Carty 1990: 131–33).[4]

It was argued, however, in the House of Commons debate, that she should be obliged to demonstrate, with relevant evidence before the Security Council, that Article 51 had been observed. This would mean producing concrete evidence that, at the least, without an air strike there would be planned raids from specific camps, putting British citizens at risk. The Foreign Secretary, Sir Geoffrey Howe, himself a Q.C., argued in reply that the right of self-defence includes the right to destroy or weaken one's assailants, to reduce his resources and to weaken his will so as to discourage and prevent further violence.

The argument by the Foreign Secretary was, then, presented in a context where the information that was supposed to ground the threat or risk and the justification for military action could not be disclosed because it would jeopardize sources of intelligence information. There was effectively a claim to determine unilaterally the scope of international obligations with respect to restraint on the use of force, not only with respect to the extent of the norm but also the factual context of its application.

Yet, from a practical point of view it can be very difficult to penetrate significantly "into the bowels of the state." It is very difficult to discuss contemporaneous events for a number of reasons. Those involved are usually still alive and may continue to be engaged in the very same events that are ongoing. Perspectives and opinions about the best course of action will remain openly contested. Furthermore, there will not usually be agreed objective and detached sources from which one can draw to determine the nature of the events. There will be much fresh, first-hand testimony, but it will be conflicting. Where official events are concerned, and state practice falls under this rubric, there will not be direct access to primary source material, and, indeed it may be wondered whether the very idea of primary source material itself is becoming archaic in the postmodern age of political spin. Contemporary events will be important to those still engaged and passions will run high in attempting to discuss them. At the same time, the objective, detached, perhaps officially agreed records for the description of the events will not be available and there will be no final authority to adjudicate contesting versions of the events.

All of this impinges directly on the practice of the international lawyer in at least two respects. The international lawyer needs, as much as the diplomatic historian, to understand state conduct and this means having reliable access to state intentions. These remain, in principle, state secrets except in so far as the state itself chooses to disclose them, or when recalcitrant officials leak them, or journalists otherwise come improperly or irregularly on state intentions. Such well-known problems pose for the theory of state practice the temptation to avoid the psychological or intentional element of state practice when collecting and analysing it. We suggest that it is a remedy a lot worse than the disease.

What is needed is a framework of analysis of state activity that allows a legal analyst to engage in effective analysis of the conduct of states as actors in international society. This entails actually penetrating the corporate veil of the state in order to understand both facts and intentions. For some purposes this might not be strictly necessary, e.g. if the matter under observation is purely one of legal/state

responsibility. Positions taken by governments would then be of more importance than understanding actions in contexts. However, investigation of customary practice is a matter of deciphering the normative significance of the behavior of collective entities, and of evaluating, comparatively, clashing collective actions. As we have seen, doctrine has virtually talked its way into the position that somehow the very idea that states have intentions, minds etc. is regarded as absurd. Instead, the notion of legal obligation of states is to be inferred from the results of their behavior, externally observed as a sort of material fact. As Akehurst (1974–5: 195) put it some time ago: "We cannot know what States believe. First of all States being abstractions or institutions do not have minds of their own; and in any case since much of the decision-making within governments takes place in secret, we cannot know what States (or those who speak for them) really think, but only what they say they think."

It is necessary to realize that there are degrees to which the internal workings of the state can be made transparent and part of the rigor which may accompany the work of the legal analyst is to realize the extent to which one is approximating total transparency. For instance purely historical work, in the sense that archives are fully open, allows one to construct an historical narrative that determines precisely whether law has formed part of the motivational structure of the action of a state.[5] This will constitute an absolute standard against which to judge whatever other explorations of state practice one may undertake. In this respect, the work of the legal analyst most closely approximates that of the diplomatic historian.

At the same time a theory of the practice of international law has also to consider the inherent possibilities of the impact of legal advising in the state structures which make up international society. This brings the legal analyst much closer to the theorist of international relations, as well as to the science of the history of political ideas. There is a widely held realist view of the nature of international society, which dictates that a state will place its subjectively considered view of its national security needs above any international legal or moral standard. There is unending controversy about the extent to which this in fact must happen. However, the legal analyst needs to be conscious of both the pressures the "in-house lawyer" will suffer within national state bureaucracies and indeed the extent to which the whole ethos and intellectual tradition of international law, as part of the European history of political ideas, is itself permeated by the language of raison d'état.[6] Nonetheless, empirical investigation of the practice of international law within state structures should throw enormous light on the "real" force of "realist" perspectives on the importance of international law. Obviously, there are many other international relations perspectives, but space does not permit consideration of them and for this reason, the "realist" theory is chosen as the one most likely to discount any place for international law in the decision-making process of a state. The discussion will not focus on elaborating on variations of "realist" theory but merely try to expose, through a study of international law practice, the actual place of international law in international society in particular cases. Through study of numerous such instances of practice, it may be eventually possible to generate new international relations theory.

Exploration of state practice with the tools of diplomatic history

In the words of the 1920s' U.K. Foreign Office Legal Adviser, Sir Cecil Hurst: "What makes international law is the practice of governments, and to know in any particular case not merely what the Government did but why it did it, i.e. the particular circumstances in the case on which its view is based, is what makes the precedent valuable as a guide for the future."[7] In other words the legal advice only becomes the position of the government when the government actually follows it. At the same time where the government has heard legal suggestions but not followed them, that fact can indicate a great deal about the political character of the state decision, even when it cannot be said that the state has acted illegally. The manner in which the legal advice is introduced can affect its character. For instance, it is not uncommon for the lawyers to have no case stated to them, but simply to be sent all the relevant dispatches. This will have the effect that the lawyers are expected to enter into all the practical considerations on which the government has to decide. However, a more usual practice is for papers submitted to the legal advisers to be minuted so as to show as clearly as possible the points on which the legal advisers' view is required. Any use of that advice must be clearly approved by the legal adviser. According to a former legal adviser, this gives the lawyer not merely a function of finding and explaining the law but also "an important control over the way in which the law is applied in particular cases" (Berman 1994: 85).

The usually understood form of international legal analysis can be actually quite alien to the way in which international law is practiced, not simply in the sense of how international lawyers understand it, but also in the sense of how it becomes the international legal practice of states. Lawyers have distinguished what they call a purely legal method of exposition of the legal advice given to governments and an historical–diplomatic approach. Clive Parry, Lord Arnold McNair and H. A. Smith have expressed themselves on this matter. Part of the difficulty is seen to be feasibility to present all relevant contextual documentation, but also lawyers doubt whether they have the competence, in McNair's words, "to pursue each incident to its conclusion and find out what happened. That would be diplomatic history, a field in which I have no experience and into which I would not dare to enter" (McNair 1956: xx).

McNair and Parry both consider that legal advice is in itself very valuable, as being impartial advice given with respect to a concrete situation. One can wonder how they feel so assured as to the impartiality of advice if they remain unaware of the context in which it is given. However, much more importantly, the lawyers here appear to be making a fetish out of the legal advice by forgetting that the only point at which international law can come into existence, or have any real existence, is through the actual practice of states, and yet they are saying that they do not have the competence as diplomatic historians to assess exactly what is the precise historical significance of state practice. Hence, there is no one who can make the distinction, crucial for the evolution of new customary international law, between state practice which is legally or not legally significant, because it is or is not attributable to a legal conviction (*opinion juris*) on the part of states. How such a determination would work out in practice can be illustrated from a contribution to this debate by Smith, with respect to the U.K. recognition of the Spanish American Republics. We use this example because we intend to illustrate the historical diplomatic method later, with respect to the U.K. government's recognition of the new Communist Chinese government in 1949. Smith (1932) says:

> Legal opinions and pronouncements have but little value except in relation to the facts which provoke them . . . Without a fairly generous selection from the political documents it would be impossible, for example, to understand the reasons which finally impelled Great Britain, after many years of hesitation, to decide upon the policy of recognizing the Spanish American Republics.

It is argued here that it is worthwhile to ask whether a state's actions in a particular instance are motivated by legal considerations among others. Whether this is the case is simply a matter of assessing whether significant state officials acted in terms that were understood subjectively to be formulated legally. That is to say, the officials considered they were acting as they were legally entitled or bound to do. This is a matter of evidence and the evidence is in the archives. House of Commons statements or other official communiqués can bind the state, in the sense of an estoppel, but they do not amount to reliable evidence of what the state's actions *mean*. For this one needs access to intentions, as much in the practice of legal interpretation as in the practice of states.

That many specialists in the field of international law should say there is no coherent legal method to directly access customary international law and so one has to await pronouncements of the World Court as to that practice is an internally contradictory view of the nature of international law. This is because it is already recognized by the foundational article 38 of the Statute of the I.C.J., that judicial opinions are merely evidence of the law and not its direct source. If no "normal" international lawyer can explain how he can unearth a state practice which constitutes customary law, the mere authority of the judiciary cannot fill the gap. At the same time international relations scholars recognize that the importance of anthropological theory for the foundations of international law rests in the fact that the meaning of legal concepts is limited by the relativity of different state or other collective community grasp of any sense of obligation outwards, whether legal or otherwise.[8] Some mechanism to explore a dialectic of disparate legal meanings has to be elaborated. The perspective on the analysis of state practice, which is offered here, has the ambition to explore in very much more detail the suspicion that concrete international legal practice, despite its ideological tones and pretence of universality, is actually very bound to national institutions that effectively determine the meaning of legal obligations. However, it is too simple to say that states, as sovereigns, give words meanings that suit state interests. This begs the question: What

87

is the state? Instead, it should be recognized that the state as an institutional framework for numerous subordinate institutions is a textual or interpretative community within which international law officials work with others to achieve certain aims.

It may be that in a particular case the lawyers are the determining factor in a decision-making process and in this case to understand the outcome as a human action, it is only necessary to trace the intentions of the lawyers and how it is that these intentions came to be adopted. However, more usually the work of the international lawyer will be entwined in a complex of attitudes and expectations also held by those who are not lawyers. The question is not whether the international lawyer nobly upholds legal principle as against a grimy national interest, as there will be a dialectic among several governments attempting to apply general principles or rules, in accordance with their own subjective interpretations. Even more significantly, within national state institutions as well as within smaller groupings or networks of states, it will be seen that the law really exists within webs of tacit understandings and arguments, whose meaning cannot be unraveled without regard to the interaction of the intentions and expectations of diplomats, politicians and lawyers. The international law practice of a country and its other standards, ethical, political or whatever, *together make up the ethos which permeates the context within which all the officials (legal and political) work.* Another U.K. Foreign Office Legal Adviser has given expression to very much these sentiments. Sir Ian Sinclair (1982: 134) has written:

> In the international legal field, there is no clear dichotomy between law and policy, particularly where, as is often the case, textbook solutions are not available. The role which the FCO Legal Advisers perform in relation to their clients is accordingly rather more creative than first appearances might suggest; it will not be confined to the

rendering of abstract advice, but will rather be designed wherever possible to afford practical guidance as to what course of action to follow in the particular circumstances, having regard to governing legal principles and to developing legal trends.

It is proposed to illustrate this theory with a concrete example from British diplomatic and legal practice, where it could be said that the lawyers had clearly a very determining role in the outcome of a very significant area of policy making where the politicians and diplomats certainly preferred to regard their options as completely open, until they were otherwise directed by the international lawyers.

The case concerns the *de jure* recognition of the Chinese Communist government following its seizure of Beijing in October 1949. There are two broad strands of documents. The first is the *Documents on British Policy Overseas: Britain and China 1945–1950* (henceforth, *Documents*) which are drawn entirely from government archival sources, which ends with the recognition of the Chinese government.[9] They provide some picture of the wider chronology of the diplomacy leading to recognition, but also mention the place of legal advice, quite unusual in such types of publications. The second strand of documents consists of unpublished archive materials, mainly from the Foreign Office. Resort is had to this for the purpose of obtaining the fullest picture of how the legal advice is developed and used. These archival material show that the legal advice was directly taken on board by the political officials and became, virtually verbatim, the position represented by the Foreign Secretary, Ernest Bevin. The archival material also indicates that the Foreign Office legal adviser also considered that the issue of recognition of governments and representation at the U.N. were related, so that the decision as to the former could be guided by how one expected to deal with the latter.

Recognition by the U.K. of the Communist government of China

The issue of recognition of a Communist regime was first broached in February 1949 when the Chinese were already in control of a large area of China and refusing to recognize foreign consuls operating within their territories on the grounds that diplomatic relations had not been established.[10] However, it did not become a pressing and clear case for a call for legal advice until August and September 1949. The first thing which clearly emerges from the archival record, but not so easily from the *Documents*, is that the Foreign Secretary and senior political officials within the Foreign Office were of a mind to make recognition of the new Chinese government dependent on various conditions, and that the contrary legal advice, particularly of Sir Eric Beckett, was, most probably, very influential in leading the government not to set conditions to its *de jure* recognition of the new Chinese government.

The story reaches its crucial stage on September 27, 1949 when officials (P. D. Coates) brought to the attention of the legal adviser, a public speech by the Secretary of State in the U.N.G.A., reported in the *Times*, that China, having entered into certain international obligations, must honor them. The *Times* correspondent added that this phrase has aroused much speculation. Reference is made to a legal adviser memorandum, saying that it is not customary to make conditions of this nature preliminary to recognition of a new government, but that the legal minute cannot be traced.[11] An extensive two-page minute from Sir Eric Beckett follows on October 4, 1949.

> The predominant and I think the right legal view is that the recognition of a government . . . is one which can be appreciated solely on whether the regime applying for recognition fulfils the qualifications for recognition laid down by international law. The political appreciation which necessarily comes in should really be limited to forming an opinion on whether the legal qualifications are fulfilled or not . . . In the recent past the conduct of a good many states and of some reputable states . . . has hardly been in accord with what I have indicated above as being the proper legal view . . . I would rather gather from these papers that the Secretary of State has decided, and is even committed to, that there shall be no recognition of the Communist Government in China as the *de jure* Government in China until it says that it will accept Chinese international obligations (query in general or with specified particular I do not know).
>
> Now the position of China and the Security Council eloquently, I think, testifies to the difficulties which are likely to occur if recognition is granted or refused on other than some legal principle. I think that . . . in an ideal world, the other members of the Security Council . . . impartially assess the practical elements of the situation and see who is legally most entitled legally to represent China.

In the course of the preparation of a draft cabinet paper for October 24, 1949 legal advice was taken solely on the question whether there could be any legal objection to the recognition of the Chinese government, and, citing Hersch Lauterpacht's views on recognition, the legal advice was that there could be no objection "having regard to the proportion of Chinese territory controlled by the Communist Government, the firmness of its control there, on the one hand and the tenuous nature of Nationalist control, where it exists, on the other hand."[12] This opinion was reproduced verbatim in the Cabinet Paper, the *Memorandum of Mr Bevin on Recognition of the Chinese Communist Government*, of October 24, 1949.[13]

However, this memorandum did not deal with the question of assurances from the Communist Chinese that they should respect China's international obligations. *Documents* point to further discussion of the issue in diplomatic exchanges and in cabinet. The Australian Minister for External Affairs,

Dr. Evatt, claimed that the U.K., the U.S., and Australia were in complete accord on this need to respect international obligations, and also that recognition would not be forthcoming unless China gave specific assurances respecting the territorial integrity of neighboring countries. Bevin replied that no such assurances had been required from the "satellite" governments in eastern Europe and added that "in the light of our bitter memories of the fate of non-aggression pacts at the hands of totalitarian states" it was "inconceivable" that the U.K. would request guarantees for the territorial integrity of China's neighbors.[14]

When it came to the preparation of a further cabinet paper in December 1949, the legal adviser was approached by Mr. Scarlett, who said the time for according *de jure* recognition is fast approaching. He notes to Beckett:

> You have minuted . . . that the granting of *de jure* recognition is in fact merely an acknowledgment of facts and in consequence that this should not be conditioned in any way. On the other hand, I have no doubt that it would be politically of some advantage to phrase our communication to the Chinese in such a way that the expressed wishes of e.g. the United States Government and the Government of Australia might be held to have been met. Both these Governments have repeatedly expressed the view that recognition should only be accorded in return for some prior undertaking of good behavior from the new regime in China.

> As I see it there are three possibilities.

> (1) Our Note to the Chinese could simply state that H.M.G. were now ready to accord *de jure* recognition . . .
> (2) We might follow our Yugoslav note which began by stating H.M.G.'s readiness etc. . . . and went on to state H.M.G.'s assumption that the new Government would respect the international obligations of its predecessor.

> (3) The Chinese say they are willing to establish diplomatic relations with any Government willing to observe the principles of equality, mutual interest and mutual respect for territorial sovereignty . . . We could echo this phrase and argue thereafter that it implied some general assurance of decent behavior.

Scarlett concluded by asking Beckett: "Do you think that forms of words along the lines of (2) or (3) would be likely to strengthen our hand in law *vis a vis* the Chinese if need arose?"[15]

Beckett replied on the same day that he considered it unnecessary and undesirable to try to make a bargain under which recognition *de jure* is given for an assurance that previous international obligations will be observed. This would certainly apply to (2), but even to the vaguer (3). Even that invites an awkward answer and you gain nothing by it. This is for reasons given in an earlier minute on the same day. Beckett suggested instead that a separate statement might be made to some else to which the Chinese government is not required to respond.[16] Such an approach recognizes the fact, insists Beckett, that:

> [N]o change in the international obligations of a state are brought about by a change of regime, and therefore it is not necessary, as the United States appear to be doing, to insist on an explicit acceptance of this principle by the new regime. Indeed, to insist on such an explicit statement has its disadvantages because it opens the way to the argument that the new regime is only bound by the previous obligations of the country if it expressly says that it will be.[17]

These legal conclusions are substantially reproduced verbatim in the final *Memorandum by Mr Bevan on Recognition of the Chinese Communist Government*, to Cabinet (December 12, 1949).[18] Given especially the fact that the legal adviser did not claim his view of the law was even frequently applied, one must suppose that the Foreign Secretary simply considered the legal advice sound in itself. The memorandum observes, on the effects of recognition, that "recognition does not itself make the Communist authorities the rulers of China. They are that already. Recognition is no more than an acceptance of a fact, which its withholding would not alter."[19] To refuse recognition when no other effective authority exists in China is to imply a boycott, which would be negative for long term relations. Politically, recognition means willingness to enter into diplomatic relations and does not signify approval of ideology. "The political advantages of recognition are calculated on the assumption that we cannot afford to ignore, however much we may disapprove its political orientation, a government which has effective authority over a vast territory and population. Similarly, it is assumed that without relations with this Government, we shall be in no position to exert influence on its future development."[20] It was recognized that such a position clearly did not guarantee treaty rights of the U.K. The final cabinet memorandum mentions that the Chinese offer of relations of equality etc. was only part of the picture. The Chinese press announced that all Kuomintang treaties were liable to re-examination and revision. The judgment was that in any case a unilateral statement by the U.K. would make no difference, will not lead to the obligations being regarded as binding and delay in recognition will not help as the treaties are valueless without diplomatic relations. Therefore recognition, followed by laborious and unpromising negotiations is what lies ahead, particularly with respect to the Sino–British Treaty of 1943.[21] More precisely, it is stated that while "the new regime is not at present so corrupt as its predecessor, its authority may well prove even more arbitrary and vexatious in its regulations."[22]

The cabinet adopted the recommendation to recognize the new Chinese government on December 15, 1949.[23] Two days later the ambassador in Washington reported the results of a meeting with the U.S. Secretary of State, Dean Acheson. Sir O. Franks reported that "They [the U.S.] now thought there was likely to be early expansion (of the Chinese) south and east beyond the borders of China. This expansion would be especially dangerous, if it took place, where there were considerable Chinese settlements." The Ambassador asked what evidence there was for this and said "The only reply I got was that the Communists would, by aggrandizement in the south, direct the gaze of the Chinese people from Manchuria."[24]

On January 6, 1950, The U.K. accorded recognition of the Chinese government, as in effective control of by far the greater part of the territory of China, as the *de jure* government and they were ready to establish diplomatic relations on the basis offered by the Chinese themselves, i.e. equality, mutual benefit and respect for territorial integrity and sovereignty.[25]

In June 1950 the Foreign Secretary produced an extensive circular on *Recognition of States and Governments* which was to remain authoritative for at least 20 years.[26] The Foreign Office was continuing to refer to it in the face of the blizzards of military coups in Africa and other parts of the "Third World" in the 1960s and 1970s. The document outlines two approaches, which it calls "doctrines" regarding the matter. It is so comprehensively and closely argued that its reproduction is advisable. Its content will only be outlined here to show the connection with how it applied in the case of the recognition of the Communist government of China, after October 1949. The document itself includes an annex of a letter of Hersch Lauterpacht to the *London Times* on January 6, 1949, "prompted by His Majesty's Government's recognition of the Chinese Communist government." The letter "refers only to the recognition of governments, but the principles applying to the recognition of states are virtually the same."

The first approach was that recognition was a matter of mixed law and fact, but mixed only in the sense that: "The law determines the conditions which entitle a state or a govern-ment to *de jure* or *de facto* recognition . . . Policy determines whether these conditions are or are not fulfilled, and there is often a margin for a political appreciation . . . But if the conditions for recognition are fulfilled, there is a legal duty to grant it." The crucial part of this argument, which was decisive to the Chinese case, comes at the end. "Recogni-tion does not necessarily imply any approval of or any friendly disposition towards the regime recognized."

The second approach was that "recogni-tion is a pure matter of policy and involves no question of law whatever . . . states recog-nizing or refusing to recognize are merely using political weapons in a political game." Again, the punchline is at the end. "Under this doctrine recognition implies a moral or political approval of the regime recognized."

It would not be fair to say that policy advantage alone led to the choice of the first approach without any constraining legal force. However, this policy was specifically evolved in the Chinese context where it was always recognized that Britain's main pro-tagonist, the United States, took the second approach while Britain was preparing to take the first one. In this memo, the arguments are expressed more abstractly and even academ-ically rather than diplomatically.

In the document, the argument is that the first doctrine "is broadly based on the general practice of states and, taken over a long period, though there are admittedly excep-tions, the balance of authority is strongly in its favor." In contrast, the second doctrine is anarchic:

> It makes almost nonsense of a great part of international law and if generally followed may render almost impossible the working of any international organization. When the greater part of international law is directed to defining the rights of States, it is not on a very sound foundation if State A can in effect avoid the greater part of its obliga-tions to State B by deciding as a pure mat-ter of policy not to recognize it, or not to

recognize what is obviously its Govern-ment. Similarly, no international organiza-tion can work if, following the purely anarchic doctrine of recognition, States are infinitely various as regards the regimes they recognize, as they are likely to be, whereas the scope of difference is reduced to narrow proportions if the first doctrine is strictly followed.

The document recognizes that it is the U.S. which virtually adopts this second doctrine although not precisely in the language pre-sented here, viz., that recognition is purely a matter of policy. The U.S. itself will present its strategy on recognition "as an instrument of policy in support of law and legal order." For instance, a regime should not be recog-nized if it is unconstitutional, e.g. the U.S. approach to certain Latin American regimes. Neither should there be recognition if a state or regime is constituted as a result of aggression, as with the Stimson doctrine, characterized by this document "as completely unsuccessful." Again, recognition may be refused to a government, unless it appears the state or regime will recognize international obligations, particularly those of its prede-cessors. The document notes such a practice of bargaining for recognition is not infrequent, but it is incoherent because new govern-ments are anyway bound by such obligations, "and to bargain about this as a condition to recognition tends to throw doubt on the legal principle."

The document is especially determined to root out evaluative elements in recogni-tion, however high sounding. The second doctrine remains just as anarchic as in its bald formulation:

> It would be possible to justify almost any non-recognition on the ground that the non-recognizing State was not satisfied that the new regime was prepared to fulfill all its international obligations, for instance recognition of *all* Communist regimes could be refused on the ground that they did not recognize human rights.

In fact, these two doctrines are being formulated as a matter of direct British opposition to U.S. policy and tactics with respect to the cold war, with Communist China as the focal point. The document itself mentions Israel and China. Israel was recognized as soon as the establishment of the new state was no longer in doubt, but "as soon as it was clear that it was sufficiently firmly established, they [H.M.G.] recognized it." More central to our present story:

> The recognition of the Chinese People's Government was a straightforward case of the application of the first doctrine . . . because the Chinese People's Government was firmly established, with control over practically all Chinese territory, they [H.M.G.] recognized it *de jure*, although the character of that Government was not one which commanded their approval and it was far from certain that it would recognize obligations under international law, as His Majesty's Government understand it.

It is important to conclude this section of the story with a remarkable passage, which shows the very careful deliberation, which is going into the choice of the word "doctrine." Bevin is arguing in his circular to U.K. representatives abroad, that H.M.G. is choosing the first doctrine as the right doctrine, which it thinks is in the interest of the development of a peaceful and stable world order. He continues:

> In view of the attitude of the United States Government, it is clear that any public discussion of this subject must be very carefully handled. Nevertheless it is the intention of His Majesty's Government to spread as widely as possible the knowledge that the doctrine set out by Professor Lauterpacht is in their opinion correct and to propagate that doctrine by all suitable means, in the hope that the contrary doctrine may thus become generally discredited and be eventually abandoned.

This very carefully constructed picture is the outcome of what the Foreign Office took to be the experience it had had in negotiating its policy of recognition of the Chinese People's government with the United States.

International relations theory and the practice of international law

The present case study focuses on the active U.K. Foreign Office discussions in July and August 1957 about the best way to present the U.K.'s relations with Oman and Muscat internationally, when an Arab bloc of states, led by Egypt, tried to place (what it called) U.K. armed aggression against Oman on the agenda of the Security Council. The legal advice of Francis Vallat and Sir Gerald Fitzmaurice played a considerable part in these discussions, which reveal a vision of governmental structures for dealing with international relations which appear very much a hangover from the period of the high renaissance. Secrecy is prized as the most reasonable option when it comes to providing public explanations of state conduct. What the case study will show is not the failure to apply international law, but rather a more constructivist, and at the same time, fragmented picture of an international society where legal discourse plays a significant part but does not grasp fully the complexities of the situations which it indeed may contribute to concealing. International law is both constrained by raison d'état and also becomes interwoven in the secrecy of the diplomacy that that requires.

The case study takes as a starting point the types of charge levied against the U.K. in works such as Mark Curtis's *The Ambiguities of Power* (1995) and the successor volume, *The Great Deception, Anglo-American Power and World Order* (1998). Curtis's view is that Britain has a clear foreign policy aim, which it follows in concert with the United States. This aim is to preserve as much as it can the economic, political and military advantages, which it possessed at the time of the Empire. In his analysis, Britain continues to be largely successful in the pursuit of this policy in the Middle East, especially in the Gulf, and in southeast Asia. Military interventions, whether covert or open, and support for friendly regimes, particularly military and other security training, will be attuned to the need to preserve these interests. Obviously, the language of international law is a potentially useful propaganda weapon in the hands of opponents and so no useful purpose is served by an explicit and provocative disregard of it.

Therefore the British rhetoric is one of continued commitment to the principles of the U.N. Charter, viz., above all, non-intervention in the internal affairs of other countries, respect for human rights and democracy, and priority to the peaceful settlement of disputes. Positions in accordance with these principles will be declared in international fora and even in public debates within national fora. The actual practice is difficult to put together because it remains largely secret and one obtains only sporadic glimpses of it.

What are the implications of these polemics for attempts to assess what contribution Britain is making to the development of international customary law on the law relating to the use of force and the right of intervention at the behest of a friendly government? For instance, the 1986 United Kingdom materials on international law contain a document produced by the planning staff of the F.C.O. in July 1984, entitled "Is intervention ever justified?" (Marston 1986: 614–20). The question is how, or even whether, such a document is to be read critically, i.e. how to assess the relationship of the document to an inevitably largely hidden practice. For instance, in paragraph II.6, intervention under a treaty with, or at the invitation of, another state is mentioned. If one state requests assistance from another, then clearly that intervention cannot be dictatorial and is therefore not unlawful. In 1976, the Security Council recalled that it is the inherent right of every state, in the exercise of its sovereignty, to request assistance from any other state or group of states. An example of such lawful intervention at the request of states might be the British aid to Muscat and Oman.

Curtis comments on this incident as follows. Oman requested British military aid to quell a revolt in the north of the territory in the summer of 1957. In fact, in Curtis' view, Oman was a de facto client state controlled by Britain as much as any former colony. Its armed forces were commanded by British officers under the overall control of a British general. The Ministries of Finance and Petroleum respectively and the director of the intelligence service were British. Banking and the oil company management were controlled by the British. The country was desperately poor, with infant mortality at 75%. The Royal Air Force and the Special Air Service together struggled until 1959 to put down a revolt against these conditions. Oman continued after its suppression to serve British financial and other interests very well. Extensive bombing of villages was an integral part of this campaign. At one point, the British political agent recommended that the villages should be warned that unless they surrendered ringleaders, they would be destroyed one by one, etc. (Curtis 1995: 98–9).

The Foreign Office paper fully recognizes the complexity and controversy surrounding this area of law. It continues, on mentioning Oman in 1957, to say in paragraph II.7 that international law does prohibit interference (except maybe humanitarian) when a civil war is taking place and control of the state's territory is divided between warring parties. At the same time, the paper claims that it is widely accepted that outside interference in favor of one party to the struggle permits counter-intervention on behalf of the other, as happened recently in Angola.

There was a very full discussion within the Foreign Office in July and August 1957 about the best way to present the U.K.'s relations with Oman and Muscat internationally, when an Arab bloc of States, led by Egypt, tried to have what it called U.K. armed aggression against Oman placed on the agenda of the Security Council. Legal advice by Sir Gerald Fitzmaurice and Francis Vallat played a considerable part. The Foreign Office was reacting to arguments put forward in a particular context, a U.N. forum. Arab States, backed by the Soviet Union, wanted to have British military action in the Sultanate characterized in U.N. Charter language as constituting aggression against the independent state of Oman, coming from British forces in Muscat.

Fitzmaurice's and Vallat's legal advice

The advice from Vallat for the benefit of the Secretary of State was that intervention, at the request of the Sultan of Muscat, to put down an insurrection by tribes in Oman was legal. Intervention is wrongful but that only refers to dictatorial interference, not assistance or cooperation. Oppenheim gives numerous examples of military assistance to maintain internal order, including Portugal in 1826, Austria in 1849, Cuba in 1917 and Nicaragua in 1926–27.[27]

Fitzmaurice is more explicit about the importance of the status of Muscat and Oman. Oman is not an independent state. In the international legal sense, it is not a state at all, but merely part of Muscat and Oman. The imam of Oman exercised no territorial sovereignty. There are no frontiers between Oman and any other state or between Oman and Muscat. An agreement, known as the Sib Agreement, was reached in 1920. During the negotiations in 1920, a request for independence was completely rejected. The Agreement worked well until 1954. The Sultan's sovereignty was recognized by the imam, in that external affairs remained in the hands of the Sultan, i.e. concerning individuals and their lawsuits with foreign administrations. The imam's adherents relied upon passports issued by the sultanate. Judgments of the Muscat Appellate Court were accepted in the interior. An attempt to assert independence in 1954 failed. No state had

regarded "Oman" as a sovereign state independent of Muscat until the Saudi and Egyptian intrigues which followed a Saudi incursion into neighboring Buraimi in 1952.[28]

This presentation of the situation was successful when the U.K. argued it before the Security Council. Sir Pierson Dixon mirrored the legal advice closely. There could be no aggression against the independent state of Oman because none existed. The Sultan of Muscat and Oman had his sovereignty over both recognized since the nineteenth century. Egypt and other countries claim that the independence of Oman was reaffirmed in the 1920 Treaty of Sib. This treaty granted the tribes of the interior a certain autonomy but did not recognize Oman as an independent state. This request was refused by the Sultan. Also the agreement was not a treaty, but merely an agreement between the Sultan and his subjects. Sir Pierson Dixon followed Fitzmaurice's line very closely about the later marks of sovereignty. He concluded by saying the U.K.'s action in supporting the legitimate government of Muscat and Oman had been in the interests of stability of this area. If the subversion there had not been checked, the consequences might have been felt beyond the sultanate and would not have been to the advantage of any of the countries in the region that signed the letter to place this issue on the agenda of the Security Council.[29]

The vote against putting the matter on the agenda was five to four, with two abstentions.[30] Only the Philippines denied the legality of an intervention at a request of a government. The Soviet Union confined itself to generalities about the oppression of the national liberation movement of the Oman people. There was little stress on the argument about outside intervention in Oman, except from France, which led the vote against adopting the Arab item on the Security Council agenda. The U.K. itself played it down because it did not want to exacerbate its relations with Saudi Arabia.[31] An item to this effect was circulated to all the British embassies in the Middle East. Although the U.K. knew of the Saudi involvement, a higher priority had to be given to drawing Saudi Arabia out of the Soviet and Egyptian sphere of political influence (see also Nolte 1999: 86–9). This goal would have been lost if one had entered into specific detail about Saudi subversive activities. Instead, the legality of a response to an invitation for assistance was stressed.

Pressure for public disclosure: Sir Ronald Wingate's counsel

However, further pressure came on the Foreign Office from quite a different source: The domestic media, in particular an article in the *Guardian* of August 7, 1957. Pressure grew within the U.K., in the media and through questions in parliament, to uncover what the exact relationship between H.M.G. and the Sultan of Muscat and Oman was. Here, the picture which emerged in Foreign Office discussions was quite different from the public face at the U.N. A focus for discussion was whether to publish the Sib Agreement which appeared to define the relations within the sultanate. This was thought not advisable, as the more the history and operation of the agreement was explored, the clearer it would become that the only coherence and stability that the sultanate enjoyed came from British support at every level. The British political agent, now Sir Ronald Wingate, who had effectively written both sides of that agreement, was still alive in 1957.

In September 1957, Sir Ronald came to see officials in the Foreign Office. He explained to Foreign Office officials, in particular a Mr. Walmsley, that the western concept of sovereignty was meaningless in the region. The Walis, whom the Sultan maintained in Oman, did nothing and could not be said to constitute a token of government. The entire sultanate of Muscat and Oman was, for all practical purposes, not administered. The situation there in 1954, as in 1920, could be

compared to the Scottish highlands before 1745. The Sultan was completely dependent on Britain and powerless outside a few coastal towns. Wingate commented on a copy of Dixon's speech to the Security Council. He said that he could see nothing wrong with it, except that he would have expressed himself more frankly. The immediate comment of Walmsley was that while one might speak reasonably to reasonable people, it was impossible to concede any point unnecessarily in the U.N.[32]

Wingate made a further detailed comment on the Agreement of Sib and Sir Pierson Dixon's speech. Treaties concluded by the Sultan did not mean he had any effective sovereignty over an undefined area. His power had always extended only to a few coastal towns and it would be impossible to hold that the Sultan exercised any sovereignty over the interior between 1913 and 1955. Indeed, the interior tribesmen, who hated the Sultan, could have driven him into the sea had it not been for a strong battalion of imperial troops. This policy cost the U.K. a lot and served no purpose. It had been there in the nineteenth century to keep the French out and to combat the slave trade. Both reasons were long defunct. In 1920, Wingate, as political agent, undertook to reorganize the sultanate, putting Egyptian personnel in charge of administration. He, Wingate, and not the Sultan, refused to acknowledge the independence of Oman. He refused to recognize the imam of Oman as imam because of the religious significance of such an act. It would have given the imam authority over the whole sultanate. However, the imam remained as head of the tribal confederation. The agreement recognized the facts of the situation in a way that permitted Muscat and the coastal Oman, on the one side, and the tribes of the interior Oman, on the other, to exist as separate self-governing units. No question of allegiance to the Sultan arose. What the Sultan did in 1955 was not to reassert his authority but to take over the interior by armed force. This could be justified as necessary for the security of the coastal regions. However, one also had to be careful about how to deal with the extraordinary rise in the Sultan's revenues, derived presumably from oil exploration rights which he had granted in the interior tribal areas, and which necessitated the provision of security for the drilling parties in the tribal territories.[33]

Wingate's comments were relevant to the advisability of publishing the Sib Agreement as a way of silencing British media controversy about the status of the Sultan, in particular the article in the *Guardian* of 7 August 1957. It was thought that, on balance, publication would merely show how uncertain the situation in Muscat and Oman was, although selected journalists were shown the agreement on a confidential basis. A further detailed internal F.O. reading of the Agreement of Sib revealed that it was difficult to use. The difficulty of the agreement was that it made no mention of sovereignty for either side, so officials reasoned that they would have to elaborate a thesis that the Sultan's authority was implicitly assumed and that the burden of proof would be on Omanites to show they had any corresponding sovereignty. The whole question was that much more prickly because of a British administration report which appeared on a F.O. confidential print on the Buraimi: "The Agreement of Sib virtually establishes two states, the coast under the Sultan, and the interior, that is Oman proper, under the rule of the Imam . . . The tribes and tribal leaders having attained in their own eyes complete independence."[34] The best one could make of this would be to stress the words "virtually" and "in their own eyes." The Sultan's interpretation of this agreement was equally valid. There was a consensus that this was also the direction of Wingate's commentary.[35]

One further difficulty is that while Wingate's report as political agent states categorically that the demand for the independence of Oman was refused, it also makes a number of uncomfortable points, if one had to rely on it by publishing it. He denigrated

the unparalleled degree of ineptitude of the Sultan and even worse, his despatch made the following "acid remarks" on British policy: "Our influence has been entirely self-interested, has paid no regard to the peculiar political and social conditions of the country and its rulers and by bribing effete Sultans to enforce unpalatable measures which benefited none but ourselves, and permitting them to rule without protest, has done more to alienate the interior and to prevent the Sultans from re-establishing their authority than all the rest put together."[36]

One might try to say that the agreement had been violated, and ceased to exist by virtue of the subversion coming from Oman and so it was quite pointless to produce it. However, if one attempts to argue that the balance of the agreement has been destroyed by the aggression of Imam Ghalib and treats the agreement as no longer valid, to do this: "[We] should have to explain how completely he was in the pocket of the Saudis, and this would conflict with the Secretary of State's decision that at present we must avoid attacking the Saudi Government over Oman."[37]

Therefore, it can be argued that in 1957, the senior Foreign Office officials did not think that there was any realistic way in which they could present publicly what they understood to be happening in the sultanate of Muscat and Oman, other than in the Charter language of friendly states and supporting internal order within them. In fact, there was no state other than what Britain undertook to maintain, but the alternative would be for Saudi Arabia, Egypt and eventually the Soviet Union to occupy a space if Britain were to vacate it. Dorril explains at length that further insurgency against the Sultan in the late 1960s convinced the Wilson government of the need for change, and the Conservative government gave the go-ahead at the end of June 1970. It was agreed to replace the Sultan with his English-educated and more competent son. It still took until 1975 to defeat Chinese and Soviet-backed insurgency (Dorril 2000: 729–35).

It is ironical that assessments of Curtis and Dorril, that the sultanate was so misgoverned in the years before the 1970 coup, are part of the implicitly official U.K. view of that period from the hindsight of post-coup developments. The two authors rely on much secondary evidence, but the secondary evidence is a book called *Oman: The Making of a Modern State* (Townsend 1977). Townsend was economic adviser to the Oman government from 1972 to 1975. Curtis (2003: 279) quotes him as arguing that, after the regime change, the Sultan's response to the rebels in the 1960s was not an alternative program with proposals for reform or economic assistance, but simply the use of even greater force. By 1970, that policy promised to lose the sultanate to communist-backed forces. This was not acceptable. Furthermore, with the Shell-owned Petroleum Development (Oman) oil company producing oil in commercial quantities by 1967, there was plenty of domestic revenue to allow scope for a more pragmatic social policy.

Conclusion: the international lawyers' perplexity

For the international lawyer, as well as the international relations theorist, the question that is most pressing is whether and how the Charter paradigm and language for the analysis and understanding of international society can retain not merely formal validity but also a significant impact on the forces at work in that society. Perhaps the least that one can say as an international lawyer is that positions taken up by the U.K., or for that matter any other government, cannot be taken at face value, or even be treated with anything other than complete skepticism. Without consistent and comprehensive access to the governmental policy-making process in which government international lawyers may also have a significant input, it is impossible to assess the process of decision making in such a way as to determine exactly how

international law is being interpreted, applied, followed or ignored.

The difficulty has already been seen to lie in part with the continuing and presumably inevitable secrecy of diplomacy where strategic interests are engaged. This is, in effect, to acquiesce to the vision that governmental structures for dealing with international relations remain a hangover from the period of the high renaissance. A typology of this world is provided by Jens Bartelson in *A Genealogy of Sovereignty* (1995: esp. chapter 5). The so-called modern state arising out of the wars of religion of the sixteenth and seventeenth centuries is silent about its origins and primarily obsessed about its own security needs. It can usefully be understood as the subject of Descartes' distinction between the immaterial subject and the material reality, which it observes, classifies and analyses. Knowledge supposes a subject and this subject, for international relations, is the Hobbesian sovereign who is not named, but names, not observed, but observes, a mystery for whom everything must be transparent. The problem of knowledge is the problem of security, which is attained through rational control and analysis. Self-understanding is limited to an analysis of the extent of the power of the sovereign, measured geopolitically. Other sovereigns are not unknown "others" in the anthropological sense, but simply "enemies," opponents with conflicting interests whose behavior can and should be calculated.

So, mutual recognition by sovereigns does not imply acceptance of a common international order, but merely a limited measure of mutual construction of identity resting on an awareness of sameness, an analytical recognition of factual, territorial separation. The primary definition of state interest is not a search for resemblances or affinities, but a matter of knowing how to conduct one's own affairs, while hindering those of others. Interest is a concept of a collection of primary, unknowable, self-defining subjects, whose powers of detached, analytical empirical observation take absolute precedence over any place for knowledge based on passion or empathy.

Within this framework of analysis international law is perceived subjectively by each state in the light of the perspective it has of its own interests. It reflects on other states an image of international law which is part of its image of itself in relation to its "others." These images clash and may occasionally break through to one another. However, the level of existing research into the practice of international law does not permit one even to imagine how this might happen. There is no credible primary source based research into the interacting practices of international lawyers simultaneously within and across state bureaucracies.

Notes

1 See, for instance, the standard chapter on "The sources of international law", by Hugh Thirlway, *International Law*, edited by Malcolm Evans, 2003, 117–44. This is devoted to commenting on article 38 of the Statute of the International Court of Justice, setting out the sources of law to which the Court will refer. Similarly the other standard textbook by Malcolm Shaw, *International Law*, 5th edition, Cambridge University Press, 2003, 68–87, also considers almost exclusively the case law of the international courts, with, in addition to what Thirlway/Evans consider, a very superficial review of some secondary literature on customary law.

2 Ibid., and the literature cited therein: a comprehensive survey of doctrine, especially "continental."

3 See further, Marston (1990: 35), saying that parliamentary sources predominate in the U.K. materials on international law, i.e. positions taken by ministers before parliament. He points out that only rarely is material made available here which has not already been released to the public.

4 Aust's 1986 *International and Comparative Law Quarterly* article is discussed here.

5 What follows draws on Anthony Carty and Richard A. Smith (2000: chapter 1, 1–40).

6 This part of the argument will draw more particularly on Anthony Carty (2007a: chapter 2,

26–78) and particularly also an article reproduced there and published in *The Singapore Year Book of International Law* (Carty 2005).

7 FO/370/203, folios 210–11 (Foreign Office File 4704), quoted by Geoffrey Marston (1990: 40, 46).

8 The present author's latest reiteration of this point is to be found in the *European Journal of Legal Studies*, vol. 1, 2007, "The yearning for unity and the eternal return of the Tower of Babel", 1–28.

9 Series I, Vol. VIII, edited S. R. Ashton, Whitehall History Publishing, Frank Cass, 2002.

10 *Documents*, Doc.58, 17.2.1949, 204–207.

11 U.K., Foreign Office, FO 371/75815, F14109.

12 U.K., Foreign Office, FO 371/75818, F6028, October 20 and 22, 1949.

13 *Documents*, No.105, 397–402, CP (49) 214, (CAB 129/37).

14 *Documents*, No.105, 402.

15 U.K., Foreign Office, FO 371/75826, F18535: 49, December 5, 1949.

16 U.K., Foreign Office, FO 371/75826, F18535: 50.

17 U.K., Foreign Office, FO 371/75826, F 18695/1023/10, December 5, 1949.

18 *Documents*, No.110, 417: 420, paragraph 12, CP (49) 248 (CAB 129/37).

19 *Documents*, No.110, 417: 421, paragraph 15, CP (49) 248 (CAB 129/37).

20 *Documents*, No.110, 417: 421, paragraph 16, CP (49) 248 (CAB 129/37).

21 *Documents*, No.110, 417: 422, paragraph 15, CP (49) 248 (CAB 129/37).

22 *Documents*, No.110, 417: 422, paragraph 21, CP (49) 248 (CAB 129/37). *Documents* provides edited notes that: "It was China's entry into the war (Korean) in October 1950 that put paid to any prospect of negotiations with the Communists to protect British firms . . . They were forced into such debt by taxes and regulations that they had to close, leave China voluntarily and hand over what remained of their assets to the Chinese Government. Their withdrawal was announced in May 1952 and subsequent U.K. losses were estimated between £200 million and £250 million," ibid., 442–3.

23 *Documents*, No. 110, 417: 426, CP (49) 248 (CAB 129/37).

24 *Documents*, No. 116, 435–6. *Sir O. Franks to Mr Bevin, telegram no. 5855*, U.K., Foreign Office, FO 800/462, December 17, 1949 .

25 *Documents*, No.121, *Mr Bevin to HM Representatives Overseas*, 448–9.

26 Original reference, L 280/1 Circular No.059, found at FCO 25/046. The author has benefited from an AHRC research grant to undertake archival research, and this document was unearthed in the course of the project by Dr. Orna Almog.

27 U.K., Foreign Office, FO/371/126877/EA1015/89.

28 ——, FO/371/126887/EA1015/365.

29 ——, FO/371/126884/EA1015/282(A), August 20, 1957.

30 ——, FO/371/126884/EA1015/283, August 20, 1957.

31 ——, FO/371/126878/EA1015.

32 ——, FO/371/126887/EA1015/371.

33 ——, FO/371/126829: FO Confidential Note on the Agreement of Sib, and Sir Pierson Dixon's Speech in the Security Council of 20/8/1957, prepared by Sir Ronald Wingate.

34 ——, FO confidential print on the Buraimi at 157.

35 ——, FO/371/26882/EA1015/235.

36 ——, FO/371/26882/EA1015/235(A).

37 ——, FO/371/26882/EA1015/235(A).

6

International law as a unitary system

Anthony D'Amato

The thesis of this chapter is that rethinking inter-national law as a unitary system will yield im-portant insights into the still controversial questions of how international law works and what role it plays in international relations. It begins by clari-fying some of the key terms used in international law, especially the distinction between consensual and nonconsensual law. It then argues the case for using a systems analysis perspective in order to build in the international legal system (ILS) as an actual player in the international relations game. The pres-ence of the ILS transforms what was previously ana-lyzable as a two-person zero-sum game (between A and B) into a three-person non-zero-sum game (A, B, and the ILS). Under game theory, two-person zero-sum games can reach a maximin result solely through conflict (acts of war). By taking active part in the game, the ILS necessitates some resort to cooperation in order to bring the game to the equi-librium point. ILS is a purposive self-regulating system hardwired in favor of cooperation.

The thesis of this chapter is, as just stated, that rethinking international law as a unitary system can yield important insights into still controversial questions of the workings of international law and the role it plays in inter-national relations. First, however, we should take a moment to make sure that we are talk-ing in the same language.

Toward a uniform terminology

The terminology of international law has become increasingly imprecise and muddled. As a result, many scholars are talking past each other. Here are some suggested clarifications of some of the more important terms.

It is convenient at the outset to divide inter-national law into consensual law and non-consensual law. The former depends on the consent of the governed. It includes treaty law and the law of title to territory (territory may no longer be acquired by conquest). The latter − law that applies irrespective of any state's consent − is usually called customary law. The term "customary" is misleading; a better name for it would be "general" inter-national law. Here is a brief summary:

CONSENSUAL LAW	NONCONSENSUAL LAW
Conventional	Customary
Written	Unwritten
Specific	General
Applies only to the parties	Applies to all states equally

Although a treaty can sometimes affect third parties indirectly, it cannot bind any state directly other than the signatories. The

101

parties are bound "by convention" insofar as their relations to other parties are concerned.

Why is general international law often called customary law? The term "customary law" was imported into textbooks of international law in the late nineteenth century for no apparent reason other than giving the writers of those textbooks something to say about the source of general international law.[1] In 1890 Pitt Cobbett (1922) invented a simile that has stuck: Custom is like footsteps across a common that eventually becomes a path habitually followed by all. Writers were quick to restate Cobbett's image as a metaphor: Customary law is formed by a norm that takes time to ripen into a binding rule of international law. Yet, it was asked, how can we pinpoint the time when the norm ripens or the footsteps become a path? And what was the status of international law *while* the norm was ripening or the footsteps were trampling out a path? Alas, the Latinism offered for curing the problem was worse than the disease: *opinio juris*. When states act under a belief that their actions are required by international law, then they are said to be acting with *opinio juris*. Thus, all that seemed to be needed to determine *when* the path formed or the norm ripened was to test or measure whether states were acting under a belief that the norm in question was legally compulsory.

However, no one in the 4000-year history of international law has ever been able to determine, even once, whether any state was acting under the belief that its action was compulsory under international law. Obviously states don't *have* beliefs; states are artificial constructs. Are a state's officials a reasonable surrogate for the state itself? These officials may have beliefs, but how are those beliefs to be ascertained? By a telephone survey of the 1000 leading state officials? By a questionnaire? Consider a current dispute. With the advent of global warming, frozen waterways in Canada are beginning to thaw and may open up the fabled Northwest Passage connecting the Pacific and Atlantic

Oceans through various Canadian Arctic rivers and lakes. Some ships that now travel through the Suez or Panama Canals would welcome the much shorter route through the Northwest Passage. However, its high economic salience almost guarantees an international controversy. The Canadian government considers the Northwestern Passage part of Canadian internal waters, whereas the United States and other countries regard it as an international strait, open to all. If we could somehow ask all Canadian officials whether they believe that there is a rule of international law that the Northwest Passage is an international strait, we can be quite certain that they will respond in the negative. If we ask the same question of officials of the United States, we can be equally sure that they will respond in the affirmative. We may well suspect that the uniformity of responses within each of the two states reflects policy and not a penchant for telling the truth to strangers. Presidents and other high government officials only say things that serve their strategic interests. Hence *opinio juris* can never be measured. It is not a test for law, for it presupposes that which it seeks.

General international law, or just plain international law, is what states invoke to defend their entitlements against illegal acts by other states. From time to time, some writers will contend that there is no such thing as general international law. Bismarck took this position in the nineteenth century, as did the Soviet Union in the twentieth century. Some officials in the Bush administration and their academic apologists assert exceptionalism – the idea that the most powerful state is not subject to international law. Every chapter in the book you are reading refutes these extreme notions. International law provides the legitimate framework within which states interact with each other. Although some of the more interesting topics of international law concern law-in-formation, it is clear that these topics would not even arise were it not for a shared framework of boundary delimitations laid down by international law. Even the most basic player in international law, namely the state, is defined by international law. We know an entity is a state when international law tells us it is a state.[2]

In short, if a new state calls itself a state, it is, in fact, scanning the panorama of legal rules that tell us what a state is. If the facts comport with its assertions, the new state is close to achieving statehood.

Analytical advantages of systems analysis

International law is often, in fact off-handedly, called a system.[3] If we take seriously the proposition that it constitutes a system, we just might change forever the way we think about international law and the role it plays in international relations.

The first change in our mindset is to regard the international legal system (henceforth "ILS") as an actual player in the international relations game. The rules of international law that are incorporated in the ILS are the resultants of vectors of compromises and dispute resolutions extending back to the beginning of recorded history 4000 years ago. A rule of international law encapsulates the aggregate interest of the states of the world. Thus if states A and B are having a dispute, the ILS insists on intruding like a busybody. It defends the collective interest of the non-participating states. In doing so it also defends the long-term interests of both A and B in international stability, even if neither A nor B is willing to acknowledge this beneficial input in the heat of their battle with each other. The bottom line is that international law should no longer be viewed as a set of background rules; rather, it is an actual player with real beliefs and objectives that participates in every bilateral or multilateral dispute among states.

The second shift in the way we think about international relations is that the presence of the ILS transforms what was previously analyzable as a two-person zero-sum game

(between A and B) into a three-person non-zero-sum game (A, B, and the ILS). Under game theory, two-person zero-sum games can reach a maximin result solely through conflict (acts of war, etc.).[4] But a three-person non-zero-sum game can only reach a maximin equilibrium by some mixture of conflict and cooperation. By taking active part in the game, the ILS necessitates some resort to cooperation in order to bring the game to the equilibrium point. This conclusion explains the large degree of cooperation through the history of international relations: we find that the non-participating states are usually the most powerful force for cooperation. If it were not for this third-party initiative, international relations over the years would be buffeted by a series of random wars with random outcomes. There would be nothing like the degree of cooperation we enjoy today in a global economy that could have ever arisen by chance out of a random process.

A third change in the way we think about the role of law in international relations follows from the "cooperation" element just discussed. We found that non-zero-sum game theory creates a kind of vacuum for the element of cooperation to fill in, for there can be no equilibrium solution of a non-zero-sum game without resort to cooperation (in addition to conflict which is always abundantly present). Why is the ILS biased in favor of cooperation when it might have consisted of a random collection of rules? The answer is that the ILS is hardwired in favor of cooperation, peace, and stability. Hence, it is necessarily biased against conflict. States are not similarly hardwired, of course; we know this from the fact that states have often resorted to war when it was unnecessary for their self-defense or even disastrous for their self-interest (e.g. Saddam Hussein's attack on Kuwait).

Of course, the hardwire explanation, standing alone, is empty. We need to know how the hardwiring came about. To go there, we first need to establish that the ILS is a purposive self-regulating system. We will then find that the hardwiring is the result of a process akin to Darwinian evolution.

Concept of a purposive system

Systems analysis has been around a long time. At first, static systems were the objects of scientific investigation: think of the steam engine or the wrist watch. The invention of the thermostat in 1885 gave rise to the first cybernetic system, one that seemed to be purposive, namely, keeping room temperature close to a desired norm. During the Second World War, John von Neumann developed a torpedo for the United States Navy that, after being aimed at its moving target, would self-adjust its direction to home in to the target as it moved (see Wiener 1948). This, too, seemed to be a purposive system. Many diverse fields, such as engineering, management, and social science, saw the value of cybernetic modeling in their own research. The definition of system has been steadily honed so that today we may define a system as a mechanical or theoretical organization of components, distinct from its environment, that adds something new, and often unexpected, to our understanding of the ensemble of components out of which it was constructed (see e.g. Ashby 1960; Beer 1959; Buckley 1968; Klir 1969; Laszlo 1972, 1973; McCulloch 1965; Sutherland 1973; but see also von Bertalanffy and Rapaport 1956).[5] One common definition that was generally accepted by researchers was that a system is a self-organized collection of elements that are interconnected in the sense that any force imparted to one of them affects the positions of all of them.[6] Ludwig von Bertalanffy (1962: 1, see also, generally, von Bertalanffy 1968) defined a system as a "complex of mutually interacting components." But a system is more than that; it is an entity in itself that is different from, and perhaps greater than, the sum of its parts.[7] Accordingly, the ILS has a role in international politics that is more than the sum of the interests of the approximately

190 states that are the creators/subjects/enforcers of international law.[8] It carries an additional "emergent" weight because it represents the precedents of previous dispute resolutions – the wisdom of the status quo in the dynamic sense described by Edmund Burke (see e.g. 1774, 1790).

An attempt was made in 1975 to apply cybernetic modeling to law (D'Amato 1975; Kiss and Shelton 1986), but what was not fully available at that time was the theory of autopoiesis. Even so, other important elements of general systems theory were being developed in interdisciplinary contexts. Prominent is the theory of the stability of complexity. Complex systems tend to be more stable than simple systems. (A tricycle is more stable than a bicycle.) The large number of states in the world in the twentieth century with their complex interactions made it possible for the international system to absorb the shocks of two world wars. By contrast, there were very few states of any significance in ancient Rome, making it possible for the Roman Empire to conquer and absorb all states within its extended reach. International law was "suspended" during the Roman era because of the absence of a plurality of nations.[9]

The concept of recursion was another significant development in general systems theory. We have to acknowledge the fact that any system containing norms (such as the ILS) will find that the norms do not precisely fit the empirical facts of the system's environment. For example, the norm specifying the breadth of the territorial sea might be three miles at a time when most states were proclaiming and enforcing a 12-mile limit. The disconnect between norm and reality must be resolved if the model system is to be accurate. This disconnect cannot be resolved a priori (who is to say that three miles is "better" than 12?). Model builders thus resort to pragmatism. They try out certain norms on the environment, and then tinker with them. The tinkering is designed to see whether the environment will react to the norms, or whether the environment is being stubborn such as to require the model to make adjustments. This back-and-forth adjustment process is called *recursion*. It reduces a large circularity into a set of tiny circles each of which can be adjusted. If the process is successful, the system will contain a rule that both explains the facts and justifies them.

To be sure, a newcomer to international law might object that a recursive process cannot be costless. Recursion dulls the edge of the rules and hence in the long run undermines their ability to draw sharp distinctions between closely argued positions. However, there is a simple evaluative test to see if there is too much recursion. Recall that the rules of international law arose from the aggregate interest of states. Thus the rules are very "close" to what the behavior of states would be if there were no rules. Or to put it another way, the rules of international law do not get in the way of important aggregate interests. For example, if a rule blocks A and B from going to war against each other, then even if both A's and B's own interest in going to war is high, once we add in the countervailing interest of the remaining 188 states in the world in preventing war, we find that the 188 swamps those two. In other words, the rule hardly budged aggregate behavior even though it highly impacted the behavior of two of the states.

It is thus clear that the development of customary international law over time has ensured the emergence of rules that do not depart appreciably from patterns of state behavior. This may seem a weakness of international law from a moralistic point of view, but it is also a strength of international law from the self-preserving point of view. To restate the important point made above, the "successful" norms in the Darwinian struggle taking place in the international arena are those that are close to the inferences we would draw from state behavior if there were no such thing as international law. The ILS is interested in an orderly and peaceful international environment that is conducive

to the maintenance and perpetuation of the ILS itself. This does not necessarily involve "moral" or "justice" considerations except to the pragmatic extent that ignoring such considerations might bring about armed conflict that could destabilize the system.[10]

Light was cast from an unlikely direction on the problem of why and how complex systems can be purposive. In 1980, Chilean biologists Humberto Maturana and Francisco Varela (1980) refined the concept of the self-organization of systems.[11] Their theory of autopoiesis defines living systems as self-producing units which maintain their essential form, perpetuating themselves *according to their internal organization*. Or otherwise stated, the system produces its own organization that maintains itself in the space in which its components exist.

As a complex system, international law closely resembles the self-regulating systems described by Maturana and Varela. It is separate from its environment but at the same time interacts with its environment. The interaction, of course, consists of providing rules of decision and guidance when conflicts arise between states, and of assessing the efficacy of those rules in conflict resolution. A recursive process modifies the rules when they need updating. The ILS makes the modifications according to its internal organization and processes. Thus when international lawyers argue the existence of a purported rule of international law and cite various precedents and events in support of their argument, they are obliquely describing the internal organization of the ILS.[12]

We can now begin to see that the ILS has no direct interest in reducing conflict or promoting cooperation in its environment – that is, in the real world – but rather is only interested in preserving and maintaining itself. Its purpose is nothing other than the preservation of its own existence. This is the same purpose we find in every animal and every plant in the world. All animals and plants that lacked this purposiveness were destroyed by their predators eons ago. The drive to self-preservation is proportional to the brain power and complexity of the animal. For example, a clam has hardly any intelligence, but it has evolved a hardwired shell that has been successful in protecting it from predators. At the other extreme, humans have not evolved a carapace, which would have required a vast investment of energy. Instead, by evolving a larger brain, Homo sapiens have been able to outrun, outbuild, or outwit their natural predators. (If humans had failed to do so, you would not be reading this sentence.)

The ILS distills the intelligences of several thousand international lawyers and statespersons. In controversies between states, the party that can show its preferred rule to be friction reducing obtains an advantage in the negotiation. Even if the advantage is slight, the cumulative effect of preferring tension-reducing rules over the centuries of conflicts and controversies is a set of well-honed rules of today's international law.

Suppose an occasional rule shows up as outdated and potentially friction producing. The three-mile limit of the territorial sea may have been an example of such a rule. It had lasted for several centuries. But after the Second World War, many coastal states began to assert control over a broader territorial sea, both for reasons of national security in the face of longer ranged weapons aboard ships, and for extending the state's monopoly over coastal fisheries. Some Latin American countries even proclaimed a 200-mile territorial sea. During the 10-year conference on the law of the sea convention, a consensus emerged among the delegates that the most stable rule would provide for a 12-mile territorial sea and a 200-mile exclusive economic zone. These rules quickly became absorbed into international practice well before the treaty on the law of the sea was ready for signing. Indeed, even if nations viewed the resulting Law of the Sea Convention as non-severable, the friction-reducing quality of the new territorial sea and exclusive economic zone was so apparent that

those rules could enjoy a severable existence in general international law.[13]

The ILS in the example just given was not interested per se in the breadth of the territorial sea. Neither was it even directly interested in reducing friction between coastal states and others that might disfavor encroachments on the freedom of the seas. Rather, the ILS was interested in preserving itself. Changing the rules of its environment thus becomes desirable from the vantage point of the ILS if there is an overall enhancement of global peace, order, and stability. If the world environment is peaceful and orderly, the ILS will grow and thrive. But if war breaks out, legality could be an early casualty. Indeed, a nation struggling for its life may view war crimes as a trap: if it holds back certain actions because it is law abiding, the enemy might well disregard legal constraints entirely and thus gain a military advantage.[14] If mankind then somehow saves itself after the global war, there could be no assurance that the old system of international law would be restored. Anarchy could bring about the permanent demise of the ILS.

Coercive systems

It is one thing to have a legal system; it is another to have people obey it. Do states actually obey international law, or do they simply act in their own interests while simulating obedience? In a chapter published in advance of her forthcoming book co-authored with Dean Harold Koh (Hathaway and Koh 2005), Oona Hathaway says that neither advocates nor skeptics of international law are looking at the whole picture:

> Both fail to consider the role of internal enforcement of international treaties on countries' decisions to accept international legal limits on their behavior and then to violate or abide by them.
>
> (Hathaway and Koh 2005)

As a defense of international law, this is very weak tea. Professor Hathaway is only talking about treaties, which have always been the clearer case of compliance with international law (compared to general international law). Second, she is only talking about an extremely limited form of compliance. She is saying in effect that if a state accepts Rule X by incorporating it into its domestic law, then that very incorporation acts as a brake on political leaders who might otherwise wish to gain a temporary advantage in international relations by violating Rule X. Although this proposition is undoubtedly true (it has been argued by American scholars for years), it amounts at best to saying that states only have to obey the rules of international law that they wish to obey. They may pick and choose, accepting the rules they like and rejecting the others. It is clear that Professor Hathaway has not taken a middle position in the debate. Whatever her intent, she has come down squarely on the side of the skeptics.

Her chapter illustrates a general malaise that younger scholars have with international law. They see the occasional but important violations and gaps that are the very tip of the iceberg while failing to see the vast and complex system of rules beneath the surface that are not only routinely obeyed by nations but are not even questioned. What nation today would attempt to extend its territorial sea beyond 12 miles? What nation would claim the right to arrest tourists and place them in indefinite detention? These and millions of other potential violations of general international law do not even come up for consideration.

However, putting aside routine considerations of compliance, the harder cases cannot be ignored. Is international law a coercive system? Are its rules enforceable against the states? How? Are they enforceable against a superpower? If not, then rules of international law are, in Professor Hathaway's words, "mere window dressing" (Hathaway and Koh 2005). We can be certain of one thing: there

has never been a legal system on this planet that allows citizens to decide which laws they will obey. It is no answer to the question of compliance to say that states internalize rules that they decide to internalize. International law skeptics such as Professor Hathaway seem to use the term "international law" as a fashionable tag, but their arguments prove that they are not talking about real law at all.

I argue that international rules are enforced in exactly the same way in which domestic rules are enforced. Every nation prescribes internal punishments for illegal acts. (Just try to argue to a prosecutor or judge that the law is mere window dressing.) The crucial point is that these punishments consist of deprivations of the defendant's legal rights. For example, a defendant who loses a civil case must pay damages; if she does not, the state may invade her right of property by seizing her car and selling it at a sheriff's auction. A defendant convicted in a criminal case may find that his rights to liberty and freedom of movement have been forcibly taken away by the judge's prison sentence. In states that allow capital punishment, a criminal defendant may find that his right to live has been taken away. Thus in all cases, whether civil or criminal, the penalty inflicted on the losing side is the curtailment of one or more of the losing side's legal rights.

When we turn to states as the subjects of international law, obviously a state that transgresses international law cannot be punished by being incarcerated or annihilated. But each state has a bundle of rights under international law. Indeed, since the state is an artificial entity, it may be said that a state is nothing more than the rights it is accorded by international law. These rights are the flipside of obligations. For example, state A has a right to a 12-mile territorial sea, and it also has an obligation to respect B's right to a 12-mile territorial sea.

We now see that the rules of the ILS form a closed loop. Rules that gives state A rights are also the rules that may be taken away (temporarily) to punish state A for violating the rights of another state. For example, the international imposition of sanctions on South Africa and Rhodesia during their apartheid regimes, which impeded their rights of international commerce and navigation, played a significant role in the eventual dismantling of the illegal (under international law) practice of apartheid.

Suppose, however, that the state committing the initial violation of international law is a superpower. The kinds of economic sanctions that worked against South Africa and Rhodesia could not realistically be enforced against a superpower. Yet if we think beyond the territorial limits of the superpower, we find that it has nationals and investments all over the world that are, indeed, vulnerable as punishments or sanctions.

For example, at any given time there are hundreds of thousands of American citizens either traveling or residing abroad. The Census Bureau reports that in 1998 there were over 56,000 Americans traveling abroad (compared to 46,000 foreign tourists visiting the United States). Even more striking are the figures of American citizens residing abroad as reported by the Bureau of Consular Affairs in 1999. There were 27,600 U.S. citizens residing in Buenos Aires, 55,500 in Sydney, 250,000 in Toronto, 48,220 in Hong Kong, 75,000 in Paris, 138,815 in Frankfurt, 45,000 in Tokyo, and 441,680 in Mexico City. Among the smaller countries that could become "hot spots," the Bureau reports 646 American citizens living in Albania, 1320 in Bangladesh, 1600 in Bosnia, 440 in Congo, 2000 in Cuba, 10,000 in El Salvador, 546 in The Gambia, 11,000 in Haiti, 18,000 in Israel (Tel Aviv), 8000 in Jordan, and 6639 in Kuala Lumpur, and those are taken from just the first half of the list.[15] To these figures must be added the many thousands of American military personnel and their dependants on foreign bases. How many American nationals must a country threaten to make the United States take notice? Just 50 were sufficient in 1978 when Iran arrested that

number of American diplomatic and consular personnel in Tehran. The hostage taking led to severe repercussions in the United States including perhaps the defeat of presidential incumbent Jimmy Carter in the election of 1980.

Superpower vulnerability is enhanced by the bluntness of the military instrument. For example, even though the United States could have annihilated Iran with a volley of nuclear ICBMs, such a wholly disproportionate retaliation would not have saved the hostages. The global scatter of assets and persons from all nations has virtually assured the universal efficacy of the international reprisal system. Indeed, in a shrinking world, the reprisal system is likely to become increasingly efficient. Perhaps there is a correspondence between the efficacy of peaceable reprisals and the recent finding that there has been a steady decline in the global magnitude of armed conflict following its peak in the early 1990s (Marshall and Gurr 2005: 1).

When Iran detained 50 American diplomatic personnel in 1978, it claimed that its act was justified by the retaliatory rule of international law. In presenting its case before the International Court of Justice, Iran claimed the detention of the hostages was just a "marginal" response to "more than 25 years of continual interference by the United States in the internal affairs of Iran, the shameless exploitation of our country, and numerous crimes perpetrated against the Iranian people, contrary to and in conflict with all international and humanitarian norms." The Court dismissed the Iranian claim in language that reaffirms the "closed loop" view of international law presented earlier:

> [L]egal disputes between sovereign States by their very nature are likely to occur in political contexts, and often form only one element in a wider and long-standing political dispute between the States concerned. Yet never has the view been put forward before that, because a legal dispute submitted to the Court is only one aspect of a political dispute, the Court should decline to

resolve for the parties the legal questions at issue between them.[16]

The Iranian hostages case has another important lesson for us regarding retaliation as punishment. When the 50 American diplomatic personnel were arrested in Tehran, the first reaction on the part of the State Department was to arrest 50 to 100 Iranian diplomats and consular officials in the United States and then offer a trade. Even though this strategy appeared as a possibility in the *New York Times*, American officials quickly realized that the United States might actually be doing Iran a favor by arresting its diplomats. The Iranian diplomats in the United States had been appointed by the Shah of Iran, who had been recently deposed. The new fundamentalist Iranian government would soon be in the process of replacing those diplomats with ones more loyal to the new regime. Therefore the Iranian government would probably welcome the indefinite incarceration of the Shah's diplomats by the United States and would not have any desire to trade them for the American hostages.

Thus, from the American point of view, a tit-for-tat retaliatory strategy would probably not work. Instead, the State Department opted for what I have called a "tit-for-a-different-tat" strategy (D'Amato 2004). Their idea was to deprive Iran of one of its international legal rights that carried an exceptionally high cost, and then trade that deprivation for the release of the American hostages. Very quickly President Carter issued executive orders freezing all bank accounts owned by Iran in American banks. In addition, most European countries cooperated by freezing Iranian bank accounts in banks in their countries. The banks were delighted to oblige, because it meant that they might avoid paying interest on the Iranian accounts. The interest rates at that time were at a peak of about 15%. Eventually Iran caved in, returned the American hostages unharmed, and received access to its bank accounts (but not the earned interest).

Conclusion

We saw in the second and third sections of this chapter that the ILS gives expression to its database of rules of general international law when the rules are relevant to a dispute or controversy. We also saw in the fourth section that the same database of rules serves the enforcement function of international law: A state that violates international law may expect that one or more of its rights in the database might be suspended as an official reprisal or punishment for the violation. Finally, in addition to its legal competences just mentioned, the ILS represents the political interests of all the states that are not directly involved in a given dispute or controversy.

Given this combination of competences, it is clear that the ILS does not have its counterpart in domestic legal systems:

COMPETENCES

International legal system	*Domestic legal system*
1 Database of all laws	1 Database of all laws
2 Control reprisals	2 Reprisals controlled by political branch
3 Represent political interest	3 Does not represent political interests

The puzzle for students of international law is not whether international law is effective or whether the ILS is a powerful player in the game of international politics, but rather why the role of international law is so underappreciated. A large part of the reason is the academic separation between departments of political science and law schools. The political scientists, encouraged by Hans Morgenthau in 1946, viewed rules of law as impediments to the national interest (Morgenthau 1946). By defining international relations as "power politics," rules of law as well as rules of morality were pushed aside as ivory-tower idealism. Meanwhile, on the other side of the campus, law schools sought but could not find points of entry into the realist carapace in which the political scientists had encased international relations.

How can the communications gap between political science and international law be bridged? The burden should perhaps be placed on international lawyers to start the construction of the bridge. The reason for assigning this burden to them is the existence of an educational imbalance: most lawyers have had courses in political science in college on their way to law school, whereas most political scientists have gone straight from college to Ph.D. programs without taking any courses in law.

By taking systems theory seriously, lawyers may find that the ILS as described in this chapter might serve as the long-awaited interdisciplinary bridge to political science. It is at the very least an intellectual vehicle for taking rules out of the background of international relations and promoting them to the status of a player in the game of international politics. This promotion dramatically changes the nature of the game from a two-person (my country versus all others) zero-sum game to a three-person non-zero-sum game (conflict *plus* cooperation) that, methodologically and analytically, offers a far more realistic understanding of international relations than either the political scientists or the international lawyers have come up with separately.

Notes

1 Customary law originated in the writings of Continental legal sociologists and then imported into international law. See the account in Anthony D'Amato, *The Concept of Custom in International Law* (1971: 47–56).

2 The status of some would-be states are at present contested under international law, such as Taiwan, Kosovo, The Vatican, Monaco, Puerto Rico, and the Isle of Man, not to mention Transnistria.

3 The term "unitary system" used in the title of this chapter is mildly redundant. It is intended to emphasize the difference between the holistic approach taken here and the recent spate of essays that label international law as "fragmented" (see e.g. Nicolaidis and Tong 2004) (nearly all participants agreeing that international law is fragmented).

4 Jack L. Goldsmith and Eric A. Posner view international relations as a two-person zero-sum game with occasional nods to a third person (e.g. the Prisoner's Dilemma) in their recent book, *The Limits of International Law* (2005). It is no wonder that they believe the rules are there just to be manipulated for the strategic advantage of whatever state is doing the manipulation. Their assumption that international rules lack a purpose simplifies their analysis: the rules, being random, simply form part of the environment. What is left is a two-person zero-sum game (the manipulating state versus all the other states) that either proceeds randomly or proceeds at the behest of the most powerful state. Clearly, they have an impoverished view of international law. Their willingness to see international law end, as expressed in the title to their book, is simply the product of their belief that international law never got started. To the contrary, we argue that the ILS is itself a significant player in a complex non-zero-sum game of politics among which nations states cannot simply manipulate the ILS; they have to take account of it. The ILS takes an active role in avoiding, reducing, or resolving conflicts. It also promotes international cooperation by fostering rules that maximize the interconnections among states. (Free trade is arguably the most important "connector.") International relations is a large complex system within which exists the ILS, a self-regulating purposive system.

5 The only "system" that has no environment is the universe; for that reason, it is probably misleading to call the universe a system.

6 A system can be open or closed, and still fit this definition. Thus, the human body is an open system (because it ingests oxygen and food and excretes carbon dioxide and waste products). But if we enlarged our definition to "human body + environment," then it could be regarded as a closed system. This frame-of-reference problem is similar to the problem of the entropy of system vs. subsystem (Nicolis and Prigogine 1989: 160–64).

7 For example, any living organism is something quite distinct – and unpredictable – from the collection of its chemical elements. "Living matter" could not have been predicted from such a collection. Or to take a case of an inert element: Imagine meeting someone living on a remote island in the equatorial zone in the

Pacific Ocean who had never seen or heard about ice. He would hardly have reason to believe you if you said that if water is cooled sufficiently it can become so hard that people can walk on it. Ice is an emergent property of water (and water is an emergent property of ice).

8 At present there are approximately 190 states in the world.

9 The Roman *jus gentium* should not be confused with international law. It involved only the extension, with modifications, of Roman law to the outlying provinces. For further details see D'Amato, 1971: 237–40.

10 The developing law of human rights is an example. Although states remain highly reluctant to outside interference in their internal affairs, human rights would hardly deserve the name if they did not constrain the actions of one's home government.

11 Autopoiesis is the process by which a system produces its own organization and then maintains itself in the space in which its components exist. See http://pespmc1.vub.ac.be/ASC/AUTOPOIESIS.html.

12 If I say I'm hungry, I am obliquely describing the medical condition of the cells of my body that objectively require for their continued functioning inputs of energy in the form of nutrition.

13 For further argument on this point, see D'Amato 1985.

14 Several decades ago there was public agitation for a no-first-use treaty regarding nuclear weapons. The United States said it would not support such a treaty because it could amount to unilateral disarmament. In other words, the United States would refrain from first use whereas its opponent might simply violate the treaty. The most notorious precedent in this respect occurred in June 1941 when Hitler suddenly invaded his treaty ally the Soviet Union. Stalin was shocked and went into seclusion for the entire first week of the invasion; he could not bring himself to believe that Hitler had done such a thing.

15 See http://www.pueblo.gsa.gov/cic_text/state/amcit_numbers.html. These numbers do not even include hundreds of thousands of U.S. military personnel and their dependants in bases all around the world.

16 *United States Diplomatic and Consular Staff in Tehran*, 1980 ICJ Rep. 3, Para. 37.

Section II
Evolution of international law

7

International law in the ancient world

David J. Bederman

This briefly assesses the historiographic literature about the idea that ancient state systems predicated their relations on the rule of law. It examines ancient practices in relation to diplomatic privileges and immunities, treaty conclusion and observance, and the initiation and limitation of armed conflict. There was a coherent sense among ancient peoples from Near East and Mediterranean traditions that state relations should be conducted in accordance with established norms and values.

An historiographic introduction

This chapter examines the idea of international law in the ancient world. At the outset one must be aware that the entire project might be condemned with the charge of anachronism (Preiser 1984: 128–31). The study of a law of nations in antiquity suffers, in essence, from a double blight. First, there is the perception that *all* law in ancient times was primitive. Ancient law was formalistic, dominated by fictions, had a limited range of legal norms, and was based solely on religious sanction. In short, it lacked the essential characteristics of a modern, rational jurisprudence (Hoebel 1954: 258–86; Vinogradoff 1920: 1: 364). Although this critique has been largely disproved by modern scholarship that

has either emphasized new, empirical research, or has adopted an anthropological attitude of moral relativism in legal relations, it remains a potent school of thought (Diamond 1971). If all of this were not enough, there is the second, and as yet largely unquestioned, belief that international law, even today, is a primitive legal order (Dinstein 1985).

The confluence of these two intellectual forces has meant that the study of ancient international law has had, of late, few advocates. Those doing serious scholarship on ancient legal systems have evinced little interest in exploring such an abstract area as legal restraints on interstate relations. The attitude of legal historians towards ancient international law has thus been one of indifference.

Alas, the same cannot be said of contemporary international law publicists writing on the subject of a law of nations in antiquity. Indeed, one can say that the opinion of a majority of modern international lawyers is that ancient states were incapable of observing a law governing their international relations. Consider the views of a few leading publicists. In Lassa Oppenheim's well-respected manual on international law, he noted that: "International law as a law between sovereign and equal states based on

the common consent of those states is a product of modern Christian civilization, and
may be said to be about four hundred years
old" (Oppenheim 1948: 68). Modern writers
have insisted that ancient states did not
possess a notion of sovereignty and that there
was no sense of universal community, and
without these two elements the idea of international law in antiquity was a nullity
(Brierly 1958: 20; Shaw 1986: 14), Other
writers have emphasized putative features
of an ancient law of nations that one would
instantly recognize as being somehow associated with any "primitive" legal system:
the emphasis on religious (and not legal) sanctions; the inability to develop consistent,
customary rules of state conduct; and the belief
that there could never be a condition of peace
between ancient states (Heffter 1881: 12;
Maury 1859: 3: 401–402).

This modern critique of the intellectual
soundness of referring to a law of nations in
antiquity has served many purposes. One, of
course, is to provide an acceptable story for
the emergence of international law, not only
as a cluster of legal doctrines, but also as a
learned study. The inability of some modern
scholars to perceive of an international law
prior to its Grotian origins has been discussed
elsewhere, and need not be repeated here.
There is also a reproach here, which I readily credit, that antiquarian pursuits in tracing
international law doctrines to some origin
shrouded in the mists of time, is a silly and
(ultimately) distracting exercise. The strong
reaction that contemporary publicists have
held to the idea of international law in antiquity may, in part, be explained as a reaction
to those earlier writers who "inordinately
extoll[ed] antiquity to the disadvantage of the
modern age" (Phillipson 1911: 2: 166). Even
worse, there were those who attempted to
use ancient authorities in the pursuit of
some instrumental historiography, particularly
those who were advancing strong, Eurocentric characteristics for modern doctrines
(Rostovtseff 1922: 32–3; Scupin 1984: 7:
132–3).

This contribution hopes to redress some of
these historiographic and intellectual deficiencies by first considering the existence of
authentic state systems in ancient times.
Next, I will briefly examine three fundamental
areas of states' relations that appeared to be
influenced by consistent rules or norms of
international behavior: (1) the sending and
receiving of ambassadors; (2) the making and
enforcement of treaties; and (3) the initiation
and conduct of hostilities. From this narration, broad patterns of ancient state practice
can be defined and analyzed, leading to the
conclusion that there did exist in the ancient
world a set of sources, processes and doctrines
that constitute the beginnings of an international legal consciousness.

Ancient state systems

The scope of this chapter is limited to three
general periods of antiquity. They are (1)
the ancient Near East including the periods
subsuming the Sumer city states, the great
empires of Egypt, Babylon, Assyria and the
Hittites (1400–1150 BCE), and a later, brief
period focusing on the nations of Israel and
their Syrian neighbors (966–700 BCE); (2) the
Greek city states from 500–338 BCE; and (3)
the wider Mediterranean during the period
of Roman contact with Carthage, Macedon,
Ptolemaic Egypt, and the Seleucid Empire
(358–168 BCE).[1] My thesis is that the traditions of statecraft that were developed at an
early time by the Sumer city states and their
Akkadian conquerors, and reformulated by the
Assyrians and Hittites, were transmitted to later
cultures through the Egyptians and Israelites
and Phoenicians, and thence to Greece,
Carthage, and Rome.

It is for this reason that I do not survey
the great international law traditions of India
and China in this chapter. The literature available on the political cultures and international
societies of ancient India (from the post-Vedic
period until 150 BCE) is large and of generally high quality,[2] as is that on the Eastern Chou

and warring states periods in China (770–221 BCE).[3] (For considerations of the general theory of international relations in ancient India, see C. H. Alexandrowicz, 41 Brit. Y.B. Int'l L. 301 (1965); Ved P. Nanda in Janis and Evans (eds) (1994).) Nevertheless, there is simply no historical evidence to suggest that there was any substantial diplomatic contact between Indian and Chinese cultures, or between these great Asian international systems and those of the Near East and Mediterranean. This is surprising in view of the extensive economic and religious contacts between all of these culture centers in the ancient world. But without that essential element of diplomatic contact and continuity, I believe it prudent to exclude from the wider consideration of this article Indian and Chinese contributions to the development of international law.[4] I recognize that this exposes the study of ancient international law to the additional charge of Eurocentrism and western cultural particularism, but I see no alternative given the current posture of scholarship in this field, and the paucity of historical sources and material.

The three time periods and regions that are examined here all had one thing in common: An authentic state system was in place for these times and places. I take as my working definition of a state system Professor Hedley Bull's formulation in *The Anarchical Society*:

> A society of states (or international society) exists when a group of states, conscious of certain common interests and common values, form a society in the sense that they conceive themselves to be bound by a common set of rules in their relations to one another, and share in the working of common institutions.
>
> (Bull 1977: 13)

Implicit in this definition is that political entities are organized and think of themselves as states, and that it is possible to discern "common interests and . . . values" in deciding whether those states deal with each other on a "conscious" basis. Both inquiries –

the existence of states and the identification of conscious value systems – are essential in the context of antiquity.

Most contemporary scholarship has accepted both the fact of the existence of ancient states and the reality of international relations in antiquity (Ago 1982: 214; Paradisi 1951: 355–6). The city states of ancient Sumer and Mesopotamia, as well as the great Near Eastern empires that subsisted between 1400–1150 BCE (including Egypt, Babylon, and the Hittite, Mitanni and Assyrian empires) had at least an inchoate identity as an authentic state system (Ago 1982: 215; Preiser 1954: 269; Scupin 1984: 133). Even better documented are the interstate relations of the ancient Greek city states, particularly in the period from 500 to 330 BCE (Adcock and Mosley 1975: 128, 144–50; Ago 1982: 222; Low 2007: 33–76; Phillipson 1911: 1: 32–7; Scupin 1984: 134–5). Lastly, the Roman Republic's rise to empire from 358–168 BCE involved competition with many state polities, including Carthage, Ptolematic Egypt, Macedon, and the Seleucid Empire (Ago 1982: 229; Phillipson 1911: 1: 106–11; Preiser 1954: 131–32; Scupin 1984: 136–7; Walker 1899: 51).

There were, in essence, two traditions of ancient state practice (Bederman 2001b: 47, 277–9). The feudal empires of the Near East created their special diplomatic argot, one that was transmitted (by contacts through the Egyptians, Phoenicians, and Israelites) to the later political cultures of the Mediterranean basin. The second heritage was produced by the querulous relations of the Greek city states. Roman statecraft was a mixture of these two manners. How these two traditions came to define the ancient conception of a law of nations – through diplomacy, treaty making, and the initiation and conduct of hostilities – will be discussed in the remainder of this chapter. What needs to be reiterated here is that there were special times and places in antiquity where political entities coalesced as states and related with their like-constituted polities on the basis of independence,

117

sovereign equality, and a respect for rules in the conduct of international relations.

Reception and protection of diplomats and embassies in antiquity

Fundamental to the idea of a law of nations in ancient times was the proper respect and protection to be accorded to the official representatives of other sovereigns. Two ancient states might have been in a condition of distrust or competition, and yet diplomatic contacts were constantly promoted and reinforced between them as long as they were not actually at war. The principles of diplomatic intercourse were surely seen as rules to be followed save in the most grievous breach. The international law of diplomats and diplomatic protection was fundamental, because without it the simplest forms of negotiation between independent polities would have been impossible. The rules of diplomatic conduct were, therefore, motivated by the highest demands of necessity.

Each of the ancient cultures surveyed in this chapter held strong notions of hospitality and the proper courtesies and facilities to be extended to strangers from afar. In a world of imperfect and dangerous communications and means of transport, where even modest distances posed incredible obstacles and difficulties for travelers, hospitality was more than a merely desirable institution of personal favor. Rather, in each of the state systems considered here, hospitality was sanctioned and ritualized. It undoubtedly possessed a private aspect: one family or household extending hospitality to a traveler from abroad (Bederman 2001b: 88–95). Of concern here is how beliefs regarding private hospitality became institutionalized and ritualized into patterns of *state* practice.

There were enormous implications of the ancient institution of hospitality: In the treatment of aliens living abroad, in the peaceful settlement of certain kinds of dispute,

and even in the conduct of hostilities between two warring nations. It is of note that the principle of private hospitality was quickly transformed into an essential feature of interstate relations. This transformation occurred quite early. Friendship and diplomacy were always inextricably linked. Strong personal relationships undoubtedly facilitated diplomatic contacts even between potentially belligerent nations. In the fourteenth century BCE, the Hittite king was vexed because one of his vassals, one Piyamaradu, was raiding his territories. The Hittite king complained to a neighbor, the king of Ahhiyawa, whose protection Piyamaradu had sought when militarily confronted by the Hittites. The Hittite king then asked the ruler of Ahhiyawa for Piyamaradu's extradition. The bearer of this message was a prominent individual well known to the king of Ahhiyawa. The historical record indicates that the well-born messenger had previously participated in diplomatic contacts between the houses of Hatti and Ahhiyawa. The selection of this envoy was apparently critical to the Ahhiyawa king's favorable consideration of the Hittite request: Piyamaradu was bound over to the Hatti. This, in spite of the fact that Piyamaradu was owed hospitality by his host. The selected envoy was privileged in his functions precisely because of the bond of friendship and hospitality that had been formed (Audinet 1914: 33; Hooker 1976: 124; Karavites 1987: 85). Likewise, Livy relates the incident where ambassadors were dispatched by King Perseus of Macedon to Rome in 171 BCE. This was apparently a delicate mission, and the only reason Perseus felt comfortable enough to send the embassy was that a bond of private hospitality existed between him and one of the current consuls in Rome, Marcius, a tie that had been formed between their fathers (Livy 12: 405 (passage xlii.38)).

These examples of "personal diplomacy" are hardly surprising. The concept of private hospitality and friendship, extended between individuals of different nationalities, surely acted as a critical facilitation of diplomacy. Even more significant was the manner in which the hereditary aspect of private hospitality was transmuted into the concept of perpetual peace between sovereigns. As seen in the examples of Roman and Hittite practice, the initiation of diplomatic relations acted, in effect, as the formation of a bond of public friendship between two states. This fiction was probably intended as an antidote to the religious particularism of many ancient nation states. The very act of receiving a foreign nation's ambassadors was seen as an acceptance of an alien religion and its national gods. The concept of perpetual peace was seen as a very public form of ritualized hospitality between two nations (Paradisi 1951: 346).

The analogue between the forms and functions of private hospitality (on the one hand) and official diplomacy (on the other) was imperfect and certainly had its limits. International diplomacy could not have proceeded on the same basis, with the same assumptions of human nature, as the laws of private hospitality and comradeship. There was simply too much at stake. The fortunes of nations could be risked on a diplomatic interchange or negotiation. Envoys could be feckless. Or, worse still, they could take advantage of the rules of hospitality to deceive a host. So ancient peoples had an alternative to seeing the rules of diplomatic conduct as the extension of the dictates of private hospitality. This choice was reflected in their substantial concern in establishing the trustworthiness of diplomatic personnel. The Greeks were preoccupied with this. Many Greek cities established laws to punish envoys found guilty of distortions or fabrications in the course of their official acts (Mosley 1973: 94–5).

One technique for assuring the integrity of visiting envoys was to hold them personally liable for their transgressions or those of their masters. This seemingly conflicted with every civilized principle of diplomatic immunity, and yet it was not really viewed as a contradictory practice by ancient peoples. Diplomats were often held as privileged sorts of hostages, particularly in Greece (Amit

1970). Envoys who violated their own bona fides were subjected, under Roman law, to noxal surrender to an enemy (Rich 1976: 109). Other examples abound of personal coercion being applied against the official representatives of foreign states, all for the purpose of preventing deception or trickery in the process of international relations.

The ancient reconciliation of diplomatic immunity with sanctioned retribution is one of the paradoxes of ancient international relations. Suffice it to say here, however, that such duress rarely achieved much success. One example is enough. In the winter of 478 BCE, Athens began rebuilding the city's fortifications destroyed in the earlier Persian invasion. Athens' neighbors fretted about this development, and sought Spartan help to dissuade the Athenians from what might have been perceived as an aggressive move. The Athenians needed to buy some time, pending the completion of their works. This they accomplished with a diplomatic stratagem. Athens dispatched to Sparta one Themistocles, a leading citizen, but extraordinarily well regarded and well trusted by the Spartans. He assured the Lacedaemonians that no such aggression was intended and allayed their fears of a new round of Athenian imperial expansion. Reports of continued building on the walls found their way back to Sparta. Themistocles assured his Spartan hosts that the accounts should not be believed, and that, instead, a high-level Spartan delegation be sent to Athens to investigate in person. But Themistocles had secretly arranged that when that Spartan embassy arrived in Athens it would be detained to act as security for his own safety, once his own fraud was discovered, which it inevitably was. Thucydides reported that since the eminent Spartans were in the hands of the Athenians, the Lacedaemonian authorities had no choice but to accept Athens' fait accompli and release Themistocles (Thucydides 1: 149 (passage i.89–92)).

This story says much about the mutual expectations of diplomatic relations by ancient states. Some level of trickery and dishonesty was acceptable, perhaps even required. What is noteworthy, however, is the extent to which the rules of diplomacy were so widely observed. Because the international law of diplomacy was inextricably linked with each of the authentic state systems considered in this contribution, a polity's acceptance of diplomatic niceties was often considered a sine qua non for its participation in the international system of state relations. There were a few, basic rules of diplomatic intercourse: (1) foreign envoys would be treated as guests, and that (2) although tolerable levels of personal coercion were permitted, the diplomats would otherwise be immune from sanctions in the host state. These basic rules were respected by nearly all of the states existing *within* the three time periods of international relations pondered here. The content of the rules was, moreover, remarkably consistent throughout the entirety of antiquity and throughout the ancient world (Bederman 2001b: 95–135). The universality of diplomatic law was a signal feature of its success.

A consistent theme of historic narratives from antiquity is the extent to which even peoples and states on the periphery of "civilization" still followed the dictates of diplomatic practice. So it was that Polybius could express surprise that the mercenary leaders of Libyan tribes observed all of the correct rituals (at least by Greco-Roman standards) in their relations with the Carthaginians in 238 BCE (Polybius 1: 229–31 (passage i.85)). In the same vein, the historical evidence is strong that Persia conformed its international conduct and behavior to Greek diplomatic standards, even as Persian kings attempted to conquer Greece in the fifth century BCE (Bauslaugh 1991: 38–43, 91; Mosley 1973: 164–5).

That leads me to consider the last general concept that motivated the development of the ancient practice and organization of diplomacy. This was the notion of *sovereign equality*. The power to dispatch and receive ambassadors, the right of legation, was typically seen as an incident of power and political independence. The Romans were particular sticklers on this point: They would not receive ambassadors from a less than free and autonomous political entity. This was codified in later Roman law, but even in the time of Roman transmarine expansion, as Polybius recorded, Roman authorities would not receive embassies from defeated peoples (Justinian Digest 4: 920 (passage 50.7); Polybius 4: 97 (passage ix.42)). In short, the privileges and immunities of diplomats came as part and parcel of the right of legation.

It made sense surely to regard those diplomatic practices as an essential part of a system of states. Envoys, as already noted, were seen as the personification of the sending state. Any offense to an ambassador was an offense against a coequal sovereign. It was also possible to see the entire system of diplomatic privileges and immunities as an outgrowth of the recognition that certain classes of entitled individuals were subject only to their own sovereign's authority, even when they traveled into the territorial realm of another ruler. Diplomatic privileges, as an outgrowth of extraterritorial immunities, were a very real way that political entities avoided conflict.

Taken together, the general principles that guided the ancient practice of diplomatic law had a profound impact on the manner in which envoys operated and the extent to which they were protected. Ritualized hospitality was balanced carefully with concerns over the probity of an envoy and that of his master. The universality of rules of diplomatic comportment was qualified by the principle that only legitimate states had the right to send and receive embassies. Despite these contradictions, the overall picture of the international law of diplomacy in antiquity was remarkably stable and predictable.

Treaty practices among ancient peoples

Enforcement was always a difficult issue of making faith in antiquity. For early Near

Eastern polities there were consistent concerns about crafting treaty terms that were truly reciprocal and recognized as equally binding on both sets of parties. For these cultures, the act of treaty making was viewed as a unilateral act: the sovereign of one nation pledged his troth on the assumption (although without the certainty) that the treaty partner was doing the same (Numelin 1950: 293; Théodoridès 1975: 105–107). The idea that treaty making was an inherently reciprocal exercise – indeed, that it had no meaning otherwise – appeared only later in the ancient Near Eastern tradition, with the covenant between Rameses II and Hattusili III being exemplary (Kastemont 1974: 47, 438–9; Langdon and Gardiner 1920: 188–98).

Once the notion of reciprocity was embraced by ancient cultures, they could then confront the problem of internal and external means of treaty enforcement. There was a dynamic tension between these two approaches. An "internal" way of enforcing an international agreement emphasized background rules of good faith, reasonable interpretation, and faithful observance over time. "External" means implicated personal surety and responsibility in the enforcement of treaty values. These included hostage taking and noxal surrenders.

Every ancient culture surveyed in this chapter vigorously debated the question of how to coerce treaty faith. This argument was typically conducted in the form of a disquisition of the morality (or at least the political wisdom) of accepting hostages as treaty guarantors. And, indeed, while commentators condemned the practice, it was followed with more or less regularity by every state system reviewed here, with the notable exception of the Greek city states. Even the Romans, despite their strong sense of bona fides in treaty observance, took hostages. The Greeks sought, instead, to put their reliance in a whole panoply of structural solutions to ensure treaty fidelity: anti-deceit clauses, rules of treaty interpretation, and refined doctrines of treaty termination (Adcock and

Mosley 1975: 191–98, 221–25; Amit 1970; Ténékidès 1956; Wheeler 1984). The Greek approach to treaties was, in a very real sense, a legal one.

The Romans conceived treaties in a legal sense of obligation as well, but their vision was formalistic. The elaborate charade of noxal surrender following a repudiated *sponsio* was emblematic of (largely) empty Roman legal forms. It also says much about Roman (and, for that matter, ancient Near Eastern) ambivalence about observing international obligations for the simple reason that they reflect a rational exchange of promises and an expectation of subsequent certainty in political and diplomatic relations (Bickerman 1952).

There may well be a correlation between the character of the state system in which diplomacy (and treaty making) is being conducted and the preferred mode of treaty enforcement. "Dynamic" state systems (those with more than five major actors) may well have resorted to more "internal" means of enforcement. Greek multipolarism was exemplary of this. Alliances were extraordinarily fluid in these state systems, and so "external" (and usually more coercive) means of enforcement were likely not to have been employed with substantial success. The more "static" state systems that prevailed during much of the ancient Near East and the period of Roman expansion, having (typically) less than four or five great powers, were more brittle. Treaties seemed to matter for less, were drafted at a higher level of abstraction, and, yet, ironically, were more often enforced by coercive, "external" means, including hostage taking and personal pledges of surety.

Problematic enforcement of international agreements did not seem, however, to interfere with the process of developing legal sophistication. A signal aspect of every state system reviewed here is that, as time went on, treaties became more diverse in the subject matters of substantive provisions, more precise in the structuring of those clauses, and (generally) more complex in the interrelation of these obligations. Treaties like the 1280 BCE instrument between Egypt and the Hittites, or the 215 BCE agreement between Hannibal and Macedon, are models both of complexity and precision (Bickerman 1952; Langdon and Gardiner 1920).

Both were treaties of alliance *and* friendship, capturing all the ambiguity and difficulty that those relationships entailed for the two treaty partners. Every legal culture considered in this article had to confront the issue of how to narrate and control diverse kinds of alliance statuses between two or more polities. Sovereign equality was always problematic, and although Greek alliance typology was certainly the most nuanced in antiquity, Roman conceptions of different kinds of affiliations were complex, and so too were Hittite and Assyrian treaty forms (Adcock and Mosley 1975: 191–93; Boak 1921; Larsen 1968; Martin 1940: 371–72; Matthaei 1907; McCarthy 1963; Mendenhall 1955; Paradisi 1951: 345–50). Alliance configurations culminated in extraordinarily complicated league patterns.

The most convincing evidence that ancient peoples conceived of international links as legal relations was that they committed their treaties to writing. The power of the written word was not to be underestimated in antiquity. The emphasis – one might say the obsession – of ancient states in properly keeping and revering treaty texts was symbolic of the power and authority of the written word to convey legal meanings for international relations (Adcock and Mosley 1975: 177–8; Karavites and Wren 1992: 188–9).

Ancient treaty making also had a strong universalist flavor. By this, I mean two distinct things. The first is that there was a single ancient tradition in treaty making, an inherent unity of conception in the way that treaties were made and observed. There were, of course, some variations in these forms, but what is surprising is the commonality. The basic Hittite treaty form, a secular contract formed out of solemnized oaths, was adopted (with some changes) by the Assyrians, Egyptians, and ancient Israelites. It was, in turn, transmitted into the Greek and Hellenistic worlds, and thence into the western Mediterranean region of Rome and her neighbors. The proof lies in those agreements made by nations at the temporal and spatial intersections of these different state systems – such as that between Rameses II and Hattusili, or that between Macedon and Carthage, or that between Rome and the Aetolians (Bickerman 1952; Langdon and Gardiner 1920; Matthaei 1907: 189; Paradisi 1951: 345–6). In each of these instances, pre-existing forms were (to be sure) altered. It may have been the dropping of elaborate preambular passages, or the inclusion of specific legal terms or provisions (such as *maiestas* clauses or qualifications regarding after-acquired allies). Regardless, there was always a synthesis of forms and motifs of legal expression in treaties, never an outright repudiation of old forms.

As developed in the ancient Near East, treaties narrated a story of relations between two or more states, and purported to tell also a story of their peaceful relations for all time to come. Although the elaborate preambular statements used by the Hittites were not replicated even in all ancient Near Eastern texts – and certainly not in Roman, Greek or Egyptian instruments – there was still a strong element of historic narration and structure to these later treaties. All political cultures reviewed here had to struggle with the fundamental dilemma of state relations: did the conclusion of treaties necessarily mean that relations with another polity could be based on the notion of perpetual peace?

There seems no doubt that ancient peoples regarded treaties as the chief means of regulating peaceful relations between states. The institutions of private hospitality and the public reception of emissaries could assist in this process, but, ultimately, it was up to states to pledge their faith to each other. This act of making faith could have many forms. It could have been a simple recognition of friendship existing between nations. Or it could be a conclusion of some sort of political alliance. Greek and Roman statecraft understood a distinction between *philia* and *symmachia*, *amicitia* and *foeda*; they also knew that the alternative to peace was a state of war or enmity (Karavites 1982; Scupin 1984: 137–8).

Commencement and conduct of hostilities in ancient times

The ancient preoccupation with war focused on applying rationality to a fundamentally irrational endeavor. The goal was nothing less than managing conflict. To the extent that ancient societies developed religious, ritual, and rational strictures on declaring war and initiating hostilities, there must have been some manifest belief that war was an exception to the normal course of international relations, an aberration in the way that peoples dealt with each other.

The nearly universal conscience of peoples in antiquity was that it was never desirable to be branded the aggressor in a conflict (Adcock and Mosley 1975: 202–203). There was a moral advantage to be won in exercising restraint before entering a condition of belligerency, or at least in appearing to do so. It was this fact that led to the development of rules for neutrality, which depended for their vitality on a status being given to those polities that chose to abstain from conflict. And if the regime of neutrality was never widely, or absolutely, recognized, it was an epitome of a legal status used in ancient state relations (Bauslaugh 1991).

As for rules governing the conduct and prosecution of hostilities, one might wonder whether there was even a need to actually manage ancient warfare. Ancient conflict was usually a desultory affair, synchronized with the turn of the seasons, limited by great distances, imperfect communications, and difficult logistics. There were battles fought

and towns besieged, for sure, but the structure of ancient warfare was such that a campaign could end very easily with a decisive engagement or a stormed city. Civilians were usually left alone, if for no other reason that if armies killed peasants and burned fields, soldiers would probably starve before the inhabitants of the district did. Total war was virtually unheard of. The Israelite doctrine of *mitzva* notwithstanding, and the dramatic, life-and-death struggles of the Peloponnesian and second Punic wars, the very process of war in antiquity succeeded in limiting its effects (Rosenne 1958: 139).

Ancient wars were fought for territory – and for glory. Most ancient states were socially organized on a footing that facilitated the marshaling of resources for armed conflict. These resources were finite. Blood and treasure came in limited supplies. The Israelites, the Greeks, and the Romans all came to understand that war depleted social and economic capital so quickly that the very integrity of the state was jeopardized. All ancient belligerents had an incentive, therefore, to make war quick and cheap. Warring nations feared defeat, but they trembled more in the face of *ataphos*, the death of the human spirit that the conditions of war produced. In antiquity, war was, at one and the same time, the great legitimizer of the state, and its greatest threat (Bederman 2001b: 208–27).

To respond to the challenges that war presented to the state, religion and ritual and reason were called on to sanction and give order to life in belligerency. These mixed and produced a distinctively legal vision of how ancient states initiated hostilities and how they conducted them. The mechanism by which religious values were transformed into rituals and thence into legal rules was achieved in two different ways, both hastened by war itself. The first was in the creation of distinctive social institutions, whether sacerdotal colleges like the Roman fetials or the Israelite high priests (Harris 1974: 269; Saulnier 1980; Watson 1993; Wiedemann 1987). Religious values, often expressed in virulently nationalist forms, were maintained and applied by these institutions. Their primary goal was to preserve the legitimacy of the state against both internal and external challenge. These institutions kept the mysteries of the state religion and carried on a discourse with the national gods concerning the state's place in the world (Bederman 2001b: 59–79). The key elements in the legitimacy of these institutions were the rituals they managed on behalf of the state and its people. The second mechanism was simply the process of secularism. Religion and ritual, after time, could not succeed in sustaining state values or legitimacy. The ancient Israelite notion of *mitzva*, as a command for divine, obligatory war, gave way to a rational notion of "optional" war (Holloday and Goodman 1986). The spear-throwing ritual of the fetials, as the dramatic *bellum indicere*, was modified as time and international conditions changed (Harris 1974: 267–9; Rich 1976: 103–104; Wiedemann 1987: 481). It was replaced by the language and rhetoric of law and legal rules of obligation (Bederman 2001b: 79–85). *Halachic* (legal) thinking influenced and moderated the Israelite approach to war. The Greeks, strongly disposed to philosophy and rhetoric already, consistently referred to the norms of conduct in warfare as a common law of mankind. After all, the final, winning argument of the Thebans was that they had "suffered contrary to law" because of the Plataeans' previous violations of those customs (Thucydides 2: 117–19 (passage iii.66)). The Romans, from their earliest period of organized political history, claimed legal right as the basis for their moral and military superiority. Remember the words of the Roman *pater patratus*, head of the college of fetials, when he remonstrated against the enemy that had failed to do right? "Let the law of heaven hear," the enemy, he said, was "unjust, and does not act agreeably to law" (Livy 1: 115–17 (passage i.32.6–10)).

It was not just that ancient peoples uttered a sense of legal obligation in warfare. The Greek *to dikaion* and the Roman *ius ad bellum* and *ius in bello* had actual, substantive content. In part this can be seen in the many dualities that were part of the ancient law of war. Ancient states made a distinction between enemies and foes (Schwab 1987: 194–5). This was the central concept of restraint and proportionality in conflict. Without the idea that public wars had to be treated differently than private feuds, there could be no rule of law in wartime, since conflict presumably dissolved all bonds of hospitality.

Ancient states also saw a difference between just and unjust, lawful and unlawful wars. Sometimes this was a matter only of internal, scriptural significance (as in the Israelite contrast of *mitzva* and *reshut*), but it also could extend to broader notions of justification. Lastly, all ancient states saw the need for limitations and immunities to be impressed on the conduct of warfare. These were the most specific, and literal, of the norms governing armed conflict. And although there were only a handful of rules of conduct in warfare, these were generally observed and respected, to a degree that was startling for a time that was supposed to be barbaric and lawless (Bederman 2001b: 242–63).

Whether there was a law of war in antiquity is the ultimate test of whether there was a cohesive idea of a law of nations at all in ancient times. I have argued here that there indeed was a common core of ideas leading to the exercise of restraint by ancient states in armed conflict. As with all of the themes considered in this contribution, the sources of legal obligation in ancient state relations were multivalent, and this is nowhere more evident than in the ancient law of war.

Conclusion

The norms of international law thus had the same purpose throughout antiquity: to promote predictability and stability, to adequately channel state conduct in ways that were conducive to maintaining power relations, and to nourish the internal legitimacy and sovereignty of polities. Despite my occasional use of the term "international law" in this chapter, the ancient law of nations was conceived only as an instrument of state relations. It had virtually no regard for other values such as human rights or dignity, the protection of common resources, or the advancement of some exogenous ideology or philosophy. The law of nations in antiquity was, first and foremost, an expression of the ancient mind's desire for *order*.

To achieve international society meant that a delicate balance had to be struck with the internal, political and religious order of individual states. This was the singular task of the law of nations in antiquity, one that it accomplished to a surprisingly effective degree. Ancient states were particularistic. Their internal political order depended on exclusion, on aggression, and on difference (Bederman 2001b: 59–61). The rules of state relations in ancient times managed to transform this particularism into cooperation. *Friendship* was achieved through the translation of hospitality practices into the institutions of diplomacy. Likewise, the ancient state was made *tolerant* by rules of conduct which permitted the movement of people, goods, and services across boundaries. *Trust* was made possible through the rituals and forms of making faith through treaties and alliances. Finally, *restraint* came to be exercised by ancient states even in wartime as a consequence of self-interest and concern for order.

We do not speak of these values today in modern international law. Perhaps we should. These are the essential ingredients of community, a notion and principle that is at the theoretical center of the modern law of nations. This contribution has, in large measure, been the story of the creation of a nascent community, one with a political structure and legal sensibility. Ancient state systems may have little to teach us about today's global world order, and they may not have much to instruct as to the substantive content of essential doctrines of international law, but the history narrated here has substantial bearing on the creation of legal communities which aspire to universality.

[Author note: This chapter is based on portions of the author's previous volume, *International Law in Antiquity* (Cambridge University Press. 2001b).]

Notes

1 "BCE" means "before the Christian era."
2 For general treatises, see, e.g. Chacko, "India's contribution to the field of international law concepts", 93 *Recueil des Cours de l'Académie de Droit International* [RCADI] 117 (1958–I); Hiralal Chatterjee, *International Law and Inter-State Relations in Ancient India* (1958); Nagendra Singh, "History of the law of nations – regional developments: south and south-east Asia", in 7 *Encyclopedia of Public International Law* 237 (Rudolph Bernhardt ed. 1984); Nagendra Singh, *India and International Law* (1969).
3 See, e.g. Britton, "Chinese interstate intercourse before 700 B.C.", 29 *American Journal of International Law* [AJIL] 616 (1935); Shih-Tsai Chen, "The equality of states in ancient China", 35 *AJIL* 641 (1941); Frederick Tse-Shyang Chen, "The Confucian view of world order", in *The Influence of Religion on the Development of International Law* 31 (Mark W. Janis ed. 1991); Iriye, "The principles of international law in view of Confucian doctrine", 120 *RCADI* 1 (1967–I); Shigeki Miyazaki, "History of the law of nations – regional developments: Far East", in 7 *Encyclopedia of Public International Law* 215 (Rudolph Bernhardt ed. 1984).
4 For much the same reasons, I also excluded considerations of African state systems and the international relations of the Byzantine Empire. For more on these, see T. O. Elias, "History of the law of nations – regional developments: Africa", in 7 *Encyclopedia of Public International law* 205 (Rudolph Bernhardt ed. 1984); Stephen Verosta, "International law in Europe and western Asia between 100 and 650 A.D.", 113 *RCADI* 484 (1964–III).

8

The age of Grotius

Edward Keene

This chapter is organised around two themes. First, it examines the changing discourse of international legal thought during the sixteenth, seventeenth and eighteenth centuries. After a brief summary of the traditional narrative of the emergence of Grotian doctrines within the context of the "Westphalian system", particular attention is paid to the ways in which more recent scholarship has opened up new chronological, geographical and philosophical perspectives on the transition from medieval to modern doctrines. The second theme concerns the comparatively neglected issue of the evolution of the international legal profession. Changes in legal education are discussed here, especially the impact of new humanist approaches and the growing focus on training in national institutes of law rather than the medieval ius commune. In this context, the chapter also discusses the professional roles that lawyers played in aspects of the conduct of international relations such as diplomacy. The changing requirements of the latter help to explain the emergence of a new genre of legal scholarship devoted to the historical analysis of treaties, which profoundly influenced the development of positivist doctrines towards the end of the eighteenth century.

The purpose of this chapter is to describe how international law changed during the sixteenth, seventeenth and eighteenth centuries. It is con-cerned with two related questions: How did the conceptual and doctrinal apparatus of the law of nations, linked to fields such as civil law, canon law, natural law, and public law, evolve during the period? And how did expert practitioners of the law of nations apply these doctrines in the course of activities such as the adjudication of disputes, diplomacy and treaty making? The former question has tradi-tionally occupied the bulk of the attention of legal historians, especially in the English-speaking world. Over the last 150 years or so (Wheaton 1845 is one of the first sustained treatments), a very large, and still growing, literature has accumulated on the changes and continuities in international legal thought from the late medieval civilians and canon-ists, such as Bartolus of Sassoferrato or Pope Innocent IV; through the sixteenth-century scholastics, such as Francisco de Vitoria; and the later theories of natural law that were influenced by the "new learning" of the humanist movement as well as the Spanish scholastic tradition, advanced by northern European scholars such as Hugo Grotius; to the positivist systems of European public law produced by eighteenth-century authorities such as Georg Friedrich von Martens. By con-trast, although the historical development of the practice of international law has by no means been entirely neglected (Durchhardt 2004; Grewe 2000; Lesaffer 2004; and Roelofsen 1989 are a few recent examples), the literature here is comparatively slight.

There are two reasons for this discrepancy. In the first place, it reflects a wider tendency in historical scholarship to focus on the evolution of disciplinary systems of thought rather than the activities of practitioners. As William J. Bouwsma remarked, we have plenty of "histories of law – indeed great classics on this formidable subject – but very little on lawyers as a profession characterized by a certain social role and a particular perspective on life and the world" (Bouwsma 1973: 304). That complaint is now over 30 years old: Bouwsma acknowledged that it was already beginning to be addressed when he wrote (for instance, Martines 1968), and it has since to a considerable degree been answered by more recent scholarship (Brundage 2004; Karpik 1999; Prest 1981, 1986). Nevertheless, most of these studies have dealt with the evolution of national professions, perhaps because they have a much tighter and more readily identifiable structure, and have touched only marginally on the education, careers and other characteristics of practitioners who concentrated on handling international disputes.

The second reason is that there is a tendency in the study of international law, and international relations more generally, to think of the historian's primary task in terms of illuminating the legal, political and moral principles that played some kind of role – often poorly defined as to exactly how – in shaping the normative structure of the international system or international society at large: the so-called "Westphalian system". The focus, in other words, is on the *structure* of the "international legal order" rather than the *agents* who made that order a reality by consistently applying legal rules to the everyday conduct of relations between princes and states. Where agents do make an appearance, it is often only in the form of a handful of almost heroically great jurists – Grotius is the obvious

example – who wrote the authoritative treatises that are said to have laid down the foundations of the international legal order that underpinned the Westphalian system. But that leaves unclear the transmission mechanism through which their doctrines were capable of influencing international affairs. To know how books affect the way people live, one cannot just read the books; one must also understand the readers. In this case, that means understanding the dispositions of trained legal practitioners involved in international affairs, without whom Grotius would have had many fewer readers, rulers would have lacked a vital source of expert assistance with which to conduct their relations with one another and the Westphalian system would quite possibly have ceased to function as a normatively regulated order.

None of this is to say that theoretical treatises on the law of nations do not matter. On the contrary, one cannot understand how international law was practised in the early modern period, or how and why its practice was changing, without an appreciation of the doctrines advanced by authorities such as Grotius; apart from anything else, they were an essential part of the education of practitioners and were commonly referred to in concrete disputes. But just as one cannot understand the practice without the theory, so it is difficult to understand the theory in isolation from the practice. With a few exceptions – Christian von Wolff, for example, who spent his entire career as a professor of mathematics and philosophy at the universities of Halle and Marburg (and whose work was, perhaps not coincidentally, notorious for its abstractness and impenetrability) – most of the people who wrote prominent works on the theory of the law of nations were also themselves practitioners. Grotius, Pufendorf, Emerich de Vattel and Martens all served as diplomats at some point in their careers, although not always with distinction. Many managed to build impressive professional careers in addition to their scholarly accomplishments: Cornelis van

Bynkershoek, for example, wrote his celebrated doctrinal treatises on the law of the sea,
rights of ambassadors and public international law while serving as the President
of the Supreme Court of Holland, Zeeland
and West Friesland (see Ittersum 2006 on
Grotius' professional activities and their
importance for understanding his scholarship;
see Akashi 1998 for a similar perspective
on Bynkershoek). That is to say, they had
received the kind of training that was common for law students at the time; where
available they often possessed appropriate
credentials or memberships of professional
groups; and they engaged in practical activities such as representing and advising clients
or serving on diplomatic missions. One of the
contexts within which their texts may be
read – although not the only context within
which they can be read – is therefore how
these occupational characteristics of practitioners of international law were being
reshaped during the late medieval and early
modern periods.

We will begin by trying to sketch in
broad outline the changing conceptual and
doctrinal apparatus of the early modern law
of nations. We will not look in detail at the
works of individual authors (Nussbaum 1947
is still a very useful study in that respect, as is
Grewe 2000) and, because there is such an
extensive literature on this topic, the discussion is to a large degree a survey of existing
work, with a particular focus on points of
current controversy and debate. We will start
by briefly describing what might be called
the standard or textbook account of the
origins of modern international law that was
originally constructed by nineteenth-century
legal historians, such as Henry Wheaton.
Their account places Grotius at the centre of
the story and depicts his work as a response
to the fragmentation of Christendom into
a system of independent sovereign states.
We will then look at some of the major
lines of criticism of this interpretive scheme
that have developed over the last 70 or so
years, concentrating on questions about the

chronological, geographical and philosophical contexts within which the evolution of modern international law may be
understood.

In the second part of the chapter, we will
turn to the issue of how international law was
practised, and especially how the community,
if we may use that possibly exaggerated term,
of practitioners of the law of nations changed
during the early modern period with respect
to how its members were trained and the
kinds of activities in which they were typically engaged. There are two main points to
the argument here. First, legal education,
including the teaching of the law of nations,
underwent a transformation during the sixteenth and seventeenth centuries that is only
partially explained by the process of state
formation that occupies such a central place
in the standard history of the origins of
the modern international legal order. The
emergence of sovereign states certainly was
important here, but so were educational
reforms introduced by religious reformers
and (especially) humanists, which reshaped
the curricula of law schools and patterns of
student mobility, and help us to understand
some of the driving forces behind the doctrinal innovations of the seventeenth century.
Second, how qualified experts on the law
of nations practised their profession also
changed. One reason was the restructuring of
the system of courts in Europe as states sought
to control and rationalise their national jurisdictions, but we will concentrate more on
the changing nature of European diplomacy
during the seventeenth and eighteenth
centuries, and in particular the tendency to
recruit diplomats not from the legal profession but from the nobility and the military.
Some training in international law was still
generally regarded as necessary for a diplomat,
but rather than formal legal qualifications,
still less a doctorate in law, candidates were
increasingly expected to have a grasp of the
history of treaties: during the early eighteenth
century a number of collections of treaties were
published to serve this need, which provided

a crucial part of the background against which positivist theories of international law developed.

The changing discourse of the early modern law of nations

Compare a famous text from near the beginning of our period, Vitoria's *De Indis* and *De Iure Belli* (originally delivered as lectures in the 1530s, and first published in 1557: see Vitoria 1917), with an equally celebrated one from near the end, Martens' *Precis du Droit des Gens Moderne de l'Europe* (first published in 1788: for the first English edition, see Martens 1795). They are different in numerous ways: in the philosophy with which they approach the study of international law, in the method according to which they determine the content of international legal rules, in the sources they use, in the political environment and audience towards which their arguments are addressed, and in numerous smaller, but by no means trivial, linguistic, conceptual and stylistic details. Vitoria saw the study of the law of nations primarily as a branch of the study of natural law, thereby associating his enquiry with a glorious and lengthy tradition of scholarship; Martens dispensed with natural law in a few paragraphs of deliberately faint praise, and described his positivist approach as a "science" that had been shamefully neglected in the past. When Vitoria drew on concrete examples, his major point of reference was the ancient world; Martens asserted that the world had changed so much that it was virtually worthless to study the ancients, and that in most cases one did not have to go back more than 100 or 150 years to know what the law of nations was. Where Vitoria appealed to faith and reason, understood through the lenses of scripture, theology, classical (mainly Aristotelian) philosophy and canon or civil law, Martens looked to treaty and custom, drawing on genres of scholarship that barely existed, if at all, in Vitoria's time: studies of the constitutional law of the various European states, statistical surveys of the European political system, works on modern history, and collections of treaties.

Why did these changes happen? For well over 100 years, the most popular answer to that question has been that it was a response to the transformation of the European political system, above all, the decline of the confessional and imperial unity of Christendom and the consequent fragmentation of western Europe into a system of independent, mutually recognising but also mutually hostile, sovereign states, divided by religious and political differences. Add into the mixture the influence of the more aggressive, competitive form of statecraft proposed by theorists of "reason of state", and one is left with a recipe for what the nineteenth-century international lawyer Thomas Lawrence described as a "tendency to utter lawlessness in international affairs" in the late sixteenth and seventeenth centuries (Lawrence 1885: 173). War on an unprecedented scale, and of an unimagined brutality, was the result. In order to keep the notion of an effective law of nations alive, jurists were forced, so the argument goes, to rethink their ideas about the sources of international legal obligation, moving in the process from a theory of natural law as a code inherent in the order of things and ordained by god, to a voluntarist or positivist doctrine that made the consent of states into the key principle for the establishment of legal rules. International law was thus cut adrift from its high purpose of promoting universal moral principles and was converted into a mere tool in the hands of statesmen; but at least it survived as a real constraint on what those statesmen thought they could legitimately do in the pursuit of their interests. The frequent but limited wars of the eighteenth century are commonly proposed as evidence of both the pliability and the strength of the early modern international legal order in the years before it was transformed yet again by the new forces unleashed by the French Revolution.

To look at this story a little more closely, it really contains two distinct movements. The first is the initial response to the collapse of the old order, which might be described as a reformulation, rather than abandonment, of the classical doctrine that the *ius gentium* was intimately linked to, and derived much of its force from, a law of nature, *ius naturale*. One of the cardinal themes in the standard history of the origins of modern international law is thus the elaboration of new conceptions of the law of nature, often relocated within a pre-Christian Stoic, or neo-Stoic, context of reason and passions (on neo-Stoicism in general, see Oestreich 1982): it is, in other words, a law of nature grounded in an idea of human nature rather than a divinely ordained, and so ultimately supra-human, code. This reconceptualisation of the natural law of nations in turn passes through several moments: from Grotius' assertion of a basic human instinct for sociability; through Pufendorf's adaptation of the bleaker Hobbesian picture of the state of nature; to Wolff's and Vattel's defence of the possibility of a rationally grounded, Enlightened law of nature based on principles of freedom and equality, the rights of man transfigured into the rights of states.

The second movement is away from natural law altogether, in the direction of a positivist jurisprudence standing alone as the foundation of the law of nations: a law made by the will of properly constituted sovereign authorities. The problem here lay not so much with the medieval theologians but with the Romans who, it is often argued (see, for example, Lawrence 1885), had confused the issue by muddling together *ius gentium* and *ius naturale* as two facets of a rational universal code, whereas, on the contrary, *ius gentium* was really only ever a special set of positive rules developed by the Romans for the resolution of disputes between foreigners (Kelly 1992: 61–62). Grotius again plays a pivotal role in this part of the story, because he was said to have admitted an unusually important role (by the standards of the sixteenth and early seventeenth centuries) to volitional law as a source of the law of nations, alongside his

arguments derived from a new way of thinking about natural law. Grotius was often described by nineteenth and early twentieth-century legal historians as an "eclectic" (for example Hershey 1912), occupying a position in between either pure naturalism (for which Pufendorf is the standard seventeenth-century exemplar) or pure positivism (Richard Zouche and Bynkershoek are the principal examples here), and drawing freely on elements of both. This fits well with the traditional idea of Grotius as the pivotal thinker in the emergence of the modern law of nations, since it presents him as a kind of bridge from the dominant naturalism of the sixteenth century to the increasingly positivist outlook of the eighteenth, Wolff and Vattel excepted. Gradually, the argument continues, the naturalist elements of the Grotian system were jettisoned, allowing yet freer play to its volitional or positivist dimension; scholars such as Martens can then be seen as having developed this potential within Grotian thought to its logical conclusion. (Although it might be noted that Martens himself does not describe either his own project or its relationship to Grotius' work in precisely these terms, a point to which I will return at the end of the chapter.)

The standard interpretation thus locates the origins of modern international legal thought firmly in the context of the "Westphalian system" of sovereign states, and points to the neat, albeit not quite perfect, synchronicity between the publication of *De Jure Belli ac Pacis* in 1625 (see Grotius 1925) – the founding text of modern international legal doctrine – and the Peace of Westphalia in 1648 – the founding act of the modern international system. As such, it is still regularly endorsed by textbooks today (for example, Cassese 2001: 19–21). Nevertheless, few legal historians would accept it without reservations, and at least three major critical themes have developed in twentieth-century scholarship.

The first questions the way in which the conventional story treats the mid-seventeenth century as the decisive turning point in the history of international legal thought, arguing that some of the most important elements of modern ways of thinking were established well before the publication of *De Jure Belli ac Pacis*. In its early form, this line of argument often turned into a debate about who, if not Grotius, should be seen as the real "father" of modern international law. In the 1930s James Brown Scott championed the claims of Vitoria to that title, on the grounds that he had developed a novel idea of "*ius inter gentes*" – law between nations – as opposed to the traditional notion of a *ius gentium* or law of nations, and thus had anticipated one of the hallmarks of the modern age, namely the idea of a legal code produced by the nations themselves through their mutual intercourse, rather than standing above them as a facet of the universal natural law (Scott 1934). Others have subsequently argued that Scott was mistaken to locate the origins of this way of thinking in the Spanish scholasticism of the early sixteenth century – often doubting whether Vitoria's *ius inter gentes* can do all the work Scott claims for it – and some scholars have pointed even further back to what they claimed were similar conceptions developed by fifteenth-century canon lawyers, such as Paulus Vladimiri, and, earlier still, the thirteenth-century Pope (and expert canonist) Innocent IV (Belch 1965 and Muldoon 1972: the latter goes well beyond a focus on Innocent IV alone, and is by no means a naive attempt to identify the "father" of modern international law, something one cannot so easily say for Belch, who often appears to be motivated as much by nationalistic pride in Vladimiri as by other concerns).

Since then, the debate about the chronological origins of modern international law has broadened out to embrace numerous other aspects of the ways in which late medieval legal thought, civilian as well as canonist, played an important role in shaping modern ideas (Berman 1983 is an important study of this theme in legal history in general; see also Post 1964). Its influence has been detected in the origins of vital elements of the modern inter-

national legal order such as the concept of sovereignty (Pennington 1993) and the principle of *pacta sunt servanda* (Lesaffer 2000). Moreover, rather than simply developing the idea of a *ius inter gentes*, there was a crucial shift in canonist and scholastic thought in the concept of *ius* itself that took jurists away from the idea of *ius* as an objective legal order, and towards the idea of *ius* as a subjective right, again paving the way for the characteristic voluntarism of the modern perspective on the *ius gentium* as a system of the "natural rights" of sovereign states, rather than a divinely ordained "natural law" operating above them and oblivious to their wills (Bauer 2004; Tierney 1997; Tuck 1979). All these arguments, by looking more closely at the specific ideas and terminologies employed by the early modern jurists, point towards the fact that the conceptual framework that made modern international law thinkable was largely created well before the early seventeenth century. The articulation of the basic concepts of the modern law of nations thus anticipated, rather than followed, the key political changes in the structure of the European system that brought Christendom crashing down in the wars of religion; we will not dwell here on the possible implications of this for our understanding of the causal relationship between ideational and material forces in the revolutionary changes that transformed international relations during the period.

A second criticism is that it is a mistake to focus only on developments within European politics, as is implied by the way the textbook story is organised around the emergence of the "Westphalian system" in western Europe. Late medieval and early modern international lawyers were equally interested in the world beyond Europe, and many of their arguments can be seen, and were sometimes explicitly intended, as attempts to justify European colonialism and imperialism overseas. This overlaps with the first line of argument discussed already, since one of the driving forces behind the focus on continuities with late medieval canon law and scholasticism was a recognition that international questions had been paramount concerns for those scholars as well, so long as one looked beyond the supposedly unified and internally harmonious world of Christendom. For Scott, it was the encounter with the New World and the legal problems raised by the conquest that had led Vitoria to rethink earlier ideas of the law of nations, while subsequent revisions to Scott's argument were similarly informed by the awareness that such encounters had been going on well before 1492, whether with respect to dealings with Muslims in Spain and the Holy Land (Muldoon 1972) or with pagan and recently converted peoples in eastern Europe (Belch 1965).

One of the pathbreaking works in understanding the importance of the extra-European context to modern international legal thought was Charles Alexandrowicz's *Introduction to the History of the Law of Nations in the East Indies*, and his subsequent study of the legal framework for European colonialism in Africa (Alexandrowicz 1967, 1973). Broadly speaking, Alexandrowicz was interested in how international legal doctrines had permitted, or even assisted, the gradual decline of Asian rulers from a position of rough parity with their European counterparts to a much more subordinate role, in some cases to the extent of their being denied international personality altogether. The sixteenth-century natural lawyers, to simplify Alexandrowicz's account somewhat, had adopted a universalist worldview, within which all peoples had equivalent rights; the emerging positivism of the eighteenth and nineteenth centuries tore up the foundations of those natural rights, leaving non-Europeans in a limbo that allowed European states to treat them as virtually non-existent for the purposes of colonial expansion (Lindley 1926 covers similar ground), but I think this kind of argument is often overstated and it is important to acknowledge the significance of treaty making with non-Europeans at least through the end of the eighteenth and into the early nineteenth

centuries (Alexandrowicz's work is a very careful treatment of these issues; see also Jones 1982; Keene 2007; Mainville 2001).

Subsequent work in this vein has explored further the various ways in which the encounter with non-European peoples shaped emerging legal ideas about sovereignty and the law of nations, often questioning the rather benign liberal interpretation that earlier historians such as Scott or Alexandrowicz gave to the supposedly universalist spirit of the sixteenth-century law of nations. As Antony Anghie points out, for example, while Vitoria championed the natural rights of Native Americans: "[H]is work could also be read as a particularly insidious justification of their conquest precisely because it is presented in the language of liberality and even equality" (Anghie 2005: 28). Vitoria proclaimed a universal and reciprocal system of rights, but in so doing he legitimated a situation where the practicalities of the Iberian–American encounter ensured that the various parties had different opportunities to exercise those rights, to the considerable disadvantage of the Native Americans (as well as Anghie 2005, see also Green and Dickason 1989; Pagden 1995). Many other early modern jurists, most notably Grotius, were if anything even more complicit in imperial activities, and their accounts of the law of nations, while often substantially different from Vitoria's, betray a similar talent for developing ideas about sovereignty and property rights that were suspiciously useful for the needs of European imperialists and colonisers (Ittersum 2006; Keene 2002; Tully 1992 is an important study of Locke's political thought in this context). We will not explore the implications of this for our view of the morality of modern international law, but merely observe that the conventional belief that the building of the modern international legal order was a project purely concerned with re-establishing peace and stability within western Europe is no longer tenable: modern international lawyers have always had a global outlook; the management of relations between peoples with radically different religions, cultures and political or economic systems, often through the application of discriminatory standards, has been a longstanding element of the law of nations – or laws of nations – that they constructed.

The final critical theme involves the exploration of the wider intellectual connections between developments in international legal thought and other currents of change in philosophy, whether natural, moral or political. The standard account of the origins of modern international law is not blind to these contexts, but in general it tends to see the works of thinkers such as Grotius as effectively de novo responses to the political crisis created by the collapse of Christian unity and the pernicious influence of reason of state: they were responding to new times by thinking up new ideas, and, in the textbook narrative, the latter often appear to have been inspired by nothing other than their functional or practical utility as solutions to the problem of lawlessness created by the failure of medieval institutions.

By contrast, following methodological innovations introduced by discursive or linguistic approaches to the history of ideas (Foucault 1972; Pagden 1989; Pocock 1973; Skinner 2002), international legal thought may be viewed in the context of an evolving discourse or language within which educated persons thought about and acted on political and legal issues more generally. Martti Koskenniemi, for example, invokes Michel Foucault in his interpretation of modern international law's voluntarism as a facet of the larger shift in political and social thought towards ascending and consensual theories of legitimacy within the state (Koskenniemi 1989). Another argument of this nature, this time with roots in Quentin Skinner's adaptations of linguistic philosophy to the history of ideas, has been made by Richard Tuck. Building on his earlier analysis of the evolution of natural rights theories, Tuck has argued that international legal thought was profoundly influenced by the need to respond

to sceptical moral philosophies, which had posed a major challenge to theological theories of a divinely ordained universal moral and legal code: the goal was not simply to respond to raison d'état and the contempt for the law that it inspired, but to develop a new, sceptic-proof moral reasoning (Tuck 1987, 1993). More recently, he has highlighted the way in which both humanist and scholastic philosophers were beginning to create an idea of human beings as autonomous agents within an originally pre-social state of nature, a condition for which, Tuck argues, they found a powerful analogue in the emerging world of independent sovereign states (Tuck 1999). As with Koskenniemi, the evolution of the modern law of nations is thus interpreted as a crucial part of the development of modern liberal political and social thought, and the one cannot properly be understood independently of the other. Parallel arguments have been made about connections to other early modern fields of thought and scholarship, for example the relationship between the scientific revolution and legal postivism, which, we might recall, was proudly hailed as a new "science" by its advocates (Berkowitz 2005 attaches a particular emphasis to the importance of Leibniz in this context).

These are mere sketches of some of the major themes and controversies within traditional and contemporary scholarship on the history of modern international legal thought. They show that the chronological, geographical and philosophical contexts of the early modern law of nations all remain issues of real debate beyond the orthodox "Westphalian" version that still dominates most textbook narratives. And that is not even to go into the controversies that surround the interpretation of individual authors: there is a small industry of specialized Grotius scholarship, for example, on which we have hardly touched here. Nevertheless, having given this overview of the changes in international legal doctrine, and indicated some of the principal lines of argument through which historians have sought to explain why international legal thought developed as it did, we now want to turn to the issue of how the practice of international law was also changing during this period.

The changing practice of the early modern law of nations

Many of the works on the changing discourse of international law mentioned earlier concern themselves, above all, with a handful of especially prominent jurists such as Vitoria and Grotius. But, of course, this is merely the top layer, so to speak, of a much larger group of experts on the law of nations who were involved in applying legal doctrines to specific cases and disputes and thus making a law-governed international society a reality. As we have said, if we are to understand how theoretical treatises such as *De Indis*, *De Jure Belli ac Pacis* or the *Precis du Droit des Gens* influenced the conduct of international affairs, we need to understand this wider community of practitioners of the law of nations: who were they, how were they trained, and what did they actually *do* when they were practising international law?

These are very large questions, for some of which, especially the sociological or prosopographical question about the composition of the international legal profession, more research is needed before we can even begin to canvass possible answers. The point is further complicated by the fact that, during the early modern period at least, practitioners of the law of nations form a much less easily identifiable group than national legal professions. Although England is perhaps an extreme case, due to the strength of its indigenous common law tradition administered through the Inns, the activities of civil and canon lawyers – from whose ranks English practitioners of the law of nations were often drawn (Helmholz 2001: 5) – were much less closely regulated than their common law counterparts. Their principal organising body, Doctors' Commons, "remained essentially an informal association of advocates that did not certify men for legal practice", and, unlike the Inns, it did not undertake an educational role, which was left to the universities, where civil and canon law continued to occupy the bulk of the curriculum (Levack 1981: 113). Moreover, the mere fact that someone was a civilian lawyer or a member of Doctors' Commons does not, of course, mean that he was involved in practising international law, since ecclesiastical disputes provided an alternative, and probably more important, source of work. Thus, while the Inns offer an obvious starting point and valuable repository of information for any survey of the English legal profession in general (as Prest 1986 demonstrates), it is harder to locate equivalent data about the sociological profiles of those English lawyers who had a special interest in the law of nations.

Although it is difficult to make generalisations about the social or personal characteristics of early modern international lawyers, one can say more about the education or training they would typically have received at universities or other specialised academies, and one can also make some observations about the kinds of professional activity in which, having gained their qualifications, they would have engaged. In terms of legal education, the principal theme of the early modern period is the fragmentation of what, by the late middle ages, had become a remarkably standardised curriculum organised around the *ius commune*: a compound of Roman civil law and canon law, the former based on Justinian's *Corpus Iuris Civilis* and the latter on Gratian's collection of papal canons, the *Decretum*; with both having accreted a large literature of glosses and interpretations (Bellomo 1995). From the perspective of international relations, the crucial feature of the *ius commune* was its continental scope: it was a common European discourse, overlying the often very different specific legal codes within countries or cities, which made it possible for lawyers from different countries, and lawyers representing different princes or foreign nationals in disputes at places such as the papal *curia*, to argue together about the merits of their particular cases, and so hope to achieve some sort of mutually intelligible, if not always mutually acceptable, judicial resolution of their claims. On this basis, numerous courts within Europe, for example courts of chivalry, although organised on a national or local basis, could presume to some kind of international jurisdiction, on the grounds that they were applying a law that was essentially the same for all everywhere (on this aspect of the courts of chivalry, see Keen 1965; something similar may be said for mercantile courts, see Cutler 2003: 108–40).

One of the most important elements that created and sustained the *ius commune* as a European code was the nature of legal education. During the thirteenth and fourteenth centuries a highly internationalised legal profession developed whose members were trained in the same ways, read the same textbooks, and, as a result, practised the law in an essentially similar manner, irrespective of the particular courts or cases in which they were engaged. Bologna, Paris and Oxford were outstanding institutions in this respect, and the first two especially attracted students from across Europe, often organised along national lines within the common university framework and making them virtual "international societies" in their own right (Kibre 1948; see also Cobban 1975). Even the proliferation of law schools across Europe during the thirteenth century did not seriously dent the unity of the profession: so great was the prestige of the first *studia generale*, above all Bologna, that they were able to transmit a standard curriculum and course of study to the newer academies, especially since the latter were eager to establish their prestige and reputation as providing suitable training (Brundage 2004: 26–63; see also García y García 1992). Moreover, because the *ius commune* was essentially the same wherever it was practised, doctors of civil or canon law (or both: *doctores utriusque iuris*) could go almost anywhere in Europe to practise; it is

not at all difficult to imagine a German student going to Paris to earn a doctorate in canon law, before pursuing a career at the Roman *curia*, quite possibly in the employ of a prince from yet another country.

The late medieval law curriculum came under attack from two main sources during the sixteenth century. One was the Reformation, which was centred around an assault on the whole apparatus of canon law: Luther's decisive break from the Catholic Church was heralded, we might recall, by his public burning of key canonist texts (Witte 2002). This had important effects on the education of lawyers by inspiring the foundation of new institutes of learning, by encouraging rulers of various confessions to control the teaching provided in "their" universities and by profoundly reshaping patterns of student mobility. Some universities, even relatively new ones, now became vital educational institutions for the members of a particular faith: for example, Leiden (where Grotius studied) "was indisputably the largest international centre for seventeenth-century Protestants . . . between one-third and one-half of all students were foreigners" (Ridder-Symoens 1996: 423). The Reformation (and the Counter-Reformation) thus did not prevent students' international mobility altogether, but they did channel that mobility down certain, confessionally defined routes, undermining the less restricted Europe-wide mobility of the later Middle Ages. In terms of the content of curriculum, however, it is easy to exaggerate the ultimate impact of the Reformation: despite the ferocity of Lutheran attacks on canon law, civil law continued in its importance, and even teaching in canon law persisted at universities in Protestant countries (Helmholz 1992; Witte 2002).

A more significant and lasting change in the curricula of law schools was produced by the other great challenge to traditional legal teaching: humanism. As Donald Kelley has explained, this worked along two main lines (Kelley 1970). The first was the development

135

of philological studies, which led to a rein-terpretation of classical texts, often to the detriment of late medieval scholarship, both canonist and civilian, whose barbarous Latinity became a refrain of advocates of the "new learning". The second, of perhaps greater long-term importance for the development of international law, was historical. In contrast with the *mos italicus* of ahistorical interpreta-tion of texts such as the *Corpus Iuris Civilis* that had been practised at Bologna (and elsewhere), the *mos gallicus* that humanist scholars developed in France demanded that legal texts be understood in terms of their specific historical context and content, and embraced the notion that legal codes de-veloped over time. Combined with princely efforts to exert control over statutory law – which provides considerable support for the traditional focus on the importance of state formation to the development of modern international law – this led to a new emphasis on the evolution of national systems of law, often from their feudal and customary origins. By the seventeenth century, to gloss over a long period of highly fruitful and original legal scholarship, it was beginning to result in the concept, if not yet codification, of institutes of national law as an essential feature of legal training: national institutes were studied in very similar ways across Europe, but the mere fact of their existence at the centre of law schools' curricula lent a new particularism to legal training and professionalisation (Luig 1972). Even Roman law was now subjected to the *usus modernus* and studied according to a comparative method, charting the various ways in which classical principles had evolved in different countries rather than insisting on the Europe-wide unity of the Roman legal heritage (Brockliss 1996: 601). Coupled with the growing importance of national institutes: "It was only a matter of time before jurisconsults in the common-law dominated regions of northern Europe would declare that the study of civil law was professionally pointless" (Brockliss 1996: 608).

The growth of a more historical and national focus in legal scholarship and educa-tion, with the concomitant decline in the relevance of civil law, had obvious implica-tions for the teaching of international law or (to use a slightly looser, but, we believe, more useful formulation) the application of the law to international affairs. Whereas the later Middle Ages had had an internationally shared *ius commune* and a highly internation-alised legal profession, by the mid- to later seventeenth century the international scope of both had been significantly reduced. Neither canon nor, *a fortiori*, civil law had entirely lost its relevance or its place on the curriculum of law schools, but the typical law student was now receiving relatively more training in a particular national legal code and he emerged into a profession that, although not completely nationalised, was increasingly becoming so and had patterns of international connections that were dictated by confessional boundaries rather than being European in extent. The *ius gentium* had been an integral part of the *ius commune* and was virtually inescapable by anyone acquiring a legal training; in a world where even the study of civil law could be derided as "professionally pointless", this was less the case.

One response, and an extremely important one in terms of the doctrinal changes of the seventeenth century that we have already discussed, was to institute chairs in natural law and the law of nations. In terms of its academic disciplinary character, it is worth not-ing that this essentially new subject field was not rooted in the old civilian or cannonist scholarship of the *ius commune* (an obvious place for the study of the *ius gentium*) but was, as Laurence Brockliss puts it, "born fully clothed, so to speak, with the foundation in the mid-seventeenth century of a number of courses in the northern Protestant univer-sities, beginning at Leiden in 1658" and expanding quickly to Lutheran and Calvinist countries (Brockliss 1996: 602–603). Not only does this help us to understand the relative freedom, intellectually speaking, with which seventeenth-century scholars were able to begin developing elaborate new schemes of natural law and the law of nations, but also one can perhaps understand why, doctrinally speaking, so many of the major authorities on the law of nations in the seventeenth and eighteenth centuries were Dutch or German – Grotius, Pufendorf, Bynkershoek, Wolff, Martens – and why one finds fewer English, French or Spanish authors discussed in conventional histories of international legal thought during that period, despite the relative importance of the last in international affairs.

The significance of these changes in the education of new generations of lawyers can be more fully appreciated if we also look at the kind of professional activities they might have pursued after they had gained their qualifications. As was, and, of course, still is, the case for lawyers in general, international lawyers represented clients in courts and advised them as to the legality of specific courses of action in cases where some aspect of the law of nations applied. Opportunities to practise in this manner continued throughout the early modern period: for example, courts of admiralty consistently threw up disputes between foreign nationals or about issues – such as the taking of prizes – where the law of nations was a crucial element of the process (this was the occasion for one of Grotius' most important early writings on international law, *De Jure Praedae*: see Grotius 1995; see also Ittersum 2006 for an excellent exploration of the concrete legal dispute about the prize in question). Since these were often disputes within what would eventually come to be known as private international law, this perhaps provides a reason why the latter field remained relatively close to the theoretical scholarship of earlier studies of natural and especially Roman law (Savigny 1880).

Nevertheless, some of the most important courts where questions of international law had been argued and judged in the Middle

Ages clearly experienced a diminishing influence in the early modern period. The obvious example is the *curia* which had been, among other things, a vital setting for the adjudication of disputes about recognition and for various forms of international arbitration (Grewe 2000). Moreover, since the Church had become increasingly dominated by trained lawyers rather than theologians (see Brundage 2004; Guillemain 1962; Partner 1990), this represented a major way in which the late medieval legal profession, greatly assisted by its internal homogeneity, was at the centre of the management of international affairs. The decline of the papacy as a site of international adjudication and arbitration during the early modern period thus implied a significant restriction on the opportunities for lawyers to play such a pivotal role in dispute adjudication and in diplomatic bargaining more generally.

The decline of the lawyer-dominated papal court's role was paralleled by other changes in early modern diplomacy. In the late Middle Ages, diplomatic missions had, from about the thirteenth century on, increasingly been staffed by counsellors and civil servants, with great hereditary nobles tending to appear in a more or less ceremonial role as the head of a mission; lawyers were especially prominent among the new, bureaucratic type of diplomat (Queller 1967: 152–7). They were not the only source from which the latter were drawn – merchants, for example, might well be employed on a mission with economic concerns – but they were one of the most important: reviewing the list of ambassadors sent to Florence during the fifteenth century, Donald Queller observes that: "The most striking factor . . . is the very large number of lawyers" (Queller 1967: 157). This was reciprocated: "Throughout the thirteenth and early fourteenth centuries, when the need arose, Florence continued to rely on the expert hand of its lawyers in relations with the Empire and with other communes and city-states" (Martines 1968: 312; Ganshof 1971; Mattingly 1955: 116).

137

One should not understate the importance of ceremonial, which clearly lent significance to the continuing noble element in diplomacy, but the detail of negotiation was increasingly the preserve of professional lawyers.

Numerous changes in diplomacy – such as the rise of the resident ambassador, charged as much with information gathering as with specific negotiations; and the growing humanist emphasis on oratorical and personal or social skills – led to significant changes in the recruitment and training of diplomats. During the seventeenth century, in France and England at least, there was a trend towards the recruitment of diplomats from the military, rather than the legal profession (Roosen 1976: 67; see Black 2001: 44). When questions about the appropriate qualifications for diplomats were raised, the kind of education that was thought useful was quite different from a detailed study of the law, still less the possession of a doctorate. David Horn remarks that, in the English service, "the one technical accomplishment demanded of young men who wished to make a career in diplomacy was a knowledge of French" and he observes that there was a general disdain for university education among serving diplomats, expressed also by key authorities on diplomatic practice such as Abraham de Wicquefort (Horn 1961: 136; but also 134–5). It is perhaps revealing, although we would be wary of overemphasising the point, that detailed studies have found little evidence of serious legal training among either the Dutch or Spanish ambassadors at Munster during the negotiations for the Peace of Westphalia, although the terms of the treaty do show some influence of technical legal concepts from Roman law (Winkel 2004: 234).

During the early eighteenth century there were a number of attempts to provide some specialised training for diplomats, most famously in Torcy's short-lived *Académie Politique*, established in 1712 but which only survived for a few years, and related institu-tions such as the academy founded at Strasbourg or the Regius professorships in Modern History at Oxford and Cambridge (Keens-Soper 1972). The curricula for these diplomatic academies, as well as emphasising languages and the study of modern European history and statistics, included a legal dimension. Grotius and Pufendorf were both standardly recommended, but a highly significant addition was the insistence that the would-be diplomat should familiarise himself with the history of treaties (and with accounts of negotiations, as well as with public – that is, constitutional – law within the various European states).

The need to study treaties helped fuel demand for a new and influential genre of legal scholarship. One of the key figures at the French Academy, Jean-Yves de Saint-Prest compiled a collection of treaties from French archives for his charges, while an even more ambitious work was put together by Jean Dumont as his *Corps Universel Diplomatique du Droit des Gens* (Dumont 1726). Dumont began his multi-volume work by making an explicit distinction between the "*corps diplomatique*" that he was trying to create and the "*corps du doctrine*" that he attributed to scholars such as Grotius. Anticipating the attitude of Martens' positivist science of public law, Dumont paid lip service to the importance of natural law, but it was very clear that he thought the study of natural law and the law of nations in the manner of the late seventeenth-century German and Dutch universities was less relevant than a familiarity with the texts of treaties, something that is virtually absent from, for example, Pufendorf's work. His approach represented a novel way of studying international law and one that, in the context of the early eighteenth century at least, was essentially outside of formal training at the universities, but which had an avowed focus on the practical needs of the diplomat.

Dumont was under no illusion about the relationship of those needs to the abstract moral principles that were increasingly informing academic studies of natural law, culminating in the work of Wolff and Vattel, and there is a frankness of raison d'état in his discussion of the way that the value of studying treaties and negotiations is to understand how princes conceive their interests, to keep score in the competitive business of international relations, to have a wealth of diplomatic formulae to manipulate to one's immediate purposes and, at the most, to be able to expose attempts by rulers to break or manipulate the terms of the treaties they have previously signed.

As with other, similar works that laid the foundations for European public law – one might point, for example, to the work of the Abbé de Mably in the mid-eighteenth century (Mably 1758) – Dumont's was an essentially practical body of scholarship, for the most part constructed outside any formal university setting: he was trying to develop an account of the law of nations that would be serviceable for potential diplomats. The practice of private international law remained basically tied to the representation of clients in courts, and so retained much of its university, civil and natural law focus; but the public activities of international lawyers became increasingly oriented towards diplomatic relationships rather than judicial processes, and so the positivist–historical approach to the study of treaties pioneered by Dumont and a few others was to become a vital ingredient of legal doctrine during the later eighteenth century, as it gradually filtered back into the universities and inspired a flurry of textbooks on public international law that, as with Martens' influential early study, cloaked their basic focus on treaties as the primary source of international legal rules beneath the scholarly respectability of an often thin veneer of natural law theory.

Conclusion

Diplomatic historians often refer to the existence of an "aristocratic international" as a crucial ingredient of the solidarity of inter-national society during the nineteenth century (for example, Anderson 1993: 121). To extend that idea, we might say that one of the essential elements of the unity of late medieval Christendom, more important than the always dubious and contested claims to "universal monarchy" made by Pope and Emperor, was an international of legal professionals, trained in similar ways to expertise in a shared *ius commune*, which could be applied in a variety of judicial and diplomatic settings to ensure the legal regulation of relations between princes. One theme that we may take from standard histories of the development of early modern international law is that this international of lawyers was undermined by the state-building efforts of absolutist princes, who, as they exerted control over law making and courts' jurisdictions, channelled the professional opportunities for lawyers down essentially nationalistic lines and made a highly specialised legal training less valuable as a qualification for diplomatic service. But it was also profoundly influenced by religious and educational reforms, especially humanism, that transformed the ways in which lawyers were trained and socialised into their profession in ways that fragmented the field. When a new common idiom was established towards the end of the eighteenth and the beginning of the nineteenth centuries, it was quite different from the old *ius commune*, being grounded instead in the comparative study of the national legal systems of "civilised" countries and the historical analysis of treaties, which, together, defined the European public law and permitted European states to exert considerable authority in redefining the terms of any extra-European law of nations that might be held to govern their relations with non-European peoples.

Changes in the professional community that practised international law were the other side of the coin to the conceptual and doctrinal changes that one may observe in the transition from Vitoria to Martens, via Grotius, Pufendorf and so on. It is not particularly helpful to ask whether one or

139

the other played the more decisive role. The doctrinal innovations of a Grotius, for which one must give credit to his phenomenally wide learning and individual brilliance at harmonising diverse sources into a coherent system, undoubtedly had a significant effect in helping to shape the new field of natural law and the law of nations that became an essential part of legal training in northern European countries in the late seventeenth century. But at the same time, if we ask why *De Jure Belli ac Pacis* was so enthusiastically received and so rapidly attained its status as a seminal work, a major part of the answer lies in the fact that a book of such stature was needed by a legal profession that had, thanks to humanist educational reforms at law schools, lost its old foundations on the *Digest* and the *Decretum*. Similarly, if we ask why the voluntarism that lurks in Grotius' system became so triumphant in the positivist legal science of the late eighteenth century, a major part of the answer to that question is that the ground was laid by changes in international arbitration and diplomacy (if not so much in private international law) that had made comparative national law and treaty histories essential: Martens' *Precis du Droit des Gens* was an ideal textbook for a field of public international law practised in such a manner.

9

The legacy of the nineteenth century

Martti Koskenniemi

The period from the late eighteenth century to the First World War shaped both the humanitarian internationalist approach to international law and, through the vocabulary of legitimacy that accompanied the consolidation of the European states system, its emphasis on sovereignty, state power and the balance of power. Different national perspectives also began to emerge over issues such as colonialism and the law of the sea, with barely disguised national rivalries shaping much of the discourse. Underlying all this, we may discern a fundamental tension between international law as "apology" for state power – which was seen as essential to an effective system of international law – and as "utopia" – or a means of constraining state power. Towards the end of the century, they were expressed in a rhetoric that envisaged international law essentially as a social phenomenon. This chapter reviews some of the intellectual debate that accompanied these developments.

The long and short nineteenth century

Much of what we recognize as distinctively "modern" about twentieth-century political culture is a development of aspects of nineteenth-century thought and experience. This applies to international law as well. Its

humanitarian internationalism draws inspiration from such nineteenth-century moments as the conclusion of the 1864 Geneva Convention for the treatment of the wounded in armies in the field, the delivery of the first important arbitral award in the "Alabama" dispute between Britain and the United States in 1872, and the convening of the first peace conference in the Hague in 1899. The establishment of the first university chairs in international law proper and the regularization of legal advice as part of the foreign policy of European powers in the last third of the nineteenth century configured the field in terms of a pervasive opposition between more or less "idealistic" and "realistic" approaches that still structure professional imagination in the field.

But like every commonplace, this involves simplification. The experience of the nineteenth century grew out of eighteenth-century European themes such as secularism, imperialism, and the tension between public law sovereignty and private rights of civil society that have accompanied and justified the expansion of diplomacy and war, on the one hand, trade, technology and European notions of "civilization," on the other. Twentieth-century lawyers have understandably looked back to the immediately preceding years as delineating, for them, the sense of political and legal possibility. The powerful post-1919 association of international law with public international institutions – establishment of the League of Nations, Permanent Court of International Justice, International Labor Organization, among others – reflects efforts and proposals that emerged during the last third of the nineteenth century but whose roots lie further back in European modernity (see, especially, Kennedy 1987). The dynamic between historicism and rationalism, statehood and the "international community" that structures nineteenth-century legal doctrine and the obsession with the balance of power that does the same for diplomatic practice, rehearse eighteenth-century themes: the specter of revolution in Europe and the universalism that animates Europe's relations with the rest of the world develop aspects of Enlightenment thought. Nationalism is certainly one legacy bestowed by the nineteenth to the twentieth century. But its roots lie further back in the vocabularies of legitimacy that accompanied the consolidation of the (European) states system.

There is thus a "long" nineteenth century that encompasses the practice and thought about international law and politics as an outgrowth of European modernity – the formation of the nation state, the tension between sovereignty and liberal individualism, influence of technology and economic growth on state power, secularism, rationalism and belief in progress as a lingua franca between international elites. The nineteenth century gives form and constancy to such (and other) themes that lead into the twentieth century's most characteristic moments: the creation of world economy and a global technological culture; totalitarianism and total war; decolonization, environmental destruction, human rights. Two ideas are particularly important constituents of international law's "long nineteenth century": the view of history as "progress" and the association of "progress" with the becoming universal of the Euro-

pean state form.[1] Joined in Immanuel Kant's famous essay from 1784 on the "idea for a universal history with a cosmopolitan purpose" (Kant 1991), these ideas lie behind the development of international law from a philosophical preoccupation in the eighteenth century to an instrument of diplomacy and an academic discipline in the nineteenth and an institutionally oriented formal–legal technique in the twentieth century[2] – each period conserving something of the memory of its predecessor as a residue of assumptions and fallback positions.

By the same token, a break should be made around the year 1870. The emergence of a united Germany after the Franco-Prussian war (1870–71) completely transformed the structures of political, cultural and also legal hegemony on the continent.[3] Outside, European powers turned from informal to formal empire. Liberal ascendancy in European governments reached its peak, and the first signs of a new great power emerged in the western hemisphere.[4] The last third of the century and the beginning of the next until 1914 famously constitute a "short nineteenth century," which, for our purposes, may be defined as the moment when the consciousness of European elites had formed around a cosmopolitan worldview, expressed in cultural and political commitment to what the lawyers called "ésprit d'internationalité" (Röben 2003: 152–6) and projected in such institutional forms as the first professional journals (the *Revue de Droit International et de Législation Comparée* in 1869, the *Revue Générale de Droit International Public* in 1894) and associations (the *Institut de Droit International* and the *Association for the Reform and Codification of International Law* [later *International Law Association*], both 1873) (Koskenniemi 2001: 39–41 and notes therein). Multilateral diplomacy took on a legislative role at the Berlin Congresses of 1878 and 1885 and the two Hague peace conferences of 1899 and 1907. Peace societies that earlier in the century had focused on economic and social issues began to make proposals for general and compulsory arbitration of international disputes and were joined by arbitration societies, national parliaments and even some governments (Hinsley 1963: 114–52). The first technical international organizations (the so-called "unions" such as the Universal Telegraphic Union of 1865 and the Universal Postal Union of 1874/1878) were set up to foreshadow what one influential international lawyer of the period already called "administrative law of an international community" (Martens 1883–87: esp. vol. 3).[5]

Much of the legal–institutional activism that emerged during 1919–39 as well as again after 1989 is inspired by or follows on initiatives made and ideas expressed in the last third of the nineteenth century. It is really that moment international lawyers remember when they speak about the nineteenth century (Kennedy 1996).[6] And yet, there is a point in retaining the years between the Congress of Vienna (1814–15) and the Franco-Prussian war (1870–71) in an account of the legacy of the nineteenth century as the *background* against which later developments should be understood. Many of the initiatives were made in reaction to the "dangerous" policy of the balance of power and the connected principle of legitimacy, translated in due course into external state sovereignty and the primacy of domestic jurisdiction. Where the beginning of the century, from the point of view of international law, was conservative and often nationalistic, the last third was liberal and cosmopolitan.[7] This is illustrated by the life of one key international law activist, the Columbia Professor Francis Lieber (1800–1872), who had come to the United States in 1827 as a refugee after having participated in revolutionary activities across Europe. By 1870 he had become the initiator of the professional organization of international lawyers and his work for the "Lieber Code" for the use of the Union armies in the U.S. Civil War was inspiring the adoption of humanitarian laws of warfare around the world (see Hartigan 1983; Röben

2003: 15–39). Lieber and his European colleagues looked for change as much as they wanted peace and stability and fitted those objectives together in an account of individual rights and the gradual civilization that would in due course extend to non-European peoples owing to what they hoped would be the increasingly enlightened policies of the powers themselves. The ambivalence of this optimism – a critique of state power and a simultaneous reliance on the beneficial effects of that power – was a major heritage passed from the fin-de-siècle to the twentieth century.

A divided legacy

But the memory of the Victorian century is far from uniform. First, it was a European century. For the world outside Europe and Europe's white settlement colonies, the nineteenth century organized itself in accordance with a different collective calendar, marked by different forms of *colonialism*. This was not a uniform experience either for the colonized or the colonizing power. The techniques of colonization varied between different moments and locations. Until late in the century, British overseas domination was maintained by private actors, usually organized in colonial companies that were chartered to carry out some administrative activities, while French and Russian colonization took place through official policy and often by military conquest. Towards the end of the century, however, the technique of the "cat's paw" had shown itself inefficient and open for flagrant mistreatment of the populations so that the British and even the Germans who as latecomers had opted for the technique of informal influence moved to formal annexation (see Anghie 2005: 32–114; Koskenniemi 2001: 98–178).[8]

The transformation from informal to formal empire is the century's principal colonial theme.[9] It is accompanied by a bewildering variety of legal forms applied in different

143

localities, ranging from unequal treaties, hinterland claims, arrangements for special "treaty ports" (Japan and China), the use of consular jurisdiction or mixed tribunals so as to exempt Europeans from local jurisdiction, to different kinds of protectorates or other kinds of dependency in Africa and the Far East. No single legal regime and thus no single experience of "colonial international law" ever emerged. The same concerns the European use of the vocabulary of "civilization" so as to mark levels of development of non-European communities. Although distinctions between "civilized," "half-civilized" (or "barbarian"), and "savage" communities were routinely made, they did not link to clearly identifiable legal forms of institutions (see Gong 1984; Koskenniemi 2001: 132–6). Colonialism began as a "science" only within the mandates system of the League of Nations in the 1920s and then in theories of "development" in the 1950s and thereafter (Anghie 2005: 182–7; see, further, Trubek and Santos 2006). Until then, the meaning of a term such as "protectorate" (or "colonial protectorate") or the relationship between local and European laws, for example, depended completely on changes of policy fashion in the capital – usually on how much money was available for administrative or commercial investment in the colony.

International lawyers were enthusiastic colonialists and, for example, greeted the allocation of the Congo to King Leopold at the Berlin Conference of 1885 with satisfaction.[10] But it says something about the overwhelming predominance of Europe that even the principal anti-colonial vocabulary was European: sovereignty, liberal humanitarianism, or the principle of "nationalities" that turned into the call for self-determination after the mid-twentieth century. In both of its forms – as memory of alien rule and a desire for collective selfhood, colonialism defined much of the international law and politics of the twentieth century so that the paradoxes and ambivalences that associate with later pursuits of "universal" international law

cannot be understood without reference to the colonial experience.

Second, the legacy of the nineteenth century is also divided inasmuch as its development in different parts of Europe and the world followed different local experiences and variations of political and legal culture. In the early years of the century most publicists continued to write about a *droit public de l'Europe*, one that was adopted from practices and writings of the pre-revolutionary period. Its focus was on the laws of warfare, diplomacy and treaty making, and it often adopted the principle of the balance of power as its starting point.[11] The continued widespread use of Emer de Vattel's *Droit des Gens ou Principes de la Loi Naturelle appliqués à la Conduite des Nations et des Souverains* (1758) remained an anachronism, however, and the old-fashioned naturalism of its theory and the uncertainty about who the subjects of the law of nations really were, reflected in its title, called out for new articulations of the field. It was one thing to argue in terms of legal theory according to which owing to the absence of a common sovereign above them, princes and nations remained in a state of nature, and another to come up with reliable rules and institutions as deductions from it. In the 1830s and 1840s publicists from different parts of Europe were voicing concern about the state of the law of nations – either, as the Germans did, lamenting the absence of "system" from the treatment of the disparate materials or then, with British students of Bentham, worrying over the absence of mechanisms of enforcement other than that of the elusive "public opinion."[12]

Alongside this old law, and with increasing intensity towards the end of the century, specific French, British, German, Russian, American, and Latin American international law themes and priorities began to emerge. There was an active internationalist legalism in small countries such as Belgium, Netherlands, and Switzerland and liberal lawyers from each became leading members of the new profession towards the end of the century (see Koskenniemi 2001: 1–97). Turkish and Italian voices put forward proposals focusing on specifically Turkish or Italian themes such as reform of consular jurisdiction or the application of the "principle of nationalities."[13] Legal attitudes towards colonization were influenced by whether one's experience had been expansion by trade (as in Britain) or warfare (as in France) and how early or late one had joined the colonial game. The way in which law of the sea issues, for example, were discussed reflected one's position either as a maritime or a non-maritime power. In the long struggle that began in 1815 against the slave trade many nations – especially France – continued to oppose the British position that navies ought to have the right of visit on suspected slavers as an attempt at illegitimate extension of Britain's maritime dominance.[14] In fact, much of the writing that came out from France in the first part of the century was programmatically oriented against British policies.[15] A self-conscious "particularism" was developed in Latin America whose colonies had used the Napoleonic incursion into Spain in 1808 to proclaim independence from the motherland. A strong bias against external intervention, supported since 1823 by the Monroe Doctrine, was buttressed by an indigenous effort to complete the "civilization" of the continent by various forms of legal cooperation undertaken between the elites of the new states, well represented in the United States and (especially) continental Europe by lawyers such as Carlos Calvo and later Alejandro Alvarez.[16]

Even differences in legal education played a part. Whether one saw public international law as a sister to private international law (as in Italy or France), or whether it was taught as "external municipal law" principally in connection with domestic constitutional principles about treaty ratification (as in Germany) was not at all irrelevant to how one saw the direction and possibilities of international reform – for example, whether one was to think of it in terms of the formal "constitutionalization" of the international

realm or whether one saw its development in common law terms (as Fredrick Pollock did) as spontaneous custom and the accumulation of case law from arbitral tribunals and a future international court.[17] Nevertheless, the predominant role of the textbook writer and indeed of the (often many volumed) textbook as a kind of functional equivalent to the code book seemed unaffected of these divisions and remained often the most tangible aspect of the profession.[18]

The legacy of nineteenth-century international law is not a uniform datum that would translate a homogeneous experience into linear causalities or associations of meaning in the subsequent political–legal world. The century itself was traversed by several important divides: between its early and late parts; between Europe (and the United States) and the rest of the world; and between different European–American experiences. The following sections are organized by way of giving an eye to themes that consolidate in the nineteenth century and become important, even decisive, aspects of the legal consciousness of the period after 1919.

Doctrines: Between apology and utopia

International law arose as an aspect of the early modern political theory of natural law – *ius naturae et gentium* – in the late sixteenth and early seventeenth centuries. In the course of the eighteenth century, it had diverged into three distinct streams. One had developed especially at universities in post-Westphalian Germany in connection with the project of consolidating the power of the territorial states.[19] For it, the law of nations was an aspect of the government of the state in its external relations in view of preserving and strengthening the security (and sometimes the welfare) of its population.[20] The view of international law as "external public law" remained influential in the German-speaking realm well into and even beyond late nineteenth century. It derived international law from the will of the state and focused on international law's connections with constitutional law and the hierarchical position of treaties in the domestic legal system. Outside Germany, it was often taken to imply a rather minimal conception of a state's international engagements and sometimes indicted as an aspect of the kind of "positivism" and sovereignty centeredness that gave legal expression to the extreme nationalism that was responsible for the First World War.[21] Because its standpoint was that of the state, it was, according to critics, unable to create a law that would be binding on the state (see Kelsen 1928).

Another stream of universalist–naturalist thought developed in France as an aspect of the criticism of the *ancien régime*. From Fénélon and the Abbé de Saint-Pierre, themes about perpetual peace and universal humankind had been taken into the writings of the *philosophes* – rarely, however, with any well-formulated institutional or legal proposals (for an overview, see Bélissa 1998). Rousseau remained skeptical of the extension of enlightenment ideas into the international world and regarded the balance of power as still the best guarantee for peace (Rousseau 1761 [1756]). Even Montesquieu's *Esprit des Lois* limited its view of international law to one abstract principle, namely that "[d]ifferent nations ought in time of peace to do to one another all the good they can, and in times of war as little injury as possible, without prejudicing their real interests" (de Montesquieu 1949: 5). In 1795 a proposal was made in the French national convention for the adoption of a declaration of the rights and duties of nations that would do for the international system what the *Déclaration des Droit des l'Homme et du Citoyen* had done at home. The declaration was never adopted but it inspired critical reflection from lawyers such as the Göttingen professor and later diplomat Georg Friedrich von Martens (1796: iii–xvi) who attacked it as an assemblage of pious wishes about equality and peacefulness that, as long

as men remained men, had no chance of ever being realized.

Revolutionary thought entered nineteenth-century France, Germany and other continental contexts (to the extent that it did) in the form of a variety of theories of individual, often constitutionally argued human rights.[22] It received little hearing from the international law theories of early nineteenth century – and even less from the diplomacy of the period – but it did gradually, in a domesticated form, become part of the professional rhetoric of the legal activism of the century's last third (see, especially, Bluntschli 1872: esp. 18–20, 26–7, Koskenniemi 2001: 54–7).

Between the *Fürstenrecht* produced and developed in older German natural law and the revolutionary abstractions of the French polemicists, the professional mainstream turned away from natural law as a set of excessively abstract (and in this sense arbitrary) maxims that could not form part of a practical *ius publicum Europaeum* and instead concentrated on systematizing and interpreting treaties and European practices, understood as a working system of largely customary law.[23] For Bentham (1843: 535–71) who famously coined the term "international law" to replace the older "law of nations" the task was to project the search of the greatest utility of the greatest number from the domestic to the international field. Neither of his students, James Mill and John Austin, continued in this vein, however, although each sought to provide a realistic view of the field, the former by stressing the role of sanction in law and imagining public opinion – public shaming – in this role, the latter more skeptically giving it up as a legal topic and relegating it into the field of "positive morality" altogether (see Austin 1954 [1832]; Mill 1825; see also discussion in Sylvest 2005: 12–18).

The success of Vattel's old *Droit des Gens* from 1758 still in the nineteenth century could also be understood in terms of the useful compromise it contained between the naturalist legitimation of the diplomatic system and the practical usefulness of the exposé of the techniques of foreign relations it contained, providing a credible interpretation of war, treaties and diplomacy as aspects of an actually operating legal system. Owing to the turn in doctrine to commentary on treaties and diplomatic practices, many historians have labeled the nineteenth century an era of "positivism" (see, e.g. Neff 2005: 169–76, 2006: 38–46; Nussbaum 1954: 232–6). The ambiguity of the expression "positivism" notwithstanding, this ignores persistent strands of "naturalism" in the century's legal doctrine, constantly referring back to the moral and civilizing force of European laws and practices. The definition of the field by the British lawyer Sir Robert Phillimore (1879) captures a widely shared understanding: "From the nature of states, as from the nature of individuals, certain rights and obligations towards each other necessarily spring . . . These are the laws that form the basis of justice between nations." The U.S. lawyer Theodore Woolsey (1879: 14) expressed the same idea by criticizing the view that international law could be understood in "narrowly" contractual terms:

> In every contract it may be asked whether the parties have a right to act at all, and if so, whether they can lawfully enter into the specific relation which the contract contemplates . . . A voluntary code of rules cannot, for this reason, be arbitrary, irrational, or inconsistent with Justice.

From such widely articulated basis, it became possible for the novel profession to subject any diplomatic rules or practices to the critique of its moral conscience. Law, mainstream lawyers were saying (or at least implying), did not come about (merely) by treaties between sovereigns (although these were an important source) but through a process of consolidation from practices of European societies, understood to reflect the increasing "civilization" of international contacts that could be laid down in works of scientific codification (see, especially, Bluntschli 1872). When

international lawyers organized themselves in 1873 in the *Institut de Droit International*, they defined their profession as the "juridical consciousness of the civilized world" and set up a program of codifying international law in scientific restatements that may have regarded European practices as authoritative (and were in this regard "positivist") but received this from a (naturalist) view of the direction of progress in the "community of civilized nations" (Koskenniemi 2001: 39–41).

While many nineteenth-century lawyers stressed the need to study international law on the basis of treaties and other European practices so as to avoid collapsing it into dubious (and inherently political) moral preaching, others used it to critique the policies of European powers, rejecting balance of power or "sovereignty" as the law's authoritative foundation. Both groups were hoping to construct space for international law beyond (mere) "politics," understood as "subjective," "arbitrary," dangerous, and so on, but conceived "politics" in contrasting ways, some associating it with moral abstractions, others with state power. To reduce international law to either would have meant doing away with its quality as "law."

This inaugurated the basic doctrinal dynamism of twentieth-century international law as well. On the one side, there has been the effort to support international law's reality and effectiveness by highlighting its close relationship with state power – on the other side, the pursuit of autonomy for the law from the policies and diplomacy of states so as to ground its moral and political appeal.[24] But neither path could be pursued irrespective of the other.

To explain international law by reference to principles beyond diplomacy and state power undermined its concreteness and the verifiability and reliability of its conclusions. To focus too intensively on state behavior or will reduced it into an instrument of shifting policies and failed to give room to the profession's civilizing ethos. The dilemma of "apology" and "utopia" thereafter came to structure the way abstract reflection about the nature and progress of international law would be conducted in the twentieth century in terms of the opposition of more or less "idealistic" and "realistic" approaches. Increasingly, however, this type of abstraction was set aside as inconclusive and was replaced by another type of vocabulary, namely the debate about international law as a "social" phenomenon. The substitution of the (old) language philosophy by vocabulary of the "social" was another legacy from the nineteenth century to the way international law has been understood and debated in the twentieth.

Practices: International law and society

That international law was a "social" phenomenon meant above all two things. First, it was to be understood *historically*, so that determining its content would have to involve reflection of how people – rulers, states and lawyers – have thought and acted in the past. The nineteenth century inaugurated the practice of treating international law as an outgrowth of European diplomatic history from the emergence of the nation state and from the Treaties of Westphalia (1648), supported by a continuum of philosophical reflection from Hugo Grotius and the Spanish scholastics to present pragmatism. Alongside specifically historical works such as those by Ward (1795) and Wheaton (1853), textbooks and monographs invariably included opening sections treating the diplomatic and literary histories as carriers of political and legal ideas from which rules were derived in a way that was specific to each context or period. Although the high point of Savigny's historical school was over by the middle of the nineteenth century, key internationalists such as Bluntschli or Westlake had been trained in thinking of the law in historical and cultural terms against what they had learned to attack

as the rationalist abstractions of their eighteenth-century predecessors. When Henry Sumner Maine (1887) replaced Westlake at the Whewell Chair of International Law at Cambridge in 1887, he had no problem in conceiving of the field in terms of European developments and Roman law techniques.

Second, the historical approach involved a *teleology* (Neff 2006: 45). Late nineteenth-century works uniformly assumed that European modernity constituted the highest point of human civilization and that it would also form the goal of developments elsewhere. This would involve cessation or humanization of warfare, advancement of economic liberalism and the all-round cultural and political progress of "modernity." History developed through "stages" to ever expanding forms of civility and culture.[25] Even the century's early writers who focused on the practices carried out under the policing eye of the great powers assumed that international law's growth would follow the increasing economic and cultural contacts between nations, their interdependence – a word that Francis Lieber (1868: 22) claimed to have invented. Public opinion would play a great role in this regard.[26] Few lawyers expressly adopted the language of Immanuel Kant's 1784 essay about the "Idea for a universal history with a cosmopolitan purpose" but almost all shared its major premise – namely that with the progress of modernity, the world would be gradually united in a community of individuals organized under peaceful republican constitutions (Kant 1991).[27] The argument about a "liberal peace" – the increasing economic cost of warfare – that had been made by Kant and Benjamin Constant became part of the educated legal common sense.[28]

Nevertheless, with the significant exception of a number of religiously inclined activists in the United States,[29] most lawyers stayed aloof from the peace movement of the 1840s and 1850s composed in part of political activists, even revolutionaries who saw no reason whatsoever to regard the mores of European elites as rudiments of a world government (see, e.g. Proudhon 1927 [1861]). For them, it was part of the problem rather than the solution. With the successful settlement of the *Alabama* Affair in 1872, however, the peace movement turned increasingly to international law and arbitration and lawyers began to participate in its ranks (see also Schou 1963: 305–37). Tension between the two groups – lawyers and pacifists – continued to be reflected for example in the almost simultaneous establishment in 1873 of the two societies, the *Institut de Droit International* and the Association for the Reform and Codification of International Law, the former consisting of a limited number of elite jurists often with close contacts to national policy leadership, the latter a more broad-ranging forum for internationalists bent on the preparation of an international code for the establishment of peace (Abrams 1957).

It was only gradually in the course of the eighteenth century that "states" came to be regarded as subjects of international law alongside kings, or "sovereigns," peoples and nations (Schröder 2000). This use was stabilized as the administrative structures of the European nation state were consolidated in the early nineteenth century. Foreign affairs were organized as part of state administration and international law turned from philosophical speculation to governmental practices of negotiation, treaty making and formal diplomacy. However, accepting that international law's proper subjects were "states" and that the law itself should be seen as an effect of "state will" gave rise to the puzzle about how international law could possibly be "real," that is, both an effect of state will and still binding on that same will, especially in the absence of a supra-state institution of law enforcement.[30]

If the theory of sovereignty arose as a tool for the internal pacification of European societies in late sixteenth and early seventeenth centuries, its external implications began to seem problematic as the naturalist frame in which it had originally been argued and limited became increasingly thin. As long as sovereignty could be seen in sociological or cultural terms and its different forms ("absolute" or "popular" sovereignty, state sovereignty) could be understood to reflect the histories of European societies, there was no problem to fit it into a teleological frame pointing to progress and future unity. Separated from such an understanding, however, and argued in universal, even logical terms as unconditional independence, on the one hand, "sovereign equality," on the other, it began to seem incompatible with any idea of a binding legal order.

Nevertheless, the idea that state sovereignty did not signify any independence from international law became part of the legal common sense towards the end of the century. The predominant way to reconcile sovereignty with a binding international order was received then (as it has been since) from the raison d'état tradition that had always separated the "arbitrary" interests of states from their "real" interests – the latter being covalent with the presence of a robust system of keeping one's promises (see, especially, de Rohan 1995 [1638]). This separation was expressed in the now odd fashion that was carried over from the eighteenth century into the nineteenth and emphasized the need of a properly "scientific" approach to international law – a view highlighting the role of academics in their role as counselors to government and of the function of law as a technical knowledge about the management of foreign affairs. Sovereigns were not to act out of short-sighted or otherwise elusive "passions" but were to follow what best comparative and historical – and of course legal – studies would suggest was in their long-term interests (see Hirschman 1997). It is perhaps no wonder that this view was most forcefully represented in German public law that had since the Peace of Westphalia been accustomed to examining the relations between the Holy Roman Empire and the territorial estates precisely in view of a sovereignty that would be compatible with the harmonious co-existence of both.[31]

149

An influential extension of these doctrines to international law was accomplished by the Austrian public lawyer Georg Jellinek in 1880 as follows. States are bound by treaties because they will so. But this does not mean that they could discard their obligations by changing their will. For that will is not free. It is limited by what Jellinek, borrowing his vocabulary from what earlier *ius publicum* used to label *Staatszweck*, the purpose of the state, namely to provide protection and welfare to its people (see Preu 1980: esp. 107–25). This was possible only in cooperation with others. The nature of the international world – *Natur der Lebensverhältnisse* – required that states keep their word (Jellinek 1880). Jellinek, a friend of Max Weber's later in life, like generations of international lawyers after him, employed a sociological naturalism to understand international law: It is binding because that is socially useful.[32]

From the late nineteenth century onwards, international lawyers have been critics of "sovereignty" as egoism, arbitrariness, and the absolutism of state power. The contrary to sovereignty was international law. Jellinek's sociological explanation to international law's binding force was only the sharpest formulation of what fin-de-siècle jurists often discussed in terms of the "Austinian challenge." Under it, being bound by one's promises was not really *derogation* from sovereignty but an *effect* of sovereignty: a construction formalized by the Permanent Court of International Justice in the Wimbledon case in 1923 (S.S. Wimbledon Case: 9–10). It also allowed the critique of *any* existing international arrangement as either too respectful of sovereignty (and thus reform in an internationalist direction) or then too far reaching derogation from it (and thus a justification for claims of autonomy and national jurisdiction). The legacy of the nineteenth century was not excessive deference to sovereignty (arguments against such deference were common then as they are today) but rather the emergence of "sovereignty" as the key *topos* of international

law, leading the law into a formal and procedural direction, away from views about the substantive rightness or wrongness of particular types of behavior (Kennedy 2006: 61–62).

Into formalism

The focus on sovereign statehood as the law's operating center made it possible to conceive the various legal institutions and principles by analogy to the domestic law of a liberal society that imagined itself as a contractual arrangement between originally free and equal individuals: The "rational and moral grounds of international law," Woolsey explained, are "the same in general with those on which the rights and obligations of individuals in the state, and of the single state towards the individuals of which it consists, repose" (Woolsey 1879: 14). The significance of the point lies in the way it proposes to end the debate about whether in matters of state the morality of individuals or a special morality of states would apply. In fact, there would be no "morality" at all, but a set of neutral and objectively determinable formal rules that would henceforth empower, coordinate and limit the activities of states in the international world to the practical satisfaction of all. To found the law on "sovereignty" instead of some substantive rights or wrongs would produce a law that would be both realistic and forword looking, a sword and a shield, as the moment might require (see also Koskenniemi 2005a: 143–54).

Accordingly, the law of territory, for example, was consolidated in the nineteenth century following domestic doctrines about the procedures to be followed in the acquisition and possession of as well as succession to property (see further Carty 1986). The rule that grounded territorial rights on effective occupation crystallized in the nineteenth century as against merely symbolic forms of annexation thus transposing a Roman law notion that had been already included in the century's German and Swiss civil law codifications at the international plane (Lauterpacht 1927 [1923]: 112–16). Although lawyers continued to make the distinction between ownership and jurisdiction, their continued overlap in argument resembled the earlier difficulties of keeping up the analytical separation between the legal notions of *dominium* and *imperium*, that is, domestic and international types of authority (Lauterpacht 1923: 91–99).

Likewise, nineteenth-century developments in the law of treaties came about as elaborations of general principles and Roman laws of contract: The right of making treaties was thought as one of the essential attributes of sovereignty in the same way as the right to make contracts is an aspect of free personhood (Davis 1908: 234). Accordingly, rules concerning the conclusion of treaties, conditions of validity, binding force, interpretation, application and termination were all derived from a contractual analogy that played on the familiar opposition of "will" and "reason," *voluntas* and *ratio* in the explanation of the binding force of treaty law and in the interpretation of treaty provisions (see, e.g. Koskenniemi 2005a: 333–45, Zoller 1977: 47–95, 202–44). Treaties are binding because and to the extent that they capture the "will" of the parties – and yet what counts as a valid expression of will and when might will cease to be binding is constantly measured against a strong set of background assumptions about the injustice of particular (types of) treaties (see Distefano 2004).

The way concentration of the law on formally equal sovereigns led to a proceduralization of its substance is easiest to see in the laws of warfare. From the outset of the century, doctrines of the just war were set aside and war became a part of the political everyday, a procedure (a "duel") within which states sometimes chose to fight out their quarrels (see, e.g. Westlake 1910: 81). For this purpose, it was conceived as a public law institution – the "state of war" – strictly limited against

"peace" and in which special rules of the game would apply. Professional lawyers concentrate in great detail on working out what those rules are, highlighting for example, that the public nature of war would no longer provide room for private armies or privateering, definitely abolished in 1856, or the indiscriminate looting or destruction of private property situated in occupied territory. As a public law procedure, war was strictly limited to activities of the belligerent parties in a way that led into detailed discussions of rights and duties of neutrality as well as efforts to keep war from disturbing private commerce. For the humanitarians, too, the strategy consisted in maintaining strict separation of war from peace so as to then diminish its scope as much as possible. It is striking in what detail nineteenth-century lawyers lay out procedures concerning the identification and treatment of contraband goods, for example, assuming that even in the midst of a war – at least war between "civilized nations" – the belligerent powers retain the ability and willingness for cool analysis and reason, a "sunny optimism" about the business of fighting (Neff 2005: 177–201).

But even in the nineteenth century, a shadow of doubt hung about the power of these formal definitions and procedures. For example, after the question of the justice of the war had been set aside, it followed for practically all the lawyers that the older right to punish the wrongdoer completely vanished. This would be contrary to the independence of them. But few, if any lawyers, once they thought about the matter, took this view to its apparent conclusion. For the world seemed also full of injustice, oppression, and violence that "civilized nations" needed to deal with. So most lawyers, too, opened the door for the use of force in situations involving an "extreme case of outrage . . . when a . . . choice to . . . protect the weak abroad, or to punish the oppressor, ought hardly to be disobeyed" (Woolsey 1879: 19; similarly Hall 1884). Both in state practice as well as in the writings of leading jurists, humanitarian considerations were continuously invoked in defense of military operations in the frontiers of the Ottoman Empire (Neff 2005: 46).

Conclusion

Perhaps it is here, in the ambivalent relationship between the legal form and the substance covered by it where the principal legacy of the nineteenth century to the subsequent years lies. The suggestion was that the problems of the world could be best dealt with in a technical way by employing a formal concept of sovereignty, juxtaposed and disciplined by formal rules and institutions. When the First World War put an end to the Victorian optimism of the preceding years, the conclusion many drew was that the law had failed because it had not gone far enough in this project. The interwar years thus saw an intensifying critique of formal sovereignty on the part of the lawyers, accompanied by an effort to bind it down to increasingly complex technical rules and institutions within and beyond the League of Nations that were intended to tie down the period's explosive energies. The repressed returned, however, and for much of the subsequent post-war era, the nineteenth century and its offspring, the interwar system, survived principally as a memory of political innocence or of cynicism in the garb of innocence, depending on the political preference of the analyst, that contained within itself the power of its undoing. The analysis may be correct but insufficient. For the nineteenth-century practice of dealing with political power – using it, disciplining it – through public law sovereignty and formal diplomacy also liberated the most powerful social forces to mold the international world in accordance with their structural logic and embedded preferences. The legal invisibility – and irresponsibility – of much that has taken place within the "empire of civil society"[33] is heavily indebted to European political, social and economic history so that among the legacies of

the twentieth century to the present has been a conception of international law that is severely limited in ambition and of marginal significance as a platform over which the struggles for the distribution of the world's economic and spiritual resources are being waged.

Notes

1 This is the so-called "domestic analogy," absolutely central to twentieth-century international legalism. See, especially, Lauterpacht 1927 and, for a famous critique, see Carr 1946: 22–62. For a general discussion, Suganami 1989.
2 For a description of the political ethos of twentieth-century international law, see Koskenniemi 2007.
3 A significant aspect of this was the force with which German public lawyers redefined the problems of international law in terms of the vocabulary of the *ius publicum*, developed after the peace of Westphalia to discuss the relations between the territorial states and the imperial centre. See Koskenniemi 2008.
4 I have tried to capture the legal sensibility at that moment in Koskenniemi 2001.
5 For an excellent review of the development, see Vec 2006: 21–164.
6 The contrast between early and late nineteenth century international law is discussed in Laghmani 2003: 161–66.
7 This contrast is made evident in Charles Vergé's introductory essay to the second French edition of Georg Friedrich von Martens' textbook of 1864 (Vergé 1864: i–lv).
8 For an older study, see Fisch 1984. For a recent analysis of the spirit of colonialism as it was received in the interwar era, see Berman 2007: 131–81.
9 The classic analysis is Robinson and Gallagher 1981.
10 See the declaration passed by the *Institut de Droit International* on the occasion of the 1885 Berlin conference (Institute de Droit International 1885: 17–18), and, generally, Koskenniemi 2001: 155–66.
11 For a provocative but not incorrect discussion, see Schmitt 1988: 111–85.
12 For the former, see von Stachau 1847 and, for the latter, Austin 1954 [1832]: 141–42; Mill 1825.
13 On the Italian tradition, see Catellani 1933.
14 The debate was waged throughout the century, and culminated in the adoption of the

so-called Brussels Declaration of 1890 that provided for a limited right of visit. France never joined the Declaration, however, instead preferring to apply the earlier set of bilateral treaties. See Kern 2004.

15 For one at the time famous example, see Hautefeuille 1868.

16 For an insightful discussion, see Obregón 2006: 247–64. A conventional account is Espiell 2001.

17 The terms of the debate as it still continues today are clearly put by Pollock 1916.

18 For a thorough, annotated overview, see Macalister-Smith and Schwietzke 2001.

19 Its most influential representative was Samuel Pufendorf who adapted the natural law theories of Hugo Grotius and Thomas Hobbes into a synthesis that could be applied to the Holy Roman Empire and its territorial states but that could also be used so as to understand the relations between European states more generally. See, especially, Pufendorf 1934 [1688].

20 For a discussion, see Koskenniemi 2007.

21 For this interpretation, see, especially, Lauterpacht 1933.

22 For an overview of the situation in Germany, see Klippel 1976: esp. 136–97.

23 Aside from Martens, see also Schmelzing 1818: esp. 9–19. From the Francophone realm, see de Rayneval 1803.

24 This is the theme of Koskenniemi 2005b.

25 A formal doctrine of the "recognition" of the situation of different communities on such stages is contained, e.g. in Lorimer 1884: 333–59.

26 See, e.g. the manifesto in Rolin-Jaequemyns 1869: 225–6.

27 For one significant expression of this cosmopolitan optimism, see von Mohl 1860: 599–636.

28 Nicely expressed in Renault 1932: 3–5.

29 For a review, see Janis 2005: 97–116.

30 For a recent reflection of this nineteenth-century debate, see Distefano 2004, esp. 126–40.

31 For an overview, see Gross 1975.

32 Although but few have used expressly sociological language to express this. Behind generalities about *ubi societas, ibi jus*, most international lawyers have persisted in speaking in formal terms about treaties, customary laws and general principles law – the three legal sources referred to in Article 38 (1) of the Statute of the International Court of Justice.

33 See Rosenberg 1994.

10

Latin American international law[*]

Liliana Obregón

This chapter points to the importance of sovereignty as a principle that helped to underwrite the international legal system that developed among the newly independent Latin American states in the nineteenth century. It shows how a distinctive Latin American International Law (LAIL) emerged that drew on the experience of the "creole" elites both during and after Spanish rule. The transnational legal consciousness that underpinned this continued to be influential with attempts to articulate a regional IL in the twentieth century: albeit one that still reflected the outlook of the (male) elites. LAIL can be understood as an expression of international legal "regionalism," which has been defined as a particular set of approaches and methods for examining the question of universality in international law, its historical development, and substantive issues or forms of legal method. After the 1960s Latin American regionalist perspectives in international law became scarce and thus gradually irrelevant and forgotten. However, the leading regional organization, the Organization of American States, and its Inter-American System of Human Rights, is often remembered as the institutional result of more than a century of Latin American regionalist thought in international law.

Latin American international law (LAIL) was a regionalist approach to international law that was most influential during the first half of the twentieth century. Inspired by several foundational ideas from the first post-independence internationalists of the nineteenth century, LAIL was the particular perspective of several Latin American internationalists that promoted it into full force.[1] LAIL can be understood as an expression of international legal "regionalism," which has been defined as a particular set of approaches and methods for examining the question of universality in international law, its historical development, substantive issues or forms of legal method. As international law became more specialized and responsive to functional differentiation with the emergence of special types of law that responded to specific concerns (such as "human rights law" or "environmental law") instead of geographical ones, the power of LAIL as a general approach gradually diminished and fell into oblivion. However, some analysts argue that for the second half of the twentieth century regionalism persisted through its institutional development with the Organization of American States (OAS) and its Inter-American System of Human Rights (IASHR) being the outcome of more than a century of regionalist practice and thinking about international law (Caicedo Castilla 1970; Puig 1984; Sepúlveda 1960). In

154

addition, LAIL has also been suggested to be a pre-TWAIL (Third World Approaches to International Law) as a form of resistance or questioning the universalism of international law (Wa Mutua 2000) from a state-centered perspective.[2]

Creole legal consciousness

In sum, though LAIL has often been presented through a history of sources (treaties and customary law, principles and doctrines) or institutions, its existence is constituted and advocated by the writings and practice of a century of Latin American internation-alists. Therefore, this article is focused on an author-based interpretation of LAIL rather than on trying to define its legal content. One unifying way of reading LAIL authors is through what we have previously argued as their participation in a "creole legal con-sciousness."[3] By a creole legal consciousness, we mean a broad set of problems, strategies, uses and ideas about the law that are shared among a group of Latin American lawyers in the post-independence era.[4] We do not include specific legal rules or theories about the law as part of this consciousness but rather a wide acceptance of a regional identity of the law, both in its American particularism as in its European roots, an adjudication practice that allowed for the reception and appro-priation of foreign ideas and theories about the law as part of a new application to local needs or interests, and a continuous "will to civilization."

Creole legal consciousness has its origins in the hierarchical social and legal structure of 300 years of Spanish rule in the Americas. Through its legislation, the colonial gov-ernment categorized people into different groups which gradually developed their own sense of identity and recognition. Although these groups legally disappeared when the newly independent nations were founded in the nineteenth century, ostensibly many of the characteristic ways of their habitus,[5] especially

of the *criollo* (or creole) elite, the most powerful of these groups, continued on to the post-independence period and early twentieth century.

The term *criollo* (from the Latin *creare* – to create) was first used in the sixteenth century to designate black slaves born in the Americas (as opposed to *bozales* or African born slaves) (Lavalle 1993). By the seventeenth century it had become a pejorative term that was applied by the Spanish conquerors to a person born in America of European heritage but suspicious of being miscegenated with the Indian and/or black population. Nonetheless, creoles shared a hierarchical superiority and legal equality with the Spaniards as part of the "Republic of the Spanish," a jurisdic-tion which also included the *castas* (mixed peoples) and free blacks at a lower level.[6] These categories were constituted in legal terms through separate jurisdictions, privileges and restrictions.[7] Therefore, racial stratification was based more on social, political, and adminis-trative categories than on strictly biological ones. Thus, despite their status as a local elite, continuous claims to whiteness, and legal superiority over the Indian, *castas*, free blacks, and slaves, creoles were perceived by the Spanish as impure Europeans (Mazzotti 2000) and were seldom allowed to hold the most important administrative posts[8] or have access to privileges reserved for the Spanish born.

This differentiation between the European-born Spaniards and Spanish Americans led the creole *letrados*[9] – a name given to lawyers but also to those who were well cultivated in the humanities – to gradually construct the idea of an American *patria* or homeland expressed not only in literature and the arts but also in social, political and legal manifestations. Indeed, during the first two centuries of the colonial era, when Spanish law (mainly the *Siete Partidas*, a thirteenth-century Castilian compilation based on Roman and canon law)[10] was not fully applicable to local situ-ations, creoles developed a form of inter-pretation and adjudication which took local laws (called *fueros* or municipal charters) into account in a process that became known as *derecho vulgar* (popular justice) (Cutter 1999). However, by the seventeenth century the increasingly complex mixture of peoples with their new social stratifications, distance from the metropolis, extensive territory, different forms of land management and economic exploitation posed many new legal issues that were not foreseeable by this method. Such particularisms soon became evident to the Crown and in 1614 New World distinctiveness was recognized officially through a royal order that ruled that only laws specifically issued for the Indies were applicable (Cutter 1999). The laws, together with the form of applied justice, became known as *derecho indiano* (law and justice of the Indies) where judicial decisions were based on the judge's ample discretion – known as *arbitrio judicial* (judicial will) – over the use of written law, *doctrina* (commentaries of Castilian or foreign jurists on Roman, canon and royal law), custom (as local usage and long-standing practice) and *equidad* (or fairness, as defined by the satisfaction of the aggrieved party together with the well-being and harmony of the community).[11] This case-by-case decision making, referred to as *casuismo* (casuistry), was the basis of an extremely flexible system of legal administration that was considered to be a distinctively American form of justice, and therefore called *derecho criollo* (creole law or justice).[12] Thus, the imperial structure (the universal) was challenged by the creole literati as they strategically adapted both the meaning and the use of the external law to local circumstances, giving it an identity of place, a sense of regional uniqueness while at the same time their flexibility was essential to maintaining the colonial enterprise and the centrality of a European legal heritage.[13]

After the independence of the Spanish American colonies, the former creole elite continued to identify themselves as superior to the rest of the national populations but still linked by a regional identity which in the 1850s was coined as *Latin* America despite the claims to nationalism and individual equality among the citizens of the new republics. Perhaps a well-known phrase from independence leader Simón Bolívar's 1815 "Jamaica Letter" best illustrates this double bind: "But we . . . who are not Indians nor Europeans, but a mixture of the legitimate owners of the country and the usurping Spaniards, . . . we, being Americans by birth and with rights equal to those of Europe, have to dispute these rights with the [natives] of this country, and [defend] ourselves against the . . . invaders. Thus, we find ourselves in the most extraordinary and complicated predicament."[14] Indeed, the newly independent creoles had an ambiguous position: on the one hand, the creoles' right to belong to the metropolitan center as descendants of Europeans, with, on the other hand, the need to be recognized as independent and distinct from Europe.

In addition, a new element came into play in post-independence creole consciousness: the "will to civilization"[15] or desire to be part of the community of civilized nations. "Civilization" was a word that came into use during the French Revolution as the idea of progress and the perfectibility of humanity.[16] In its plural form, it meant the existence of various social groups in development, whose unity and perfection were synthesized only in *European* civilization. Therefore, barbarism, its opposite, was outside of Europe (Elias 1994). The civilizing discourse was appropriated by the newly independent elites who appealed to their European heritage in order to avoid being excluded from the rights and entitlements assigned (by Europe) to other members of the so-called "community of civilized nations." But from their colonial tradition of autonomy and proud identity, independent creoles did not view themselves as outside of civilization, as barbarians, but rather as part of their national (and regional) mission to do everything necessary to *complete* the civilization that the Spanish colonizers had brought with them but left lacking. More than a consequence of colonization, the creoles' will to civilization was self-imposed, one of the factors they knew to be essential to the recognition of their new nations as sovereign states.

Nineteenth-century foundational authors

In the memory of twentieth century LAIL advocates, the nineteenth century is historically important because it marks the end of more than 300 years of Spanish colonial rule and the beginnings of independence.[17] Nationally, it is the era of different models of statehood and state consolidation, civil wars, *uti possidetis iuris*, *caudillismo*, the struggle over local interpretations of liberalism, the appropriation of indigenous lands, and the abolition of slavery. Internationally, the nineteenth century marks the entrance of more than 20 new republics into a "community of civilized nations," until then only understood as reserved for European states. For LAIL, it is the century of the Monroe Doctrine, the American and Pan-American Congresses, U.S. imperialism, European interventions, and the transfer of the Anglo (England and the U.S.) civilizational model to the Latin (France) one, and therefore the shift of identities from "Americans" during the first half of the nineteenth century to "Latin Americans" in the second half. The nineteenth century for Latin American internationalists is a long and turbulent one, remembered for its stories both of foundational achievements and for the ones of oppression and resistance.

Nineteenth-century Latin American writers of international law thus part from a collective understanding of their particular moment of independence. Although Henry Wheaton (1845), the renowned U.S. international legal scholar of the nineteenth century wrote in 1845 that European international law was simply extended by the accession of the "new American nations that have sprung from the European stock," a close reading of the precursors of LAIL shows that they were not simply following or copying the international law that was produced in

Europe or the United States, but rather were also participants and producers of a transnational legal consciousness that they re-created and transformed with their regional interests in mind and directed back as acceptable to the metropolitan center. In the nineteenth century, *criollo* lawyers and intellectuals received and articulated international law as part of their nation-building projects and their search for recognition and legitimate participation of the new states in the "community of civilized nations."

The most representative pre-LAIL authors are Andrés Bello (1781–1865) and Carlos Calvo (1822–1906). Bello participates in what has been called the "early professional" or pre-classical period of international law and Calvo is part of the professional or classical period.[18] Bello published the first international law textbook in the Americas in 1832, titled *Principios del Derecho de Gentes* where he acknowledged the most recognized European authors of his time as well as the U.S. jurisprudence on maritime law and prize courts of Justice Story and the writings on international law of Chancellor Kent, Joseph Chitty, and Henry Wheaton. In fact, his book anticipated Henry Wheaton's *Elements of International Law* by 4 years. Bello wrote his textbook as a treatise that condensed the most important works of the time: a codification of principles from which he anticipated legal outcomes could be deduced. Although Bello's sources were in several languages, he translated what was relevant into Spanish and edited them and rewrote what he considered appropriate to the purpose of teaching international law to the law students of the newly independent states. In his treatise, Bello purposely incorporated references to the new states as undeniable members of the community of civilized nations and participants in the making of international law. He went as far as to make commentaries in the footnotes that questioned principles upheld by the foreign sources he embraced in the mainstream of the text.[19] Bello justified this as the right that the peoples of the new states had to access to an intellectual tradition of which they were naturally part of:

> Our Republic is certainly just been born to the political world; but it is also true that since the moment of her emancipation she can access all the . . . political and legislative wisdom that Europe and North America have added to this opulent {intellectual} heritage. All the peoples that have distinguished themselves on the world scene before us, have worked for us . . . The independence we acquired has put us in immediate contact with the more advanced and cultured nations; nations rich in knowledge, of which we can participate just by wanting to.[20]

Thus Bello saw himself as improving on the recognized writers of international law. He says he wrote the book to give "uniformity" of ideas and of language to the doctrines of recognized European and U.S. publicists that were "spread out and confusing." His own text is self-described as "comprehensive" and representative of "the current state of the science" claiming to have put into "one single body *all* of the elementary and indispensable notions" of international law by incorporating only what is "useful," "substantial," and "educational." Nonetheless, he also incorporated his own critique of the principle of sovereign inequality among nations as well as repositioned and placed forth principles or issues that he felt were important to the American nations such as the need to codify international law, the principle of non-intervention, the use of arbitration as a form of resolving conflicts among states, the status of combatants in civil wars, the rights of nationals and foreigners, and the most-favored nation status for trade among Spanish American nations, all of which were later held to be unique Latin American contributions to international law.

Later in the same century, Carlos Calvo, who had studied international law through Bello's book, made an effort to acknowledge the field as *scientific* by writing manuals and dictionaries of international law, presented almost all international legal issues in a historicist narrative, and proposed a distinction between public and private international law. Although he also wrote in Spanish, Calvo published most of his work in French, the language of international diplomacy and culture at that time, so that he would reach a broader European audience. He compiled treatises and other documents dating back to the period of conquest to present positive sources of international law that originated in Spanish America as well as a manual and dictionary of international law which were later translated and used by French and U.S. authors. In a similar move to Bello's, Calvo inserted the names of several Latin American publicists and the history of the region and its role in international law into his widely read treatise and dictionary. In fact, Calvo is one of the first to adopt the term '*Latin America*' as a post-independence effort to defend the region's interest. Calvo (1862) was concerned that Latin American nations were not taken seriously as active participants of international law because of the "absolute ignorance in Europe of our state of civilization and progress."[21] Stressing that the negative judgments of Europeans were not based on facts, Calvo (1862) pointed to the obligation of "any American" to demonstrate the truth of the continents progress in a way "that will not leave any doubt in the spirit of the European reader."

Even Bello's seemingly systematic treatise of international law is full of references to the Latin American context of the time. Bello's particular role as the region's foremost nation builder does much to explain why he gave such attention to international law. In fact, many of his disputes with European legal scholars are based on an intense relation with events that happened in Latin America. The same is true of Calvo. Both intertwined regional events with those of Anglo and European international histories as a way to include their view of a corrective, more balanced account of the Latin American

nations' participation in the further development of international law, guided by a
complex dialectical relationship between
globality and locality, international prestigious
authorities and local demands and contesta-
tions. Contrariwise, the texts' structure shows
that these early Latin American scholars were
very familiar with the contemporary canon
of international law and participated in a common vocabulary shared by European and
North American writers despite that they are
not remembered as such or that the memory
of their existence is limited to their particu-
larity as Latin Americans.

Despite the fact that these pre-LAIL
authors did not develop a rejectionist stance
of international law their writings could
also be read as presenting the perspective of
former colonial subjects that questioned the
balance of power in the world but at the same
time had immense faith in their capacity to
participate in the adaptation of international
law to accept the needs of the newly independent states. This does not mean that
Bello and Calvo, as other authors of their
time, were aware of their own colonial attitudes towards the subaltern subjects of their
new states or that they did not embrace the
European move of restricting the right to
sovereignty of those considered "uncivil-
ized" during the colonial enterprise of the
nineteenth century. Indeed, the development of a doctrine of state sovereignty was
one of the principal concerns of nineteenth-
century Latin American internationalists but
in accordance with what benefitted their
own particular situation in the world with
respect to the issues of recognition, the principle of non-intervention, the notion of
regional unity and the limitation of borders
among neighboring countries.

Twentieth-century rise and fall of LAIL

Soon after the publication of Carlos Calvo's
book *Le Droit International Théorique et*
Pratique (*Theoretical and Practical International
Law*) Amancio Alcorta, an Argentine internationalist, wrote an article complaining
that Calvo's work did not mention the possibility of a LAIL (Alcorta 1883). Calvo
responded that though he had a regional
approach to his writings, LAIL as such did not
exist because international law should be
about general principles and not about particular problems and LAIL should not be
understood as a branch of law because it only
referred to a particular set of regional problems (Calvo 1883).

Two decades later, however, Alejandro
Álvarez,[22] a young Chilean internationalist
argued for a LAIL in a paper titled "Origen
y desarrollo del derecho internacional
americano" ("Origin and development of
American international law") presented at the
third Latin American Scientific Congress
in Rio de Janeiro.[23] Álvarez (1910) began to
claim for himself a foundational role as sole
theorizer of LAIL:

> In spite of the obvious existence of this law
> . . . it has not been studied nor even clearly
> stated by the publicists either of Europe
> or of America . . . The only publicist who
> seems to have grasped the idea of the exist-
> ence of the matters constitutive of [an
> American International Law] is Alcorta[24] but
> he never expressly affirmed its existence, nor
> indicated its foundations, nor the subjects
> that constitute it.[25]

Although Álvarez was later followed by several other internationalists, the debate on the
existence or not of a LAIL continued well into
the twentieth century. Indeed, a Brazilian
diplomat and professor of international law,
Manoel Álvaro de Souza Sá Vianna (1860–
1924) published a book titled *De la non
Existence d'un Droit International Americain*,[26]
which was presented at the Fifth Latin
American Scientific Congress of 1912 in an
effort to challenge Álvarez's (1905, 1907b,
1909a, 1910) earlier proposals for a general
recognition of the existence of a LAIL.[27] Sá
Vianna's intention was to put an end to the

notion of a regional international law, arguing that problems common to the countries of Latin America or to the American continent did not and could not constitute a basis for an autonomous or separate sphere of international law. For Sá Vianna international law was based on principles, laws, and rules observed by the international society and not on common historical experiences among a group of countries, as Álvarez had argued.

Nonetheless, Álvarez continued to publicly defend in his writings and oral presentations the need to recognize a regional version of international law.[28] In addition, several other Latin American internationalists followed Álvarez and published books and articles on the characteristics, history, proposals and future of LAIL during the first half of the twentieth century.[29] The proposal of a LAIL, as well as the debates about its existence, bring forth the underlying story of a regional sensibility and it troubles the common assumption that the discourse of international law went unchallenged when received and appropriated by Latin American nations peripheral to European and U.S. economic and political dominance.[30]

Although Álvarez broke away from the classical period and became modern by embracing and promoting social legal thought in international law, he still inhabited a creole legal consciousness reflected in three areas in which Álvarez worked: in his own reading of local events and texts, in the production of a theory of LAIL and in the project of institutionalization of a regional law. First, from 1905 to 1910 Álvarez wrote extensively for the recognition of a LAIL. His historical exposition referred to the regional treaties and conventions, the Latin American and Pan American conferences, and Scientific Congresses that occurred throughout the nineteenth century. He claimed that all these events revealed the particular character of problems *sui generi's*, which were the basis of a LAIL that European publicists did not account for.

Second, Álvarez claimed to be the first to theorize LAIL in an effort not to follow

European writers. Álvarez critiqued European internationalists for not taking into account the social, economic and technological transformations of the nineteenth century. He also criticized them for continuing with the same conception of the nature and extension of the rules of international law and for giving excessive credence to sovereignty and to the universality of all principles. Thus Álvarez proposed that by studying the states of the Americas in their particular situations and history of institutions, it would be possible to proclaim that there were different or contrary principles from those of the European states, and that they would reveal a different character of the rules of international law.

Third, Álvarez was able to access and master the centers of academic and institutional production of international law in order to promote his work in French and English, languages that were more broadly read. When the U.S. began to promote the Pan-American Congresses he changed his first text titled "Latin America and international law" to "American international law" and figured the U.S. as an important hegemon in the region, despite the charges of U.S. imperialism by several of his colleagues. From 1916 to 1918 he spoke at nearly 30 U.S. universities in order to promote the unification of what he called the Anglo-American and Latin American schools of international law into a single Pan-American School. In Latin America he promoted his theory in the Scientific Congresses and when he was challenged by Sá Vianna and others he adapted by changing his titles to "American problems in international law" or "International law . . . from the point of view of the American continent." He also managed to promote a motion in the First Panamerican Scientific Congress in which all the discussions of the sciences (including political science and legal science) would be done from "an American point of view." Álvarez was also concerned about institution building. He co-founded the American Institute of International Law in

1912 and its French counterpart in 1919. On one side of the ocean, he promoted the consolidation of an American juridical conscience, on the other, he promoted an international juridical conscience. Álvarez preached his project of codification both at the American and international levels, managing to get conferences and discussions started at each.

In sum, it would not be difficult to prove that Álvarez was making generalizations that only apply to his specific experience as member of a particular male, educated, "white" elite group that during the colonial era was denominated as *criollo*. It is obvious that Álvarez essentialized characteristics from nations that have different ethnical and historical compositions inside of their national boundaries. He so adamantly believed in these claims that he had presented them (and more) in previous texts and would continue to do so for the next 50 years (Álvarez 1905, 1907a, 1907b, 1909a, 1909b, 1910, 1911a, 1911b, 1917). Álvarez argued such a position unabashedly and with utmost convincement because he was thinking, writing and speaking from his particular creole habitus and arguing the need for a regional perspective on international law from a creole legal consciousness.

Conclusion

A regional consciousness of international law is evident in the representative works of Andrés Bello, Carlos Calvo and other Latin Americans during the nineteenth century, but it wasn't until the beginning of the twentieth century that a "Latin American international law" (LAIL) was theorized and promoted by its main proponent Alejandro Álvarez. Many other internationalists followed Álvarez in defining and promoting a LAIL, but after the 1960s Latin American regionalist perspectives in international law became scarce and thus gradually irrelevant and forgotten. However, the strength of

these regionalist perspectives (as well as the fissures in their homogeneity) every now and then resuscitate in the political discourse of Latin American leaders, from grassroots advocates to presidents. In addition, the leading regional organization, the Organization of American States, and its Inter-American System of Human Rights, is often remembered as the institutional result of more than a century of Latin American regionalist thought in international law.

Notes

* This chapter is drawn in part from the following: "Noted for Dissent: the International Life of Alejandro Alvarez", Special edition of the *Leiden Journal of International Law*, Vol. 19, No. 4, Cambridge University Press 2006. "Between Civilization and Barbarism: Creole Interventions in International Law", special issue, *International Law and the Third World*. Guest editors Richard Falk, Balakrishnan Rajagopal and Jaqueline Stevens in *Third World Quarterly*, Vol. 27, No. 4, Taylor & Francis 2006. "Creole Consciousness and International Law in Nineteenth Century Latin America" in *International Law and its Others*, edited by Anne Orford, Cambridge University Press 2006.
1 For other recent readings on LAIL see Becker Lorca 2006; Gros Espiell 2001.
2 LAIL scholarship like TWAIL I scholarship (or the first wave of TWAIL scholars of the 1960s and 1970s) was state centered and believed in the future of the United Nations as the institutional embodiment of the development of international law.
3 I have developed the idea of a creole legal consciousness previously in Obregón 2002: 200, 2006.
4 Although there have been myriad legal consciousness studies since the 1980s my definition is based on Duncan Kennedy's as a "particular form of consciousness that characterizes the legal profession as a social group, at a particular moment. The main peculiarity of this consciousness is that it contains a vast number of legal rules, arguments, and theories, a great deal of information about the institutional workings of the legal process and the constellation of ideals and goals current in the profession at a given moment." This definition is part of Kennedy's manuscript of 1975 reformatted

in 1998 (Kennedy (1998 [1975], first chapter published as Kennedy 1980)). In a more recent article, Kennedy clarifies his borrowing from the linguist Ferdinand de Saussure by explaining that a legal consciousness is "understood as a vocabulary of concepts and typical arguments, as a langue, or language," which contain an infinity of laws or "phrases" that can be formulated in the conceptual vocabulary of that consciousness as "*parole*," or speech. Therefore to identify one writer as participating of a consciousness (i.e. creole) does not mean that others of the same consciousness (*langue*) will utter identical forms of speech (*parole*) nonetheless, they participate by combining and recombining the general policy "argument or sound bites" of that language. Kennedy has recently revived the concept of legal consciousness in a global dimension in Kennedy (2003) and as noted in the "legal history" section of his new web page http://www.duncankennedy.net. The idea of argument bites is more extensively explained in Kennedy (1994b). For an analysis of the legal consciousness literature in the law and society scholarship see the articles by García-Villegas (2003) and Silbey (2005).

5 I am referring to Pierre Bourdieu's notion of habitus, as an "habitual, patterned ways of understanding, judging, and acting which arise from our particular position as members of one or several social 'fields,' and from our particular trajectory in the social structure (e.g. whether our group is emerging or declining; whether our own position within it is becoming stronger or weaker). The notion asserts that different conditions of existence – different educational backgrounds, social statuses, professions, and regions – all give rise to forms of habitus characterized by internal resemblance within the group (indeed, they are important factors which help it to know itself as a group), and simultaneously by perceptible distinction from the habitus of differing groups. Beyond all the undoubted variations in the behaviours of individuals, habitus is what gives the groups they compose consistency. It is what tends to cause the group's practices and its sense of identity to remain stable over time. It is a strong agent of the group's own self-recognition and self-reproduction" [translator's note in Bourdieu (1987)].

6 As African slavery was introduced into the Spanish colonies, distinctions grew in importance in multiple and ever increasingly complex ways. The colonial system of *castas* (castes) ranked individuals hierarchically according to the amount of visible (skin color), perceived (education, language, religion, culture) and acquired (through political or economic influence) European "blood." Edicts and other colonial legislation determined the limits of the *castas* in accessing certain jobs, holding public office or receiving public education. A mixed person could ascend beyond his skin color by adopting as many European traits as possible (see Jackson 1999; Seed 1982).

7 Precisely because of the creoles' characteristic ambiguity some scholars have suggested the term "agency" rather than "subject" as a marker of their political will within the public sphere. See José Antonio Mazzotti's (2000) collection on different studies of creole agency and ways in which the category of the *criollo* was constituted during colonial times. Although creoles in Spanish America were often portrayed as "white," it is constraining and misleading to describe the creole as a monolithic subject based only on a racial or social category. Other elements such as honor, purity of blood, legitimacy of birth, social status, economic and political power were more significant when defining differences that were legally, institutionally, and socially enforced. It is more appropriate to say that he (the creole is undoubtedly a male subject) represented certain positions taken in the public sphere. In this sense, it is easier to understand why "honor" rather than "race" would be important to a person positioning himself or being positioned as creole (see for example, Uribe Urán 2000).

8 Such as those of viceroys, bishops or *oidores*. *Oidores* were judges who were part of one of the *audiencias*: "a governmental body with administrative and judicial functions, usually the highest level appellate body located in a geographic area governed by a viceroy or other royal official magistrates" (Mirow 2001).

9 *Letrados* has been translated as "lettered men" or literati (Rojas 2001). Ángel Rama in *The Lettered City* describes the literati as "the restricted group of intellectual workers who learned the mechanisms and vicissitudes of institutionalized power and learned, too, how to make irreplaceable institutions of themselves ... their services in the manipulation of symbolic languages were indispensable ... servants of power, in one sense, the *letrados* became masters of power, in another" (Rama 1996).

10 These codes or compilations are the Ordenamiento de Alcalá (1348) restated in the Leyes de Toro (1505), Nueva Recopilación

de Castilla (1567) and the Novísima Recopilación de Castilla (1805).

11 I have taken these categories as conveniently simplified by Cutter (1999).

12 Even today, when contemporary legal issues are discussed based on local circumstances the charge is of *casuism* or of giving a creole interpretation to the law. Diego López Medina (2004) has done much to give new value to these Latin American transformations or transmutations of what he calls a "transnational legal theory" coming from "prestigious sites of production" by showing them as creative and often brilliant local appropriations. I would add that these transformations could be read as part of a modern creole legal consciousness. In fact, López's book may be read in the same tradition: López is appropriating (and criticizing) European- and Unitedstatesean-produced theory to propose a novel reading inscribed in the region, which would not have been possible from a monologist view from the center.

13 Joseph Lund (2001: 54–90) describes this as typical of Latin American exceptionalist discourse: that it proclaims its difference and distance but at the same time it only is able to legitimize itself through a Eurocentric point of departure.

14 As translated in Álvarez 1924.

15 I have borrowed the concept of the "will to civilization" as described by Cristina Rojas as "a place of [violent] encounter between the colonial past and the imagined future, as a passage between barbarism and civilization" (Rojas 2001). I also had in mind Walter Benjamin's statement: "There is no document of civilization which is not at the same time a document of barbarism" (Benjamin 1973: 256).

16 Civilization was understood as a "universal fact," and, with it, the trust that law and institutions would be able to mold the human character. The word "civilization" originated in the use of the French words *civilité* (civility) and *poli* (polished, refined, courteous, to emit prudent laws). For more about the etymology of the word see Goberna Falque (1999), Starobinski (1993), Lochore (1935), Febvre et al. (1930).

17 Depending on what countries are included in the imagery of "Latin America," independence dates can range from as early as 1791 for Haiti or as late as 1898 for Cuba. If only the continental former Spanish colonies are included in the regional reference these dates range roughly from 1810 to 1825.

18 Although these classifications are rough sketches of a time period they help to describe different moments of legal consciousness. Martti Koskenniemi uses the term "early professional," or "early classical" to describe international law publicists for the first half of the nineteenth century, roughly for the same period that Duncan Kennedy uses the term pre-classical to describe legal consciousness in the United States. The classical or professional period for both authors refers to the late nineteenth century, and the modern moment refers to the twentieth century (see Kennedy 1998 [1975]; Koskenniemi 1989). However, I, like Koskenniemi or Kennedy, do not use these terms to present a progress narrative of legal consciousness.

19 Bello's work is better explained in the chapter "Andrés Bello's principles of international law" in Obregón (2002) or in Obregón (2006).

20 The original quote in Spanish is taken from Hanisch Espíndola (1983).

21 Calvo's work is better analyzed in the chapter "Carlos Calvo's theoretical and practical international law" in Obregón (2002).

22 For a recent and extensive analysis of Alvarez's oeuvre, see Several 2006.

23 The paper was later modified and published as an article in Álvarez 1907b. In the revised edition, he enlarged the geographic domain to include the United States, therefore changing the name from "Latin American" to "American" (as in the continent).

24 Amancio Alcorta (1883) complained that Carlos Calvo's work on international law did not mention the possibility of an American international law (*derecho internacional americano*). Calvo (1883: 629–31) responded by saying that there was no American international law because international law treats principles and not problems. This debate initiated a series of discussions on the existence or not of an American international law. Among others who cite this debate, see Yepes 1938 and Jacobini 1954. For a contemporary analysis of these debates, see Becker Lorca 2006.

25 Bello and Calvo also felt that they were being original from an American point of view though they did not promote the idea of a regional version of international law. Nonetheless, they, like Alvarez, used rhetorical strategies to place their work at the center of production of international law. Doris Sommer (1999) has masterfully shown how minority writers often use "rhetorics of particularism" in order to engage admiration while at the same time resist control.

26 "[N]'existe pas, et ne peut exister un Droit International Latino-Américain . . . ni un

Droit International Américain" (Sá Vianna 1912). All translations are mine unless otherwise stated.

27 The usage of the term "Latin America" only began in the mid-nineteenth century but became more commonly used in the twentieth. Most writers refer to American as pertaining to the former Spanish colonies or to the entire continent but not solely to the United States. Sá Vianna makes the distinction of Latin American or American to clarify that he is referring to an international law pertaining to the former Spanish colonies and to a continental international law. Throughout this work, I will comply with a similar usage and make the distinction of Anglo American or U.S. when I refer to someone or something pertaining to the United States.

28 In 1909 Álvarez published two texts in English: "American problems in international law" and "Latin America and international law" in the *American Journal of International Law*. In 1910 he published a book titled *Le Droit International Américain: Son Fondement, sa Nature: d'apres l'Histoire Diplomatique des États du nouveau Monde et leur Vie Politique et Économique*, which he presented at the Fourth Panamerican Conference held in Buenos Aires, Argentina. A year later, still before the First World War, Álvarez released a book on the Monroe Doctrine and its impact on the American nations. After the First World War, he published *Le Droit International de L'Avenir* (*International Law of the Future*) a book which proposed to renovate a failed international law backed by the moral strength of a Latin American perspective. During the interwar period, Álvarez also published several papers and articles on an American need to codify international law. After the Second World War, Álvarez continued his belief that it was necessary to place the American continent's role at the forefront of the drastically changed international environment and expressed these views in several of his dissenting opinions as a judge on the International Court of Justice.

29 Álvarez 1923; American Institute of International Law, Pan American Union and Scott 1925; Arroyo Rivera 1952; Baez 1936; Castro Ramirez 1915; Checa Drouet 1936; Cock Arango 1948; Henriquez 1948; Henriquez Vergez 1966; Labra 1912; Mackenzie 1955; Nielsen Reyes 1934; Oro Maini 1951; Orrico Esteves 1956; Paredes 1924; Planas Suarez 1924; Puig 1952; Quesada 1916; Restelli 1912; Rueda Villareal 1948; Sanchez I Sanchez 1941; Sanchez I Sanchez 1958; Scott 1930; Uriarte 1915; Yepes 1930; Yepes 1952; Zárate 1957.

30 Latin America has been traditionally identified by comparative legal scholars as a place where legal imports are borrowed and well received. See Esquirol and López Medina's S.J.D. dissertations (Esquirol 2001; López Medina 2001, 2004).

11

Religion and international law: an analytical survey of the relationship

Mashood Baderin

This chapter provides a general but contextualized and critical analytical survey of the relationship between religion and international law from four main perspectives: historical, theoretical, empirical and doctrinal. The historical perspective generally analyzes how religion has featured in the evolution of international law over time and its consequences for modern international law. The theoretical perspective analyzes the main theoretical viewpoints on whether or not religion ought to have any normative role in international law, while the empirical and doctrinal perspectives examine the practical and legal parameters of the relationship respectively.

Introduction

Religion[1] has played, and continues to play, a significant role in the evolution of international law, even though the relationship between the two is often perceived to be complex and controversial for different reasons. On the one hand, the controversy surrounding the relationship may be attributed to the apparent differences in the nature of religion (sacred) and that of international law (secular). Carolyn Evans (2005: 3) has noted in that regard that: "The place of religion in the international legal system, or indeed any legal system that purports to be secular, is likely to be controversial and complex." On the other hand, religion and law are identical in some other ways. Generally, both religion and law are important social phenomena that relate to fundamental social issues in human society, which has often stimulated "passionate disagreement about their proper content and functions"[2] in that regard (Jamar 2001: 609). Also, both religion and law can be politicized and manipulated by the elite to achieve particular intended objectives, which also adds to the complexity and controversy in their relationship. Owing to its complexity, the relationship between religion and international law can be analyzed from different perspectives depending on one's objective.

As a chapter in a handbook on international law, this essay aims at providing a general but contextualized analytical survey of the relationship from four main perspectives: historical, theoretical, empirical and doctrinal. These four perspectives are not strictly mutually exclusive, but are intrinsically interrelated as, for example, the theoretical perspective must, as a matter of necessity, not only be historically aware, but empirically meaningful and also doctrinally relevant. The historical perspective will generally analyze how religion has featured in the evolution of international law over time and its consequences for modern international law. The theoretical perspective will analyze the main theoretical viewpoints on whether or not religion ought to have any normative role in international law. The empirical and doctrinal perspectives would examine the practical levels of the relationship and explore the legal scope of the relationship respectively. It is necessary to state that the term "religion" is used here in a very general sense, but reference would be made to specific religions where necessary to illustrate and provide context to relevant arguments.

Historical perspective

The history of international law is usually delineated by the Peace of Westphalia, which is often depicted as the beginnings of modern international law and international relations, and thus conventionally divided into the pre-Westphalian and post-Westphalian periods. This traditional division of the history of international law is essentially Euro-Christian in nature and has been described as being "to a certain extent, old fashioned" (see Steiger 2001: 180). The important point, nevertheless, is that religion has played a significant role in both historical periods.

Before the Peace of Westphalia in 1648, religion constituted a fundamental basis for the normative rules regulating the relationship between the political powers of that period in different parts of the world (see e.g. Bantekas 2007: 115; Bederman 2004). For example, while the earlier writings on rules of the law of nations by jurists in Europe relied heavily on Judeo-Christian religious sources, similar writings by jurists in the Muslim world also relied mainly on Islamic religious sources (see, e.g. Khadduri 1966). After Westphalia, international law materialized as an essentially secular and European construct but remained very much influenced by Christian religious dictates generally.[3] Heinhard Steiger (2001: 183) has observed

in that regard that the epoch of international law from the thirteenth to the eighteenth centuries was an epoch of "international law of Christianity," with the law deeply rooted in religious or divine law. He noted that: "Christianity formed the major intellectual foundation of legal order for the entire epoch," which, *inter alia*, "brought Europe together, not only into an intellectual-religious unit, but also under the political idea of *res publica Christiana*," a term he identified as still "used in treaties as late as the 18th Century" (Steiger 2001: 184).

Writing from an Islamic perspective, Muhammad Hamidullah (1977: vii, emphasis in original text) had earlier made a similar observation in 1941, stating that what passed as international law in Europe up to the mid-nineteenth century was "a mere public law of *Christian nations*" and noted that it was "in 1856 that for the first time a non-Christian nation, Turkey, was considered fit to benefit from the European Public Law of Nations, and this was the true beginning in internationalizing the public law of Christian nations." To highlight however that the concept of international law was not limited to Europe in those times, Hamidullah (1977: vii) further observed notably that international law existed long before then within Islamic law, based principally on Islamic religious sources. There have also been observations by other scholars highlighting the existence in other religions of relevant rules for the regulation of the "interstate" relationships between political powers in the form of law of nations prior to the Peace of Westphalia in 1648 (see, e.g. Jain 2003; Weeramantry 2004: 17–30).

Over time after Westphalia, emphasis on the substantive role and influence of religion in international law declined gradually in Europe, until modern international law became perceived strictly as a secular positivist legal system with its foundation regarded as lying "firmly in the development of Western culture and political organization" (Bederman 2001a; Brierly 1963: 1; Shaw

2003: 13–22; Stumpf 2005). Carolyn Evans (2005: 2) refers notably to Mark Janis' observation in that regard that "by 1905, when Oppenheim published his classic *International Law*, religion no longer played the important role that it had in earlier texts: 'rather religion was part of the history of international law, something that once had mattered'" (see also Janis 2004: 138; Kennedy 2004: 145–53).

The adoption of the United Nations (UN) Charter in 1945 can be described as the climax in the formal substantive secularization and positivization of modern international law, as none of its provisions refers directly to religion as a legal or normative source of international law, except for its provisions on prohibition of non-discrimination on grounds of religion.[4] Christoph Stumpf (2005: 70) has, however, observed that this secularization of international law has European traditional underpinnings, and that this creates a source of "potential conflict in the relationship between secularized legal cultures which are customarily labeled 'Western', and other legal cultures that wish to uphold their religious root." Stumpf's observation is reflective of the fact that the world is today constituted of states that operate different legal cultures, with religion still playing a very visible role in the public sphere and legal culture of many states, particularly Muslim states. In the words of Ilias Bantekas (2007: 116): "To be certain, the world is divided into secular and non-secular countries." That, in essence, continues to have significant impact on the relationship between religion and international law at their different levels of interaction.

Thus, despite the substantive secularization of modern international law, the discourse on the relationship between religion and international law is no longer merely historically relevant, i.e. "something that once had mattered" (Evans 2005: 2) but has become, in the last few decades, relatively more substantively relevant, i.e. "something that still matters" (see, e.g. Hackett 2005: 661;

Haynes 2005; Petito and Hatzopoulos 2003),[5] particularly after the 1979 Islamic Revolution in Iran and the al-Qaeda terrorist attack of September 11, 2001, both of which invoked Islamic religious sources as their basis of action and both of which have had important impacts on international law respectively. While this has placed Islam in the forefront of the contemporary discourse on the relationship between religion and international law, as will be reflected in the context of this chapter, it is by no means the only religion relevant in the discourse. For example, Richard Falk (2002: 4–5) has referred to the Falun Gong movement in China and the current political leverage of the religious right in the United States of America as relevant examples of the current religious dynamics in different parts of the world impacting on the relationship between religion and modern international relations and international law.

In the face of diverse contemporary international challenges, especially regarding issues of international peace and security, some international law scholars and jurists have proposed a general return to relevant principles of natural law as well as religious and cultural values to find ways of expanding the scope of the principles of modern international law to meet those challenges (see, e.g. Falk 2001; Meron 2000: 278; Weeramantry 2004). Also, many other commentators have, especially from an Islamic perspective, specifically challenged what they consider to be the continued European and Christian underpinnings and influences on modern international law and called for an appreciation of the necessary inputs that other religions, especially Islam, can offer to the development of modern international law (see, e.g. Abou-el-Wafa 2005; Baderin 2008; Shihata 1962). Thus, while Christianity had played an almost unilateral role in the historical development of modern international law, other religions now tend to be asserting their respective values as relevant factors to be considered in its continued evolution. This brings us to the examination of the different

167

theoretical perspectives around which the debate on the relationship between religion and international law are being diversely framed today.

Theoretical perspectives

The main theoretical question in the debate about the relationship between religion and international law centers on whether or not religion ought to have a normative role in modern international law. The complex aspect of the debate is that there are diverse views based on different worldviews and theoretical arguments. Richard Falk has noted in that regard that: "There are those who view religion as disposed towards extremism, even terrorism, as soon as it abandons its modernist role as a matter of private faith and belief that should not intrude upon governance . . . [and their] opponents argue the opposite thesis, which contends that without rooting governance in the dictates of religious doctrine, the result is decadence and impotence" (Falk 2002: 6–7). There is a third viewpoint in between. Thus, the current literature generally reflects three main theoretical perspectives on the subject, which may be classified as the "separationist," "accommodationist," and "double-edged" theoretical perspectives respectively.

Separationist theory

The separationist theoretical perspective reflects a secular positivist view of international law, which advocates a strict separation between religion and law and argues that religion should have no normative role in international law at all. It draws mainly from the western, particularly American, liberal concept of the separation of church and state, which asserts that religion should be a personal matter restricted to the private sphere of individuals, "solely between Man and his God," and not allowed into the public sphere of governance generally and of law

particularly (Jefferson 1802: para. 2). Scott Thomas (2005: 151) calls this the "Westpahlian presumption" in international relations, "which says religious and cultural pluralism cannot be accommodated in a global multicultural international society, and so must be privatized or nationalized if there is going to be domestic or international order." It advocates a pure theory of international law aimed at ensuring neutrality of the law and devoid of religious and cultural reductionism or influence. Thus, the main logic of the separationist theory is the "neutrality argument," which asserts that a secular positivist international law is necessary to ensure neutrality in the operation and application of international law in a manner that ensures equality and non-discrimination in a multicultural and multi-religious global system.

Today, most scholars of international law, particularly from the western world, adopt the separationist theory and advocate a secular positivist international law that is separated from any religious persuasion. For example, in his critique of the arbitration tribunal's reference to Islamic law in the case of *Eritrea vs. Yemen (Phase Two: Maritime Delimitation)*,[6] Michael Reisman (2000a: 729) argued, *inter alia*, that: "The essential function of general international law, as a secular *corpus juris*, is to provide a common standard and to play a mediating role between states with different cultures, legal systems, and belief systems," and that international tribunals "would be well advised to stick to international law" in that secular form. A similar point, but in a different context, was made by Antonio Cassese (1988: 78) in his criticism of the Israeli Commission of Enquiry's reference to rabbinic law in the *Sabra and Shatila Inquiry* of 1982 and its shunning of international law in that regard. Also in his comments on the observation of the International Court of Justice (ICJ) in the *Case Concerning United States Diplomatic and Consular Staff in Tehran* (ICJ Reports 1980: 41) that the traditions of Islam has made substantial contribution to the principle of the inviolability of the persons of diplomatic agents and premises, Ilias Bantekas (2007: 127) contended that there was no need for the court to have made a reference to Islam on this point as there was sufficient substantive international law the court could have relied on in that regard.

I submit to the contrary and argue that such complementary references to religious law by international tribunals in relevant cases, as seen earlier, reflect an accommodationist perspective, which can contribute to the development of customary international law. It must be emphasized however that this should not extend to the total jettisoning of international law for religious principles as appeared to have been the approach of the Commission in the *Sabra and Shatila Inquiry* as analyzed by Cassese. He noted that the Commission had set aside relevant international law and "referred exclusively *to moral and religious imperatives*" to formulate its reasoning on the question of "indirect responsibility" in that case (Cassese 1988: 79). Rather than completely sidelining international law, our argument here is that relevant religious law can be persuasively cited to complement international law for the purpose of establishing the existence of customary international law in relevant cases, especially where such religious law is a formal part of national law. There is no rule of international law that prohibits doing so. Actually, it is recognized under international law that states' municipal laws may in certain circumstances form the basis of customary rules (Shaw 2003: 79). I will further elaborate this point in the section on doctrinal perspectives in a later part of this chapter. Mark Janis (1993: 321–22) has advanced a similar argument to the effect that international law needs to "draw on the many different religious, political, economic and social traditions to find values common to the many nations, which may be adopted as norms in customary [international] law."

The neutrality argument of the separationist theory has however been challenged, both in its national and international context, on the contention that the argument is itself based on certain presumptions that are not really neutral in themselves. For example, Douglas Laycock (1990: 994) has referred, in that regard, to Michael McConnell's challenge that "neutrality is not a self-defining concept, because properly defined, it is often at odds with religious liberty," while according to David Cinotti (2003: 500), "neutrality is an indeterminate and vacant idea because one may always counter neutrality-based arguments by reframing the definition of neutrality or by making counterarguments also from neutrality" (see also Ravitch 2004).[7] The problem with the neutrality argument is that there is always the need for establishing an appropriate baseline from which deviations from neutrality can be assessed, the choice of which, especially in relation to the separationist theory, is itself not absolutely neutral (Ahdar and Leigh 2005: 90–92; Esbeck 1997: 5; Ravitch 2004: 493–506). Thus one of the main challenges to the separationist theory in respect of the relationship between religion and international law is that a strict secular system of international law may not necessarily be neutral in every sense of the word, as is often presumed. Carl Esbeck (1997: 1, 5) has argued in that regard that:

> Separationism is a value-laden judgement that certain areas of the human condition best lied with the province of religion, while other areas of life are properly under the authority of civil government. Separationism, this most dominant of theories is in no sense the inevitable product of objective reason unadulterated by an ideological commitment to some higher point of reference. Separationism cannot stand outside of the political and religious milieu from which it emerged and honestly claim to be neutral concerning the nature and contemporary value of religion or the purposes of modern government. The same must be said for its primary competitor, the neutrality theory. Indeed, to demand that any theory of church/state relations transcend its pedigree or its presuppositions and be substantively neutral is to ask the impossible.

The historical awareness of the separationist perception of international law is based on the fact that it is generally motivated by a post-Reformative and post-Westphalian interpretation of international relations informed by the European historical experience of the long years of religious wars of the sixteenth and seventeenth centuries. The Peace of Westphalia was reached after a century of religious wars that ravaged Europe between 1550 and 1650. Scott Thomas (2005: 22) has noted that this experience has led to the general impression in modern international relations that "when religion is brought into domestic or international public life . . . it inherently causes war, intolerance, devastation, political upheaval, and maybe even the collapse of the international order," and thus must be excluded from both the political and legal realms of international relations generally and international law specifically.[8] He described this interpretation of the wars of religion in Europe as both a "political mythology of liberalism," and the "myth of the modern secular state" which continues to affect "the way culture and religion are interpreted in international relations today" (Thomas 2005: 22), and thereby proposed the view that "[a] new approach to international order is required which overcomes this 'Westphalian presumption'" (Thomas 2000: 815).

Thus, while the separationist theory is historically aware, its historical awareness is not necessarily universal but based on a European experience, which has been challenged in the contemporary debate on the relationship between religion and international law. The general contention in that regard is that the war of religions experienced in Europe may not necessarily reflect the religious experiences of other civilizations in relation to the accommodation of religious norms within the public sphere of law and governance and does not thus, necessarily, reflect a universal worldview on the subject. Furthermore, a strict dichotomy between the private and the public sphere, as required under this theory, is not easily determinable

in a clear way because the private and public spheres overlap extensively in all societies, which makes it difficult to separate the two spheres in relation to issues regarding religion and international law in many societies today (Thomas 2005: 35). Christine Chinkin has noted that: "The location of any line between public and private activity is culturally specific and the appropriateness of using Western analytical tools to understand the global regime is questionable" (Chinkin 1999: 390). Carolyn Evans (2005: 2) has thus observed that:

> [E]ven if religion is often distinguished from law in Western legal and political philosophy, and largely ignored in legal writing, no such division can be neatly maintained in the real world. This is particularly the case in many parts of the world . . . where the law and religion are often deeply intertwined and religion may play a more meaningful and significant role in influencing behavior than does law.

Practically, the separationist theory does not yet have a universal reception, as religion still plays a significant public role in many states today and the world still divided into secular and non-secular countries. This brings me to the second theoretical perspective – accommodationist theory.

Accommodationist theory

In contrast to the separationist theory, the accommodationist theoretical perspective advances the view that religion can play an important normative role in international law and must therefore be accommodated in that regard. This perception is based generally on a naturalist view of international law, which was traditionally underpinned by religion as analyzed in the historical perspective earlier. Proponents of this view assert that religious considerations are too important for the majority of the world's population to be considered irrelevant or problematic for accommodation in the public sphere of law generally and of international law particularly.[9] The main argument of this theory is that since many aspects of international law, such as human rights, humanitarian law, environmental law, disarmament and maintenance of international peace and security, are all underpinned by humaneness, considerations of morality and human dignity, religious norms and values can make an important contribution in that regard and must therefore be normatively accommodated within the principles of international law. For example, Christopher Weeramantry (2004: 15), a former judge of the ICJ, has observed:

> Given the strength in the modern world of religious traditions, such as the Buddhist, Christian, Hindu and Islamic, and that they command the allegiance of over three billion of the world's population, there cannot be any doubt that future thinking on international law can benefit deeply from the teachings contained in these traditions.

Similarly, in answering the question of whether religion has served as a catalyst or impediment to international law, Mark Janis (1993: 321–22) identified that religion could play three important facilitative roles in international law as follows:

> First, religion traditionally has been one of the most fertile sources of the rules of international law. It may well be that all religious traditions have norms that are applicable to the relations of states and their peoples . . . One of the major tasks confronting international lawyers in the modern era is to draw on the many different religious, political, economic and social traditions to find values common to the many nations, which may be adopted as norms in customary law. This should be a mission, not only for scholars of international law, but also for scholars of all the world's religious faiths.
>
> Secondly, religious belief has been one of the chief motivations for enthusiasts of

international law. Religious principle and dedication were, for example, at the heart of the movement in the nineteenth century for the promotion of international arbitration and adjudication. Many twentieth-century achievements of international law and international organization stem from the nineteenth-century religious enthusiasts of international law. That such religiously based enthusiasm for international law still exists is easily seen by an observation of the record religious groups surrounding such international causes as human rights law, disarmament and environmental law.

> Thirdly, the morality of religion has provided some of the glue that has made international law stick. The binding force of any law, international law included, cannot rest solely on force. The legitimacy of international law and international organizations ultimately is a function of widespread individual beliefs that the law and its authorities are right and appropriate. International lawyers have long recognized the potential of religious and moral belief for building a sense of international community whereby the peoples of the globe will be concerned with the fate of all the nations, not just their own.

With specific reference to international humanitarian law, Carolyn Evans (2005: 2) has equally argued that religion "can have persuasive value to those who are, or who consider themselves to be, outside the scope of traditional international law, particularly the ever more important non-state actor. It can add an important moral or emotional dimension to reasons for compliance with international law. Even a pragmatic, secular advocate of international humanitarian law may see strategic advantages to the selective use of aspects of religious traditions to bolster compliance and commitment to the laws of war."

The accommodationist theory has often been found useful by other religious advocates who seek to challenge the European and Christian foundations of modern international law and its perceived continued

171

influence on many aspects of the system despite its formal post-UN secularization. The contention is that through the accommodationist theory, other religions can contribute positively to the development of international law in a way that makes its principles much more universally persuasive to all religions. Ibrahim Shihata (1962: 101–102) has argued in respect of Islamic law that through the accommodationist theory, "contemporary international law will probably prove to be a more readily accepted system to [the] vast part of the international community vaguely referred to as the 'Muslim world'."

The main shortcoming and challenge to this theory is that it is usually one sided and most of its advocates do not often acknowledge that there are provisions in almost all religions that are evidently inimical to some principles of international law. There are many contemporary examples of violations of some fundamental principles of international law by states and non-state actors invoking religious provisions and viewpoints to justify their actions. Thus in his answer to whether religion has served as a catalyst or impediment to international law, Mark Janis (1993) further noted that apart from its potential of facilitating international law religion also has the potential "to complicate the work of international lawyers," which, in essence, brings us to the examination of the third theoretical perspective of the relationship between religion and international law – double-edged theory.

Double-edged theory

The double-edged theoretical perspective lies between the separationist and accommodationist theories. It generally reflects a realist view of the relationship between religion and international law and argues primarily that religion is like a double-edged sword that could be utilized either positively or negatively in its relationship with international law. In advancing the double-edged theory in relation to international humanitarian law,

Carolyn Evans (2005: 2) argued that in addressing the relationship between religion and international law "[s]ome writers focus only on the positive aspects of a particular religious tradition and dismiss any negative role played by that religion as a misinterpretation of its true meaning," while "[o]ther writers choose only to focus on the more dangerous and divisive aspects of religion" without acknowledging the positive aspects. That demonstrates a one-sided approach that does not present a full perception of the relationship. The double-edged theory remedies that one-sided approach by advocating, on the one hand, the important need to recognize that there are religious provisions that are international law friendly and can be utilized to promote compliance with international law, while emphasizing, on the other hand, the need to also acknowledge that there are religious provisions that are apparently conflicting with international law.

In addressing the relevance of religion to modern global governance, Richard Falk not only advances the double-edged theory but also points out the effect of each of its two edges and proposed how to deal with each of them. He noted that:

> [A]ll great religions have two broad tendencies within their traditions: the first is to be universalistic and tolerant toward those who hold other convictions and identities; the second is to be exclusivist and insistent that there is only one true path to salvation, which if not taken, results in evil. From such a standpoint, the first orientation of religion is constructive, useful, and essential if the world is to find its way to humane global governance in the decades ahead, while the second is regressive and carries with it a genuine danger of a new cycle of religious warfare carried out on a civilizational scale. The hope of the future is to give prominence and support to this universalizing influence of religion and, at the same time, to marginalize religious extremism based on an alleged dualism between good and evil.
>
> (Falk 2002: 7)

While Falk's proposition for dealing with each of the two edges of this theory (i.e. "give prominence and support to [the] universalizing influence of religion" and "marginalize religious extremism based on an alleged dualism between good and evil") is logical, the problematic aspect is with the latter point on how to marginalize religious extremism. Realistically, it would be extremely difficult to achieve such marginalization of religious extremism at the grassroots level in many religious societies as long as the principles and application of secular international law are continued to be seen at the grassroots, especially in the developing world, as being politically manipulated by the political elite in the developed world, and consequently regarded as incapable of impartially resolving long-running international crisis such as the Israeli–Palestinian crisis in the Middle East. For example, the Israeli–Palestinian crisis continues to influence the religious attitude of many Muslim states, organizations and individuals in ways that have impacted seriously on the relationship between religion and international law. Marc Gopin has emphasized the need for the international community to appreciate the fact that religion plays an important role in the Israeli–Palestinian crisis. He argued that international law's failure so far in resolving the crisis "stems in large part from its complete neglect of cultural and religious factors," and thus called for "greater integration of the religious communities of the region into the peace-building efforts" asserting that "only by including religion in the peace process can we move past fragile and superficial agreements and toward a deep and lasting solution, to the crisis" (Gorpin 2002: inner front jacket).

Thus, it is important to note that, similar to religion in its relationship with international law, international law can equally have a double-edged effect in its relationship with religion. On the one hand, international law can positively facilitate the flourishing of religion through its guarantee of international religious freedom and international religious

non-discrimination, but could, on the other hand, also be negatively applied to restrict religious beliefs and norms that may be indiscriminately considered incompatible with relevant principles of international law. A strict and indiscriminate secular interpretation of international law may sometimes have negative impacts on personal religious beliefs and practices of individuals and groups, which could diminish their confidence in a strictly secular system of international law. This is exemplified, for example, in the current jurisprudence of the European Court of Human Rights on the wearing of headscarves by Muslim women as required by their religious beliefs,[10] which has been criticized by some commentators (see, e.g. Ali 2007; Hoopes 2006; Vakulenko 2007). The possible negative impacts of an indiscriminate international secularism on the relationship between religion and international law are well reflected in Elizabeth Hurd's (2004: 240) observation that:

> [I]n an interdependent world in which individuals draw from different sources of morality, an indiscriminate secularism leads to three risks. There is the potential of a backlash from proponents of non-secular alternatives who are shut out of deliberations on the contours of public order. There is a risk of shutting down new approaches to the negotiation between religion and politics, in particular those drawn from non-Western perspectives. Finally, there is a risk of remaining blind to the limitations of secularism itself.

Richard Falk (2002: 7) also advances a similar view regarding what he calls "secular intolerance" in his own observation that:

> [S]ecular views that hold the line against their perception of religion also can adopt fundamentalist canons of belief, and view those who seek to center their identity on religious affiliation as intrinsically evil. Such secular intolerance is as unwelcome with respect to informing patterns of

global governance as its religious counter-part. Both religionists and secularists can only contribute to the emergence of humane forms of global governance if they adhere to an ethos of tolerance.

The double-edged theory thus provides us with an important perceptive tool for a critical evaluation of the relationship between religion and international law. It serves as a very practical and objective analytical process for understanding and managing that relationship in a manner that can lead to a mutually beneficial interaction between the two, leading to the realization of a more humane and universal international law. This theory, however, calls for pragmatism and legal dynamism, which brings us to the examination of the empirical and doctrinal perspectives of the relationship.

Empirical and doctrinal perspectives

Empirically religion, and international law may interact at four main levels as analyzed in this section. While the formal public role of Islam in the domestic laws of many Muslim states makes it feature prominently in the illustrations that follow, the analyses applies similarly to other religions in that regard.

The first level of interaction is in relation to the domestic laws of states where religion plays a formal role in national laws and policies. Owing to its public role in such domestic systems, religion becomes directly relevant in the interaction of international law with the domestic law of such states. Currently, this level of interaction between religion and international law occurs mostly in Muslim states whose constitutions formally recognize Islam as the religion of the state and Islamic law as part of state law. There are currently a significant number of Muslim states in that regard (see, e.g. Stahnke and Blitt 2005: 7–12). The formal role of Islam in such states has often influenced the state practices of the

relevant Muslim states in relation to international law in different ways, sometimes positively and sometimes negatively (see, e.g. Baderin 2001). I have analyzed, elsewhere, the different approaches and perspectives to such interaction between Islam and international human rights law in Muslim states and argued that such relationships need not necessarily be negative and adversarial but could be positive and harmonistic in ways that can facilitate the realization of the ideals of international law in Muslim states (Baderin 2007). The formal interaction between religion and international law at this level is relatively limited in states where religion has no direct formal role in the domestic law. For example, Ilias Bantekas (2007: 117) has noted in that regard that while Christianity as the dominant religion does inevitably influence a variety of policies in some western countries, the policy of those countries remains essentially and formally based on secular principles in relation to international law.

The second level of interaction is in relation to regional inter-governmental organizations (RIGOs) in which religion plays a formal role. The importance of RIGOs in international law is very well reflected in Chapter 8 of the UN Charter, thus where religion plays a formal role in the objectives of a RIGO that can inevitably create possible interaction between such religion and international law at the regional level. Similar to the example of domestic law in Muslim states above, the Organization of Islamic Conference (OIC) is a distinctive example in that regard. The OIC Charter provides that the organization is, among other objectives, to promote Islamic spiritual, ethical, social, and economic values among the member states as an important means of achieving progress for humanity.[11] The OIC has in that regard adopted instruments that make reference to Islam as a relevant factor in relation to international law in the Muslim world. However, it has also consistently expressed its commitment to international law and cooperation with the UN but usually emph-asized the role of Islam in that regard. In 2004 the organization made a submission to the UN General Assembly in respect of proposed reforms of the UN Security Council stating that "any reform proposal, which neglects the adequate representation of the Islamic Ummah in any category of members in an expanded Security Council will not be acceptable to the Islamic countries."[12] This obviously reflects an accommodationist approach. Formal interaction between religion and international law at this level is also relatively limited in RIGOs where religion does not play a formal role in the system. For example, a proposal by European churches for a formal recognition and reference to Christianity in the Constitution of the Euro-pean Union (EU) during the drafting and consultation stages of the constitution was discarded in the end, which was obviously a reflection of the separationist theory (Bantekas 2007: 129–30).

The third level of interaction is in relation to the religious freedom of individuals and groups, while the fourth level is in relation to other non-state actors such as religious non-governmental organizations (NGOs) and institutions. As international law has, today, moved beyond its traditional state-centric nature, it applies not only strictly to states but may impact directly or indirectly on the lives and activities of individuals, groups and other non-state actors respectively. Thus the interaction between religion and inter-national law occurs not only in relation to the practices of states and inter-governmental organizations but also in relation to the reli-gious beliefs and practices of individuals and groups. Relevant aspects of international law, such as human rights, environmental law, refugee law, and humanitarian law brings international law into direct contact with the religious beliefs and practices of indi-viduals and groups in different parts of the world today. As earlier noted, international human rights law acknowledges the import-ance of religion in human society by provid-ing for the right to freedom of religion, which includes the right to collective practice and public manifestation of religion by indi-viduals and groups as long as this does not violate public order or the fundamental rights of others.[13] It also prohibits religious dis-crimination against individuals and groups,[14] which apparently facilitates the flourishing of religion and enables individuals and religious groups to plead the right to religious freedom in defense of their religious beliefs and values, which augurs for a harmonious relation-ship. By the same token, international law does challenge religious norms in different ways, which equally raises the possibility of a conflicting relationship between the two in relation to individuals and groups. A common example is the possibility of conflict between the limits of freedom of expression and free-dom of religion under international human rights law.

Apart from the relationship at the level of individuals and groups, there are also today many non-governmental organizations (NGOs) motivated mainly by religious prin-ciples and values into participating actively and positively in different areas of international law. The need for interaction between religion and international law at the level of NGOs and other religious institutions was demonstrated in the hosting of a conference on interfaith cooperation to promote world peace within the context of international law at the UN headquarters in June 2005 at the end of which the conference recommended "an expansion and deepening of the rela-tionship between the United Nations and civil society, including religious NGOs."[15] The relationship at this level is also demonstrated by the active involvement and influence of religious institutions such as the Roman Catholic Church on issues such as abortion, death penalty, use of force, human rights and other important issues of international law (Bantekas 2007: 131–32).

The consequential question from the empirical perspective is whether these differ-ent levels of interaction between religion and

175

international establish any legal basis for religion as a possible source of obligation or right under international law, which brings us to the doctrinal perspective of the relationship.

As stated earlier, the UN Charter makes no direct reference to religion as a source of international law. However, the Charter also does not contain any provision prohibiting relationship or interaction between religion and international law. Under Article 38 of the ICJ Statute,[16] the main sources of international law are international treaties, customary international law and general principles of law recognized by civilized nations.[17] Certainly, where state parties to an international treaty consent to the inclusion of a religious principle or norm as a provision in a treaty, this would be binding on the parties as long as such religious principle or norm does not violate a norm of *jus cogens* under general international law.[18] A good example of this is the provision in Article 20(3) of the UN Convention on the Rights of the Child (1989b) which includes "*kafalah* of Islamic law" as a recognized means of alternative care for a child temporarily or permanently deprived of his or her family environment. This inclusion of a relevant principle of Islamic law in a substantive provision of a treaty under international law demonstrates the practicality of the accommodationist theoretical perspective analyzed earlier.

With regards to customary international law, I argued earlier that the approach of the international tribunals in the *Eritrea vs. Yemen* and *United States Diplomatic and Consular Staff in Tehran* cases, each of which referred to relevant religious principles respectively, can contribute to the development of customary international law especially in relation to the identification of local custom among a group of states that follow particular local practices accepted as law between them. For example, in the *Eritrea vs. Yemen* case the tribunal had referred to Islamic religious principles to establish that "the traditional fishing regime around the Hanish and Zuqar Islands and the islands of Jabal al-Tayr and the Zubayr group

is one of free access and enjoyment for the fishermen of both Eritrea and Yemen," which must be preserved for their benefit.[19] That approach was, in my view, a relevant and valid means of establishing the local custom in that context between the parties based on the facts before the tribunal. Similarly, in the case of *Saudi Arabia vs. Aramco* the arbitrator referred to relevant principles of Islamic law to support the customary nature and the universal recognition of the principle of *pacta sunct servanda* in international law by observing that "Muslim law does not distinguish between a treaty, a contract of civil or commercial law" and that "[a]ll these types are viewed by Muslim jurists as agreements or pacts, which must be observed . . . as expressed in the Koran: 'Be faithful to your pledge, when you enter into a pact'."[20] Another significant example can be cited of Judge Weeramantry's (as he then was) dissenting opinion in the case concerning the *Legality of the Threat or Use of Nuclear Weapons*,[21] in which he referred notably to different religious traditions as follows:

It greatly strengthens the concept of humanitarian laws of war to note that this is not a recent invention, nor the product of any one culture. The concept is of ancient origin, with a lineage stretching back at least three millennia. As already observed, it is deep-rooted in many cultures – Hindu, Buddhist, Chinese, Christian, Islamic and traditional African. These cultures have all given expression to a variety of limitations on the extent to which any means can be used for the purposes of fighting one's enemy. The problem under consideration is a universal problem, and this Court is a universal Court, whose composition is required by its Statute to reflect the world's principal cultural traditions. The multicultural traditions that exist on this important matter cannot be ignored in the Court's consideration of this question, for to do so would be to deprive its conclusions of that plenitude of universal authority which is available to give it added strength – the strength resulting from the depth of the tradition's historical roots and the width of its geographical spread.[22]

The learned judge then went on to provide detailed analysis of the relevant principles of the different religions to accumulate universal support for his opinion that the use or threat of use of nuclear weapons is illegal in all circumstances.

All these cases and references by the different international tribunals just examined establish that while religion may not serve directly as sources of obligation under international law, it could nevertheless serve as a valid complementary means of establishing customary international law in relevant cases as confirmed by the tribunal in the *Eritrea vs. Yemen* that "in today's world, it remains true that the fundamental moralistic general principles of the Quran and the Sunna may validly be invoked for the consolidation and support of positive international law rules in their progressive development towards the goal of achieving justice and promoting the human dignity of mankind."[23] The same is true of relevant "moralistic general principles" of all other religions, as was eruditely reflected by Judge Weeramantry in his dissenting opinion in the *Legality of the Threat or Use of Nuclear Weapons* case earlier cited.

Similarly, there have been representations for indirect reference to religious principles through "the general principles of law recognized by civilized nations" as well as through Article 9 of the ICJ Statute, which provides that in electing the judges of the ICJ "the election shall bear in mind not only that the persons to be elected should individually possess the qualifications required, but also that in the body as a whole the representation of the main forms of civilizations and of the principal legal systems of the world should be assured." In a memorandum presented by delegates of Muslim states to the League of Nations in September 1939 and to the UN Conference in San Francisco in April 1945, it was submitted that Islam constituted one of the main forms of civilization and Islamic

law one of the principal legal systems of the world referred to in Article 38 of the Statute of the Permanent Court of International Justice under the League of Nations, which was subsequently adopted as Article 38 of the ICJ Statute (Mahmassani 1966: 222). A survey of different statements by Muslim states and by the OIC reflects that this perception is still held by many Muslim states today. A similar assertion has been made by Shabtai Rosenne (2004: 63), in the context of Judaism and the development of international law, to the effect that the provisions of Article 9 of the ICJ Statute is a positive acknowledgment of the need for international law to "draw upon the general legal experience of mankind," which, he argued, "draws attention to certain features of what might be termed the intellectual components of public international law, and as such, as is being increasingly recognized, it has wider implications."

Conclusion

The current growing wave of scholarship on religion and international law is a strong indication that religion is still very relevant to the modern evolution and future development of international relations and international law, even though this, as observed by Jonathan Fox (2001), is often overlooked by the mainstream literature on international law and international relations. However, it has been asserted notably that if international law must achieve its aim of developing "a legal framework that emphasizes our common humanity and dignity" in today's world, then "international lawyers can no longer afford to ignore the importance that religion plays for many individuals and many societies" (Janis and Evans 2004: vii).

[Author note: I thank Professor Robert McCorquodale and professor Mathew Craven for reading through the draft of this chapter and for their kind comments. Responsibility for the views expressed herein is, however, mine alone.]

Notes

1 For an analysis of the complexity of defining religion in international law, see, e.g. Gunn 2003.

2 Jamar (2001: 609) observes eloquently that: "Religion is like law: the more closely we try to define it, the more it slips through our grasp. Religion is like law: both address fundamental issues about ordering society and the status and nature of the individual within it. Religion is like law: both engender passionate disagreement about their proper content and functions."

3 See Peace Treaty of Westphalia of 24 October 1648, http://www.yale.edu/lawweb/avalon/westphal.htm.

4 See, e.g. United Nations Charter (1945) Art. 1 (3); Art. 13(1)(b); Art. 55(c) and Art. 76(c).

5 For example, Haynes (2005) observed that "[r]eligion's role in international relations has recently become an increasingly important analytical focus," and Hackett (2005: 661) observed that "the early 1990s marked an upsurge in literature recognizing the role of religion in the public sphere."

6 *Eritrea vs. Yemen* 119 ILR, 417.

7 See also Ravitch 2004, who asserted that "neutrality, whether formal or substantive, does not exist."

8 See also Ahdar and Leigh 2005: 73, where the authors argue that: "For Enlightenment separationists, separating church and state ensured that dangerous religious passions and 'superstitions' would be confined to the private sphere. When religion and government mixed the outcome could be disastrous as the Wars of Religion testified."

9 See, e.g. Weeramantry 2004: 368, who observed that more than 4 billion of the world's population are inspired by religious beliefs and norms.

10 See the case of *Layla Sahin vs. Turkey* (2005).

11 See the Preamble and Article II(A)(1) of the OIC Charter.

12 UN Doc. A/59/425/S/2004/808 (11 October 2004), para. 56.

13 See, e.g. Article 19 of ICCPR.

14 See, e.g. Art. 2 of ICCPR.

15 "Report of the Convening Group of the Conference on Interfaith Cooperation for Peace: Enhancing Interfaith Dialogue and Cooperation towards Peace in the 21st Century", 22 June 2005: 2.

16 The ICJ Statute is annexed to the UN Charter, of which it forms an integral part.

17 The subsidiary sources are "judicial decisions and teachings of the most qualified publicists of the various nations" and are not considered here.

18 This is pursuant to Article 53 of the Vienna Convention on the Law of Treaties (1969).

19 Award of the Arbitral Tribunal in the Second Stage of the Proceedings between Eritrea and Yemen (Maritime Delimitation), 17 December 1999, para. 101.

20 *Saudi Arabia vs. Aramco* 1963: 27 ILR 117.

21 *Legality of the Threat or Use of Nuclear Weapons* 1996: 35 ILM.

22 Dissenting Opinion of Judge Weeramantry, para. 2.

23 *Eritrea vs. Yemen* 119 ILR, 417.

12

The struggle for an international constitutional order

Marc Weller

International law has come under pressure in recent years. The possible rise in unilateral action by the United States, claims of exceptionalism in relation to "rogue states," the failure to respond effectively to man-made humanitarian disasters and genocide, and the Asian values debate have all undermined the credibility of the universal legal order. However, although somewhat obscured by these day-to-day developments in international politics, very significant advances have taken place in international law. These changes are driven by the readjustment of the international system to new, postmodern realities. They include a questioning of state sovereignty, the increasing role of non-state actors in the international public realm, the ever increasing need for transnational cooperation in the face of common challenges and the entrenchment of certain universal core values. Gradually, these factors are combining to establish a global constitutional order.

Set against this background, this chapter analyzes recent trends in the international legal order relating to issues of statehood, sovereignty, democracy, the law-making process, international competencies and institutions, and compliance management. It argues that these developments, when taken together, reveal far more advanced structures of international life than are generally presumed to exist. The international constitutional law approach offers a unifying framework for understanding

these advances, both to international legal experts and to scholars of international relations.

International law appears to exist in two parallel universes. On the one hand, recent events have pointed to a risk of, and a possible rise in, unilateralism, exemplified mainly in U.S. action in relation to Iraq and in NATO's aerial campaign against Kosovo. The two episodes also appear to have undermined the credibility of core rules of the international system, such as the prohibition of the use of force and non-intervention. Moreover, in this context, arguments were made based on so-called exceptionalism that seemed to erode the universal ambition of the international legal order. Negative exceptionalism would purport to exclude "rogue" or otherwise unreliable or dangerous states from the protection of international legal rules. Positive exceptionalism would remove states claiming to act on behalf of what they claim to be global community values from certain international legal constraints. While this approach may have characterized what may have been a rather brief "unipolar moment" for the U.S., other states may follow this example. The Russian Federation, in reasserting its position as a great power, has started to exhibit ambivalence towards key international legal rules. Others may follow.

There is also an argument about the fragmentation of the international legal order, purportedly evidenced by a divergence in the jurisprudence of a variety of specialized or regional international courts and tribunals, that has contributed to this development. Indeed, the debate about "national or regional particularities," recently sparked by certain Asian states, has called into question the assumption that the most fundamental values enshrined in international human rights and humanitarian rules are, indeed, universally shared. Moreover, the basic constituent unit of the classical legal order, the state, has come under threat from disintegrative tendencies, such as violent dissolution or opposed unilateral secession. Non-state actors demonstrated on September 11, 2001 that they, too, can wield a decisive influence in global politics that is unlikely to be significantly constrained by the classical rules of the international system, including in particular humanitarian law.

These disintegrative tendencies are counterbalanced by the steadier, long-term development of the international system since 1945. These developments consist of the consolidation of international core values, the move away from the principle of strict consent in the creation of international legal rules with universal ambition, the increasingly complex variety of international actors, and the management of compliance with international legal obligations. Taken together, it is argued by a steadily increasing number of legal scholars that we are heading towards an international constitutional system based on common core values, the international rule of law and mechanisms for law enforcement (albeit largely decentralized ones). Indeed, a bibliographic search in support of this chapter has revealed in excess of 100 recent major scholarly articles addressing international constitutionalism (see, among others, Caldani and Ángel 2004; de Wet 2006a; Fassbender 2007; Fischer-Lescano 2003;

Frowein 2000; Habermas 2005; Kolb 2001; Ku 2005; Opsahl 1961; Peters 2005, 2006; Tomuschat 1997; and von Bogdandy 2006).

The question arises therefore of whether the international constitutional approach is, indeed, grounded in the modern realities of international life, and whether it is likely to retain or gain credibility in the light of the disintegrative challenges to which reference was made at the outset.

International constitutional approaches

A distinction is often drawn between international constitutionalism and international constitutional law. International constitutionalism is seen as a proactive, future-oriented campaign, agitating in favor of the development of an international constitutional system of world governance. It is a programmatic movement, building on other approaches, including "world federalism" and other essentially Kantian projects that have occupied thinkers for several centuries. On one hand, the long tradition of projects to build perpetual peace through world law imbues this approach with intellectual weight. On the other, the very fact that projects of this kind have tended to be formulated over several centuries, without implementation, is also seen as an indication of a lack of promise. The failure to achieve full implementation of such designs, often proposed at times of significant change or upheaval within the international system, has reduced the credibility of constitutionalism in the eyes of some who consider it an "idealist" construct. This view has also been extended to more recent arguments in favor of the international constitutional organization of the world, for instance at the end of the First and Second World Wars (Clark and Sohn 1958; Verdross 1926).

In contrast to international constitutionalism, which is essentially a movement agitating in favor of global social change, the international constitutional law approach is significantly more pragmatic. Previously, this latter approach was dominated by Austro-German scholars educated in Kelsen's strictly logical theory of the hierarchy of legal competences, and a civil law belief in the centrality of statutes and their literal application (hence, the heavy emphasis on the U.N. Charter as "the" international constitution). Seen from this perspective, international constitutional legal studies are devoid of a romantic campaigning element – the concern is principally with the present state of affairs and not with an imagined future. The school of international constitutional law is rooted in empiricism. It claims that key elements of an international constitution can already be observed in operation – to observe them we need only to shift our vantage point, our analytical paradigm.

Of course, there are various incarnations of the international constitutional law approach (see for example, Fassbender 2005; Johnston 2005). At its most all-encompassing, international constitutional law concerns itself with all public decisions. Such a system would be similar to the vision articulated in Philip Allott's *Eunomia* – a self-regulating global structure managing the exercise of public authority, in which the significance of the state has been much reduced (Allott 2001, 2002). At the other end of the spectrum, by contrast, one finds rather narrow and restrictive approaches. For instance, a significant amount of energy has been expended in arguing whether or not the U.N. Charter itself can be described as an international constitution (see, for example, Crawford 2002b; Dupuy 1997; Fassbender 1998a, 1998b; Franck 2003). Clearly, taken alone, this view is too mono-dimensional and simplistic to describe accurately the complex international constitutional processes of the global legal system. The U.N. Charter does not offer much insight into the regulation of public power outside the narrow context of international peace and security. Moreover, it is somewhat outdated in its identification of the core values underpinning the universal international

constitution, and in its emphasis on the purportedly inherent rights of states.

Others have attempted to construct a picture of international constitutionalism by observing the development of self-contained legal regimes at the international level (Álvarez 2001). For instance, at the regional level, the EU has been taken as a model of international constitutional development (Pernice 1999, 2002; Ruiz-Fabri and Grewe 2004; Uerpmann 2003). In terms of sectoral regimes, much scholarship has been applied to the WTO as a functional constitutional order at the international level (Petersmann 1996/7). Moreover, in the absence of the kind of advanced institutionalization apparent in the WTO, other sectoral regimes of international co-operation, such as the environment, have been regarded as the seeds of constitutionalization (Scheyli 2002). Of course, these regional or sectoral approaches alone do not make a persuasive case in favor of a genuinely universal and comprehensive international constitutional order either. After all, part of the reason for the formation of special regional or sectoral regimes may well be the very absence of effective regulation at the universal or general level. Furthermore, it is not always clear whether the mechanisms of regional or sectoral integration are, in fact, capable of being transferred to the universal level in all respects. Quite clearly, the organized global community does not yet function in all, or even most, of its aspects as a supranational organization, ordered according to one constitutional text and equipped with a single set of interlocking institutions. Instead, we are witnessing the development of a system that is becoming ever more complex. Still, this approach also adds to our growing understanding of the "legalization" and "constitutionalization" of international life.

Still other approaches focus on the interaction between national and international law (Bryde 2003; de Búrca and Gerstemberg 2006; Cottier 1999; Kadelbach and Kleinlein 2006; Rensmann 2006). This resurgence of "monist" approaches to law, with the addition of the more recently discovered concept of multilevel international governance, is another useful instrument in the analysis of international constitutional law. This analytical toolbox is further complemented by advances in international relations theory, drawing, in particular, on regime theory, liberal and democratic theory and the growing international governance literature. In fact, there are several points of contact between developing theories of global multilevel governance and the international constitutional law approach, both in law and in international relations. Indeed, the international constitutional law approach, in its more modest form, can well be considered an evolution of the "international community" doctrine, shared by both disciplines and advanced by some of their most venerable exponents.[1]

While there remains a diversity of perspectives, it is nonetheless possible to discern a gradual convergence of approaches. The dichotomy between "idealist" constitutionalism and the positivist international constitutional law approach is gradually being bridged. Clearly, the core elements of an international constitution already exist and can be described in positivist terms. However, it is also evident that the international constitutional system is still evolving. Hence, it is legitimate to foster visions for its future development without being exposed to the charge of being naively "idealist."[2] Moreover, international constitutional investigations that draw on regional or sectoral legal regimes, or a reevaluation of the relationship between national and international law, fit usefully within a broader emerging picture of an evolving international constitutional system. Indeed, Erika de Wet, first Professor of International Constitutional Law in the University of Amsterdam, defines international constitutional law as:

[A] system in which the different national, regional and functional (sectoral) constitutional regimes form the building blocks of the international community ("international polity") that is underpinned by a core value system common to all communities and embedded in a variety of legal structures for its enforcement.

(de Wet 2006a: 53)

The diverse approaches to international constitutional law can thus be regarded as the distinctive parts of a puzzle that, when fully assembled, reveals the overall picture of international constitutional law today (Weller 1997). That picture, it has to be admitted, remains a rather complex one. This complexity is due, in part, to the proliferation of constitutionally authorized non-state actors empowered to fulfill certain public functions within the universal system.

The particular elements constituting this multifaceted international constitutional system might, of course, be contested, depending on the respective legal tradition and background of the scholars contributing to the debate. Indeed, the question of whether or not the international legal system may now be considered an international constitutional one is contingent on the definition one adopts of a constitutional system more generally. Much like the ancient debate of whether international law is a legal system proper, a rigid transposition of legal concepts and terms from the domestic sphere is not of much use here.[3] Hence, those who believe that a constitution must be contained within a single constitutive document, generated in a revolutionary or otherwise singular constitution-making act, and must provide for a fully institutionalized system of lawmaking, adjudication and enforcement, will inevitably conclude that international law does not qualify. However, the very significant body of literature referred to above tends to agree on the essential elements of a constitutional system outside of the strictly domestic context. It is generally agreed that the international constitutional structure consists of formal and material rules, and of institutions. Formal rules concern the assignment and exercise of public authority at the international level. Material rules are substantive rules of governance. This chapter will concern itself with the formal constitution, mentioning the substance of material law only by way of example when considering the law-making process.

The formal international constitution

If formal international constitutional law concerns the organization of public power, then it must contain a number of key elements. First, the very concept of an international constitutional system implies that we are concerned with a system based on the rule of law. This means that all public decisions must be generated according to a constitutionally established process. The conduct of public and private actors must comply with the essential core values underpinning the constitutional system and with the rules it generates. Where disputes arise, all actors must have the right, ultimately, to have the dispute resolved on the basis of the law.

The first point to consider, therefore, concerns the assignment and exercise of public authority, or competence. In order to understand the fundamental shift that has taken place in this respect, it is necessary first to consider briefly the classical origins of the modern state system.

Classical antecedents

In classical doctrine, the sole constituents of the classical international system were states, represented exclusively by governments. These states were born nominally equal and free, and were endowed with imprescriptible rights (the so-called fundamental rights of states, purportedly enshrined in U.N. General Assembly Resolution 2625 (XXV)). Derogations from this natural state of freedom were only possible through consent, or perhaps through the actions of "great" states which dominated the system, despite the

existence of the nominal rule of sovereign equality.

The doctrine of absolute sovereignty which underpinned this classical system was expressed in Jean Bodin's *Six livres de la République*. Sovereignty denotes the supreme authority over all subjects and objects within a given territory. Thus, the very person of the prince, through divine right or social contract, was the ultimate source of all secular authority. Louis XIV really meant it when he said, "*l'etat c'est moi.*" Hence, public authority is only genuine if its origin can be traced back to a pronouncement by "the sovereign."

The absolute right to exercise public authority within the realm, and the exclusive right to represent all within its claimed jurisdiction in relation to other states, remained unchallenged, even when the Enlightenment transferred the source of sovereign authority from the very person of the prince to the abstraction of the state. Although political philosophers asserted a sphere of autonomy on behalf of those trapped within this all-powerful state, nineteenth-century nationalism consolidated their effective disenfranchisement. A population could only actualize its historic potential if it acted as a Hegelian nation, through the institutions of the state.

By contrast, the modern state system of the twentieth century purported to embody the principle of popular sovereignty. Sovereignty was no longer held uniquely by the person of the prince or the abstraction of the state, but rather was vested collectively in all the constituents of the state. The authority to govern, and to represent the governed internationally, was to be based on the will of the population of the state in question. However, this process of transmitting the will of the people and thus of legitimizing public acts was generally illusory, as the international legal rules crafted by governments continued to assert that any effective administration reflected, by definition, the will of the people. Hence, governments which could maintain themselves through whatever means were entitled to benefit from the fundamental rights which attached to the concept of the state, such as the right of non-intervention, the right to receive assistance in engaging internal and external enemies, and so on.

The legitimizing myth of the universal principle of popular sovereignty was maintained through the adoption of the concept of human rights. These were international guarantees of governmental conduct which purported to protect individuals who remained submerged within the state and the international system as a whole. However, as Philip Allot has so convincingly demonstrated, the very concept of human rights is one which brings the disenfranchisement of the domestic constituents into relief. By agreeing to accept human rights obligations, governments confirm that the existence of such rights is in fact contingent on an act of will on their part. Hence, the state, represented exclusively by the government, confirmed the principle of absolute power over its constituents through the very act of "granting" them certain rights.

Similarly, the modern feature of the development of relative international personality of non-state actors did not fundamentally attack the theory of the concentration of sovereignty within the state. The powers of public international organizations, for example, were explained in a way which left intact the view that all public authority must ultimately emanate from the state structure. Hence, it was argued that those international organizations which enjoyed some form of autonomous decision-making powers in relation to states and other actors did so precisely because they had been endowed with such authority by their member states.

Reassessment of public power in the international realm

At present, we are witnessing the destruction of the legitimizing myth of classical and modern sovereignty. It is becoming increasingly evident that the sovereign state,

exclusively controlled and represented by an internationally unaccountable government, no longer exists. The term "state" no longer describes a metaphysical entity endowed with supreme internal and external authority. Instead, it is a technical term which modestly represents one of many layers of competence to which individuals have transferred public powers. Other such layers of competence might have been created in the form of non-governmental organizations exercising public functions; regional structures of governance, the authority of which is not derived from a grant of authority from above; supranational structures, such as the European Union (EU); or universal mechanisms of public administration, including the United Nations Security Council.

Just as the "loyalty" of its constituents is no longer necessarily focused exclusively on the state itself, sovereignty is no longer a commodity located uniquely in the abstraction of the state. Instead, "sovereignty" is constantly being exercised by all, through the infinitely complex process of assigning authority to appropriate and often overlapping structures of governance, from the local to the universal.

At present, of course, this assignation of powers still favors the state as the principal layer delegated competence. However, and crucially, it is not a creature which, simply by virtue of its existence, enjoys all powers that it has not positively relinquished through an act of consent. Instead, the state can exercise only those powers specifically delegated to it by its constituents or, expressly or impliedly, by the international legal order. In addition, the administration of state powers is subordinated to the universal constitutional process, both externally and, in some respects, even internally. That is to say, the state is always embedded within the international constitution and cannot, even through an act of unanimous will by its constituents, give itself powers inconsistent with that constitutional order. For instance, if the population of a state were to vote overwhelmingly to authorize their governing authorities to commit genocide against a minority on the state territory, such action, however democratically legitimate, would offend the international constitutional order and attract its condemnation, sanction and even the possibility of armed intervention.

If the exercise of public powers must be derived from the international constitutional order or from a grant of authority from constituents, two difficult issues arise. First, there is the increasingly complex issue of the authoritative assessment of the competence of individual actors on the international scene. Second, there arises the question of the legitimacy of a grant of authority. According to the international legal principle that the authority to govern must be based on the will of the governed, one might expect a process of validation of governmental authority according to the democratic principle.

Measuring competence

Classically, the state was presumed to enjoy all public authority, including the full and complete right of representation and action at the international level. According to the international constitutional model, the powers of the state must be founded in the vesting of authority within it by its constituency. When engaging in international contact, it would therefore, at least in theory, be necessary to verify the extent of competence enjoyed by each and every individual state. In reality, however, internal constitutional assignments of power (for instance the power to engage in foreign relations, conclude treaties, participate in the work of international organizations, and so on) remain fairly similar across the major regions of the globe. Nevertheless, a number of interesting and new particularities can be observed. For instance, the member states of the EU no longer exercise authority in relation to issue areas that fall within the competence of the Union. They lack the legal capacity to enter international agreements with regard to certain problems. For instance, the

EU sought membership in the International Food and Agricultural Organization (FAO) based on the argument that its own members (also represented in the organization) no longer had the competence to act on all matters falling within its purview.

While this phenomenon relates to the upward move of sovereignty to a supranational structure, a parallel trend of downward delegation can also be observed. For instance, in several recent internationalized constitutional settlements, the central government no longer enjoys the power to make binding agreements in relation to certain autonomous regions without their specific consent. The process of evaluating the extent of competence enjoyed by actors on the international place will therefore increase in relevance, including in relation to the state.

Moreover, the material international constitution denies altogether the right of representation to states whose very existence offends the international constitutional order. This is achieved through the subjective criteria of statehood which prevail over the traditional, objective elements of the definition of a state. Hence, an entity which exists, or has come into existence, in violation of material rules of constitutional standing (see below) will never be able to attain statehood, however vigorously it displays effective control over a defined territory and a permanent population. Thus, the Turkish Federated Republic of Northern Cyprus, brought into being through an unlawful use of force, has not attained statehood. Southern Rhodesia, created to negate the claim of the indigenous population to self-determination, was denied statehood and subjected to international sanctions. The Bantustans of South Africa, contrived to facilitate the continuation of the crime of apartheid, never achieved statehood. The Republika Srpska had to content itself with status short of statehood, as it had come into being as a result of armed intervention and possible genocide.

Other aspects of quality control for new entities claiming a cluster of competences

185

which are presumed to attach to statehood relate to their acceptance of the fundamental rules of the universal constitutional order. Participation in that order may be denied to entities which fail to commit themselves to the material rules of constitutional standing and to essential mechanisms for their implementation. The EU rules on the recognition of states, adopted at the time of the dissolution of the former Yugoslavia, confirm this trend.

Processes and mechanisms for assessing the authenticity and the extent of authority of actors within the system will gradually expand to cover not only states and governments, but also non-state actors (Schachter 1997: 7).

The authoritative external assessment of the scope or extent of competence, once it has been granted by the internal constituents of the relevant political system or sub-system, can be demonstrated once again in relation to the EU. Other actors have had to devise means of determining whether it is the Union, its member governments, or both, which are internationally entitled to represent the constituents of the European system in relation to matters in which the Union claims either parallel or exclusive competence. This need will increase as more substantive powers migrate to regional or functional organizations featuring elements of supra-nationality.

The emerging universal constitution is also moving gradually towards recognition of the fact that "private" actors, in particular NGOs and corporations, are increasingly involving themselves in the administration of public functions. Similar mechanisms for the confirmation of the authenticity and the extent of authority claimed by such actors have yet to be established.

Democratic legitimacy

The problem of democratic legitimacy has not eluded writers on international constitutional law (Charnovitz 2003; Kumm 2004). It is, of course, not possible here to rehearse

the entire debate over democratic entitlement in international law. Briefly, this entitlement consists of two main elements: on the one hand, there is the right of populations to be governed internally and to be represented externally by authorities established on the basis of, and acting in accordance with, their will; on the other, there is the question of the democratic functioning of international constitutional processes at the international level (Bryde 2005). For the purposes of this short introduction, it is sufficient merely to note a number of developments concerning the former – the legitimacy of acts of governance at the domestic level.

First, there is a growing recognition that the existence of the state itself must be based on an exercise of the will of the people. Where a major constitutional change, such as dissolution, secession or merger, occurs, a referendum, or at least an authentic decision by the democratically elected parliament, is required. Similarly, where a new constitution is generated, for instance after a period of violent upset due to internal conflict, it will often now be endorsed through referendum or a decision by a popular assembly. Moreover, international peace support operations will, in such circumstances, invariably be involved in generating at least a first round of democratic elections aimed at ensuring that the new democratic consensus will indeed result in governance on the basis of the will of the governed.

This process is also in operation in relation to entities such as the institutions of the European Union. The referenda required in states which recently joined the EU, and which thus transferred significant public power to another layer of authority, can be used as an example in this respect as they can be said to reflect the acceptance of a legal rule requiring the validation of a significant transfer of competence from one layer to another though an act of choice by the relevant constituents.

Classically, international law treated the effective government as the exclusive entity entitled to exercise public authority within the state, and to represent it externally. The principle of periodic and genuine elections was not implemented with any seriousness. Effectiveness trumped democratic legitimacy. This, too, is now changing. There is significant international opposition to manifestly undemocratic practices of government, although it has to be admitted that the picture remains mixed. However, in a number of instances, the fundamental international constitutional principle that the authority to govern must be based on the will of the people is being acted upon. These are cases where effectiveness and legitimacy are so far apart that the structural requirement of representativeness must prevail over effectiveness.

Hence, the test of the legitimacy of the conduct of constitutional agents applying competences through public administrative acts, including governments especially, is no longer restricted to the mechanical and circular validation through the effectiveness criterion. Instead, the abstract principle of legitimacy in the exercise of authority has already been translated into substantive rules of fundamental dissociation. Accordingly, an effective authority can no longer claim to represent its constituents, either generally or in relation to specific functions of the state, if:

- the constituents have directly manifested this dissociation in elections that were actually held and which demonstrated clearly that the effective authorities did not represent the population (Haiti, Burundi)
- the effective authorities are actively exterminating a constitutionally relevant segment of the population (Iraq, Rwanda, Bosnia)
- the effective authorities are denying a population that which is necessary for its survival (Iraq, Somalia, Liberia)
- the central government has effectively disappeared and civil war has led to a need to re-establish constitutional legitimacy (Liberia, Somalia)

- the effective authorities have been established as the result of an unlawful use of force, or as the result of, or in pursuit of, international criminal conduct (Southern Rhodesia, South Africa, etc.).

Under those circumstances, the universal constitution permits action on behalf of a population, in the absence of consent from the effective authorities, directly in line with the express or implied desire of the population or a constitutionally relevant segment of the population. While this process of direct action on behalf of populations should, in principle, be conducted under a collective security mandate, recent practice indicates that provisional action can also be taken by regional organizations or even coalitions of states, provided the need for such action has been confirmed by an international objective agency and the action does not exceed that which is strictly necessary to counter the immediate emergency.

Within the international constitution, therefore, all public power is derived from a popular mandate. Its exercise is bounded by international legal constraints. State competence is no longer absolute and inherent. Instead, sovereignty is relative, if the term retains any meaning at all in a system where public power is attributed to innumerable potential layers of decision-making. Moreover, where *de facto* authorities effectively dissociate from the populations they claim to represent, direct action can be taken on behalf of these disenfranchised constituencies by other international actors, be they universal or regional organizations, or even states or collations of states.

Core values and law making

Classically, the state retained full control over the legal obligations to which it wished to be subjected. However, even during the heyday of positivism, most states also recognized that they were embedded in a rudimentary system of public order law – general international (or customary) law. International constitutional law is rooted in the presumption that states, as well as other actors, can only exist within a deep international constitutional legal order. This legal order establishes a mandatory, non-derogable environment for international action that operates irrespective of specific consent.

Hierarchy

Over the last 50 years, a rather sophisticated international constitutional mechanism has been generated to protect and promote core values of the international system. This mechanism does not offer merely a hierarchy of the so-called sources of law, which places those of constitutional standing at the top. Instead, it has devised a comprehensive set of interlocking doctrines and mechanisms to ensure that its core values are transmitted throughout the system and are not transgressed. This system consists of:

- the doctrine of general (or universal) law
- the doctrine of *erga omnes* obligations
- the doctrine of fundamental rules (*jus cogens*)
- the doctrine of serious breaches of obligations under peremptory norms of general international law
- the doctrine of crimes in international law.

General international law makes it possible to establish legal obligations that are truly universal and apply throughout the system. New states are deemed to be born into the obligation to comply with general rules of international law. Existing states will also be bound, even if their specific consent cannot be demonstrated. Without the authentic universality created through the doctrine of general international law, it would not be possible to speak of an international constitutional system.

If general international law renders legal obligations universally opposable, the *erga omnes* effect ensures that all states can profess a legal interest in compliance with those obligations of all other states. Hence, if Iraq invades Kuwait, all states are legally affected, as all states share an equal interest in maintaining an effective prohibition of the use of force. This phenomenon is also particularly relevant in relation to obligations contracted into by states, but the beneficiaries of the obligation are individuals or groups. For instance, if Myanmar/Burma persistently violates the human rights of its citizens, all other states can exhibit a legal interest in this conduct.

The next level of legal entrenchment of core international obligations is *jus cogens*, or the doctrine of peremptory norms of general international law. Peremptory norms are those rules of international law that apply to all under all circumstances. States can never suspend their obligations in relation to, or effectively conclude treaties that are inconsistent with, *jus cogens*. Moreover, facts or circumstances brought about in violation of *jus cogens* rules do not enjoy the protection of the international legal order that would ordinarily arise. Hence, if a state occupies territory in violation of the *jus cogens* obligation relating to the non-use of force, or the doctrine of self-determination, this administration, no matter how effective, can never mature to legal title.

The effect of rendering a legal nullity an act offensive to *jus cogens* is strengthened further by the doctrine of "serious breaches of obligations under peremptory norms of general international law." According to an influential document produced by the United Nations International Law Commission (ILC), gross or systematic failure by a state to comply with *jus cogens* rules triggers obligations incumbent on all other states. The latter must cooperate in seeking to bring to an end the breach in question. They must not recognize as lawful the situation brought about by the breach, nor can they render assistance to the offending state in maintaining that situation.

The final element in this cascade of mechanisms to protect international core values concerns individual crimes. Some offenses against *jus cogens* obligations are so abhorrent to the peace and security of mankind that they trigger direct and immediate international criminal responsibility of the individuals concerned. This may be the person or persons actively engaged in the acts, or those who ordered their commission. Hence, in addition to holding the state responsible for the conduct of those representing it, individual perpetrators may find themselves exposed to criminal liability administered by any other state, by specialized international courts or tribunals, or by the newly established International Criminal Court at The Hague.

These general mechanisms are capped by the emerging institutional architecture to protect and preserve core values of the international system. In particular, the U.N. Security Council has expanded its remit of action. It can now consider not only breaches of international peace, but will also consider threats to peace and security stemming from the internal conduct of governments or authorities. According to Article 103 of the U.N. Charter, such action trumps competing treaty obligations.

The core values of the international system of protection, evident in these doctrines and mechanisms include:

- prohibition of the use of force
- armed intervention
- colonialism, armed occupation, racist regimes and other violations of the right to self-determination
- slavery, torture and other crimes of humanity, including politically motivated rape
- forcible ethnic displacement and genocide.

It is noteworthy that these obligations can also be applied in relation to non-state actors, such as rebel movements or effective authorities that are denied the status of a government. The overall interest of the international constitutional order is, after all, to prevent or punish activities of this kind, irrespective of the identity of the perpetrator.

Consent

Classically, states could micro-manage the obligations to which they were subject by giving their consent only very selectively. Through the doctrine of reservations, states could even claim the benefit of membership in conventions with a universal aim, while still micro-tailoring contingent obligations in accordance with their wishes. Moreover, general international custom could only develop if it attracted virtual uniformity of practice and *opinio juris* (the subjective knowledge of being required to follow that practice as a matter of law), including states representing the major geographic and ideological systems of the world and states specifically affected by the rule in question. Moreover, states could exempt themselves from the application of individual rules seeking universal acceptance through the doctrine of persistent objection.

Even under this restrictive, consent-based regime, it was possible to generate an impressive body of general international law, whether it was of a formal constitutional kind (say the customary international law on treaties) or material (for instance, the customary law of the sea). Indeed, in some instances requiring rapid international regulation, the doctrine of "instant (general) custom" facilitated the informal establishment of universal legal regimes that had suddenly become necessary, for example, due to unexpected advances in technology (i.e. space travel bringing the moon within human reach). More recently still, it has been proposed that it is not sufficient to rely on universal conventions or the emergence of rules of custom in order to address issues of concern to all mankind. For instance, it is difficult to accept that a handful of "specifically affected states"

189

should be able to obstruct the development of environmental legal rules that are of essential importance for the well-being of the planet at a whole (Buzzini 2004; Charney 1993; Mosler 1974; Nadelmann 1990; Simma 1994; Tietje 1999; Tomuschat 1993; de Wet 2006b). Similarly, it has recently become apparent that it may be necessary to enforce certain obligations concerning proliferation of weapons of mass destruction even in relation to states that may not have contracted into the relevant proliferation regime, given that the threat posed by such weapons and technologies cannot be contained by national boundaries. The creation of "objective legal regimes," that is, of legal obligations created by some, but rendered opposable to others, has therefore taken place in some areas of international constitutional relevance.

Stability, change and the rule of law

In the past, international law appeared to some to be composed of rules of convenience, subject to the ever-changing interests of the state. The international constitutional order has addressed this problem by developing a system of rules governing the stability of international obligations. This development has taken place in large part through the work of the ILC, which has addressed the law of treaties and that of responsibility of states for internationally wrongful acts. While some legal regimes are immune from challenges (stability of borders) on account of changing circumstances, a cautious balancing of interest can take place in relation to those where continuous performance of previously established obligations would be manifestly unreasonable. Hence, by regulating the possible accommodation of changing interests, the stability of legal rules has been enhanced more generally. The previously fairly open doctrines of fortuitous event, *force majeure*, distress, necessity and *rebus sic stantibus* have been tamed through this codification, which subjected them to the general principle of *pacta sunt servanda*.

Compliance management

If legal rules within the international constitution are stable, the question of compliance with them still needs to be addressed. Given the absence of a central law-enforcement agency, this issue has traditionally been considered the weak spot of international law.

Rules of state responsibility

States and other internationally authorized actors have traditionally claimed that only they are competent to determine by which international legal obligations they are bound, and whether or not they are in compliance with these legal obligations. The freedom of states in assessing this level of compliance has been reduced somewhat through the codification of the law on state responsibility by the ILC.

A move away from auto-interpretation

The constituents of the international system retain, of course, considerable freedom in structuring their relations with other actors within the overall bounds of the international constitution. However, any actor is at all times entitled to insist on the application of legal rules in relation to all other actors. In particular, all actors have a right to have disputes with other actors decided on the basis of law, rather than on considerations that might be advanced by the other party. Even an actor which itself has violated essential principles of the universal constitutional order is entitled to the protection of its fundamental principles. For instance, a state that has violated the prohibition of the use of force remains protected by the rule of proportionality, which must govern the collective security response triggered by its conduct. Humanitarian principles also remain in operation in relation to that state, and its constituents. Individuals who commit international crimes retain the right to insist that they themselves do not suffer from violations of their non-derogable human rights, such as the freedom from torture or the right to a fair trial.

Of course, traditionally it was a significant structural deficit of the modern international order that there existed no comprehensive, compulsory jurisdiction. This meant that all disputes, of whatever kind, not settled through some other means, would ultimately be subject to the jurisdiction of a particular court or tribunal, such as the International Court of Justice at The Hague. This deficit has not yet been rectified through a universal obligation to submit all disputes not settled elsewhere. The Statute of the International Court of Justice contains an optional clause, permitting states to declare that they submit to the jurisdiction of the Court in relation to any other state making a similar declaration.

With the end of the Cold War, the number of submissions to this clause rose significantly, to its present number of 65 (although some declarations are restricted through certain reservations). However, perhaps more important is the proliferation of international conventions that now come equipped with dispute settlement clauses. Many of these conventions refer disputes relating to their interpretation or application to the jurisdiction of the World Court. Others will provide for conciliation or arbitration. Indeed, several universal sectoral (U.N. Convention on the Law of the Sea) or regional instruments come equipped with their own court or tribunal (for example, the European Court of Justice). Indeed, this development has been so pronounced that there is now debate over the risk of divergent jurisprudence emerging from this multitude of dispute settlement mechanisms. It is also to be noted that internationalized arbitrations between governmental and non-governmental (commercial) actors are on the rise. Hence, instead of having achieved comprehensive compulsory dispute settlement through one World Court, we are moving towards an ever denser network of dispute settlement mechanisms,

significantly reducing the ability of states to evade their legal obligations (Vicuña 2004; Warioba 2001; Watts 2001).

Moreover, other means of providing authoritative guidance on the existence and extent of international obligations are constantly being added and developed, be they U.N. or treaty-based specialist committees on human rights or other types of obligations, High Commissioners with remits over certain subjects, joint consultative commissions, and so on. Furthermore, many of these mechanisms are accessible not only to states but to other constituents as well, including individuals, groups, minorities, non-governmental organizations and multinational companies.

Enforcement techniques

With the exception of matters concerning international peace and security, there is no centralized international enforcement system. Even where international peace and security is concerned, allegations of double standards and selectivity in the practice of the U.N. Security Council remain relevant. Suggestions of reining in the application of the veto in the Security Councils through certain procedural innovations have not borne fruit. Instead, the use of force against Iraq in 2003 undermined the primacy of the Council in this respect. On the other hand, in instances where the attitudes of the permanent members have permitted it, the Council has engaged in an impressive series of actions. It has taken action in around 30 cases of internal armed conflict or humanitarian emergency, expanding its remit through such engagement. Moreover, it did fulfill its enforcement role, to an extent, in relation to the Kuwait crisis – the instance that was taken by some to define collective security within a new constitutionally-based world order. In addition, it has addressed new security challenges, such as international terrorism in the wake of the 9/11 attack, and it has found new modalities of action, including increasingly sophisticated sanctions regimes and other enforcement measures. These include the establishment of a border demarcation commission, disarmament commissions, very significant post-conflict state-building operations and the establishment of two *ad hoc* international criminal tribunals.

Of course, it is a mistake to focus principally or exclusively on the area of the use of force when considering international enforcement mechanisms. In the area of routine international interaction, the proliferation of international dispute settlement bodies noted above has contributed significantly to the implementation of international obligations. Where such a body has made an authoritative pronouncement on the law in any given case, instances of non-compliance have remained very rare. The expanding reach of international jurisdiction has therefore substantially reduced the classical problems within international law of auto-interpretation and of auto-enforcement. Traditionally, international law provided for the opportunity of self-help through the doctrine of reprisal, or counter-measures. In a prolonged debate, the ILC came close to proposing the virtual abolition of counter-measures by attaching to their application the submission of the dispute in question to third party settlement. In the final version of the ILC text on state responsibility this vision could not be maintained. However, the conditions for the adoption of counter-measures were stated in very restrictive terms, including the obligation not to infringe on the essential rules of international constitutional standing in the process.

Institutions

The ever-expanding reach of substantive legal regulation is paralleled by a growth in international institutions to administer this developing body of law. Of course, many international institutions remain very much under the control of member governments. However, other institutions have developed

functions and powers that remove them from such supervision. In fact, it is not possible in this short article to give even a flavor of the vast expansion of the role of international institutions, including the rise of very powerful non-governmental organizations, some of which have started to engage in the exercise of public functions.

The executive functions of public international organizations are already well known to scholars and practitioners. Obvious examples include the European Commission, the activities of the International Atomic Energy Agency, and the various U.N. High Commissioners and Special Rapporteurs charged with implementing mandates derived from the United Nations or regional organizations, including the Organization for Security and Cooperation in Europe. The range of executive functions of such institutions can be very extensive and include the authority to take and to implement public decisions, at times in the absence of the consent of states, of other international actors, or of the individuals at whom the decision is directed.

The authority of such institutions has generally expanded beyond that which was originally provided for in the constitutional documents that created them. The doctrines of implied powers and the presumption of the *intra vires* nature of decisions adopted by organs of international institutions led to an autonomous expansion of the public authority exercised by them, not only in respect of executive action but also in respect of the creation of legal regulation that is opposable to the members of the institutions.

In fact, there have been cases where institutions, rather than individuals or even states, have created other institutions that might themselves exercise significant powers. The establishment of the Iraq Claims Tribunals, the Iraq Boundary Delimitation Commission and the Yugoslavia and Rwanda Criminal Tribunals furnishes perhaps the most striking example of this practice. These institutions also illustrate the fact that international organizations no longer operate exclusively within one layer of substantive universal competence. Such institutions will not only address other institutions, but will interact across the universal system, with states, companies, NGOs and individuals. Some institutions will take decisions which pierce through layers of public authority and are directly applicable to individuals, companies and other actors. In the examples just mentioned, the exercise of public functions by international institutions directly interferes with, and partially displaces, state competence, precisely in the areas of their so-called "exclusive domestic jurisdiction."

The functioning of the United Nations Security Council and of regional organizations and mechanisms is now gradually being placed within the context of the substantive law of constitutional standing. Instead of open-ended powers to respond to threats to the peace, these institutions are gradually becoming enmeshed within the constitutional administration of the collective response to *jus cogens* violations.

The actions of international institutions also contribute in an important way to the identification of other rules of law, either in the general interpretation of, or in application to, concrete circumstances. Some institutions have been endowed with, or have arrogated to themselves without a specific grant of authority, the power to take a legally binding decision of a judicial or quasi-judicial character. The proliferation of institutions dedicated specifically to the authoritative identification of facts and law and the settlement of disputes has already been alluded to.

The vast importance of institution-building in relation also to the development of substantive legal standards has recently been demonstrated by the transformation of the Conference on Security and Cooperation in Europe into the organization it is today, and by the creation of the WTO. The latter case demonstrates with great force the fundamentally norm-creating function of institutionalized cooperation among actors, including increasingly non-state actors.

It must be noted, however, that the rapid growth in the exercise of constitutional functions by international institutions has not only undermined the classic or even modern paradigm of international relations, but also poses difficulties for the emerging universal constitution. Precisely because these institutions have arrogated so much authority for themselves, it will soon become a constitutional necessity to contemplate ways to ensure that their activities are indeed based on a grant of authority by their constituents, and that they comply with the rule of law and operate transparently and in a publicly accountable way.

Conclusion

It is not possible to list all of the recent developments relating to the emerging constitutional order within the confines of such a short chapter. Nevertheless, even this brief survey might help to establish that there exists a gradual movement towards a universal constitutional system which can be described and analyzed in legal terms. Such a change is unavoidable, in the light of the collapse of traditional concepts of essential importance to the classical, or even the modern, international system, especially the doctrine of unipolar sovereignty.

The proliferation of constitutionally empowered actors other than the state will make it necessary to create structures to manage their participation in the system effectively. This relates to the law-making process, to the process of authoritatively identifying legal obligations, including their general content and the concrete circumstances of their implementation, and to the mechanisms for ensuring compliance with such obligations.

In addition to the redistribution of authority away from the state, the need for genuinely global approaches to global problems will foster a climate for the development of the international system into a universal constitutional system. In this context, the increased role of international institutions in the administration of constitutional processes will reinforce and accelerate the development of formal and material constitutional law. However, there will remain the difficult challenge of ensuring the rule of law, transparency and accountability at all levels of public administration. The subordination of all levels of public authority, including international institutions, to the rule of law and democratic accountability will be a key element in this process. The ordering of the respective competences of the emerging actors, in terms of their geographic scope, their subject matter, the other constituents to which the competences relate, the hierarchy of obligations, and so on, will also require a significant intellectual effort.

Of course, the process of constitution building will not be a linear one, nor is it necessarily a conscious one. In this phase of global reordering, some actors have actually reverted to patterns of conduct which would be more comfortably situated within the classical paradigm of international relations than in a post-modern concept of a constitutional order. Some of the advances in the architecture of the international system were not intended as the building blocks of the emerging constitution, but rather as pragmatic solutions to immediate and practical problems. These developments furnish the elements, as it were, of an unconsciously or intuitively derived architecture for the future, and much of the practice which evidences the emergence of constitutional structures is still being conducted from the perspective of the modern, state-based system.

We are therefore at an intermediate stage in the development of the international constitutional order, one of international (or inter-state), rather than global, constitutionalism. That process of constitution building is being sustained through the activities of traditional and non-traditional actors within the system, often in a haphazard, semiconscious way. However, the melting away of the modern state system into a regime of increasingly complex structures of relative authority or competence will make the definite and intellectually organized transition towards a universal constitutional system unavoidable. In fact, many of the relevant actors are beginning to come to the Allottian realization that they are already engaged in the creation of just such a system.

Notes

1 The origin, or rediscovery, of this doctrine in international law may be traced back to Sir Hersh Lauterpacht's work on "The Grotian Tradition" in the field. The communitarian view was also significantly developed by leading German scholars, such as Hermann Mosler and, most recently, Christian Tomuschat. The latter argued for this extension of communitarianism into constitutionalism *in extenso* in his groundbreaking Hague Academy Lectures of 1974, a concept which he developed in his later work (1997). In the IR field, it is of course Hedley Bull, followed by David Held, who are associated with the gentle 'English school' approach to, initially, international society, and then the international community.
2 Of course, Philip Allott is right to point out that idealist perspectives are entirely appropriate and valid approaches, given the transformative power of law and legal studies.
3 Those who denied the legal quality of international law would ordinarily do this on the basis of the Austinian definition of law as a command backed by a sanction, arguing that the lack of institutionalized enforcement precluded the legal quality of international law.

Section III

Law and power in international society

13

Law and force in the twenty-first century

Gerry Simpson

In this chapter, the law of force (or the ius ad bellum) is represented as the performance of an argument between three competing and potent visions of international legal order. These can be characterized as an absolutist view that seeks to approach war and peace through non-negotiable, universalizable and unqualified moral truths, a sovereigntist perspective that holds the desires or fears of the sovereign to be the single source of legitimacy in assessing decisions to go to war or engage in diplomacy and (an occasionally militant) legal pacifism that wants to use law to abolish war. This may help account for the law's thematic ambiguities, its textual evasions, its judicial agonies and its interminable crises. It may explain also why its primary organs repeatedly move from institutional paralysis to hyperactivism and back. The Iraq war, for example, rather than being viewed as an extraordinary challenge to the future of international law, can be reinterpreted, in these terms, as part of the perpetual crisis of law, war and peace.

Three fantasies

On February 6, 2004 in the German city of Munich, Donald Rumsfeld, then Secretary of Defence in the Bush Administration, was asked during a press conference whether there is a code of international rules. He replied: "I honestly believe that every country ought to do what it wants to do . . . it is either proud of itself or less proud of itself."[1] Some days later, at his Sedgefield constituency, former British Prime Minister, Tony Blair, announced the end of the Westphalian era of international relations.[2] It was time, according to Blair, to usher in a new interventionist period in which force would be used to avert or end humanitarian catastrophe: "I was already reaching for a different philosophy in international relations from a traditional one that has held sway since the treaty of Westphalia in 1648; namely that a country's internal affairs are for it" (Blair 2004).

The United Nations Charter in Article 2(4) prohibits the use of force among states and the Charter's preamble speaks of eliminating the scourge of war altogether. International law, indeed, may be associated in the public mind with a form of pacifism. To be on the side of international law is to be on the side of peace, or, at the very least, the peaceful resolution of disputes.[3] This legalist–utopian insistence on the virtues of peace is pervasive but it co-exists in international relations and, more importantly, in our intuitions about security and survival, with two other fantasies. In one, war is imagined as a radical solution to

197

the problem of social evil. Tony Blair's Sedge-field speech and his whole humanitarian-military ethos, first articulated in Chicago in 1999, are built around this idea (Blair 1999). So, too, in a different vein is George Bush's war on terror, a self-conscious and publicly proclaimed effort to destroy all those who would do evil (or commit (certain) acts of terrorism) (U.S. National Security Strategy 2002). The second fantasy is reflected in Donald Rumsfeld's response to his European interlocutors. Here, sovereignty is anterior to, prior to and transcendent of any concepts of community or law or obligation. War is a question of pride (or, vanity) or strategic calculation or revenge, or the product of some neurotic urge. Whatever the case, sovereignty is its own justification; there is no normative universe outside the state or its elite capable of reining its (often violent) appetites. This sovereigntism sometimes is combined with a knowing realism about the true nature of international relations (Hobbesian) and the inclinations of nation states (cold hearted monsters). As Churchill put it:

> War is too foolish, too fantastic, to be thought of in the 20th Century . . . civilisation has climbed above such perils . . . the interdependence of nations . . . the sense of public law have rendered such nightmares impossible. Are you quite sure? It would be a pity to be wrong.
>
> (Woodward 2007: 44)

Often, the debate about the use of force is conducted in terms of a contest between international law's commitments to peace and constraint, and a world of violence and politics in which law struggles for footing. Most often, this image is accompanied by a sense that law is weak and ineffectual (but the product of essentially decent inclinations). Arrayed against this timid repository of our best hopes and most creative ideas are the brute conditions of international anarchy and the programmatic impulses of charismatic leaders and exceptionalist nation states. In 1970,

Thomas Franck asked "Who killed Article 2(4)?" (Franck 1970). According to this view, there are myriad possible perpetrators (they include the great powers, "sovereignty", political cynicism and the lack of a community or society in international relations). In the end, even the most ardent internationalist begins to ask: Who would want to keep it alive?

In this chapter, I want to represent the law of force (or the *ius ad bellum*) a little differently and, perhaps more representatively, as the performance of an argument between these three competing and potent visions of international and social order sketched earlier. These can be characterized as an absolutist view that seeks to approach war and peace through non-negotiable, universalizable and unqualified moral truths, a sovereigntist perspective that holds the desires or fears of the sovereign to be the single source of legitimacy in assessing decisions to go to war or engage in diplomacy and (an occasionally militant) legal pacifism that wants to use law to abolish war. These three are ideal types, of course. Most scholars, for example, tend to offer some combination of the three approaches in their work (e.g. Cassese 1999). It is important, however, to understand the *ius ad bellum* as embedding, articulating and accommodating these three sets of claims. This may help account for the law's thematic ambiguities, its textual evasions, its judicial agonies and its interminable crises. It may explain also why its primary organs repeatedly move from institutional paralysis to hyper-activism and back. The Iraq war, for example, rather than being viewed as an extraordinary challenge to the future of international law, can be reinterpreted as part of the perpetual crisis of law, war and peace.

To put this a different way, because wars are occasions for national invigoration, political reinvention or personal heroism as well as moments of collective horror, mass psychosis and individualized evil, it is not at all clear what we want to do with, and about, war.

Public international law, while it promises the resolution of this angst, is instead an expression of it. This angst is found in three doctrinal debates concerning the regulation of force and violence in the international system. These revolve around, first, the nature of the prohibition itself (what exactly is made illegal by the UN Charter and customary international law?), second, the limit and extent of the right to use force in self-defense and, third, the parameters of properly authorized collective or individual action (including the validity and desirability of wars for humanity (or humanitarian interventions)). This chapter will consider each of these in turn.

Prohibiting force, permitting violence

In 1907 the international community of states, under the influence of Latin American nations anxious about the regional ambitions of the United States, resolved to outlaw a particular form of violence in the international system. The *Hague Convention Respecting the Limitation of the Employment of Force for the Recovery of Contract Debts* made it unlawful for states to use military force against each other for the purposes of securing repayment of outstanding loans (contract debts). This fin-de-siècle moment of legal regulation marks the opening move in a century-long project to outlaw certain types of violence. Of course, the significance of the 1907 Convention lies, also, in the narrowness of its range of operations; most uses of force remained perfectly lawful and indeed, the 1907 Convention can be reread as imposing a duty to attempt arbitration prior to embarking on a reparative war.

Most interstate force at this time was still constrained only by the inclinations of sovereignty or the prerogatives of conscience. This was made explicit at Versailles with the ill-starred attempt to criminalize war (or at least certain types of war). Article 227

of the Versailles Peace Treaty proposed the arraignment of the Kaiser on charges of having initiated a war of aggression or a war against the sanctity of treaties; the trial did not take place (largely because of the refusal by the Dutch government to surrender the Kaiser to the victorious Allies). The international law position is best articulated, however, by a commission on the authorship of the war (established by the Versailles delegates and made up of a group of diplomats and eminent international lawyers) (Commission on Responsibilities 1920). This Commission states, in its final report, that the criminalization of war is novel and unprecedented, and has no place under international law. War is to be left to the judgment of history and conscience; states do what they must do and the consequences are a matter for sovereigns and philosophers not lawyers (the Commission was particularly keen to preserve the immunity of these sovereigns).

The interwar period was marked by a series of haphazard initiatives largely made up of unequivocal prohibitions lacking status (a draft League of Nations *Treaty of Mutual Assistance* in 1923) or treaties with some force that, nonetheless have an ambiguity at their heart (the *Kellogg–Briand Peace Pact* outlawing recourse to war but omitting to delineate any possible exceptions based on self-defense: the inclusion of self-defense being unnecessary according to Kellogg–Briand's American sponsors because it was self-evident that sovereigns could use violence to defend themselves, see discussion, *infra*).

The year 1945, then, was a constitutional moment for law and force. At Nuremberg, the IMT declared war of aggression to be the supreme international crime, one "containing the accumulated evil of the whole". This time, in a reversal of the Commission on Responsibilities at Versailles, rather than insisting that law vacate authority to ethics, the conscience of mankind demanded that the law criminalize war. The IMT Charter Article 6 made it a crime "to plan, prepare, initiate or wage a war of aggression or wars in contravention of international treaties". The formula is repeated in the Charter of the International Military Tribunal for the Far East, Article 6(a) and in Law No. 10 of the Control Council for Germany (20 December 1945) and restated in subsequent UN General Assembly resolutions in 1965, 1970 and 1974.

At San Francisco, meanwhile, the newly created UN Charter contains a prohibition on the use of force (and a preference for pacific forms of dispute resolution) at its center. Article 2(4) makes it unlawful for member states to use force against the territorial integrity and political independence of other states or in any manner contrary to the principles and purposes of the UN Charter. This provision has become part of customary international law and is regarded as a norm of *ius cogens*, (*Nicaragua*, para. 190) applying to non-member states also.

Article 2(4) is a bold statement for an international system where military force had hitherto been a sovereign prerogative. But it is striking how much violence is left untouched by Article 2(4). This article (and its twin at Nuremberg) are directed at a particular and, increasingly, marginal genus of violence involving the formally invasive war making of sovereign states against one another. Article 2(4) has nothing to say about wars conducted by states against their own populations (e.g. Guatemala, 1960–96, Rwanda, 1994), or about wars within states between two or more collective groups (e.g. conflict between Bosnian Croats and Bosnian Serbs within Bosnia-Herzegovina) or wars between the state and internal armed opposition (sometimes with a self-determination cast) (e.g. Biafra 1967–70). Neither is Article 2(4) concerned with the sorts of violence perpetrated on human beings under repressive economic orders or because of the maldistribution of economic goods within the global political order.[4]

Even in the case of its putative field of application, interstate war, there is, inevitably, an elasticity at the margins (sometimes at the core)

of these provisions. For example, in the case of the UN Charter, it is not clear the extent to which the qualifiers "territorial integrity and political independence" have real interpretive purchase. Did the Israeli raid on Entebbe Airport in Kampala (to free hostages taken by a Palestinian group) in 1976 have an adverse effect on Ugandan integrity and independence? Many legal experts took the view that this action fell foul of Article 2(4) but the US, for example, in debates at the Security Council, emphasized the limited nature of the intervention as a way of excusing it (Gray 2004: 30). Similarly, was the 2003 war in Iraq an effort to restore Iraq's political independence (by removing a tyrant) (Soefer 2003)? Or was it an egregious breach of that independence (the imposition of foreign-emplaced government to replace an indigenous one?) (Sands 2006). Then there is the question of scale and intensity. How is the provision to be interpreted in such a way as to avoid its application to trivial cases of force while at the same time maintaining its integrity (this is an issue taken up in the discussion of self-defense)? Thomas Franck has considered these questions in his illuminating discussion of legitimacy (Franck 1990). The problem for international lawyers lies in coming up with prohibitions that offer clarity and flexibility at the same time. The twin dangers of the idiot rule (the rule that allows for no margin of appreciation, the norm that looks foolish if applied rigidly to a complex moral problem) and the vague rule (the rule that allows for myriad exceptions, provides for every possible nuance and ends up emptied of content) are with us at all times in this area.

Self-defense, armed attack

The law of self-defense, too, is constructed around the dilemmas of sovereignty, law and virtue. The legalist–utopian fantasy of abolishing war confronts, at the same time, the necessity of defending the state and statism in its abstract formal sense (Koskenniemi 1991) and the intuition that some state-based ideological projects are worth defending and others are not (Rawls 1999; Tesón 1992).

Prior to 1945, self-defense was an unstated exception to any principle making war unlawful. Curiously, self-defense pre-dates the prohibition itself, receiving what is regarded as its first thorough diplomatic airing in an exchange of letters between Lord Ashburton (the British Foreign Secretary) and Daniel Webster (the American Secretary of State) in 1837. This came to be known as the *Caroline Incident*, an early instance of a purported exercise of preemptive self-defense against the activities of terrorist non-state actors. The US and the UK, while disagreeing on the specific case (involving the destruction, by the British, of a Canadian rebel ship operating from US waters and alleged to be engaged in an attack on British interests in British North America (Canada)), arrived at a joint declaration as to the content of self-defense. Such action was permitted in cases involving "a necessity for self-defence, instant, overwhelming, leaving no choice of means and no moment of deliberation". This case continues to exercise power over the legal (Jennings 1938) and political (US National Security Strategy 2002) imagination.

If Caroline elaborates a principle of constraint, then almost a century later, Kellogg–Briand's silence around self-defense was just as eloquent. The renunciation of war as a means of settling disputes and as a national policy choice was unaccompanied by any qualification in regard to self-defense. For the Americans, at least, such a reference was otiose. The right to self-defense, an inherent sovereign prerogative, was simply a fact of international political life. This rendering of self-defense as simply "there" – a fact of sovereignty – was restated 70 years later in the *Nuclear Weapons case*. The ICJ, contemplating the legality of nuclear devices, found it difficult to conceive of an instance in which such weapons could be used without offending principles of proportionality, necessity and

humanity. Yet, always self-defense and the requirements of sovereignty were in the background threatening to unpick the near complete prohibition. Famously, then, the Court stated it could not "conclude definitively whether the threat or use of nuclear weapons would be lawful or unlawful in an extreme circumstance of self-defence, in which the very survival of the state would be at stake" (*Nuclear Weapons* 1996: para 105, dispositif E). The Court was engaged in a tragic struggle to reconcile an overwhelming human instinct (for survival, for humanity, for law) with the potent formulations of sovereignty.

This assumption that self-defense is somehow present (and therefore not requiring articulation) in a way that the prohibition itself is not, is found in Article 51 of the UN Charter: "Nothing in the present Charter shall impair the inherent right of individual or collective self-defence if an armed attack occurs against a Member of the United Nations."

The word "inherent" has generated a fair bit of commentary. In *Nicaragua*, it was used to establish that the law on the use of force was part of customary international law independent of the Charter itself (this was important for the purpose of escaping the US reservation to its declaration accepting the jurisdiction of the International Court). In the work of many expansionists (those who wish to extend the right to self-defense), it is used to justify readings of self-defense that take it some way beyond the text of Article 51 itself (Bowett, 1958) and, more radically, it preserves the idea that sovereignty is prior to law, that the natural right to use force in self-defense pre-exists the law of self-defense.

Of course, there are sovereigntists who take the view that some aspects of self-defense are beyond law (there is a hint of this in *Nuclear Weapons*). Dean Acheson said of the Cuban Missile Crisis:

> The power, position and prestige of the United States had been challenged by another state; *and the law does not deal with*

201

such questions of ultimate power – power that comes close to the sources of sovereignty.
(Acheson 1963b)

Mostly, however, contours of the relationship of law, sovereignty and virtue are conducted through legal texts and discourse. The central doctrinal debates in relation to self-defense turn respectively on the definition of an "armed attack", the constraints on any response to an armed attack (implicating questions of "necessity" and "proportionality"), the extent of any right to use force preemptively and the existence of a right to exercise force against non-state actors (particularly those located in foreign state territory).

In order to activate a right to use force in self-defense, there must be an armed attack (*Oil Platforms*: paras 51, 61–64 and 72; *Nicaragua*: para. 195) or, at least the imminent threat of one. What, though, *is* an "armed attack"? The consensus appears to be in favor of requiring the use of military force of a certain degree of intensity (*Nicaragua*: 191 and 195; *Oil Platforms*: 63–64; Brownlie 1963: 278) against a state's territory, armed forces or embassies (and in the absence of that state's consent) and the existence of some sort of intention on the part of the attacking state to bend the target state to its will (Chatham House Report 2005: 5). The aim, then, is to exclude minor or trivial uses of cross-border force (a rifle fired across a frontier) as well as more substantial but accidental infringements of territory (inadvertent overflights by military aircraft or missiles). In *Nicaragua*, the ICJ made further, and more contentious, distinctions between "uses of force" (arming and sending irregulars or rebels into foreign territories) and "armed attacks" (invasions or the arming and sending of irregulars when such action acquired the gravity of an armed attack). The Court held that only the latter gave rise to a right to self-defense. These, apparently, semantic distinctions accord with the different language used in Article 2(4) and Article 51 of the UN Charter and they are attempts to restrict the latitude for responsive

violence (particularly the sorts of collective self-defense that might have the effect of widening a conflict). The Court, however, has been criticized (sometimes ridiculed) for making these distinctions (Higgins 1994).

On the one hand, this could be characterized as a contest between a restrictionist tendency (present among judges at the ICJ) to reduce the scope for legitimate interstate violence as much as possible, and an expansionist effort to limit the constraints on defensive force or maximize the range of permissible responses to threats and infringements. But, on the other hand, this debate is also about the relationship between and among sovereigns (Koskenniemi 2002).

These struggles re-emerge in three further doctrinal debates. In *Oil Platforms*, the Court found that any use of force in self-defense must be "necessary and proportionate" (*Oil Platforms*: para. 51). This was held to be a "rule of customary international law" (*Legality of Nuclear Weapons*: para. 41). The *Nicaragua* court, rather unhelpfully, emphasized that action in self-defense ought to be "proportional to the armed attack and necessary to respond to it" (*Nicaragua*: para. 176). Necessity, then, refers both to the lack of a reasonable alternative means of ending or averting the attack and the reasonableness of the military measures taken.

This rule was given some elaboration in the discussion of the US attack on the Iranian oil installations in 1986 and 1988. Here, the Court found that this use of force was disproportionate because *Operation Praying Mantis* (encompassing widespread attacks on Iranian interests) was an incommensurate response to a single assault on one US ship, which damaged but did not sink the ship, killed no US personnel and was of unknown origin (*Oil Platforms*: para. 77). The Court found, too, that there was a lack of necessity for the attacks (they were not required to prevent Iranian mining of the Straits, there were no demands made to the Iranians requiring them to cease employing force from the platforms and some of the US attacks had been merely "opportunistic"). The Court rejected also the US argument in this case that there is a "measure of discretion" when undertaking good faith evaluations of essential interests (*Oil Platforms*: para. 73). For the Court, such evaluations were not a matter of subjective tests (para. 43) but law.

Questions of proportionality and necessity, however, are most often auto-interpretive thereby affording precisely this sort of discretion. There always will be a clash of sovereigns or a conflict between restriction-ist and expansive reading of the law. In the case of the Afghanistan intervention, some scholars (viewing the matter from the perspective of Afghan sovereignty) argued that the invasion and occupation of a whole country could not possibly be proportionate to the destruction of two buildings in New York City (e.g. Myjer and White: 2002). Another group of scholars argued that proportionality and necessity had to be considered from the perspective of the attacked state (e.g. Lowe, Chatham House 2005: 44). For the United States, it appeared perfectly reasonable to occupy the country in order to eliminate the Taliban, a government that had given succour to the group responsible for the attack on the Twin Towers. It is difficult to know how such arguments about proportionality and necessity ought to be resolved except by courts making the sorts of sometimes arbitrary and assertive judgments found in some ICJ jurisprudence on the matter.

A second doctrinal debate has been preoccupied with the relationship between Afghanistan's responsibility for the attacks on the United States and the US right to use force in self-defense against terrorists operating from Afghan territory. In relation to terrorism and state responsibility generally, there are two relatively straightforward cases and one much more complicated matter. The two simple cases involve terrorists operating from non-sovereign territory (e.g. outer space or, more likely, the high seas) or from bases in a state where that state has actively supported, or failed to take reasonable measures to prevent, such activities. In each of these cases, the exercise of self-defense is uncontroversial.

The difficult case occurs when there is an armed attack emanating from a state territory where that state does not incur state responsibility for the attack (i.e. the actions of the non-state group cannot be attributed to the state in question). Again, two views emerge. One group of commentators and judges point to the problems inherent in permitting a use of military force in self-defense against a state that has committed no wrong under international law (*Armed Activities* 2005: 146–7). Another group wonders how it can be that the necessity of self-defense can turn on the responsibility of the host state rather than the sovereign rights of the attacked state (Chatham House 2005: 8; *Armed Activities, Separate Opinion of Judge Simma*: 7–12). This latter view suggests that if it is necessary for the US to invade Afghanistan in order to prevent further attacks on US territory, then such force constitutes lawful self-defense. Once again, though, it is unclear how such a dilemma ought to be resolved from within a legal tradition in which there is an allergy to choosing one set of sovereign rights over another.

The final doctrinal debate concerns preemptive self-defense. The Bush administration placed this debate center-stage with its National Security Strategy initiative in 2002 but lawyers have wrestled with this problem since, at least, the *Caroline* case. Strict constructionists have argued that since Article 51 permits self-defense only when there is an "armed attack", there can be no right to use force in *anticipation* of an armed attack. This position has been seriously eroded from at least three directions. Another group of textualists have argued that the word "inherent" in Article 51 incorporates either a pre-existing right to anticipatory self-defense (*Caroline*) or an equivalent post-1945 customary right. Others have argued that an "armed attack" begins from the moment a decision to use force has been made or from the moment such a use of force has become imminent (this collapses altogether the distinction between self-defense and anticipatory self-defense) (Dinstein 2001: 172).

Finally, there are those who have taken a pragmatic or "policy-oriented" approach to argue that the advent of nuclear weaponry or the speed of modern armies or some radical change of circumstances have made it impossible to reject a right to anticipatory self-defense. In each case, however, the formula for anticipatory self-defense has been yoked to a finding of imminence and this, in turn, has been linked to some notion of immediacy or temporal proximity.

The Bush Doctrine departed from all of these traditions to develop an expanded idea of self-defense based on preventative war. As President Bush put it in his West Point speech in 2002: "We must take the battle to the enemy, disrupt his plans, and confront the worst threats before they emerge" (Bush 2002b). Imminence remains relevant; indeed there is considerable effort made to ground the new doctrine in old precedents (notably *Caroline*): "We must adapt the concept of imminent threat to the capabilities and objectives of . . . rogue states and terrorists."[5] However, this form of preemptive self-defense relies on a modified version of "imminence". It is no longer the imminence of the attack that is controlling but instead the likely emergence of an irreversible threat. This conception of self-defense is heavily weighted in favor of the responding state. This may explain why it suits the dominant hegemon. The 2003 intervention in Iraq is often cited as an example of the Bush Doctrine in practice, although the emphasis throughout the period immediately prior to the war was on issues of collective security. Still, it is no doubt true that figures in the Bush administrations and prominent voices in the political and media establishments in the US believed this was a test of preemption's credibility (Soafer 2003). In this sense, the existence or non-existence of WMDs was somewhat beside the point from the per-

spective of preemption. What counted was the possibility or probability of Iraq emerging at some point in the future as a threat to US security. The preemptive war was about Saddam's psychology not Iraq's current capability.

Needless to say, this invocation of a rather distant prospect of emerging danger failed to attract many adherents to the idea of preemption in Iraq. No doubt, the current weight of legal opinion favors heavily the existence of a right to anticipatory self-defense in cases of imminent attack (this has been confirmed in the Secretary-General's *In Larger Freedom* Report 2005: para. 124) or "irreversible emergency" (Chatham House 2005: 5) but there is precious little support for any expanded right to engage in preventative wars (a short-lived and roundly condemned "Howard Doctrine" says something about the status of this form of self-defense; more tellingly still, the UK Attorney-General, Peter Goldsmith, condemned the doctrine in a statement to the House of Lords in April 2004 (UK Attorney General 2004).

It may be, of course, that what is being argued for, most often implicitly, by the United States in its National Security Strategy and by some (largely western) expansionists are exceptional rights to employ force in self-defense (Simpson and Wheeler 2007). One way to understand the doctrine of self-defense is to see it as constructed around an asymmetrical distribution of rights (Simpson 2004). No longer a universal right to use force when attacked, it becomes a right subject to expansion when the great powers (say, the United States or Russia) act in the name of security, or international community or democracy, and contraction when less virtuous or powerful states (say, Iran, or Vietnam in 1979) claim to employ it as part of their repertoire of sovereign rights. The elasticity of the language used makes this tendency less visible than it might otherwise be. It becomes possible both to justify and condemn virtually every act. Thus, even relatively sophisticated articulations of the self-defense norm, such as those found in the Chatham House statement, rely on open-ended phrases such as "each case will necessarily turn on its facts" or "depending on the circumstances" and on subjective references to "good faith" (Chatham House 2005: 7–8).

To conclude, the law of self-defense is a painfully constructed abstraction. It embodies an effort to constrain war through law while at the same time permitting wars in the name of (self-judged) sovereign rights. It purports to yield generalizable norms of behavior and yet has been regularly interpreted to support expansive readings where elite powers use defensive force and restricted readings where outlier states respond to perceived aggressions. The law of self-defense is a conversation between legal pacifism (or abolitionism), sovereign vanity and self-preservation, and the sense that justifications for defensive force turn, to an extent, on the virtuousness of those employing this form of force.

Collective security, humanity

Along with self-defense, Security Council-authorized uses of force represent the other uncontroversial exception to the prohibition on non-consensual uses of armed force between states.[6] Indeed, the UN founders in San Francisco envisaged the eventual eclipse of self-defense altogether as the Council took full responsibility for international security. In fact, the reverse occurred, at least initially. By the turn of the century, scholars such as Michael Reisman were calling for expanded forms of unilateralism to compensate for the moribund nature of the collective security order (Reisman 2000b).

This security order, articulated in Chapter VII of the Charter, was based on the assumption that the Council, on finding that a threat to the peace, breach of the peace or act of aggression had occurred (Article 39), would take measures (first provisional (Article 40) then coercive (Article 41) and finally military (Article 42)) to restore or maintain international peace and security. These "measures" might be effected by a state or group of states acting with the authorization of the Council or, in the case of military force, under Article 42, the UN's own would-be standing army (to be established under a UN Staff Command in Article 43–47) might deploy to confront an aggressor state. FDR believed that this system would work best where the great powers acted in concert to regulate or discipline a largely disarmed world (this was the "Four Policemen" model).

A law of unintended consequences began to operate almost immediately. Prior to the Gulf War in 1991, US–Soviet strategic rivalry paralyzed the Council and meant that a UN standing army could not be created. The Council authorized various activities but these were either exceptional Chapter VII interventions (in Korea in 1950) or consent-based peacekeeping activities not even envisaged by the drafters of the Charter (Congo 1960; Kosovo 1999).

The Iraq crisis may be regarded in retrospect as a crisis for collective security but it was an opportunity, too. In 1991 the Security Council authorized, in Resolution 678, collective action to expel the Iraqi army from Kuwait. A coalition of largely western forces, acting in combination with the Kuwaitis, launched a successful and brief war against Iraq. This was the Charter's paradigm case of collective action: perhaps its only one. Saddam Hussein's Iraq was the Charter enemy from central casting. The Charter had, after all, been designed around the idea that there would be no repeat of the inaction of the League in the face of the insidious interwar aggressions of middle powers (Italy in Abyssinia, Japan in Manchuria). It was this inaction that was thought to have emboldened Hitler (this explains the talk of appeasement in relation to Iraq). Saddam's Iraq precisely was a middle power: weak enough to be overborne in brief war but powerful enough to pose as a plausible threat to international peace and security.

The Gulf War in 1991 initiated a change in the UN's self-image and in the potential uses of collective security. Paradoxically, this one paradigm instance of intervention heralded a shift in Council policy towards all sorts of action unanticipated at San Francisco and of debatable constitutionality. In the case of Somalia, the Council authorized a humanitarian intervention, and the war in the former Yugoslavia resulted in resolutions embroiling the UN in a civil war and the establishment by the Council, acting under Chapter VII, of a war crimes tribunal (Security Council Resolution 827). The Council has in recent years initiated its own war on terrorism establishing oversight committees (e.g. Resolution 1373) and placing individuals on lists of known terrorists. Most of this has been politically contentious (is it prudent for the UN to become engaged in humanitarian interventions (see Blackhawk in Somalia) or in civil wars (the Srebrenica debacle)?). And, despite the Council's apparently unconstrained powers in Articles 25 and Chapter VII of the Charter, there are concerns that it may have overreached its constitutional authority (Álvarez 1995; *Lockerbie* 1998; *Tadic* 1995).

The Iraq and Kosovo interventions presented quite different and rather unexpected problems for collective security. Up until this point, disagreement turned on the desirability of collective security and, in a less visible debate, on the extent of the Security Council's powers under the Charter. Few questioned whether the Council *had* authorized war in 1950 or in 1994 or in 1991. It seemed clear that a combination of the appropriate voting pattern and language (the Council invariably referred to using "all necessary measures" in resolutions authorizing war) would activate a right to intervene. The Kosovo war, however, raised two further, unexplored, possibilities. First, could a sequence of resolutions characterizing a situation as a threat to the peace but not giving explicit authorization to use force be inter-

preted as an implicit authorization? Second, might it be the case that an intervention illegal under the rules of the UN Charter could still be deemed legitimate because of some combination of necessity (i.e. the necessity to end a humanitarian catastrophe) and Security Council condemnation or censure of the offending state?

For the time being, it is premature to say that a doctrine of implicit authorization has emerged from only a handful of cases (*House of Commons Foreign Affairs Committee* 2000), particularly given the opposition of China and Russia to this interpretation of the resolutions passed shortly before the Kosovo war in 1999. Legitimacy, too, is underdeveloped (Tom Franck's *The Power of Legitimacy* is a notable exception (Franck 1990)) as a norm capable of explaining or justifying interventions.[7]

The war initiated by the "Coalition of the Willing" in Iraq in 2003 received very little backing from international lawyers around the world (a small group of US academics and government lawyers defended the war). In this case, the problem was one of interpretation rather than doctrine. The collective security argument for the war, superbly articulated on March 7 by the UK Attorney-General, Lord Goldsmith, in a memorandum that was kept from the British people and Cabinet until several years later, turns on the existence of a resolution (678) expressly authorizing war (but passed in 1991) and allegedly revived by a later resolution (1441) passed in October 2002. What lawyers, and it is fair to say also many politicians, argued over was the form of words contained in Resolution 1441. The Americans and British argued that since this resolution had afforded Iraq "a final opportunity" to comply with earlier resolutions and avoid a serious breach of its obligations, and since Iraq had failed to take the opportunity and had continued to be in serious breach, the US and the UK had been authorized by the Council, prospectively, to take action on March 20, 2003. Put in different terms, the original authority contained in Resolution 678 had been revived by the failure to comply with Resolution 1441. The French position (shared to an extent by the Russians, the Chinese and many international lawyers) was that Resolution 1441 contained no "automaticity" and, indeed, required the Council to reconvene to consider Iraq's behavior. This, and the UN's repeated reference to its prerogatives on the question of Iraq, made any unilateral action by a small group of Council members acting without a specific, explicit and contemporaneous resolution, unlawful.

The intensely contested nature of the Iraq war and collective security in general can be explained partly by the existence of the three models of law and war discussed at the beginning of this chapter. Legalists concerned with the integrity of the Charter and the need to preserve the constraining power of law have worried that Council activism has strayed into areas where the Council has no writ or where the Council has become a tool to promote hegemonic ends through war. Sovereigntists, meanwhile, have encouraged the Council to act in cases where state security is threatened but have been less enthusiastic about more muscular or programmatic forms of intervention to promote human rights or counterterrorism. Finally, there is a humanitarian–aspirational camp that views the Council as a vanguard organ capable of pursuing all sorts of designs for enlarged security or humanity or peace.

These threads have come together over the difficult question of humanitarian intervention. To what extent should the international community protect vulnerable populations located in oppressive states? This is an ancient question; Grotius and Suarez were each engaged with it and it has re-emerged at different points in the history of international law. In the 1970s international law academics debated the desirability of unilateral humanitarian interventions and developed "criteria" for interventions (scale of suffering, likelihood of success, duration and scope of

intervention and so on). Cases of possible humanitarian interventions were discussed (Bangladesh 1971, Cambodia 1979) and the development of a customary right of intervention was mooted. Scholars disagreed and then they lost interest.

Twenty years later the Security Council intervened to protect civilians in Mogadishu. This, however, ended badly and there was no significant intervention in the Rwandan genocide. Humanitarian intervention had become a troubling idea. The Security Council had the power to authorize interventions along these lines but, commonly, lacked the will. States acting unilaterally sometimes possessed the inclination but lacked legal authority to intervene. Meanwhile, argument raged between those eager to engage in wars for humanity (Blair 1999), those who were worried that this would be cover for new variants of hegemony, those who continued to hold on to the idea that sovereignty remained a barrier to such interventions and those who believed that concerns about humanity were fraudulent (as Carl Schmitt put it: "He who invokes humanity cheats" (Schmitt 1996)).

In 2000 the International Commission on State Sovereignty, a Canadian-sponsored group of elite policymakers and lawyers, published a document outlining a "Responsibility to protect" (ICISS 2000). This idea received further elaboration and status in the Secretary-General's High-Level Panel on Threats, Challenges and Change in 2004 and was endorsed by Kofi Annan himself in his major reform statement, *In Larger Freedom* (2005). The doctrine is grounded in two uncontentious propositions and two more novel formulations. Advocates of a responsibility to protect argue that sovereign states have a duty to protect the human rights of their own citizens (this seems self-evident given the slew of human rights conventions to which states have signed up) and that the Security Council has a right to authorize humanitarian interventions to protect acutely vulnerable people (this, too, is unremarkable given the language of Chapter VII and, in particular, Article 39). These two norms, of course, give no protection at all to the victims of Rwandan- or Guatemalan-style genocides. They are the victims of pathological sovereign states (their own sovereign state) and passive international organizations. The High-Level Panel, then, suggests two supplementary norms. The first provides a duty or responsibility on the part of the international community to take action against states. In particular, the Security Council is required to engage in a policy analysis, guided by a normative framework, not unlike that developed by the 1970s' scholars, discussed earlier. The second norm, barely adverted to, might permit states to act unilaterally where there has been no response from either the host state or the responsible international organization.

This "responsibility to protect" norm is preoccupying international lawyers at present precisely because it draws together the three thematics that form the core thesis of this chapter. It negotiates with a legalist pacifism that wants to constrain force through law and forbid uses of force whose justification is derived from supervening and highly contested notions of humanity. It offends a sovereign centrism that insists on the inviolability of borders and is suspicious of the motives and intentions of the great powers. And, finally, it advances a programmatic, cosmopolitan conception of community, and furnishes that community with reasons and justifications for using military violence to advance or protect its key values. This is the very stuff of the *ius ad bellum* and represents the past, present and future of collective security discourse.

Arguing about war

Law and force in the twenty-first century will be shaped to some extent by technological developments (computer-attacks, new weaponry, soldier-robots), environmental transformations (the much discussed resource wars over oil, water and minerals) and political pathologies (the decline of reflective democracy in western industrialized nations, the rise of a post-democratic Russia, the increasing military assertiveness of an economically emboldened China). However, there is an equally significant terrain of language and law that will determine how wars are understood and when they might be fought. At the beginning of the twenty-first century, it might be said that war has been abolished or that the abolitionist tendency has prevailed in Martin Wight's domain of eternal recurrence and repetition. But this is not the legalist utopian–pacifism with which one branch of international law will always be associated. Instead, this termination is a linguistic, rhetorical and juridical turn embedded in the practice of war and the repositioning of international legal and political institutions (most notably the United Nations). At one level, war as a method of control has been displaced by political, economic and cultural hegemonies. To reverse von Clausewitz, politics is the continuation of war by other means. More significantly, in some of our linguistic and institutional practices, war has become peace. Previously (in some respects) oppositional, the language of peace has displaced entirely the language of war. The international community now deploys its military forces in peacekeeping, peace building, peace enforcement and so on. The great powers, meanwhile, no longer fight wars but are instead engaged in what Carl Schmitt called "pest control" (usually termed anti-insurgency operations or counterterrorism).

It has always been the case that such wars have been justified as exceptions to the prohibition on the use of force. Increasingly, however, the policing wars of the contemporary era are regarded as having transcended the prohibition altogether. Pacifism, sovereignty and humanity are conjoined in a legal order dedicated to abolishing wars by fighting them.

Notes

1 Donald Rumsfeld at Munich Press Conference, February 6, 2004 at http://www.guardian.co.uk/comment/story/0,3604,1145413,00.html and http://italy.usembassy.gov/viewer/article.asp?article=/file2004_02/alia/a4020905.htm.

2 Prime Minister Blair, Speech to Sedgefield Constituency Party, March 5, 2004 at http://politics.guardian.co.uk/iraq/story/0,12956,1162991,00.html.

3 Article 33 of the UN Charter obliges states to resolve conflicts peacefully. This is a background to the more specific prohibitions and exceptions found elsewhere.

4 Of course, international law has developed to cover these activities (antiterrorism conventions, human rights standards, the application of war crimes law to internal armed conflict).

5 *National Security Strategy of the United States* (September 2002), part I.

6 The use of force by invitation of the host government is deemed to be lawful. See *Armed Activities (Congo vs. Uganda)* at paras 42–54 for an interesting discussion of consent or invitation in this context.

7 For example, a Whitehall spokesman was quoted as saying, in relation to the proposed invasion of Iraq: "What will be important is that what we are being told to do has legitimacy. Legitimacy can derive not just from a UN mandate. Lawful and legitimate are not necessarily the same thing" (Richard Norton Taylor, "Threat of war: Blair to order invasion this month: tanks will form the core of British contingent", *The Guardian*, October 8, 2002: 12.

14

The nature of US engagement with international law: making sense of apparent inconsistencies

Shirley V. Scott

The attitude of the US towards international law often appears full of contradictions, which critics tend to characterize as hypocrisy. This chapter seeks to move beyond criticism or defense of the nature of US engagement with international law in order to make better sense of the apparent inconsistencies. Three features of the US engagement are identified and explored: the US uses international law to disseminate its policy preferences; the US seeks to protect its own policy choices and legal system from external influence via international law; and, with some provisos, the US takes legal obligations seriously. Individually and in combination, these three factors can help account for many seemingly anomalous actions or inactions of the US as well as provide a basis on which to identify elements of change and continuity in the nature of the US engagement with international law.

The United States has in recent years come under considerable criticism for its seemingly undesirable attitude towards international law. Given that the US is known as a legalistic country whose rhetoric has made much of the ideals of democracy and the rule of law, displays of apparent US disregard for international law have been disappointing and virtually incomprehensible to many observers, particularly in countries closely allied with the US. The US treatment of detainees during the war on terror, the failure of the Bush administration to join the new International Criminal Court, its rejection of the Kyoto Protocol, and the fact that the US has yet to become a party to a number of the key global human rights treaties, are typically interpreted as a sharp divergence from strong US support for international law in the early post-Second World War years. Beyond recognizing that some practices of which the US is accused, such as torture – are not open to justification – this chapter does not aim to excuse or condemn the US. Rather, the chapter seeks to provide the context within which to make sense of apparent anomalies and to highlight elements of both continuity and change in the US approach towards international law. Three features of the US engagement are identified and explored: the US uses international law to disseminate its policy preferences; the US seeks to protect its own law and policy from external influence via international law; and, with some provisos, the US takes legal obligations seriously.

Is there an identifiable US approach to international law?

There are numerous seeming contradictions and anomalies in the US approach to international law. The US has long been regarded as the leading protector of human rights, but the US has ratified few of the major human rights instruments; the US has supported most moves towards international courts and tribunals but is rarely prepared to itself be subject to a third party adjudication; the US constitution appears to accord high status to international law but the US legal system is in practice relatively closed to the influence of international law; and the US refers often to the importance of the international rule of law in its foreign policy rhetoric but does not always seem to want to support the further development of that system. One of the most common criticisms of the US in relation to international law is that the US is hypocritical – it does not want to behave in relation to international law as it tells others they should. The US justified its invasion of Iraq in part on Iraqi non-compliance with international law and yet the US invasion was itself in blatant breach of the international law on the use of force.

Attempts to explain recent undesirable actions of the US in simple dichotomous terms as a shift from multilateralism to unilateralism, or from embracing to rejecting, are inadequate, for there are always exceptions. While much recent US action has been of a unilateral nature, there is considerable multilateral law with which the US still engages and, while unilateralism is often referred to in negative tones, unilateralism may on occasion be a positive and effective mode of action. It is difficult to claim that the US has "rejected" international law when in 2006 alone it entered into 429 new international agreements and treaties (Bellinger 2007). The question thus arises as to whether it is possible to identify any patterns in the nature of the US engagement with international law or whether it is simply a mix of contradictions, excuses, and anomalies. If there appears to have been a shift in the US attitude towards international law during the Bush administration or since the end of the cold war, is it simply a case of the US going from being an ardent supporter of international law and its further development to an avoider and spoiler, or is it possible to at least in part reconcile recent behavior with traditional US rhetoric and actions highly supportive of international law? The objective of this chapter is to try to articulate some of the patterns in the nature of the US engagement with international law so as to make better sense of the apparent inconsistencies and changes.

Some scholars of IR might object to the task of defining a set of characteristics of the US engagement with international law. Talk of the US as a single unit might be considered problematic because such an approach appears to be treating the state as a monolithic entity, overlooking the fact that the US includes several branches of government as well as numerous interest groups and individuals with strikingly divergent understandings of what international law is all about. While the fullest explanation at the lowest level of analysis of any specific US action or inaction in relation to international law would undoubtedly be made at the sub-state level, it is indeed worthwhile to seek to identify patterns in US behavior, if only because the US participates in the system of international law as a single unit; the United States is a single "subject" of international law. Providing a picture of what the US "usually does" in relation to international law will not only facilitate reconciling apparent contemporary inconsistencies in US actions but will provide a basis on which to discern elements of continuity and change over time. Three such characteristics will be defined and explored.

The US uses international law to disseminate its policy preferences

The use of international law to disseminate US policy preferences was a very strong feature of the international order established in the wake of the Second World War. In his writing on "liberal hegemony", John Ikenberry (2000) has emphasized that the success of post-1945 US foreign policy owed much to the spread of international law and institutions. In the case of some treaties, such as the UN Charter and the Antarctic Treaty, the US provided the draft text. In some instances the draft was based on recent US legislation and so reflected a shift in US policy. The 1972 Convention on the Prohibition of the Development, Production and Stockpiling of Bacteriological (Biological) and Toxin Weapons and on Their Destruction followed the unilateral 1969 US announcement that the US would renounce the possession and use of lethal and incapacitating biological weapons and destroy its entire stockpile (Tucker 2002: 107). The US took unilateral action in the 1970s to control aerosol emissions of CFCs ahead of the negotiation of the 1985 Vienna Convention for the Protection of the Ozone Layer (Scott 2004a: 268). In a number of cases, international law can thus be understood to have in effect extended US policy foci to other countries. Negotiations have still taken place, but the initiative, the issue and approach adopted in the resultant treaty came from the US.

The 1972 Marine Mammal Protection Act provided for a moratorium on the taking of all marine mammals and products in the United States and prohibited their importation. The Act required United States officials *inter alia* to endeavor to negotiate a binding international convention that would ensure comprehensive protection for marine mammals. The US took its new anti-whaling policy to the United Nations Conference on the Human Environment in Stockholm, and from there to the International Whaling Commission (Scott 2004b: 130–43). The Commission finally agreed to a moratorium on commercial whaling, which took effect in 1986. In 1977 the US Congress passed the Foreign Corrupt Practices Act (FCPA), which was aimed at curbing overseas bribery of public officials by US corporations. Out of concern that US corporations had been put at a competitive disadvantage by the FCPA, Congress in 1988 urged the executive branch to negotiate prohibitions on bribery within the OECD (Glynn, Kobrin and Naím 1997: 19). This generated the momentum that in 2003 gave rise to the UN Convention against Corruption.

This first identified feature of the US relationship with international law is one regarding which there appears to have been some shift in recent years. Many people hoped that the end of the cold war would usher in an era of enhanced international cooperation and reliance on international law. But in the US there was in some quarters a sense that the US, as the sole superpower, could now achieve its objectives without incurring formal legal obligations (Taft 2006: 504). A number of academic commentators in the US have promoted the idea that international law is a strategy used by the weak against the strong, the implication being that the most powerful only stand to lose through participation in the international legal system (Rivkin and Casey 2000/2001: 35). This contrasts strikingly with the notion of international law as an effective means for the powerful to disseminate their policy preferences. Paul Kahn wrote in 2000, for example, that "appeals to international law have been one of the tools available to weaker States in their battles with more powerful states" (Kahn 2000: 1). Such ideas have permeated official thinking. According to the 2005 National Defense Strategy (at 5): "Our strength as a nation state will continue to be challenged by those who employ a strategy of the weak using international fora, judicial processes, and terrorism."

US use of international law to disseminate its policy preferences has during the Bush administration been overshadowed by a prominent use of non-treaty forms of policy dissemination. The Introduction to the 2002 US National Security Strategy referred to coalitions of the willing which can "augment" longstanding alliances such as the UN, the WTO, the OAS and NATO. Critics charge that in the case of Iraq, the "coalition of the willing" was not used so much to augment the United Nations but to replace UN authorization. One significant area of policy in which the US has drawn on non-treaty forms of cooperation, developing a loose coalition within which it negotiates a series of bilateral rather than multilateral agreements, is climate change. On July 28, 2005 the US, Australia, China, India, Japan, and the Republic of Korea presented a "Vision Statement for an Asia-Pacific Partnership for Clean Development and Climate". Although the US denied that what came to be known as the AP6 and more recently the APP was intended as a replacement for Kyoto, the fact that the Bush administration had categorically rejected Kyoto and favored such a coalition meant that in practice the US was proposing the AP6 as a substitute means of tackling the issue on a multilateral level.

The US use of non-law approaches to issues requiring a collective or widespread response has in practice not been an outright rejection of law in favor of non-law because non-legal methods may serve as an impetus to legal developments and legal and non-legal processes have often been used in conjunction with each other. The US reaction to the threat of maritime terrorism post-9/11 offers a useful example. The US responded to the heightened awareness of the threat of a maritime terrorist attack on a major US city by reviewing its domestic laws and policies and used both treaty and non-treaty methods to disseminate these policy preferences at a global level. Non-treaty initiatives included the Container Security Initiative, aimed at identifying potentially dangerous containers well before

they entered the US, and the Proliferation Security Initiative, designed to interdict ships suspected of carrying WMD and missile-related technologies. The US also initiated and led a drive to improve international law on the subject. In January 2002 the US submitted a proposal to the International Maritime Organization on measures to strengthen maritime security on ships and in ports. By the end of that year the Conference of Contracting Governments to the International Convention for the Safety of Life at Sea had adopted a new International Ship and Port Facility Security Code, which was incorporated as a new Chapter of the 1974 International Convention for the Safety of Life at Sea (SOLAS) (Beckman 2005: 250 fn 1).

In acknowledging that the Bush administration has made strong use of non-legal mechanisms to disseminate its policy preferences it must be recognized that multilateral treaties have rarely solved the problems they were negotiated to solve. It is true that the use of ad hoc coalitions and agreements with no legal status does nothing to further the development of the system of international law, but it does avoid institutional blockages. The US can limit membership to a small group of like-minded states and then expand the group once momentum has been achieved (Byers 2004: 544). Constructing coalitions on an ad hoc basis may be more effective than large-scale multilateral treaty approaches, the documented deficiencies of which include the slow speed of negotiations, the lowest common denominator impact of large negotiating groups, and creative ambiguity in the treaty text (Kellow 2006: 290).

In some situations in which observers might have anticipated that the US would promote a multilateral treaty approach, the United States has in recent years sought resolutions of the UN Security Council. Security Council Resolution 1373 (2001), based on a US draft, required all states to take certain actions against the financing of terrorist activities and established a committee of

213

the Council to monitor implementation of the resolution. Unlike previous Council decisions commanding states to take specific actions, there was no explicit or implicit time limit to the actions required of states; hence the resolution could be said to establish new binding rules of international law (Szasz 2002: 902). Resolution 1540 (2004), requiring states to take certain specified actions to prevent non-state actors acquiring weapons of mass destruction, prompted some lawyers to argue that such legislative resolutions are beyond the powers of the Council (Elberling 2007).

There are obvious practical advantages to the US of using Security Council resolutions in this way, including the relative speed of the negotiating process and the fact that by article 25 of the UN Charter, members have agreed to accept and carry out the decisions of the Security Council. The introduction of "legislative" resolutions has sparked concern at the potential scope for this autocratic mode of imposing new law on the international community in contrast to the relatively more democratic method of multilateral treaty negotiations. To be perceived as legitimate, such law making requires trust on the part of the less powerful states that the permanent members of the Security Council will not abuse their powers but trust in US foreign policy, methods, and motives has in recent years been in short supply.

The US seeks to protect its own policy choices and legal system from external influence via international law

A second feature of the US engagement with international law is that the US guards keenly against other actors using the international legal system as a means of influencing US law and policy, both foreign and domestic. The net effect of a lot of US-led multilateral treaty law has been that the US has influenced the laws and policies of others

in a way that is not true vice versa (Scott 2004c). The US has been strongly resistant to anyone else attempting to use international law as a way of changing US law or policies. The US did not support the Landmines Convention that, if ratified, would have impacted on US policy on the Korean Peninsula; neither has the US accepted the need for a new arms control treaty for outer space as has been promoted by China. According to the 2006 US national space policy, the US will "oppose the development of new legal regimes or other restrictions that seek to prohibit or limit US access to or use of space" (US National Space Policy 2006: 2). Within the US there have in recent years been strong voices warning US policy makers to guard against the "threat" of international law (Spiro 2000b); Rivkin and Casey have, for example, claimed that "international law may prove to be one of the most potent weapons ever deployed against the United States" (Rivkin and Casey 2000/2001: 36).

US resistance to the imposition on US society of external law can be said to have a long history:

> For the American Revolution was a rebellion against the imposition of transnational law, the precise issue being whether the British Parliament possessed the rightful authority to make laws for the internal affairs of the colonies. The colonists insisted that, as they had never been represented in the British Parliament, they could not accept such authority. The British disagreed, and so brought on a revolutionary conflict.
> (Rabkin 1999: 31)

There has long been a view that leaving US law unsullied could strengthen US cohesion and identity and guard against foreign meddling in US affairs. While liberal internationalists might point out that engagement in the international legal system inevitably involves some loss of national sovereignty or policy control, it is worth bearing in mind that the fact that the US took the lead in drafting so many of the significant post-Second

World War treaties together with its careful monitoring of the international law commitments it assumed subsequently, has meant that US participation in the system of international law has not involved nearly such a loss of independent decision-making capacity as it has for the average participant.

This longstanding US care to protect its law and policy choices from external encroachment can help us understand recent reluctance on the part of the US to participate in some significant new developments in international law. In the case of US hostility to the ICC, for example, it is true that there were specific aspects of the Statute that the US did not like, foremost among which was that it left open the possibility of a US national being brought before the Court despite the fact that the US had never ratified the Statute (Elsea 2006). The underlying grounds for US hostility towards the Court can, however, be understood to be that international judicial bodies and interested states would be able to use the Court to shape American policy. "An American president would be far less likely to use force if there were a genuine possibility that US soldiers or officials, including himself, would face future prosecution in a foreign court" (Rivkin and Casey 2000/2001: 40).

The US has with few exceptions always guarded against the possibility of the US and its citizens being brought against their will before an international court or tribunal. Despite the fact that the Permanent Court of International Justice, established in 1922, "owed something to the example of the US Supreme Court and much to the inspiration and leadership of American legalists" (Bailey 1974: 629), the US never ratified its Statute. The US did ratify the Statute of the International Court of Justice, but did so with the Connolly reservation by which the US declared exempt from the Court's compulsory jurisdiction "disputes with regard to matters which are essentially within the domestic jurisdiction of the United States of America as determined by the United States

of America". The United States has not only "unsigned" the Rome Statute of the ICC but has through its negotiation of bilateral "impunity agreements" actively sought to ensure that no US citizen ever appears before the Court. A notable exception to the pattern of the US shielding itself from being brought against its will before an international court is the US preparedness to be subject to the compulsory and highly legalized dispute settlement system of the World Trade Organization, in whose establishment the US was a leader.

Article VI of the US Constitution of 1789 declares that not only the Constitution and the Laws of the United States, but all treaties, "shall be the Supreme Law of the Land"; "the judges in every state shall be bound thereby, anything in the Constitution or laws of any state to the contrary notwithstanding". The fact that the Constitution declares treaties to be the supreme law of the land might appear to suggest a much greater domestic acceptance of international law than, say, the UK system in which treaties have no domestic force unless explicitly incorporated into the national legal system via an act of parliament (Denza 2006: 434). Indeed, the Supremacy Clause is generally understood as having been intended to reverse the British rule, which the US would have otherwise inherited (Vazquez 2008). In practice, the apparent openness of the US legal system to international treaties has led to considerable focus being placed on ways of resisting what might potentially have been an overwhelming impact of international law on the domestic legal system.

One means by which this has taken place has been through the judicially developed doctrine of non-self-executing treaties. As early as 1829, Justice Marshall attached a proviso to his statement affirming that in declaring treaties to be the law of the land, the US constitution was providing that in courts of justice, a treaty is to be regarded as equivalent to an act of the legislature. A treaty was to be regarded as equivalent to an act of the legislative "whenever [the treaty] operates of itself without the aid of any legislative provision. But when the terms of the stipulation import a contract, when either of the parties engages to perform a particular act . . . the legislature must execute the contract before it can become a rule for the Court" (*Foster vs. Neilson* (27 US 253 (1829)). A self-executing treaty is thus one to which the executive and courts are to give effect without awaiting an act of Congress. Non-self-executing treaties are treaties by which the US government has promised to take a specific course of action such as to enact a law and these require congressional implementing legislation. An example of a non-self-executing treaty is the Genocide Convention by which the US undertook to make genocide a crime in the US. Although it need not necessarily have done so, the doctrine of non-self-executing treaties has, in practice, functioned as a mechanism by which the impact of international law on US law and policy has been considerably constrained (Henkin 1996: 291–92).

The fact that any treaty into which the US was going to enter was going to be "supreme" within the US legal system meant that particular care was to be taken before committing to any treaty obligations. Treaties were to be entered into by the president only if two-thirds of the Senate were to concur.[1] Because a political party rarely commanded a two-thirds majority, this constitutional provision required that a treaty have received broad political support before the US became party to it. Failure to achieve a two-thirds Senate consent to ratification of a treaty has constituted another means by which the impact of international law on US law and policy has been minimized. It is not that the Senate has rejected a large number of treaties; in many cases a treaty has stalled before even being voted on in the Senate when the extent of opposition to the treaty has become apparent.[2]

One whole category of treaties that the US has ratified at a very low rate is that of human rights treaties. The United States has signed but not ratified the International Covenant on Economic, Social and Cultural Rights, the Convention on the Elimination of all Forms of Discrimination against Women, and the Convention on the Rights of the Child. It has neither signed nor ratified the two Optional Protocols to the International Covenant on Civil and Political Rights and the Convention on the Rights of the Child. The reluctance of the Senate to lend its consent to ratification of human rights treaties is exacerbated by the fact that these treaties typically address subjects that are primarily a matter of state law in the United States (Murphy 2004: 101).

When it *does* ratify human rights treaties, the United States generally does so with a number of reservations, understandings and declarations (RUDs) that have the effect of severely limiting any independent influence of international law on US law or policy. Kenneth Roth has described how a treaty is subjected to systematic analysis by Justice Department lawyers, who:

[C]omb through it looking for any requirement that in their view might be more protective of US citizens' rights than pre-existing US law. In each case, a reservation, declaration, or understanding is drafted to negate the additional rights protection. These qualifications are then submitted to the Senate as part of the ratification package.

(Roth 2000: 348)

Hence, for example, although the United States ratified the International Covenant on Civil and Political Rights (ICCPR), its accession was accompanied by five reservations, four interpretative declarations and five understandings. The US has entered the highest number of reservations by states parties to the Torture Convention, the Convention on the Elimination of Racial Discrimination and the ICCPR (Redgwell 2003: 394). In the case of the ICCPR, three out of four states have ratified the treaty without a single reservation, whereas the US has entered 11. While article 7 of the ICCPR states, *inter alia*, that no one shall be subjected to torture or to cruel, inhuman or degrading treatment or punishment, the US has entered a reservation that: "[T]he United States considers itself bound by article 7 to the extent that 'cruel, inhuman or degrading treatment or punishment' means the cruel and unusual treatment or punishment prohibited by the Fifth, Eighth, and-or Fourteenth Amendments to the Constitution of the United States." The practice of seeking to limit acceptance of a treaty to only those provisions already provided for in US law serves to narrow the difference, in practical terms, between those human rights treaties the US has or has not ratified. The US has difficulties in relation to any treaty, such as the Rome Statute of the ICC, which do not permit reservations; John Bolton, who served as the Assistant Secretary of State for International Organization Affairs at the Department of State from 1989 to 1993, has asserted that the US should never agree to such a clause (Bolton 2000: 190).

In the 1950s Senator Bricker mounted an unsuccessful campaign to amend the Constitution to ensure that all treaties would be non-self-executing and to deny Congress the power to implement certain treaties in domestic law, apparently so as to guard against racial discrimination and segregation being ended by international treaty (Henkin 1995b: 348). Contemporary would-be protectors of the US legal system from international human rights law intrusions on US domestic policy include Jack Goldsmith, author of such titles as "Should international human rights law trump US domestic law?" (Goldsmith 2000a). Human rights treaties come in for particular criticism because this group of treaties imposes limits on the basic powers of a state to establish what constitutes permissible conduct in that society and what consequences should flow from a breach of those rules; human rights circumscribe a government's power to define its relations with its own citizens (Schou 2000).

It is in relation to customary international law that fear of the potential impact on US law of international law has been most strongly expressed. Speaking in 2006, Secretary of Homeland Security, Michael Chertoff, emphasized the fairness of the US living up to the letter of a treaty ratified by the Senate, yet cautioned against "an increasing tendency to look to rather generally described and often ambiguous 'universal norms' to trump domestic prerogatives that are very much at the core of what it means to live up to your responsibility as a sovereign state". He explained the value of the Senate adopting a cautious approach through the use of reservations:

> And yet again, the experts and sometimes the foreign adjudicators simply view those limitations as minor impediments to insistence that we accept the full measure of the treaty as ratified by others, or perhaps as not ratified by anybody, but as having its source in that vague and fertile turf of customary international law.
>
> (Chertoff 2006)

The fact that the Supreme Court has in some cases relied on international and foreign law in its interpretation of the Constitution has fueled considerable scholarly output concerning the legal status of customary international law and the validity of using foreign and international law in constitutional interpretation (e.g. Goldsmith and Posner 2005; McGinnis 2006; Neuman 2006).

The US takes legal obligations seriously

It may make for a pithy press release on the part of an NGO to claim that the US simply does not care about international law – indeed, there are undoubtedly many individuals in the US who do not, but if the breadth of US state behavior is held up to analytical scrutiny, such an assertion does not hold up. With the twin provisos that US national security must come above all other considerations and that the US seeks to guard against external influencing of US policy via international law, the US can be said to take legal obligations seriously. This is true whether the obligations are US obligations or those of others. US respect for international law can be said to be an extension of US respect for its own legal system. President Abraham Lincoln declared in 1838:

> As the patriots of seventy-six did to the support of the Declaration of Independence, so to the support of the Constitution and Laws, let every American pledge his life, his property, and his sacred honor; – let every man remember that to violate the law, is to trample on the blood of his father, and to tear the character of his own, and his children's liberty . . . let [a reverence for the laws] become the political religion of the nation; and let the old and the young, the rich and the poor, the grave and the gay, of all sexes and tongues, and colors and conditions, sacrifice unceasingly upon its altars.
>
> (Lincoln 1838)

It has often been noted that the United States is a country built on law. "We are a nation bound together not by ties of blood or religion, but by paper and ink. The Declaration of Independence itself was, at its heart, an appeal to law" (Rivkin and Casey 2000/2001: 35). "American law is not merely one social system among many. It is the central instrument of the self-constituting of American society" (Allott 2003: 131). Respect for the rule of law has traditionally been perceived as a core ingredient of US strength. President Lincoln declared in 1838 that: "[W]hile ever a state of feeling, such as this [a reverence for the laws] shall universally, or even, very generally prevail throughout the nation, vain will be every effort, and fruitless every attempt, to subvert our national freedom" (Lincoln 1838).

There are several, perhaps unexpected, implications of the US taking legal commit-

ments seriously. One is that the US shies away from committing to treaties that other states may readily ratify but then not implement. John Bellinger III, US Legal Adviser, commented in 2007 that: "[U]nlike certain countries, we do not join treaties lightly, as a good will gesture, or as a substitute for taking meaningful steps to comply" (Bellinger 2007). It may be the state that has the least intention of complying with a treaty that is most ready to ratify it. China, for example, has a much worse record in terms of torture than the United States, and the Convention against Torture a relatively low participation rate, yet China was an early ratifier of the Torture Convention (Kent 2007: 202–204). While the US may be the only country other than Somalia not to have ratified the UN Convention on the Rights of the Child, this is presumably not indicative of the typical childhood experience in the US and Somalia relative to that in the rest of the world.

The US is ready to hold other states fully accountable in terms of their legal obligations and is particularly unhappy when members of an international committee or organization use that participation to provide cover for actions that may not be compatible with the legal obligations they have assumed. In rejecting the proposed Verification Protocol for the Biological Weapons Convention, the US argued that the Protocol was inadequate to the task and would enable states to gain credibility from ratifying the Protocol even if in breach of their obligations under the Convention (Murphy 2001: 899–901). This is not to say that the United States is never itself in breach of international law; indeed critics accuse the US of grave breaches, including on such high-profile issues as use of force, torture, provisional measures of the International Court of Justice, and the Treaty on the Non-Proliferation of Nuclear Weapons.

How can such apparent lapses in the legal credentials of the US be reconciled with an assertion that the US takes legal obligations seriously or is this identified characteristic no more than an apology for US behavior? One perhaps rather simplistic answer would be that the US takes its legal obligations seriously but, from a lawyer's perspective, perhaps not seriously enough. Or, to express it differently, the US is prepared to put its policy choices, particularly those involving the "national interest", ahead of an obligation in international law. A lawyer might believe that a state should comply with international law no matter what, but from a political or even ethical perspective, many questions other than that of legality need to be taken into account in evaluating policy choices.

While it is extremely rare for a state to openly admit that it intends to breach international law, it would be fair to state that the US has gone to extraordinary lengths to try to reconcile its policy choices with contemporary international legal standards. This has on occasion produced contrived legal justifications that lose sight of the spirit if not the letter of the relevant law. The use of force against Iraq offers one example, but the strain in other legal justifications proffered by the US in recent years has been as great if not greater. Particularly given that the prohibition against torture exists in customary international law as well as in treaty law, the US explanation to the Committee against Torture as to how the infamous "torture memos" were compatible with an abiding US commitment to the prohibition on torture would appear to most readers as an exercise in semantics (List of issues). The US has entered into the same definitional acrobatics in terms of who can be regarded as a prisoner of war under the Convention Relative to the Treatment of Prisoners of War (see Aldrich 2002). Such acrobatics may or may not have been performed cynically – the point here is not that US officials necessarily believed in the legal arguments they were putting forward – but that they at least recognized the importance of having a legal rationale and hence the seriousness of legal obligations.

Although the US engages on occasion in contorted legal justification for a policy or action that is not compatible with existing US obligations in international law, it would be fair to say that this is not the preferred position. Where practical, US officials would probably prefer to withdraw from the relevant legal obligation. On December 13, 2001 the US submitted formal notification to Russia of its intention to withdraw from the Anti-Ballistic Missile Treaty of 1972. The treaty had been premised on the cold war doctrine of mutually assured destruction and US defense policy had moved on. While Russia's President Putin recognized that the US was within its rights to withdraw from the Treaty, there was widespread concern that the withdrawal could spark a fresh arms race, particularly with China ("US quits ABM Treaty" 2001).

Following the Avena Case in which the International Court of Justice found that the US had violated article 36, paragraph 1(b) of the Vienna Convention on Consular Relations in its treatment of Mexican nationals on death row in the United States, the US Secretary of State on 5 March 2005 announced the US withdrawal from the Optional Protocol to the Vienna Convention on Consular Relations Concerning the Compulsory Settlement of Disputes (Death Penalty Information 2005). Mexico had invoked the Optional Protocol as the basis of the Court's jurisdiction in this case, as had Paraguay and Germany in two previous cases brought against the United States on the question of consular access for foreign nationals arrested in the United States and sentenced to death.[3] Although withdrawal from a legal obligation with which the US is not complying may be an expedient means of ending US non-compliance, the US cannot simply withdraw from all legal obligations that become inconvenient because the system is premised largely on the principle of reciprocity and the US still wants and needs the international legal system both to promote stability and to provide a means for the dissemination of US policy preferences.

Most US observers would believe that this third feature of the US engagement with international law is one that has changed significantly in recent years. Whether the US does in fact take its legal obligations less seriously now than it did 30 or 40 years ago would be difficult to measure. It is not new for the US to engage in acts of non-compliance, even with the international law on the use of force and it is true that higher standards are expected of the US than of other countries. This underscores the importance of perception. The US under the Bush administration appears on occasion to have deliberately fostered a perception of a reduced US commitment to its international law obligations through its rhetoric. This may be one of the ultimate anomalies in the contemporary US engagement with international law, for it would most readily be assumed that a state would want to "talk up" rather than "talk down" its commitment to international law. Joseph Nye has led an effort to warn Washington of the consequences of disregarding the importance of "soft power". Global opinion polling now suggests that majorities around the world assume that China will one day be as powerful as the US and that the US is not concerned by that fact (WorldPublicOpinion.org 2007).

Conclusions

Our starting point in this chapter was the many anomalies and apparent inconsistencies that pervade the US engagement – and disengagement – with international law. In an attempt to reconcile some of those anomalies, this chapter has identified three features of the US relationship with international law. In combination, these features help make sense of many actions and inactions of the US. The US may like to use international law to disseminate its policy preferences, but what then appears as support for the system of international law is weakened by the fact that the US also wants to prevent others from using international law to impose their

policy preferences on the US. The US may support the development of international human rights law as a means of disseminating its policy preferences but the fact that it has such faith in its own legal system and respect for the legal obligations its citizens incur thereunder gives rise to a belief that the US has no need for external standards of human rights.

The three identified features of the US engagement also provide a basis on which to tease out aspects of change and continuity in US practice in relation to international law. The US failure to ratify the Rome Statute of the ICC might, for example, appear to reflect a recent downturn in US concern for international law, but it can at the same time be viewed as reflecting continuity with the US reluctance to submit itself or its citizens to the compulsory jurisdiction of an international court. That reluctance remains. While the fact that the US did not veto a 2005 Security Council resolution referring the situation in Darfur to the ICC is interpreted by some observers as another shift on the part of the US, this time toward greater acceptance by the US of the Court, the US has never opposed criminal accountability before an international court or tribunal – at least so far as others are concerned.

Although it would be difficult to sustain an argument that acts of US non-compliance are a new feature of the US relationship with international law, the claim that the US takes legal obligations seriously has in recent years been challenged by a number of high-profile cases of non-compliance, including, most prominently, the 2003 invasion of Iraq. The use of international law to disseminate preferred policy options has been overshadowed by the use by the Bush administration of non-legal means of policy dissemination. This suggests that of the three identified features of the US engagement it is the US determination to protect its own legal system from external influences via international law that has remained most constant. This feature gives rise to many of the inconsistencies in the US attitude towards international law, for it tempers both the use of international law to disseminate policy preferences and the seriousness with which the US accepts its international law obligations.

It is interesting to note in conclusion that attaching great importance to respect for sovereignty is also a hallmark of the Chinese attitude towards international law (Xue 2007: 84). As a rising power, China has worked hard to make effective use of soft power (Kurlantzick 2007). The argument that the US should show greater deference towards international law now so that China will do the same if and when its power equates with that of the US may not be entirely convincing (Posner and Yoo 2006). It is nevertheless difficult to see how the US stands to benefit from fostering a perception that it no longer cares about international law.

Notes

1 US Constitution, article II, section 2. This differs from normal legislation, which requires approval by simple majorities in both the Senate and the House of Representatives.
2 Not all treaties are put through this process. Because of the difficulty of acquiring 2/3 Senate approval, a practice arose early on of referring to some of what would in international law be treaties, by other names such as presidential agreements and Congressional–Executive agreements and gaining approval for their ratification via different processes.
3 The first of these cases did not reach the merits stage, after the US executed Angel Francisco Breard in defiance of the provisional order issued by the ICJ. In its decisions in both the LaGrand and Avena Cases, the ICJ found that the US had violated the Consular Convention. Case Concerning the Vienna Convention on Consular Relations (*Paraguay v. United States*), 1998 ICJ Rep. 248; LaGrand Case (*Germany vs. United States*), 2001 ICJ Rep. 466.

15

The Iraq war and international law

Wayne Sandholtz

The 2003 war in Iraq, perhaps more than any other event since the Second World War, touched on the historic core issues of public international law, as well as twentieth-century developments in international human rights. Existing rules on the use of force and the treatment of detainees appeared to be under strain; some governments argued for their revision or replacement. This chapter examines the implications of the Iraq war and its aftermath for three areas of international law: the use of force, the treatment of detainees, and occupation. The legal debates surrounding the invasion and occupation of Iraq have largely reaffirmed existing fundamental norms but also highlighted areas of the law in need of further development.

Rarely, if ever, has the spotlight of public attention shone on international law as intensely as it has since the March 2003 invasion of Iraq. Leading stories in the newspapers and on television have regularly discussed, for example, The Hague and Geneva Conventions, and debated the interpretation of Security Council resolutions. International law has been at the heart of some of the vital controversies of the day – war, occupation, the treatment of prisoners.

The war in Iraq, perhaps more than any other event since the Second World War, touched on the historic core issues of public

international law – sovereignty, the use of force, the rules of war, occupation – as well as twentieth-century developments in international human rights. Traditional norms of international law seemed to be under strain; indeed, some American officials asserted that the challenge of global terrorism necessitated the revision or replacement of existing rules on the use of force and of parts of the Geneva Conventions. International lawyers joined the debate with passion and insight.

How have the events of the Iraq war and the legal arguments surrounding them affected the development of international law? For example, was the invasion of Iraq the first step in the emergence of new norms on the use of force, or did it largely reaffirm existing rules? Comprehensive answers may be decades away, when legal analysts will be able to assess patterns of state practice and legal interpretation since the Iraq war. But it is possible now to distill preliminary conclusions, and this chapter aims to suggest some. It examines the implications of the Iraq war and its aftermath for three areas of international law: the use of force, the treatment of detainees, and occupation. The legal literature on each of these topics is already voluminous. This chapter cannot, therefore, cite every relevant work, but it does strive to represent the key controversies and the principal arguments. To preview, it concludes that the legal debates surrounding the invasion and occupation of Iraq have, on balance, reaffirmed existing fundamental norms but also highlighted areas of the law in need of further development.

The use of force

On March 19, 2003 a U.S.-led coalition began bombarding selected targets in Iraq and coalition troops crossed the border the following day. According to U.S. officials, the coalition included 30 states, with another 15 countries privately expressing support for the action (Guynn and Infield 2003). The United States supplied the greatest share of the troops (over 250,000), followed by the United Kingdom (45,000) and Australia (2000); these three countries were the only ones whose forces participated in the land invasion. The slenderness of the coalition was directly connected to the breadth of international opposition to the war. Important traditional allies of the United States, including Canada, France, and Germany, not only refused to participate in the coalition but criticized the war as unjustified. Middle Eastern countries that had actively contributed to the coalition that drove Iraq out of Kuwait in 1991 (like Kuwait and Qatar) declined to join in 2003. Turkey, a NATO partner, refused to allow coalition troops to attack Iraq through its territory. Russia, China, and other states from every region of the world condemned the invasion. The opposition to the Iraq war may have been tied to political, strategic, or economic interests, or to pragmatic concerns, but it also had a vigorous legal component: for much of the world, without authorization from the United Nations Security Council, the use of force against Iraq was illegal and illegitimate.

That the United States and its allies attacked Iraq without a mandate from the Security Council might seem to weaken the Charter system for regulating the use of force

in international affairs. But the reliance of both advocates and opponents of the Iraq war on the Security Council process, with Security Council resolutions at the heart of the debates, may in fact reinforce the Council's role. Although the United States claimed Security Council authorization for its actions in Iraq, it did not assert a general, unilateral right to decide on the use of force. The legal dispute, therefore, centers on the interpretation of Council resolutions, not on the viability (or non-viability) of the Security Council as the central international mechanism for overseeing peace and stability. The U.S.-led coalition may well be judged, ultimately, to have waged an illicit war. But, for the system of international rules, it is far better that such a judgment be made in a context of interpreting and applying Council resolutions than in a setting in which the survival of Article 2(4) and of the Security Council role in regulating the use of force are in question (Murphy 2004: 176–7).

The key international law controversy surrounding the use of force against Iraq, then, centers on the contention that a series of Security Council resolutions provided a legal basis for the invasion. This is the only law-based claim that the United States and the United Kingdom articulated in a formal (that is, United Nations) setting. U.S. officials did, however, suggest a second justification for military action against Iraq, namely, that the United States could in any case exercise its right to preventive self-defense.[1] The language of self-defense may have had largely political purposes, but it did contain a legal claim, which international law commentators seized on and explored.

Security Council resolutions and the use of force against Iraq

In their formal communications to the Security Council, the governments of both the United Kingdom and the United States argued that Iraq's ongoing refusal to comply with Security Council resolutions justified the use of force. U.S. Secretary of State Colin Powell's extended presentation to the Security Council on February 5, 2003 repeatedly invoked Resolution 1441 as Iraq's "one last chance" to rid itself of weapons of mass destruction (WMD); presented evidence that Iraq remained in "material breach" of its obligations under Resolution 1441 (2002); and intimated that it was time for the Security Council to use force to compel Iraqi compliance (United Nations 2003d). The following month, after it became clear that the Security Council would not pass a new resolution explicitly authorizing the use of force, the leading coalition members claimed that Iraq's failure to comply with Resolution 1441 left it in ongoing material breach of disarmament obligations contained in Resolution 687 (1991). Because Resolution 687 was the basis for the ceasefire that ended the Persian Gulf war, Iraq's violation of its provisions terminated the ceasefire and revived the original authorization of force contained in Resolution 678 (1991). Resolution 678 "authorizes Member States co-operating with the Government of Kuwait . . . to use all necessary means to uphold and implement resolution 660 (1990) and all subsequent resolutions and to restore international peace and security in the area."

The British government delineated the legal argument prior to the invasion. A secret memorandum of March 7, 2003 (later leaked and subsequently released officially) from Lord Peter Goldsmith, British Attorney General, to Prime Minister Tony Blair, offers what is probably still the most nuanced analysis of the Resolution 1441 argument in favor of using force against Iraq. Goldsmith concludes that, at a minimum, the Security Council would have to discuss evidence that Iraq had failed to comply fully with Resolution 1441. He leans toward the interpretation that, ideally, a second resolution (even a vague one) would then trigger the use of force, but notes that the United States had made a forceful argument that the mere fact of continued Iraqi non-compliance was suf-

ficient to reactivate the "all necessary means" clause of Resolution 678, even without a new Security Council resolution. The memo also warns that regime change by itself could never provide legal justification for using force against Iraq (Goldsmith 2003b).[2]

Ten days later, Lord Goldsmith submitted to parliament a more succinct and far less qualified legal justification for attacking Iraq. Presumably, by then the British government needed not an exploration of legal subtleties but as solid a justification as possible for a decision to go to war. The March 17 statement declares that Iraq's continued non-compliance with its disarmament obligations revived the Resolution 678 authorization to use force, without the need for a new resolution (Goldsmith 2003a). A letter of March 20, 2003 from the United Kingdom's Permanent Representative to the President of the Security Council offered the same legal justification as the Goldsmith memoranda (United Nations 2003c). A letter from the Permanent Representative of the United States on the same date made the same case (United Nations Security Council 2003b). The Australian government had also received from the Attorney General's office and the Department of Foreign Affairs and Trade a legal opinion justifying the use of force in identical terms. Iraq's refusal to rid itself of all weapons of mass destruction was a material breach of Resolution 687; "[c]onsequently, the cease-fire is not effective and the authorisation for the use of force in SCR 678 is reactivated" (Australia 2003).

The question is whether the coalition's invocation of prior resolutions was a legally sound basis for using force against Iraq. Despite some supportive analyses by academic lawyers (see Yoo 2003) the overwhelming conclusion of the commentators is that the coalition arguments are strained and untenable. The principal problems with the coalition legal argument are the following.

First, when Resolution 678 mentions Resolution 660 "and all subsequent resolutions" (paragraph 2), the most plausible reading is that it refers to the 10 resolutions identified in the preamble, all of them prior to Resolution 678. Resolution 678 authorizes the use of force if Iraq failed to comply with those resolutions by 16 January 1991. That authorization could not apply to later resolutions, like 687, for the simple reason that Iraq could not possibly comply by 16 January 1991 with resolutions that would not yet exist as of that deadline (Murphy 2004: 181). Furthermore, it seems implausible in the extreme that the Security Council would grant permission to use force against Iraq to all members of the 1991 Persian Gulf war coalition, into the unbounded future. Similarly, the Resolution 678 mandate "to restore international peace and security in the area" cannot create an open-ended authority to use force against Iraq for any purpose. "Restore" logically refers to a return to the situation before Iraq's invasion of Kuwait; it does not confer a license to install a new regime in Iraq. Moreover, Resolution 687 established a new mandate for the "restoration of peace and security in the region," superseding that of Resolution 678 (Murphy 2004: 183–4).

Second, as Murphy notes, the U.S. (and British) argument regarding Resolution 687 ignores the context created by Resolution 686. In Resolution 686 (1991), the Security Council lists the steps that Iraq must take in order to "permit a definitive end to the hostilities" (United Nations Security Council 1991a). On March 3, 1991 Iraq indicated its acceptance of the obligations detailed in Resolution 686, and one month later the Security Council adopted Resolution 687, which was the "definitive end to the hostilities" foreseen by Resolution 686 (Murphy 2004: 192). Resolution 687 then establishes a ceasefire and a new, post-conflict set of conditions on Iraq. It further declares that it would be up to the Security Council – not individual states – to "take such further steps as may be required for the implementation of the present resolution and to secure peace and security in the region" (United Nations Security Council 1991b: 34). Finally, rather than announcing

that Resolution 678 (specifically, its provisions on the use of force) remained in effect, as Resolution 686 had done, Resolution 687 details a new set of mechanisms (not including military force) for compelling Iraq to meet its obligation to disarm.

Third, even if military means of enforcing Resolution 687's disarmament provisions appeared to be required, any use of force would have to be proportionate to the Iraqi offense. Force could be used to destroy Iraqi WMD production facilities or storage sites, for example, or to compel access for inspectors. If regime change appeared to be the only way to achieve Iraqi compliance, then the decision to replace the government by force would have to be made by the Security Council (Murphy 1992; Murphy 2004: 197). Fourth, resolution 687 is not an armistice or ceasefire treaty (as argued by Yoo (2003)) whose violation would permit the offended states to resume hostilities. In fact, Resolution 687 is not a treaty at all.[3] The coalition argument that Iraqi non-compliance with Security Council resolutions entitled coalition members to suspend the 1991 ceasefire is thus inapposite. Yoo's argument that the coalition was justified by its right to suspend or abrogate treaties is likewise unsustainable (Yoo 2003, contending that Iraq's breach of Resolution 687 was equivalent to material breach of a treaty obligation, permitting the coalition states to set aside their obligations under it). But no treaty between Iraq and the coalition members existed. Resolution 687 is not a treaty; it is a decision of the United Nations Security Council, binding on all member states. When a Security Council resolution is the obligation in question, only the Council can decide on appropriate responses to a state's non-compliance with its terms.

Fifth, Resolution 1441 did not in itself authorize the use of force. The United Kingdom and the United States argued in the weeks leading up to the invasion that Resolution 1441 (November 2002) constituted Iraq's last chance. Resolution 1441 required of Iraq a full and accurate declaration regarding all of its WMD programs. The United States argued that if either the International Atomic Energy Agency (IAEA) or UNMOVIC (the United Nations inspection team), or a member state, reported to the Security Council that the Iraqi declaration was incomplete, the Security Council needed only to meet to consider that submission. Crucially, the coalition leaders asserted that once the Council had met, member states could use military means to enforce U.N. resolutions in Iraq – no further, explicit decision (or "second resolution") was required.

Despite the ambiguities in Resolution 1441, ambiguities traceable to the difficult political compromises required to obtain consensus on its adoption, one thing is certain: the resolution does not explicitly authorize the use of force. It threatens unspecified "serious consequences" (United Nations Security Council 2002b). In the debates over earlier drafts of the resolution, the United States pressed for language that would have directly authorized the use of force. A solid majority of the Council resisted. In the discussion immediately following passage of Resolution 1441, nine countries expressed their understanding that, in the words of the French representative, the resolution reflected their "request that a two-stage approach be established and complied with," and that "all elements of automaticity have disappeared" (United Nations Security Council 2002a: 5).[4] In the same meeting the British delegate acknowledged that "there is no 'automaticity' in this resolution," and the U.S. representative agreed that the resolution contained "no 'hidden triggers' and no 'automaticity' with respect to the use of force" (United Nations Security Council 2002a: 3, 5). In other words, the Security Council adopted Resolution 1441 on the basis of a solid consensus that a second resolution would be required to authorize military action. In January and February 2003 U.S. and British efforts to gain passage of a second

resolution failed. Again, the solid majority of Security Council members were not willing to pass a second resolution that, they had agreed, alone could permit the use of force against Iraq. Thus arguments to the effect that Resolution 1441 implicitly authorized the use of force, or that the members of the Security Council understood it to do so, do not stand up to the factual record. If the Council members that voted in favor of Resolution 1441 had intended it to authorize force, they could simply have reaffirmed that decision in a second resolution, as the United Kingdom and the United States urged them to do.

Despite the Security Council's refusal to authorize the use of force against Iraq, the United States appeared committed to war. In the same meeting in which the Security Council passed Resolution 1441, Ambassador Negroponte of the United States warned that if the Security Council "fail[ed] to act decisively . . . this resolution does not constrain any Member State from acting to defend itself against the threat posed by Iraq or to enforce relevant United Nations resolutions" (United Nations Security Council 2002a: 3). As the now-famous "Downing Street Memo" reveals, the Bush administration had decided on war, well before the Security Council debates.[5] Even so, on balance, it is better for international law that the United States worked through the Security Council and offered legal justifications based on Security Council resolutions. Ignoring the Security Council process, or dismissing it as irrelevant, would have been more damaging to international order.

In summary, the balance of legal arguments weighs against the U.S. and British interpretation of Resolutions 678, 687, and 1441. The Security Council did not, either in 1991 or in 2002, authorize the 2003 invasion of Iraq. The war in Iraq was therefore a significant violation of one of the fundamental norms of international law, the Article 2(4) prohibition on the use of force.

The debates surrounding the invasion of Iraq did generate questions regarding Security

Council practices and the interpretation of Security Council resolutions.[6] For example, what significance should we attach to language the Security Council omits from its resolutions? What is the meaning of silence? Taft and Buchwald argue that because Resolution 1441 omitted proposed clauses that would have required a second decision, a second resolution was not necessary and the use of force was therefore justified by Resolution 678 (Taft and Buchwald 2003: 561–62). In other words, in this view, the omission of language authorizing the use of force should not be seen as a decision to withhold such authority. But the omitted language argument must work both ways. If the absence of an explicit authorization to use force should not be seen as a decision to withhold such authority, then the absence of an explicit requirement for a second resolution should not be seen as a decision to dispense with the need for a second Council decision.

In any case, both omissions would be consistent with a Council that assumed that explicit authorization was necessary to use force and that, as a consequence, a second resolution was required.

More generally, requiring that the authorization to use force always be explicit best serves international law and international order (Murphy 2004: 172). Otherwise, arguments will inevitably arise about whether a particular resolution was or was not meant to authorize the use of force. In the absence of specific language, actors would be forced to infer the intentions of members of the Security Council. Arguments would revolve around what Council members "really" meant or were thinking. Not only would such a setting be more open to political maneuvering, it would also be more susceptible to unilateral use of force, with states claiming that they alone were carrying out the "true" intentions of the Security Council. A bright line of explicit authorization is the best bulwark for the Charter norms regulating the use of force.

Preventive self-defense

Although it is true, as commentators have noted, that the United Kingdom and the United States did not offer a self-defense justification in the Security Council (Brunnée and Toope 2004: 794; Kritsiotis 2004: 248; Murphy 2004: 174–7), various U.S. officials did raise such an argument in other settings. The U.S. government's September 2002 National Security Strategy had declared that "[t]o forestall or prevent such hostile acts by our adversaries, the United States will, if necessary, act preemptively," before such threats are fully realized or imminent (United States of America 2002: 15). President Bush seemed to be preparing the way for such preventive action when, in his January 2003 State of the Union address, he declared, "America will not accept a serious and mounting threat to our country"; if "Saddam Hussein does not fully disarm," he continued, "we will lead a coalition to disarm him" (Bush 2003).

In a speech immediately following the invasion, William Howard Taft IV, Legal Adviser to the Department of State, invoked the Security Council resolutions argument but also remarked that "the President may also, of course, always use force under international law in self-defense" (United States Department of State 2003). Similarly, in a memorandum to the Council on Foreign Relations, John B. Bellinger III, of the National Security Council, invoked a U.S. "right to use force in its inherent right of self-defense . . . in anticipation of an armed attack" (Bellinger 2003).

Traditional international norms permitted states to use force against an attack that was about to occur; this "imminence" criterion was generally seen as fundamental, at least since the exchange of letters between the United States and Great Britain regarding the British use of force in the Caroline incident. The four overlapping Caroline criteria, which have generally been taken as expressing customary international law on anticipatory self-defense, require, for the use of force to be lawful, that:

1 the threat be imminent, that is, about to be realized, leaving "no moment for deliberation" (quoted in Jennings 1938: 89)
2 the use of force be necessary, in that no other means could prevent the imminent attack from occurring
3 the force used be proportionate to the threat, "limited by that necessity and kept clearly within it" (quoted in Jennings 1938: 89)
4 the use of force be a last resort, after peaceful means have been exhausted or proven impracticable.[7]

Some commentators have advocated the adaptation of the Caroline criteria to the modern dangers of international terrorists and weapons of mass destruction, granting states greater leeway in the use of force for anticipatory self-defense. Wedgwood, for example, calls for new rules, arguing that states may have a responsibility to act against "terrorist *capability* before it is employed and, better yet, before it is acquired" (Wedgwood and Roth 2004: 282–3). Yoo contends that the right of self-defense justified the invasion of Iraq, independently of Security Council resolutions (Yoo 2003: 563–4). He argues, first, that "imminence" should refer not just to the "temporal proximity of a threat" but also to "the probability that the threat will occur," and, second, that "the threatened magnitude of harm must be relevant." Yoo also contends that overthrowing the Ba'athist regime in Iraq was a proportional response to the threat Iraq posed, as Saddam Hussein himself was the source of Iraq's "hostile intentions" (Yoo 2003: 572–4).[8]

Most commentators, however, have seen serious risks in the prospect of more permissive rules of anticipatory self-defense. The notion of a right to preventive self-defense – against a threat that might emerge at some indefinite time in the future – replaces the imminence criterion with subjective judgments that are liable to abuse. The proposed right of self-defense against potential threats could, to the extent that other states concur that such a right exists, form the basis in the future for the unilateral use of force. The result would be the obliteration of normative limits on anticipatory self-defense (Brunnée and Toope 2004: 792). Indeed, permissive rules of anticipatory self-defense would undermine international law constraining the use of force. If states are free to identify potential future threats and to take military action against them, virtually any unilateral use of force could be justified as anticipatory self-defense.

The prospect of unwinding modern international legal restraints on the use of force has provoked considerable commentary affirming the continued validity and utility of the Caroline criteria. Even members of the U.S. administration sometimes expressed support for the traditional principles. In a November 2002 memorandum to the Council on Foreign Relations, State Department Legal Adviser William H. Taft IV, although touching on the need to adapt the rules of preemptive self-defense to the era of weapons of mass destruction and global terrorist groups, affirms the core of the customary norms: "Within the traditional framework of self-defense, a preemptive use of proportional force is justified only out of necessity. The concept of necessity includes both a credible, imminent threat and the exhaustion of peaceful remedies" (Taft and Buchwald 2003). Wippman (2004) suggests that the traditional criteria invoked by Taft continue to be widely shared internationally, arguing that the "further the United States moves from self-defense" against actual or imminent attacks, "the harder it will likely be to convince others of the legitimacy of military intervention" (Wippman 2004: 46).

Even the United States' most fervent ally, the United Kingdom, was not prepared to abandon the Caroline criteria. In fact, the British Attorney General's March 7, 2003 advice to Prime Minister Tony Blair summarizes the traditional norms and then declares: "I am aware that the USA has been arguing for recognition of some broad doctrine of a right to use force to preempt danger in the future. If this means more than a right to respond proportionately to an imminent attack . . . this is not a doctrine which, in my opinion, exists or is recognised in international law" (Goldsmith 2003b: ¶ 3). Prime Minister Blair himself, responding to questions in a meeting of the Liaison Committee of the House of Commons, explicitly rejected the preventive self-defense basis for using force against Iraq (United Kingdom Parliament 2003: ¶¶ 51–52).

Although there is a right to self-defense against an attack that is not yet occurring but is imminent (the Caroline context), there is no right under international law to use force against future threats. Greenwood points to the Nuremberg Tribunal decision on Germany's invasion of Norway and to international reaction to the 1981 Israeli bombing of an Iraqi nuclear reactor as affirming the principle that anticipatory self-defense is justified only when the threat is imminent (Greenwood 2003: 13–14). Greenwood concludes that: "[I]n so far as talk of a doctrine of 'pre-emption' is intended to refer to a broader right of self-defense to respond to threats that might materialize at some time in the future, such a doctrine has no basis in law" (Greenwood 2003: 15). Lowe criticizes the notion of self-defense against potential future threats as a "dangerous doctrine . . . patently lacking in any basis in international law" (Lowe 2000b: 865).

In sum, the more persuasive arguments support the conclusion that the Caroline criteria remain viable and necessary as safeguards against self-interested exploitation of the doctrine of anticipatory self-defense. That said, international rules regarding anticipatory self-defense could be adapted to deal with the threat of terrorist groups. In fact, Reisman and Armstrong point out that many of the states claiming a right to preemptive attacks assert it in the context of an imminent threat, and

that most do so with respect to terrorist groups, not states. They conclude that the Caroline criteria for anticipatory self-defense continue to apply, although they have been "relaxed" with respect to terrorism (Reisman and Armstrong 2006: 538–48). Brunnée and Toope argue that an actual or imminent attack from a terrorist group, with convincing evidence of "direct support or at least tacit approval" from a harboring state should be necessary in order to justify preemptive use of force in the territory of that state (Brunnée and Toope 2004: 415).

Occupation

On May 1, 2003, President Bush famously, and theatrically, proclaimed the "end of major combat operations" in Iraq (New York Times 2003). The U.S. and British governments quickly established a Coalition Provisional Authority (CPA), headed by L. Paul Bremer III, President Bush's envoy to Iraq. In mid-May, Bremer issued the CPA's first Regulation, which announced that the CPA would "exercise powers of government temporarily" and that it was "vested with all executive, legislative and judicial authority necessary to achieve its objectives" (Coalition Provisional Authority 2003). The CPA shut down on June 28, 2004 and the Iraqi Interim Government (IIG) assumed authority. Iraqi voters ratified a new constitution in an October 15, 2005 referendum and elections in December 2005 filled the new Iraqi Council of Representatives.

The application of occupation law to Iraq under the CPA was non-controversial. A joint U.S.–U.K. letter to the Security Council (May 8, 2003) affirmed that the coalition members would "strictly abide by their obligations under international law" (United Nations Security Council 2003d). Furthermore, the Security Council adopted Resolution 1483 (May 22, 2003), which refers to the coalition members as "occupying powers" and, under Chapter VII authority, "calls upon" them to comply with, "in particular," the 1949 Geneva Conventions and the 1907 Hague Regulations (United Nations Security Council 2003a), those being the fundamental instruments of international occupation law. Both the United Kingdom and the United States voted to approve Resolution 1483.[9]

The beginning of an occupation depends on empirical conditions defined by Article 42 of the 1907 Hague Regulations: "Territory is considered occupied when it is actually placed under the authority of the hostile army" (*Hague Convention (IV), Convention Respecting the Laws and Customs of War on Land*). Thus, in Iraq, occupation was a factual state of affairs, not a matter of coalition policy or labeling. The fall of Baghdad on 9 April 2003 marked the end of organized resistance by Iraqi armed forces and the collapse of the Iraqi government. As of that date, therefore, coalition forces were in de facto control of the country as occupiers. A plausible date for the end of the occupation is June 28, 2004, when the CPA passed governing authority to the Iraqi Interim Government (IIG) and dissolved itself. In fact, the Security Council, in Resolution 1546, endorsed in advance the "sovereign" IIG, noting that it would "assume full responsibility and authority . . . for governing Iraq" and declaring that the occupation would end by June 30, 2004 (United Nations Security Council 2004a: ¶¶ 1, 2).

In any case, the period between April 2003 and June 28, 2004 was clearly that in which the CPA exercised full legislative, executive, and judicial authority in Iraq and issued far reaching orders and regulations regarding the country's political, legal, and economic institutions.

The deep and extensive reforms decreed by the CPA have raised questions regarding the degree to which the coalition occupation conformed with international law. The fundamental tension is between international rules that grant narrowly limited powers to occupiers, on the one hand, and the ambi-

tious reformist acts of the CPA, on the other. At the heart of international law on occupation is the "conservationist principle" that is codified in the 1907 Hague Regulations, especially Article 43, and the 1949 Geneva Convention IV.[10] Both the Hague and Geneva Conventions are now accepted as customary international law, binding on all states (Yoo 2003).[11] Under the conservationist principle, occupying powers exercise temporary, de facto control over the occupied territory. They may exercise that control for essentially administrative purposes – to "restore, and ensure, as far as possible, public order and [civil life]" (*Convention (IV) respecting the Laws and Customs of War on Land and its Annex: Regulations concerning the Laws and Customs of War on Land. The Hague, 18 October 1907* 1907).[12] The occupier, because it does not exercise sovereign authority, cannot engage in fundamental restructuring of the legal and political institutions of the occupied territory. Article 43 of the Hague Regulations requires the occupying power to respect, "unless absolutely prevented, the laws in force in the country." GC IV supplements and reinforces the Hague Regulations in this respect. Article 47 provides that citizens of the occupied territory shall not be deprived of their rights under the Convention by any changes introduced by the occupation into "the institutions or government of the said territory" (*Convention (IV) Relative to the Protection of Civilian Persons in Time of War, Geneva, 12 August 1949* 1949). The International Committee of the Red Cross commentary on Art. 47 declares that "international law prohibits such actions" as "changes in constitutional forms or in the form of government, the establishment of new military or political organizations, the dissolution of the State, or the formation of new political entities" (International Committee of the Red Cross: 273). Article 64 of GC IV further specifies that the occupier must maintain in force the penal laws of the territory, subject only to suspension or modification when necessary to ensure security or to meet the occupier's obligations under the Convention.

The reforms enacted by the Coalition Provisional Authority in Iraq went far beyond the minimal, custodial role set out by Hague and Geneva law and these major reforms can be usefully grouped under the following headings:

1 *De-Ba'athification*: abolished the Ba'ath Party and banned its members from government positions and public sector employment.
2 *Security and military organizations*: dissolved the Iraqi army and created new army and law enforcement organizations.
3 *Human rights*: created a new Ministry of Human Rights, to ensure that Iraq complied with its obligations under human rights treaties.
4 *Criminal law and law enforcement*: reformed criminal law, police procedures, and the court system, though all remained under CPA authority.
5 *Economy*: the most ambitious part of the reform program aimed at creating a market economy, and notably removed restrictions on foreign investment.
6 *Good government*: to promote transparency and reduce corruption (Fox 2005: 208–225).

Although there is little question that the CPA reforms exceeded the circumscribed authority conferred by occupation law, commentators have explored other potential legal bases for the restructuring of Iraqi institutions. The most prominent alternative legal justifications for far reaching reform of occupied Iraq emphasize Security Council resolutions or international human rights law:

▪ *Security Council resolutions endorsed extensive reforms.* It can be argued, for example, that Resolutions 1483 and 1511 "remove any doubt" that altering Iraq's constitution and political structures was part of the U.N.-

approved program (see Yoo 2004: 10–12).[13] Indeed, Resolutions 1483 (May 2003), 1511 (October 2003), and 1546 (June 2004) do endorse the establishment of a new (and representative) political system in Iraq (United Nations Security Council 2003a: ¶¶ 1, 22; 2003a; 2004a).[14] What is striking about the resolutions, however, is that, although they support the creation of new governing institutions in Iraq, they do not confer on the CPA the authority to effect those institutional reforms. Rather, the Security Council places the competence to devise new institutions in the Iraqi people themselves, with an assisting role for the United Nations (see United Nations Security Council 2003a: ¶ 7; and 2004: Preamble). Resolution 1546 also declares that the IIG will refrain "from taking any actions affecting Iraq's destiny" (¶ 1) before the election of a transitional government. If the IIG was not authorized to undertake long-term reforms, surely the CPA, as a foreign actor, would be under a similar limitation.

In short, Resolutions 1483 and 1546 mention the United Nations as having a vital role in assisting the people of Iraq to build democratic institutions, while reminding the coalition authorities of their duty to respect Hague and Geneva law, which limit the prerogatives of occupying powers.

▪ *Many of the structural reforms in Iraq were consistent with international human rights law, which might create obligations superior to those of occupation law.* In several cases since 1945, national and international bodies have held that occupiers did have an obligation to apply human rights law in occupied territories. Indeed, it would be absurd to require the coalition to preserve the governing institutions under which hundreds of thousands of Iraqis were detained

231

arbitrarily, tortured, executed without trial, or subjected to military attack, including with chemical weapons, by their own government. Thus the Hague and Geneva Conventions should be interpreted in light of modern human rights law (Fox 2005: 270–274). In this perspective, the CPA's human rights reforms in Iraq are compatible with international human rights norms, for example, those established by the Universal Declaration of Human Rights (UDHR) and the International Covenant for Civil and Political Rights (ICCPR).

The establishment of representative democracy in Iraq, an objective of the CPA endorsed by Security Council resolutions, is also consistent with what is increasingly seen as a right to democracy under international law (Fox 1992; Franck 1992; Fox and Roth 2000). Brown Weiss argues that such a right under international human rights law attenuates the obligation of an occupying power to respect or preserve the legal order of the defeated regime (Brown 2004: 41–44). It can also be argued that states have not always been willing to condemn changes in the form of government of an occupied country, especially when the reforms aimed at the establishment of constitutional democracy, or when, after a war, the former rulers of the occupied territory were not going to return to power.

The authority of the occupiers to impose democracy, however, is limited by the right of the local population to self-determination. That is, a new set of political institutions, even democratic ones, must be accepted as legitimate by Iraqis (Brown 2004: 41–44). The Transitional Administrative Law, promulgated by the CPA and the Iraqi Governing Council, led to a process that was congruent with the Iraqis' right to self-determination: election of an assembly to draft a constitution, a national referendum to approve the constitution, and a government elected under the new constitution.[15]

Still, human rights norms cannot provide a legal basis for all of the reforms enacted under the CPA. The CPA's refashioning of Iraq's military and security organizations, its ambitious economic reforms, and its good-government reforms may not be justified by the demands of human rights law. The thorough transformation of Iraq's economy in particular has provoked legal controversy. Iraq's prior constitutions had established national control over natural resources and the means of production, prohibited foreign (non-Arab) ownership of enterprises, and instituted state planning of the economy (McCarthy 2005: 52). The aim of the CPA reforms was to create a market economy, through new laws for banking and securities, trade, foreign investment, privatization, incorporation and bankruptcy, the currency, and taxation. The market model is clearly the dominant one in today's world. The major international economic institutions – the World Trade Organization, the World Bank, and the International Monetary Fund – explicitly promote market liberalization. But there is no international legal requirement (under human rights law or any other body of law) that states must adopt the liberal, market model.

Some commentators in the field of IL have thus concluded that the CPA's economic reforms in Iraq are harder to justify under international law than, for example, the legal reforms while others argue that the transformation of Iraq's economy exceeded the authority conferred by the international law of occupation. Furthermore, the reforms, especially the removal of restrictions on foreign ownership and repatriation of profits, appear self-serving, especially given the prominent role of U.S. firms in Iraqi reconstruction. The economic restructuring will be difficult for a future Iraqi government to modify or reverse, imposing durable restrictions on the country's economic sovereignty.

The controversies surrounding the legality of the institutional reforms carried out by the coalition in Iraq highlight the need for further development of occupation law.

Scheffer suggests that a new body of occupation law would provide much needed international standards for permissible institutional and legal changes in the rebuilding of failed or formerly repressive states. New rules could apply both to belligerent occupations and to U.N. peacekeeping and intervention missions (Scheffer 2002). Ratner has further developed that theme, arguing that occupation by states and occupation by international organizations share a common legal framework. Both operate at the intersection of international humanitarian law, international human rights law, local law, and mandates from international organizations (Ratner 2001–2002). It could, furthermore, be argued that the gap between conservationist occupation law and the need for institutional transformation in many post-conflict societies could be bridged by the application of human rights law to military occupations and by a formal Security Council role in specifying the goals of an occupation and authorizing specific reforms.

Treatment of detainees

The worldwide dissemination in April and May 2004 of photographs from Abu Ghraib prison revealed appalling abuses committed by U.S. personnel against detainees in Iraq. The mistreatment of prisoners in Iraq had actually begun much earlier. Beginning in May 2003, the International Committee of the Red Cross (ICRC), Amnesty International, and the Special Representative of the Secretary General had reported to U.S. authorities numerous instances of detainee abuse (International Committee of the Red Cross 2005: sec. 3.4; Amnesty International 2003: sec. 5; United Nations 2003d: ¶ 47).

The Red Cross had also expressed concern over mistreatment it observed during visits to Abu Ghraib in October 2003. The U.S. military responded by asserting that many Iraqi prisoners were not covered by the Geneva

Conventions and by attempting to curtail Red Cross visits to the prison (Jehl and Schmitt 2004). A number of NGO reports[16] and official investigations[17] have since detailed various categories of physical and psychological mistreatment of Iraqi prisoners. This analysis focuses on detainee abuse,[18] as well as on "ghost detainees" and renditions.

At all times in Iraq, the applicable international rules included, at a minimum, the Geneva Conventions. All persons detained by coalition forces in Iraq are therefore protected either as prisoners of war (GC III, Relative to Prisoners of War) or as civilians (GC IV, Relative to the Protection of Civilian Persons in Time of War) (Sadat 2007: 325). GC III covered Iraqi combatants captured by the coalition during the hostilities (that is, until May 2003). GC IV protected all other categories of detainees, namely, persons arrested for crimes, persons arrested for hostile acts against coalition forces, and persons detained for "imperative reasons of security."

After the end of combat operations, the coalition faced armed resistance from various groups and militias. Because these groups did not represent the Iraqi state or its armed forces (both of which had ceased to exist), their members were not covered by GC III (Prisoners of War). They were, however, protected by GC IV, whose Article 4 extends its protections to all those "who, at a given moment and in any manner whatsoever, find themselves, in case of a conflict or occupation, in the hands of a Party to the conflict or an Occupying Power of which they are not nationals" (*Convention (IV) Relative to the Protection of Civilian Persons in Time of War* 1949).[19] Coalition troops are still, as of this writing, fighting various kinds of insurgents in Iraq, which means that they are engaged in ongoing "armed conflict not of an international character" (GC IV, Article 3). GC IV therefore continues to apply to suspected insurgents detained by coalition forces in Iraq. GC IV requires that all detainees "be treated humanely" and prohibits, "at any time and in any place whatsoever . . . violence to life and person, . . . cruel treatment and torture," and "outrages upon personal dignity, in particular humiliating and degrading treatment" (Article 3). In short, the Geneva Conventions ban any abuse of detainees in Iraq, from the date of the invasion to the present.

The detainee abuses documented at Abu Ghraib and other sites clearly violated these norms. The *Taguba Report* concludes that U.S. military personnel had "committed egregious acts and grave breaches of international law" (*Article 15-6 Investigation of the 800th Military Police Brigade (The Taguba Report)* 2005: 50), and repeatedly recommends that detainees, guards, interrogators, and their officers all be instructed in the requirements of the Geneva Conventions and that the Geneva rules be clearly displayed in detention facilities. The *Schlesinger Report* likewise declares that the war in Iraq "is an operation that clearly falls within the boundaries of the Geneva Conventions and the traditional law of war. From the beginning of the campaign, none of the senior leadership or command considered any possibility other than that the Geneva Conventions applied" (*Schlesinger Report* 2004: 82).

The same report also determines that coercive interrogation techniques had been applied unlawfully in Iraq to "detainees who did fall under the Geneva Convention protections" (*Schlesinger Report* 2004: 14).

Whereas U.S. officials condemned the physical mistreatment of detainees in Iraq, they have sought to justify two other highly controversial practices: "ghost detainees" and renditions. "Ghost detainees" are prisoners held by coalition (in practice, U.S.) forces but whose names are not entered on prison records and whose detention is therefore kept secret. According to all of the reports, the Central Intelligence Agency (CIA) was responsible for the problem of ghost detainees. The CIA brought "high value" detainees (that is, prisoners suspected of belonging to Al Qaeda or other terrorist groups) to Abu Ghraib for interrogation.

These prisoners were kept "off the books." The *Taguba Report* found that on at least one occasion, military police at Abu Ghraib moved 6–8 ghost detainees around within the facility "to hide them from a visiting . . . [Red Cross] survey team," a practice that the report condemned as a "violation of international law" (*Taguba Report* 2004: 26–27). The Department of Defense reportedly acknowledged that the number of ghost detainees may have reached 100. The *Jones-Fay Report* criticized the CIA's ghost detainee program as leading to a "loss of accountability." The report strongly recommended that military personnel ensure that the CIA follow Department of Defense procedures for registering detainees, so that military personnel would "never be put in a position that potentially puts them at risk for non-compliance with the Geneva Convention or Laws of Land Warfare" (*Jones-Fay Report* 2004: Executive Summary). The *Schlesinger Report* notes that Defense Secretary Donald Rumsfeld "publicly declared he directed one detainee be held secretly at the request of the Director of Central Intelligence" (*Schlesinger Report* 2004: 87).

The existence of ghost detainees in itself violates the Geneva Conventions, as the *Taguba Report* noted. GC III requires that prisoners of war "be enabled to write direct" to their families, immediately on capture or no more than one week after arrival in a camp (Article 70). Prisoners must be allowed to correspond to the outside via letters and cards (Article 71). Representatives of the Red Cross are entitled to visit all detention and transit facilities, to determine the length and frequency of such visits, and to interview prisoners without witnesses present (Article 126). GC IV creates identical rights and obligations with respect to all other categories of detainees (Articles 76, 108, and 143). By holding ghost detainees, U.S. personnel violated these provisions.

"Rendition" (sometimes also called "extraordinary rendition") is a practice by which U.S. agents have secretly transferred detainees to the custody of another country. The purpose of such transfers is to allow the detainees to be subjected to coercive inter-rogation techniques, including torture, in the receiving country. Through renditions, the United States has sent persons seized or detained in Afghanistan, Iraq, and several European countries to Egypt, Jordan, Morocco, Saudi Arabia, Syria, and Yemen – all of which have been cited by the U.S. State Department for interrogations involving the use of torture (Association of the Bar of the City of New York and Center for Human Rights and Global Justice 2004: 8–9). The U.S. government, not surprisingly, is offici-ally silent with respect to renditions, but numerous officials have acknowledged the practice obliquely or informally. In Iraq, about 12 detainees were transferred to other countries through rendition prior to Octo-ber 2004.

International humanitarian law prohibits such transfers. Article 49 of GC IV stipulates that "individual or mass forcible transfers, as well as deportations of protected persons from occupied territory to the territory of the Occupying Power or to that of any other country, occupied or not, are prohibited, regardless of their motive". Article 76 of the same convention requires that the detaining power notify the ICRC of any transfers of protected persons, even those of brief dura-tion and within the occupied territory. The rendition of detainees from Iraq violates Article 49; the secrecy of the transfers con-travenes Article 76.

A draft opinion prepared by the Office of Legal Counsel in the U.S. Department of Justice opens an exception to the U.S. gov-ernment's oft stated position that all persons detained in Iraq are fully covered by the Geneva Conventions. The draft opinion, dated March 19, 2004, concludes that the United States may legally transfer protected persons "who are illegal aliens from Iraq pursuant to local immigration law" and may relocate protected persons (whether or not they are illegal aliens) to other countries "to

facilitate interrogation, for a brief but not indefinite period" (Goldsmith 2007: 2). Although the opinion was a draft, the CIA reportedly has relied on it as the legal basis for its program of renditions. That reliance appears to be misplaced: there has been a com-prehensive refutation of the opinion's inter-pretation of Article 49, arguing on the basis of the plain meaning of the text, linguistic considerations, the historical context of the Geneva conventions, and customary law and international practice (Sadat 2006: 237–38). Indeed, commentators have concluded that extraordinary renditions are a grave breach of the Geneva Conventions and that they violate various international human rights conventions, including the Convention against Torture, the ICCPR, the Universal Declaration of Human Rights, the Conven-tion and Protocol Relating to the Status of Refugees, and the Vienna Convention on Consular Relations (Sadat 2006: Weissbrodt and Bergquist 2006).

Conclusions

The coalition invasion of Iraq was an imper-missible use of force. The invasion did not fall within either of the two exceptions to the general prohibition (U.N. Charter Article 2(4)) on the use of force: it was not an exercise of the right of self-defense in response to an imminent threat, neither was it authorized by the Security Council. States decisively rejected the U.S. and British contention that the use of force was authorized by prior Security Council resolutions; legal scholars have pointed out any number of crippling flaws in the U.S. and British arguments. The more speculative assertion, that a doctrine of anticipatory self-defense actually justified the attack on Iraq, has similarly suffered from telling critiques. Indeed, the debates seem to have strengthened the traditional Caroline criteria governing anticipatory self-defense: the use of force is permitted in advance of an actual attack only if such an attack is about to occur, other modes of responding would be unavailing, and the use of force is both necessary and proportionate.

The occupation of Iraq raised pressing questions regarding the tension between traditional international rules that narrowly limit the prerogatives of occupying powers and the need for transformation in Iraq's political, legal, and economic institutions. More than anything, the legal debates have highlighted the need to adapt occupation law to take into account modern human rights law, thereby establishing international standards for the reform and restructuring of failed and formerly repressive regimes. The new norms should govern transformative occupations whether the agents of change are international bodies (such as the United Nations) or coalitions of states.[20]

Issues relating to the treatment of detainees are of more than historical or doctrinal interest; they raise ongoing questions of responsibility for violations of international law. Torture; cruel, inhuman, or degrading treatment; ghost detainees; and renditions have occurred in Iraq, Afghanistan, Guantánamo Bay, and secret sites on several continents. The global pattern of U.S. conduct with regard to detainees suspected of terrorist connections disproves the Bush administration's assertions that the crimes committed at Abu Ghraib were the work of a small number of "bad apples." More troubling, the unlawful practices documented in Iraq have been, and continue to be, at the heart of the U.S. government's approach to dealing with captives in its so-called "war on terror." Recent reports reveal that Justice Department memoranda from 2005 authorized the CIA to employ "painful physical and psychological tactics, including head-slapping, simulated drowning and frigid temperatures." (Shane et al. 2007) The existence of the still unpublished opinions, approved by then Attorney General Alberto Gonzales, shows that the Bush administration continues, to the date of this writing, to authorize torture and related abusive practices.

Indeed, in its quest to gain intelligence on terrorist groups and their plans, the Bush administration has systematically sought to evade international rules governing the humane treatment of detainees. From September 2001 on, the Bush administration has claimed that coercive interrogation techniques, including methods that are widely regarded as torture, are necessary in order to extract from suspected terrorists timely information that could prevent further attacks. The documentary trail is by now conclusive in establishing that the Bush administration has based its policies and operational directives on its own decisions that:

1 Existing international law on torture is an outmoded obstacle to gaining useable intelligence from detainees.

2 The President of the United States, when acting as Commander-in-Chief of the armed forces, is unbound by international law, the U.S. Constitution, or domestic statute.

3 The president is acting under his commander-in-chief power when taking actions under the so-called "global war on terror."

4 Iraq is a "central front" in the war on terror.

5 The president may therefore authorize harsh and coercive interrogation techniques to be used on detainees in Afghanistan, Iraq, Guantánamo Bay, and elsewhere.

6 Techniques that intentionally inflict physical or mental "severe pain or suffering" (*Convention against Torture*, Art. 1) do not fit within the U.S. government's narrow definitions of torture.

7 U.S. personnel who employ such techniques are immune from prosecution under U.S. law.

8 In any case, certain categories of detainees – "unlawful combatants" – fall outside Geneva and other legal protections.

236

In other words, both the White House and the Department of Defense, through a series of official policies and interpretations, have made it clear that, when interrogating detainees, traditional limits no longer apply; the end of gaining intelligence justifies the coercive means needed to obtain it. Even if high-level military and government leaders did not openly order torture, their subordinates down to the operational level (at Abu Ghraib, for example) could not help but understand that they were expected to extract information from detainees even if it meant employing cruel, inhuman, or degrading methods, or torture. Thus one (unnamed) U.S. official could still go on record to declare: "If you don't violate someone's human rights some of the time, you probably aren't doing your job." The official reports issued in the wake of Abu Ghraib all establish that the legal and policy decisions that justified and encouraged abusive interrogation practices filtered down to the units guarding and interrogating detainees. The *Jones-Fay Report* concludes that U.S. personnel at Abu Ghraib felt "intense pressure . . . from higher headquarters, to include CENTCOM, the Pentagon, and the DIA [Defense Intelligence Agency] for timelier, actionable intelligence" (as reproduced in Danner 2006: 47–8). The *Schlesinger Report* affirms that coercive interrogation techniques authorized by the Secretary of Defense for use at Guantánamo Bay "migrated to Afghanistan and Iraq where they were neither limited nor safeguarded" (as reproduced in Danner 2006: 37; see also the *Jones-Fay Report*).

A substantial body of analyses overwhelmingly concludes that the legal bases for the Bush administration's authorization of torture and cruel, inhuman, or degrading treatment are profoundly and irreparably flawed.[21] By justifying and promoting harsh detention and interrogation practices, the U.S. government has encouraged conduct that violates the Geneva Conventions and therefore constitutes war crimes. Specific officials responsible for authorizing, ordering, or providing legal cover for illegal activities may thus have participated in a common plan to permit war crimes, or abetted the commission of war crimes, raising the prospect of individual civil or criminal liability. Legal action against U.S. officials is unlikely, given current political realities. But, as the *Pinochet* case reminds us, realities can change.

Notes

1 Both legal commentators and public officials deploy a variety of words to capture the idea referred to here. The terms "preemptive," "preventive," and "anticipatory" are all in common use, sometimes interchangeably. For the sake of clarity, I use "anticipatory self-defense" to refer to any use of force by a state against a threat, before that threat has produced an actual attack. "Preemptive self-defense" is a subcategory of anticipatory self-defense, in which a state uses force to counter an attack that is imminent (about to occur). "Preventive self-defense" is another subcategory of anticipatory self-defense, in which a state uses force to halt the development of a threat that could, at some future time, produce an armed attack (that attack not yet being imminent).

2 This conclusion assumes significance in light of repeated post-war U.S. assertions that, despite the absence of weapons of mass destruction and links to al Qaeda, the war was justified because "the world is better off without Saddam Hussein in power."

3 Papastavridis argues persuasively against the applicability of standard principles of treaty interpretation, including the Vienna Convention on the Law of Treaties, to Security Council resolutions (see Papastavridis 2007).

4 The other eight countries expressing similar convictions were Bulgaria, Cameroon, China, Colombia, Ireland, Mexico, Russia, and Syria.

5 The "Downing Street Memo" was first published in the *Sunday Times* on May 1, 2005. The document, dated 23 July 2002, summarizes the report of British director of foreign intelligence Sir Richard Dearlove following a visit to Washington, DC. Dearlove reported that, in the U.S. government, "military action was now seen as inevitable," and that the "intelligence and facts were being fixed around the policy."

6 The controversies have generated calls for clearer standards for interpreting Security

Council resolutions. For one such appeal, and a proposed set of interpretive principles, see Papastavridis 2007.

7 The discussion here presumes that the customary criteria for anticipatory self-defense continue as international law alongside the U.N. Charter rules on the use of force, especially Art. 2(4). An alternative view is that Art. 2(4) supplants previous customary law and permits the use of force only in the case of an actual armed attack. The debate on this point is beyond the scope of this essay, but Shaw (2003) offers overviews of the main positions.

8 Dinstein adopts yet a different view. He asserts that there is no right to preventive self-defense under either the Charter or customary international law; force is justified only against an attack actually occurring. Dinstein argues that no Security Council resolutions were necessary for the Persian Gulf war (1991), which was justified simply as collective self-defense; that the coalition had been in a continuous state of war with Iraq since then, with an extended period of ceasefire (1991–2003); that Iraq's violation of Resolution 687 released the coalition from its obligation to observe the ceasefire; and that, therefore, the 2003 invasion of Iraq was fully justified under the inherent right to collective self-defense that initially justified the war in 1990 (see Dinstein 2005).

9 As various commentators have observed, U.S. officials consistently avoided referring to the U.S. presence in Iraq as an "occupation" or to U.S. forces there as "occupiers." U.S. officials preferred to describe coalition troops as "liberators." Yet it has been pointed out that the choice of terms was a rhetorical tactic rather than a meaningful legal distinction. In any case, the United States never questioned the applicability of occupation law.

10 Yoo contends that occupation law permits far reaching reforms of the institutions of the occupied territory, especially given state practice in the 1940s and since (Yoo 2004).

11 Although Yoo argues that the Hague Regulations do not apply in Iraq because Iraq is not a party to that convention; see ibid.

12 The authentic French text of Hague Regulations Art. 43 establishes the obligation of the occupier "de rétablir et d'assurer, autant qu'il est possible, l'ordre et la vie publics." The French version thus requires the occupier to *restore* and *maintain* both public order and public, or civil, life. The (non-authentic)

English version still in use incorrectly translates the relevant phrase as "public order and safety."

13 Dorosin was at the time Attorney-Adviser in the U.S. Department of State, speaking in his private capacity.

14 The discussion here avoids the vexed question of the extent to which Security Council resolutions adopted under Chapter VII can override general international law. Dorosin cites Article 103 of the U.N. Charter to support his argument that the resolutions regarding Iraq did supersede traditional occupation law.

15 Wheatley argues that the creation of the transition government was not compatible with the right of Iraqis to self-determination, though the establishment of a constitutional government was; see Wheatley (2006), arguing that imposition of democracy by an occupying power violated Article 43 of the Hague Regulations (533).

16 Both Amnesty International and Human Rights Watch have published numerous reports on torture and other abuses of detainees.

17 The principal official investigations of the prisoner holding area at Abu Ghraib and other instances of detainee abuse are the *Taguba Report*, the *Fay-Jones Report*, and the *Independent Panel Report* (also known as the *Schlesinger Report*). The *Taguba Report* is available online at http://www.fas.org/irp/agency/dod/taguba.pdf. The *Jones-Fay Report* is available at http://www4.army.mil/ocpa/reports/ar15-6/AR15-6.pdf, and the *Schlesinger Report* is available at http://www.defenselink.mil/news/Aug2004/d20040824finalreport.pdf.

18 This category includes physical and psychological mistreatment of detainees, including punching, kicking, and beating detainees; prolonged forced nudity; sexual humiliation; simulation of electric torture; use of unmuzzled dogs; and rape and threatened rape; see *Article 15-6 Investigation of the 800th Military Police Brigade (The Taguba Report)* (2004).

19 Both Geneva Conventions also applied during the period of occupation; Article 2 of each Convention stipulates that each "shall also apply to all cases of partial or total occupation."

20 Unilateral occupation for the purpose of regime change and institutional transformation would be indistinguishable from the illegal, unilateral use of force.

21 For a sample of such analyses, revisit any of the references already given in this chapter.

16

The International Criminal Court

Beth Simmons and Allison Danner

This chapter describes the history and structure of the International Criminal Court (ICC), a permanent court, created in 1998, dedicated to prosecuting individuals for violations of war crimes and genocide. With limited exceptions, the ICC will only hear cases in which either the state where the crime occurred or the state whose national is accused of committing the crime has ratified the ICC treaty. Simmons and Danner argue that the most puzzling question about the ICC is why states created the Court and why any state – particularly those whose leaders may be at risk for prosecution – would join the institution. Based on empirical analysis of the states that joined the ICC in its first 5 years, they advance a tentative hypothesis, developed more extensively elsewhere. They argue that the ICC serves a mechanism by which leaders may make a costly commitment both to the international community and their domestic supporters and opponents to ramp down the level of violence in a civil war setting, thus setting the stage for peaceful resolutions to domestic conflicts. Their evidence suggests that governments in power in countries with weak accountability mechanisms that have recently experienced a civil war are much more likely to ratify the ICC statutes than countries with civil wars that do have relatively strong accountability mechanisms in place. They also find that ICC ratification is associated with interruptions in civil war violence and a somewhat higher tendency for

these states to sign peace agreements to address domestic war.

The International Criminal Court (ICC) is one of the newest, most ambitious, and most controversial of international organizations. The Court is designed to prosecute a small number of exceptionally serious crimes at the international level. Its ultimate justification lies in the hope that it will prevent future occurrences of mass atrocity. Whether the Court can accomplish this lofty goal, however, is far from certain. Although on paper the ICC has serious enforcement powers – it can, for example, send convicted individuals to jail for the rest of their lives – the ICC depends on state cooperation for its principal tasks. It relies on states to provide logistical support for its investigations, to arrest its defendants, and to provide its funding. This dependence on state cooperation provides a political reality check on the Court's function and constitutes one of the ICC's greatest weaknesses. The Court opened its doors in 2002 and has investigated a modest number of cases since that time. Given the difficulty of building cases involving international crimes, a slow start was to be expected. For many observers, the most startling fact about the ICC is that it came into being at all.

History of the ICC

The ICC traces its roots to the international military tribunals at Nuremberg and Tokyo set up in the waning days of the Second World War. These tribunals, established by the Allies to try defeated members of the Axis powers, each conducted one "mega trial" and then was closed (Bass 2000). In 1947, the United Nations General Assembly instructed its Committee on Codification of International Law to prepare a draft code for an international criminal court. In the heat of the cold war, however, neither the United States nor the Soviet Union found an international court to be in its interest, and the movement died a quiet death.

In 1989, Trinidad and Tobago introduced a suggestion in the United Nations General Assembly for the establishment of a specialized international court to combat transnational drug trafficking. The General Assembly, in turn, requested that the International Law Commission (the successor of the Committee on Codification of International Law) draft a proposed statute (Bassiouni, et al. 1999). This draft became the negotiating text for the ICC treaty.

The quest for a permanent international criminal court also gained steam from the creation of two temporary tribunals by the United Nations Security Council in the early 1990s. These tribunals, the International Criminal Tribunals for the Former Yugoslavia (ICTY) and the International Criminal Tribunal for Rwanda (ICTR), were set up in The Hague and in Arusha, Tanzania, respectively, to prosecute international crimes associated with the brutal wars that occurred in the Yugoslavia and Rwanda in the 1990s. The ICTY and ICTR, which are still in existence as of 2007, have proved expensive and slow. The jurisdiction of each court is limited to crimes committed in those countries. But they have also demonstrated that international criminal justice can be accomplished outside of the Second World War context. The ICTY and ICTR have

made dramatic strides in the development of a body of international criminal law and procedure that existed only in skeletal form after Nuremberg and Tokyo. As of October 2007 the ICTY had sentenced 52 individuals and a further 53 others were in custody in the ICTY's jail and facing ongoing proceedings.[1] As of this date, the ICTR had completed proceedings against 27 individuals, six cases were on appeal, and 35 others were ongoing.[2] The qualified success of the ICTY and ICTR gave new impetus to the negotiations over the ICC. The establishment of the ICTY and ICTR was relatively uncontroversial. This was due, in part, to the fact that no members of the Security Council (with the exception of Rwanda, which voted against the ICTR) had any concern that their nationals would face prosecution in these courts. Indeed, one of the most persistent criticisms lodged against international criminal justice has been that its punishments fall solely on individuals from militarily defeated and regionally weak countries. Supporters of the ICC intended for this court to be quite a different animal. In their vision, nationals of all countries would potentially be subject to the strictures of international criminal justice. Whether this goal would be reflected in the court's jurisdiction was the principal bone of contention during the ICC treaty negotiations.

Negotiating the ICC Treaty

The final text of the ICC Treaty was hammered out in a conference held in the summer of 1998 in Rome, Italy.[3] Based on the place of its location, the ICC treaty is widely known as the "Rome Statute." Negotiators worked from the draft text that had been prepared by the International Law Commission. This text was deferential of state sovereignty and set up an enforcement scheme that has been described as "jurisdiction à la carte" (Williams 1999: 337). Like the jurisdictional scheme of the International

Court of Justice, it essentially required state consent for prosecutions on a state-by-state basis, even for states that had ratified the treaty. It also provided that the Court would not have jurisdiction over crimes arising out of any situation being considered by the Security Council under its Chapter VII authority (Williams 1999). These two considerations – the relationship of the Court to the Security Council and the prerequisites for all cases not referred by the Security Council – were the central jurisdictional questions in the negotiation of the ICC treaty.

Unsurprisingly, the permanent members of the Security Council (P-5) wanted a strong role for the Security Council. These countries advocated that the Security Council be able to refer cases to the Court and block the Court's investigation or prosecution of cases under its consideration. Essentially, the Security Council members, and particularly the United States, wanted the ICC to function as a type of permanent ad hoc criminal tribunal in the model of the ICTY and ICTR.

The drive for a strong court was led by the "Like-Minded Group" (LMG), an influential group of states composed of approximately 60 members. Led by Canada, it also included most members of the European Union (but not France), Australia, Brazil, and South Africa. The LMG shared a "commitment to an independent and effective Court" (Kirsch and Robinson 2002: 70). It generally accepted a role for the Security Council in referring cases to the Court but argued that the Court should have jurisdiction over other cases on the basis of universal jurisdiction. In this context, universal jurisdiction meant that the Court would have jurisdiction over any individual who committed a crime within the jurisdiction of the Court anywhere in the world, as long as a state party to the ICC treaty had custody over the individual. The LMG was supported to a significant degree by the hundreds of NGOs that were working at Rome during the negotiations and who are widely seen as having an influential role in the ultimate outcome of the treaty (Lee 1999: 14). The remaining states took various positions between those of the P-5 and the LMG.

Beyond the jurisdictional scheme of the court, other major debates centered on whether to have a prosecutor with the independent authority to bring cases, whether to criminalize crimes committed in civil wars, how to define crimes against humanity, and whether to include the crime of aggression within the court's jurisdiction. The United States' objective with regard to the jurisdictional scheme was simple and inflexible: No U.S. national should be vulnerable to prosecution by the ICC. When it became clear that most states wanted the Court to have jurisdiction over cases even if some members of the Security Council objected, the permanent members of the Council put forth a proposal that would have allowed states to opt out of the Court's jurisdiction over their nationals for crimes against humanity and war crimes (but not genocide) for a renewable ten-year period. This proposal did not garner significant support. The treaty's key points remained highly contentious until the last hours of the Rome Conference. The final text was presented to the delegates in the waning hours of the conference as a package deal not subject to renegotiation. The treaty was ultimately adopted by a vote of 120 states in favor, 7 against, and 21 abstentions. Among those voting against the treaty were the United States, China, and Israel (Lee 1999).

Jurisdiction and structure of the ICC

Prosecutions at the ICC are limited to cases involving three crimes, as defined in the Rome Statute: genocide, crimes against humanity, and war crimes.[4] So-called "treaty crimes," including drug trafficking and terrorism, were not included in the final treaty. Furthermore, the Court has jurisdiction only over crimes that occur after July 1, 2002, the date of entry into force of the Rome

241

Statute.[5] Unless the Security Council has referred the relevant situation to the Court, the ICC will not have jurisdiction unless either the state where the crime occurred or the state whose national is accused of committing the crime has ratified the Rome Statute.[6]

Three sets of entities have the ability to trigger investigations and prosecutions in the ICC. The first is States Parties to the treaty. Any state that has ratified the Rome Statute may refer a "situation" to the ICC's Prosecutor if "one or more crimes within the jurisdiction of the Court appear to have been committed."[7] The United Nations Security Council may also refer a situation to the Prosecutor under its Chapter VII powers, which are implicated by threats to or breaches of the peace and aggression.[8] Finally, the Prosecutor may trigger the jurisdiction of the ICC by commencing an investigation on the basis of information he has received; the source of the information is irrelevant.[9] The Court's prosecutor is elected by the Assembly of States Parties (ASP), the representative body composed of one member from each state. He serves for one, nonrenewable nine-year term.[10] The International Criminal Court has eighteen judges, who will each serve one, non-renewable nine-year term, although the terms of the first judges elected are of staggered lengths.[11] They are elected by supermajority vote of the ASP.[12] Any State Party to the statute has the authority to nominate a judge to the Court. The judges must be of different nationalities and must either be experts in criminal law or international law. They are also required to "possess the qualifications required in their respective states for appointment to the highest judicial offices."[13]

The most important innovation of the ICC lies in the "complementarity" regime. The complementarity system established by the Rome Statute reveals states' unwillingness to vest the Court with unfettered discretion over international crimes. The ICTY and ICTR, and the Nuremberg and Tokyo tribunals before them, had "primary jurisdiction,"

meaning that prosecutions at these international courts took precedence over domestic prosecutions. The scheme is reversed with the Rome Statute. Under the ICC, states with domestic jurisdiction over any possible crime first have the option of adjudicating the case in their domestic courts before the ICC can address it.[14] In technical terms, a case is not "admissible" in the ICC if a state is itself investigating or prosecuting it.[15] The admissibility procedures attempt to balance states' desire to control the Court's docket with concerns that states would exploit the complementarity regime as a way of precluding the Court from hearing a case that the state itself had no intention of pursuing. The Prosecutor can challenge the state's assertion that the case is inadmissible in the ICC because of an ongoing domestic investigation or prosecution. The Court's judges may find a case admissible in the face of a domestic investigation or prosecution if the Court determines that "the state is unwilling or unable genuinely to carry out the investigation or prosecution,"[16] or the state's decision to investigate but decline to bring charges "resulted from the unwillingness or inability of the state genuinely to prosecute."[17] The ability of the ICC to override a domestic prosecution, notwithstanding the complementarity principle, is one of the reasons cited by U.S. officials for the country's refusal to join the Court.

Membership and first cases

To many observers' surprise, many states have already joined the ICC. As of October, 2007, the Court had 104 members. There are more members from Africa than from any other continent, and Asia has the fewest. As of this writing, twenty-nine members are from Africa, twelve from Asia, sixteen from Eastern Europe, twenty-two from Latin America and the Caribbean, and twenty-five from Western Europe and "other," which includes Canada, Australia, and New Zealand.[18] There are many notable omissions from the list of members. Non-members include China, the United States, Russia, Israel, Iran, Iraq, India, and Pakistan.

As of October 2007, the Court is investigating four "situations" involving four countries. All four of the situations arise from central Africa, a point of some controversy among court observers. The situations involve crimes committed in the Democratic Republic of the Congo, Uganda, the Central African Republic, and Darfur (Sudan).[19] The first three situations all resulted from "self-referrals," meaning that these countries themselves asked the Court to prosecute the cases. This is a surprising development, because the possibility that courts would refer situations occurring in their own countries was seen as highly unlikely during the treaty negotiations. Self-referrals are less surprising when one realizes that all these cases involve crimes allegedly committed by groups rebelling against governmental authority.[20] The Security Council referred the situation involving Darfur to the ICC. This development, like many in the history of the ICC, was also a surprise. Most observers had assumed that the United States would veto any Security Council resolution referring a situation to the ICC. With regard to Darfur, however, the United States ultimately chose to abstain in the vote over the referral.

With the exception of the situation in the Central African Republic, the ICC's prosecutor has issued arrest warrants against at least one individual in all of the situations under investigation. Symptomatic of the Court's weakness, however, only one person – of the seven for whom arrest warrants have been issued – has been arrested. The ICC's complex institutional apparatus, therefore, has thus far produced only one case that has moved beyond the preliminary phases. While early weaknesses also marked the beginnings of the ICTY and ICTR, this lack of progress provides fodder for those who accuse the ICC of being ineffectual. Supporters counter that the Court needs more time, and that the

Court's success can only be measured over the long term.

Research on the probable effects of the ICC

Thus far, few social scientists have given this innovative institution close scrutiny.[21] Those who have are often skeptical of its ability to deter international crime and encourage peace and stability. Jack Snyder and Leslie Vinjamuri argue that institutions bent on doling out universal justice are likely to cause more harm than good.[22] Michael Gilligan offers a formal model that shows this is not necessarily true, however, and shows formally that an institution such as the ICC might be able to deter some atrocities "on the margins" (2006). International lawyers are characteristically (though not uniformly) more optimistic. On the one hand, those such as David Scheffer or Payam Akhavan who have had close involvement with such tribunals are likely to attribute deterrent properties to them (Akhavan 2001; Scheffer 2002). By contrast, more removed legal scholars such as Julian Ku and Jide Nzelibe argue that international criminal tribunals are hardly likely to deter crimes by government opponents, whose calculations are overwhelmingly more likely to be influenced by harsh local sanctions than by lighter and less likely international ones (Ku and Nzelibe 2006).

Optimists are likely to view international criminal tribunals as important influences on domestic values and cultural orientations toward violence (Kiss 2000); pessimists (more plentiful among international relations scholars and increasingly vocal in the legal academy (Goldsmith 2003) remain largely unconvinced of such tribunals' transformative potential (Bloxham 2006). New research is beginning to examine the empirical patterns of support for and opposition to the Court in an effort to infer motives for joining, and from those, forecasts about its probable operation. Beth Simmons and Allison Danner have modeled the ICC as a mechanism by which leaders may make a costly commitment both to the international community and their domestic supporters and opponents to ramp down the level of violence in a civil war setting, thus setting the stage for peaceful resolutions to domestic conflicts (Simmons and Danner 2007). Their evidence suggests that governments in power in countries with weak accountability mechanisms that have recently experienced a civil war are much more likely to ratify the ICC statutes than countries with civil wars that do have relatively strong accountability mechanisms in place. Simmons and Danner also find that ICC ratification is associated with interruptions in civil war violence and a somewhat higher tendency for these states to sign peace agreements to address domestic war.

Research by Judith Kelley shows that many states have maintained their commitments to cooperate with the Court despite potentially costly pressure by the United States not to do so. Kelley argues that these states often cite a normative commitment to the principles of justice and the rule of law (2007). Although it is too early to project too much based on these findings, their research suggests that the motives many states have for submitting to the ICC may closely parallel those hoped for by its early supporters.

Conclusion

The International Criminal Court represents a significant innovation in international criminal law. For the first time, a significant number of states have been willing to acknowledge the authority under limited circumstances of the international community to prosecute nationals who have committed some of the most egregious war crimes and crimes against humanity. It is not an institution that supersedes national sovereignty in this respect; it is clearly designed to complement it. The effort to enhance the international regime for criminal justice has been quite

controversial, but now over one hundred states have formally committed themselves to cooperate with and become legally bound by the ICC's statutes. Scholars are divided on the probable effects of the institution on peace and justice, although some early research suggests the potential for positive consequences. Given that the Court is still in its infancy, it is easier to establish the Court's innovative ambitions than to confirm the scope and nature of its influence.

Notes

1 "Key figures of ICTY cases." Available at http://www.un.org/icty/glance-e/index.htm.
2 "ICTR status of cases." Available at http://69.94.11.53/default.htm.
3 For a more extensive description of the Rome negotiations, see Danner 2006.
4 Rome Statute, art. 5. The Rome Statute also gives the Court jurisdiction over the crime of aggression. The delegates at Rome, however, could not agree on a definition of aggression. Aggression will come within the jurisdiction of the Court once the Assembly of states parties amends the Rome Statute to include a definition of aggression. Rome Statute, art. 5(2). According to the terms of the Rome Statute, the earliest such an amendment can occur is in 2009, 7 years after the entry into force of the Treaty. Rome Statute, art. 121(1).
5 Rome Statute, art. 11(1). If a state ratifies the Rome Statute after July 1, 2002, the ICC will only have jurisdiction over crimes committed after the entry into force of the Treaty for that state. Rome Statute, art. 11(2).
6 Rome Statute, art. 12(2). A state may also accept the jurisdiction of the Court on an ad hoc basis with regard to that particular situation. Rome Statute, art. 12(3).
7 Rome Statute, art. 14.
8 Rome Statute, art. 13(b).
9 Rome Statute, art. 15(1).
10 Rome Statute, art. 42. The ASP elected an Argentian, Louis Moreno-Ocampo, to serve as the ICC's first prosecutor.
11 The ICC's first group of judges was elected in February 2003. The following judges were elected (country of origin in parentheses): Rene Blattman (Bolivia), Maureen Harding Clark (Ireland), Fatoumata Dembele Diarra (Mali), Adrian Fulford (United Kingdom),

Karl T. Hudson-Phillips (Trinidad and Tobago), Claude Jorda (France), Hans-Peter Kaul (Germany), Philippe Kirsch (Canada), Erkki Kourula (Finland), Akua Kuenyehia (Ghana), Elizabeth Odio Benito (Costa Rica), Gheorgios M. Pikis (Cyprus), Navanethem Pillay (South Africa), Mauro Politi (Italy), Tuiloma Neroni Slade (Samoa), Sanghyun Song (Republic of Korea), Sylvia H. de Figueiredo Steiner (Brazil), and Anita Usacka (Latvia). The full listings are available at http://www.un.org/law/icc/elections/results/judges_results.htm. There have since been additional elections.

12 Rome Statute, art. 36(6).
13 Rome Statute, art. 36.
14 See Rome Statute, Preamble (emphasizing that the ICC "shall be complementary to national criminal jurisdictions").
15 See Rome Statute, art. 17. One commentator has labeled Article 17, which sets out the admis-sibility procedures, as "one of the most sensitive provisions of the Rome Statute." (See Holmes 2001: 335.)
16 Rome Statute, art. 17(1)(a).
17 Rome Statute, art. 17(1)(b).
18 States parties to the Rome Statute, http://www.icc-cpi.int/statesparties.html.
19 International Criminal Court, Situations and Cases. Available at http://www.icc-cpi.int/cases.html.
20 A state that refers a situation to the Court, however, cannot limit the subject of the referral to particular individuals, so these countries run the risk that the prosecutor may choose to prosecute individuals affiliated with these states' governments.
21 Exceptions include Fehl 2004.
22 Snyder and Vinjamuri 2003–04. For a contrary view, arguing that the ICC in fact sets parameters in which political settlements can take place, see Méndez 2001.

Section IV

Key issues in international law

17

Fidelity to constitutional democracy and to the rule of international law

Russell Powell and Allen Buchanan

Until recently, international law was almost exclusively concerned to regulate the behaviour of states toward one another. In contrast, what may be called robust international law (RIL) claims the authority to regulate matters within states and even to prescribe how the state is to treat its own citizens within its own territory. International human rights law is RIL par excellence, but international criminal law and some international environmental and trade law also regulate conduct previously thought to be reserved for state control. In this chapter, we focus on a fundamental question: Is the commitment to (domestic) constitutional democracy compatible with the commitment to robust international law? In the first section, we examine the question of whether RIL is compatible with democracy, examining claims that a state's recognition of the supremacy of RIL is inconsistent with democratic principles. We then go on to ask the same question about constitutionalism that we asked in the first section about democracy: Is recognition of the supremacy of RIL consistent with the principles that comprise the political ideal of constitutional government?

Over and above its astonishing proliferation, perhaps the most remarkable development in international law in the last few decades has been the emergence of what might be called robust international law (RIL). Until recently, international law was almost exclu-

sively concerned to regulate the behaviour of states toward one another. In contrast, RIL claims the authority to regulate matters within states and even to prescribe how the state is to treat its own citizens within its own territory. International human rights law is RIL par excellence, but international criminal law and some international environmental and trade law also purport to regulate conduct previously thought to be reserved for state[1] control.

International law, like all law, claims authority. Yet international law does not recognize domestic[2] law, even domestic constitutional law, as limiting its authority. It claims supreme authority on those matters it addresses.[3] Such a claim is remarkable, given that the constitutions of most states either explicitly claim unlimited legal supremacy or are implicitly regarded as enjoying it.[4] How can domestic constitutional law and international law both be supreme with regard to the same domains of control?

That question has become urgent with the development of effective RIL – law that not only claims the authority to regulate matters hitherto regarded as the prerogative of the state, but that is also increasingly backed by significant sanctions, including, in some cases, a credible threat of coercion. In brief, both the reach and the grasp of international law have been augmented, even if the former still exceeds the latter. The question of compatibility is no longer a curiosity of abstract jurisprudential theory; it is a pressing practical matter.

RIL has emerged in an environment in which those who advocate the rule of international law generally also endorse constitutional democracy at the level of the state. But some who claim to be friends of domestic constitutional democracy now raise serious doubts about its compatibility with RIL. These worries about incompatibility, as we shall show, extend far beyond the question of how to make international law's unlimited claim to supremacy consistent with the claims of supremacy that domestic constitutions make. Some of the more serious worries would remain even if every state constitution explicitly recognized the supremacy of international law or of certain types of international law, such as human rights law. The problem of compatibility does not admit of a purely formal solution.

Conflicting claims of legitimacy

Concerns about the relationship between RIL and domestic constitutions can be formulated as issues of competing claims to legitimacy, where legitimacy is understood as the right to rule. International law claims legitimacy and does not qualify this claim by acknowledging any superior legal authority, even where it purports to regulate the internal affairs of states. Domestic constitutions typically make a similarly unlimited claim regarding internal affairs. Thus there are conflicting claims of legitimacy. So far as their plausibility is concerned, however, there seems to be a stark asymmetry. The dominant view is now that democracy is a requirement of legitimate government. But RIL is not the product of democratic institutions. In the form of treaty law, it is the product of a process of negotiation among states some

of which are not democratic, and in which enormous inequalities of power among states can call the voluntariness of state consent into question. In the form of customary international law, RIL is also a far cry from law made by representative legislatures: whether a norm becomes customary international law depends upon whether it gains sufficient support from powerful states (some of which are not democratic), from unelected judges in international tribunals, and from prominent legal scholars. The norms promulgated by global governance institutions, such as the WTO, the Security Council, and various international environmental and regulatory regimes also lack the legitimacy that democratic law-making processes are thought to confer at the domestic level; these institutions are not democratic in anything like the way that legitimate states are expected to be. From this perspective, RIL's claim to unlimited authority is especially problematic because it amounts to the assertion that institutions of dubious legitimacy have the authority to override the norms of institutions that have a much stronger claim to legitimacy — namely, democratic states.

The scholarly debate about the compatibility of RIL and constitutional democracy has chiefly taken place in two venues: the rich literature on the expanding authority of European Union (EU) institutions and the much less developed literature that revolves around the critique of RIL advanced by a group of American constitutional and international law scholars sometimes referred to as the "new sovereigntists". The American side of the debate has been hobbled by three self-imposed limitations: (1) an unwillingness to learn from the EU literature, (2) a failure to distinguish clearly between the question of whether RIL is compatible with constitutional democracy and whether it is compatible with the current American constitution or American-style democracy and (3) a refusal to consider the possibility that when there are tensions between RIL and a state's constitution, one option worth considering is whether the tension could be relieved by constitutional amendment. The first and third self-imposed limitations, we will argue, are related: If the new sovereigntists paid more attention to the EU literature, they would find it more difficult to ignore the option of constitutional amendment to accommodate RIL, because several EU countries have in fact made such an adjustment. It is perfectly appropriate, of course, for scholars to focus on the impact of RIL on the US Constitution or on American democracy, but it is wrong to slide from claims about what is incompatible with that constitution or detrimental to that form of democracy to more grandiose assertions about what is incompatible with constitutionalism or with democracy themselves.

In this chapter, we focus on the most fundamental question: "Are the commitments to (domestic) constitutional democracy and to robust international law compatible?", while trying to avoid the limitations of the American side of the debate. In the first section, we consider whether RIL is compatible with democracy, examining claims that a state's recognition of the supremacy of RIL is inconsistent with democratic principles. Here we argue that the charge of inconsistency relies on implausible assumptions about democracy. We also argue, however, that the expansion of RIL poses a fundamental problem for democratic states, a problem that democratic principles, including the principle of subsidiarity, which has figured so prominently in the EU literature, cannot answer: How much self-government should a democratic people relinquish to international institutions? In the second section, we ask the same question about constitutionalism that we asked in the first about democracy: Is recognition of the supremacy of RIL consistent with the principles that comprise the political ideal of constitutional government? In this section, we argue for two conclusions: First, although RIL and constitutionalism are formally consistent in the sense that a constitution can consistently acknowledge a superior legal authority, there are circumstances in

which acknowledging the supremacy of RIL can impair the functioning of a state's constitution; and, second, that when the acceptance of RIL involves either serious impairment of a state's constitution or a significant loss of self-determination for the people whose constitution it is, then principles of democratic constitutionalism require a special form of democratic authorization – either a new constitution, constitutional amendment, or a special super-majoritarian legislative act.

Before turning to the question of compatibility, it is important to be clear about why it matters. The possibility that the commitment to RIL is incompatible with the commitment to constitutional democracy is disturbing because both seem morally compelling. Since the case for constitutional democracy is better known, here we will only sketch, in broad strokes, the chief reasons for acknowledging the authority of RIL.[5] Our purpose is not to make the case for RIL but simply to indicate the costs of abandoning the development of RIL in the name of protecting constitutional democracy.

There are two types of reason for the citizens of constitutional democracies to urge their leaders to acknowledge the authority of RIL. The first may be called self-regarding: These are reasons that apply independently of any cosmopolitan commitments on the part of the citizenry. By "cosmopolitan commitments" here we mean commitments grounded in a direct concern for the well-being or protecting the interests of persons who are not members of one's own polity.

Self-regarding reasons

Acknowledging the authority of RIL can improve the functioning of constitutional democracies in at least four ways, independently of whether it happens to fulfil cosmopolitan commitments. First, by acknowledging the authority of RIL, governments can provide benefits that their citizens have demanded, but which cannot be provided by unilateral action or by traditional-style bilateral international agreements that do not commit states to RIL. Robust international legal regimes help solve coordination problems, provide global public goods, and avoid or reduce negative externalities.[6]

Second, even the best constitutional democracies sometimes fail to provide equal protection of the rights of some of their citizens. Furthermore, every constitutional democracy is at risk for unjustifiably infringing civil rights generally, not just those of minorities or women, when there is a perceived national emergency, such as war or terrorist attacks. If a state acknowledges the authority of international human rights law, this can help mobilize political support, both within the country and from without, for the protection of domestic constitutional civil and political rights. In some cases, types of international law that are not typically categorized as human rights law, including law affecting economic development, can also have a significant positive impact on the security of citizens' civil and political rights, to the extent that states acknowledge their authority in the domestic sphere.

Third, all constitutional democracies include various institutional mechanisms for reducing the persisting risk that policy will unduly reflect the preferences of powerful special interests; but when such interests are concentrated and the opposition to them is diffuse, these domestic mechanisms may be insufficient. When this is the case, participation in international institutions that claim robust legal authority may help counter the power of special interests. For example, the binding rules of the WTO that prohibit trade discrimination have helped the US Congress resist pressure from domestic protectionist groups.

Fourth, by participating in robust international legal regimes, states can improve public deliberation in domestic policymaking across a wide range of domestic policy areas: they can more effectively draw on more exten-

sive pools of experts and can identify and learn from "best practices" developed elsewhere. In some cases, acknowledging the authority of RIL is a necessary condition of reaping these epistemic gains.

The foregoing four reasons to accept RIL should appeal to citizens of constitutional democracies because of their positive effects on domestic politics. Their force does not depend on the assumption that the citizens of a constitutional democracy are or ought to be influenced by cosmopolitan commitments; it does not presuppose a non-instrumental concern for the rights and interests of foreigners. In addition to these self-regarding reasons, there are reasons for acknowledging the authority of RIL that carry considerable weight from a cosmopolitan point of view.

Cosmopolitan reasons

First, a commitment to robust international human rights law and to the emerging institutions of international criminal law can enhance the effectiveness of the efforts of the citizens and leaders of a constitutional democracy in promoting the protection of the basic interests of all persons. By promoting human rights through participation in international institutions, as opposed to acting unilaterally, a state can also assure others that its efforts are sincere and not a guise for the pursuit of narrow national interest. The perception of legitimacy can increase cooperation and to that extent can make it more likely that the goal of better protection for all will be achieved.

Second, participation in robust international legal regimes can help to counter the parochial bias of democratic politics. Constitutional democracies are typically structured to ensure that legislators and government officials are accountable to – and only to – their own fellow citizens. Foreigners have no votes and in some cases domestic law is explicitly intended to prevent "foreign influences" on the policymaking process.[7]

Thus constitutional democracies systematically exclude from proper consideration the legitimate interests of others that are affected by their actions. Acknowledging the authority of RIL can help correct this bias by requiring state policy that affects the basic interests of foreigners to take those interests into account. In the next section, we will argue that it is a misunderstanding of democracy to hold that the government of a democracy must be accountable exclusively to its own citizens.

Third, acknowledging the authority of RIL can be an expression of the commitment to the ideal of the rule of law. One of the chief moral attractions of the rule of law is that it embodies a commitment to not settling conflicts of interests and preferences by recourse to sheer power. This commitment does not rule out the resolution of conflicts by force, of course, but it does require that force not be the first resort and that when it is employed it is justified by publicly available reasons of the right sort, what might be called principled reasons, as distinct from mere threats or appeals to the interests of those who happen to be the stronger. In international relations, where disparities of power are great, the moral case for the rule of law is correspondingly strong.

There are several reasons to repudiate the rule of sheer power. The need to protect the vulnerable and to avoid unfairness are among the most obvious, but there is also the idea that respect for persons requires an appeal to their capacity to act on the basis of principled reasons rather than relying solely or primarily on their capacity to respond to threats. All of these reasons qualify as cosmopolitan, because they all assume the fundamental equal moral status of persons: all are to be treated fairly; vulnerable persons generally, not just the vulnerable who are one's fellow citizens, are to be protected; all are to be respected by appealing to their capacity for being moved by principled reasons.

These basic moral attractions of the rule of law have always been one chief element in the case for having international law (the other

being the realist idea that the system of restraint that international law provides is in the interest of every state because no state can reasonably expect to maintain a position of domination). The question at hand, however, is not whether the ideal of the rule of law supports a commitment to international law as it was traditionally conceived, but whether it supports a commitment to robust international law. More precisely, do the basic moral values that ground the commitment to the rule of law give the citizens and political leaders of a constitutional democracy reason to acknowledge the authority of international law even within domains that were previously thought to be protected by the veil of sovereignty?

The question is still insufficiently precise, because the answer may depend on what sort of international law is involved. Consider the case of international human rights law. It is appropriate to focus on human rights law because it is perhaps the type of RIL that has been viewed with the greatest suspicion by those who say that fidelity to constitutional democracy and to RIL are incompatible. Disputes arise as to the meaning, scope and institutional implications of particular human rights norms. Presumably the principle that conflicts should not be settled by sheer power applies to this sort of dispute; to exclude it seems arbitrary. If this is the case, then the idea of repudiating the rule of sheer power, which as we have seen lies at the heart of the commitment to the rule of law, provides a reason in favour of a powerful state such as the US not claiming the unqualified right to determine how human rights norms will be interpreted and applied to its own actions or the conduct of its citizens or officials. When a powerful state claims the right to do this, it is in effect asserting that it is permissible for it to be a judge in its own case, to decide whether complaints that it has failed to protect human rights are valid. Because it is a powerful state, its vulnerability to sanctions by other states or international organizations or world public opinion will be relatively inconsequential, at least in cases in which it has a strong interest in the outcome, and this means that effective checks on its acting in a self-serving, biased fashion will be absent. There will be a significant risk that the conflict will be settled by sheer power – that is, in accordance with the interest of the powerful simply because they are powerful – rather than in a principled, publicly justifiable way. At the very least, such a state bears a burden of argument to explain why the usual rule of law considerations that speak in favour of not being a judge in one's own case are not dispositive in case of disputes over the interpretation and application of human rights norms.[8]

One could, of course, argue that at present the burden of explaining why the principle that one shouldn't be a judge in one's own case cannot be met in some areas of international law that most significantly challenge state sovereignty. For example, some have argued that the defects of the current International Criminal Court process are so great as to outweigh the rule of law reasons for acknowledging the authority of the Court. Our aim here, however, is not to show that the commitment to the rule of law supplies a conclusive reason to support any particular area of RIL, but only to show that it can provide a reason to support RIL, depending on the circumstances. Moreover, when it does, the reason it supplies is one that should carry significant weight with those committed to constitutional democracy, so far as the idea of constitutional democracy subsumes or presupposes that of the rule of law.

Taken together, the four self-regarding and the three cosmopolitan reasons show that there is a strong case for acknowledging the authority of RIL when certain conditions are satisfied. These reasons do not purport to provide a blanket endorsement for all international law that claims robust authority. Rather, whether any of the reasons apply and the weight they carry may vary depending on what sort of law is involved and on whether the benefits that acknowledging the authority of

the law brings can be gained in some other way. Nonetheless, we hope that this brief discussion makes clear the attractions of having an international legal system that includes mechanisms for creating RIL. Keeping the potential benefits of RIL in mind, we will now consider whether a commitment to RIL is incompatible, with either democracy or constitutionalism.

Are fidelity to constitutional democracy and fidelity to robust international law compatible?

Whether these two commitments are compatible depends, of course, on what democracy is. Remarkably, the new sovereigntists who deny compatibility offer no explicit conception of democracy and tend to assert, rather than to argue, that acknowledging the supremacy of robust international law offends democratic principles. Even more frustrating, they are sometimes unclear as to whether the alleged incompatibility is with democracy or with constitutional democracy or with some particular constitutional democracies or with only one constitutional democracy (namely, the United States). To begin to assess charges of incompatibility we must first settle on a serviceable conception of democracy. In doing so, we must avoid controversial conceptions of democracy in order not to prejudice the issue of compatibility.

Democracy, in the most general and least controversial sense, is a process for making decisions that will be binding on all members of a group, each of which has an equal say at some important stage or level of the process.[9] When applied to modern, large-scale states, the term usually connotes as well the requirement that important government officials, or at least legislators, are held accountable through periodic elections in which citizens have equal votes. We will refer to this core idea of democracy as equal popular electoral accountability or popular accountability for short.

It is crucial to note that this definition does not assume that all of the laws to which the citizens of a democracy are subject must be made by their elected representatives (or voted on directly by the citizens themselves, as in referendum). So it is compatible with some domestic law being created through judicial decisions and/or administrative processes. This seems unexceptionable, if the goal is to settle on a moderately realistic conception of democracy, one that can at least be approximated, under reasonably favourable circumstances, by the clearest examples of actual states that are generally regarded as democratic.

With this broad and relatively uncontroversial conception of democracy in mind, let us now consider four arguments – or in some cases, reconstructions of intimations of arguments – that purport to show that the commitment to democracy at the domestic level and the commitment to RIL are incompatible. It should be emphasized that our purpose here is analytical, not exegetical. In each case we will reference work by new sovereigntists that at least suggests a given argument, but we make no effort to document conclusively who advances which argument. One reason for this approach is that some of the theorists in question are unclear as to which arguments for incompatibility they are advancing in a given context. Another reason is that each scholar who is sceptical of delegations to international institutions has her own nuanced view of the constitutionally appropriate scope of delegation, and consequently it is difficult to bring all of these authors under a single, uniform conceptual umbrella.

The exclusive accountability argument

This is the claim that democracy requires that every official who exercises political authority over the citizens of a state must be accountable solely to those citizens. The concern here is primarily with the delegation of legal authority over the domestic citizenry

to officials of global governance institutions or to judges of international tribunals. For example, John Yoo (2000: 1715) appeals to broader, normative principles of constitutionalism to justify the priority of the Appointments Clause of Article II of the US Constitution in its conflict with the new international law, stating that:

> The Framers . . . centralized the appointments power because they feared the vesting of power in officeholders who were not accountable to the electorate, as had occurred during the colonial period . . . A centralized appointments process prevents the national government, as a whole, from concealing or confusing the lines of governmental authority and responsibility so that the people may hold the actions of the government accountable. Allowing the transfer of command authority to non-U.S. officers threatens this basic principle of government accountability. International or foreign officials have no obligation to pursue American policy, they do not take an oath to uphold the Constitution, nor can any American official hold them responsible for their deeds.[10]

If this first objection is understood to apply only to the US Constitution, the claim is that acknowledging the authority of RIL, or some instances of RIL, violates the constraints on delegation of executive authority set out in the Appointments Clause of the US Constitution. As we have already emphasized, however, our focus in this chapter is not on whether RIL is compatible with distinctive features that particular democratic constitutions may or may not have, but on the more basic question of whether it is compatible with constitutional democracy itself. In this section, we are sorting out incompatibilist objections that pertain to the democracy part of constitutional democracy. So the question is whether democracy requires that all political authority exercised over citizens of a democracy must be accountable exclusively to those citizens.

According to the broad and relatively un-controversial definition of democracy adduced earlier, the answer is clearly "no". Democracy, on this definition, requires that any official who wields political authority over the citizens of a democracy must be accountable to those citizens and it also imposes a requirement of equality among citizens – all citizens are to have an equal say, at important stages or levels of group decision making – but it does not rule out the possibility that such officials may also be accountable to non-citizens.[11] At most the non-controversial definition implies that those exercising authority over citizens of a particular state be accountable equally to all of them and to whomever else they are accountable, but it does not require accountability only to those citizens.

It is worth noting that even when the Exclusive Accountability Argument is restricted to the US case, it is implausible. The US Constitution authorizes the president, with concurrence of two-thirds of the Senate, to enter into and ratify treaties. In some cases, treaties set up mechanisms for dispute resolution through arbitration by third parties who are not exclusively accountable to the citizens of the contending states (if they can be said to be accountable to them at all). The clause of the Constitution that authorizes treaty making includes no suggestion that such treaties are prohibited. Moreover, not only the United States, but also other states that are commonly regarded as democratic, routinely enter into such treaties. So if exclusive accountability is a necessary condition for democracy, then there are few, if any, democracies in the world. A more reasonable conclusion is that exclusive accountability is not a requirement of democracy. This conclusion is reinforced by the realization that neither the idea of equal electoral accountability nor other notions usually associated with democracy (such as the idea that government has no rights on its own account, but instead only has the authority that is conferred on it by those whose interests it is supposed to serve) require exclusive accountability.

The democratic deficit argument

One theme common to the EU literature and the American literature is the idea that international legal regimes suffer a "democratic deficit", although this term seems to be more commonly used in the EU context. As we shall understand it here, the phrase "democratic deficit" refers to the international (or, in the EU case, regional) version of a problem that has preoccupied democratic theorists for some time: the problem of bureaucratic distance. In the domestic case, the complaint is that officials of the modern administrative state make important decisions and in some cases even make laws, yet are not subject to electoral accountability. In the supranational context, the charge is that chains of authority stretching from democratic publics to officials of international or EU institutions are too attenuated to warrant the title of democratic accountability.[12]

It is crucial to distinguish between the charge that robust international legal institutions lack exclusive accountability to particular domestic publics and the charge that bureaucratic distance undercuts adequate accountability, because adequate accountability need not be exclusive. If it were the case – contrary to what we have argued already – that democracy requires exclusive accountability, then fidelity to RIL and to democracy would be incompatible in principle, because legitimate international institutions could not be accountable solely to the people of any particular country.[13] The bureaucratic distance problem, in contrast, is remediable, so long as adequate accountability mechanisms can be developed. In that sense, the democratic deficit argument is not capable of showing that there is any inherent incompatibility between RIL and constitutional democracy.

Moreover, incompatibilists who wield the democratic deficit argument must tread a razor-thin line: They must make the case that the problem of bureaucratic distance is so severe and intractable in the international case that democratic states should deny the authority of RIL, but, at the same time, they must provide reasons to believe that the same problem in the domestic case is not so severe as to undermine domestic legal authority. That is a tough order to fill, because it requires either (1) a principled identification of a point along the continuum of bureaucratic distance that undercuts authority, along with convincing reasons for concluding that domestic bureaucratic distance falls below it and international bureaucratic distance above it or (2) good evidence for thinking that the problem of bureaucratic distance can be adequately ameliorated in the domestic case but not in the international case.[14]

At any rate, the key point is that the democratic deficit or bureaucratic distance argument is incapable of showing that domestic democracy and RIL are incompatible in principle. Just as important, those who advance this argument fail to consider the possibility that its shelf life may be rather short; they do not even entertain the possibility that better accountability mechanisms for international agencies and officials can be and ought to be developed.[15]

None of this is to deny that the problem of bureaucratic distance is serious at the supranational level or that it should be especially troubling to those who endorse democracy at the domestic level. To a large extent the case for democracy at the domestic level rests on the idea that democratic institutions provide popular accountability, where this includes accountability of officials to all those they govern. So those who endorse democracy at the domestic level should be very disturbed when governing officials, domestic or supranational, are not adequately accountable to those they govern.

Rather than saying that the commitment to domestic democracy and the commitment to RIL law are presently incompatible due to the relatively underdeveloped popular accountability of those international legal institutions that assert robust authority, it

would be more accurate to say that in these circumstances there is a tension between the two commitments. This language better conveys the possibility that trade-offs between the two commitments may be in order. The possibility of trade-off should not be dismissed; after all, as we have already argued, there are a number of reasons why democracies should find the availability of institutions for creating RIL attractive. More specifically, if such institutions are to develop greater popular accountability, it may be necessary, especially for more powerful and influential democratic states, to participate actively in them and to that extent acknowledge their authority *pro tanto* – that is, provisionally on the expectation that they can be improved and conditionally on their actually showing promise of improvement. Temporary toleration of an international institutional democracy deficit may be a reasonable price to pay in order to reap the benefits of RIL while working for better accountability.

The unacceptable loss of self-government argument

The self-governance of a democratic people can be diminished in several ways. One way we have just discussed: To the extent that officials, whether domestic or international, govern citizens without being adequately accountable to them, there is a loss of self-government, because self-government requires popular accountability. A democratic people also experiences a diminution of self-government if important decisions previously made by officials exclusively accountable to them are now made by officials who are accountable to other constituencies as well, as occurs when international institutions exert robust legal authority. When this second sort of diminution of self-government occurs, the problem is not that something has transpired that is inherently incompatible with democracy at the domestic level; as we have seen, democracy

is not incompatible with a people being subject to authority that is not exclusively
accountable with them. Rather, the worry is
that if increasingly more authority is transferred
to officials who are not exclusively accountable to a particular people, then a point will
eventually be reached at which it is no
longer meaningful to say that the polity is self-
governing. To put the same point in a
slightly different way, democracy does not
require that all authority over a democratic
people be exclusively accountable to them,
but it does require a significant domain of
authority that is characterized by exclusive
accountability to them. If a state transferred
virtually all important governing functions to
some other political entity, so that its people
had no exclusive control over any area of
policy, we would no longer regard it as self-
governing, or, hence, as a democracy. Clearly
those who value democracy at the state level
have a right to be concerned about the
extent of the transfer of authority to supranational institutions, even though they can and
should acknowledge that it is not the case that
a people can only be subject to the authority of officials that are exclusively accountable to them.

The loss of self-government worry is not
to be confused with the democratic deficit
argument noted earlier. Even if all international institutions exhibited better popular
accountability than any existing democratic
states, the question would still remain: Is their
exercise of power compatible with meaningful domestic self-government? International
institutions with a great deal of popular
accountability – accountability to the citizens
of all states – could be described as providing global self-government, but depending on
the scope of its powers this might come at
the price of an unacceptable loss of self-
government at the level of individual states.

The critical issue, then, is this: At what point
does the diminution of self-determination
in a state become so great as to be incompatible with it warranting the title of a democracy, a territory whose inhabitants are in

some meaningful sense self-governing?[16] The
answer to that question depends upon an
account of what makes political self-determination valuable. Political self-determination
is valuable for a number of reasons, which need
not be rehearsed here. Because it is valuable
for a number of different reasons, reasons that
will have greater weight for members of various groups, and because self-determination
is not an all or nothing matter, but rather
comes in many forms and degrees, there is no
single or easy answer to the question: How
much self-determination is enough for a
constitutional democracy?

An intuitively plausible response to this
quandary is to appeal to the value of self-
determination itself and simply say that the
citizens of democracies should decide how
much self-governance they will relinquish
to global governance institutions.[17] But even
if we grant that the decision to relinquish
some dimensions of self-determination to a
robust international legal order ought itself
to be viewed as a matter of rightful self-
determination, we still need to know how
this choice is to be made. For even if it is
permissible or even obligatory to relinquish
a great deal of self-governance to the international legal order – for example, to promote
peace or to achieve better protection of
human rights or to safeguard the environment
– it would not follow that just any way of
transferring political power is appropriate.
More precisely, we need to ask whether the
same values that undergird the commitment
to democracy also place constraints on how
powers of self-government can be transferred to international institutions.

The lack of democratic authorization argument

It should not be assumed that the ways in
which RIL is actually being created satisfy reasonable constraints on the relinquishing of self-
determination. Consider an analogy. There
is much to be said for the idea that when existing political units come together to form a

federal state, as occurred in what became the US, or when a centralized state devolves into a federal state, these are such significant constitutional changes as to require some form of democratic authorization that is more robust than the ordinary legislative process. In brief, for such major changes in the character of a polity, public constitutional deliberation and popular choice seem to be required.[18] Similarly, if the development of RIL continues to reduce the domain of self-determination for a democracy, the point may be reached at which proper appreciation of the value of self-determination requires public deliberation and popular choice, or at least some sort of authorization that is more directly democratic than an ordinary legislative act or the ratification of a treaty.

The argument thus far can now be summarized. When a democracy transfers authority to supranational institutions, it thereby relinquishes the right to exclusive accountability for its exercise and this constitutes a diminution of self-determination. But there is no inherent incompatibility here between democracy and RIL, because it is not part of the idea of democracy that the scope of self-determination must be unlimited. However, if a democracy either (a) transfers so much authority to supranational institutions that it can no longer be said to be self-governing or (b) relinquishes significant dimensions of its self-determination without doing so by a process of authorization that is consonant with the core ideas of democracy, then its citizens thereby compromise their commitment to their democracy.

The idea that some processes for relinquishing self-government may be compatible with democratic principles while others may not be warrants elaboration. Consider three quite different types of process by which a democracy might subject itself to international legal regimes that significantly limit the scope of its self-government. The first, to which we have already alluded, is through public constitutional deliberation and popular choice, by processes that give more

weight to the popular will than ordinary legislative processes and which are preceded by special public deliberations designed to reflect the fact that issues of significance for the fundamental character of governance are at stake. Here the mechanisms for accepting RIL that entails a significant diminution of self-government would be a new constitutional convention, constitutional amendment, or perhaps some form of referendum in which all citizens could vote. The second alternative is some form of special supermajority legislation: recognition of the supremacy of international law that qualifies as constitutional change would require approval from the national legislature by considerably more than a bare majority. Variants of the first and second processes have in fact been utilized by states joining the EU or acceding to its evolving structures of authority. The third alternative is a process of accretion in which no public constitutional deliberation or popular choice occurs and no special legislative approval is required – a process that might be characterized rather uncharitably as a democracy's slow death by a thousand cuts. The accretion can occur through a combination of:

- executive agreements
- automatic incorporation of ratified treaties into the law of the land (so-called self-execution)
- recognition of international law as federal common law
- judicial borrowing from international law
- the development of more robust global governance institutions that increasingly create policies through their own bureaucracies without the "specific" consent of states.

The process of accretion is deeply problematic from the standpoint of democracy: there are significant losses of self-determination, but without deliberation by the people as to whether to incur them and there is no special process of authorization that reflects the fact that changes of this sort require robust popular support. There is not even any special national legislative act to signal that this is not just law making or treaty making as usual.

The processes by which European Union governance has developed have included, at several critical junctures, something approaching the first model for accepting international law that is sufficiently robust to result in significant diminutions of self-government – the public constitutional deliberation and popular choice model. But in the case of most states outside Europe, including the US, the process of accepting RIL has been one of accretion: public constitutional deliberation and popular choice have been conspicuously absent. To accept the process of accretion, when other, more democratic processes for acknowledging the authority of RIL are available, is to indulge in an unjustified departure from the commitment to domestic democracy.

The principle of subsidiarity and its limitations

The principle of subsidiarity has played a prominent role in the EU debate about the compatibility of constitutional democracy with RIL, but is largely absent in the American debate. Our aim here is not to do justice to the sophisticated literature on subsidiarity in the context of EU politics and legal development, but rather to try to determine whether an appeal to subsidiarity can answer the question posed in the previous subsection: At what point does the relinquishment of authority by a state to international legal regimes violate the commitment to domestic democracy?

The basic idea of subsidiarity is that political authority should be exercised at the "local" level except when it is "better" exercised at a higher level. Subsidiarity is perhaps more accurately described as a mode of practical reasoning for decisions about the allocation of political authority rather than

as a principle of jurisdiction. Where the allocation of authority is between a state and a supranational entity, the idea is that the default allocation is to the state and that proponents of an allocation to a supranational entity bear a burden of justification. Matthias Kumm notes that subsidiarity is a central principle of European constitutionalism, and he characterizes the process of reasoning that subsidiarity entails as follows:

[S]ubsidiarity analysis . . . requires a two-step test. First reasons relating to the existence of a collective action problem have to be identified. Second the weight of these reasons has to be assessed in light of countervailing concerns in the specific circumstances.

(Kumm 2004: 921)

The reference to collective action problems suggests what might be called the narrow understanding of subsidiarity, namely, that it is a principle of efficiency. Collective action problems arise when two or more agents who prefer some outcome, O, that can only be attained by their joint action are barred from achieving it because the structure of incentives is such that if each acts so as to optimize, the result is suboptimal from the standpoint of achieving O. On the narrow understanding, subsidiarity is a principle of efficiency because following the process it prescribes simply allows agents to better achieve outcomes they (all) prefer. As such, subsidiarity has nothing to say about cases in which groups with different preferences must decide how to allocate authority. It cannot provide guidance, for example, when the people of a state value self-governance in some area of life so highly that they are willing to sacrifice some efficiency to preserve it, while others prefer more robust international authority.

Kumm makes it clear that he does not construe subsidiarity in this narrow way as a principle of efficiency. He says that it is compatible with there being exceptions to the rule that authority should be allocated to the higher level political entity only if doing so is necessary for solving collective action problems. This suggests that, on a broad understanding of the principle, subsidiarity gives considerable but not exclusive weight to efficiency but also permits other values to be taken into account. The only other value Kumm mentions is "the protection of minimal standards of human rights" (2004: 921). However, to limit departures from an exclusive concern with efficiency in this way seems arbitrary. Why consider only the protection of minimal standards of human rights (given that human rights typically are themselves thought of as minimal moral requirements) and not other values as well, such as self-determination?

Those who would invoke subsidiarity to determine what sorts of relinquishments of self-determination are compatible with a commitment to domestic democracy confront a dilemma. They can either construe subsidiarity narrowly as a principle of efficiency, in which case it is silent on the question at issue; or they can construe it broadly, so as to accommodate values other than efficiency, in which case they must either provide a principled account of why only certain other values (such as the protection of human rights, but not self-determination) are relevant or acknowledge that the "principle" of subsidiarity is the unhelpful truism that we are to allocate authority to the local entity, except when not doing so is better all things considered.

Our conclusion is not that subsidiarity is useless as a constitutional principle, but rather that it provides little or no guidance for answering the question "How much authority should those committed to their own democracy be willing to give up for the sake of acknowledging the authority of robust international law?"[19] Even more clearly, the notion of subsidiarity sheds no light on the other major concern about the impact of RIL on self-government at the level of states; it is silent on the question "Which processes for relinquishing powers of self-government to supranational entities are most consonant with the commitment to democracy?"

The results of this section can now be summarized. There is no in principle incompatibility between fidelity to robust international law and fidelity to democracy at the domestic level. Those who have suggested that there is have apparently done so on the basis of a controversial and problematic, but unarticulated conception of democracy as either requiring that all those who exercise authority over the citizens of a democracy must be accountable exclusively to them or as permitting no diminution of self-government. Nonetheless, although fidelity to RIL and domestic democracy are in principle compatible, both the bureaucratic distance that characterizes international institutions and the undemocratic processes by which some states have relinquished self-government to these institutions raise serious concerns for those committed to democracy at the domestic level. Finally, the principle of subsidiarity sheds limited light on either the question of how much authority a democratic people ought to be willing to cede to international legal regimes and no light whatsoever on the question of how they should authorize whatever transfer of authority they are willing to make.

Are fidelity to constitutionalism and fidelity to robust international law compatible?

The second prong of our investigation of whether RIL and constitutional democracy are compatible focuses on the constitutionalism side of the issue, as the first focused on the democracy side. In the first section, we began with a relatively uncontroversial and moderately realistic conception of democracy; here we do the same for constitutionalism.

According to what may be the leanest plausible definition, constitutionalism is the view that if government is to be legitimate its powers must be subject to entrenched legal limitations. Entrenched legal limitations need not be irrevocable – they can be removed by constitutional amendment, for example. But removing them must be more difficult than changing ordinary laws and the validity of ordinary laws depends on their consistency with existing limitations. According to this view, the constitution of a polity is a public (although not necessarily written) specification of the entrenched legal limitations on government power.

A somewhat thicker, but still relatively uncontroversial definition includes everything in the narrowest definition but adds the idea that legitimate government requires a public specification of the basic structure of government, a specification that makes clear the entrenched legal limitations on government's power, while taking into account that government requires a plurality of distinct institutions. This additional element is most clearly expressed in written constitutions that distinguish legislative, executive, and judicial "branches of government" or "powers" and assign them each distinctive functions.

According to what might be called the liberal conception of constitutionalism, whatever else the specification of the structure of government encompasses, it must include the idea that the judiciary is "independent" of the executive. On most accounts, liberal constitutionalism adds to this the idea that among the entrenched limitations on government power, individual civil and political rights are prominent and that one function of the "independence" of the judiciary is to help uphold these rights. However, the liberal constitutionalist conception of an independent judiciary does not itself include a requirement of American-style robust judicial review of legislation.

In the case of federal states, constitutionalism also includes the idea that the public, entrenched specification of the structure of government and the limits on government power includes an allocation of powers among two or more distinct polities. Standard definitions of federalism include the idea that this allocation of power must rec-

ognize domains of supremacy for the distinct polities, in other words, that each has the "final say" on some matters (Karmis and Norman 2005; Waluchow 2007). (Without this added condition, it would not be possible to distinguish merely decentralized states from federations.)

Constitutionalism and the "supremacy" of constitutional law

At the outset of this chapter we noted that states' constitutions typically claim supremacy. Some would argue that the concept of constitutionalism itself grounds this claim, that constitutional law, by definition, is supreme. There are, however, two quite different ways in which to understand the claim that constitutionalism includes the idea that when governance is legitimate the constitution is supreme, that is, that it has the "final say" on legality. On the first construal, the supremacy of constitutional law is internal only: The constitution is the supreme legal authority within the polity of which it is the constitution. On the second construal, the supremacy of constitutional law is unbounded: The constitution is supreme not only with respect to other sources of law within the polity, but also with respect to all other sources of law.

The core idea of constitutionalism, the thesis that legitimate government requires entrenched limitations on government power, does not itself imply unbounded constitutional supremacy; at most it implies that it is supreme with respect to the ordinary law of the polity. In fact, none of the definitions of constitutionalism listed above includes the idea of unbounded constitutional supremacy. Yet at least the richer variants seem to capture what is essential to constitutionalism. So the assertion that constitutionalism is incompatible with a state's constitution recognizing the supremacy of supranational law is dubious at best.

There is an inconsistency between constitutionalism and the supremacy of supranational law over domestic constitutional law, then, only if we add to the idea that legitimate government requires entrenched legal limitations on its power the further requirement that the entrenched legal limitations must not be subject to the supremacy of law from any other source. It may be the case that constitutionalism is often implicitly understood as including this stronger notion – that constitutionalism is thought to include the idea that the constitution of a polity is supreme in the strong, unbounded sense. But it bears emphasizing that this stronger notion adds something to standard definitions of constitutionalism that appear to be quite unexceptionable without it.

One final point about constitutional supremacy is worth noting. Even on the unbounded construal, there is an important sense in which constitutional supremacy allows for the subordination of the constitution to supranational law. A constitution can contain an explicit recognition of the supremacy of international law over its other provisions, as is the case with Austria and the Netherlands.[20] Of course, so long as this constitutional provision is itself subject to revocation by processes of constitutional amendment, there is a sense in which the constitution remains supreme with respect to supranational law. Nonetheless, this ultimate supremacy of the constitution is compatible, from the standpoint of constitutionalism, with an existing constitution recognizing the supremacy of international law even with respect to some of its most significant provisions, including its enunciation of civil and political rights. Such acknowledgement occurs when a state's constitution provides that in cases where international human rights law contains a broader scope for a particular right, that understanding trumps a narrower interpretation that has developed in domestic constitutional law.[21]

So far we have argued that even on the dubious assumption that constitutionalism includes unbounded constitutional supremacy, rather than merely internal supremacy of the constitution, there is no inconsistency between the commitment to constitutionalism and acknowledging the supremacy of supranational law over a state's constitutional law, if two conditions are satisfied: (1) the constitution provides for the supremacy of the RIL in question and (2) the constitution also provides for revoking that supremacy. We now want to argue that in spite of this in principle compatibility, in practice the acknowledgment of the supremacy of RIL can be highly problematic from the standpoint of the commitment to domestic constitutionalism, under certain circumstances.

Potential negative impact of RIL on constitutional structures[22]

Even if the supremacy of a certain area of RIL, such as international human rights law, is explicitly acknowledged in a state's constitution and that constitution provides for revoking the acknowledgement of supremacy, there is still the worry that RIL may have a negative impact on domestic constitutional structures. The potential damage is of two sorts: (1) the undermining of the constitutional allocation of power among the branches of the government and (2) the undermining of federalism, by encroaching on the authority that the constitution accords to federal units ((US) states, cantons, provinces, etc.). The general point is that constitutional acknowledgement of the supremacy of supranational law, whether it is revocable or not, does not itself guarantee practical compatibility.

The first type of risk to constitutional structures can be illustrated briefly by reference to the US case, but the problem, with variations, applies much more broadly. RIL can become binding domestic law in the US chiefly in two ways: through the ratification of treaties and when international customary law is regarded as federal common law.

Some US constitutional scholars charge that in either case the incorporation of RIL into domestic law diminishes the rightful authority of the legislative branch.[23]

According to the US Constitution, international law created through treaties automatically becomes the "law of the land": When the US ratifies a treaty, its provisions take precedence over both the law of the states (federal units) and prior federal law with which it is inconsistent, without the requirement of federal legislation (US Const. Art. VI). The executive's power to make treaties is not unlimited of course, because ratification requires Senate approval; but the latter is a much weaker form of legislative control than in the ordinary creation of federal law. Moreover, the US Constitutional provision that makes ratified treaties federal law without federal legislation was drafted in a world in which international treaties did not include RIL – law that extends to matters previously thought to lie at the core of the protected sphere of state sovereignty, as is the case with modern human rights law.

Nevertheless, given that the US Constitution unconditionally declares the supremacy of treaty law over states' laws and inconsistent prior federal law, and given the unqualified nature of its provisions for the creation and ratification of treaties, it is implausible to argue that RIL created by treaty is contrary to the US Constitution.[24] It might still be the case, however, that the acceptance of RIL through treaty ratification effects a reallocation of power away from the legislative branch that is suboptimal from the standpoint of constitutional design and perhaps contrary to the intentions of the framers of the constitution as well.

The second risk that RIL can pose to domestic constitutional structures applies to cases of federal states. It can be argued that treaty-created RIL, at least in the area of human rights, reallocates power from the state legislatures to the federal executive and the Senate, when human rights treaties are ratified and take precedence over the states'

laws. The charge here is that the acceptance of RIL changes the constitutional structure of the federation by weakening self-government in the federal units. The same sort of change could be effected by according customary international human rights the status of federal common law. For example, acknowledging the authority of customary international human rights law could result in a diminution of federal units' control over the nature of punishments under their own criminal laws or could overturn provisions of marriage law, even though the federal constitution allocates the power to make laws in these areas to federal subunits.

The more general point is that for states whose constitutions were drafted prior to the era of RIL and which have not been carefully modified to accommodate this development, the possibility that domestic legal acknowledgement of the authority of RIL may damage the state's constitutional structures cannot be dismissed. The introduction of new legal norms from the outside – norms that regulate matters previously assigned by the constitution to various branches and levels of government or that allocate power between the federal government and federal subunits – may well be at odds with existing constitutional design. To assume that they will be harmonious would be unduly optimistic. A constitutional provision acknowledging the supremacy of RIL does not guarantee compatibility.

However, when the acceptance of RIL does impair existing constitutional structures, the proper conclusion to draw is not that constitutionalism is incompatible with RIL per se, but rather that the acceptance of the particular RIL in question is incompatible with the optimal functioning of those particular constitutional arrangements. Showing that this or that existing constitutional structure is impacted negatively by the acceptance of some type of RIL is a far cry from establishing that constitutionalism and RIL are incompatible, because there is a plurality of forms of constitutional democracy.

Further, constitutional structures rarely if ever work either optimally or not at all; instead, they do the jobs they were designed to do with greater or lesser effectiveness. When the acceptance of RIL does have a negative impact on the constitutional structures of a particular state, the impact may be of greater or lesser seriousness. In cases where the impact is limited, accepting some detriment to the functioning of existing constitutional arrangements may be a reasonable trade-off, if this is the only way to secure the important benefits that RIL can bring. For example, some loss of legislative authority on the part of the subunits of a state might be a reasonable price to pay, under certain circumstances, if this is necessary for achieving better protection of basic human rights. Constitutionalism may require that where acknowledging the authority of RIL disrupts constitutional structures, either the constitution must be changed or the authority of RIL must be denied, but it cannot tell us which the proper course of action is. The answer to that question depends upon the resolution of contested issues in political philosophy.

Notes

1   Obviously, the word "state" can refer both to countries (e.g. Spain, Thailand, the UK) and to federal subunits (e.g. California, Maryland, etc., in the case of the United States, and Chiapas, Chihuaha, etc., in the case of Mexico). No differentiation is made in spelling here, however (i.e. State or state).

2   By "domestic law" we mean the law of particular countries. The term "national" law is unfortunate because it helps perpetuate the myth of the nation state, that is, the false belief that all countries are mononational, when in fact most include two or more nationalities.

3   For example, Article 46(1) of the Vienna Convention on the Law of Treaties (the "treaty of treaties"), provides that: "A state may not invoke the fact that its consent to be bound by a treaty has been expressed in violation of a provision of its internal law regarding competence to conclude treaties as invalidating its consent unless that violation was manifest and concerned a rule of its internal law of fun-

damental importance." Thus, even a manifest conflict with domestic law does not invalidate international treaty obligations, unless it amounts to the violation of a domestic law that is of fundamental importance. According to the constitutionalist tradition, if constitutional officers exceeded their competence or authority in concluding a treaty, the treaty is deemed to be invalid. The internationalist tradition, however, maintains that while treaty obligations may be invalid *within* a state if they conflict with domestic law, they remain unimpaired at the international level insofar as a treaty claims to supersede state law.

4   For example, one of the central dogmas of US constitutional jurisprudence is that the Constitution is the supreme law of the land, not to be superseded by any other law. See *Reid vs. Covert*, 354 US 1 (1957) (holding that "no agreement with a foreign nation can confer power on the Congress, or on any other branch of Government, which is free from the restraints of the Constitution"). Similarly, the German constitution is the paramount law of the land, claiming priority over any other government act. Emerging from the fall of the totalitarian Nazi regime, German constitutional supremacy was designed as a safeguard against dictatorship and human rights abuse (Limbach 2001).

5   We develop reasons for acknowledging the authority of RIL in more detail elsewhere (see Buchanan and Powell 2008). In the present paper, we focus more on examining the question of just which principles of constitutionalism or democracy are supposed by some to be incompatible with states acknowledging the supremacy of RIL.

6   See Keohane, et al. (unpublished paper). These authors cover the "self-regarding" reasons, but not the cosmopolitan ones.

7   For instance, federal election law in the US prohibits a foreign national, which includes foreign businesses and governments, from making election campaign contributions to any candidate (federal or state) for public office – and it prohibits public officials from accepting the same.

8   Kristen Hessler (2005) has argued that democracies have epistemic virtues – in particular, resources for public deliberation – that create a presumption that they should have the authority to interpret human rights norms in their domestic application. This is compatible with the claim that there are circumstances in which the authority of international human rights law should supercede the authority of the state.

9 This definition is based on that offered by Thomas Christiano (2006).

10 See also Ku (2000) (following Yoo in arguing that insofar as treaties establish independent verification regimes (such as chemical weapons inspections), they violate basic constitutional principles of accountability in the enforcement of federal law).

11 Presumably, the equality element of this basic idea of democracy as equal electoral accountability would at the very least require that if some officials exercising political power over the citizens of a democracy are accountable not only to them but also to others, then the citizens must have at least an equal say in the processes of accountability, that is, that their ability to control the conduct of the officials must not be inferior to that exercised by the others to whom the officials are accountable. If this is so, the conclusion to draw is not that RIL is incompatible with democracy, but that those who make, apply, and execute international law ought to be equally accountable to the citizens of all states.

12 Thus American constitutional scholar Curtis Bradley (2003: 1558) complains that: "By transferring legal authority from US actors to international actors – actors that are physically and culturally more distant from, and not directly responsible to, the US electorate – these delegations [of authority under RIL] may entail a dilution of domestic political accountability." This concern may be heightened by a lack of transparency in supranational decision-making. Notice that Bradley does *not* assert that those exercising authority over Americans must be *exclusively* accountable to them, but only expresses a concern that those officials may not be *sufficiently* accountable to them. However, in the passage by John Yoo (2000) quoted earlier (see note 10 and accompanying text), there is a slip from the idea that international officials are not sufficiently accountable to American citizens to the idea that they must be exclusively accountable to them, when Yoo remarks that such officials "have no obligation to pursue American policy". If international officials are accountable to the citizens of other states as well as to those of the US, then *of course* they cannot have an obligation to pursue American policy as such. Yoo does not offer an argument to show why those who exercise authority over the citizens of a particular state must be accountable solely to them. If his remarks are supposed to show that RIL is incompatible with constitutional democracy, they simply beg the question by assuming exclu-

sive accountability, a condition which, as we have already argued, has been routinely violated by the US and virtually all other states in the practice of treaty making and which in no way contradicts the core ideas of democracy.

13 See for example, John Yoo's (2000: 1715) apparent indignation at the fact that officials of international institutions "have no obligation to pursue American policy, they do not take an oath to uphold the Constitution, nor can any American official hold them responsible for their deeds".

14 For an attempt to articulate a conception of accountability suitable for international legal regimes that assert robust legal authority, see Buchanan and Keohane (2006).

15 A distinct objection to acknowledging the authority of RIL relates to the so-called "sovereign source" requirement, and is rooted in the Madisonian idea that the Constitution is a document of power granted by liberty, rather than a doctrine of liberty granted by power. This was the essence of the US Supreme Court's reasoning in the seminal case of *Erie R.R. vs. Tompkins* (1938), which famously held that federal judge-made law is illegitimate insofar as it is not grounded in a sovereign source. The sovereign source argument assumes a similar form in the context of the subordination of domestic to international law. The new sovereigntists assume that international law must be grounded in sovereignty, since all law depends on sovereignty for its legitimacy. See e.g. Rabkin (1998, 2005). They perceive a lack of sovereignty vis-à-vis the authority of RIL in numerous contexts, such as judicial decision making that involves appeals to international human rights norms, self-executing treaties that govern traditionally domestic affairs, and the incorporation of customary international law into federal law sans legislative mediation. The sovereign source problem takes on an added dimension when the people of a democratic state are subjected to laws created not by them or their representatives, but by agent delegatees conferred with legislative, executive, or judicial authority. This is the problem of sub-delegation, which entails that the powers delegated by "the people" to a particular component of government are then sub-delegated to another government body without direct participation or authorization of the original sovereign source, severing the link between the exercise of power and the constituency which authorized its exercise.

The new sovereigntist appeal to the sovereign source argument is ambiguous on many fronts – it is unclear about the nature and conditions of sovereignty itself, and its relation to the exclusive accountability and democratic deficit arguments addressed earlier. We will consider the sovereign source argument in more detail in the third section, where we take up the question of whether RIL is compatible with constitutionalism and (more specifically) the idea that all sources of political authority must be identified in the domestic constitution.

16 The remainder of this subsection draws on Section II of Buchanan and Powell (forthcoming).

17 On reflection, this intuition may not stand scrutiny, because, at least in principle, it seems that the citizens of a democracy could mistakenly cede authority beyond the point at which it could be said that they are self-governing.

18 In order to ratify treaties of major importance, such as those which establish or pave the way for accession to robust supranational organizations, many nations require special majority legislation (e.g. Austria, Croatia, Finland, Greece, *inter alia*) or constitutional revision (e.g. France), while others hold referendum (e.g. Denmark, Sweden and Switzerland) (Vereshchet 1996).

19 It is important to note that Kumm does not think that subsidiarity is to be employed in isolation from other considerations. He thinks that the legitimacy of international legal regimes depends on three other principles: the presumptive bindingness of international law, a procedural principle of adequate participation and accountability and a substantive principle according to which outcomes must not violate fundamental rights and must be "reasonable". Although space precludes pursuing this matter here, we believe that even the combination of these principles does not provide an answer to the question of how much authority a democratic people ought to cede to supranational institutions or the question of which modes of ceding authority are consonant with democratic values.

20 For instance, under Article 91(3) of the Netherlands' Constitution adopted in 1983, treaties that conflict with the Constitution may be approved by the chambers of parliament by a 2/3 vote; as per Article 94, statutes that are inconsistent with treaties are not applicable. Similarly, Articles 9, 44, and 50 of the Austrian Constitution allow international law to modify constitutional law by 2/3 majority vote in the house. Likewise, Article 17 of the Russian Constitution declares that: "[I]n the Russian Federation rights and freedoms of per-

son and citizen are recognized and guaranteed pursuant to the generally recognized principles and norms of international law and in accordance with this Constitution" and Article 46(3) provides the right to appeal to interstate bodies for the protection of human rights if all domestic means have been exhausted. (See Vereshchet 1996 for a comparative constitutional review.)

21 For example, Article 11 of the Slovak Constitution (1992) provides that international instruments on human rights and freedoms ratified by the Slovak Republic and promulgated under statutory requirements "shall take precedence over national law provided that the international treaties and agreements guarantee greater constitutional rights and freedoms". Similar provisions are contained in the Czech Constitution (1992, Article 10) and the Moldova Constitution (1994, Article 4(2)). See ibid.

22 Some new sovereigntists also worry about domestic court judges "borrowing" from international law, especially human rights law. The concerns here are of two sorts. First, there is the worry that judicial borrowing will be unprincipled "cherry picking". We regard this as a worry about the rule of law, not about the compatibility of RIL with constitutionalism or democracy, so we do not discuss it here, though we do so at length in Buchanan and Powell (forthcoming). Second, there is the claim that "borrowing" from international law may disrupt the normative coherence of domestic law, because international law may express values that are alien to the domestic society. We address this issue in the same article.

23 The tripartite separation of powers is allegedly vitiated by the federal incorporation of international law in several ways. The judicial branch is said to exceed its constitutional mandates by incorporating customary international law into federal common law and by invoking foreign precedent as persuasive authority in US constitutional jurisprudence. The executive is claimed to exceed its constitutionally enumerated powers by entering into "self-executing" treaties which regulate subject matter reserved to the Congress and or to the several states. Finally, the entire federal government is held to exceed its legitimate authority by incorporating into US law international norms which regulate content constitutionally reserved for state regulation (see Bradley and Goldsmith 1997).

24 This case is persuasively made by David M. Golove (2000, 2002).

18

International crimes

William A. Schabas

The conception of international crimes, as mala in se or mala prohibita, is considered against the background of the early efforts at codification. The distinction between crimes that have been internationalized in order to facilitate their repression, such as piracy, and the more recent categories such as crimes against humanity and genocide, whose defining characteristics include the fact they are "crimes of state" is considered. Drafting of the International Law Commission Code of Crimes against the Peace and Security of Mankind is considered, as well as judicial contributions to the evolving definitions. The consequences of international criminalization are examined, such as the possibility of exercise of universal jurisdiction, the impact upon immunities recognized at customary international law and the obligation to prosecute or extradite.

Many crimes prosecuted by national justice systems, such as murder and rape, are universal in nature. Although formulated with slight differences, they appear in all penal codes. These are crimes that are *mala in se*. Their presence in criminal law is not the result of a policy choice by legislators, but rather the consequence of profoundly important values that are deeply rooted in all human societies. Moreover, international human rights law now imposes obligations with respect to investigation and prosecution of such crimes.

That is to say, they must now be included in national justice systems as a result of international legal obligation. In a line of early cases, international human rights law dealt with the obligation to legislate and prosecute where state complicity in such crimes was suspected.[1] More recently, it has extended this logic to cover "ordinary" crimes involving individual delinquents, without any hint of state involvement.[2] To the extent that prosecution of such crimes is dictated not only by the consistent practice of all states but also by rulings of international human rights bodies applying universal norms, it might be said that murder, rape and similar crimes against the person are "international crimes." Indeed, there is evidence of attempts by academics in the past to prepare an international or universal codification of criminal law on this philosophical basis.[3] Yet murder, rape and similar serious crimes against the purpose do not generally figure in enumerations of "international crimes," neither do they mandate the application of various principles applicable to international crimes, such as the permissibility of universal jurisdiction, the prohibition of statutory limitations, and the restriction on sovereign immunities.

Many crimes are recognized as "international" because they are declared to be criminal in an international treaty. Cherif Bassiouni (2004: 46) has identified 28 categories of crime set out in 281 international conventions concluded between 1815 and 1999. Crimes appearing on the list include piracy, unlawful use of the mail, counterfeiting, destruction of submarine cables, and bribery of foreign public officials. Their designation as international crimes, and the obligations that result from this, are set out in treaties that apply, in principle, to the parties only.

In a certain sense, such crimes have less of a claim to international status than do murder and rape. They often do not threaten human life and dignity, they do not offend fundamental human values, and they attract penalties that would not necessarily be at the highest end of the scale. Their prosecution is not required so as to conform with international human rights obligations. As a general rule, these crimes are outlawed by international treaty essentially because they require international cooperation in order to ensure repression. Often their commission is more transnational than international in nature. In some cases, such as piracy, they pose jurisdictional problems because the crimes are committed on the high seas and therefore escape the territory reach of any given states. This was explained by the Permanent Court of International Justice in *SS Lotus*: "As the scene of the pirate's operations is the high seas, which is not the right or duty of any nation to police, he is denied the protection of the flag which he may carry, and is treated as an outlaw, as the enemy of all mankind – *hostis humani generis* – whom any nation may in the interest of all capture and punish."[4] These are crimes that are most certainly *mala prohibita*, but not, as a general rule, *mal in se*.

Finally, there are international crimes that concern "atrocity." These are of more recent vintage than the transnational crimes such as piracy and trafficking in persons. The first suggestions of their prosecution date to the time of the massacres of the Armenians during the First World War, when Britain, France and Russia announced "[I]n the pres-

ence of these new crimes of Turkey against humanity and civilization, the allied Governments publicly inform the Sublime Porte that they will hold personally responsible for the said crimes all members of the Ottoman Government as well as those of its agents who are found to be involved in such massacres."[5] Comprehensive attempts at codification of these "new crimes" had to wait another 30 years, for the *Charter of the International Military Tribunal*,[6] the *Convention on the Prevention and Punishment of the Crime of Genocide*[7] and the *Geneva Conventions*.[8] The "new crimes" differ from the earlier generation of international crimes in that they are generally concerned with "crimes of state," that is, serious violations of human rights committed by a state against its own civilian population, or that of a territory that it occupies. The difference was also recognized, albeit implicitly, in the original draft resolution on genocide in the United Nations General Assembly, proposed in 1946: "*Whereas* the punishment of the very serious crime of genocide when committed in time of peace lies within the exclusive territorial jurisdiction of the judiciary of every State concerned, while crimes of a relatively lesser importance such as piracy, trade in women, children, drugs, obscene publications are declared as international crimes and have been made matters of international concern."[9] These are crimes that are most definitely *mala in se* rather than *mala prohibita*.

Precise distinctions between these different types of international crime are not simple to establish. When destruction of submarine cables and genocide are compared, the difference in nature seems evident enough. The former is a "transnational crime" that is *mala prohibita* whereas the latter is an offense *mala in se* that is in principle confined to a single territory, but one where the state is involved in perpetrating the acts and is therefore unwilling to prosecute. When crimes such as terrorism and trafficking in persons are considered, however, it is not as easy to draw the line.

269

Crimes against the peace and security of mankind

Since the period of initial codification of international war crimes, crimes against humanity, crimes against peace and genocide, in the 1940s, there have been various attempts at explaining the nature of these "new crimes." In 1947 the United Nations General Assembly charged the International Law Commission with identifying and codifying "offences against the peace and security of mankind."[10] The expression is attributed to Francis Biddle, one of the judges at the International Military Tribunal, who had referred to them in this manner in a letter to United States President Truman in the aftermath of the Nuremberg trial. Biddle was attempting to characterize the subject matter jurisdiction of the Nuremberg tribunal.[11]

In his 1950 report on the subject of an international criminal jurisdiction submitted to the International Law Commission, Special Rapporteur Ricardo Alfaro spoke of "crimes which affect the community of States and hence should be subject to an international jurisdiction."[12] Alfaro thought an international tribunal should exercise jurisdiction not only over crimes derived from the Nuremberg proceedings and the crime of genocide, but also over "certain offences which have always been known as 'crimes against the law of nations,' such as piracy, slave trade, traffic in women and children, traffic in narcotics, currency counterfeiting, injury to submarine cables. To these might be added terrorism of an international character, as defined by the Convention of 1937 on the Prevention and Punishment of Terrorism."[13]

But Alfaro was preparing the special part of a criminal court statute, not a codification of "offences against the peace and security of mankind," and his approach was therefore rather broad. The International Law Commission expert charged with launching work on the draft code of offences against the peace and security of mankind, Special Rapporteur Jean Spiropoulos, insisted on a distinction

between "crimes against the law of nations" and "crimes against the peace and security of mankind." Spiropoulos described the latter concept as:

> [A]cts which, if committed or tolerated by a State, would constitute violations of international law and involve international responsibility. The main characteristic of the offences in question is their highly *political* nature. They are offences which, on account of their specific character, normally would affect the international relations in a way dangerous for the *maintenance of peace*.[14]

For this reason, Spiropoulos insisted that "the draft code to be elaborated by the International Law Commission cannot have as its purpose questions concerning conflicts of legislation and jurisdiction in international criminal matters. Consequently, such topics as piracy (*delicta juris gentium*), suppression of traffic in dangerous drugs (opium), in women and children (white slave traffic), suppression of slavery, of counterfeiting currency, protection of submarine cables, etc., do not fall within the scope of the draft code with which we are concerned here."[15] The draft codes prepared by the Commission in 1951[16] and 1954[17] confined themselves to enumerations of crimes that constituted, in practice, a rather detailed development on the three categories of offense that were prosecuted at Nuremberg.

The Commission did not return to the draft code until the early 1980s. In one of its early discussions of the nature of crimes against the peace and security of mankind, the issue was presented as follows:

> Among the several possible criteria suggested were the following: the inspiration of the criminal act (for example an act based on racial, religious or political conviction); the status of the victim of the criminal act (for example, a State or a private individual); the nature of the law or interest infringed (the interest of security appearing more important than a purely material

interest); or lastly, the motive, etc. Interesting as those suggestions were, none of the criteria proposed sufficed by itself to identify an offense against the peace and security of mankind. The seriousness of an act was judged sometimes according to the motive, sometimes according to the end pursued, sometimes according to the particular nature of the offense (the horror and reprobation it arouses), sometimes according to the physical extent of the disaster caused. Furthermore, these elements seemed difficult to separate and were often combined in the same act.[18]

The Commission observed that since the 1954 draft of its code, many new crimes had been defined by international legal instruments. These included colonialism, *apartheid*, use of nuclear weapons, environmental issues, mercenarism, taking of hostages, violence against persons enjoying diplomatic privileges and immunities, economic aggression, and aircraft hijacking. The Commission even considered including such crimes as forgery of passports, dissemination of false or distorted news and insulting behavior towards a foreign state.[19] In the end, however, it recognized that there was a danger that it might "blur the distinction between an international crime and an offence against the peace and security of mankind."[20] For the Commission, "not every international crime is necessarily an offence against the peace and security of mankind."[21] It therefore decided that:

> [T]he code ought to retain its particularly serious character as an instrument dealing solely with offences distinguished by their especially horrible, cruel, savage and barbarous nature. These are essentially offences which threaten the very foundations of modern civilization and the values it embodies. It is these particular characteristics which set apart offences against the peace and security of mankind and justify their separate codification.[22]

The Commission agreed that in addition to the crimes prosecuted at Nuremberg and

included in the early draft codes of 1951 and 1954, these criteria were met by colonialism, *apartheid*, "possibly serious damage to the human environment and economic aggression," mercenarism, and international terrorism.[23]

As its work evolved, the Commission tended to concentrate on expanding the concept of crimes against humanity, listing under that heading, rather than as autonomous categories of offense, a number of acts that had not been part of the definition at Nuremberg, including *apartheid*,[24] serious damage to the environment, drug trafficking, trafficking in women and children, and slavery.[25] In its 1991 draft, the Commission abandoned entirely the concept of crimes against humanity. In distinct provisions, it defined specific crimes of genocide and *apartheid*, and then provided a list of acts whose origin can be traced to the crimes against humanity definition found in the *Charter of the International Military Tribunal* in a separate provision entitled "Systematic or mass violations of human rights."[26] The 1991 draft also contained provisions entitled "[c]olonial domination and other forms of alien domination," "[r]ecruitment, use, financing and training of mercenaries," "[i]nternational terrorism," "[i]llicit traffic in narcotic drugs," and "[w]ilful and severe damage to the environment."[27] But by 1996, when the final draft code was submitted to the General Assembly, the International Law Commission had come back down to earth. There were only five provisions, dealing with aggression, genocide, crimes against humanity, "Crimes against United Nations and associated personnel and war crimes."[28] A summary explanation accounted for the dramatically reduced ambitions of the Commission:

> With a view to reaching consensus, the Commission has considerably reduced the scope of the Code. On first reading in 1991, the draft Code comprised a list of 12 categories of crimes. Some members have expressed their regrets at the reduced scope

of coverage of the Code. The Commission acted in response to the interest of adoption of the Code and of obtaining support by Governments. It is understood that the inclusion of certain crimes in the Code does not affect the status of other crimes under international law, and that the adoption of the Code does not in any way preclude the further development of this important area of law.[29]

With the exception of "[c]rimes against United Nations and associated personnel," the draft code was essentially confined to crimes that had been recognized by international law in the late 1940s, although there had been some significant evolution in terms of their scope.

Judicial attempts to define international crimes

Explaining the nature of international crimes is a matter that has also confronted the judiciary. The District Court of Jerusalem, in *Eichmann*, said that crimes that have "offended the whole of mankind and shocked the conscience of nations are grave offences against the law of nations itself ('*delicta juris gentium*')."[30] On appeal, the Supreme Court of Israel said that: "[T]hese crimes constitute acts which damage vital international interests; they impair the foundations and security of the international community; they violate the universal moral values and humanitarian principles that lie hidden in the criminal law systems adopted by civilised nations."[31] Eichmann was prosecuted in accordance with Israeli laws that were modeled on article VI of the *Charter of the International Military Tribunal* and article II of the *Convention on the Prevention and Punishment of the Crime of Genocide*.

When the Security Council established the ad hoc tribunals in the early 1990s, subject matter jurisdiction was limited to war crimes, crimes against humanity and genocide.[32] These were described collectively as "serious violations of international humanitarian law."[33] The Security Council did not include "aggression" or "crimes against peace," although the idea of an international tribunal to deal with Iraqi aggression in 1990 had been seriously mooted by the United States, the United Kingdom and the European Union (Gerald 1990, 1991; Weller 1990). According to the Appeals Chamber of the International Criminal Tribunal for the Former Yugoslavia, "serious violations of international humanitarian law" consist of breaches of "a rule protecting important values," whose breach "must involve grave consequences for the victim."[34]

The Appeals Chamber of the International Criminal Tribunal for the Former Yugoslavia has described the subject matter jurisdiction of the ad hoc tribunals as encompassing "Universally Condemned Offences."[35] The judges actually capitalized the three words, suggesting that they were attempting to coin a new umbrella term that would subsume genocide, crimes against humanity, and war crimes. Citing Judge Rosalyn Higgins (1995: 72), of the International Court of Justice, the Appeals Chamber said that "Universally Condemned Offences are a matter of concern to the international community as a whole." On other occasions, the Appeals Chamber has noted that its subject matter jurisdiction is exercised over offenses that "do not affect the interests of one State alone but shock the conscience of mankind."[36] Citing the Supreme Military Tribunal of Italy, in a post-Second World War case, the Appeals Chamber said:

These norms [concerning crimes against laws and customs of war], due to their highly ethical and moral content, have a universal character, not a territorial one . . . The solidarity among nations, aimed at alleviating in the best possible way the horrors of war, gave rise to the need to dictate rules which do not recognise borders, punishing criminals wherever they may be.[37]

The *Rome Statute* uses the expression "the most serious crimes of concern to the international community as a whole" in four places to describe the subject-matter jurisdiction of the International Criminal Court.[38] It also speaks at one point of crimes that "shock the conscience of humanity."[39] Because the Court has jurisdiction over genocide, crimes against humanity, war crimes, and aggression, it can be assumed that these four categories fall within the rubric of "most serious crimes of concern to the international community as a whole." But the line becomes blurred when reference is made to the Final Act of the Rome Conference. It notes that it was not possible to reach agreement during the Diplomatic Conference on a definition of terrorist acts, which are "serious crimes of concern to the international community," and international trafficking of illicit drugs, which is a "very serious crime." According to the Final Act, these "scourges . . . pose serious threats to international peace and security."[40] The Final Act recommended that terrorist acts and international drug trafficking be considered for inclusion in the *Rome Statute* by amendment, implying that both fit the concept of "most serious crimes of concern to the international community as a whole" that "shock the conscience of humanity."

This discussion is not intended to provide a comprehensive theoretical framework for identifying international crimes, or for classifying them in categories. Rather, it attempts to highlight some of the difficulties involved in the exercise. This is a matter on which modern international law lacks limpidity. In fact, the approaches appear somewhat muddled and confused. Although there is much to support a distinction between crimes that are international for essentially practical reasons, such as piracy and trafficking in counterfeit currency, and those "atrocity crimes" that are prosecuted because they "shock the conscience of humanity," there are cases that fall between and that seem to defy such attempts at classification, such as drug trafficking. But lack of clarity about these distinctions does not mean they can be ignored. Drawing the line between international crimes that are *mala prohibita* and those that are *mala in se* has significant legal effects.

In the negotiations leading up to the adoption of the *Rome Statute*, the distinction was often made between "core crimes" and "treaty crimes." The implication here is that the "core crimes" owe their existence to customary international law. The legal consequences of classifying a crime as international under customary international law cannot necessarily be the same as those that result from inclusion of the crime within an international treaty. In the latter case, the legal effects of codification of international crimes are set out in the treaties themselves, and will only bind those states that are parties to the instruments in question. The analysis is not made any easier by the fact that many of the serious international crimes that "shock the conscience" have also been codified. Referring to the first great international criminal law treaty, the *Convention on the Prevention and Punishment of the Crime of Genocide*, the International Court of Justice said:

> The origins of the Convention show that it was the intention of the United Nations to condemn and punish genocide as "a crime under international law" involving a denial of the right of existence of entire human groups, a denial which shocks the conscience of mankind and results in great losses to humanity, and which is contrary to moral law and to the spirit and aims of the United Nations. The first consequence arising from this conception is that the principles underlying the Convention are principles which are recognized by civilized nations as binding on States, even without any conventional obligation.[41]

There would be little disagreement that the four crimes over which the International Criminal Court has jurisdiction, in accordance with article 5(1) of the *Rome Statute*, are also international crimes whose prohibition is "recognized by civilized nations as binding on

States, even without any conventional obligation." It is not so obvious, however, that the multitude of acts considered by the International Law Commission over the years, and the crimes of terrorism and drug trafficking being studied as possible amendments to the *Rome Statute*, also belong in the category. The distinction is important because of the legal effects that flow from recognition as an international crime belonging to the category variously described in this chapter as "new crimes," "atrocity crimes," "crimes against the peace and security of mankind," "crimes that shock the conscience of humanity," "serious violations of international humanitarian law," and "the most serious crimes of concern to the international community as a whole."

Legal consequences of international criminalization

There are several important consequences that result from the characterization of acts as an "international crime" of the "new crimes" variety: they can be prosecuted retroactively; they can be prosecuted by courts that would not normally exercise jurisdiction; they impose duties on states with respect to mutual legal assistance in the investigation, extradition and prosecution of such offenses; defenses that may exist for ordinary crimes, are eliminated or reduced; traditional rules concerning immunity of heads of state and other senior officials are relaxed; statutory limitations are prohibited. Although some of these features may also apply to certain other "treaty crimes" of the *mala prohibita* genus, this is not an automatic consequence of their designation as international crimes.

Retroactive prosecution operates as an exception to the general rule that prevents a person being tried for an offense that was not prohibited by law at the time of its commission. There is a long history of this norm in national constitutions, which was recognized in international law as early as 1935

in the Permanent Court of International Justice case concerning legislative decrees in Danzig.[42] When challenged by the Nazi defendants who argued that "crimes against peace" had never before been punishable, the Allied judges at Nuremberg tried to demonstrate that acts of aggression had indeed been universally condemned in past decades. The Nuremberg judges also conceded that such crimes should be punished because it would violate principles of justice to let the offenders go free.[43] But this argument is today less tenable because of the quite clear terms of international human rights law: "No one shall be held guilty of any penal offence on account of any act or omission which did not constitute a penal offense, under national or international law, at the time when it was committed."[44] In other words, it is not enough to argue that the act was universally abhorrent and that it would be unjust not to punish offenders. Where a crime is not provided for under national law, retrospective punishment is only acceptable if it can be demonstrated that the act itself was condemned by international law.

The second consequence of characterizing an act as an international crime is that this authorizes prosecution by courts that would not normally be allowed to exercise jurisdiction. The exercise of jurisdiction over crimes is a facet of national sovereignty. Pursuant to principles of international law, as a general rule states have only exercised jurisdiction over crimes when they could demonstrate an appropriate link or interest. Normally, this consisted of a territorial connection, either because the crime was committed on the state's territory or because it had significant effects on that territory. More exceptionally, international law has also allowed states to exercise jurisdiction over acts committed by their nationals, and over acts of which their own nationals are victims,[45] even outside their own territory.

Defining an offense as an "international crime" authorizes some type of international jurisdiction. This may take the form either of an international tribunal as such, or of prosecution by courts of a state that has no significant connection with the offense, under the universality principle. Views on this subject have evolved considerably over the years. There is now much support for the position that international law entitles the exercise of universal jurisdiction for the core international crimes, although the views of judges of the International Court of Justice were inconsistent when they were canvassed on this subject in early 2002.[46] A case now pending before the Court confronts this issue directly.[47] It is useful to recall that in 1948, the United Nations General Assembly rejected the concept of universal jurisdiction over genocide.[48] This had been proposed by the authors of the original resolutions in the General Assembly, who lamented in their first draft the fact that "genocide when committed in time of peace lies within the exclusive territorial jurisdiction of the judiciary of every State concerned."[49] They failed in their efforts to obtain a declaration from the General Assembly that would change this situation, with the result that article VI of the *Genocide Convention* says: "Persons charged with genocide or any of the other acts enumerated in article 3 shall be tried by a competent tribunal of the State in the territory of which the act was committed, or by such international penal tribunal as may have jurisdiction with respect to those Contracting Parties which shall have accepted its jurisdiction."[50] Fifteen years later, the District Court of Jerusalem, in *Eichmann*, said: "It is the consensus of opinion that the absence from this Convention of a provision establishing the principle of universality (and, with that, the failure to constitute an international criminal tribunal) is a grave defect in the Convention which is likely to weaken the joint efforts for the prevention of the commission of this abhorrent crime and the punishment of its perpetrators."[51] The Court held that Israel was entitled to exercise universal jurisdiction over genocide because this was authorized by customary international law.

Among recent indications that states generally accept universal jurisdiction over genocide and similar international crimes are the growing application of the principle in national law. More and more states enact legislation permitting them to prosecute on this basis. Even the United States of America, which has been historically rather reticent about the concept, enacted a statute in late 2007 permitting its courts to prosecute genocide on the basis of universal jurisdiction.[52] Further evidence is provided by debates in the Security Council, where there has been at least tacit endorsement of the referral of cases by the International Criminal Tribunal for Rwanda to states prepared to hold trials of genocide suspects using universal jurisdiction.[53]

The third significant result of the recognition of an offense as an international crime is that it imposes duties on states with respect to investigation, prosecution and extradition. This is sometimes expressed with a Latin expression, *aut dedere aut judicare* (literally, extradite or prosecute). While related to the concept of universal jurisdiction, the two should not be confused: *aut dedere aut judicare* imposes an obligation, whereas universal jurisdiction is merely an option available to states. The duty to prosecute or extradite is recognized in some major treaties, and it is therefore beyond question that in these cases states have willingly and intentionally accepted such obligations. The grave breach provisions of the four *Geneva Conventions* require that "[e]ach High Contracting Party [. . .] search for persons alleged to have committed, or to have ordered to be committed, such grave breaches, and [. . .] bring such persons, regardless of their nationality, before its own courts." Alternatively, a state may, "if it prefers, and in accordance with the provisions of its own legislation, hand such persons over for trial to another High Contracting Party concerned, provided such High Contracting Party has made out a prima facie case."[54] The *Convention against Torture and Other Cruel, Inhuman or Degrading Treatment or Punishment* imposes something similar.[55] It has been argued that these obligations to prosecute or extradite are also required by customary international law with respect to a much broader range of international crimes. While this may be a desirable result, from the standpoint of the protection of human rights, it is difficult to find any real evidence in the practice of states to suggest that they consider themselves to be under such obligations.

The fourth significant result of the classification of an act as an international crime is the reduction or elimination of certain defenses that are generally available under national law with respect to ordinary crimes. The *Charter of the International Military Tribunal* declared that "[t]he fact that the Defendant acted pursuant to order of his Government or of a superior shall not free him from responsibility,"[56] and a similar provision has been included in the statutes of the more recent generation of international criminal tribunals.[57] The *Rome Statute of the International Criminal Court* takes a slightly less absolutist view, allowing the defense to the extent that orders are not "manifestly unlawful,"[58] a position that probably corresponds to that of customary international law.[59] Similarly, official capacity as a head of state or government, a member of a government or parliament, an elected representative or a government official is not a defense to an international crime.[60]

The legal position on some defenses with respect to international crimes remains unclear, however. The *Rome Statute* appears to allow a defense of duress,[61] whereas a majority of the Appeals Chamber of the International Criminal Tribunal for the Former Yugoslavia has ruled that the defense is inadmissible to a charge of crimes against humanity.[62] The latest international justice instrument to be adopted by the United Nations Security Council, the *Statute of the Special Tribunal for Lebanon*, has no such rules concerning the exclusion of defenses, but this is easily explained by the fact that the Special Tribunal for Lebanon does not have jurisdiction over international crimes.[63]

Principles concerning immunities are relaxed to some extent when prosecution of international crimes is concerned, although not as much as some would like. According to the International Court of Justice, the immunity of heads of state and other high officials is not a bar to prosecution before "certain international criminal tribunals." The judgment offered the International Criminal Court and the two *ad hoc tribunals* for the former Yugoslavia and Rwanda as examples. However, the International Court of Justice also confirmed that such immunities persist in prosecutions before courts of third states even when it is international crimes that are being prosecuted.[64] The logic of the Court's position is not entirely clear. The elimination of immunity before the ad hoc tribunals is a reasonable consequence of their establishment by the United Nations Security Council. Nowhere in the statutes of the ad hoc tribunals is it actually stated that there can be no immunity, and the finding that immunity does not exist before such international tribunals is a matter of judicial construction.[65] The *Rome Statute of the International Criminal Court* has an explicit provision eliminating any immunities.[66] But this may be explained as the result of a conventional agreement by sovereign states. It cannot be set up against heads of state of third states, who preserve their immunity before the Court. These distinctions are not, unfortunately, considered in the famous pronouncement of the International Court of Justice in the *Arrest Warrant case*.

Neither does the International Court of Justice consider the situation with respect to criminal tribunals established by the United Nations but with the authority to prosecute crimes that are not international in nature. Here there is a tension between form and content. The Special Court for Sierra Leone, for example, has jurisdiction over certain crimes recognized in the national criminal law of the country, such as sexual relations with a minor and arson.[67] The Secretary-General of the United Nations explained that they should be included precisely because they are "either unregulated or inadequately regulated under international law."[68] The Special Court for Sierra Leone has been held to be an "international court"[69] but that does not serve to make such crimes international in nature. The issue is posed even more acutely in the case of the Special Tribunal for Lebanon, whose subject matter jurisdiction is entirely drawn from Lebanese national law and has no claim to encompass international crimes.[70]

Finally, international crimes may not be subject to statutory limitations. During the 1960s, as the application of statutory limitations in national penal codes to Nazi war criminals seemed imminent, there was a movement to amend norms by which such prosecutions could be time barred. Accordingly, there were some changes to domestic legislation.[71] On an international level, these developments took the form of General Assembly resolutions,[72] and treaties within both the United Nations system[73] and that of the Council of Europe.[74] Both of the latter instruments refer to the crime of genocide and to crimes against humanity as offenses for which there shall be no statutory limitation. The French *Cour de Cassation* determined, in the *Barbie* case, that the prohibition on statutory limitations for crimes against humanity is now part of customary law.[75] The *Rome Statute* declares that the crimes within the Court's jurisdiction are not subject to a statute of limitations.[76] Given that the *Rome Statute* has no statutory limitations, the provision appears to be directed at national legislation. It effectively prohibits domestic justice systems from establishing or maintaining statutory limitations with respect to the four crimes within the jurisdiction of the International Criminal Court.

Conclusion

The internationalization of criminal law has brought with it developments of both a structural and a substantive nature. At the structural level, there is a panoply of mechanisms

designed to assist the repression of crimes, such as arrangements for extradition and mutual legal assistance as well as the establishment of international bodies such as Interpol. These apply to a variety of criminal acts under national law, of varying degrees of seriousness, as well as to transnational and genuinely international crimes. International law has also seen the establishment of international criminal tribunals.

The international criminal tribunals mainly exercise jurisdiction over "international crimes," but there are exceptions – the cases of the Special Court for Sierra Leone and the Special Tribunal for Lebanon have been discussed – indicating that a precise equation cannot be made between the international nature of the institution and the international nature of its subject matter jurisdiction. Moreover, the concept of "international crime" is also extremely important at the level of national jurisdictions, where it authorizes a number of derogations from general rules applicable in criminal law such as those concerning territorial jurisdiction, immunities, the permissibility of statutory limitations and the prohibition of retroactive offenses.

For this reason, it is important to have a theoretical construct permitting the identification of international crimes and their distinction from crimes that are merely national or transnational in nature, or that are international crimes recognized for practical reasons rather than because they "shock the conscience" of humanity or are "Universally Condemned Offences." The task is complex and confusing, and there is no generally accepted set of conditions permitting such classification. Some categories are beyond debate, of course. These include genocide, crimes against humanity, war crimes and aggression. Their status would seem to be confirmed by inclusion within the subject matter jurisdiction of the International Criminal Court, were it not for the fact that amendment of the *Rome Statute* is being considered so as to include crimes whose claim as cognates to the existing crimes is far from obvious. No single set of criteria appears to provide an adequate framework. We agree that genocide is, of course, a "Universally Condemned Offence," but doesn't murder also belong to this category?

The exercise is perhaps no simpler in national law, where efforts to classify crimes as *mala prohibita* and *mala in se* have always been imprecise. Perhaps the real difficulty is that we have embarked on a process of globalization that is still very incomplete. The state monopoly on criminal law jurisdiction is slowly being eroded. What are today known as "international crimes" may be simply manifestations of the beginning of this phenomenon. Perhaps at some point in the future, criminal jurisdictions throughout the world will have the authority to prosecute all serious crimes, wherever committed and by whomever. Why, indeed, should borders make any difference when a serious crime has been committed against a fellow human being?

Notes

1 *Velázquez Rodriquez vs. Honduras*, July 29, 1988, Series C, No. 4, (1992); *Bautista de Arellana vs. Colombia* (No. 563/1993), UN Doc. CCPR/C/55/D/563/1993; *Laureano vs. Peru* (No. 540/1993), UN Doc. CCPR/C/56/D/540/1993; *Streletz, Kessler and Krenz vs. Germany*, March 22, 2001; *Akkoç vs. Turkey*, October 10, 2000.

2 See, e.g. *MC vs. Bulgaria* (Application no. 39272/98), Judgment, December 4, 2003.

3 On the efforts of Garofalo and others, see the report by Vespasian Pella to the United Nations International Law Commission: "Memorandum présenté par le Secrétariat," UN Doc. A/CN.4/39, para. 30.

4 *France vs. Turkey, S.S. Lotus* (1927) PCIJ Ser. A. (Judgments) No. 10 (Judgment No. 9) (1929).

5 English translation quoted in United Nations War Crimes Commission 1948: 35.

6 *Agreement for the Prosecution and Punishment of Major War Criminals of the European Axis, and Establishing the Charter of the International Military Tribunal (IMT)*, annex, (1951) 82 UNTS 279, art. 6.

7 *Convention on the Prevention and Punishment of the Crime of Genocide* (1951) 78 UNTS 277.

8 *Geneva Convention for the Amelioration of the Condition of the Wounded and Sick in Armed Forces in the Field* 1950: 75 UNTS 31, art. 49; *Geneva Convention for the Amelioration of the Condition of the Wounded, Sick and Shipwrecked Members of the Armed Forces at Sea* 1950: 75 UNTS 85, art. 50; *Geneva Convention Relative to the Treatment of Prisoners of War* 1950: 75 UNTS 135, art. 129; *Geneva Convention Relative to the Protection of Civilians* 1950: 75 UNTS 135, art. 146.

9 United Nations 1946: UN Doc. A/BUR/50.

10 United Nations 1947: GA RES. 177 (II).

11 United Nations N.D.: UN Doc. A/CN.4/25, para. 9.

12 United Nations 1950: para. 95.

13 United Nations 1950: para. 97; also para. 100.

14 United Nations N.D.: para. 35, original emphasis.

15 United Nations N.D.: para. 35, original emphasis.

16 United Nations 1951: para. 59.

17 United Nations 1954: para. 54.

18 United Nations 1984: para. 34.

19 United Nations 1984: paras. 52–63.

20 United Nations 1984: para. 63.

21 United Nations 1984: para. 63.

22 United Nations 1984: para. 63.

23 United Nations 1984: para. 65. See also: United Nations 1985: paras. 61–94; United Nations 1988: paras. 262–7.

24 *Apartheid* had already been defined as a crime against humanity in the *Convention on the Non-Applicability of Statutory Limitations to War Crimes and Crimes against Humanity*, (1968) 754 UNTS 73, art. 1(b), *International Convention on the Suppression and Punishment of the Crime of Apartheid*, (1976) 1015 UNTS 244, art. I(1).

25 United Nations 1986a: paras. 93–102; United Nations 1986b: paras. 199–210.

26 United Nations 1991: para. 176.

27 United Nations 1991: para. 176.

28 United Nations 1996: para. 50.

29 United Nations 1996: para. 46.

30 *AG Israel vs. Eichmann* 1968, 36 ILR 5 (District Court, Jerusalem): para. 12.

31 *A.G. Israel vs. Eichmann* 1968 , 36 ILR 277 (Supreme Court of Israel): 291–93.

32 UN Security Council 1993b: annex, arts. 2–5; UN Security Council 1994: annex, arts. 2–4.

33 UN Doc. S/RES/808 (1993a), para. 1; United Nations 1993: para. 33; UN Security Council 1993a: annex, preamble, arts. 1, 9(1), 10(1)–(2), 23(1), 29(1).

34 *Prosecutor v. Tadić* (Case No. IT-94-1-AR72), Decision on the Defence Motion for Interlocutory Appeal on Jurisdiction, October 2, 1995, para. 94.

35 *Prosecutor v. Nikolić* 2003 (Case No. IT-94-2-AR 73), paras. 24, 25.

36 *Prosecutor v. Tadić* (Case No. IT-94-1-AR72), Decision on the Defence Motion for Interlocutory Appeal on Jurisdiction, October 2, 1995, para. 57.

37 *Ibid.* (citing Sup. Mil. Trib., Italy, 1950; unofficial transcript).

38 *Rome Statute of the International Criminal Court*, (2002) 2187 UNTS 90, preamble, paras. 4 and 9, art. 1, art. 5(1).

39 *Ibid.*, preamble, para. 2.

40 United Nations Diplomatic Conference of Plenipotentiaries on the Establishment of an International Criminal Court (1998) "Final Act of the United Nations Diplomatic Conference of Plenipotentiaries on the Establishment of an International Criminal Court", UN Doc. A/CONF.183/10.

41 *Reservations to the Convention on the Prevention and Punishment of the Crime of Genocide (Advisory Opinion)* (1951) ICJ Reports 16, p. 23.

42 *Consistency of Certain Danzig Legislative Decrees with the Constitution of the Free City, Advisory Opinion* [1935] PCIJ 2, Series A/B, No. 65 (December 4, 1935), p. 51.

43 *France et al. vs. Göring et al.* (1946) 22 IMT 203, 13 ILR 203, 41 *American Journal of International Law* 172, p. 217.

44 *Universal Declaration of Human Rights*, GA Res. 217 A (III), UN Doc. A/810, art. 11(2). Also: *International Covenant on Civil and Political Rights* (1966) 999 UNTS 171, Art. 15.

45 *S.S. Lotus (France vs. Turkey)* [1927] PCIJ Ser. A. No. 10 (Judgment No. 9) (September 7, 1927).

46 See: *Democratic Republic of Congo v. Belgium (Arrest Warrant of 11 April 2000)*, Separate Opinion of Judge Bula-Bula, February 14, 2002; *Democratic Republic of Congo vs. Belgium (Arrest Warrant of 11 April 2000)*, Separate Opinion of President Guillaume, February 14, 2002; *Democratic Republic of Congo v. Belgium (Arrest Warrant of 11 April 2000)*, Joint Separate Opinion of Judges Higgins, Kooijmans and Buergenthal, February 14, 2002; *Democratic Republic of Congo vs. Belgium (Arrest Warrant of 11 April 2000)*, Separate Opinion of Judge Koroma, February 14, 2002; *Democratic Republic of Congo vs. Belgium (Arrest Warrant of 11 April 2000)*, Dissenting Opinion of Judge Oda, February 14, 2002; *Democratic Republic of Congo vs. Belgium (Arrest Warrant of 11 April 2000)*, Declaration of Judge Ranjeva, February 14, 2002; *Democratic Republic of Congo vs. Belgium (Arrest Warrant of 11 April 2000)*, Separate Opinion of Judge Rezek, February 14, 2002; *Democratic Republic of Congo vs. Belgium (Arrest Warrant of 11 April 2000)*, Dissenting Opinion of Judge Van den Wyngaert, February 14, 2002. These were individual opinions and, strictly speaking, only *obiter dicta*. The matter is raised directly in pending litigation before the International Court of Justice: *Republic of the Congo vs. France (Case Concerning Certain Criminal Proceedings in France)*, Application, December 9, 2002.

47 *Republic of the Congo vs. France (Case Concerning Certain Criminal Proceedings in France), Request Provisional Measure, Order of 17 June 2003*, [2003] ICJ Reports 102.

48 UN Doc. A/C.6/SR.100. See the discussion in Schabas 2000: 353–8.

49 Draft Resolution, U.N. Doc. A/BUR/50.

50 *Convention on the Prevention and Punishment of the Crime of Genocide* (1951) 78 UNTS 277.

51 *AG Israel vs. Eichmann* (1968) 36 ILR 5 (District Court, Jerusalem), para. 24.

52 S. 888, 110th Cong. § 1; 153 Cong. Rec. S 4150; H.R. 2489, 110th Cong. § 1; 153 Cong. Rec. H 14207.

53 United Nations Security Council (2007) "United Nations Security Council", 62nd year: 5796th meeting, Monday, 10 December 2007, New York, UN Doc. S/PV.5796.

54 *Geneva Convention Relative to the Protection of Civilian Persons in Time of War* (1950) 75 UNTS 287, art. 146. Also: *Geneva Convention for the Amelioration of the Condition of the Wounded and Sick in Armed Forces in the Field* (1949) 75 UNTS 31, art. 49; *Geneva Convention for the Amelioration of the Condition of Wounded, Sick and Shipwrecked Members of Armed Forces at Sea* (1950) 75 UNTS 85, art. 50; *Geneva Convention Relative to the Treatment of Prisoners of War* (1950) 75 UNTS 135, art. 129.

55 *Convention against Torture and Other Cruel, Inhuman or Degrading Treatment or Punishment*, GA Res. 39/46, annex, art. 5(2). See also *International Convention for the Protection of All Persons from Enforced Disappearance*, UN Doc. A/RES/47/133, annex, art. 9(2).

56 *Agreement for the Prosecution and Punishment of Major War Criminals of the European Axis, and Establishing the Charter of the International Military Tribunal (IMT)*, (1951) 82 UNTS 279, annex, art. 8.

57 UN Security Council 1993b: annex, art. 7(4); UN Security Council 1994: annex, art. 6(4);

Statute of the Special Court for Sierra Leone (2002) 2178 UNTS 138, annex, art. 6(4).

58 Rome Statute of the International Criminal Court, (2002) 2187 UNTS 90, art. 33.

59 Empire vs. Dithmar and Boldt (Hospital Ship "Llandovery Castle"), (1921) 2 ILR 437, 16 American Journal of International Law 708; German War Trials, Report of Proceedings before the Supreme Court in Leipzig, Cmd. 1450, London: HMSO, 1921, pp. 56–7.

60 Agreement for the Prosecution and Punishment of Major War Criminals of the European Axis, and Establishing the Charter of the International Military Tribunal (IMT), (1951) 82 UNTS 279, annex, art. 7; Convention on the Prevention and Punishment of the Crime of Genocide, (1951) 78 UNTS 277, art. 4; Rome Statute of the International Criminal Court, (2002) 2187 UNTS 90, art. 27(1); UN Security Council 1993b, annex, art. 7(4); UN Security Council 1994: annex, art. 6(4); Statute of the Special Court for Sierra Leone, (2002) 2178 UNTS 138, annex, art. 6(4).

61 Rome Statute of the International Criminal Court (2002) 2187 UNTS 90, art. 31(1)(d).

62 Prosecutor vs. Erdemović 1997a: para. 75; Prosecutor vs. Erdemović 1997b: para. 12.

63 Statute of the Special Tribunal for Lebanon, UN Doc. S/RES/1757 (2007), Attachment.

64 Democratic Republic of Congo vs. Belgium (Arrest Warrant of 11 April 2000), Judgment, February 14, 2002, para. 61. This largely overturned a somewhat more liberal ruling by the United Kingdom's House of Lords in the celebrated Pinochet case. In R. vs. Bartle and the Commissioner of Police for the Metropolis and others, ex parte Pinochet Ugarte, (1999) 2 All. ER 97 (HL), a majority of the House of Lords said "[s]uch immunity is only in respect of 'official' acts performed in the exercise of his functions." There is a gap between the two tests, as dissenting Judge Van den Wyngaert observed: Democratic Republic of Congo v. Belgium (Arrest Warrant of 11 April 2000), Dissenting Opinion of Judge Van den Wyngaert, February 14, 2002, para. 36.

65 Prosecutor v. Milošević (Case No. IT-02-54-PT), Decision on Preliminary Motions, 8 November 2001, paras. 26–34; Prosecutor v. Taylor (Case No. SCSL-2003-01-I), Decision on Immunity from Jurisdiction, May 31, 2004. It is widely believed that article 7(2) of the Statute of the International Criminal Tribunal for the Former Yugoslavia, and the equivalent provisions of the other statutes, operate to this effect. But careful reading of the provision shows that it deals with the defense of official capacity, which is not the same thing. The distinction between the defense of official capacity and immunities can be seen clearly in the two paragraphs of article 27 of the Rome Statute. It is also apparent with reference to paragraph 61 of the Arrest Warrant case, which cites article 27(2) of the Rome Statute but no corresponding provision in the statutes of the ad hoc tribunals.

66 Rome Statute of the International Criminal Court, (2002) 2187 UNTS 90, art. 27(2).

67 Statute of the Special Court for Sierra Leone (2002) 2178 UNTS 138, annex, art. 5.

68 United Nations 2000a: para. 19.

69 Prosecutor vs. Taylor (Case No. SCSL-2003-01-I), Decision on Immunity from Jurisdiction, May 21, 2004.

70 United Nations 2000: paras. 19–25.

71 Germany seems to have had a 20-year limitation period on Nazi crimes not contemplated by Control Council Law No. 10. On March 25, 1965 the Bundestag extended the limitation date for murder to December 31, 1969, which was the twentieth anniversary of establishment of the German Federal Republic. But this was inadequate and the date was again extended until December 31, 1979. On July 3, 1979 the Bundestag voted to eliminate any limitation date for murder (see Monson 1982).

72 G.A. Res. 3 (I); G.A. Res. 170 (II); G.A. Res. 2583 (XXIV); G.A. Res. 2712 (XXV); G.A. Res. 2840 (XXVI); G.A. Res. 3020 (XXVII); G.A. Res. 3074 (XXVIII).

73 Convention on the Non-applicability of Statutory Limitations to War Crimes and Crimes Against Humanity, 754 U.N.T.S. 73 (1970) (see Miller 1971).

74 European Convention on the Non Applicability of Statutory Limitation to Crimes against Humanity and War Crimes of January 25, 1974, E.T.S. 82.

75 Fédération Nationale des Déportés et Internés Résistants et Patriotes et al. vs. Barbie, (1984) 78 ILR 125, 135. Also France, Assemblée Nationale, Rapport d'Information déposé en Application de l'Article 145 du Règlement par la Mission d'Iinformation de la Commission de la Défense Nationale et des Forces Armées et de la Commission des Affaires Étrangères, sur les Opérations Militaires menées par la France, d'autres pays et l'ONU au Rwanda entre 1990 et 1994, p. 286 (1999).

76 Rome Statute of the International Criminal Court, (2002) 2187 UNTS 90, art. 29.

19

Challenges of the "new terrorism"

John F. Murphy

An especially disquieting aspect of the "new terrorism" is the increased willingness of terrorists to kill large numbers of people and to make no distinction between military and civilian targets. Another facet is the extraordinary extent to which it has been able to globalize itself. Still another is the debate over the appropriate legal regime to apply to it. Prior to the September 11, 2001 attacks, international terrorism had been treated primarily as a criminal law matter with emphasis placed on preventing the commission of the crime through intelligence or law enforcement means, or, if prevention failed, on the apprehension, prosecution and punishment of the perpetrators. After September 11, however, the criminal justice approach was de-emphasized and to a considerable extent supplanted by the use of military means. A decision to employ the military model of counter-terrorism in place of the law enforcement model, or vice versa, may have serious functional consequences. For example, under the law enforcement model, it is impermissible to pursue and kill a suspected criminal before his capture, unless it is necessary to do so as a matter of self-defense. Under the military model, it is permissible to pursue the enemy with the intent to kill. Under normally applicable criminal law, moreover, conviction may be difficult because of the requirement that the crime be proved "beyond a reasonable doubt" and other barriers posed by criminal procedure and constitutional standards.

Because of the nature of the new terrorism, it has proved to be necessary to employ some modern approaches to combating terrorism. For example, it is clear that terrorists in several locations have now moved beyond conventional tactics to engage in well supplied and well-planned insurgencies. Whether one approaches counterterrorism from the military or the law enforcement model, it is clear that an ideological struggle is a key part of the counter-terrorism effort. The most important ideological struggle, however, is not likely to be that between al Qaeda and the west. Rather, it is the struggle within Islam itself. Other important methods of combating terrorism, such as the gathering of intelligence, recent resolutions of the U.N. Security Council, efforts to block the financing of terrorism, and civil lawsuits against terrorists, terrorist organizations, and states that sponsor terrorism, are also briefly explored in this essay and in some concluding observations.

> We have cause to regret that a legal concept of "terrorism" was ever inflicted upon us. The term is imprecise; it is ambiguous; and above all, it serves no operative legal purpose.
>
> (Baxter 1974: 380)

The trenchant observation of Richard Baxter, late Professor of Law at Harvard and

Judge on the International Court of Justice, published in 1974, has stood the test of time. The term "terrorism" is imprecise, it is ambiguous, and, furthermore, serves no operative legal purpose. But above all, the hard school of experience has shown, it has constituted, and continues to constitute, a major barrier to efforts to combat the criminal acts often loosely described as "terrorism."

In practice, the terms "terrorism" and "terrorists" have been used by politicians and diplomats as labels to pin on their enemies. The cliché "One man's terrorist is another man's freedom fighter" is a notorious reflection of this game of semantics. It also reflects a serious conflict of values between those who believe that the end always justifies the means and those who do not. Thus, in the current environment especially, there are those, apparently increasing dramatically in number, who, in an effort to reach their end or goal, are perfectly willing to engage in the deliberate targeting and massive slaughter of civilians, employ suicide bombers, use children as shields, and behead helpless hostages before a worldwide audience.

This clash of fundamental values has been a major factor contributing to the failure to agree on a definition of terrorism in the United Nations and in other international fora.[1] Some countries believe that the causes of terrorism or the political motivation of the individual terrorists are relevant to the problem of definition. For example, the position of some governments has been that individual acts of violence can be defined as terrorism only if they are employed solely for personal gain or caprice; acts committed in connection with a political cause, especially against colonialism and for national liberation, fall outside the definition and constitute legitimate measures of self-defense. Another variant but closely related approach is to define as terrorism only the use of terror by governments, or so-called "state terrorism." Indeed, the word "terror" was first used in connection with the Jacobin "Reign of Terror" during the French Revolution.

Because of these varying approaches and the "clash of values" among its member states, with the result being an inability to reach agreement on a definition, the United Nations has been unsuccessful in its efforts to conclude a comprehensive treaty against terrorism.[2] Instead, the world community has attempted to resolve the question of definition largely by ignoring it and focusing instead on identifying particular criminal acts to be prevented and punished and on particular targets to be protected. The result has been a "piecemeal" approach to combating international terrorism, an approach followed at several different levels. That is, a number of global treaties and conventions have been adopted at the United Nations and in other fora. At the same time, several regional conventions have been drafted to reflect the particular needs and perspectives of the states in the region concerned. Finally, a number of bilateral agreements have been adopted. Some of these deal specifically with a particular manifestation of international terrorism; others are relevant to international terrorism, although they cover a wide variety of other crimes as well.

At this writing, the United Nations or its specialized agencies have adopted 13 global, multilateral antiterrorist conventions. These include: Convention on Offences and Certain Other Acts Committed on Board Aircraft (1963); Convention for the Suppression of Unlawful Acts against the Safety of Civilian Aviation (1971); Convention on the Prevention and Punishment of Crimes against Internationally Protected Persons, including Diplomatic Agents (1973); International Convention against the Taking of Hostages (1979); Convention on the Physical Protection of Nuclear Material (1979); Protocol for the Suppression of Unlawful Acts of Violence at Airports Serving International Civil Aviation, supplementary to the Convention for the Suppression of Unlawful Acts against the Safety of Civil Aviation (1988); Convention against the Safety of Maritime Navigation (1988); Protocol for the Suppression of Unlawful Acts against the Safety of Fixed

Platforms Located on the Continental Shelf (1988); Convention on the Marking of Plastic Explosives for the Purpose of Detection (1991); International Convention for the Suppression of Terrorist Bombing (1997); International Convention for the Suppression of the Financing of Terrorism (1999);[3] and, most recently, International Convention on the Suppression of Acts of Nuclear Terrorism (United Nations 2005b), which entered into force in 2007. Most of these conventions contain no definition of terrorism whatsoever. A few, such as the International Convention for the Suppression of Terrorist Bombings and the International Convention for the Suppression of the Financing of Terrorism, contain definitions of the crime they cover that contain elements of the crime of terrorism, but they are limited in effect to the conventions in which they appear and do not represent agreement on a comprehensive definition of terrorism per se.[4]

Despite the world community's inability to agree on a definition of terrorism, and despite the many practical problems definitions of terrorism pose, it is necessary at a minimum to have a rough working definition of the subject we are discussing. To this end, one might consider the definition of "international terrorism" that appears in the U.S. federal crime code's chapter on terrorism. According to this definition, "international terrorism" means activities that:

- involve violent acts dangerous to human life that are a violation of the criminal laws of the United States or of any state, or that would be a violation if committed within the jurisdiction of the United States or of any state
- appear to be intended:
  - to intimidate or coerce a civilian population
  - to influence the policy of a government by intimidation or coercion
  - to affect the conduct of a government by mass destruction, assassination, or kidnapping

- occur primarily outside the territorial jurisdiction of the United States or transcend national boundaries in terms of the means by which they are accomplished, the persons they appear intended to intimidate or coerce, or the locale in which their perpetrators operate or seek asylum.[5]

With this brief background to some of the definitional problems of terrorism, let us consider some of the salient aspects of the "new terrorism."

The "new terrorism"

Back in the (relatively) halcyon days of the "old terrorism," the conventional wisdom was that terrorists had little interest in killing large numbers of people because it would undermine their efforts to gain sympathy for their cause. An especially disquieting aspect of the new terrorism is the increased willingness of terrorists to kill large numbers of people and to make no distinction between military and civilian targets.[6] A major cause of this radical change in attitude has been aptly pinpointed by Jeffrey D. Simon (2002: 11):

Al Qaeda . . . is representative of the emergence of the religious-inspired terrorist groups that have become the predominant form of terrorism in recent years. One of the key differences between religious-inspired terrorists and politically motivated ones is that the religious-inspired terrorists have fewer constraints in their minds about killing large numbers of people. All nonbelievers are viewed as the enemy, and the religious terrorists are less concerned than political terrorists about a possible backlash from their supporters if they kill large numbers of innocent people. The goal of the religious terrorist is transformation of all society to their religious beliefs, and they believe that killing infidels or nonbelievers will result in their being rewarded in the

283

afterlife. Bin Laden and Al Qaeda's goal was to drive U.S. and Western influences out of the Middle East and help bring to power radical Islamic regimes around the world. In February 1998, bin Laden and allied groups under the name "World Islamic Front for Jihad Against the Jews and Crusaders" issued a fatwa, which is a Muslim religious order, stating that it was the religious duty of all Muslims to wage a war on U.S. citizens, military and civilian, anywhere in the world.

Another facet of the new terrorism is the extraordinary extent to which it has been able to globalize itself. Although in many ways al Qaeda has been severely undermined, with many of its leaders dead or in jail, it has succeeded in promoting its violent fanaticism on a worldwide basis and thereby gaining substantial numbers of new militants to its cause. The result has been, in the words of some commentators, "terror by franchise" (see, e.g. Khalaf and Fidler 2007: 5, col. 1). That is, while the jihadi threat has been suppressed in some countries – for example, Saudi Arabia and Indonesia – it is increasing in places in North Africa and in Lebanon. These al Qaeda inspired groups in turn have established links with a new breed of home-grown terrorist. The problem is especially acute in the United Kingdom where radicalized British Muslims have established links with Al Qaeda- and Taliban-sponsored training camps in Pakistan (Fidler 2007: A1, col. 1). In continental Europe, home-grown terrorists have established links with radical cells in North Africa.

The current headquarters of Al Qaeda is reportedly in Waziristan and the Baujur region, wild tribal areas on the borders between Pakistan and Afghanistan (see Bokhari and Fidler 2007: 5, col. 8). The Pakistani government has been unsuccessful in its efforts to suppress the activities of al Qaeda and the Taliban in these areas, and a peace arrangement in 2006 between the Pakistani government and the tribal chiefs may have allowed al Qaeda more freedom to operate.

Indeed, on July 17, 2007, the U.S. White House released a National Intelligence Estimate, which represents the consensus view of all 16 agencies that make up the American intelligence community (see Mazzetti and Sanger 2007: A1, col. 1). The report concludes that the United States is losing ground on a number of fronts in the fight against al Qaeda and that the terrorist front has significantly strengthened over the past 2 years. One of the main reasons for al Qaeda's resurgence, according to intelligence officials and White House aides, is the "hands-off approach toward the tribal areas by Pakistan's president, Gen. Pervez Musharraf" (Mazzetti and Sanger 2007: A1, col. 1). As a result, American officials have reportedly been meeting and discussing "an aggressive new strategy, one that would include both public and covert elements" because of "growing concern that pinprick attacks on Qaeda targets were not enough" (see Mazzetti and Sanger 2007: A6, col. 1).

The implication in this report that it might be necessary for U.S. military forces to take action in the tribal areas of Pakistan illustrates another facet of the "new terrorism": the debate over the appropriate legal regime to apply to efforts to combat terrorism after the September 11, 2001 attacks. Prior to those attacks, international terrorism had been treated primarily as a criminal law matter with emphasis placed on preventing the commission of the crime through intelligence or law enforcement means; or, if prevention failed, on the apprehension, prosecution and punishment of the perpetrators. After September 11, however, the criminal justice approach was deemphasized and to a considerable extent supplanted by the use of military means. (On this point, see Power 2007: 1.)

This shift to the military model of counterterrorism has engendered considerable controversy. Critics of this approach argue that it threatens fundamental human rights and that it is unnecessary because normal law enforcement measures can effectively combat the terrorist threat (see, e.g. Roth 2004: 2).

In sharp contrast, supporters of the military model contend that criminal law is "too weak a weapon" and that it was inadequate to stop al Qaeda from planning and carrying out the attacks of September 11 (see, e.g. Wedgwood and Roth 2004: 126).

A decision to employ the military model of counterterrorism in place of the law enforcement model, or vice versa, may have serious functional consequences.[7] For example, under the law enforcement model, it is impermissible to pursue and kill a suspected criminal before his capture, unless it is necessary to do so as a matter of self-defense. The goal here is to capture the suspect, subject him to trial in accordance with due process, and then, if he is convicted, impose an appropriate sanction, which, in some cases, especially under U.S. law, could include the death penalty. Under the military model, it is permissible to pursue the enemy with the intent to kill. Capture in place of killing is required only when the enemy has surrendered. If the enemy surrenders, and he qualifies as a prisoner of war, he may not be subject to sanction unless he has committed a war crime. He may, however, be detained until the end of the conflict to prevent him from returning to the battlefield; if the law enforcement model applies, he normally cannot be detained after trial unless he has been convicted of a crime. Under normally applicable criminal law, moreover, conviction may be difficult because of the requirement that the crime be proved "beyond a reasonable doubt" and other barriers posed by criminal procedure and constitutional standards.

Because of these and many other differences between the law enforcement and military models of counterterrorism, a heated debate has arisen, especially in the United States, between those who favor trying alleged terrorists in civilian courts and those who favor military commissions as the appropriate forum.[8] For its part, the Bush administration, through an executive order issued by President George W. Bush providing for the creation of special military commissions to try members of al Qaeda,[9] has opted, at least in significant part, for the military model. The President's order and subsequent developments from it have raised a host of international and constitutional law issues. Space limitations preclude a discussion of these in this essay. For present purposes, suffice it to note that in *Hamdan vs. Rumsfeld*,[10] by a 5–4 majority, the U.S. Supreme Court decided that the military commissions established by the President lacked the authority to try suspects like Hamdan because their structure and procedures violated both the Uniform Code of Military Justice and the Geneva Conventions. In response, after strenuous negotiations, the Bush administration convinced Congress to pass the Military Commissions Act of 2006,[11] which, among other things, authorizes "the use of military commissions to try alien unlawful enemy combatants engaged in hostilities against the United States for violations of the law of war and other offenses triable by military commission"; precludes *habeas corpus* review on behalf of any detainee classified as an "unlawful enemy combatant"; and permits only D.C. Circuit Court of Appeals review of such determinations by Combatant Status Review Tribunals; and provides that "no person in any *habeas* action or any other action may invoke the Geneva Conventions or any protocols thereto as a source of rights, whether directly or indirectly, for any purpose in any court of the United States." Shortly after the passage of the Military Commissions Act, the Court of Appeals for the D.C. Circuit, in *Boumediene [and Al Odah] vs. Bush* (2007), rejected, by a 2–1 vote, petitions filed for writs of *habeas corpus* filed by aliens captured abroad and detained as enemy aliens at the Guantanamo Bay Naval base in Cuba, on the ground that it had no jurisdiction in such cases. It is likely that this and other issues will ultimately be decided by the U.S. Supreme Court.

Parenthetically, it should be noted that since September 11 European states have largely reacted to the new terrorism threats by means of traditional law enforcement methods (see Warbrick 2004). Recently, however, there has been some recognition in Europe that the law enforcement model may not suffice in all circumstances to cope with the new terrorism.[12] It has been suggested, moreover, that, with the United States beginning to recognize that the early post-September 11 position that terrorist detainees have few enforceable legal rights is unacceptable, a "global convergence on terror" may be developing (Goldsmith 2007: 11, col. 2).[13]

The concern that terrorists may resort to the use of weapons of mass destruction – nuclear, chemical, or biological – is of long standing (see, e.g. Jenkins and Rubin 1978). Since September 11, however, this concern has been greatly heightened. Moreover, Osama bin Laden and al Qaeda have made plain on many occasions their desire to obtain weapons of mass destruction, especially nuclear weapons, and their use of civilian aircraft on September 11 and their effective employment of the internet since have demonstrated their technological competence. Their competence with computers has led one commentator to suggest that they now have the capacity for hijacking satellites. "Capturing signals beamed from outer space [it is alleged] terrorists could devastate the communications industry, shut down power grids, and paralyze the ability of developed countries to defend themselves" (see Wright 2004: 40, 50).[14]

We turn now to examine some modern approaches of counterterrorism.

Counterinsurgency

Staying with the military model of counterterrorism for the moment, it is clear that terrorists in several locations have now moved beyond conventional tactics to engage in well-supplied and well-planned insurgencies. This is most evident in Iraq and Afghanistan, but significant terrorist insurgencies are also present in such countries as the Philippines and Malaysia. Indeed, according to the U.S.

Department of State (2007: 2): "Al-Qaeda openly describes itself as a transnational guerrilla movement; it applies classic insurgent strategies at the global level."

Unfortunately, it is also clear that, when the magnitude of the September 11 attacks demonstrated the seriousness of the threat al Qaeda had become, the United States military was woefully unprepared to cope with insurgencies. As noted by Samantha Power (2007: 9): "[T]he Army counterinsurgency manual had not been updated since 1986 and the Marine Corps guide had not been revised since 1986." Power (2007: 9) further elaborates on the impact of such lack of preparation: "In Afghanistan and Iraq, the armed forces did not have the appropriate intelligence, linguistic capabilities, weapons, equipment, force structures, civil affairs know-how or capacity to train security forces in other countries."

In 2006 a new *U.S. Army/Marine Corps Counterinsurgency Field Manual*[15] was published. In the new foreword in the University of Chicago version of the Manual, Lt. Colonel John A. Nagel writes that: "It is fair to say that in 2003 most Army officers knew more about the U.S. Civil War than they did about counterinsurgency" (Department of the Army 2007: xv).

The primary architect of the Manual was General David Petraeus, who currently is the overall American commander in Iraq. At the time of writing there is some evidence that the military aspects of the counterinsurgency in Iraq are going well (see, e.g. O'Hanlon and Pollack 2007: A17, col. 2), but, as General Petraeus and other military officers have noted, success in counterinsurgency requires more than military capability, and there is so far little evidence that the Iraqi government has the capacity or the will necessary to take the steps required for quelling the insurgency (see Mazzetti 2007: A11, col. 1).[16]

There is also the crucial issue of the time required, in both Iraq and Afghanistan, for a well-run counterinsurgency strategy to work. Sara Sewall (2006: xxi, xxxviii–xxxix), a former Pentagon official who wrote the introduction to the University of Chicago edition of the manual, for one is skeptical that the U.S. public will be willing to "supply greater concentrations of forces, accept higher casualties, fund serious nation-building and stay many long years to conduct counterinsurgency by the book."

The ideological struggle

Whether one approaches counterterrorism from the military or the law enforcement model, it is clear that, to quote a phrase that borders on being a cliché, an ideological struggle for hearts and minds is a key part of the counterterrorism effort. It is, moreover, a struggle that fundamentalist terror is wining.

According to *The 9/11 Commission Report* (2004: 50): "[T]he extreme Islamist version of history blames the decline from Islam's golden age on the rulers and people who turned away from the true path of their religion, thereby leaving Islam vulnerable to encroaching foreign powers eager to steal their land, wealth and even their souls." In the modern context, the rulers who have turned away from the true path of Islam include the rulers of Muslim countries, most especially the rulers of Saudi Arabia, where Mecca, the birthplace of Mohammed and Islam's most holy city, is located. The primary encroaching foreign power is the United States, with its placement of troops in Saudi Arabia (now removed) being a particular source of outrage. In the view of bin Laden and al Qaeda, according to the *9/11 Commission Report* (2004: 51):

> America is responsible for all conflicts involving Muslims. Thus, Americans are blamed when Israelis fight with Palestinians, when Russians fight with Chechens, when Indians fight with Kashmiri Muslims, and when the Philippine Government fights ethnic Muslims in its Southern islands. America is also held responsible for the governments of Muslim countries, derided by

al Qaeda as "your agents." Bin Laden has stated flatly, "our fight against these governments is not separate from our fight against you." These charges found a ready audience among millions of Arabs and Muslims angry at the United States because of issues ranging from Iraq to Palestine to America's support for their countries' repressive rulers.

Al Qaeda and other Islamic fundamentalist terror groups have made good use of modern technology, especially the internet, in propagating their message (see Wright 2004: 40, 50). They were also successful in portraying both the U.S. invasion of Afghanistan and that of Iraq as a "war against Islam." As a result, Bruce Hoffman of Georgetown University, an eminent authority on terrorism, has recently been quoted as saying that "Al-Qaeda is not on the run. It is on the march" (2007: 72).

The most important ideological struggle, however, is not likely to be that between al Qaeda and the west. Rather, it is the struggle within Islam itself. At the present time "those Muslim preachers with authenticity tend to be the street preachers–firebrands, who gain legitimacy by spewing hatred at both their own regimes and the western powers that support them" (Friedman 2006: A23, Col 5). Unless and until more moderate voices within Islam succeed in getting their message across, al Qaeda's recruitment of converts to its cause is likely to continue to enjoy substantial success.[17]

Prevention of terrorism

Ideally, the goal of law enforcement and, for that matter, the use of military force, is to prevent international terrorism from being carried out. With the advent of the "new" terrorist's willingness to kill large numbers of people, perhaps through the use of weapons of mass destruction, fulfillment of this goal has become of crucial importance. There are two primary methods for preventing the commission of terrorism: (1) hardening of possible targets; and (2) use of intelligence gathering by intelligence agents and of information resulting from investigations by law enforcement officials to intercept terrorists before they can commit their crimes. Examples of the hardening of possible targets are the barricades that surround Congress and key governmental agencies in Washington, D.C. and other primary possible targets such as financial institutions in New York City or nuclear facilities in various locations in the United States. Screening of passengers and baggage on civilian aircraft flights for weapons or bombs is another example. Special problems surround efforts to harden computer networks against attack because of their vulnerability (see United States 1996: 5).

The gathering of intelligence and investigations for law enforcement purposes have both an international and domestic dimension. On a global basis, an important player is Interpol, the international police organization. According to Interpol: "[S]trict limits on intelligence sharing are hindering efforts by law enforcement agencies to understand how the global threat is changing" (see Huban 2004: 5, col. 3).

At the domestic level, in the United States, there has long been a separation between intelligence gathering agencies, such as the Central Intelligence Agency, and investigation for law enforcement purposes, such as by the Federal Bureau of Investigation. The *9/11 Commission Report* (2004: 73–82) emphasizes the failure of intelligence agents and law enforcement officials to share information ("connect the dots") that might have resulted in apprehending the 9/11 hijackers prior to the commission of their acts. To resolve this problem, the Commission (2004: 417) recommends that: "[I]nformation procedures should provide incentives for sharing, to restore a better balance between security and shared knowledge."

In both intelligence gathering and investigation for law enforcement purposes, there has been concern that there not be arbitrary or unlawful interference with privacy, family, home, or correspondence. The issue recently came to a head in the United States when it was revealed that surveillance was being conducted in secret by the National Security Agency and outside the Foreign Intelligence Surveillance Act,[18] which requires the government to seek approval from a special court to eavesdrop on Americans. After substantial debate over the legality of this practice, on August 5, 2007, President Bush signed into law legislation that amends the Foreign Intelligence Surveillance Act and greatly expands the government's ability to eavesdrop international telephone calls and email messages of U.S. citizens without warrants.[19] It allows intelligence agencies to intercept telephone calls and emails of foreign terror suspects routed through the United States, without a warrant. The law remains in effect for six months, at which point it will be revisited.

Interrogation of persons suspected of terrorism, either to prevent the commission of future terrorist acts, or to ascertain the whereabouts of perpetrators of terrorism, since 9/11 has raised storms of controversy. Revelations, for example, that the U.S. Department of Justice's Office of Legal Counsel sent memoranda to the White House in January and August of 2002 (superseded in December of 2004)[20] approving interrogation tactics that stopped just short of a prisoner's death and arguably constituted torture precipitated a flurry of sharp reactions from both ends of the political spectrum, rejecting the arguments set forth in the memorandums. The Detainee Treatment Act of 2005,[21] while not expressly referring to torture, does require that persons in the control of the Department of Defense shall be subject only to interrogation techniques or treatment included in the U.S. Army Field Manual[22] and states that "no individual in the custody or under physical control of the United States Government shall be subject to cruel, inhuman, or degrading treatment or punishment."[23]

It is arguable that the U.S. Government has violated provisions of the Convention against Torture and Other Cruel, Inhuman, or Degrading Treatment or Punishment (the Torture Convention) through a program know as "extraordinary rendition," whereby an individual suspected of terrorism is transferred from one state to another for purposes of interrogation, detention, and possible prosecution. A Canadian commission of inquiry, for example, found that Maher Arar, a dual national of Canada and Syria, was detained by U.S. officials as he changed planes in New York on September 26, 2002, and subsequently deported to Syria where he was tortured (see Zagaris 2006). Reportedly, other governments also have engaged in extraordinary renditions.[24] Article 3(1) of the Torture Convention provides: "No State Party shall expel, return ('refouler') or extradite a person to another State where there are substantial grounds for believing that he would be in danger of being subjected to torture." Condoleezza Rice, U.S. Secretary of State has "repeatedly insisted that the U.S. did not deliver prisoners to governments it believed would torture them" (Dinmore 2006: 3, col. 1).

Prosecution and punishment

If a suspected terrorist is apprehended abroad, the issue arises whether, and if so where, he will be prosecuted. If the United States wishes to prosecute him, it will seek his return, either through extradition or some other process of "rendition" such as exclusion, deportation, or, in extreme cases, abduction. (For further discussion, see Gilbert 1998.) The so-called antiterrorism conventions of the United Nations normally contain, as a basic provision, an "extradite or prosecute" requirement. That is, a state party that apprehends a person who allegedly committed a terrorist act covered by the convention must either extradite him to a state party seeking his extradition or submit his case

to its authorities for prosecution. Normally, the decision whether to extradite or prosecute is in the sole discretion of the state party that has the accused in custody. The primary goal of the antiterrorist conventions is that persons accused of crimes covered by the conventions be prosecuted before the national courts of states parties in accordance with procedures that safeguard their due process rights.

It is not at all clear, however, that this goal is met with any degree of consistency. A major part of the problem is the lack of adequate data on the extent of successful actions to prevent terrorist acts and of successful prosecutions of terrorists. (For further discussion of this problem, see Murphy 2005: 465–8.) The crucial issue is the extent to which the global antiterrorist conventions have been or will be vigorously implemented. Conclusion of antiterrorist conventions is only the first step in the process. Unfortunately, many states parties seem to regard it as the last. But recent action by the U.N. Security Council has made it more difficult for states in general and states parties in particular to persist in this attitude.

Security council resolutions 1373 and 1540

U.N. Security Council Resolution 1373[25] "[c]alls upon all states" to take a number of steps in cooperation with other states to combat terrorism.[26] These steps include, "intensifying and accelerating the exchange of operational information," becoming parties to the relevant antiterrorist conventions and ensuring, "in conformity with international law," that refugee status is not abused by terrorists, and that "claims of political motivation are not recognized as grounds for refusing requests for the extradition of alleged terrorists."

Significantly, to monitor implementation of Resolution 1373, the Council established the Counter-Terrorism Committee (CTC) and called on all states to report to the committee – no later than 90 days after the date of adoption of the resolution – on the steps they have taken to implement the resolution.[27] The Council further "[e]xpresse[d] its determination to take all necessary steps in order to ensure the full implementation of this resolution, in accordance with its responsibilities under the Charter."[28] Similarly, Ambassador Jeremy Greenstock, the first chairman of the CTC, emphasized the importance of implementing antiterrorist measures. According to Ambassador Greenstock (2002), prior to the resolution "[governments] were already familiar with what needed to be done. But few had done it. Resolution 1373 drew on the language negotiated by all U.N. members in the twelve Conventions against terrorism, but also delivered a strong operational message: get going on effective measures now."

Although the record is somewhat mixed, Resolution 1373's "strong operational message" has been heard. According to Eric Rosand (2005: 548–9): "[P]artly as a result of Resolution 1373, and the work of its offspring, the Counter-Terrorism Committee ('CTC'), almost every country has taken steps to enhance its counter-terrorism machinery, whether in the form of adopting anti-terrorism legislation, strengthening border controls, becoming party to international treaties related to terrorism, or becoming proactive in denying safe-haven to terrorists and their supporters."

As noted by Rosand, in adopting Resolution 1540:[29]

> Again, faced with a global threat potentially emanating from both non-State actors as well as any State, the Council decided to adopt a resolution that imposed a series of far-reaching obligations on all States. It required them to refrain from providing support to non-State actors attempting to manufactures, possess, transport, or use WMD [weapons of mass destruction] and their means of delivery. It further required them to prohibit in domestic law any such activities by non-State actors, particularly for terrorist purposes, and prohibit assistance or financing of such activities. It obligated States to adopt measures to prevent the proliferation of WMD and their means of delivery, including by accounting for and physically protecting such items, establishing effective border controls and law enforcement measures.
>
> (Rosand 2005: 547)

Following the lead of Resolution 1373 in establishing the CTC, the Security Council decided, in adopting Resolution 1540, to create a similar committee to monitor the implementation of the latter Resolution.[30]

Space limitations allow only a (very) brief consideration of two other modern methods of counterterrorism.

Efforts to block the financing of international terrorism

As a follow-up to Resolution 1373, which had as its primary focus the financing of international terrorism, the Security Council adopted Resolution 1390,[31] which directs members of the United Nations to freeze without delay the financial assets or other economic resources of a lengthy list of individuals, groups, undertakings and entities in the annex to the resolution. Moreover, reportedly, between September 2001 and March 2002, $103.8 million in assets had been frozen on a worldwide basis, with roughly half of the funds connected to Osama bin Laden and al Qaeda. This amount pales, however, in comparison with the between $500 billion and $1 trillion reportedly laundered every year and illustrates how difficult it is to dry up terrorist funding.[32]

Civil suits

Using civil lawsuits against terrorists, terrorist organizations, and states that sponsor terrorism as a legal response to international terrorism has only recently been undertaken and largely only in the United States. Traditionally, the emphasis has been on punishing terrorists with criminal penalties, not on holding them liable for their actions. Moreover, civil litigation in the United States as an alternative to criminal prosecution for the commission of international crimes or egregious human rights violations is a highly controversial subject. Subjecting foreign governments to such suits has been, if anything, even more controversial. Barriers to successful litigation in this area are formidable, and include, *inter alia*, resistance by the U.S. government, limits on the lifting of immunity of foreign states under the Foreign Sovereign Immunities Act, difficulties in collecting judgments in the United States and abroad, and possible hostile and retaliatory reaction on the part of foreign governments.

To the extent that actions against terrorist organizations are successful,[33] plaintiffs may have more success in collecting on their judgments because such organizations are likely to have substantial assets in the United States. But the debate continues on the desirability and feasibility of civil suits as a method of combating terrorism (see, e.g. various essays in Moore 2004).

especially, counterinsurgency and effective use of "soft power," i.e. the ability to persuade others of the appeal of one's culture, values, and institutions,[34] to meet the ideological onslaught of Islamic fundamentalism.

An especially salient challenge of the new terrorism is that it requires a major effort to strike a proper balance between the need to safeguard national security, on the one hand, and to promote and protect human rights, on the other. Failure to prevent a future terrorist attack of the magnitude of 9/11 or greater would shift the balance alarmingly away from the concern to protect human rights.

It will also be necessary to make more effective use of international institutions, including the much maligned United Nations, to ensure the close international cooperation required to counter the globalization of terror. Recent reports that the United States and the United Nations are discussing a possible return of the United Nations to Iraq are a step in the right direction.

Lastly, it will be a challenge not to overreact to the threat of the new terrorism. We must not give in to the temptation to create a garrison state or interfere excessively with international travel and business (see Buck and Sevastopulo 2007: 1, col. 3).[35]

Conclusion

This chapter has attempted to identify some of the major challenges of the new terrorism. Perhaps the overarching challenge is the complexity of these challenges and the heated debate that has arisen as to how best to meet them. The resolution of this debate is crucially important because, unlike traditional terrorism, the new or modern terrorism arguably constitutes the major current threat to the national security of numerous states, especially in the west.

Moreover, western governments, including that of the United States, are not particularly adept in some of the methods required to combat the new terrorism. These include,

Notes

1 For a more extensive discussion of the obstacles to reaching agreement on a definition of terrorism, see Murphy 1990. Some recent writings on the issue of definition include Beres (1995); Byford (2002: 34); Tiefenbrun (2003); Young (2006: 23).

2 See, e.g. the Statement of Brigitte Mabandia, South Africa's Minister for Justice and Constitutional Development, on July 5, 2007, reported in AllAfrica, Inc., Africa News. In her statement, Ms. Mabandia reportedly said that the South Africa Government was of the view that the lack of consensus on the definition of terrorism in the U.N.'s Ad Hoc Committee established by the General Assembly Resolution 51/210 of December 17, 1996 was "problematic." She further reportedly said that with regard to the Comprehensive

Convention against Terrorism, South Africa "supported the early finalization of this convention but it was disappointing that the work of the U.N.'s Ad Hoc Committee was deadlocked." The reason for the deadlock, she said, "was a principled difference between states on whether or not national liberation movements should be exempted from the scope of the convention."

3 The texts of the foregoing conventions may most conveniently be found in United Nations 2001a.

4 Article 2 of the International Convention for the Suppression of Terrorist Bombing provides:

> Any person commits an offence within the meaning of this Convention if that person unlawfully and intentionally delivers, places, discharges or detonates an explosive or other lethal device in, into or against a place of public use, a State or governmental facility, a public transportation system or an infrastructure facility:
> a. With the intent to cause death or serious bodily injury; or
> b. With the intent to cause extensive destruction of such a place, facility or system, where such destruction results in or is likely to result in major economic loss.

Article 2 (1)(b) of the International Convention for the Suppression of the Financing of Terrorism comes closer to being a general definition of terrorism:

> Any . . . act intended to cause death or serious bodily injury to a civilian, or to any person not taking an active part in the hostilities in a situation of armed conflict, when the purpose of such act, by its nature or context, is to intimidate a population, or to compel a Government or an international organization to do or to abstain from doing any act.

For a variety of definitions of terrorism or terrorist acts, drawn from a variety of national and international sources, see van Schaack and Slye 2007: 541–44.

5 *United States Federal Crime Code* 18 U.S.C. section 2331 (1).

6 It is worth noting that in 1998 Osama bin Laden told ABC News that "he made no distinction between American military and civilian targets, despite the fact that the Koran itself is explicit about the protections offered to civilians" (see Bergen 2002: 28).

7 For an especially thoughtful treatment of these distinct consequences, see Feldman 2002: 466.

8 For various views on this issue, see Koh 2002.

9 Administration of George W. Bush (2001) Military Order, Detention, Treatment, and Trial of Certain Non-Citizens in the War against Terrorism, 66 Fed. Reg. 57,833 (November 16, 2001).

10 *Hamdan v. Rumsfeld* (2006)126 S.Ct.2749.

11 United States (2006b) Pub. L. No 109-366, 120 Stat. 2600.

12 According to Jack Goldsmith, the German Interior Minister, Wolfgang Schauble, recently told the German magazine *Der Spiegel* that: "The old categories no longer apply. The fight against international terrorism cannot be mastered by the classic methods of the police . . . We have to clarify whether our constitutional state is sufficient for confronting the new threats" (see Goldsmith 2007: 11, col. 2).

13 See also Feldman 2002: 479: "More generally, however, what can we say about the use and the meaning of the categories of crime and war in this complicated situation . . . The key point . . . is surely that terror fits both categories – and neither."

14 For some of my views on the threat of computer attacks by terrorists, see Murphy 2002.

15 See Department of the Army, *Counterinsurgency* (December 2006). Because of high demand for the Manual, it also was published by the University of Chicago Press, with a new foreward by Lt. Colonel John A. Nagel and an introduction by Sarah Sewall (Department of the Army 2007).

16 Based on the testimony of Michael G. Mullen, nominee for chairman of the Joint Chiefs of Staff.

17 For a provocative thesis that modern Islam is an imperialist force, see Karsh 2006.

18 *United States Foreign Intelligence Surveillance Act* (1978) 50 U.S.C. sections 1801–1863.

19 See *United States Protect America Act of 2007* (2007) Pub.L. No 110-55, 121 Stat. 552.

20 See Memorandum for Alberto R. Gonzales, Counsel to the President, and William J. Haynes II, General Counsel of the Department of Defense, Re: Application of Treaties and Law to al Qaeda and Taliban Detainees (January 25, 2002), available at http://msn.com/id/4999148/site/newsweek; Memorandum for Alberto R. Gonzales, Counsel to the President, Re; Standards of Conduct of Interrogation under 18 U.S.C. Sections 2340–2340A (Dec. 30, 2004), available at http://www.usdoj.gov/olc/18usc23402340a2.htm (superseding August 1, 2002 opinion outlining applicable Standards of Conduct).

21 On December 30, 2005, President Bush signed into law H.R., the Department of Defense, Emergency Supplemental Appropriations to Address Hurricanes in the Gulf of Mexico, and Pandemic Influenza Act of 2006, Pub. L. No. 109-148. Title X of Division A of the Act is the Detainee Treatment Act of 2005. 10 U.S.C. section 801 Note.

22 Detainee Treatment Act, 2005: section 1002(a).

23 Detainee Treatment Act, 2005: section 1003(a).

24 Amnesty International has claimed Bosnia, Germany, Italy, Macedonia, Sweden, Turkey, and the United Kingdom have engaged in such practices (see Dinmore 2006: 3, col. 1).

25 U.N. Security Council, S.C. Res. 1373, U.N. SCOR, 56th Sess. 4385th mtg., U.N. Doc. S/Res/1373 (2001b).

26 U.N. Security Council, S.C. Res. 1373, 2001b: section 3, (a)–(g).

27 U.N. Security Council, S.C. Res. 1373, 2001b: section 6.

28 U.N. Security Council, S.C. Res. 1373, 2001b: section 8.

29 U.N. Security Council, S.C. Res. 1540, U.N. SCOR, 59th Sess. 4956th mtg., U.N. Doc. S/1540 (2004b).

30 U.N. Security Council, S.C. Res. 1540, 2004b: paragraph 6.

31 U.N. Security Council, S.C. Res. 1390, 57th Sess., 4452d mtg., U.N. Doc. S/Res/4452 (2002).

32 For a recent consideration of the difficulties in controlling the financing of terrorism, see Scott 2007.

33 For a recent example of such a case, see *Almog vs. Arab Bank, PLC*, 471 F. Supp. 2d 257 (E.D.N.Y. 2007).

34 For a discussion of the possible uses of soft power, see Nye, Jr. 2002.

35 Reporting on European objections to a new U.S. visa law requiring travelers to the U.S. to give U.S. authorities at least 48 hours' notice of their plans to visit the country and to a U.S. law requiring the screening of all air and sea freight at foreign ports before being shipped to the U.S.

20

Law and legitimacy: the World Trade Organization

Amrita Narlikar

In this chapter, I investigate the puzzle why increasing legalization of the multilateral trading regime has not been accompanied by increasing legitimacy. I argue that increasing legalization can in fact trigger a process of de-legitimization if a legal system upholds rules that are perceived to be poorly negotiated. The paper presents a discussion of the concepts of legitimacy and legalization, analyzes the mechanisms whereby the processes of de-legitimization have occurred, and finally suggests ways whereby the legitimacy of the World Trade Organization might be reclaimed.

The creation of the World Trade Organization (WTO) in 1995 not only heralded the replacement of the General Agreement on Tariffs and Trade (GATT) with a full-fledged organization, but also the creation of a dispute settlement mechanism that was dramatically more powerful than the GATT's. Increasing legalization of the multilateral trading regime, however, has not been accompanied by increasing legitimacy. Outside major ministerial level meetings of the WTO, demonstrations led by anti-globalization protestors are commonplace. Inside the WTO too, the rumblings of discontent from members have grown louder, and are most patently manifest in the recur-

rent deadlocks that have plagued the negotiations of the Doha Development Agenda.

In this chapter, I investigate the sources of the diminished legitimacy of the WTO in comparison to the GATT's. Both the legalization and the legitimacy of the WTO are examined in the first section. I then argue in the second section that increasing legalization can in fact trigger processes of de-legitimization if a legal system upholds rules that are perceived to be poorly negotiated. I identify the mechanisms whereby these processes of de-legitimization have occurred. In the third section, I go on to argue that if the WTO is to reclaim its legitimacy, it will have to move from processes of passive to active legitimization, and suggest ways in which this might be achieved.

Increasing legalization, declining legitimacy?

The multilateral trading regime presents me with a high level of legalization, not least since the creation of the WTO and its dispute settlement mechanism. Yet what is legal need not necessarily enjoy legitimacy. In this section, I briefly discuss the phenomenon of increasing legalization of the WTO, and further illustrate that this legalization has not been accompanied by increasing legitimacy of the organization.

Judith Goldstein, et al. assess levels of legalization along three dimensions: obligation, precision, and delegation. They further describe the international trade regime as "usually accepted as one of the most legalized global economic regimes" (Goldstein et al. 2000: 11; also see Goldstein and Martin 2000). Particularly on the first two dimensions – obligation and precision – evidence of high legalization of the WTO (particularly in comparison to the GATT) is easy to find. Members of the WTO are legally bound to honor their obligations, with fewer exemptions than the GATT allowed.[1] Its rules are precise in that they "unambiguously define the conduct they require, authorize, or proscribe" (Abbott 2005: 17). These rules are listed in detail in the agreements of the WTO that number over 550 pages of printed text.

On the third dimension – delegation – the case for high levels of legalization is less straightforward. The WTO retains the member-driven nature of the GATT, and there is no delegation of powers to a secretariat or an alternative governing body that makes the rules. The onus of negotiating and implementing agreements lies with the members themselves. But the WTO does show a much higher level of delegation of powers as far as the interpretation and enforcement of its agreements are concerned. In the WTO (unlike the GATT), the findings of the dispute settlement panels need consensus to be overruled, thereby facilitating a greater automaticity of the WTO's dispute settlement mechanism and the enforceability of the rules of the organization. The successes of the dispute settlement mechanism of the WTO are borne out by the sheer number of cases – 369 between January 2005 and September 2007 – that have been filed under it.[2] And yet, despite having one of the busiest dispute settlement

mechanisms in the history of international law, the WTO's increasing legalization has not been accompanied by an increase in its legitimacy.

For this paper, I use a broad definition of legitimacy, as provided by Mark C. Suchman (1995: 574): "Legitimacy is a generalized perception or assumption that the actions of an entity are desirable, proper, or appropriate within some socially constructed system of norms, values, beliefs, and definitions." Unpacking the concept into its various components provides us with useful foci against which the legitimacy of any institution might be assessed. To this end, we turn to Andrew Hurrell's conceptualization of the five dimensions of legitimacy (Hurrell 2005):

1   legitimacy as process and procedure or "input legitimacy"
2   legitimacy as substantive values
3   legitimacy and its links to specialized and specialist knowledge
4   legitimacy as effectiveness or "output legitimacy"
5   legitimacy as giving reasons and persuasion.

On four of the five dimensions, the legitimacy of the WTO is under challenge. Before I discuss the mechanisms whereby the legitimacy of the WTO has declined, a brief application of these five dimensions of legitimacy to the WTO follows.

The "input legitimacy"[3] of the WTO has come under challenge from not just the anti-globalization protestors outside but from member states within. Non-governmental organizations attack the WTO on the grounds that its system of legalized and intrusive rules is negotiated by states rather than the people who are directly affected by these rules and yet have little say in their making. Within the WTO, member governments particularly from developing countries have complained about the lack of transparency in the proceedings of the WTO and further constraints on their participation. The dissatisfaction of both sets of constituencies came to the fore in 1999 at the Seattle Ministerial Conference. It is worth noting that WTO has attempted to address both sets of concerns. Its outreach to NGOs has expanded significantly, as have access points that NGOs now enjoy into the organization (for instance, through *amicus curiae* briefs that they can submit in disputes, and through the process of accreditation whereby they can attend ministerial meetings). Additionally, improvements in the participation of developing countries in the organization are most patently manifest in the transformation of the old GATT "Quad" (which comprised Canada, the EU, Japan and the U.S.), into a new core group of countries comprising Brazil and India along with the EU and the U.S. The legitimacy of the WTO does not seem to have improved, however. NGOs continue to fault the WTO for its chain of delegation being far too removed from people who are affected by it, and smaller developing countries continue to claim marginalization from the process.

The second dimension of legitimacy pertains to "substantive values." It is defined by Andrew Hurrell in the following terms: "In order for an institution or political arrangement to be legitimate, its core principles need to be justifiable on the basis of shared goals and values." (Hurrell 2005: 20) At one level, few would dispute the goals of the WTO as stated in the preamble to the Agreement establishing the World Trade Organization, which include raising standards of living, full employment, expansion in the production of and trade in goods and services, sustainable development, and attention to the needs of developing countries and especially least developed countries (LDCs). However, there exists disagreement on how these shared goals are to be implemented, exactly which areas the agreements of the WTO should extend to achieve these sometimes inconsistent goals, and exactly what the rules negotiated to these ends should comprise.

These disagreements are manifest in the debates over the mandate of the WTO (for instance, the controversy surrounding the "Singapore issues"). Neither are these controversies limited to the expanding remit of the organization; some scholars point to the costs that multilateral trade liberalization entails in terms of the policy space of developing countries.[4]

The third dimension of legitimacy – the basis that the WTO-led trade liberalization enjoys in "specialized and specialist knowledge" (Hurrell 2005: 22) – is perhaps the least contested of the five. Note that Hurrell takes the opposite view, and argues, "As with claims to legitimacy based on technocratic knowledge (for example, in the cases of the IMF or the WTO), such arguments have suffered heavily in the face of both intelligence failures, manifestly insufficient knowledge of the countries under analysis, and the political manipulation of such intelligence." This may have been true of the GATT in the 1970s, particularly when the developing world argued its case using a different epistemic alternative based on import-substituting industrialization, resulting in the call for the New International Economic Order in the UNCTAD. Today, few developing countries would appeal to such arguments, while most scholars would agree that trade is a necessary (although not sufficient) condition for development.[5] The WTO too seems to take a similar view, with trade as not the panacea for all problems, but as only one of the conditions necessary for promoting development. This recognition is visible not only in the Doha Ministerial Declaration, but also in the Aid for Trade agenda that attaches considerable importance to capacity building (including productive capacity and economic infrastructure) in developing countries.[6]

The fourth dimension of legitimacy – output legitimacy or effectiveness – is under severe challenge. I find evidence of this in the increasing disengagement of politicians in the developed and developing worlds, and the turn away from multilateral trade agreements to regional and bilateral ones. This disengagement is not surprising given the recurrence of deadlocks and missed deadlines in the DDA: The short electoral cycles of politicians are not in synch with the long negotiating cycles of trade, and the WTO does not seem to be coming up with the promised deliverables in time. It is worth recalling that the DDA was due for completion in January 2005. Even as late as mid-2008, an agreement was nowhere in sight.[7] It is worth noting that the goal of input legitimacy is often at odds with that out of output legitimacy: improving the transparency of decision-making processes can generate costs in terms of the effectiveness of decision making (especially when the organization is governed by consensus-based rule making wherein all 152 members can, in principle, cast a veto).

Finally, even if all the legitimacy concerns raised in the previous paragraphs were resolved and the legitimacy of the organization were established indisputably in a normative sense, it would still not ensure the legitimacy of the institution in a sociological sense, i.e. when "it is widely *believed* to have the right to rule."[8] To achieve legitimacy in the latter sense requires giving reasons, persuasion, and justification; this notion of legitimacy is related in part to the notion of input legitimacy insofar as it attempts to improve the internal and external accountability of the organization. Internally, given the member-driven character of the WTO and its role as a bargaining forum, such justification is perhaps less necessary than it would be in other organizations with higher degrees of delegation. Externally, however, the role of such reason giving is key: The WTO needs to justify what it does, first and foremost because of the enforceability of its rules. It is true that the WTO's engagement with different constituencies has improved dramatically, especially since the Seattle Ministerial conference of 1999. This engagement takes the form of its Public Forum, and various online mechanisms that give voice to non-state actors (in addition to mechanisms

already mentioned in the context of input legitimacy). And yet, public support for the institutions of the WTO is low: worldwide, respondents to a poll expressed concerns about the impact of trade on environment and labor, and further showed considerable variation on whether their country should comply with any WTO rulings that might be brought against it.[9]

The mechanisms of de-legitimization

Increasing legalization, in the case of the WTO, has not been accompanied by increasing legitimacy of the organization. At first glance, this observed negative relationship between legalization and legitimization is counterintuitive. One would expect that the increasing precision of rules, and their greater enforceability via delegation to dispute settlement panels, is likely to improve the legitimacy of the organization due to the rising importance of due process (covering certain aspects of input legitimacy), more efficient enforcement mechanisms (covering certain aspects of output legitimacy). The reasons why this is not the case are twofold – domestic and international.

The first relates to the impact that legalization has on domestic support for trade liberalization. Judith Goldstein and Lisa Martin (2005) point to three important effects of legalization:

1 Greater legalization, which results in the availability of greater information about the distributional effects of agreements, increases the incentives of antitrade groups to mobilize and deters the conclusion of cooperative deals.
2 Exporter groups targeted with precise threats of retaliation are more motivated to organize in favor of the trade regime than those facing imprecise threats.
3 A stronger enforcement mechanism with penalties and reduced flexibility

297

may further undermine domestic support for an open trade policy.

Using these mechanisms, they argue: "Evidence suggests that the effects of legalization may not be as glowing as proponents argue. First, legalization may be one reason for the increased attention and activity of anti-trade groups . . . Second, some evidence suggests that changes in WTO rules undermine the incentive for export groups to mobilize in defense of free trade. In that the WTO makes retaliation more difficult, both because of changes in the rules on safeguard provisions and because of the process of dispute resolution, we expect exporters to mobilize less often to balance the action of rent-seeking import-competing groups" (Goldstein and Martin 2000). In other words, legalization changes the incentives for domestic groups, and may well result in declining domestic support for international trade. But the reason for the declining legitimacy of the WTO does not work at the domestic level alone.

At the interstate level, the WTO is caught between a rather cumbersome rule-making system (which it inherited from the GATT), and an increasingly legalized rule enforcement system. Herein lies the second reason for the declining legitimacy of the WTO: increasing legalization has not been accompanied by a commensurate ability or authority of the organization to negotiate agreements. Negotiations are perceived to be unfair or inefficient (or both in certain instances) by different negotiating parties and their key constituencies. The discrepancy between its rule-making and rule enforcement functions heightens the legitimacy deficit of the WTO.

There are three mechanisms that explain why the WTO's negotiation processes have begun to unravel, particularly when compared against the days of the GATT. The first and foremost has to do with the rise in the expanded and increasingly active membership of the organization. The GATT started out with 23 members and functioned like a club.

Developing countries sat on the margins of the GATT; with certain exceptions like Brazil and India, most were not privy to the Green Room meetings where consensus was shaped. The bargain worked, nonetheless. Even while sitting on the periphery, developing countries managed to free ride on the concessions that were exchanged by the larger countries via the most favored nation status that they enjoyed qua contracting parties to the GATT.

Today, the WTO comprises 152 members. The expanded reach of the organization into behind-the-border measures, the Single Undertaking, and the enforceability of its rules mean that developing countries can no longer afford to be sleeping partners in the trade negotiations. However, it is important to bear in mind that even though the membership and mandate of the WTO have expanded significantly, its decision-making processes are still closely related to that of the GATT. Besides other similarities to the GATT, decisions in the WTO are arrived at through consensus, which is defined in the following terms: "if no Member, present at the meeting when the decision is taken, formally objects to the proposed decision."[10] Consensus is extremely difficult to reach in the WTO, and not only because each one of its 152 members may, at least theoretically, exercise a veto and hold up an agreement. Rather, it is also because many developing countries, acknowledging the new imperatives generated by the very existence of the WTO, have demonstrated a greater proclivity to participate much more actively and also exercise their potential veto power.[11]

Several factors – new opportunities and also new challenges – have contributed to the improved participation of developing countries (Barton et al. 2006; Gruber 2000; Narlikar 2003; Odell 2006). At least some credit must go to institutional reform within the WTO, which has responded to criticism about its lack of internal transparency in the late 1990s by improving the accessibility and openness of small-group consultations and also providing technical assistance and capacity-building for weaker members.[12] However, with such a large number of members now at the negotiating table, and much more willing and able to bargain, this transparency has come at the price of efficiency. One significant cost of this inefficiency is the time it now takes to reach any agreement – the recurrence of deadlock in the Doha negotiations provides an indication of this. Declining political commitment to the multilateral process and the turn to regional and bilateral alternatives – by developed and developing countries alike – are reactions to these costs. A vicious cycle ensues: As the available alternatives expand, the commitment of countries to the long-drawn multilateral process declines further.

Second, and closely related to the problem of growing numbers, is the changing balance of power in the core of the WTO. Previously, consensus was shaped predominantly by the "Quad" group of industrialized and high-income countries comprising Canada, the EU, Japan, and the U.S. The Doha negotiations today, and perhaps indicative of the opening up of the process of rule making to the developing world, are conducted among a new "Group of Four". Brazil, the EU, India, and the U.S. form the core of WTO decision making. The presence of Brazil and India on this "New Quad" makes it significantly more diverse than the old one, and it has been expectedly difficult for even this small core group to arrive at the beginnings of a consensus (let alone sell it to the rest of the membership). Admittedly, this small group is more representative of the economic and political realities today than the old "Quad" would have been, and reflects a commendable democratization in the workings of the WTO. But the "New Quad" lacks the efficiency of the old one due to its diversity. Equally, it has also been challenged on the grounds of its representativeness and legitimacy, particularly by the LDCs who do not have a direct voice in this group.

Third, the reach of the WTO goes considerably further than the GATT in terms of the coverage of its rules. The GATT dealt primarily with trade in goods, with other behind-the-border issues such as standards (e.g. sanitary and phytosanitary barriers to trade) entering its purview only through plurilateral agreements that members could pick and choose to sign on to or not. The WTO is different. When the WTO was created, all members agreed to sign onto the entire package of agreements via the Single Undertaking, even when these agreements extended to rules relating to TRIPs, TRIMs, services, sanitary and phytosanitary barriers to trade, technical barriers to trade, and so forth. Perhaps this expansion could have enjoyed greater legitimacy had there existed a consensus on it among members, or if it could have been clearly justified through the existing agreements, or if there existed a clear epistemic consensus on it, or even if members eventually came to recognize the virtues and concrete gains from an agreement that they might have resisted in the negotiation process. However, the expansion in the mandate of the WTO has seldom been driven by any of these legitimizing mechanisms.[13] Most negotiators recognize the politics that drives the evolving mandate of the WTO; at least a few negotiators from the developing world see it driven predominantly by power politics, where the areas of interest for the powerful make it onto the agenda while those of the weak are either bypassed completely or enter only in name rather than generate actual results.[14] The failed promises of the Uruguay Round lend further credence to the power politics interpretation.[15]

It is partly as a reaction to these criticisms that the current round of trade negotiations has taken the shape of a development round. But even these attempts to put development at the forefront have left most major constituencies dissatisfied. With the removal of the Singapore issues from the agenda and the primary focus on development issues, the zone of agreement has shrunk as far as developed countries are concerned. For developing countries – be they the middle-income developing countries or LDCs – the current negotiations focus insufficiently on development. These countries are thus even more reluctant to make any concessions, thereby reducing the commitment of the developed world to the multilateral trade negotiations even further.

The rules that the WTO embodies, and the new ones that are currently under negotiation, are contested in terms of substance or outcomes, as well as process. This questioning of outcomes is reflected, for instance, in the criticism of the "Bum Deal" of the Uruguay Round, or the substance of the current negotiations. The process leading to these outcomes is challenged from all sides – by smaller developing countries for still failing to meet some simple standards of democracy and internal transparency, by NGOs for still failing to meet standards of accountability and external transparency, and by the developed countries for failing to meet minimal standards of efficiency and effectiveness. And it is these rules, which are deeply contested in terms of both process and substance, that the WTO implements via the dispute settlement mechanism.

The problem lies not only in the fact that the DSB implements and enforces rules that are under challenge. Rather, the Appellate Body has a tendency to engage in considerable judicial interpretation and activism. This creates a backdoor entry for new legislation on which there is no consensus among trade negotiators. Rules developed in this manner are likely to undermine the legitimacy of the organization even further (Barton et al. 2006). Besides principled objections to this tendency to litigate when states fail to negotiate, there is also the practical consideration that most developing countries do not have the resources to use the DSM effectively nor the strength to retaliate even if the DSB rules in their favor (Busch and Reinhardt 2003). As such, developing countries, which

have only recently begun to reap the payoffs of learning to negotiate more effectively, once again risk marginalization if rules are made via the Appellate Body rather than negotiated.

Reclaiming legitimacy: the way forward

As argued in the previous section, the legitimacy deficit of the WTO lies in the growing divergence between its flailing negotiation processes and its legalized dispute settlement mechanism. Reclaiming this legitimacy is not easy, but it is critical if the multilateral trading system (and the many gains that it has generated for countries rich and poor) is to survive.

Marc Suchman provides a useful discussion of legitimacy as seeking passive acquiescence or active support, or legitimacy as "cognitive taken-for-grantedness" or legitimacy as "evaluative approval." He writes: "To avoid questioning, an organization need only 'make sense'. To mobilize affirmative commitments, however, it must also 'have value' – either substantively, or as a crucial safeguard against impending *non*-sense" (Suchman 1995: 575). Particularly in the face of failed promises of the past and availability of regional and bilateral alternatives, the WTO needs to signal its value for its states (and their people), and thus seek active legitimization.

Most challenges to legitimacy "ultimately rest on failures of meaning: Audiences begin to suspect that putatively desirable outputs are hazards, that putatively efficacious procedures are tricks, or that putatively genuine structures are facades" (Suchman 1995: 597). The first step towards reclaiming the legitimacy of the WTO would be to address the question of its function – what is the role of the WTO today, and why should it be regarded as the institution most suited to serve this end? This is not just a second-order matter of reason giving and persuasion catered to audiences ill informed about the WTO (though a strategy of re-legitimization would need to incorporate such tasks as well). Rather, to implement this strategy successfully, negotiators within the WTO, along with the assistance of its Secretariat and experts outside, would need to come up with principles that would define the mandate of the WTO and also anticipate its future development.[16] This process would need to be intellectually rigorous and also politically acceptable. Negotiations based on a mandate clearly established through agreed principles would significantly improve the efficiency and perceived fairness of the everyday workings of the organization. It would also help deal with the problem of unrealistic expectations.[17]

Rethinking the mandate and functions of the organization through internal and external engagement would improve the legitimacy of the WTO along all the five dimensions discussed in the first section. Input legitimacy would be improved through the consultative process; substantive legitimacy would be improved through a precise and principled definition of the mandate and its purpose; the epistemic consensus that underlies the negotiations would be reinforced (after reconsideration and revision if necessary); output legitimacy would be greatly enhanced with a clearer definition of the WTO's functions against which it could be evaluated and held explicitly accountable; finally, simply a rethinking along such lines would signal the willingness to work towards the reclaiming of its legitimacy.

Second, negotiation processes, i.e. the legislative function of the WTO would need to be directly addressed in terms of both input legitimacy and output legitimacy. Admittedly, reform measures to improve input legitimacy can undermine those directed to improving output legitimacy. For instance, greater transparency in the proceedings and more effective voice for developing countries has improved the input legitimacy of the organization, but it has also undermined its effectiveness by making it much more difficult to arrive at an agreement.

Types of solution to balance these difficult and divergent goals lie beyond the scope of this chapter. But negotiators will need to arrive at such a balance, and will also need to be able to justify it by providing reasons to constituencies within and outside the WTO. Addressing the limitations of its rule making would provide the key to restoring the balance between the legislative and judicial functions of the WTO, and thereby get to the heart of the legitimacy deficit that afflicts the organization today.

Third, it is not only the legislative end of the multilateral trading system that needs to be reformed; dispute settlement also needs to be rethought. Here the core question lies in the costs and benefits of legalization, suggesting two, sometimes diverging solutions. First, some flexibility could be built back into the WTO's DSM, through measures that would include building in constitutional restrictions on the power of the Appellate Body. Such a solution would suggest some dilution in power of the DSM. Not entirely in contradiction to this though, certain aspects of the DSM could be strengthened, particularly in terms of improving its access for weaker countries that lack resources for its use or retaliatory power. Any reform of the DSM would have to be carried out hand in hand with the first two sets of reform of mandate and process.

Finally, even a program of far reaching reform would be unsuccessful if it were not *seen* to be improving the fairness and efficiency of the system. To ensure the legitimacy of the WTO in a sociological sense, constant engagement would be necessary on the part of the negotiators and the Secretariat with politicians, NGOs, and the private sector. This would include giving of reasons regarding the functions of the multilateral trading system, justification of its mandate, and demonstration of the fairness of its process and outcomes. Equally however, and perhaps even prior to reform, more awareness needs to be created as regards the merits of multilateralism and the benefits that developed and developing countries have reaped from it over the past 60 years.[18]

There may be little overlap between the legal and the legitimate. But the law and legitimacy can be used to reinforce each other, and build a system that is fairer and also more effective. Balancing the legislative and legal functions of the WTO will provide initial steps in this direction.

Notes

1 The expiry of the Protocol of Provisional Application or the "grandfather clause" is an example of the increased obligations that members are required to take on under the WTO. The Protocol of Provision Application allowed contracting parties to exempt themselves from GATT rules if they were inconsistent with pre-existing domestic legislation; the members of the WTO are no longer allowed to appeal to grandfathering rights.
2 www.wto.org. Also see Chapter 2 of the Warwick Commission Report (2007).
3 On "input legitimacy" and "output legitimacy," see Scharpf 1999.
4 For instance, see Wade 2006.
5 For an accessible analysis to these debates, see Chapter 3, Warwick Commission Report 2007.
6 www.wto.org.
7 Warwick Commission Report 2007.
8 On legitimacy in a normative versus sociological sense, see Buchanan and Keohane 2006.
9 http://www.worldpublicopinion.org/pipa/pdf/apr07/CCGA+_GlobTrade_article.pdf. Also see Scheve and Slaughter 2007.
10 See the Agreement establishing the WTO: http://www.wto.org/english/docs_e/legal_e/04-wto.doc.

11 This veto power has manifested itself in different forms and on different occasions. The Africa group, for instance, threatened to walk out of the Seattle Ministerial Conference in 1999; several members of the WTO including the EU, the Africa Group, South Korea and Japan refused to make any concessions on the Singapore issues at the Cancun Ministerial in 2003 thereby providing the immediate cause for the failure to reach agreement there.
12 On the various institutional reforms taken on within the organization, see Narlikar 2005.
13 Recall, for instance, the controversy that surrounded attempts to include services, TRIPs, and TRIMs in the Uruguay Round, or the failed attempts to include the Singapore issues in the DDA. For further details, see Narlikar 2005. Specifically on the issue of the mandate, see Evenett 2007.
14 For some interesting anecdotes on this, see Jawara and Kwa 2003.
15 On the problems of implementation that emerged after the completion of the Uruguay Round, see Narlikar and Odell 2006.
16 The Warwick Commission Report (2007) takes an important step in this direction.
17 Sylvia Ostry 2001 argues persuasively that "overzealous proponents of 'free trade' or globalization unleashed unrealistic expectations. If you promise but can't deliver Nirvana it's bound to evoke cries of Armageddon from the disapproving and the disappointed." The same argument could be made about the attempt to couch the current trade negotiations entirely within a development framework, without any clarification on what this means or what countries might expect from it.
18 Such a strategy would fit with Suchman's "Don't panic" recommendation; drawing on the work of Ashforth and Gibbs, he writes: "Delegitimated organizations that seek too frantically to re-establish legitimacy may dull the very tools that, if used with patience and restraint, might save them" Suchman (1995: 599).

21

Attainments, eclipses and disciplinary renewal in international human rights law: a critical overview

Obiora Chinedu Okafor

This chapter provides a critical overview of the con-temporary state of the international human rights law discipline. It does so chiefly through the expli-cation of patterns revealed and insights gained by training three kinds of conceptual lens on the texts, discourses, contexts, and praxis of the discipline. These lenses are devoted to the capture and assess-ment of the attainments that have uplifted the dis-cipline, the eclipses that trouble it, and the bouts of disciplinary renewal that it has experienced from time to time as it struggles with the possibility or otherwise of enduring self-transformation. The chapter maps and examines, albeit in a measured way, the attainments that have advanced the dis-cipline to date; teases out and explicates most of the eclipses (full or partial) that have inhibited the discipline's optimization; explores what is referred to in the paper as the dualistic deep structure of human rights, and the relationship of this deep structure to the characteristics and ultimate utility (or otherwise) of the discipline's constant drive to renew itself. In the end, it is suggested that while human rights' renewal has, of course, always been possible, even the entailed ebb and flow of the zone or band of international human rights protection, the observable expansion and contraction of the borders of the living human rights law, and the mobility of the boundary of protection that human rights offers, does not erase entirely the margin that is too often inhabited by those who have been left in (nay, shifted

to) the human rights cold. This is why the discipline is in danger of being unable to achieve real sustained transformation in our time.

Introduction

This chapter provides a critical overview of the contemporary state of the international human rights law discipline. It does so chiefly through the explication of patterns revealed and insights gained by training three kinds of conceptual lens on the texts, dis-courses, contexts, and praxis of the discipline. These lenses are devoted to the capture and assessment of the *attainments* that have up-lifted the discipline, the *eclipses* that trouble it, and the bouts of *disciplinary renewal* that it has experienced from time to time as it struggles with the possibility or otherwise of enduring self-transformation.

In order to develop systematically the main argument that is made in it, the chap-ter is divided into three main sections. Each section corresponds to one of the three organizing sub-themes of the chapter: that is, attainments, eclipses, and the question of the (im)possibility of disciplinary renewal. These three organizing sub-themes are considered in the chronological order in which they have been stated here. The second section maps and examines, albeit in a measured way, the attainments that have advanced the discipline to date. In the third section, most of the full or partial eclipses that have inhibited the discipline's optimalization are teased out in an extensive way. The last section concludes the chapter by pondering what is referred to as the dualistic deep structure of the discipline and its relationship to the characteristics, and ultimate utility or otherwise, of the discipline's constant drive to renew.

Due to space constraints, not every important attainment or eclipse could be discussed in this chapter.

Attainments

Up on the "moral plateau"[1]

As praxis, *human rights* have come a very long way from the time when Jeremy Bentham felt able to declare that they were nothing more than "rhetorical nonsense – nonsense upon stilts" (Bowring 1843: 501). Even as late as 1937, the principal international law authors still denied that there were any such thing as international human rights law (Buergenthal 2006: 783–5). Today, despite persisting legitimate doubts about the coherence of the conceptual and practical enterprises that have been spawned by the introduction of this concept into social life (Sen 2004: 316), few, if any, serious commentators can refer so dismissively either to the concept of human rights or to the sub-discipline of international law that is devoted to its study. This is so much so that even its most articulate critics have recognized the dizzying heights which it has attained in our time. For example, Upendra Baxi has gone as far as arguing that as contingent, contradictory and contested as international human rights norms too often are, they "remain perhaps *all that we have* to interrogate the barbarism of power" (Baxi 2006: 4). This, in Balakrishnan Rajagopal's words, means that human rights discourse is now

the sole *approved* discourse of resistance (Rajagopal 2003: 165). And if Amartya Sen is right in declaring that human rights are quintessentially ethical articulations (Sen 2004: 321), Makau Mutua's now famous conclusion that these norms now sit on a "moral plateau" is as revealing in this respect (Mutua 2002: 40). So is Louis Henkin's oft cited description of the respectability that international human rights norms have attained in our time in terms of its constitution of "*the* age of rights" (Henkin 1990: 26–9). For a set of ideas, texts and praxis that had endured centuries of excessive discursive skepticism, this ascent to the dizzying heights of widespread rhetorical acclaim is a significant – if in itself insufficient – attainment; not least because of the "rights consciousness" (in the formal sense) that it has helped to highlight and foreground.

Rights consciousness

At the very least, a certain consciousness about the potential utility of much of the formal corpus of international human rights law for the prosecution of their various emancipatory or repressive agendas seems to have emerged among almost all elite classes almost everywhere in the world (Robinson 2003). This exponential rise in the circulation of a relatively elite version of human rights law discourse has led Michael Ignatieff to identify the post-1945 generation as one that currently encounters a significantly heightened "juridical revolution" (Ignatieff 2001: vii). To paraphrase Cassel, many respected scholars have claimed – with some justification – that there has been a *triumph* of rights consciousness; one that has both contributed to and stimulated an explosion in international human rights law (Cassel 2004: paras 40–4).

Standard setting and vindication mechanisms

Most knowledgeable observers of the discipline will easily agree that international human rights law has achieved considerable, if narrow ranging and insufficient, success in the standard-setting and mechanism-constituting areas. In the last five or six decades, literarily hundreds of human rights documents of varying legal force have been adopted, and scores of institutional mechanisms established (Buergenthal 2006). Before and after the adoption of the Universal Declaration of Human Rights in 1948, the corpus of international human rights law has been immensely expanded in size and range to include a large number of basically global (usually U.N.) human rights treaties and soft law documents. This process has also resulted in the adoption and entry into force of the regional human rights treaties and in the establishment of the corresponding monitoring bodies. The dismantling of the United Nations Commission on Human Rights and its replacement with a new United Nations Human Rights Council is only the latest event in a long list of post-1945 developments in the institutional expansion of the international human rights area (Lauren 2007: 335–43).

Focusing beyond the state

It is indisputable that, after decades of neglect international human rights law is *beginning* to pay significantly more attention to non-state actor human rights violators than it historically did. Although, as we shall see in the third section, this incipient turn away from state centrism has been painfully slow and inadequate (Agbakwa 2003; Baxi 2006), it has been steady nevertheless. This is not, of course, to suggest that international human rights law has in fact captured non-state actor violations in an adequate way, but merely to point out that given the extent of the prior neglect, it is a relatively significant attainment for it to begin to focus on the issue at all.

In a noticeable, if cautious, departure from the historical tendency among the mainstream authors of the sub-discipline to ignore the rampant violations of human

rights by non-state actors (such as local "private" actors, multinational corporations and the international financial institutions), the Human Rights Committee has of recent paid some attention to the need for greater scrutiny of the activities of so-called private actors in relation to activities that affect the enjoyment of human rights (Alston 2005b: 769–70). The committee now requires states to ensure as much as they can that these non-state actors do not impair the enjoyment of human rights within their territories.[2] However, as Alston has correctly lamented, nothing in the committee's work has so far suggested that in the absence of effective action by states in the area of reining in these non-state actors, international human rights law imposes *direct* obligations on private actors such as private healthcare providers or multinational corporations. Needless to say therefore, and as significant as they are in relative terms, the attainments of the sub-discipline in this area have not been all that robust.

Correspondence

Critical as he is of the tendency of international human rights law to, in part, encode and reflect global power asymmetries, and to exclude the subordinated from its inner driving rooms, Baxi has correctly recognized that:

> Through myriad struggles and movements throughout the world human rights has become an arena of transformative political practice that disorients, destabilizes, and, at times, even helps destroy deeply unjust concentrations of political, social, economic, and technological power.[3]

How does international human rights law, a law which applies in a largely sheriff-less globe, achieve this mild feat?

As I have argued elsewhere (Okafor 2007), the principal way in which international human rights law has diffused and percolated around the world is through its remarkable capacity to induce something I have referred to as *correspondence*. This occurs both within and way beyond the compliance-focused radar, so much so that those who train their lenses exclusively on the incidence of state compliance with international human rights law tend to miss far too many of its significant effects. Thus, were one to be largely concerned with the capture and measurement of state compliance, one would be likely to see a far less developed, intricate, and robust picture of the attainments of international human rights law than would be revealed were one to adopt a more holistic focus on the generation of correspondence by international human rights praxis. This is, of course, not an argument against the measurement of state compliance as such. Rather, what is being suggested here is that the state compliance measure too often produces too limited a picture of the actual concrete workings and attainments of international human rights law.

An example of the way in which a broader focus on correspondence tends to produce a more holistic and thus more accurate picture of the operations and effects of international human rights law is the way in which the African human rights system, which is widely regarded in the literature as weak (Steiner and Alston 2000: 920), and with whose views states do not comply that often (Viljoen and Louw 2007), has nevertheless helped induce far stronger *correspondence* within a significant number of African states, especially Nigeria and South Africa (Okafor 2007: 91–154, 155–219). A couple of examples from both countries will serve to concretize and illustrate this point. In Nigeria, a group of ethnic minority rights activists escaped execution at the hands of a military regime in part as a result of the influence of a decision of the African Commission on a local high court judge (Okafor 2007: 98–101). In South Africa, some recent decisions of the Constitutional Court, such as the *Kaunda* and *Bhe* cases have been significantly

influenced by the African Charter on Human and Peoples' Rights[4] (Okafor 2007: 157–65). In both examples, the desired effect occurred not because of state compliance as such but more or less in its absence. Yet their impact was most significant in each case. What is more, in regard to both countries, a wealth of similar evidence exists.

In both states, a process of *transjudicial communication* that was brokered and facilitated by local activist forces (including varying arrays of NGOs, women's groups, activist judges, journalists, and so on) enabled African system norms to percolate (beyond the state compliance radar) into local executive, legislative and judicial decision-making processes in a way that produced a range of impact on state and society alike. Were one to focus on Nigeria's or South Africa's formal and direct compliance with the decisions of the African Commission on Human and Peoples' Rights, one would not tease out as rich and extensive a picture of the attainment of this key institution of international human rights law. The resulting picture would be incomplete, and as such, inaccurate on the whole.

As such, it is only logical to suggest that a full appreciation of international human rights law's attainments is not really possible without the aid of a correspondence-focused set of tools. It is also in this way that both the promise and limits of the sub-discipline can be more accurately mapped and analyzed.

Full and partial eclipses

Origins and development of conceptions of human rights

The historiography of human rights has been a site of intense and continuing contestation. While all too many of the dominant western accounts of the origins of human rights locate its origins *exclusively* within the west (for example, Afshari 2007: 3–4; Donnelly 1995: 246–7; Howard 1993: 315; Ignatieff

2001: 4; Schulz 2003: 43), many critical scholars have, over the years, warned against this tendency to erase the "Third World" from the story of the origins and development of human rights. For instance, Balakrishnan Rajagopal has quite understandably lamented the rather unfortunate fact that the Third World rarely figures in what he has referred to as the mainstream "tellings" of the extant story (Rajagopal 2003: 172). Tiyambe Zeleza has pointed to the conscious or unconscious failure to in part root the international human rights movement and the legal regime it has spawned in the long histories of the struggles of Third World peoples against slavery, colonial despotism, and postcolonial misrule (Zeleza 2004: 3). And Paulin Hountondji has warned against the conflation (by those to whom the Third World's hand in the development of human rights appears invisible) of the question of the *origins of the idea* of human rights with that of the *origins of a particular conception* of human rights (Hountondji 1986).

Against the tendency in mainstream human rights historiography to skip the difficult but imperative prior ethnographic work that needed to be done before any viable conclusions can be drawn as to the historical presence or absence of the idea (as opposed to the narrow liberal western conception) of human rights in at least some Third World societies, some scholars have now demonstrated, conclusively in my view, that at the very least functionally equivalent conceptions of human rights have existed for very long periods of time in many Third World societies (for example, Bell 1996: 650–1; Deng 1990: 288; Quashigah 1999: 43, 66; Wiredu 1990: 257). Thankfully, there seems to be increasing recognition of this position among both historians and historiographers of the discipline (Arat 2006: 419; Lauren 2003).

As importantly, critical Third World approaches to international law (TWAIL) scholars have identified and situated the contrary position – that is, the partial eclipse

of Third World agency that is performed whenever its contributions to the origination and development of the human rights idea is deliberately or accidentally denied – as part of a now familiar broader set of discursive techniques through which the Third World is objectified and treated almost exclusively as "a domain or terrain of deployment" of "universal imperatives" that have been constructed elsewhere by supposedly far more advanced minds (Anghie 1996: 331; Mutua 2001: 205; Rajagopal 2003: 171). This points squarely to a serious "lack" in the way the dominant international human rights discourse understands and treats the Third World; one that must be redressed if the discipline is to transcend its many other limitations.

Neglect of pro-human rights Third World cultural norms

Despite the fact that some of the most discerning observers of the discipline have recognized that its attainment of cultural legitimacy within the relevant societies is a necessary precondition for the abridgement of the often wide gap between theory and practice in international human rights law (An-Na'im 1992: 431; Donnelly 1995: 249; Robinson 1993: 632; Zeleza 2004: 13), local culture – especially non-western culture – is all too often constructed within the human rights discourse in purely oppositional terms, as an obstacle to be surmounted and as a huge part of the problem. Rarely is it imagined as an important part of the human rights solution (Nyamu 2000: 392–5). So in this rather simplistic binary typology, human rights norms (which are seen as a fixed already known quantity) are an unalloyed good and local culture (which is seen in a similar monolithic light) is unqualifiedly bad.

No wonder then that there has been such scant mainstream ethnographic research into the nature and properties of the cultural norms that operate within Third World and other societies; and that systematic knowledge of the positive capacity of some of these norms to modify, shape and advance the enjoyment of human rights is almost entirely lacking in the dominant international human rights discourse (Zeleza 2004: 11). Even more worrisome is the fact that such neglect of the necessity of producing knowledge about the nature and properties of the pro-human rights local cultural norms that exist in many non-Western societies also characterizes the work done and literature produced by all too many of the local human rights NGOs that operate in the Third World (Okafor 2006: 106–11).

This situation is extremely problematic from the point of view of the attempt to ensure widespread respect for human rights. It eclipses in part the sunlight that could help energize the pro-human rights struggle in most of the world's societies. For, if as Ibhawoh has noted, every cultural tradition contains some norms and institutions that are supportive of human rights, as well as some that are antithetical to its enjoyment (Ibhawoh 2000: 859), why has the dominant international human rights discourse concentrated almost all of its energies on the analysis of the negative dimensions of local culture? Why has far more attention not been devoted to the crucial task of "finding the space that local contexts provide" for the advancement of international human rights law (Nyamu 2000: 417)?

Women's rights

Although, as Hilary Charlesworth has noted, the rhetoric of women's rights seems to have achieved widespread formal public legitimacy on the global plane (regardless of what many states and societies actually believe), it is difficult to sound as positive with respect to the concrete practice in this area (Charlesworth 1998: 791). Despite the fact that over 90 percent of the world's countries have ratified the Convention on the Elimination of all Forms of Discrimination against Women (CEDAW),[5] in spite of the rapid and impressive response of the United Nations to the challenge posed to it by women's movements around the world (Charlesworth 1998: 791), the world is still nowhere near putting an end to the more or less undeniable reality in every human society of unjustifiable discrimination against women on the basis of their gender (Apodaca 1998: 139–40). Clearly, this is a disturbing situation.

Yet, even within the international women's movement, Third World women activists and scholars have, while accepting that women everywhere have some common concerns, tended to express a sense of partial eclipse by a dominant western agenda (Nesiah 1993: 199; Oloka-Onyango and Tamale 1995: 701) that too often merely consigns them to the role of paradigm receivers who simply *apply* feminist international human rights theories developed in the west.

Rights of indigenous peoples

Judged from the overall profusion in the production of U.N. treaties and soft law standards in the international human rights area, the U.N.'s failure over the last 12 years or so to adopt even one dedicated treaty in the indigenous rights area (Corntassel 2007: 138; Williams 1990: 696–8) is a profound reflection of the severity of the partial blind spot and sheer lethargy that afflicts international human rights law with respect to the recognition and advancement of the rights of indigenous peoples. Worse still, it was only in June 2006 that the U.N. Human Rights Council adopted the formally non-binding *Declaration on the Rights of Indigenous Peoples.*[6] And although, in its case, it was adopted before the commencement of the U.N. Decade on Indigenous People, the existence of the International Labor Organization's *Indigenous and Tribal Peoples Convention No. 169 of 1989* does not remedy this problem.[7] The fact that it has been ratified by precious few countries (Quane 2005: 655) and is therefore of very limited applicability around the world, suggests this conclusion.

Ethnic minority rights

Despite the relative robustness of the corpus of regional treaty law aimed at the protection of ethnic minorities,[8] and the availability at the global level of Article 27 of the International Covenant on Civil and Political Rights (ICCPR) and of even the common Article 1 of both the ICCPR and the International Covenant on Economic, Social and Cultural Rights (ICESCR),[9] the fact that the principal U.N. legal text in the area, the *U.N. Declaration on the Rights of Persons Belonging to National or Ethnic, Religious and Linguistic Minorities* is "merely" a soft law document is one good pointer to the relative disfavor and neglect that the protection of ethnic minority rights has suffered in the post-1945 world order.

The other pointer to the relative neglect of ethnic minority rights in the U.N. system is the largely ideological insistence in most of the relevant global and regional treaties (with the notable exception of the *African Charter on Human and Peoples' Rights*)[10] on conceptualizing and crafting what are meant to be ethnic minority rights in terms of the rights of persons belonging to ethnic minorities (Jovanovic 2005: 628–9). This tendency has its roots in the dominance of a particular version of liberal thought in this area; one that has long insisted on the inadmissibility of collective rights (Donnelly 2003: 204–6; Kymlicka 1989; McDonald 1991). Yet, it is becoming clear that certain human rights – such as the right to speak one's minority language – do not make all that much sense when conceived as *individual* rights (Klabbers 2006: 205; Newman 2007: 231–2).

Thus, despite the urgency of instituting effective ethnic minority rights protections around the world as a key way of addressing the injustices that constitute the root causes of many violent and costly civil conflicts, the dominant international human rights discourse has tended to reproduce the disdain for collective rights that flies in the face of the imperative social necessity for the deployment and vindication of such rights.

Sexual orientation

There is no doubt that the rights of sexual minorities have been marginalized in international human rights law (Murray and Viljoen 2007; Sanders 1996: 78–87). For one, when they feature at all these rights sit very low on the priority listing of the human rights of the U.N. (Morgan 2000: 208; Sanders 1996: 68). Even U.N. soft law instruments are hard to find in this area (Heinze 2001: 298–300). This is therefore another area of the discipline in which a partial eclipse is detectable.

Mental disability rights

In general, although the regional human rights systems have paid some attention to mental disability rights,[11] hard law texts are all non-existent in this area of international human rights law. The global norms governing this subject matter are to be found in formally non-binding and often generally obscure soft law instruments.[12] In sum, the area is only just beginning to recover from decades of neglect and inattention by international human rights law.

Economic, social, and cultural rights

Despite the contingently useful international rhetoric of rights indivisibility and interdependence (Agbakwa 2002: 178), it is now beyond serious debate that so-called economic, social, and cultural (ESC) rights have been historically marginalized in international human rights law and practice in favor of so-called civil and political rights (Donnelly 1995: 241–5; Oloka-Onyango 1995: 1; Woods 2005: 103–4). In part as a result of their continued marginalization of ESC rights work, the dominant actors within the human rights movement still fail to address or address adequately "the most pressing issues of poverty, inequality, and marginalization affecting large majorities in most countries" (Jochnick 2004: 90; Khan 2004: 16). Thus, despite their critical relevance to the struggle to uplift the world's impoverished majority (Felice 2003: 2–7), ESC rights have been partially eclipsed over time by, among other factors (Vizard 2005: 4), the relatively disproportionate attention that has been paid in both text and practice to civil and political rights.

Neo-liberal globalization and "trade-related market friendly human rights"

Focused as it has largely been on the advancement of civil and political rights, and as skeptical as it has tended to be of the necessity of the struggle for ESC rights, the capacity of the living international human rights law to defend and protect the rights of the impoverished and socioeconomically marginalized majorities of most countries has, at best, been significantly weakened by the march of a particular (if historically recognizable) form of socioeconomic globalization: neo-liberal globalization. Largely via the operation of market discipline, which operates with little or no coercion and "imbues the individual with particular ways of thinking, knowing, and behaving, thus instilling modes of social consciousness that make social action predictable" (Evans 2005: 1054–5), neo-liberal globalization has authored a so-called "second great transformation" in world conditions and affairs (Howard-Hassmann 2005: 3) in which the validity and applicability of normative and other claims tends to be judged against the normative referent of a set of "liberal freedoms" (Evans 2005: 1057–1062).

This has resulted in the ascendancy (although not exclusive dominance) of a particular conception of international human rights law that is at the very least "friendly" to market discipline (Baxi 2006: 235). In its unfortunate praxis, the resultant trade-related, market friendly (TREMF) human rights paradigm (Baxi 2006: 132) tends to privilege the rights of capital over the rights of impoverished humans; construct the progressive state as one which is much more soft than hard toward global capital; imagine the ideal state as one that is market efficient in suppressing and de-legitimating the human rights-based practices of resistance of those of its own citizens who actively oppose that state's excessive softness toward global capital; and coerces and/or encourages states to free as many spaces for global capital as possible, initially by pursuing the three Ds of contemporary neo-liberal globalization: near relentless deregulation, denationalization, and disinvestment (Baxi 2006: 234–75).

This has led to all too many serious and increasingly well-recognized negative effects (Howard-Hassman 2005: 4–7), including its reproduction within international human rights law.

Global power matrixes and the displacement of alternative human rights narratives

As Jack Donnelly has correctly observed in his recent critique of "arrogant and abusive 'universalism'," the precious few countries of the world which currently hold and exercise the greatest global political, economic, and cultural power too often confuse and conflate the interests of the dominant segments of their societies with universal values (Donnelly 2007: 304–5). When coupled with the vastly disproportionate power which is available to this small group of mostly western actors to project their parochial world views and preferred historical record onto the world stage and construct and normalize them into *the* human rights gold standard which every other society ought to aspire to attain, the material and cultural power of these actors has all too often (although not always) produced a range of negative consequences, especially for the vast majority of the world's peoples who inhabit the Third World. Some of these consequences are discussed later.

One of the most harmful features of this kind of western-style "global dominance is the perpetual rediscovery of its own perceived innocence" (Falk 2000: 87). The myth of western innocence has been so normalized and is so powerful that it is now encoded in the living international law of human rights; that is the law as it is actually concretized and experienced. And so, despite a long history of abuse and exploitation of non-western peoples – from the dispossession of the indigenous peoples of North America, to slavery and anti-black racial abuse, to the atrocities of colonial rule in Afro-Asia, to Hiroshima and Vietnam, to French atrocities in Algeria, to CIA and other government-sanctioned killings in the Third World, to Abu Ghraib and Guantanamo Bay, and so on and so forth (Falk 2000: 87; Woods 2005: 487) – the human rights savior is still almost always understood as western while the human rights savage is almost exclusively constructed as non-western (Mutua 2002: 11–14; Okafor 2001). Needless to say, the construction of this myth of western innocence serves to foreground a narrow and incomplete narrative that backgrounds what ought to be in the foreground of the human rights story, thus displacing alternative human rights narratives.

The construction and normalization in international human rights law of this kind of heaven/hell binary (Okafor 2001) and its propagation of the myth of western innocence has fed much life sap into the idea of western (especially U.S.) exceptionalism, thus rendering it much more plausible than it would otherwise seem (Forsythe 2006: 466; Zeleza 2004: 9–10). In its U.S. iteration, this idea has been deployed to justify U.S. self-exclusion (nay, near immunity) from international human rights law. The unfortunate logic here has been that if U.S. behavior is already the gold standard in every human rights area, then why would it need any international standards to shape its behavior? This stance has led to the failure of the U.S. to ratify a number of important international human rights treaties (Ignatieff 2001: 13); its reluctance to apply international human rights law within its domestic legal system (Wu 2006: 140–5), and the rather frequent failure of far too many of its own international human rights advocates to assess the policies of their own government against the same international human rights standards that they deploy in their frequent criticism of Third World governments (Okafor 2001: 576; Tomasevski 2005: 713).

The relentless attempts of the current U.S. administration to exploit the tragic 9/11 events to "eviscerate basic rights" not just within the U.S. but also in its treatment of persons accused of terrorism or captured on the battlefield in Iraq or Afghanistan (Dickinson 2002: 1410; Tolley 2004: 540) and the fact that the U.S. still manages not just to retain its self-image (however diminished) as the "city on the hill" to which all other peoples ought to look for direction, but also continues to shape in a somewhat disproportionate way the human rights behavior of key U.N. committees (Foot 2007: 490), is another example of the negative effects that can be exerted in human rights discourse (and, by implication, in international human rights law) by the tendency of global power matrixes to operate in ways which displace and partially eclipse alternative human rights narratives in favor of the more dominant human rights stories. In this way, a particular preferred human rights picture is constructed and projected; one that inevitably shapes the living international human rights law.

The overall point that is made in this section is not that one wishes that there were no powerful actors in the world. It is not being suggested either that there can ever be a world that is *completely* devoid of power asymmetries. Power asymmetries can be radically reduced but are not likely to ever be totally erased from global social life. For is not power, after all, relational? Does not every actor exercise power in relation to some other actor in some context? Thus, there can be no international human rights praxis that

311

operates safely beyond the reach of global power. What is being suggested in the preceding paragraphs is that human rights need not be as amenable to global power as it currently is, and that the fact that it is currently so has produced far too many ill effects for all too many of the world's peoples.

"Historical" wrongs

International human rights is, at best, extremely weak at righting so-called historical wrongs (especially those of a material kind) to the reasonable satisfaction of most within the wronged subaltern group.

Massive historical atrocities such as slavery and colonial dispossession/abuse currently go unpunished or not redressed in part because the perpetrators and victims are too easily constructed as long dead, and the current *individual* citizens of the responsible countries are too readily portrayed as innocent of the crimes committed by their ancestors. Yet, almost all of the responsible *states* currently exist intact. Is the real issue not the responsibility of the collectivity (the state) for the acts that it (the state) indisputably authorized, albeit many years before? In any case, do not current citizens of those states enjoy the exponentially compounded material and other benefits (such as centuries of net free labor) extracted through slavery and colonial abuse? Of course, some could deploy more technical international law arguments such as the operation of inter-temporal law in the hope of defeating arguments that suggest that these sorts of historical wrong ought to be righted with the help of international human rights law. But the unmitigated fallacy of the inter-temporal law argument is that it projects onto the colonized Third World peoples an inter-European (and therefore geographically limited) law that they had not accepted and which clearly did not govern their affairs until much *after* the very atrocities complained of had been committed.

The story of the attempt, over the last decade or so to redress more recently inflicted historical wrongs such as land dispossession in Southern Africa further illustrates this weakness of international human rights law at contributing to the righting of so-called historical wrongs. As different as the two societies are today, in both South Africa and Zimbabwe, despite their respective successes at ending the formal political subjugation of the vast majority of their populations by a white settler colonial class, over the periods they have been so freed, there has not been all that much significant change in the racialized structure of ownership of the arable land in those societies.[13] Now, international human rights law is not, of course, chiefly responsible for this scenario. The point that is being made here is that when the living international human rights law has engaged this issue at all – at least as seen from the commentary of scholars (Boyle 2001; Shirley 2004) and the statements of civil society groups (one good example is Human Rights Watch), they have – to some extent quite understandably – focused on lamenting the (corrective) dispossession of those who currently hold the very lands that were dispossessed from the vast black majorities of both of these countries. Worrisomely far less, if anything at all, is said in this literature about the initial dispossession of the black majorities or the critical need to urgently redistribute their lost lands to them, so as to create more equitable, egalitarian, and just societies in these countries

In the end, the point is that it is as if international human rights law can only function well when fundamental historical wrongs have already been addressed and/or are not all that salient anymore. It does not itself show more than an extremely limited capacity to help reconfigure grossly unjust fundamental socioeconomic and political arrangements. Here, the deepest ideological underpinnings and moorings of international human rights law combine with the operation of particular forms of global power to eclipse alternative human rights narratives and practices.

Beyond disciplinary renewal

In conclusion, it is important to consider, even if briefly, the possibility of international human rights law pushing back against and ameliorating the harmful effects of the full and partial eclipses that are discussed here; thereby strengthening its coherence, legitimacy, and effectiveness. In other words, after taking stock, can the discipline renew itself without repeating the mistakes of the past (Kennedy 2000)? Is this even possible?

A key path to disciplinary renewal that has been suggested by a diverse bunch of some of the most established international human rights scholars of our time is a turn to "cross-cultural dialogue" or some such conversation or communicative praxis (for example, see An-Na'im 1992; An-Na'im and Deng 1990; Baxi 2006: 125–68; de Sousa Santos 1995: 337–53; Donnelly 1995: 250–2; Mutua 2002: 113). The basis of this call for dialogue is the recognition of these scholars of what Mutua has termed the incompleteness of every culture, including the predominantly western cultures from which most of mainstream global human rights proselytism emerges (Mutua 2002: 113). The expressed intention of most of those who have made this call is to encourage the development of what Donnelly has recently referred to as a partial and incomplete but "functional overlapping consensus" around the "relative universality" of the conceptual frameworks that ground international human rights law norms, while avoiding as much as is possible the imperialistic undertones and effects of all too many articulations of the universality of human rights (Donnelly 2007: 289–92).

It is also becoming increasingly recognized that for this cross-cultural dialogue to be as meaningful as it could be, it must include far more than a complex series of bi- and multilateral interstate conversations. As Rajagopal's germinal work has demonstrated, the living international human rights law (as it is experienced by most peoples in the world) is in part written and limited by

the resistance and struggles of Third World and other social movements (Rajagopal 2003: 245–71). These social movement struggles have been waged by "protest coalitions" comprised of varying arrays of trade unions, professional associations, women's groups, community and non-governmental organizations, religious leaders, environmentalists, and human rights activists (Zeleza 2004: 1–3), and have sometimes helped produce important, even remarkable, social changes. This is a fact that has not been all that easily received into the routine analytic processes through which stories of the discipline are written. In tending not to take adequate account of these struggles and their effects (Rajagopal 2003: 245–71), international human rights lawyers have too often labored under the mistaken impression that international human rights law is simply what international human rights lawyers make of it (Rajagopal 2006: 1091). Yet, in truth, as Rajagopal has told us, international human rights are what an expanded group of its practitioners (including social movements, the masses, etc.) make of it (Rajagopal 2006: 1091). This is precisely why the suggested cross-cultural dialogue must include and take seriously the popular "human rights talk" of the so-called ordinary citizens of the very cultures that are to participate in the dialogue.

Regardless of the considerable merits of cross-cultural dialogue as a *renewal* strategy in international human rights law, it is doubtful that it is likely to result in an adequate and sustained *transformation* of the discipline – at least not any time soon. Examined closely enough, the historical evidence simply does not support much optimism in that direction. For, although over its relatively long career the international human rights law discipline as we now know it has experienced many bursts of renewal, it has never adequately transformed itself. To put it rather crudely, no matter how far human rights law has expanded its zone of protection, someone has always been left out in the human rights cold. The *American Declaration of Independence* loftily proclaimed that all humans were born free and should remain so while slavery remained conceptually legitimized in the praxis of the very drafters of that document and went on largely unhindered for over a century afterward (Morgan 1972). Even today, when studied closely it becomes apparent that the living mainstream human rights praxis is still based to a significant extent on the deep conceptual structure of the oppositional competition between the deserving and the undeserving, and the displacement of suffering from the deserving to the undeserving. Landless black Southern Africans must suffer so that their landholding white counterparts can enjoy their economic human rights (Mutua 2002: 142–4). Here, the landless blacks are constructed as undeserving while the landholding whites are positioned as deserving; with the result that the potential white suffering that could result from more deeply egalitarian land reforms are displaced toward the landless blacks. The anticipated suffering of the "deserving" beneficiaries is thus displaced toward the "undeserving" victims.

The point is not, of course, that in the process of its renewal, international human rights law cannot find some middle ground or accommodation with respect to each of these cases. What is being suggested is that even such an accommodation is unlikely to escape the deep conceptual structure that the discipline has exhibited over its career. For some displacement of suffering from those who are viewed as deserving toward those who have been forced into the strait-jacket reserved for the undeserving will still occur. The accommodation will most likely only reduce the *extent* of this displacement of suffering. And so, the zone or band of international human rights protection may ebb and flow, may expand or contract, but this mobility of the boundary of protection does not erase entirely the margin that is inhabited by those who have been left in (nay, shifted to) the human rights cold. What occurs instead is a shifting of coordinates, an adjustment in the conceptual or even concrete

location of the zone of protection, in order to capture or release another who has been either "mainstreamed" or "othered."

Such then is the nature of the duality of the deep structure of human rights law – be it international or local – that it is driven, to a significant extent, by the construction of boundaries and binaries (such as the worthy and the unworthy) that allow it to displace and shift suffering from one to its "other" without fundamentally *transforming* (as opposed to renewing) the nature of suffering in that context, the nature of local or global social life, or itself as a local or global discipline.

Notes

1 I owe this term to Makau Mutua's fecund imagination. See Mutua 2002: 40.
2 See *General Comment No.31 on Article 2 of the Covenant: The Nature of the General Legal Obligation Imposed on States Parties to the Covenant*, adopted March 29. 2004, Human Rights Commission, 80th Session, 2187th Meeting, 8 U.N. Doc. CCPR/C/74/CRP.4/Rev.6 (2004).
3 See Baxi 2006: 4.
4 Supra note 10.
5 Supra note 4.
6 Human Rights Council Res. 2006/2.
7 72 ILO Official Bulletin 59.
8 See the following: *Document of the Copenhagen Meeting of the Conference on the Human Dimension of the Conference on Security and Co-operation in Europe*, adopted 29th June 1990 and reproduced in (1990) 11 *Human Rights Law Journal* 232; Recommendation 1134 on the rights of minorities, EUR. Parl. Ass., 42d Sess., 2d part (1990); the Council of Europe *Framework Convention for the Protection of National Minorities*, C.E.T.S. No. 157, reprinted in 34 I.L.M. 351 (1995), adopted February 1, 1995.
9 Supra note 6.
10 Supra note 10.
11 See *Aerts vs. Belgium*, App. No. 25357/94, Eur. Ct. H.R. (1998); *Keenan vs. United Kingdom*, App. No. 27229/95, Eur. Ct. H.R. (2001); *Varbanov vs. Bulgaria*, App. No. 31365/96, Eur. Ct. H.R. (2000); *Autism-Europe vs. France*, European Committee of Social Rights, Complaint No. 13/2002, Decision on the Merits transmitted to the Committee of

Ministers on 22 May 2003; *Rosario Congo vs. Ecuador*, Case No. 11.427, Inter-Am. C.H.R., Report No. 63/99, OEA/Ser.L/V/II.102, doc. 6 rev. (1998); *Purohit and Moore vs. Gambia*, African Commission on Human and Peoples' Rights, Communication No. 241/2001 (2003).

12 See the following: World Programme of Action concerning Disabled Persons, G.A. Res. 37/51, U.N. GAOR, 37th Sess., Supp. No. 51, U.N. Doc. A/37/51 (1982), adopted December 3, 1982; Declaration of Caracas for the Restructuring of Psychiatric Care in Latin America, adopted November 14, 1990 at the Regional Conference on the Restructuring of Psychiatric Care in Latin America, convened by PAHO/WHO; Principles for the Protection of Persons with Mental Illness and the Improvement of Mental Health Care (MI Principles), G.A. Res. 46/119, U.N. GAOR, U.N. Doc. A/RES/46/119 (1991), adopted December 17, 1991; Standard Rules on the Equalization of Opportunities for Persons with Disabilities, A/RES/48/96, 85th plenary meeting, adopted December 20, 1993; Council of Europe's Recommendation 1235

(1994) on Psychiatry, EUR. Parl. Ass. 10th Sitting, Rec. No. 1235, adopted April 12, 1994; Human Rights and Recommendation Rec (2004) 10 on the Protection of the Human Rights and Dignity of Persons with Mental Disorder, Comm. Of Ministers, 896th Meeting, Rec. No. (2004) 10, adopted September 22, 2004); and Montreal Declaration on Intellectual Disability, adopted October 6, 2004.

13 As at 2005 only about 3% of commercial farmland in South Africa was redistributed between 1994 and 2004. Some 60,000 commercial farmers (mainly white farmers making up about 5% of the total population) own between 67–87% of the total area (Moyo 2004: 7; Wisborg and Rohde 2005: 400–10). In pre-redistribution Zimbabwe, approximately 4500 white commercial farmers (0.03% of the population) controlled 31% of the country's land under freehold tenure, or about 42% of the agricultural land, while 1.2 million black families in Zimbabwe subsisted on 41% of the country's area of 39,007,600 hectares (Moyo 2004: 9). While changes have since occurred to this landholding structure, it has not changed all that significantly.

22

Colonial origins of intellectual property regimes in African states

Ikechi Mgbeoji

This chapter analyzes the colonial roots of intellectual property rights (IPR) regimes in African states and argues that the inability of contemporary African states to internalize some of the key doctrines of IPR regimes can be linked to the underlying differences between African worldviews and the Eurocentric philosophies underpinning IPR regimes. Using the general concepts of patent law as the analytical framework, it argues that unreconstructed Eurocentric IPR in Africa may be blamed for the perverse phenomenon wherein legal provisions in the statute books have failed to translate to compliance with IPR in many African states. It contends, in summation, that colonial rivalries between decolonized African states are responsible for the institutional fissures and balkanization of continental regulation of IPR in Africa.

This chapter is divided into four sections: The first queries the general assumption that IPR are universal verities divorced from local truths, in particular, the Eurocentric worldview and value systems of modern IPR. The second section traces the origins of IPR and relates the European origins of the patent system to its unsuitability for African realities. In the third section, we examine the features that make modern patent systems uniquely Eurocentric and argue for a reconsideration of those doctrines that impede

domestication of IPR in the African continent. The final sections summarizes the arguments put forward in the chapter by examining how the cultural disconnection between patent systems has influenced the inability of modern IPR laws to influence social and economic behavior in African states.

The local as universal

Although IPR regimes are often promoted as universal verities (Drahos 1998: 13), scholars are increasingly aware that standardized global IPR regimes affects various societies in different ways (Endeshaw 2002: 55). Indeed, in the past decade, the local impulses and characteristics of IPR in various states and across different historical timeframes have all become subjects of legitimate inquiry (Grundmann 1976; Penrose 1951). IPR regimes are, indeed, susceptible to the perceived changing demands of industrialized states and the power relations between states (Chiappetta 2000).

Yet, for a long time, especially in the heydays of colonial domination of Africa, Eurocentric scholars and institutions pretended that IPR are universal verities lacking

in local differences and historical contingencies. As Endeshaw (2002: 55) has observed:

> [T]his trend is evident in standard IP textbooks and even WIPO publications. Pick up any of these writings and you will see a discussion beyond the concrete; an outpouring of rules and policies that do not tie in with specific conditions of countries. Perhaps this had to do with the misfortune of IP being in the suffocating care of lawyers and not economists.

Despite the grudging admission by IPR scholars of the varieties and different temperaments if not doctrinal differences, among IPR in several states, an often ignored dimension of the local nature of IPR is the influence of the colonial origins of IPR in Africa. Yet, it cannot be seriously doubted that the nature and content of IPR laws and institutions, especially patents, trademarks, and copyrights clearly show that the dominant IPR have their origins in the cultural, legal, and economic traditions of continental Europe and of western jurisprudence and economic systems (Mgbeoji 2003). Consequently, it would be problematic for scholars to persist in the myth that local economic, technological, and cultural conditions do not influence the structure and content of IPR laws and institutions (see, e.g. Beier 1980). Thus, I argue in this chapter that the prevailing notion that Eurocentric varieties of IPR regimes should be universally accepted as symbols of civilization is a notion that needs to be scrutinized (Endeshaw 2002).

The European origins of copyrights, trademarks, and patents regimes is widely acknowledged but scholars have hardly inquired into the subject of whether the philosophical and cultural underpinnings of dominant IPR may have implications for the efficacy of such IPR in the African landscape (Lowenstein 2002). It needs to be borne in mind that the diffusion and spread of IPR regimes from Europe to other parts of the world followed distinct patterns derived from the single template of European economic, political, and cultural conquest of the globe. A combination of certain historical factors facilitated and encouraged the diffusion of IPR regimes from Europe to many parts of the world including Africa.

As a colonial transplant and imposition on African societies, Eurocentric IPR were part of the cultural, economic, and legal instruments for the control and subordination of colonized peoples and economies (Sagoe 1992; Sklan 1978). As I have argued elsewhere (2006: 13), the transplanting of IPR from Europe to Africa was an essential part of the racist and exploitative repertoire of the colonial project. The colonization of native Africans by European states was premised on two main grounds, namely, a sense of European innate superiority over colonized peoples, and, of course, economic exploitation of the colonized. On the former, colonial Europe sought to justify its suppression of native African laws and institutions on the hypothesis of racial superiority of Europeans and the inferiority of "the savages and primitives" of Africa (and Asian, natives of the Americas, aboriginal Australian and the Maoris of New Zealand). It was largely on the notion of a racial ordering of that the colonialist enterprise justified the acquisition and colonization of large swathes of lands and cultures occupied by peoples considered by the colonizing European Christians as "backward territories" and primitive peoples (Lindley 1969).

On the latter, European colonization of Africa was designed as machinery for the looting and dispossession of the colonized peoples of Africa of valuable natural resources (Wa Mutua 2000), and to create a ready market for European goods. To achieve both ends, the colonial enterprise had to create legal and social structures that ensured not only a racist ordering of cultures and societies, but a violent imposition of foreign legal norms and institutions on conquered peoples and cultures for the purposes of European economic supremacy. The obvious implication is that Eurocentric IPR regimes such as patents, copyrights, trademarks, etc., like other manifestations of European values, norms, and institutions, had to be internalized by colonized societies if such colonized societies were to be regarded as "developed" and "civilized."

It must be emphasized that the imposition of Eurocentric IPR on African societies operated on the prevalent notion that colonized African peoples and cultures had no civilization, no jurisprudence, institutions, or methods of governance worthy of respect, let alone deserving of legal protection (Bedjaoui 1978: 153). To all intents and purposes, the colonized territories and peoples were treated as cultural *tabula rasa* (Coombe 1995), on which the colonialists proceeded to inscribe European institutions, norms, and systems, including IPR regimes. This project was facilitated and justified by diverse legal theories and methods which need not detain us here but it will suffice to note that the entire process was executed without the consent or input of colonized peoples.

Accordingly, it has to be understood that the colonial project was not merely the unprecedented robbery of Africa, but also the near annihilation of autochthonous legal systems and protocols. Conversely, Eurocentric laws and instruments were promoted as the highest attainments of rationality, empiricism, and justice: universal truths and ideals attainable by all societies regardless of differences in culture (Shiva 1988). As Wa Mutua (2001) has observed, within this prevailing logic of the colonial project, "history is a linear, unidirectional progression with the 'superior' and 'scientific' Western civilization leading and paving the way for others to follow."

Today, there is hardly one African state that does not have IPR regimes copied from the template of the former colonial overlord. Beyond the colonial origins of IPR, a corollary issue is the marginal roles played by colonial and newly decolonized African states in the creation of international and global IPR legal doctrines and institutions. Historically, the structure and process of international intellectual property regulation has margin-

alized the Third World,[1] especially, Africa (Gervais 2002). This phenomenon is currently epitomized by the limited participation and near irrelevance of African countries in global IPR law-making processes (Endeshaw 2002).

As some scholars have observed, in the development of global IPR and trade frameworks,[2] a constant phenomenon is the marginal roles played by African states (Blakeney 1996; see also Gervais 2003). Despite its enormous size – the African continent is four times the size of the United States (Mallet 1999) – Africa has contributed little to the emerging global regimes on IPR (Correa 2002). The questions raised by the continued marginalization of African states in the global production and regulation of IPR norms and institutions echo the unfortunate global notion that Africa is a dumping ground for foreign goods, foreign laws, and foreign norms (Mgbeoji 2004).

Despite the successful globalization of IPR (F. Abbott 1999), the transplantation of Eurocentric IPR to African countries has not been matched with success, at least in terms of internalization of IPR norms by a reasonable proportion of African businesses (Mgbeoji 2007). Rather, IPRS in Africa have been beset with several challenges including domestic economic difficulties, cultural dissonance, and institutional incapacities. There is emerging scholarly speculation that the inability of modern IPR to take root in many African states may be related to the failure of policymakers to adapt Eurocentric IPR to local needs and worldview. Using the patent system as a model, the next part explores the viability of this school of thought (Adewopo 2002).

Colonial origins and migration of the patent system

The patent system is not new to controversy. Conceived in circumstances that Lippert (1999: 129) described as "blackmail," the concept of patents[3] are traceable to Filippo Brunelleschi's successful blackmail of the medieval Italian city state of Florence. According to Bruce William Bugbee, in 1421, Filippo Brunelleschi, the Italian architect and painter, announced his invention of an iron-clad vessel, the *Badalone*, which he claimed could carry marble across Lake Arno for the construction of the now famous cathedral of Florence. Contrary to scientific tradition (Bugbee 1961: 76),[4] Brunelleschi refused to disclose the *Badalone* to the public. In addition, he rejected the idea of putting the vessel at the service of the city unless he was granted a limited right to an exclusive commercial exploitation of the vessel. Florence yielded to his unprecedented demands and on June 19, 1421, the city issued him the first recorded patent in history. To Brunelleschi's embarrassment, the *Badalone* sank on its inaugural trip and the Florentine patent idea sank with it (Kaufer 1989) – at least, for a long time.

Recovering from the rather inauspicious debut in Florence, the patent concept migrated to Venice where it acquired legislative imprimatur and substantive features. For instance, the Venetian patent law of 1474 provided for patent duration of 10 years, examination of patent applications for novelty, and punishment for infringement of patent rights (White, Jr. 1967). However, with increasing papal intolerance and the frequent political conflicts in the Italian peninsula, Italian artisans, and craftsmen began a process of migration to central and western Europe (Macleod 1988). Naturally, they did not leave the concept of patents behind them in Italy. They took the patent concept with them. Netherlands in 1817, Spain in 1820, the Vatican in 1833, Sweden in 1834, Portugal in 1837 (F. Abbott 1999: 228). Thus, it is fair to say that the modern patent concept owes its original inspiration to the Italian city states of medieval times. From central Europe, the patent concept spread with European immigrants to North and South America; and by colonialism and diffusion, to the rest of the world.

Defining patents

At this stage, a definition of the patent concept is apposite. Although there is no universal patent law per se, Article 27 (2) of the TRIPS agreement defines patents in terms of a legal protection for products or processes which are *new, involve an inventive step*, are *useful*, and *capable of industrial application* (Gervais 2003, emphasis in original). The United States Patents Act provides that "whoever invents or discovers any new and useful process, machine, manufacture, or composition of matter, or any new and useful improvement thereof, may obtain a patent therefor."[5] Machlup (1958: 2) has defined a patent as "that which confers the right to secure the enforcement power of the State in excluding unauthorized persons, for a specified number of years, from making commercial use of a clearly defined invention."

Certain inferences may be made from the various definitions of patents. First, in spite of several theories on patents, especially, attempts to couch the arguments for and against patents in the discourse of human rights, there is no such thing as a human right to patents. A patent is a discretionary grant of a state on an invention which excludes unauthorized persons, for a specified number of years, from making commercial use of a clearly defined and specified invention.[6] Second, the patent system is anchored on a capitalist worldview. In recognition of these, particularly, the latter, the patent system, especially in western societies, is ostensibly designed to recompense investors by its offer of a temporary monopolization of the commercial benefits of a clearly defined invention. Third, the system of patents purports to celebrate creativity or authorship as an individual effort. This approach discounts immense societal contributions and the incremental basis of most inventions.

For African societies, the crux of the matter here is whether the patent system is inherently universal in its philosophy, and if so, whether it offers the best economic incentive for protecting and rewarding inventions in the realms of activities that are peculiarly communal and where innovations occur in an incremental nature, for example, in plant genetic resources. Law, as most jurists have restated, is a mirror of societal values. In other words, does the Eurocentric patent concept reflect non-European values? In resolving these difficult questions, certain factors must be taken into consideration. Primarily, the passage of time and contemporary realities have modified the jurisprudence on property ownership, the social nature of the inventive process, notions of legal personality, etc., which underpin the patent system. The crucial task thus is to locate the areas of abiding difference. This issue may best be examined within the context of the provisions of the CBD, Article 27 (3) of the TRIPs Agreement,[7] and perhaps, other international instruments purporting to deal with the subject, especially, the Food and Agriculture (FAO) Undertaking of 1983 (as clarified or amended by a number of other resolutions).

The patent system may be malleable in some respects but the question remains whether African states have the political and economic clout to create doctrinal deviations that best serve their own peculiar needs and aspirations (Coulter 1991; see also David 1993). It seems to me that unlike the powerful industrialized countries,[8] developing countries lack the economic and political machinery needed to create an effective but parallel global regime on Plant-related Resources Knowledge. As Lara Ewens (2000: 307) notes: "[B]ecause of the immense investment western corporations have made in plant genetic resources and plant genetic research, and of the important potential biotechnology offers for increases in global food supply, modification of the system is likely to come from within, if [it comes] at all."

The eurocentricity of the patent system

Before examining in relative detail the main doctrinal obstacles to the internalization of the patent system by traditional African societies, it is imperative that the social and institutional biases against traditional knowledge in general be addressed. The first socio-cultural obstacle is the notion that bio-cultural knowledge is common knowledge possessed by every African villager. This is a simplistic and indefensible dismissal of the intelligent and labor-intensive interventions of millions of people working across the millennia.

With particular reference to plants and food crops, it is known that domestication of plants leads to increased varieties. This is principally due to the phenomenon of polyploidy: a process by which chromosomes of any particular specie are increased or multiplied to yield new varieties or species (Isaac 1970). Over the centuries, small-scale farmers and local peoples have contributed to plant diversity by breeding assorted crop varieties to suit particular local conditions (Friends of the Earth 1995: 2).[9] For instance, Indian farmers have grown over 30,000 different varieties of rice during the past century. The native Andeans have developed hundreds of species of tomatoes, potato, maize, and beans. Indeed, scientists reckon that the "the total genetic changes achieved by farmers over the millennia was far greater than that achieved by the last hundred or two years of more systematic science-based efforts" (Shiva 1988: 259).

Apart from developing new varieties, the knowledge of biological resources for medicinal and other uses by local farmers and healers are often phenomenal and pragmatic. For example, in Sierra Leone, local farmers can differentiate between 70 different varieties of rice based on several criteria including: length to maturity, ease of husking, proportion of husk to grain size and weight, susceptibility to insect attack, behavior in different soils and moisture levels, cooking time, and qualities (Nijar 1994: 17).

This knowledge is not merely of academic or theoretical importance; it serves practical ends. For instance, in Rwanda, farmers have cultivated mixtures of beans that perform better in their poor soil conditions (Friends of the Earth 1995). The Aguarana Jivaro community in the Peruvian Amazon has developed 61 distinct cultivars of cassava and in the Philippines 123 rice varieties have been found at just five sites. In both cases, the varieties are designed to suit certain specific requirements and needs. Thus, the abundance of multitudinous varieties and species of plant resources and the knowledge of the uses thereof among the so-called traditional societies are not merely dependent on geographical quirks but partly a result of deliberate and cumulative efforts spanning thousands of years.

Intellectual feats such as the aforementioned cannot be adequately protected by modern patent law. Modern international law has equally come to terms with the reality of traditional input into the improvement, conservation and diversification of biological resources.[10] The preamble of the CBD recognizes the "close and traditional dependence of many indigenous and local communities embodying traditional lifestyles on biological resources."[11] Article 10 (c) of the CBD obliges Contracting Parties to "protect and encourage customary use of biological resources in accordance with cultural practices that are compatible with conservation or sustainable use requirements."[12]

Recognition of the mutually reinforcing nature of human culture with biological diversity is expressed in Article 8 (j) of the CBD which obliges contracting parties to:

> [R]espect, preserve and maintain knowledge, innovations and practices of indigenous and local communities embodying traditional lifestyles relevant for the conservation and sustainable use of biological diversity and their wider application with

the approval and involvement of the holders of such knowledge, innovations and practices and encourage the equitable sharing of the benefits arising from the utilization of such knowledge, innovations and practices.[13]

The salient points from our analysis thus far are that the links between rational human impact on and mutual interaction with plant resources is enormous and profound. Second, the notion that plant resources in the gene-rich countries are resources of a "wild" character is often generalized and exaggerated. A considerable portion of the so-called wild plant resources and ecosystems are, in fact, products of centuries of human impact on the ecosystem and particularly, plants (Hochberg 1996; Kaufman and Mallory 1993; Young 1990). Thus, to determine the boundary, if any, between the so-called wild plant species or "unknown" varieties thereof and the "domesticated" versions and the uses thereof requires a substantial degree of circumspection and open mindedness. Of course, the mischaracterization of traditional biological resources as "raw materials" for western biotechnology denies and delegitimizes the enormous intellectual contributions made over the centuries by the so-called informal breeders, farmers and other local people. Given the preceding arguments on the human impact on the improvement and sustenance of biological resources by local people in Africa and elsewhere, the next task issue is to examine doctrinal and institutional obstacles that continually make it difficult for modern IPR such as patents to be internalized by contemporary African societies.

For the purposes of securing patent protection on biological resources, for example, it is not enough that an innovation has been wrought. The threshold for legal protection under the patent regime is whether the invention has surpassed obvious or prior art in the field of that invention (de Valoir 1995; Seay 1988–9). In attempting to apply patent-like protections to biological resources, the modified test is to ask: When do such innovations, private or collective, surpass obvious knowledge or prior art (Caillaux 1994: 10)? And whose prior art is relevant?

In addressing this question, two misconceptions on the "traditionality" of bio-cultural knowledge and "naturalness" of traditional knowledge deserve our attention. First, references to the innovations and knowledge of traditional societies, especially on the issue of biological resources as "traditional" are often misconstrued to imply or mean that such inventions and innovations are static, antiquated, and wrapped in mythology. That is to say, there is a pervasive notion that African traditional knowledge or bio-cultural knowledge are intellectual relics of a bygone era handed down to modern successors by unreliable oral history. Of course, there exists "traditional knowledge" elements both in the western and non-western paradigms that are long-known. However, the notion of antiquity associated with traditional knowledge, especially, on bio-cultural knowledge is supported neither by common sense nor by international law. As the Four Directions Council points out,

> [W]hat is "traditional" about traditional knowledge is not its antiquity but *the way it is acquired and used*. In other words, the *social process of learning and acquiring which is unique to each indigenous group, lies at the heart of its "traditionality."* Much of this knowledge is actually quite new, but it has a social meaning and legal character, entirely unlike the knowledge indigenous people acquire from settlers and industrialized societies.
> (Dutfield 1999, emphasis added)

The second common misconception about traditional knowledge is the notion that traditional knowledge of biological resources is mere discovery of "natural phenomena" waiting for the lucky discoverer. As Gurdial Nijar has observed:

> [T]raditional uses, although based on natural products, are not "found in nature"; as

such. They are products of human knowledge. To transform a plant into a medicine, for example, one has to know the correct species, its location, the proper time of collection (some plants are poisonous in certain seasons), the part to be used, how to prepare it (fresh, dried, cut in small pieces, alcohol, the addition of salt, etc.), the way to prepare it (time and conditions to be left in the solvent). And finally the posology (route of administration and dosage).
> (Nijar 1996: 16)

Put simply, it would be erroneous and too sweeping to characterize all traditional bio-cultural knowledge as mere "raw materials" or as fortuitous revelations of nature. The naturalness of bio-cultural knowledge does not necessarily mean that there is an absence of human intellectual input in the improvement and modification of its relevance or utility. As the Sierra Leonean example indicates, innovations within the traditional African farming contexts, particularly, in plant breeding, can be quite complex and thus is not a process of mere conservation or knowledge of gene pools. It is, in fact, a mechanism for enhancement of natural genetic resources, albeit slow and laborious.

In order to achieve these sophisticated results in the improvement of plant varieties or cultivars, it has been observed that those farmers:

> [E]mploy taxonomic systems, encourage introgression, use selection, make efforts to see that varieties are adopted, multiply seeds, field test, record data and name varieties [and in fact] ... do what many Northern plant breeders do.
> (Friends of the Earth 1995: 4)

It is from such intricate innovation systems and processes that often yield the stupendous varieties and holistic knowledge of bio-cultural knowledge which traditional farmers and healers have been reputed for. According to a World Resources Institute report:

[I]ndians dwelling in the Amazon River make use of some 1300 medicinal plants, including antibiotics, abortifacients, contraceptives, anti-diarrheal agents, fungicides, anesthetics, muscle-relaxants, and many other most of which has not been investigated by researchers.

(Panjabi 1993)[14]

Seventy-four percent of the pharmacologically active trees reported by an indigenous group correlated with laboratory tests whereas in contrast only 8 percent of random samplings showed any activity. In short, absent "the aid of indigenous groups, it is estimated that for every commercially-successful drug, at least five thousand species must be tested" (Jenks 1995: 646). Michael Balick of the New York Botanical Gardens found that using traditional knowledge increased the efficiency of screening plants for medicinal properties by more than 400 percent (Nijar 1994: 3). It is therefore no coincidence that a decisive number of drugs derived from plant resources have been with the help of local peoples operating outside the dominant western framework of what constitutes "scientific knowledge" (Roht-Arrioza 1996).

It seems clear that the opposition by the "scientific and industrial" community to the scientific worth or merit of traditional bio-cultural knowledge has nothing to do with the innate inferiority of the latter but a reflection of a socially constructed relegated status of innovations arising from the so-called traditional or informal sectors. As the environmental activist Pat Mooney has stridently posited, "the argument that intellectual property is only recognizable when performed in laboratories with white lab coats is fundamentally a racist view of scientific development" (Shiva 2000: 259). Every bio-cultural innovation, regardless of the cultural framework from which it springs, deserves to be judged on its own merits and not to be peremptorily categorized as "raw material" or automatically elevated to the status of an invention merely because of the respective cultural setting from which it is made or derived.

With particular reference to enduring Eurocentric patent law doctrines that impede the internalization of patent systems by African societies, perhaps, the most remarkable doctrine of patent law is the fiction that inventions are necessarily the result of individual, spontaneous creativity and genius. Thus, a concept of reward and recompense on the idea of *individual* inventiveness discounts the daily African reality that most inventions are the result of incremental insights into what already exists in society. In the extremely perverse manifestation of the Eurocentric myth on inventive genius, the "inventive genius," and thus property in the inventions, belongs not to the actual "inventor," but to the capital investment made by a multitudinous number of corporate or public stakeholders. This pandering to modern capitalism affords juridical basis for ownership by corporate entities of thousands of inventions. For farmers and native healers in the traditional African setting who produce new plant varieties or discover medicinal remedies from biological sources, this is a juridical and institutional impediment.

The myth of the inventor as a lone ranger leads to the common notion that the patent concept is, *inter alia*, incompatible with the inventive process in traditional communities. The communal/collective nature of the development and improvement of bio-cultural knowledge in traditional social structures and units has been posited as one of the grounds why such units of legal *persona* may not secure patent protection for their intellectual contributions to biological resources (Gana 1995). This school of thought points to the individualistic structure of western societies. The contention is that the patent system is partly predicated on the concept of the inventor as an individual and the inventive process itself, as an exercise in solitude (Hannig 1996; Petersen 1992). In addition to the obvious generalization inherent in this categorization of the inventive process in non-western societies, there are problems of misapprehension of the modern social structure of the inventive process in western societies.

First, the impression created by the notion of an individualized inventive process in the western world is that of an inventor working alone and the invention, a product of *his* own genius. Without this individual inventor, the invention would probably never materialize. The invention is thus the "sweat of *his* own genius." The theory is that the patent grant is designed to compensate *him* – the individual inventor. This idealized, in fact, perverse narrative of the character of the inventive process, albeit heroic, is a fiction; indeed, a myth.

The individualism in western societies is probably a social fact but to suppose that the social structure of the inventive process has remained static since the days of Benjamin Franklin and James Watt is erroneous. The notion of the solitary western scientist and inventor in his isolated basement or garage has become a legal anachronism. What baffles the mind is the longevity and obduracy of this myth. Indeed, the contemporary reality is that since the legal fiction of an employer's ownership in the employee's invention,[15] and the economics of scale of group research, a community of scientists working away in huge laboratory complexes has driven the concept of the solitary inventor to virtual extinction. Yet, modern patent law persists to sustain the myth of the individual inventor.

Were Leonardo da Vinci, Thomas Edison, James Watt, and Benjamin Franklin alive today, they would in all probability be working in commercial/multinational or public-funded laboratories, bouncing ideas off one another and seeking solutions to complex problems. As Alfred Kuhn (1996) noted in a groundbreaking treatise:

> [T]he transformation of technology and of economic society during the last century negates completely the patent law assumption as to the nature of the inventive process . . . in the modern research laboratories, tens, hundreds of men focus, upon single, often minute problems; inventions become increasingly inevitable.

According to David Safran (1983: 117):

> [I]n this age, most inventions result from corporate research efforts . . . a growing number of these research efforts are the result of the work of several research and development teams that are located in different countries.

As this army of inventors are put to work, it is no coincidence that an overwhelming proportion of global patents on inventions are owned by corporate institutions and public-funded research institutions including universities, where researchers and inventors routinely work in groups. Assuming that the hypothesis of a collective inventive process in traditional societies holds, the transformation of the inventive process in western societies is in several material respects similar to the inventive process in the so-called informal sector. As Stephen Brush (1996: 145) notes, "collective invention is a common and determinant force in both local economies and the world economy."

Interestingly, it has not been suggested such collectively invented products in western societies cannot be patented because of a perceived inability to pin down the critical "flash of genius" involved in the invention to a member of the collegial team in a western laboratory. Rather, the patent law has been adjusted in western countries to create a convenient legal fiction of an employer's ownership in the employees' invention and the attendant consequence of reducing the individual inventor to a hired worker.

The inescapable conclusion is that like the "scientists" in the laboratories of the industrialized states who exchange information, collective groups of traditional knowledge holders and practitioners also exchange ideas to resolve and find solutions to deep and complex problems relating to biological resources. As the Crucible Group recently observed: "Farmer's fields and forests are laboratories. Farmers and healers are researchers. Every season is an experiment." If corporate inventors are honored with patents, *a fortiori*, their informal counterparts deserve the same privileges.

Further, just like the modern patent law created the fiction of corporate "creative or inventive" genius to serve social and economic imperatives, non-western jurisprudence has legal personalities serving same or similar ends. These artificial legal personas or juridical entities are usually designed for the regulation of diverse functions including land ownership, succession, inheritance, etc. Indeed, the category of legal persons is not closed. Yet, domestic laws in Africa have largely maintained colonially inspired categories of legal personalities, thus further enabling the irrelevance of the patent system to local needs and realities.

The alleged boundary between individual and collective creativity is a conflation of communalism with the notion of collective inventions. Often, an individual in the community of persons may derive inspiration from pre-existing knowledge, just like his western counterpart, and from thence, invent something "of intricate detail and complexity, reflecting great skill and originality."[16] In short, "gross generalizations about the irreconcilability of collective and individual" rights or contributions towards inventiveness can no longer be maintained in the context of present realities (McDonald 1998).

Another Eurocentric aspect of the patent regime is the conception of what constitutes public domain for the purposes of evaluating novelty. The prevalent notion is that bio-cultural knowledge is a matter of common knowledge and resides in the public domain. Despite its strong basis in contemporary patent law, it is argued that this tenet of patent law when uncritically applied to African settings is flawed on three grounds. First, not all traditional or informal bio-cultural knowledge is in the public domain. For instance, native healers, in particular, hardly reveal the secrets

of their medicinal knowledge and herbal remedies. Secrecy of their knowledge guarantees their power and influence in the local communities. Indeed, the rituals, magic, and spirituality that often surround the practice of traditional healing is, in addition to myriad other societal functions, a critical aspect of the "secrecy regimes"[17] imposed on such bio-cultural knowledge by herbalists and healers.

Second, assuming, but not conceding that all traditional bio-cultural knowledge is in the public domain, placement of such knowledge in the public domain by overzealous researchers without the consent of native healers, does not, *ipso facto*, extinguish a right of ownership to intellectual property. This principle is the rationale for the regime of prior informed consent (PIC) in contemporary international law on access to traditional and bio-cultural knowledge. Ironically, it is often the same information or knowledge construed to be in the "public domain" in the so-called traditional societies, which affords the basis for some patents on bio-cultural resources in some other countries, particularly, Japan and the United States. Third, the concept of public domain is an occidental legal principle that should not be foisted on traditional societies without informed consent.

Beyond the problem of what constitutes public domain, another aspect of the problem of novelty is the mistaken assumption by many policymakers that there is a universal consensus on the concept of novelty as a criterion in granting patents. A careful analysis of international patent law and practice does not support the notion of absolute global novelty in the determination of what constitutes a patentable invention. The criterion of novelty is regrettably, geographically relative and arbitrary. While this situation is to be decried and needs to be changed, it remains the law in many jurisdictions. Neither the TRIPs Agreement nor any other relevant international legal instrument contains any definition of the concept of novelty. As the United Nations Conference on Trade and Development (UNCTAD) recently observed: "[T]here is no agreed international standard of absolute novelty and, *within limits*, member countries may apply the different approaches recognized in domestic patent laws" (UNCTAD 1996: 32).

The problem is that no binding international custom or legislative instrument has yet demarcated the boundaries of the acceptable "limits" of domestic jurisdictional prerogative in defining novelty and prior art. As Richard Gardiner (1994: 256) has lamented:

> [I]n the light of uncertainty as what it is that is protected by patent law (both in the case of what required element of inventiveness is central to patentability and the extent of what the patent actually protects), readers of the Reports of Patent cases might well reach the conclusion that the state of the law in this field depends on how key concepts strike the judge hearing a cause or fit the line of reasoning . . . invention . . . idea . . . ingenuity . . . and discovery are used by the courts in conjunction with novelty and the notion of what is inventive or not obvious in unpredictable ways.

In addition to the definitional anarchy on novelty, an international juridical bifurcation arising from the United States and European patent law jurisprudence on novelty and prior art has not yet been bridged. As the United States Supreme Court held in *Gayler vs. Wilder* (1850, emphasis added):

> [I]f the foreign invention had been printed or patented, it was already given to the world and open to the people of this country as well as of others, upon reasonable inquiry . . . *but if the foreign discovery is not patented, nor described in any printed publication, it might be known and used in remote places for ages, and the people of this country be unable to profit by it. The means of obtaining knowledge would not be within their reach; and as far as their interest is concerned, it would be the same thing as if the improvement had never been discovered.*

This technical and geographically relative approach to construing the concept of novelty and prior art is hardly dissimilar to the medieval and eighteenth-century patent

policies of the fledgling European industrial states; yet it has legislative force by virtue of section 102 of the United States Patent Act (1982; see also Gratwick 1972).[18] The trouble with Section 102 of Title 35 of the United States Code and similar provisions elsewhere is that it confers juridical sanctity on the phenomenon of bio-piracy by legalizing the process by which traditional or bio-cultural knowledge may be appropriated from one country without acknowledgment or compensation. The existence of a dual regime on novelty is therefore a blemish on the international patent system. Commenting on this, Jain (1999: 781) notes that:

> [P]articularly worrisome are the ramifications of Section 102 of the United States Patent Act. Under this provision, whereas prior knowledge, use or invention in the United States can be used as an evidence to invalidate a U.S. patent for lack of novelty, similar foreign activity can not be used against a U.S. patent. The only foreign evidence which qualifies to invalidate U.S. patents is an actual patent, a known or used invention or an invention that was described in a printed publication. This technically narrow interpretation of "novelty" remains wedded to the concept of tangibility and blind to the oral traditions and knowledge of genetic resources, resources which largely flourish in biodiversity-rich areas.

In effect, for the purposes of determining novelty of invention, there are parallel regimes on publication, that is, *de facto* publication and *de jure* publication.[19] Given that innovations in the informal paradigm are largely conducted in traditions where the keeping of formalized data in books is the exception rather than the rule, the seeming triteness of such biocultural knowledge in such societies would not debar such bio-cultural knowledge from being construed as "novel" in another country like the United States (Oddi 1989). The paradox is that such bio-cultural knowledge would be ineligible for patent protection in the home country.

Hence, what is an obvious invention or prior art in India, as the controversy over *Neem* derivatives and *Turmeric* patents demonstrate (Jain 1999), may be construed as a novel art in the United States of America for the purposes of obtaining a patent grant. Yet, in both cases, the bio-cultural products were unjustly patented in the United States. Consequently, the blurring of the law on novelty permits, or even encourages some biotechnology and pharmaceutical firms to privatize traditional bio-cultural knowledge through a cosmetic repackaging of those resources and knowledge. This phenomenon often brings disrepute to the patent system in Third World countries. Thus, it is evident that at the doctrinal level, the ideological values and worldview encoded in the IPR of the colonizing European powers were often alien to indigenous African ethos and economic traditions (Farley 1997).

Echoes of the past

Leaving doctrinal obstacles aside, at the institutional level, the complications resulting from the colonial scramble for Africa are reflected in the discordant and often competing IPR laws and institutions prevalent in decolonized African countries. For example, English common law countries in Africa are structurally different from Francophone African countries. While the latter operate the French civil law system, the former apply common law plus a mix of contemporary legislation. Another layer of colonial fissure is evident in the Roman-Germanic legal system operating in lusophone countries in Africa. The result is a gaggle of IPR laws and institutions in Africa that are, in several instances, verbatim reproductions of IPR laws in the colonial states plus a mix of recent domestic legislation.

As already noted in the foregoing paragraphs, European IPR laws were often re-enacted in African colonies without regard to local sensibilities and practical realities.

For example, until 1962, patent law in French Africa was governed by French laws. Administratively, the French National Patent Rights Institute (INPI) was the national authority for members of the African French Union.[20] Similarly, barely two decades ago, a person wishing to obtain patent protection in most British colonies in Africa could do so by reregistering a British patent in the local office in the particular African country. In effect, both the substance and process regulating IPR governance in Africa were appendages to colonial dictates and preferences.

Clearly, the internationalization of IPR which started in Europe in the nineteenth century and culminated with the conclusion of the Paris Convention and the Berne Conventions was an extension of colonial diktat in African IPR governance (Adewopo and Oguamanam 1999). African countries did not participate meaningfully in the law-making process at the international level. African states have largely played the role of passive recipients of laws and norms rather than co-participants in the creation of both the content and structure of international IPR regimes. It seems obvious that the alienation of African states from IPR law-making processes is implicated in the non-protection of indigenous categories of IPR such as folklore (Kuruk 1999).

Regrettably, the process of political independence for African colonial states marked by the retreat of most European settlers to Europe in the 1960s did not bring about radical changes. Indeed, shortly after formal decolonization, with the singular exception of South Africa, none of the newly-decolonized African states operated functional patent offices. Save for trademarks, which were used to protect merchandise from the imperial states, there was little domestic efforts on the protection of IPR.

At the continental and macro levels, the colonial rupture of Africa left in its wake fissured and competing continental institutions and frameworks for the regulation and governance of IPR. The two continental organizations that deal in IPR are (1) African Intellectual Property Organization (OAPI)[21] and (2) the African Regional Industrial Property Organization (ARIPO). The former comprises 14 French colonies in Africa (North Africa excluded). The French colonies decided in 1962 to create the African and Malagasy Patent Rights Authority by the agreement known as the Libreville Agreement. The Libreville Agreement was signed to form the African Malagasy Patent Rights Authority (OAMPI). The Libreville Agreement was based on three fundamental principles: (1) the adoption of a uniform legislation by the putting in place and application of common administrative procedures resulting from a uniform system of patent rights protection; (2) the creation of a common authority for each of the member states; (3) centralization of procedures.

Following the withdrawal of Malagasy and the need to expand coverage to other categories of intellectual property, the Libreville Agreement was revised and a new convention signed in Bangui on March 2, 1977 gave birth to the African Intellectual Property Rights Organization (OAPI).[22] The Bangui Agreement deals with the following categories of intellectual property: patents; utility models, trademarks and service marks; industrial designs, trade names; appellations of origin; and copyright. With respect to trademarks, the OAPI Agreement provides that only visible marks are registrable (Kongolo 1999). The OAPI office also serves as the registration office for OAPI members of the Trademark Registration Treaty.[23] In addition, members of OAPI submit notifications of their domestic legislation to the WIPO.[24] The Bangui Agreement was amended in 1999 to make it TRIPs compliant. The revised version of the Bangui Agreement entered into force for all OAPI members in early 2002 following ratification by 16 OAPI member states.

For most of Anglophone Africa, there was the Lusaka Agreement of 1976 which came into effect in 1978. In December 1985,

the Lusaka Agreement was amended in order to admit all African states interested. This change gave birth to the African Regional Industrial Property Organization (ARIPO).[25] The Harare Protocol adopted by ARIPO members in 1982 empowers the ARIPO office to receive and process patent and industrial design applications on behalf of states party to the Protocol. A patent granted under the Harare Protocol has the same effect in the designated contracting state as a national patent. The Banjul Protocol on marks was adopted by the administrative council of ARIPO in 1993. It establishes a trademark filing system similar to the Harare Protocol. The Protocol came into effect on March 6, 1997.

Northern African countries are a reflection of historical patterns of conquests, colonialism, Arabization, and Islamization of the Maghreb, Nile Valleys, and the Saharan parts of the African continent. The Arab conquests of the seventh century AD, European (mainly French) colonialism of the eighteenth century have largely defined the legal framework of northern African countries. With specific reference to Algeria, there are various legislations dealing respectively with patents,[26] trademarks,[27] industrial designs,[28] copyrights,[29] appellations of origin,[30] and layout designs of integrated circuits.[31] Morocco was until 1953, a French colony. Consequently, Morocco has been largely influenced by French civil law traditions.

The colonial imprint on West African countries is palpable in contemporary times. Throughout the colonial era, Britain controlled a wide swath of West Africa including The Gambia, Ghana, Nigeria, and Sierra Leone. By way of contrast, France controlled Burkina Faso, Cote d'Ivoire, Guinea, Mali, Niger, and Senegal. The remaining territories were controlled by Portugal (in Guinea Bissau) and Germany (Togo until the end of the First World War). Liberia is the only country in West Africa to escape direct imperial control although it saw itself as an American outpost in Africa.

Eastern Africa is comprised of Burundi, Comoros, Djibouti, Eritrea, Ethiopia, Kenya, Madagascar, Malawi, Mauritius, Mozambique, Rwanda, Seychelles, Somalia, Uganda, United Republic of Tanzania, Zambia, and Zimbabwe. In many instances, national laws on IPR were hitherto anchored on colonial British laws that have now been reformed to meet the minimum standards set out in the TRIPs agreement.

Central Africa comprises Angola, Cameroon, Central African Republic, Chad, Congo, Democratic Republic of the Congo, Equatorial Guinea, Gabon, and the twin islands of Sao Tome and Principe. The contextual circumstances and experiential exigencies in Central Africa are imperative factors in any useful analysis of the colonial impact of domestic IPR regimes in Central African states. The situation in Cameroon is somewhat different, largely because Cameroon has been one of the most politically stable countries in Africa. The situation in Gabon is akin to what obtains in Cameroon, CAR, Chad, and the Congo. Gabon's laws on patents, trademarks, and industrial designs are premised on the Bangui Agreement as last amended in February 1999. Southern Africa is composed of Botswana, Lesotho, Namibia, South Africa, and Swaziland. Save for South Africa with a very diverse industrial base, much of southern Africa is dependent on mining, agriculture, and tourism.

Conclusion

From the foregoing, it seems clear that the origins of IPR in African states are directly traceable to the colonial conquest and domination of Africa. While the arguments made in the 1800s for the imposition of Eurocentric IPR laws and institutions in Africa have faded and lost their appeal, it remains a paradox that African states have not re-examined the utility and relevance of those colonial legal regimes. The hope that Eurocentric laws must ipso facto give rise to

"development" and "civilization" in Africa is increasingly becoming untenable. The chasm between the promises of IPR laws and industrial development in Africa may also be a result of institutional problems and challenges rather than a demerit in the laws themselves. However, the analysis here does suggest that IPR laws are not enough in and of themselves to transform a politically unstable and economically dysfunctional continent into an innovative and technologically advanced society.

In sum, it seems that the colonial origins of IPR in Africa have cast a shadow on the contemporary development of IPR regimes in the continent. Perhaps it is time for African countries to focus on those industrial and economic activities in Africa that would best respond to certain types of IPR. For example, many African state economies are largely agrarian (Reichman 1995). In this regard, it would be sensible to adopt and implement IPR regimes that are proven to be responsive to agriculture. The existence of colonial IPR laws in Africa has not positively impacted on the lives of ordinary Africans. What is perhaps needed is a frank appraisal of the costs and benefits of those colonial IPR laws in Africa. Where necessary, such regimes should be re-structured to respond to local needs and imperatives (Oddi 1996).

Notes

1 For a definition of the Third World, see Rajagopal 1998–1999. (Contending that the concept of global south or Third World should not be inflexibly moored to a fixed geographical location.) For a consideration of the complexity of the Third World, see Mickelson 1998: 360.

2 *Agreement Establishing the World Trade Organization*, April 15, 1994, 33 I.L.M. 81, Available at http://www.wto.org/english/docs_e/legal_e/04-wto.pdf.

3 The term "patent" as an adjective derives from the Latin word *patere* which means, "to be open." When used as a noun, it means an open letter addressed to the public.

4 Prior to the modern era of serious inroads by the patent system into scientific discourse, open exchange of scientific discoveries and ideas was the norm. As Stephen Brush (1996: 149) has noted: "[S]cience is the long conversation among members of . . . community . . . the glitter of science to many practitioners is its alternative to pecuniary reward."

5 United States Patent Act (1982) 35 U.S.C. 101. (See also Gollin 1991.)

6 *Attorney-General vs. Adelaide Steamship Co.* [1913] Appeal Cases 781.

7 The literature on this burgeoning school of thought is quite remarkable. See, generally, Greaves 1994.

8 For example, when it became obvious to the industrialized states that the existing patent regime could not protect computer chip makers, the Washington Semiconductor Treaty was quickly concluded and ratified. Meanwhile, as Peter Drahos (1997) has noted: "[I]n contrast, the issue of protection for indigenous knowledge has largely remained just that, an issue."

9 Traditional ecological knowledge may be defined as "a body of knowledge built by a group of people through generations living in close contact with nature. It includes a system of classification, as set of empirical observations about the local environment, and as a system of self-management that governs resource use" (Johnson 1992: 2).

10 Preamble, CBD, supra.

11 CBD, supra.

12 CBD, supra.

13 Article 8(j) of the CBD, supra.

14 But see Merges 1988; Scalise and Nugent 1995.

15 In virtually every patent jurisdiction in the world, an employer owns the patent right to an employee's invention if the employer is hired to invent or the invention is made in the course of the employment using his employers' tools. However, under some narrow circumstances, the employee may own the invention. Similarly, governments and their research institutions can acquire the inventions of their empoyees (See Vaver 1997: 147–9.)

16 See Justice von Doussa, in *Milpurrurru vs. Indofurn* 1995: 216. In the preparation of this chapter, Tomme Rosanne-Young opined that corporate inventions are put into use when such inventions are completely invented whereas (as she argues), traditional knowledge inventions seem to come into existence after being in use. Second, that corporate membership, unlike traditional societies is fixed and determinate. With due deference, the suggested distinctions, if at all they exist, are not insur-

mountable problems capable of defeating the concept of community patents. Rules of membership of a corporate organization, like traditional societies are not necessarily uniform but a prerogative of national laws and the internal constitution of that corporate body or traditional society.

17 World Intellectual Property Organization (2007) WIPO Report.

18 Further to the WTO, the United States has amended this section but the amendment limits it to WTO member states only!

19 There is a commonly held view that traditional knowledge is uncodified. This is far from the truth, in addition to the Ayurvedic System which is codified in 54 authoritative texts, the Siddha System is codified in 29 authoritative texts, and the Unani Tibb tradition in 13. In India, the First Schedule of the Drugs and Cosmetics Act, No. 23 of 1940, as amended by the Drugs and Cosmetics (Amendment) Act No. 71 of 1986, specifies the authoritative books of the three systems.

20 Otherwise known as Union Française, the group is composed of 16 French-speaking African colonies except French North Africa. These are Benin, Burkina Faso, Cameroon, Central African Republic, Chad, Congo, Cote d'Ivoire, Equatorial Guinea, Gabon, Guinea, Guinea Bissau, Mali, Mauritania, Niger, Senegal, and Togo.

21 The acronym OAPI is derived from the French name of the organization, which is *Organisation Africaine de la Propriété Intellectuelle*. OAPI is constituted by French-speaking countries.

22 Article 19 Paris Convention permits members to belong to regional IP groupings provided there is no contradiction between the Paris norms and the obligations created by such regional groupings.

23 Art. 2(3)(4) of the Trademark Registration Treaty.

24 Benin, Congo, Cote d'Ivoire, Gabon, Guinea, Guinea Bissau, Mali, Mauritania, Niger, Senegal, and Togo have all notified WIPO on their domestic legislations. Chad simply affirmed that it will abide by the terms of the TRIPs Agreement.

25 There are currently 15 members of ARIPO. See www.aripo.wipo.net.

26 Law No. 03-19, November 2003.

27 Law No. 03-18, November 2003.

28 Decree No. 66-87, April 1966.

29 Executive Decree No. 98-366, November 1998.

30 Decree No. 76-121, July 1976.

31 Law No. 03-20, November 2003.

23

Indigenous rights claims in international law: self-determination, culture, and development

Karen Engle

This chapter examines the emergence and application of the human right to culture as the primary legal and political strategy for making rights claims on behalf of indigenous peoples. It discusses the different ways in which advocates invoke the right to culture, presenting a typology ranging from claims that make a relatively small claim on the state in terms of resource sharing and development (culture as heritage) to those that pose significant challenges to the neo-liberal state (culture as land and culture as development). I consider the successes and dark sides of each of these uses of the right to culture and caution indigenous rights advocates against the temptation to embrace "strategic essentialism."

For the past 20 years, tribal representatives, indigenous rights activists, lawyers, anthropologists, and even most states have largely coalesced around an understanding that the right to culture provides an effective means to protect the rights of indigenous peoples. This chapter traces how that coalescence occurred by studying how the human right to culture replaced the right to self-determination as the primary legal and political strategy for indigenous rights advocates. In doing so, it raises the question whether the human right to culture is robust enough to achieve the types of economic and political goals that

its advocates often seek. Imbedded in that question is another, about the similarities and differences between right to culture and self-determination claims made by indigenous advocates.

The right to culture has not totally replaced calls for self-determination in indigenous advocacy, but it has provided the dominant discursive and legal vehicle for making political and economic (as well as cultural) rights claims on behalf of indigenous peoples. When advocates invoke the right to culture, however, they do so in multiple ways. I devote much of this chapter to examining and delineating those different uses of culture, presenting a typology ranging from those claims that make a relatively small claim on the state in terms of resource sharing and development to those that pose significant challenges to the neo-liberal state. Nearly all of these claims rely to a certain extent on overly stereotyped and essentialized ideas of indigenous culture.

Through an exploration of potential costs and benefits of each of these uses of culture, I aim to urge advocates away from the acceptance and deployment of essentialized notions of culture. I argue that "strategic essentialism," the intentional use of essentialized versions of indigenous cultures to claim indigenous rights under a right-to-culture framework, often has the effect of restricting rather than broadening indigenous economic, political, and territorial autonomy.[1] I therefore call for a consideration of constructivism in legal and political advocacy alongside a more explicit statement of or at least debate over the types of economic and political claim to autonomy that advocates aim to achieve.

Indigenous advocacy based on assimilation and self-determination

When, in the 1970s, indigenous groups began to organize around a pan-indigenist ideology, they had three primary legal tools available to them for consideration: (1) the 1957 International Labor Convention (No. 107); (2) the right to self-determination, with or without a right to state sovereignty; (3) human rights. While ILO Convention (No. 107) was the only international legal document specifically focusing on indigenous peoples, it was rejected as a tool for indigenous liberation because of its integrationist and assimilationist aims. Self-determination arguments were dominant for some time but, as they gradually moved away from an insistence on statehood, the claims began to be articulated in human rights terms, even as a human right to self-determination. The human rights rubric that seems to have achieved the most traction, however, has been the human right to culture.

That said, self-determination continues to be advocated and was at the heart of many debates over the recently adopted United Nations General Assembly Resolution on the Declaration on the Rights of Indigenous Peoples. Thus, before turning to the uses of culture in the next section, I briefly consider here these first two options and the reasons they seem to have been rejected as strong tools for indigenous rights advocacy.

International Labor Convention (No. 107)

In the 1950s, the ILO became concerned with the failure of indigenous peoples to integrate into the national population. Failure of such integration was seen to have social and economic effects, on indigenous populations as well as on the nation states they inhabited. In 1957, the ILO drafted Convention (No. 107), which, according to Douglas Sanders, saw "indigenous populations as 'less advanced' than other sectors of national society. They were seen as archaic lumps in the body politic, in need of modernization and integration" (Sanders 1983: 19).[2]

Although most of the Convention was aimed at measures to integrate indigenous populations, it did not call for complete assimilation. In fact, an often overlooked provision is Article 4, which calls for "due account" to be "taken of the cultural and religious values and of the forms of social control existing among these populations" and "the danger involved in disrupting the values and institutions of the said populations" (International Labor Organization No. 107 1957: Art. 4(a), 4(b)). Moreover, it recognized indigenous peoples' right to collective lands they had traditionally occupied (International Labor Organization No. 107 1957: Art. 11). That said, a new economic order was clearly imagined, and eventually – it was thought – indigenous peoples would not require attention to their cultures or traditions. Neither would they need special protections provided by the Convention (International Labor Organization No. 107 1959: Art. 3). The idea was to "mitigat[e] the difficulties experienced by these populations in adjusting themselves to new conditions of life and work" (International Labor Organization No. 107 1959: Art. 4(c)). Similarly, land rights were subject to the "interest of national economic development or . . . the health of the said populations" (International Labor Organization No. 107 1959: Art. 12).

In the 1970s pan-indigenous movement advocates largely rejected the Convention. These advocates were explicitly anti-assimilationist and sought consciously to reclaim and preserve cultural practices seen by settlers and missionaries as "backward." From their perspective, ILO Convention (No. 107) represented a perpetuation of the civilizing mission because of its support for conventional models of industrialized economic development and its explicit attempt to assimilate indigenous people(s) into those models. In the context of Latin America, the Convention was considered to be a reflection of *indigenismo*, an ideology that dictated many Latin American state policies toward indigenous peoples in the first half of the twentieth century. Peter Wade explains *indigenismo* in the context of Mexico and Peru: "From the 1920s, the indian became a prime symbol of national identity . . . both countries created government departments for indigenous affairs, while Peru recognised the 'indigenous community' as a legal entity and Mexico created academic institutions dedicated to the study of indigenous peoples . . . [T]he central notion was that indians need special recognition and that special values attached to them" (Wade 1997: 32).

The ILO revisited its approach, and produced a new Convention on indigenous peoples in 1989, ILO Convention (No. 169). As discussed in the next section, that Convention largely approaches indigenous rights from a cultural rights perspective.

Self-determination

Self-determination as state sovereignty

Somewhat surprisingly from today's vantage point, in the 1970s, the right to self-determination – including the right to secession or state sovereignty – seemed a viable alternative for indigenous peoples. Coming on the heels of a large wave of decolonization, many indigenous advocates saw the possibility for a similar future for indigenous peoples. Particularly in former British colonies, self-determination – meaning a right to secession and statehood – was the prevailing paradigm for much indigenous advocacy throughout the 1970s and continued to struggle for dominance into the late 1980s. Advocates for this state-end model sometimes argued that indigenous groups constituted independent states under the Montivedeo Convention of 1933 or "peoples" under Chapter XI of the UN Charter. Such recognition would have entitled them to exclusive dominance over territory and (at least to the extent decolonized states were getting it) control over their natural resources. This argument met with strong resistance by states with indigenous populations and, as early as the meeting of the first United Nations Working Group on Indigenous Populations, was a major point of contention. It continues to animate debates about the meaning and appropriateness of defining indigenous rights in self-determination terms.

Until September 2007, when the United Nations General Assembly passed the Declaration on the Rights of Indigenous Peoples, there were no internationally accepted documents or instruments that applied the language of self-determination to indigenous peoples. Indeed, although the ILO reconsidered its integrationist approach toward indigenous peoples in the 1980s, states refused to agree to a Convention that included the term "self-determination." Neither that term nor "autonomy" appears in ILO Convention (No. 169) (International Labor Organization No. 169 1989: 8(2)). In contrast, Article 3 of the newly adopted Declaration on the Rights of Indigenous Peoples repeats the language of common Article 1 of the International Convention on Civil and Political Rights and the International Convention on Economic, Social and Cultural Rights, stating: "Indigenous peoples have the right of self-determination. By virtue of that right they freely determine their political status and freely pursue their economic, social and cultural development" (Declaration on the Rights of Indigenous Peoples 2007: Art. 3). The earlier Conventions had declared this right one that belonged to "all peoples" (ICCPR 1966: Art. 1; ICESR 1966: Art. 1); by replacing the word "all" with "indigenous," the Declaration placed indigenous peoples among those entitled to self-determination. Debate over the potential meaning of self-determination in that context was central to the failure of states to agree on a text for the Declaration for over two decades, and to the final opposition to the Declaration by the four states that voted against it – United States, Canada, Australia and New Zealand. These states, and many others along the way, have expressed concern that the term might be read to grant the right of statehood.

Article 3 has been in every version of the Declaration over the years, but its qualifying and limiting language has been the subject of much controversy. In 2005 the chair of the Working Group on Indigenous Populations suggested a list of compromises on the Draft Declaration to push its adoption through the new Human Rights Council. Many of the compromises limited the meaning of self-determination. This new draft of the Declaration was presented to the Human Rights Council, adopted by the Council in June 2006, and sent to the General Assembly.

Ultimately the compromises were not sufficient for the General Assembly. In late November 2006 the Third Committee voted in favor of a non-action resolution on the Declaration, deferring consideration of the Declaration for a later date. The non-action resolution was formally proposed by Namibia, on behalf of the Group of African States, in part on the ground that "the vast majority of the peoples of Africa are indigenous to the African Continent," and that self-determination "only applies to nations trying to free themselves from the yoke of colonialism" (Cherrington 2006; Lutz 2007a).

The concerns expressed by the African states were echoed in the statements of others who opposed the Declaration. The New Zealand representative, for example, issued a statement on behalf of Australia, New Zealand, and the United States expressing concern that "[s]elf-determination . . . could be misrepresented as conferring a unilateral right of self-determination and possible secession upon a specific subset of the national populace, thus threatening the political unity, territorial integrity, and the stability of existing UN member states" (Banks 2006).

Yet another compromise ensued to respond to these concerns. Article 46 of the resolution that finally passed added language specifically indicating that the Declaration should not be "construed as authorizing or encouraging any action which would dismember or impair totally or in part, the territorial integrity or political unity of sovereign and independent States." Although this compromise language gave a number of activists pause, most ultimately supported it. At the same time, it was not sufficient to convince all countries concerned about sovereignty issues to vote in favor. In its official observations on the Declaration, the United States explained that, despite limitations to Article 3 expressed in the Declaration: "We find [the] approach [of reproducing common Article 1 in Article 3] on a topic that involves the foundation of international relations and stability (i.e. the political unity and territorial integrity of nation-states) to be ill advised and likely to result in confusion and disputes" (Hagen 2007).

Self-determination as autonomy within a state

As the preceding discussion indicates, to the extent that indigenous peoples are considered to possess the right to self-determination, the term has taken on a new hue from that which initially animated indigenous rights advocacy. The consensus today, even among most advocates, is that self-determination does not include a right to statehood. Rather, self-determination is generally invoked to make claims for various forms of autonomy within (and sometimes across) already defined state boundaries. The Indigenous Peoples of Africa Coordinating Committee, for example, attempted to assuage the African Union's recent opposition to the Declaration on the Rights of Indigenous Peoples by making it clear that it had no intention of reading self-determination broadly. The Committee stated emphatically "that no single African indigenous community claims statehood." (Indigenous Peoples of Africa Coordinating Committee 2006).

The deployment of this softer form of self-determination in the indigenous context is not new. The Martinez Cobo Report, commissioned by the UN in 1971 and eventually fully published in 1984, for example states that "self-determination, in its many forms, must be recognized as the basic precondition for the enjoyment by indigenous peoples of their fundamental rights and the determination of their own future" (Martinez Cobo 1984: para. 2). Yet the Report distances itself from the strong self-determination claim through its definition of the term. For the Report, self-determination "constitutes the exercise of free choice by indigenous peoples who must, to a large extent, create the specific context of this principle, which [does] not necessarily include the right to secede. This right may in fact be expressed in various forms of autonomy within the State" (Martinez Cobo 1984: para. 581).

In Latin America, indigenous groups have rarely made strong demands for self-determination. Even at the beginning of panindigenous movements in Latin America in the 1970s, indigenous groups and coalitions tended to make claims for territorial autonomy for indigenous peoples in those states in which indigenous peoples constituted a minority, and for control over existing state structures where they made up a majority of the population.[3] Perhaps for this reason, no Latin American states voted against the

Declaration, and only Colombia abstained. There seems to be little threat in Latin America that indigenous groups will deploy self-determination in a way that would challenge "territorial integrity."

The Martinez Cobo Report, in its call for self-determination, concluded that human rights standards were inadequate for the protection of indigenous peoples (Martinez Cobo 1984: para. 580). Over the ensuing years, nevertheless, many of those who supported this version of self-determination that was divorced from secession began to advocate for legal recognition under human rights models. These models included the human right to self-determination, but much of the energy went toward a human right to culture.

Indigenous advocacy's turn to the human right to culture

Although the human right to culture might today seem an obvious and accepted mechanism for the protection of indigenous rights, it was not an obvious choice for indigenous rights advocates. If human rights are "a product of modern, post-Enlightenment, liberal secular humanism . . . elevat[ing] the individual to the point that the group is forgotten" (Zion 1992: 211), they would seem not only to conflict with, but to threaten indigenous culture. Or put another way, to the extent that human rights are inseparable from the civilizing mission of colonial days or the liberalizing mission of neocolonialism, they would appear to offer little (but a site of resistance) to those whose aim is to reject assimilation.

For these reasons, indigenous rights advocates were skeptical of human rights legal and political discourse from the beginning. In 1947, for example, the American Anthropological Association warned the United Nations against adopting a Universal Declaration on Human Rights that would fail to take into account the extent to which cultures varied in their values and norms (American Anthropological Association 1947: 539). Such a

335

failure, the association suggested, would simply perpetuate the "white man's burden" assumed under missionary practices and colonialism (American Anthropological Association 1947: 540). In this view, human rights was a modernizing move that would strip indigenous groups of their culture by imposing apparently universal values on their ways of life.

As human rights law developed, little attention was paid to indigenous rights. In fact, rights were seen to be individual as well as universal, primarily conferred upon individuals vis à vis the state. Although indigenous rights were not on the table either explicitly or implicitly, significant consideration was given early on to the issue of whether to include minority rights in human rights treaties. Advocates for ethnic minorities, particularly those within European states in the post-war period, sought to claim a right to culture during the drafting of the Universal Declaration of Human Rights (Morsink 1999: 301). Specific protection of collective cultural rights for minorities was rejected, however, for language saying that "everyone" has a right to culture (Universal Declaration of Human Rights 1948: Article 27).

In 1966, when the United Nations adopted the International Covenant on Civil and Political Rights (ICCPR), it adopted language on cultural rights that was more specific than that in the Universal Declaration. Article 27 of the Covenant reads: "In those States in which ethnic, religious or linguistic minorities exist, persons belonging to such minorities shall not be denied the right, in community with the other members of their group, to enjoy their own culture, to profess and practice their own religion, or to use their own language." Although this language was considered a victory by those concerned with the rights of ethnic minorities, indigenous rights advocates did not treat the language as applicable to their needs until the 1980s.

In the 1980s, indigenous advocates began to see the value of the right-to-culture

model. They mediated the tension they had earlier experienced between human rights and culture by calling for a human right *to* culture. For some, this move was precipitated by decisions by the Human Rights Committee, the body that considers claims brought under the Optional Protocol of the ICCPR. Advocates brought a number of indigenous rights claims to the Committee under Article 1's self-determination provision. The Committee denied admissibility under this provision, stating that self-determination could not provide the basis for a claim, given that the Optional Protocol only allows for individual claims. In one case, however, it decided *sua sponte*, to consider the claim under Article 27's protection of the right to culture (Scheinin 2000a: 179–94).[4] Advocates also began to use various protections of the right to culture embodied in the ILO Convention (No. 169).

Today, the human right to culture strategy is the most often used terrain on which individuals (on behalf of or sometimes even against the group) bring their legal claims. Importantly, indigenous rights advocates have not generally considered the use of the right to culture as a compromise. Instead, they have conceived of the right and its potential for protection rather broadly. James Anaya, for example, even while advocating for a shift from a sovereignty to a human rights focus in the early 1990s, did so in part because he believed that Article 27 of the ICCPR, the Convention against Genocide, and the UNESCO Declaration on Cultural Cooperation all evinced an "emergent human right of cultural survival and flourishment" (Anaya 1990: 841). James Zion, who saw human rights as a western enlightenment construct, also encouraged the support for indigenous rights through "the liberal construction to the concept of 'the right to culture'" (Zion 1992: 209). Even in Chiapas, Mexico, where indigenous communities have declared their autonomy, they often defend against threats to that autonomy at least in part by using ILO Convention (No. 169) provisions protecting indigenous peoples' right to the possession of their traditional lands, which is one part of the right to culture for that document.

But what does the right to culture mean for indigenous groups, their advocates and the UN? Unlike with the right to self-determination, there have been few overt debates about what constitutes the right to culture. In the next section, I briefly unpack what is meant by culture.

Indigenous advocacy and the meaning of the right to culture

In this section, I identify and trace three different understandings of culture in indigenous rights advocacy: culture as intangible heritage (like a museum piece or scarce natural resource to be preserved), culture as materially grounded in land (requiring communal and inalienable land rights to protect indigenous culture), and culture as development (specifically ethnodevelopment). While the first understanding of culture does little to question the neo-liberal state, the last two approaches, at least in principle, pose greater challenges to it. Their support for communal over individual property arrangements and their interrogation of modern forms of development would seem, at least at one level, to be in direct opposition to neo-liberalism.

I would argue that, despite their radical potential, strategies based on these understandings of culture have either failed in their resistance or have been co-opted by states and international institutions. The latter is especially true with regard to ethnodevelopment – a concept that is now supported and promoted by today's World Bank (van Nieuwkoop and Uquillas 2000). This co-optation, I would argue, is in part a consequence of strategic essentialism. Indigenous movements have unwittingly set themselves up for certain expectations about their "nature" and their conduct. In doing so, they have often both raised the bar for who

counts as indigenous and have limited the autonomy of those who do count.

Thus, each of these understandings of culture has its dark sides and unintended consequences with which I encourage advocates to grapple. The first, culture as heritage, threatens to alienate indigenous people(s) from their heritage; the second, culture as grounded in land, makes land inalienable; and the third, culture as development, combines with the second to limit the forms of development available to indigenous peoples.

Culture as heritage

Perhaps the most commonly invoked and understood meaning of culture in indigenous rights advocacy is that culture is comprised of practices, knowledge, and ways of seeing the world (cosmovision) of those societies that predated the settlers. In this usage, culture is something to be preserved, much like a museum piece or a scarce natural resource.

Culture as heritage is largely intangible, and, in one version, is much like intellectual property. It constitutes those things that were at some point thought to be produced by indigenous peoples. It is the conception of culture that is most consistent with the neo-liberal state, unlikely to require power-sharing arrangements or significant resources from the state. Importantly, it is the things, and not the peoples, that are the primary object of protection. One example of this version of culture as heritage is the UNESCO Convention for the Safeguarding of Intangible Cultural Heritage, which protects "oral traditions and expressions, including language as a vehicle of the intangible cultural heritage," "performing arts," "social practices, rituals, and festive events," "knowledge and practices concerning nature and the universe," and "traditional craftsmanship" (Convention for the Safeguarding of Intangible Cultural Heritage 2003a: Article 2(2)). It says nothing about ownership.

To the extent that they have argued for the protection of indigenous heritage – including both material and intangible items that reflect their understanding of indigenous culture – indigenous rights activists have had relative success. At least in principle, heritage is something that states and their non-indigenous citizens often seem to want to protect. As Ronald Niezen explains:

> The moral persuasiveness of indigenous peoples' claims to recognition derives not just from local grievances, but ultimately from a near-universal perception of cultural loss and nostalgia as well . . . It draws upon those who may have nothing to do with indigenous communities or international agencies, but who nevertheless feel strong stirrings of sympathy for those who represent a lost time of unhurried simplicity.
>
> (Niezen 2005: 593)

Although what Niezen refers to as a "near-universal perception of cultural loss and nostalgia" has led to a variety of international, regional and local protections, it has its dark sides as well. At times, the cultural heritage becomes revered over and disembodied from the peoples. The cultural heritage and the values it is seen to hold become the objects of protection. And what is considered the cultural heritage of a state's or region's initial inhabitants might be treated as the property and identity of the state in a contemporary form of the ideology of *indigenismo* found in many Latin American states in the early decades of the twentieth century. As Peter Wade explains of *indigenismo*: "Very often, it was a question of exotic and romantic symbolism, based more on the glorification of the pre-Columbian indian ancestry of the nation than on respect for contemporary indian populations" (Wade 1997: 32).

That heritage can be alienated from the groups from which it is seen to emanate provides the basis for another perhaps unintended consequence of this understanding of culture. It permits states and even international institutions to pick and choose the parts of the heritage they believe is worth protecting, and even to suppress those of which they do not approve. UNESCO's protection of cultural heritage, for example, only extends to those practices that are "compatible with existing international human rights instruments, as well as with the requirements of mutual respect among communities, groups and individuals, and of sustainable development" (Convention for the Safeguarding of Intangible Cultural Heritage 2003a: Article 1(1)).

In the context of Australia, Elizabeth Povinelli has called this type of limitation "an invisible asterisk, a proviso, [which] hovers above every enunciation of indigenous customary law: '(provided [they] are not so repugnant)'" (Povinella 2002: 12).

Finally, heritage makes the least demand on states of the various understandings of culture we explore. It asks states to be "tolerant," but it also makes it so that states can both appropriate and easily accommodate "heritage" without acknowledging or attending to underlying economic, social and political inequalities.

Culture as grounded in land

In contrast to the heritage idea, where knowledge is alienated for all to use, this understanding of culture often considers possession or use of a particular land or territory as the very basis of indigenous cultural identity. Taking seriously the material implications of a cosmovision centered on land, this conception belies the distinction between intellectual and real property by seeing indigenous peoples as key to the protection of those lands. Hence, indigenous peoples must be permitted to stay on, perhaps even control, if not own, their traditional territories because the land (and the peoples) both hold and carry forth the heritage. It is also used to argue for indigenous control of territory in order to protect the land in accordance with the environmentally friendly cosmovision indigenous peoples are thought to have. This argument is based on an assumption that real Indians will use the land in traditional and sustainable ways, and are therefore its proper guardians.

This idea is often reinforced by the claims of indigenous peoples themselves. Citing statements by indigenous people, James Anaya claims that there is the wide acceptance of "indigenous peoples' articulated ideas of communal stewardship over land and a deeply felt spiritual and emotional nexus with the earth and its fruits" (Anaya 1996: 104). If the cosmovision sounds too essentialist or monolithic or alienated from the everyday life of many indigenous peoples, it is a deliberate, but not inauthentic, strategy.

The strategy has led to some successful land claims. But there are potential downsides to it, which reflect more generally some of the difficulties with the ways in which strategic essentialism is often deployed. Basing indigenous rights on a human right to culture as land effectively prohibits indigenous peoples from ever choosing to alienate the property they own communally. Alienation is a complicated issue, and it is not clear that indigenous peoples want a right to alienate property. Were they to attempt to argue for such a right, however, they would find themselves in a serious bind. The moment they were to articulate a desire for the right, they would be seen as potentially exercising it, which would go against their perceived cosmovision (communal property and environmental stewardship) and thereby devalue their claim. That is, they are largely dependent on capitalist states for recognition of their right to culture, which these states view as genuine only if the culture includes a pre-capitalist/communal use-based understanding of land. If they were to aim to participate in the market with regard to land, they would be seen as going against their assumed culture and beliefs, potentially losing their claim to indigeneity.

Similarly, particularly without a strong understanding of self-determination, indigenous peoples are not always given much flexibility with regard to the use of their own land. Because of their "special relationship" to the land, they are meant to be its protectors and guardians. In some instances, states have prohibited indigenous groups from using land

in a manner that goes against their claimed attachment to it, limiting the groups' possibilities for development. The UN Report on Indigenous Peoples and their Relationship to Land, for example, lists Canada's refusal to allow indigenous groups to use land they consider hunting ground in any way that would destroy or decrease its value for hunting as an example of discriminatory treatment with regard to land title. Despite its seeming criticism of the practice, the Report does not include in its recommendations a suggested change to the practice.

There are even more potentially serious political consequences, at least for some groups, to the pursuit of a political and legal strategy based on such a special relationship to the land. When groups do not behave towards the land in this idealized manner, they might not be considered real Indians. The focus on occupation and use of land often leads to successful claims for those groups who have maintained and can prove their existence on their ancestral lands for centuries. But it misses the experience of many groups that consider themselves indigenous and are considered by others to be indigenous because of the language they speak, the traditions they practice, the ways and groupings in which they live, their internal administrative functioning or their local control, but who nevertheless live on land to which they have no proven ancestral ties. Such groups are often on land to which they were forcibly relocated or that they occupied as a result of dislocation from another territory. In such instances, these groups do not necessarily have the knowledge or means to subsist in ways that might be considered traditional. Although Martin Scheinin refers to such groups as "pathological," in fact they are quite common (Scheinin 2000b: 171–72).

In Chiapas, for example, the Mexican government has been threatening to dislocate or "relocate" groups of indigenous people living in the Montes Azules Integral Biosphere Reserve in the heart of the jungle which, likely not coincidentally, is also the home of the

339

Zapatista army. The allegation that indigenous peoples have been using "slash and burn" farming techniques has been tied into an argument about those indigenous peoples not being entitled to live on the land because they are not native to it.

This focus on culture as land often displaces a focus on the reason that indigenous peoples are in need of land and resources. It could be said that the ILO's attempt through Convention (No. 107) to integrate indigenous people and make them a productive part of economic modernization at least recognized the extent to which they had long been deprived of economic resources. If the current anti-assimilationist/pro-culture arguments recognize how neo-liberal land reform policies have in many instances destroyed communal forms of ownership and weakened the ability of indigenous peoples to control their own natural resources and maximize the productivity of the land, they respond in a limited way, both in terms of the parts of the bundle of rights that are recognized and in terms of the groups and locations where such rights are grounded.

Culture as development

Culture and development have long been linked. Western expansion – whether through Christian proselytizing, increasing of trade routes, or industrialization – was seen as a way to civilize or modernize indigenous peoples. Even when world opinion would seem to have moved away from at least an explicit goal of either conquest or forced acculturation of indigenous peoples, integration was considered to lead to progress. ILO Convention (No. 107), for example, states that part of its intent is to "assure the protection of the populations concerned . . . and the improvement of their living and working conditions" (International Labor Organization No. 107 (1959): Preamble). Some argued that it was based on an understanding that development would lead to assimilation, and eventually to greater prosperity (Kastrup 1997: 120).

By the 1970s anthropologists and indigenous rights advocates began to take a critical view of even the seemingly benevolent forms of development and of capitalism in general. Capitalism began to be viewed by some of its critics as a form of "cultural genocide" (Burger 1987: 105). Economic exploitation and cultural extermination, therefore, were inextricably connected. A critique of development projects from the 1980s elaborates at least one way of viewing the connection:

> The impact of such developments on indigenous peoples, however, is not merely economic. The displacement and environmental degradation brought about by mining, deforestation, dam building or unsuitable large-scale farming, may cause hardship; but more importantly, they also sever the vital link between indigenous peoples and their environment. When indigenous peoples are separated from their land, the social and cultural cohesion of their communities is eroded.
>
> (Burger 1987: 105)

Even if indigenous peoples were not always separated from their land, capitalism required that they have a different relationship to it. Often transforming them into laborers, it alienated them from the work as well as the land. The UN Report on the Relationship to Land explains: "National economic development schemes not only dispossess indigenous peoples of their lands, but also convert indigenous peoples into cheap labourers for industry, because the exploitation of the lands and environmental degradation have deprived them of their livelihood" (para. 64).

Indigenous peoples had available to them two potential strategies in the 1970s to combat the economic threat to their culture: they could ally with the third world and its class-conscious postcolonial struggles, or they could assert their own indigenous cultural identity. Just as many advocates chose the right to culture over self-determination in the late 1980s and early 1990s, many ultimately chose cultural identity over class conscious-ness. For movements in the English-speaking world (particularly Canada and the United States), a "fourth world" identity provided a means to ensure that the struggles of indigenous peoples were not subsumed or ignored by Third World politics. In Latin America, many indigenous and African-descendant struggles had their roots in peasant movements, and thus the tension between impulses to organize around cultural and class identity continued for a significant time. Different movements mediated the tension in different ways, but ultimately cultural identity prevailed.

As they began to consider what would replace western development, many advocates called for ethnodevelopment, or development based on the traditional culture of indigenous groups. Many argued for taking advantage of culture, resources, and sustainable atti-tudes towards the earth to permit indigenous groups to develop in culturally sensitive ways. They hoped that, without western-style industrialized development, indigenous groups would be able to return to a traditional and sustainable livelihood through, for ex-ample, engaging in sustainable forms of agri-culture, hunting whales, herding reindeer, and fishing from natural habitats. These attempts overlapped with many of the arguments based on indigenous relationship to land, and share some of the same potential benefits and dark sides.

Ethnodevelopment has met with mixed success. On one hand, it has appealed to environmentalists and even to international financial institutions such as the World Bank. It has provided a rubric for consider-ing and promoting sustainable means of development, often based on what are con-sidered to be an indigenous understand-ing of and relationship to land and the environment. On the other hand, indigenous peoples have not been granted control over development to the extent that they have gen-erally advocated. Rather, their development decisions are often subject either to govern-ment decision-making processes or to per-ceived ideas about how they can and should live their lives.

With regard to government decision making, questions about the extent to which indigenous peoples should be consulted in development decisions on or affecting in-digenous lands has been at the heart of dis-agreements over the interpretation of ILO Convention (No. 169) and the drafting of the Declaration. In both instances, indigenous peoples are meant to be consulted with regard to development decisions affecting the areas they occupy and use, but the provisions stop short of granting them autonomy over those decisions.

ILO Convention No. 169 gives indigen-ous peoples "the right to decide their own priorities for the process of development as it affects their lives, beliefs, institutions and spiritual well-being and the lands they occupy or otherwise use" (International Labor Organization 1989: Art. 7). Yet, national and regional entities continue to be able to make decisions that affect indigen-ous lands, so long as they allow indigenous peoples to "participate in the formulation, implementation and evaluation of plans and programmes for national and regional devel-opment which may affect them directly" (International Labor Organization 1989: Art. 7). Much debate has ensued over the requirements of this "prior consultation." Indigenous groups often claim that, even when governments technically comply with the requirement to consult with them, the con-sultations in fact have little effect on govern-ment decision making.

The Declaration would seem to grant indigenous peoples less autonomy than ILO Convention (No. 169) in this regard. Article 20 offers a broad statement about indigenous peoples' right to development, recogniz-ing their right "to engage freely in all their traditional *and other* economic activities" (Declaration on the Rights of Indigenous Peoples 2007: Art. 21) Yet, while earlier drafts of the Declaration granted indigenous peoples the "right to determine and develop priorities and strategies for exercising their right to development," one of the compromises made to push the Declaration through the Human Rights Council changed the wording to give them the right "*to be actively involved in* developing and determining" (Declaration on the Rights of Indigenous Peoples 2007: Art. 23; United Nations Commission on Human Rights 2005). That wording is in the final Declaration that passed the General Assembly, and arguably falls short of the participation required in ILO Convention (No. 169).

Indigenous peoples' autonomy is often limited in another way, which would seem to be more explicitly tied to the success of ethnodevelopment as a strategy. That is, their own development is often only protected to the extent that it is done in ecologically sustainable ways. In ILO Convention (No. 169), for example, governments commit to "take measures, in co-operation with the peoples concerned, to protect and preserve the environment of the territories they inhabit" (International Labor Organization No. 169 1989: Art. 7(4)). This and similar provisions might sometimes put the brakes on forms of unsustainable development by non-indigenous peoples on indigenous land, but it also limits the types of development in which indigenous peoples can engage. Indeed, the assumption that real Indians treat their land in sustainable ways sometimes comes back to haunt them and limit their possibilities for economic growth or is used to define certain groups as non-Indian.

As with culture as land, then, culture as development often depends on and requires an ongoing link between economic activity and traditional means of livelihood. Ethno-development seems most appropriate as a strategy for those groups that have a nice fit between how they in fact make their livelihood and their traditional ways of life. But it is more difficult to make the required link when groups have been displaced from their traditional lands or no longer have the popu-lation or ability to sustain themselves economically through traditional means.

Conclusion

Although the dark sides I have discussed in this chapter lead me to be skeptical of many aspects of contemporary models for the protection of indigenous rights, I also recognize the extent to which these models have been seen as aspirational and powerful. In perhaps its most radical form, the right to culture makes heritage, land and economic development inseparable; the three constitute a rights package that promises to challenge dominant distribution of wealth and resources. The stakes to claiming indigenous identity are thus increased. Some claim indigeneity to get the rights package, while others attach the package to some other form of minority cultural alterity. For those who have not experienced the protection of even some of the most basic rights included in the package, the model is particularly promising. Especially for those minority groups who do not desire to pursue strong claims to self-determination, the right to culture model is attractive for its promises for respect for difference, collective title, and economic resources for development.

Based on the apparent attraction of this rights package, many advocates express an understandable objection to or skepticism of advocacy work that deconstructs "culture" or questions particular uses of strategic essentialism. Some believe that exposing the incongruencies or conflicts in narratives of cultural unity is risky, perhaps opening it up to use by those who hope to deny claims to the cultural rights package. At some level, this concern is persuasive. But given the ways in which the right to culture claims, if taken seriously, threaten to limit the groups that might qualify for protection, overstate the cultural cohesion that other groups maintain, and limit indigenous economic, political and territorial autonomy, I would argue for a willingness to "risk" exposure. Indeed, I would argue for advocates to bring constructivism to their advocacy in a way that would expose not only the fragile nature of the culture claims, but the background distributional inequality that both underlies and structures the claims.

Without denying the power of cultural identity and the extent to which ideas about culture organize our understandings about and presentations of ourselves and others, I suggest we consider how assertions of cultural (and other) identity claims often function as a defense mechanism to protect against real vast material and political inequalities. As with most defense mechanisms, identity assertions work at some level to stave off or at least diminish the impact of daily threats, but they accept as ongoing and unchangeable the threats against which they are initially created.

Studying defense mechanisms can be useful because defense mechanisms often provide gateways for understanding underlying pathologies. In exploring the multiple deployments of culture, I attempt better to understand the threats to which they are responding. Imbedded in assertions of culture are multiple understandings about indigenous peoples and their traditions, but also about their relationship to and ongoing service to states, civil society and even the future of mankind. They are more complex and at times even more radical than they might originally appear. To the extent, however, that they function to *protect* the group, rather than transform the underlying power structures *against* which they are protecting the group, I suggest that they might be short sighted and even counterproductive. Perhaps more importantly, they appear unsustainable. To the extent that the dominant societies in which indigenous peoples or their territories reside have expressed an acknowledgment of a right to indigenous culture, including "special" protections for that culture, few indigenous groups can live up to the cultural purity

and ideal that the state and its non-indigenous citizens have come to expect in the bargain.

Far from playing into the hands of those who might aim to deny indigenous rights, my hope is that this constructivist approach to culture would not conclude that indigenous groups that do not meet the expectations of cultural performance, territory or ancestry that have come to be expected by many settler societies are inauthentic. Rather, it would demonstrate the impossibility of that performance, and aim to create more, not less, autonomy within and among groups by rejecting the assumption that they should only be empowered to the extent that they are carriers of a culture worth preserving for the good of humankind.

Notes

1 The term "strategic essentialism" was coined by Gayatri Spivak in 1984. Although generated in the context of post-colonial feminist theory, it has been employed in various disciplines and taken on a number of meanings. Spivak has since distanced herself from the term. For the interview in which the idea of strategic essentialism was introduced by Spivak see Grosz and Spivak (1985: 10–12. For one of the first discussions in which Spivak publicly abandons the term, see Danius, Jonsson, and Spivak) 1993: 34–5.

2 For an analysis of ILO Convention (No. 107) that argues that the Convention saw indigenous peoples as "ignoble primitives," as opposed to the more modern understanding of Indians as "noble primitives," see Tennant 1994.

3 For a collection of manifestos from the late 1970s and early 1980s from various indigenous organizations throughout Latin America, see Bonfil Batalla 1981.

4 Scheinin's analysis is based on *Ominayak vs. Canada* (1984), *Kitok vs. Sweeden* (1988), and *Mikmaq vs. Canada* (No. 1) (1989). In each of these cases, the Art. 1 claims were considered inadmissible because the Committee found that the Optional Protocol under which complaints are brought only recognizes individual rights and, further, that individuals cannot be victims of a collective right to self-determination (Scheinin 2000a: 179–80).

24

International refugee law: dominant and emerging approaches

Hélène Lambert

International refugee law scholarship has long been dominated by a positivist tradition within which the human rights approach has now become the dominant approach. However, states and their formal agreements get us only so far in explaining how refugee law is created and how it develops. There is another layer of explanation that looks into transnational activities and their effect on how law is shaped, interpreted, applied and developed. This chapter therefore also explores two further emerging approaches in refugee law: the transnational approach and the participatory approach. It argues that whereas the dominant human rights approach focuses mainly on sources and contents of rules (and their enforcement), both the transnational and participatory approaches are useful in capturing the complexities of the process of law formation and law development by looking more specifically at networks and other participants in the process of law making. The challenge of contemporary international refugee law is to recognize more explicitly the role of such networks and the soft law and norms that they often produce.

There is little doubt that "international refugee law has long occupied centre stage in refugee studies"[1] (Wilde 2001: 140; Zetter 2000) and that traditionally "its scholarship has been dominated by a positivist tradition"

detached from political reality (Chimni 1998: 352). Accordingly, international refugee law has long been viewed as a set of rules (e.g. the 1951 Convention Relating to the Status of Refugees) dominated by states in their application but helped by an international organization (i.e. UNHCR) in their development. However, the world has moved on and so has the way in which we theorize (refugee) law. Most significantly, the human rights approach has now become the dominant approach in refugee law. This scholarly school has not only had an impact on the content of refugee law, it has also changed the boundaries within which refugee law operates. However, the human rights approach has had little impact on the "formal scheme of the Convention [which] remains one of *obligations between States*" (Goodwin-Gill 2004: 7). This is because the human rights approach maintains a primary focus on rules as applied by states and relevant international organizations. Hence it fails to challenge the way international lawyers are trained to think "in normative and institutional hierarchies" (Byrne et al. 2004: 356). This chapter therefore also explores two further emerging approaches in refugee law that undertake such a challenge: the transnational approach and the participatory approach.

Both these approaches originate in liberal theory of international law which focuses on the importance of non-state actors and progressive values in the world legal order (Lasswell and McDougal 1943; McDougal 1960; McDougal and Lasswell 1959). The transnational approach highlights the role of processes, networks and discourse involving actors that operate within and across state boundaries (Slaughter 2004a). These transnational networks and processes clearly contribute to international normative activity (Boyle and Chinkin 2007), and to a changing conception of the world less dominated by a vertical notion of international law and domestic law; one speaks of epistemic community, transgovernmentalism, and governance. The participatory approach highlights the imperative for wider participation in this discourse (from non-western states to the refugee themselves) as being essential to build the trust necessary for international refugee law to develop further. Through this discourse, our conception of the world is changing, and so is the law relating to refugees (Chimni 1998; Harvey 1998, 1999; Hathaway and Neve 1997). Both approaches are attractive because they offer a more *prescriptive* approach to international refugee law quite unlike the *descriptive* approach of legal positivism. From the point of view of scholarship, therefore, the task is not to ascertain the content of law but to advocate law that promotes core community values. These emergent approaches therefore provide a dynamic picture of the evolution of refugee law in a world increasingly characterized by globalization and the emergence of a "common public order" (Goodwin-Gill 2006). Beyond these theoretical approaches, refugee law scholarship has also become more sensitive to the moral and ethical dimension of refugee studies (Gibney 2004; Juss 2004) as well as to sound historical foundations (Nathwani 2000; see also Abuya 2007).

Positivism and the human rights approach

Positivism views international law as "an abstract system of rules which can be identified, objectively interpreted, and enforced" (Chimni 1998: 352; see also Hart 1998: 214; Armstrong et al. 2007: 9–33, 74–83). The positivist tradition limits the possibility of engagement with politics (a good illustration of this is Hathaway 2007 and Hathaway and Neve 1997). From this perspective, refugee law has been viewed as a self-contained regime of international law with roots in extradition law and the laws relating to nationality laws and aliens (Grahl-Madsen 1966: 79; Weis 1953: 480),[2] so very much "hooked on to traditional concepts of state territorial jurisdiction, i.e. the sovereign right of states to decide on admission and expulsion of all those not linked by the bonds of nationality" (Gowlland-Debbas 1996: x).

The Refugee Convention was drafted at a time (1951) when the cold war took off, hence it has been labeled as the "child of the Cold War" (Bertrand 1993: 498). As its name indicates, the Convention Relating to the Status of Refugees is about defining who is a refugee (article 1), and the rights and benefits which persons recognized as refugees are entitled to, including the guarantee against *refoulement* (articles 2–34). *Non-refoulement* prohibits the return of refugees to any country where they are likely to fear for their life or freedom (article 33(1)). It has been described as "a cardinal principle of refugee protection" (Lauterpacht and Bethlehem 2003: 107). Issues of procedures (i.e. how to make a decision on refugee status) were never directly a matter for international law, thus states have been left with the choice of means as to implementation at the national level (Lambert 2006: 162–3). The principle of good faith in international law nonetheless requires that states provide fair and efficient asylum procedures in their compliance with the Refugee Convention, if not in terms of states' intent, at least in terms of the effect of states' action (Goodwin-Gill and McAdam 2007: 458).

In its early days, the definition of a refugee (article 1A(2)) was limited to persons who were escaping events that took place before 1951 (essentially in Europe). A Protocol Relating to the Status of Refugees (1967) extended the application of the Refugee Convention to *all* refugees. Both instruments have been described as "the foundation of the international regime for the protection of refugees" (UNHCR 2005: 1). To maximize accession, "they were carefully framed to define minimum standards, without imposing obligations going beyond those that States can reasonably be expected to assume" (UNHCR 2001: 29). There are currently 141 states parties to both instruments.[3] The underlying values of the Refugee Convention are clearly stated by UNHCR as being: humanitarian, human rights and people oriented; non-political and impartial; international cooperation; and universal and general character (UNHCR 2001: 2–3).

According to article 1A(2), Refugee Convention:

> The term "refugee" shall apply to any person who owing to a well-founded fear of being persecuted for reasons of race, religion, nationality, membership of a particular social group, or political opinion, is outside the country of his nationality and is unable or, owing to such fear, is unwilling to avail himself of the protection of that country.

It follows from this definition that the conceptualization of refugeehood in international law is based on the restrictive concepts of persecution and alienage (Shacknove 1985). This definition has been the subject of intense scrutiny through refugee determination procedures and a substantial body of jurisprudence has been created. But in the absence of an independent international body competent to interpret the Refugee Convention, each contracting party is free to adopt its own interpretation. This means

that at present considerable divergence exists in the way international refugee law is interpreted and applied. In an effort to improve implementation of the Refugee Convention, UNHCR has suggested a more regularized system of reporting, periodic meetings of states parties to review implementation issues, and harmonized regional processes for interpretation and application of the principles (UNHCR 2001: 30). Meanwhile, some lawyers have called for the establishment of an international body competent to monitor the application of the Refugee Convention by contracting states and to interpret provisions of the Refugee Convention (Chimni 2001: 157; Hathaway 2002; Macmillan and Olsson 2001; North 2005). Arguably, such proposals may be presented as attempts to claw back some of the legal space occupied by states in this area of law (Chimni 2001: 158).

It has been argued that the dominance, in particular positivist, of refugee law within refugee studies during the cold war resulted in a "depoliticized approach" which was not without consequences (Chimni 1998: 354). One such consequence was the attention given by scholars to the basic activities, structure and legal status of UNHCR in preference to its "knowledge and dissemination functions" (Chimni 1998: 366). However, international refugee law has been significantly expanded through U.N. General Assembly's resolutions and EXCOM conclusions as well as customary international law and Security Council resolutions (Gilbert 2005: 5; Goodwin-Gill and McAdam 2007: 5–7, 20–50; Gowlland-Debbas 2001; Lewis 2005). Furthermore, UNHCR has, since the end of the cold war, become an operational agency and through this has come to recognize the importance of human rights in its work (Stoltenberg 1991: 150).[4] Thus, today protection has been described as comprising "both a legal framework [i.e. international and regional refugee law and human rights law treaties] and a solutions framework [i.e. refuge/ asylum, voluntary repatriation, and assistance]" (Goodwin-Gill 2006: 6). That said, the move by UNHCR towards the protection of internally displaced persons and its activities regarding refugee status determination in nearly all the developing countries have raised serious concerns under international human rights law (Chimni 2006; Pallis 2006). Another consequence (which will be discussed later) was the fragmentation and isolation of refugee law which became seen by many as *sui generis* (Chimni 1998: 354). Finally, the positivist approach to international refugee law has also been relied on to explain states' reluctance to recognize a subjective right of asylum. Goodwin-Gill and McAdam observe that when article 14(1) of the Universal Declaration of Human Rights (UDHR) was being drafted, states were divided between those "that regarded asylum as their sovereign prerogative [e.g. the UK], and those which saw it as a duty of the international community [e.g. France]" (Goodwin-Gill and McAdam 2007: 358). The former view won over the latter, indicating that "States had no intention to assume even a moral obligation in the matter" (Goodwin-Gill and McAdam 2007: 358). As a result, article 14(1) as adopted in the UDHR reads: "[E]veryone has the right to seek and *to enjoy* [as opposed to *be granted*] . . . asylum from persecution."

Today, Goodwin-Gill and McAdam maintain that "the individual still has no right to be granted asylum. The right itself is in the form of a discretionary power" (2007: 414). In practice, many states have used the refugee definition in article 1A(2) of the Refugee Convention as the basis for granting asylum but asylum "as an obligation on States to accord lasting solutions, with or without a correlative right of the individual, continues to be resisted" (Goodwin-Gill and McAdam 2007: 415). That said, states have certain legal obligations under refugee law, human rights law, and humanitarian law, in particular they have a duty of *non-refoulement*. Furthermore, international law, which until 1991 supported the doctrine of non-intervention (article 2(7) U.N. Charter) in countries of origin producing refugees (Baer

1996: 246; Goodwin-Gill and McAdam 2007: 2), has dramatically transformed under Security Council's action. So, it has been argued that we may be witnessing an "emerging international community interest" or "common public order" based on the following elements: a right of refugees and the displaced to return to their homes in freedom and dignity with a correlative states' responsibility to protect such right; an expansion of the recognition of criminal responsibility against individuals found to have committed genocide, war crimes or crimes against humanity; and a right of access to refugees and civilian populations at risk (Goodwin-Gill and McAdam 2007: 6–7; see also, more generally, CSW 2007; Jaquemet 2001).

The formal acknowledgement that international refugee law is indeed part of international human rights law has been traced back to the adoption of the Refugee Convention as a U.N. treaty (Gowlland-Debbas 2001: 193, 200–203; Weis 1995: 1).[5] This is because the Refugee Convention became an instrument intended to contribute to the achievement of the purposes and principles of the U.N. (articles 1(3) and 55, U.N. Charter). Crucially, this commitment to human rights, as enunciated in the U.N. Charter but also in UDHR, is explicitly stated in the Preamble of the Refugee Convention. Yet, a number of factors (such as, the lack of a subjective right of asylum, traditional concepts of sovereignty and the cold war) created a narrow conception of refugee law, one that became "segregated from the development of international human rights law" (Gowlland-Debbas 1996: x; see also McNamara 1998: 175). Flauss speaks of ambiguous and contradictory relationships between international refugee law and international human rights law (Flauss 2001: 94). He gives as an example, the fact that it took 30 years for the International Institute of Human Rights (Strasbourg) to introduce a course on refugee law as part of its annual teaching program (Flauss 2001: 94). Also, one has to wait for the 1990s to see any significant references made to human rights in UNHCR EXCOM Conclusions (UNHCR 2005) and for law scholarship to articulate fully the relationship between refugee law and human rights law (Anker 2002; Harvey 1998, 1999; Hathaway 1991, 2007; Hathaway and Neve 1997; Helton 2002: 124). Gowlland-Debbas speaks of a veritable "rediscovery" that refugee law *is* human rights law (Gowlland-Debbas 1996: xiii). There is now clear understanding that international human rights law serves to reinforce refugee protection and that it gives meaning to the "right to enjoy asylum" in international law (Edwards 2005; Gil-Bazo 2006: 600). Should an inconsistency occur "between the two bodies of law, the higher standard must prevail" (Edwards 2005: 330).

Predictably, this "rediscovery" has not gone unchallenged. First, it has been argued that human rights law is not without its own problems and that some of these problems will simply transfer to refugee law, such as the domestic/international jurisdictional debate, the sovereignty/humanitarian intervention debate, the lack of self-interest as a motivating force, the proliferation of human rights coupled with the lack of a hierarchy of human rights, and the problem of institutional coordination and overlapping mandate (Gowlland-Debbas 1996: xiii; Kennedy 2005; Nathwani 2000: 364–7).[6] Second, it has been observed that the juridical link between these fields is mostly in the form of *soft law* (Gowlland-Debbas 1996: xiii). One notable exception is the adoption of the EU Qualification Directive (that is a binding legal instrument) which combines both refugee protection status and subsidiary protection status (Lambert 2006).

These criticisms notwithstanding, the human rights approach is currently the dominant one in refugee law. This approach explains that refugee law operates on the premise that a human rights violation has taken place or is going to take place imminently (Nathwani 2000). It also takes human rights law as a benchmark for the quality of protec-

tion provided by states (and by UNHCR) to refugees in countries of origin (e.g. internal protection) and in countries of refuge (in terms of the rights granted to asylum seekers as well as the rights granted upon recognition of refugee status and complementary protection status) (Goodwin-Gill 2004; Hathaway 2005; Lambert 1999, 2005). Finally, it is being used to tackle issues of states' responsibilities (Gil-Bazo 2006: 600) as well as UNHCR's accountability (Pallis 2006). Viewed from this enlarged perspective, the debate about the linkage between refugee law and human rights law has revealed a number of issues that had remained largely unaddressed in refugee law, such as the right to leave, to return, and to remain, the obligations of the receiving state to meet certain standards of treatments, the obligations of UNHCR to act in accordance with international human rights law in its refugee status determination activities, and the human rights situation in the country of origin (e.g. state responsibility, root causes).

The human rights approach is by no mean incompatible with a positivist tradition; it may indeed sit quite squarely with legal positivism (and its unilateralism and state-centered approach). Hathaway, for instance, argues that "a positivist understanding of international law is an important means to advance both refugee rights, and the more general international human rights project" (Hathaway 2005: 24). This approach may nonetheless be contrasted with a recent trend towards more dialog and wider participation. This trend is *not* incompatible with the human rights approach, but it is in the transnational approach and in the participatory approach that the full depth and breadth of such dialog is best captured.

The transnational approach and the participatory approach

The previous section discussed *international refugee law* based on the assumptions that

"International law has traditionally been just that – international" (Slaughter and Burke-White 2006: 327; see also Lauterpacht 1931: 31). However, globalization and new transnational threats have "changed the nature of governance and the necessary purposes of international law" (Slaughter and Burke-White 2006: 328). And refugee law has not been immune from these changes. Lubbers, for instance, observed that "In a globalizing world and a rapidly changing political environment, the Convention faces many challenges. These include new forms of persecution and conflict, complex mixed migration movements, the reluctance of many states to accept refugees, and restrictive interpretation of the Convention" (Lubbers 2003: xv). *International* refugee law therefore must contend with an increase in transnational activities and with calls for wider participation in these activities. This is not surprising since "the system of international protection of refugees remains a unique combination, bringing together states, international organizations, non-governmental organizations and the refugees themselves in the pursuit of common ends" (Goodwin-Gill 1999: 221).

This section discusses a few key transnational activities undertaken in this area of international law. It also discusses calls for widening participation in the process of refugee law making. Both these trends are reflected in the transnational approach and the participatory approach, respectively. As highlighted by scholars, these approaches are non-exclusive. Anker, Fitzpatrick, and Shacknove, for instance, talk about "pluralism in refugee law" (i.e. the existence of an increasing number of networks) *and* the need for refugee voices (in particular women refugees) to be taken into account in refugee law reforms (Anker et al. 1998). And Chimni talks about increasing and widening dialog between states and others actors, including refugees, in an "emerging global state" (Chimni 2001, 2004).

Transnational networks and processes in refugee law

More and more networks are working together to tackle cross-borders issues, such as refugee flows, immigration, crime, and terrorism. These networks have different shapes and sizes, and different aims. Single-issue networks focusing on one particular issue are constituted side by side with broader, more general refugee law networks. Government networks, constituted of judges and policymakers, and networks of intergovernmental organizations (IGOs) are established alongside networks of academics and activists. Chimni argues that this increase in networks and activities is creating a "global state" (Chimni 2004). An alternative perspective offered by Slaughter is that the concept of states is not disappearing, so much as it is "disaggregating" in an age of global governance with states now confronted to a new range of actors that they themselves have created (Slaughter 2004b). With the exception of the EU, all these networks and processes have contributed to the development of refugee law through *soft law* (and norms). This section looks at three kinds of transnational network: judicial, based around an IGO-UNHCR, and based around the EU.

The International Association of Refugee Law Judges (IARLJ) was established at Warsaw in 1997 to facilitate communication and dialog between refugee law judges around the world in an attempt to develop "consistent and coherent refugee jurisprudence" (Storey 2003: 422).[7] This need was felt particularly strongly in this area of law because of the lack of a supranational court competent to develop authoritative legal standards based on the Refugee Convention. Hathaway has described the IARLJ as "One of the most exciting recent developments in refugee law" because it provides clear evidence of the existence of an "ongoing transnational judicial conversation" (Hathaway 2003: 418; see also Slaughter 1994: 121, 127; Slaughter

2003). He further notes that refugee law has recently evolved mostly under the influence of judges and that refugee law has "become fundamentally judicialized" (Hathaway 2003: 418). During the last 10 years, several decisions of superior courts in states parties to the Refugee Convention have indeed contributed to the advancement of international refugee law.[8] Storey even called for the application of "a *principle of convergence*, i.e. that tribunals and courts in different countries should seek as far as possible to apply the same basic principles" (Storey 2003: 423). The role of high courts as "agents of normative change" has been recognized in other areas of law, e.g. aliens' rights (Guiraudon 2000: 1107). In the area of refugee law, this role is particularly strong in light of the coordinating work of IARLJ with many of these decisions (mostly from western states) finding a place on the IARLJ database. This role is nonetheless limited because "of necessity those cases are dependent on their own facts and have no binding qualities outside their own jurisdiction" (Gilbert 2005: 3).[9] However, the EU harmonization process of refugee law is reshaping our understanding of "persuasive authority" and cross-referencing between common and civil law jurisdictions in refugee law is on the increase. So, it may indeed be the case that refugee law judges are increasingly becoming "independent actors in the international arena" (Slaughter 2004a: 68; see also Slaughter 2003).

It has been argued that networks of national governments officials are useful in building trust and establishing good relationships among participants. In particular, looking at the judiciary, it has been argued that judges not only exchange information about different approaches to common legal issues, they also "offer technical assistance and professional socialization to members [. . .] from less developed nations" (Raustiala 2002; Slaughter 2000). Such learning experience has been identified as a two-way street when cross-referencing between high courts happens from the developed world to the developing

world and vice versa (Slaughter 2004a: 65–103). This is something that could be developed further in refugee law as it would go some way in addressing some of the criticism raised regarding these networks. Chimni, for instance, argues that a growing network of international institutions – economic, social, and political – is creating a global state of an imperial character (Chimni 2004) and that this "emerging global state" notably lacks the elements necessary for a strong dialog between south and north (Chimni 2001).

There are also a number of networks based around UNHCR. One such network is the Global Consultations Process, launched in October 2000 with the purpose of provoking "both reflection and action to revitalize the international refugee protection regime" (UNHCR 2002: 1). As a process, particular attention was given to dialog and cooperation, and to broad-based participation. So, the participation of refugees as key stakeholders in the system and of NGOs was promoted through an international dialog with 50 refugee women in Geneva and a debate bringing together over 500 refugees in the French National Assembly as well as a forum of refugees in Europe (Rouen, France) (UNHCR 2001: 31). This process lasted 18 months and led to the universal reaffirmation of the Refugee Convention as the basis of refugee protection. A first outcome of the Global Consultations Process was the adoption of the Agenda for Protection, i.e. a program of action drafted by UNHCR (approved by EXCOM in 2002) to improve the protection of refugees and asylum seekers by highlighting existing gaps in the refugee protection regime. Since then UNHCR has drafted several guidelines to complement its now quite outdated Handbook on Procedures and Criteria for Determining Refugee Status. A second outcome of the Global Consultations Process was the publication of the debates (i.e. papers and conclusions) that took place during the Global Consultations expert roundtable consultations (Feller et al. 2003). Lewis has described the Global

Consultations Process and the Programme of Action (in the Agenda for Protection) as "novel methods for contributing to the development of international refugee law" (Lewis 2005: 90). And Chimni sees UNHCR Consultation Process as one step in the direction of UNHCR's new advocate role (between south and north, and between states and other participants, including refugees) (Chimni 2001). He also calls for such initiative to be more sustained if one is to see any change in UNHCR's existing deference towards northern states (Chimni 1998: 365–71).[10] The Convention Plus Process is yet another step in that direction.

Convention Plus started as "an *ad hoc* response to the Agenda for Protection" (Betts and Durieux 2007), the essence of which (i.e. north–south responsibility sharing) had already been floated in North American legal scholarship (Betts 2005).[11] Its specific aims were twofold: "to increase the level and predictability of burden-sharing" and "to channel this new, abstract commitment into finding durable solutions to specific protracted refugee situations." Its overall purpose was to discuss "creating a normative framework for global burden-sharing" (Betts and Durieux 2007: 516; see also Betts 2006: 655). As an interstate process, Convention Plus involved creating structures to facilitate dialog between countries in the south (i.e. host states) and countries in the north (i.e. donor states). It also encouraged coalition and convergence between particular states (i.e. "plurilateralism"). As a multilateral negotiation process, Convention Plus involved states, NGOs and UNHCR in an open and structured dialog. Convention Plus was supposed to lead to the development of special agreements (in either binding or *soft law* form). Sadly, by the end of 2005, all that was achieved was the Multilateral Framework of Understanding on Resettlement and two joint statements relating to targeting development assistance and irregular secondary movements (Betts and Durieux 2007: 514). Nonetheless, Betts and Durieux have praised

Convention Plus for its norm-setting role. In particular, they see Convention Plus as representing "a significant new departure for UNHCR" within its approach to facilitating norm creation and as contributing "to the development of a range of ideas that speak to a broader debate on the role of norms within both the refugee regime and global governance broadly" (Betts and Durieux 2007: 515). Thus, they argue that "A mutually shared understanding of 'the rules of the game' [i.e. asylum, assistance and burden-sharing] may therefore offer a basis for beginning to change behaviour" (Betts and Durieux 2007: 515). More generally, Betts and Durieux highlight the key role that UNHCR can play in facilitating "the creation and development of new norms" (Betts and Durieux 2007: 516). Substantively, they identify two complementary models of norm creation in this context: the "institutional bargaining model," which is top down and which is most appropriate when trying to develop universal norms, and the "good practice model" which is bottom up and which provides examples of good practice to be followed in future.

Finally, the European Union can be described as a set of rules (i.e. treaties and secondary legislation), networks (e.g. policy networks on how to implement the asylum EC Directives to achieve harmonization) and processes that are substantially transnational because they go into states (Burley and Mattli 1993: 43)[12] (e.g. the formation of EC asylum measures, their adoption as EC law, and their implementation in domestic law). Europe is now the only region in the world to legislate (through legally binding instruments) on substantive (and procedural) matters of interpretation of the Refugee Convention. While the "power of law" clearly plays a role in these processes, the interaction of "Individual actors – judges, lawyers, litigants – [. . .] with specific identities, motives, and objectives" has been crucial in the further developments of the EU (Burley and Mattli 1993: 53). In the area of refugee law, however, individual actors have so far mostly been states. The adoption of four key directives and two regulations on matters of asylum concluded the first phase towards the establishment of a Common European Asylum System (CEAS).[13]

The formulation of these legislative acts was a result of political negotiations between key EU member states. Indeed, NGOs, academics and some key non-EU states (e.g. the U.S. and Canada) were only invited by the European Commission to participate in the early drafting stage of this process. Chimni thus describes the harmonization process in Europe as "the positivist methodology taken to its logical conclusion with Eurocrats framing the law in secrecy, away from democratic pressures" (Chimni 1998: 355). Byrne, Noll, and Vedsted-Hansen offer a more comprehensive picture of this process towards harmonization by re-orienting the debate onto the lateral process of refugee law formation, transformation, and reform, i.e. on the activities between domestic, sub-regional and regional forces (Byrne et al. 2004). For instance, having located the formative stage of the "safe third country" notion into Danish legislation, they show how 10 years later, this notion came to be implemented in practically every western European state, and how, again 10 years later, it became EU law. Crucially they note that this process of formation (in Denmark followed by other western European states), transformation (in mostly *soft law*) and reform (in EU law) followed its own dynamic in spite of opposition from the European Court of Human Rights, national courts and UNHCR. They thus conclude that "In reality, norms are transformed in a constant interplay between domestic, sub-regional and regional forces, rather than replicated from the acquis into domestic legislation" (Byrne et al. 2004: 357). So, "bilateralism accounts for a greater degree of normative development and proliferation than multilateralism at EU level" (Byrne et al. 2004: 358). Byrne et al. have thereby

revealed a transnational legal process whereby up until 2004-05, "domestic legislation [was] sending norms to, rather than receiving them from, the asylum acquis" (2004: 366). Following the adoption of the necessary directives and regulations necessary to establish a CEAS (as well as the move to the qualified majority voting and the co-decision procedure), this upward state-centrist transnational legal process is only now starting to feed back downward from Brussels to the member states.

The creation of a CEAS and its full establishment by 2010 means that implementation of refugee law is no longer only an area of national concern, it has also become a European issue. So, the Commission has recently embarked into an evaluation of the first phase, i.e. a monitoring program of activities on the implementation of all the instruments adopted so far in the field of asylum pursuant to articles 211 and 226 EC Treaty. This evaluation should help facilitate a convergence in interpretation between member states and arrive at levels of harmonization beyond what is stipulated in the directives. The European Commission has also initiated a series of cooperation measures of a practical nature (or networks), such as "contact committees,"[14] Eurasil[15] and the General Directors' Immigration Services Conference (GDISC).[16] Some of these implementation-related activities have been coordinated by the Odysseus Network.[17]

Beyond this political role, the European Court of Justice (ECJ) will ensure that national judicial interpretation of these instruments is indeed correct. Crucially, its rulings on interpretation will contribute to uniform interpretations of EU asylum law, as well as more largely to links, desperately needed in this new area of European law, between the ECJ and subnational actors.[18] The recognition of certain provisions of European Directives as having direct effect should further strengthen the legal protection of persons in need of protection in the national courts.

More dialog, more participants

Most scholars sympathize with the idea that refugee law should develop through dialog between a wide range of participants world-wide (Pallis 2006). Chimni notably argues that dialog is crucial to arrive at "a consensus on the changes to be introduced in the post-war regime" (Chimni 1998: 369). This dialog must not be limited to between scholars, lawyers, states, UNHCR, NGOs from the north but also include the south, and it should be based on the principles of deliberative democracy (i.e. on the basis of good argument as opposed to one's own interest) (Chimni 2001: 152). However, looking at the EU, Chimni denies that such dialog already exists. He relies on the fact that the EU is developing its common asylum system without entering into dialog with other regions, in spite of the influence that this regime will have on other regions (e.g. the practices of non-entrée that undermine the principle of burden sharing).

The more specific argument has also been made that refugee voices should be heard.[19] For instance, it has been argued that the participation of refugees should be enhanced in the context of UNHCR's refugee status determination activities and accountability for such activities (Pallis 2006), when discussing legal solutions (such as repatriation) to the refugee problem (Aleinikoff 1992: 134–8), or when looking at the impact of refugee law and policy (Polzer 2007).

The participatory approach therefore suggests a culturally sensitive approach to refugee law (Wilde 2001: 148). Juss even called for refugee rights to be located within a broader system of immigration rights that would be more humane and more culture sensitive (Juss 1998).

Conclusion

States and their formal agreements (e.g. the Refugee Convention and EU asylum laws)

get us only so far in explaining how refugee law is created and how it develops. There is another layer of explanation that looks into transnational activities and their effect on how the law is shaped, interpreted, applied and developed. Whereas the dominant human rights approach focuses mainly on the sources and contents of rules (and their enforcement), both the transnational and the participatory approaches (as emerging approaches) are useful in capturing the complexities of the process of law formation and law development by looking more specifically at networks and other participants in the process of law making. The challenge of contemporary international refugee law is to recognize more explicitly the role of such networks and the soft law and norms that they often produce.

[Author note: I would like to thank Professor B. S. Chimni and Professor James C. Hathaway for their valuable comments on an earlier draft of this chapter.]

Notes

1 Other disciplines such as anthropology, politics, sociology, economics, and international relations are playing an increasing role.
2 Paul Weis, for instance, argues that the lack of diplomatic protection is an essential element for the status of refugee. Whereas for Atle Grahl-Madsen, it is the rupture of the ties between a national and the authorities of his own country (i.e. de facto statelessness) that constitutes an essential element of being a refugee.
3 http://www.unhcr.org/protect/PROTEC-TION/3b73b0d63.pdf. In this chapter, all references to the "Refugee Convention" are meant to include the 1967 Protocol.
4 This publication contains excerpts from the Statement by Stoltenberg to the 46th session of the U.N. Commission on Human Rights, February 22, 1990.
5 Weis notes that the initial impetus for a Convention relating to the status of refugees originated in an initiative from the U.N. Human Rights Commission.

6 Nathwani instead suggests a "necessity approach" but admits nonetheless that both the human rights approach and the necessity approach share a common space.

7 One other objective of the association is training to improve "judicial decision-making on refugee issues."

8 E.g. *Islam v Secretary of State for the Home Department, R vs. Immigration Appeal Tribunal and another, ex parte Shah*, House of Lords, March 25, 1999, and *R vs. Special Adjudicator, ex parte Hoxha*, House of Lords, March 10, 2005.

9 For this reason, Gilbert considers UNHCR guidance (although equally non-binding) as offering "more general and far reaching analysis that, by definition, ought not to be as concerned with state interests."

10 Chimni gives two examples: UNHCR's reliance on "the language of security to recommend solutions to the global refugee problem" and "the relationship of UNHCR to human rights." Both examples illustrate UNHCR's practice in borrowing concepts developed by northern states and scholars.

11 Betts refers in particular to Hathaway's York-based Refugee Law Reformulation Project of the 1990s.

12 Or in the words of Burley and Mattli, the EC is a process of "gradual penetration of EC law into the domestic law of its member states."

13 http://ec.europa.eu/justice_home/doc_centre/intro/docs/acquis_1006_en.pdf. The European Commission's Green Paper on the Future Common European Asylum System (June 6, 2007) starts the second phase (due to end in 2010). The Eurocrats' drive is clearly for total harmonization of procedures, protection status, and asylum decisions, and for all states' discretion to be removed.

14 "Contact committees" are informal networks of experts meetings between the EU member states, with UNHCR as an observer. Meetings take place to discuss practical issues relating to the implementation of the Directives on asylum and immigration and to reach a common interpretation on the basis of best practice. The European Commission then drafts a non-binding report that is circulated only between the Member States (and UNHCR).

15 Eurasil was created in 2002 as an EU network of asylum practitioners (asylum experts, member states representatives, and UNHCR) from the member states administration. It is the main network for discussing countries of origin information. The purpose is one of exchange of information, of common interpretation, and of common usage. This network is now developing further to coordinate more activities, such as common guidelines on the use of countries of origin information and fact-findings missions, and the development of a European Asylum Curriculum (as a joint practical training and education of asylum service personnel): www.ulb.ac.be/assoc/odysseus/EAC.doc.

16 The General Directors' Immigration Services Conference was established in 2004 as a network of the General Directors of European Immigration Services to promote operational cooperation between the immigration services responsible for the implementation of migration and asylum issues through the exchange of experience and best practice and by building up networks of experts. In particular, it organizes activities funded by the European Refugee Fund and the European Commission, such as the European Asylum Curriculum.

17 The Odysseus Network was created in 1998 (at the initiative of Philippe de Bruycker – Université Libre de Bruxelles – with the financial support of the Odysseus Programme of the European Commission) to carry out legal research and offer expert opinions, and to exchange and diffuse information in the field of immigration and asylum law in Europe http://www.ulb.ac.be/assoc/odysseus/odnetuk.html. As an academic network for legal studies, it brings together experts from the 27 member states of the EU and collaborates closely with judges, governments' officials and EU institutions' officials. It is currently involved in establishing the European Asylum Curriculum: http://www.ulb.ac.be/assoc/odysseus/index2.html. It is also involved in the monitoring of the implementation of 10 Directives in the field of immigration and asylum law in the 27 member states: http://www.ulb.ac.be/assoc/odysseus/CallTenDirectives.html.

18 Note that the article 234 procedure in the area of asylum/refugee law contains some inherent limitations.

19 E.g. the Mexico Declaration to Strengthen the International Protection of Refugees in Latin America states "the importance of fully involving uprooted populations in the design and implementation of assistance and protection programs, recognizing and valuing their human potential." Mexico City, November 16, 2004, reprinted in *International Journal of Refugee Law*, 17(4), 2005: 802–807.

Sustainable development in international law

Marie-Claire Cordonier Segger

Of the 192 states that exist today, a vast major-ity are considered "developing countries". The definition of development, however, remains unclear both in fact and in law. Many economic development decisions have significant environmental and social impacts, and the notion of "sustainable development" has gained currency in international legal debates over recent decades. However, when states commit "to promote sustainable development" in a treaty, or agree to conduct their relations in accordance with a "principle of sustainable devel-opment", the implications of this commitment are not always clear. In this chapter, the origins of sus-tainable development as a concept are reviewed. The status of sustainable development in international law is then discussed. While it may not yet be gen-erally accepted as a customary principle, it is clearly agreed as a policy objective in many treaties, sup-ported by other principles. And further, sustainable development, as an objective of international law, can and does serve to reconcile interstitial tensions between economic growth, social development and environmental protection in the interest of a com-mon future.

We assume a collective responsibility to advance and strengthen the interdependent and mutually reinforcing pillars of sustain-able development – economic development, social development and environmental protection – at the local, national, regional and global levels.

(Johannesburg Declaration,
World Summit for Sustainable
Development 2002)

Introduction: making development "sustainable"?

Many economic development decisions have environmental and social impacts, and the notion of "sustainable development" has gained great currency in international debates. Sustainable development has been the topic of a world summit and is now the subject matter of many international treaties. Sustainable development issues have also been argued before many prominent inter-national tribunals. Through the 1992 United Nations Conference on Environment and Development (UNCED), the 1997 United Nations General Assembly Special Session on Sustainable Development and the 2002 World Summit on Sustainable Development, and in a recent series of significant interna-tional, regional and bilateral environmental, economic and development agreements, states have made sweeping commitments to sustainable development. However, what does this commitment mean? In particular, what does it mean in international law?

Sustainable development refers to state efforts to achieve progress (development), in a way that can be maintained over the long term ("sustainable"). The Preamble to the 1986 *Declaration on the Right to Development*, defines development as:

> [A] comprehensive, economic, social and cultural process which aims at the constant improvement and well-being of the entire population and of all individuals on the basis of their active, free and meaningful participation in development and in the fair distribution of the benefits resulting therefrom.
>
> (United Nations 1986a)

Development can be described as an iterative process which seeks to improve human conditions and find viable livelihoods for peoples in developing countries. In UNGA debates, many states have argued for a "right to development" (United Nations 1974; see also United Nations 1986a).

Concerns about the sustainability of development patterns have gained currency and are influencing the positions of many countries. Scientists are worried that if populations continue to increase and all human beings adopt the extraction, production, consumption and pollution patterns common in most developed countries, humanity will quickly exceed the carrying capacity of the world's resources. In short, there is a concern that current models of economic development are unsustainable. They cannot be maintained and their benefits will not last over time. However, as states hold sovereignty over their own natural resources, and most developing countries are understandably unwilling to accept internationally imposed limits on the exploitation of these resources. As developed countries achieved present standards of living through exploitation of resources, it appears unworkable to prevent others from adopting the same patterns, no matter the impact

on the environment or long-term survival, unless viable alternatives are offered.

Timeline of global sustainable development debates

In 1972, the United Nations (1972a) called an international Conference on the Human Environment (UNCHE), which resulted in the *Stockholm Declaration on the Human Environment*, the creation of the United Nations Environment Programme, and increased impetus to agree on certain multilateral environmental agreements (MEAs) such as the 1973 *Convention on International Trade in Endangered Species* (CITES).[1] The Stockholm Declaration recognizes, in Principle 14, the need to reconcile conflicts "between the needs of development and the need to protect and improve the environment." However, key elements of the Declaration also underlined deep divides between developed and developing countries on a global environmental protection agenda (United Nations 1972a: 11, 23).

In 1983, responding to increasingly heated debates between developed and developing countries, the United Nations General Assembly established the World Commission on the Environment and Development (WCED) mandating it "[t]o propose long-term environmental strategies for achieving sustainable development to the year 2000 and beyond" (United Nations 1983). The WCED delivered its Report to the UNGA, *Our Common Future* in 1987. The most generally accepted definition of sustainable development is found in this "Brundtland Report" where it is defined as "development that meets the needs of the present without compromising the ability of future generations to meet their own needs" (WCED 1987: 43). In Resolution 42/187, "Report of the World Commission on Environment and Development", the UN member states noted the need for "a reorientation of national and international policies towards sustainable development patterns" and emphasized "the need for a new approach to economic growth, as an essential prerequisite for eradication of poverty and for enhancing the resource base on which present and future generations depend". Though the conservation adgenda remained key, this moved international discourse beyond simply protection of the environment.

In 1992, the UN convened a global conference in Rio de Janeiro – the *United Nations Conference on Environment and Development* (UNCED, or the Rio "Earth Summit") (Kiss and Shelton 1994: 67). Specific outcomes included the 1992 *Rio Declaration*, a short consensus declaration agreed by the heads of state assembled in Rio; the 1992 *Agenda 21*, which is annexed to the Declaration and contains an extensive global action plan on specific environment and development issues; and three international treaties signed by a record number of countries: the 1992 *United Nations Framework Convention on Climate Change*, the 1992 *United Nations Convention on Biological Diversity*, and the 1994 *United Nations Convention to Combat Desertification* (United Nations 1992c, 1992d, 1994). The 1992 *Rio Declaration*, a short document of 27 principles, affirms the focus on human development that is central to the concept of sustainable development, and lays out a series of "principles" which can help to achieve sustainable development (United Nations 1992a, 1992b). *Agenda 21*, which was negotiated by the States engaged in the UNCED process, complements the *Rio Declaration* by providing an 800 page "blueprint" for sustainable development. The purpose of this "blueprint" was to halt and reverse the effects of environmental degradation and to promote sustainable development in all countries (Robinson 1993). Agenda 21 also noted, as means of implementation of sustainable development, the need for international action to codify and develop "international law on sustainable development" (see, in particular, United Nations 1992a: [39.1]–[39.10]). The Earth Summit contributed to

global understanding of the concept of sustainable development. However, most of the details on sustainable development goals and standards, remained to be worked out through, and the new obligations and institutions recommended by, the Conference. In particular, the global treaties signed at the UNCED became one of the principal areas where new standards, rules and regimes helped to clarify the content of a commitment to sustainable development. Follow-up mechanisms were set in place, including a Global Environment Facility (GEF), hosted by the World Bank, the UNEP and the UNDP (as implementing agencies) and a United Nations Commission for Sustainable Development (UNCSD) on November 25, 1992. Meeting on a yearly basis, the UNCSD reviewed implementation of the *Agenda 21* at national, regional and international levels. After Rio, the UNCSD mandate was fairly broad (see United Nations 1993a: [3]–[5]). In 1997, a special session of the United Nations General Assembly, the "Earth Summit+5", was held in New York to review progress toward the objectives set in Rio. The resulting Declaration, the *Programme of Further Action to Implement Agenda 21*, acknowledged that progress had been insufficient, called on governments, international organizations and major groups to renew their commitment to sustainable development and emphasized that economic development, social development and environmental protection are three interdependent and mutually reinforcing "pillars" of sustainable development (United Nations 1997b).

In this context, in 2002, the World Summit on Sustainable Development brought together 12,625 accredited in Johannesburg, South Africa with over 45,000 attending related events. The United Nations sought to reinvigorate global commitment to sustainable development.[2] States focused on how best to *implement* sustainable development in a context of globalization and renewed commitments to overseas development assistance.

Outcomes included a 2002 *Johannesburg Declaration*, and a *Johannesburg Plan of Implementation*. The Johannesburg Declaration simply provides a political commitment to sustainable development from Heads of State.[3] The 2002 *Johannesburg Plan of Implementation* (JPOI) is designed as a framework for action. It includes 11 chapters covering poverty eradication; consumption and production; the natural resource base; health; small island developing states (SIDS); Africa; other regional initiatives; means of implementation; and the institutional framework (governance). The JPOI contains over 30 specific time-bound targets for action (including reaffirmations of target agreed in the *Millennium Development Goals* and other instruments).[4] Specific attention was focused on certain important priorities identified by the UN Secretary General, in the areas of water and sanitation, energy, health, agriculture and biodiversity (the so-called "WEHAB" issues).

Unlike in the 1992 Rio "Earth Summit", the Johannesburg Summit process did not produce new treaties. Instead, in the JPOI, states specifically highlighted over 60 existing economic, environmental and social international agreements that play a role achieving sustainable development, and mentioned more than 200 others. It reinforced international recognition of certain key principles of international law on sustainable development, including the principles of common but differentiated responsibility, precaution, and openness, transparency and public participation and profiled international instruments and techniques to put these principles into practice (Cordonier Segger and Khalfan: 2004). At the insistence of the South African and other governments, the Summit also shifted the focus of sustainable development towards social issues, giving full priority to strategies to address poverty eradication, sanitation and health, not just environmental protection and development.

In sum, therefore, over the past 30 years, there has been an extensive "soft law"

policy-making process related to sustainable development, engaging nearly all 192 states of the world. The United Nations sought a bridge between developed and developing countries in order to resolve serious problems of environmental degradation and lack of social and economic development. The concept of sustainable development provided that bridge. However, states have not agreed on one definition for sustainable development. Rather, they have focused on developing greater global consensus on how to achieve it, signing and ratifying international treaties where necessary.

Sustainable development in international law: re-conceptualizing the debate

The most accepted short description of sustainable development continues to be the one adopted by the UN General Assembly: "meeting the needs of the present without compromising the ability of future generations to meet their own needs". This is not particularly helpful to determine the exact parameters of an international treaty commitment to "sustainable development", or the precise normative content of sustainable development in international law.

One international accord does provide an agreed definition of sustainable development. In the 2002 *Convention for Cooperation in the Protection and Sustainable Development of the Marine and Coastal Environment of the Northeast Pacific* at Article 3(1)(a), states agree that:

> [S]ustainable development means the process of progressive change in the quality of life of human beings, which places them as the centre and primary subjects of development, by means of economic growth with social equity and transformation of production methods and consumption patterns, sustained by the ecological balance and life support systems of the region.

This process implies respect for regional, national and local ethnic and cultural diversity, and full public participation, peaceful coexistence in harmony with nature, without prejudice to and ensuring the quality of life of future generations.[5]

This definition emphasizes certain aspects of the concept that have been recognized by states in the global policy-making process. First, it focuses on sustainable development as human centred, in that it involves finding new ways to improve quality of life for people. Second, it focuses on the need to reconcile and integrate environmental protection and social development with economic development. Third, it notes that development that is sustainable should be able to last over the long term, although the environmental limits of ecosystems and resources are dynamic and the relevant time horizon depends on the resource and ecosystem in question. However, this is scarcely a universally recognized or agreed definition, neither are the normative consequences straightforward.

In global summits and other processes, there are repeated calls for better law and policy to realize complementary objectives of environmental protection and socioeconomic development. For these calls to take best effect, it is important to understand the legal status of a commitment to sustainable development.

The legal status of sustainable development

How to characterize a commitment to sustainable development in international law? At least three views currently provide different pictures of the status of sustainable development in international law each with different normative consequences.

First, some states and non-governmental organizations have argued that sustainable development is a new customary principle of international law, one that is in the process of being established as binding on all but a few persistently objecting states (Hunter et al. 2001; Kiss and Shelton 1994; Sands 2003). Second, others note that international law on sustainable development has mainly emerged in international treaties and accords. It is a common purpose among many states when they sign international environmental, economic and other treaties. In some cases, such as recent treaties related to energy, desertification or food and agriculture, it might even be seen as a primary objective of the international agreements themselves (Cordonier Segger and Khalfan 2004; Agenda 21 1992). Viewed in this light, sustainable development is a purpose of treaty law rather than a single customary principle in itself. Third, even if sustainable development were mainly an objective rather than principle of international law, its invocation by states may still engage a certain interstitial normativity,[6] helping to push or pull other principles into play, and encouraging states to use certain legal or institutional mechanisms to secure progress toward sustainable development as a policy objective (Lowe 1999: 27). Each of these characterizations has different normative consequences.

Sustainable development as a customary principle of international law

"Binding" principles can be found in treaties, but they can also be discerned as principles of international customary law. Such principles are important as they can establish obligations for all states except those which have persistently objected to a practice and its legal consequences. Customary international law rules can be derived from the consistent conduct of states acting in the belief that international law required them to so act (Thirlway: 2006: 121–27). Jurists, to prove an international customary principle, must show general state practice (by demonstrating the widespread repetition by states of similar international acts over time) and *opinio juris* (by demonstrating that states acted in this way because they believe themselves to be obligated). Such acts must be taken by a significant number of states and not be rejected by too many others with an interest in the matter (Akehurst 1974–5; D'Amato 1971; Mendelson 1995).

Fundamentally norm-creating character

First, to prove a norm of customary law, there is a need to show that the state practice and *opinio juris* has been extensive and virtually uniform *in the sense of the provision invoked*. This element relates to the requirement that a principle have the "fundamentally norm-creating character such as could be regarded as forming the basis of a general rule."[7] Here, as observed by Vaughan Lowe, the concept of sustainable development in itself might encounter certain difficulties in being recognized as a principle of customary law. In 1995, Gunter Handl (1995: 96) stated baldly that: "[N]ormative uncertainty, coupled with the absence of justiciable standards for review, strongly suggest that there is as yet no international legal obligation that development must be sustainable." Some suggest, essentially, that the concept may not be sufficiently specific and normative to become a customary norm of international law, in itself.[8] As Lowe (1999: 30) notes wryly: "[T]he argument that sustainable development is a norm of customary international law, binding on and directing the conduct of states, and which can be applied by tribunals, is not sustainable."

A commitment to promote sustainable development should be specific – or at least normative enough to form the basis of a claim against a state. What would commitment "to promote sustainable development" actually prescribe, prohibit, exempt or permit states to do?

With regards to prohibitions, it appears unlikely that there exists a blanket prohibition against developing unsustainably. Or even against actions by a state to promote unsustainable development. However, these may be prescriptive or permissive elements. International tribunals have considered this issue in several ways. H.E. Judge C. G. Weeramantry, as Vice-President of the International Court of Justice, argues that sustainable development is a principle of international law in his Separate Opinion in *Gabčíkovo vs. Nagymaros*. In particular, he stated that it is "more than a mere concept, but as a principle with normative value which is crucial to the determination of this case".[9] Indeed, as he further explains, after reviewing many international commitments:

> The concept of sustainable development is thus a principle accepted not merely by the developing countries, but one which rests on a basis of worldwide acceptance . . . The principle of sustainable development is thus a part of modern international law by reason not only of its inescapable logical necessity, but also by reason of its wide and general acceptance by the global community.

Should this view be accepted, the question remains as to what such a principle permits and requires, in effect. The 2005 *Iron Rhine* (*Belgium vs. Netherlands*) award of the Arbitral Tribunal struck under the auspices of the Permanent Court of Arbitration provides some guidance in this regard. In its decision, the Tribunal first recognized that:

> There is considerable debate as to what, within the field of environmental law, constitutes "rules" or "principles"; what is "soft law"; and which environmental treaty law or principles have contributed to the development of customary international law . . . The emerging principles, whatever their current status, make reference to conservation, management, notions of prevention and of sustainable development, and protection for future generations.

The Tribunal then continued to explain:

> Today, both international and EC law require *the integration of appropriate environmental measures in the design and implementation of economic development activities.*

Principle 4 of the Rio Declaration on Environment and Development, adopted in 1992 which reflects this trend, provides that "environmental protection shall constitute an integral part of the development process and cannot be considered in isolation from it." Importantly, these emerging principles now integrate environmental protection into the development process. Environmental law and the law on development stand not as alternatives but as mutually reinforcing, integral concepts, which *require that where development may cause significant harm to the environment there is a duty to prevent, or at least mitigate, such harm . . .* This duty, in the opinion of the Tribunal, has now become a principle of general international law.[10]

(emphasis added)

This determination was directly relevant for the decision of the Tribunal in this case:

. . . economic development is to be reconciled with the protection of the environment, and, in so doing, new norms have to be taken into consideration, including when activities begun in the past are now expanded and upgraded.[11]

Applying the principles of international environmental law . . . [the] *reactivation of the Iron Rhine railway cannot be viewed in isolation from the environmental protection measures necessitated by the intended use of the railway line. These measures are to be fully integrated into the project and its costs.*[12]

(emphasis added)

Such a finding shows that there is a "fundamentally normative" element of the principle, in that its application persuaded the Arbitral Panel that the costs of impact assessments and mitigation measures should be borne by the party carrying out the development (as an integral part of the reactivation of the Iron Rhine Railway), rather than by the party through whose territory the railway would pass. A principle of sustainable development would require states to integrate environmental protection considerations (and costs) into the development process. Such a principle might be somewhat weak, but it is normative. It might even be extended, by states, to include cases where the "development process" consists of defining new trade rules, or establishing new norms to govern transboundary investments. This said, surely it has limits. "Constituting an integral part" is not the same as "becoming a trump card".

Further, defined this way the principle might actually press states, *à l'envers*, ensure that environmental protection laws and programmes not be advanced without taking social and economic development norms into account. A recent decision in the International Court of Justice does suggest the outer boundary for such a principle, in the form of a *permissive* norm – a right of states to promote sustainable development. As such the principle would mean, as highlighted in Principle 4 of Article 3 of the 1992 *United Nations Framework Convention on Climate Change*, that states "have a right to, and should, promote sustainable development." As noted by Wesley Hohfeld (2001: 11–21), such a permissive right, to mean more than a simple privilege, would need to impose a corresponding duty upon another. In this case, the other would be a state or other actor under international law. For instance, another state would be under a duty not to prevent, through their action or inaction, the sustainable development efforts of the first. This would suggest that states have accepted, over time, a prescription not to prevent the efforts of other states to promote sustainable development by integrating environmental protection into their socioeconomic development processes.

And indeed, positive claims based on a state's "sovereign right to implement sustainable economic development projects" were recently used by states in the 2006 *Pulp Mills on the River Uruguay* case. In pleadings on Provisional Measures of July 2006, the ICJ notes that Uruguay "maintained that the provisional measures sought by Argentina would therefore irreparably prejudice Uruguay's sovereign right to implement sustainable economic development projects in its own territory"; and asked the Court:

> [I]n particular to preserve its sovereign right ... to implement sustainable economic development projects on its own territory that do not, in its view, violate Uruguay's obligations under the 1975 Statute or the anti-pollution standards of CARU.[13]

It is possible that a concern for this right of a state, forms the outer boundary of the principle of sustainable development and was a principal element in the ICJ's reasoning in its first Order with regards to provisional measures in the *Pulp Mills on the River Uruguay* case,[14] where it stated:

> [T]he present case highlights the importance of the need to ensure environmental protection of shared natural resources while allowing for sustainable economic development.[15]

This echoes the "concise restatement of the *Trail Smelter* principle coupled with an affirmation of the principle of permanent sovereignty over natural resources" (Lowe 2007) in Principle 21 of the 1972 Stockholm Declaration and Principle 2 of the 1992 Rio Declaration:

> States have, in accordance with the Charter of the United Nations and the principles of international law, the sovereign right to exploit their own resources pursuant to their own environmental and developmental policies, and the responsibility to ensure that activities within their jurisdiction or control do not cause damage to the environment of other States or of areas beyond the limits of national jurisdiction.

Such a right and its attendant responsibility were reaffirmed numerous times in the "soft law" 2002 Johannesburg Plan of Implementation from the World Summit on Sustainable Development. Indeed, elements of such a right, held by indigenous peoples against their own countries, and by states against other states, also appear to be gaining recognition in the recent decisions of regional human rights tribunals.[16] The tension between these two elements is, nonetheless, clear, and neither of them provides a "sustainable development principle" alone. Rather, references to a principle of sustainable development could be a form of "legal shorthand" for Principle 4 of the Rio Declaration, which states that:

> [I]n order to achieve sustainable development, environmental protection shall constitute an integral part of the development process and cannot be considered in isolation from it.

A principle of sustainable development viewed in this light would require that where development may cause significant harm to the environment or to societies, states have a duty to prevent, or at least mitigate, such harm as an integral part of the development process. The outer boundary of the principle would be a right to sustainable development, as an extension of a well-recognized sovereign right of states to exploit their own natural resources.[17]

This definitely provides a fundamentally normative character that is binding on states, though as a double-edged sword. It would not forbid development as such. Rather, it would require states not to prevent or frustrate each other from promoting sustainable development, and "where development may cause significant harm to the environment" would require states to take steps to address a duty "to prevent, or at least mitigate, such harm". While the application of the principle in international law would suggest that this norm would only be relevant in a transboundary context, it should be noted that ecological systems are globally and regionally interrelated in complex ways that science and technology have only begun to explore. Still, if a state can show that it *has* taken measures to take environmental protection into consideration in a development process, and that it has sought to prevent, or at least mitigate, harm to the environment and the community, the state might well evoke the same principle to defend its right to sustainable development. Bounded on one side by the *Iron Rhine Railway* award, and on the other by the *Pulp Mills on the River Uruguay* order, such a principle of sustainable development might possess the fundamentally normative character to be identified as an emerging principle of customary law. However, in order to suggest that this principle could be recognized as a customary norm in international law, two elements must be shown in particular.

General practice of states

The International Court of Justice has stressed the importance of "general practice" in the construction of customary law.[18] A rule of customary law must be above all "a constant and uniform usage practised by the States in question",[19] with the sole (somewhat theoretical) exception of instant custom.[20] "It is how states behave in practice that forms the basis of customary law, but evidence of what a state does can be obtained of numerous sources" (Shaw 2003). State practice demonstrating that a principle has become part of international customary law could be discerned from many sources (ILC 1950: 368–72). For a principle of sustainable development, this might include broad ratification of treaties on sustainable development; the records or *travaux préparatoires* of international negotiations and conferences which document formal notes or statements by state representatives; votes and other acts in the UN General Assembly and other international organizations; the pleadings of states before national and international tribunals and legal opinions by government lawyers; and national legislation and the decisions of national courts.

And indeed, the evidence of some form of international commitment by states to promote sustainable development is significant and weighty. There have been near universal ratifications of treaties such as the *United Nations Framework Convention on Climate Change* (UNFCCC) which has 192 parties, the *United Nations Convention on Biological Diversity* (UNCBD) which has 190 parties, and the *United Nations Convention to Combat Desertification and Drought* (UNCCD) which has 191 parties. As will be further discussed below, these treaties (among many others) contain significant obligations on sustainable development relating to the integration of environmental protection into the development process (and vice versa). While it is not clear whether states are integrating environmental protection and development due to their obligations under these treaties in the context of climate change, biodiversity and desertification, or simply as a general practice (which could be evidence of a customary principle), the practices themselves are certainly being undertaken.

There is evidence of state practice in the universality of official announcements from heads of state and governments supporting and committing to sustainable development *as the integration of environmental protection and socioeconomic development* from Stockholm, Rio and Johannesburg. There are records of statements and formal notes from ministers and senior officials expressing their country's commitments to sustainable development through fifteen years of meetings by the United Nations Commission on Sustainable Development in New York. The National Assessment Reports of States presented to the United Nations Commission on Sustainable Development recognize sustainable development in this light, as well. Such Reports are not simply generated by a few Western or other States. For instance, the Report of Micronesia notes that ". . . sustainable development entails balancing the economic, social and environmental objectives of society in decision making".

A brief survey of State pleadings (and the decisions of judges) from international courts in the *Nuclear Tests* cases,[21] the *Certain*

Phosphate Lands in Nauru case,[22] the *Gabčíkovo-Nagymaros* case,[23] the *Iron Rhine* Arbitration,[24] and the recent *Pulp Mills on the River Uruguay* case[25] demonstrates that a broad array of States are willing to argue for the integration of environmental, economic and social concerns for sustainable development in international tribunal processes. In the *Gabčíkovo-Nagymaros* case, Slovakia argued that "there is if anything an even greater emphasis today on the need to allow States the freedom to develop their natural resources pursuant to their own policies, and in a way that is sustainable."[26] In recent cases, the arguments of states have been more explicit, for instance Belgium argued in the aforementioned *Iron Rhine* Arbitration that "the reactivation of the Iron Rhine is of major international interest, in that it will contribute to sustainable development in each of its ecological, economic and social pillars."[27] In the same fashion Alan Boyle, as Counsel for Uruguay before the ICJ in the public sitting for provisional measures in the aforementioned *Pulp Mills on the River Uruguay* case, argued that:

> This is not a dispute in which the Court has to choose between one party seeking to preserve an unspoiled environment and another party recklessly pursuing unsustainable development, without regard to the environment, or to the rights and interests of neighboring States. It is a case about balancing the legitimate interests of both parties. It is a case in which Uruguay has sought – without much co-operation from its neighbor – to pursue sustainable economic development while doing everything possible to protect the environment of the river for the benefit of present and future generations of Uruguayans and Argentines alike.[28]

There is also increasing state practice in national legislation on sustainable development that seeks to integrate environmental and social concerns into the development process. Nearly every state has, at the least, some form of environmental law in place which commits to sustainable development, and several states have now also set further laws in place,

at national or sub-national levels, that are specifically aimed at integrating environment and development considerations for sustainable development. Documented *National Strategies for Sustainable Development* exist for states such as Australia, Brazil, the Dominican Republic, China, the European Union, Japan, Mexico, South Africa, South Korea, among nearly 90 others. These strategies typically contain local activities to promote sustainable development, and even some include international measures. There is also a growing body of national jurisprudence in which courts indicate that sustainable development is legally relevant, referring to the need to reconcile or integrate environment and development objectives.[29]

In sum, there is ample, significant and voluminous evidence of state practice making commitments to sustainable development, and linking this to the integration of environmental and social considerations into development decision-making. While the evidence does not necessarily point to one specific and clear principle, in the sense that a prohibition of armed attack provides a clear "thou shalt not" or a permission of hot pursuit provides a clear "thou canst", it certainly demonstrates more than mere repetition of a term. States make commitments to sustainable development, and they do so seriously and near universally. The answer to the question of *opinio juris* is, however, not quite so straightforward.

Opinio juris – *believed to be binding by states*

It is not necessarily easy to find evidence of *opinio juris*, as this requires demonstrating the actual motives underlying a state's words and actions. Such evidence can be found in expressions of belief regarding acts of international organizations and other international meetings; statements made by representatives of states, and the conclusion of treaties and the same sources which provide evidence of state practice.[30] The problem, here, is uncovering specific formal announcements which evince that states have committed to either realize, or even promote sustainable development, *believing their decision to have been required by a binding international principle or obligation*, rather than some other form of commitment (for instance, a political commitment to a common global purpose).

Unlike international treaties, or clearly recognized international customary law, the 1992 *Rio Declaration* and the *Agenda 21*, along with the 2002 *Johannesburg Declaration* and *Johannesburg Plan of Implementation* are not binding. Rather, such consensus declarations by states are usually described as "soft law."[31] UN General Assembly resolutions, while they can be considered evidence of an emerging customary principle and while they can reflect treaty law, are similarly not considered legally binding as such. However, this does not mean that such consensus declarations of states are without legal relevance. Indeed, "soft law" declarations may give rise to legitimate expectations, in that states, assumed to be acting in good faith when they agree to such statements, might be precluded from deliberately violating agreements or commitments assumed in soft law without notice or at least assumed to be acting in accordance with such commitments (Allott 2002a: 308). In a related manner, "soft law" can provide evidence of emerging customary norms (Boyle 2006: 149–53).

One "soft law" statement on state beliefs is found in the UNGA Resolution which accepted the *Brundtland Report*, in which UN member states solemnly note the "accelerating deterioration of the human environment and natural resources and the consequences of that deterioration for economic and social development" and then declare:

> . . . sustainable development, which implies meeting the needs of the present without compromising the ability of future generations to meet their own needs, should become a central guiding principle of the United Nations, Governments and private institutions, organizations and enterprises . . .
> (United Nations 1987)

This Resolution, however, uses hortatory language – "should become" rather "can be recognized as". This implies that the members of UN General Assembly, in 1987 at least, did not yet recognize sustainable development as a guiding principle. Further, the UNGA does not actually declare that sustainable development should become a binding principle of customary international law. Rather, it uses slightly different terms – a "central guiding principle" and casts its net wider than states to include private institutions, organizations and enterprises. This suggests that the UNGA was not necessarily seeking to recognize sustainable development as binding law in the *opinio juris* sense.

However, it could be argued that a binding commitment to sustainable development has emerged since the days in 1987 when the UNGA stated that it *should become* a central guiding principle of governments and others. To do this successfully, it is necessary to show that while sustainable development was not yet accepted in 1987, it has since (quite rapidly) evolved into a customary principle of international law.

Certain evidence can be found in the pleadings and decisions of international tribunals since 1987. For instance, in the 1997 *Gabčíkovo-Nagymaros (Hungary vs. Slovakia)* case, Hungary states in its pleadings that: "Hungary and Slovakia agree that the principle of sustainable development, as formulated in the Brundtland Report, the Rio Declaration and Agenda 21 is applicable to this dispute."[32] A series of bilateral treaties also provide evidence that further states are committed to sustainable development as a principle. For instance, the treaty of the *Basis for Relations between Finland and the Russian Federation*, calls for the mutual "implementation of the principles of justice, basic universal human values and sustainable development in accordance with the Charter of the United Nations".[33] The consolidated version of the *Treaty on European Union* among 27 European states also calls "to promote economic and social progress for their peoples, taking into account the principle of sustainable development".[34]

Further, if it was formulated as a binding legal "right to promote sustainable development", it is possible to argue that several near-universal treaties actually do recognize sustainable development as a principle of international law among the parties. As noted earlier, one of the most significant is the *United Nations Framework Convention on Climate Change* (UNFCCC). In Article 3 of the UNFCCC, entitled Principles, states recognize that:

> 4. The Parties have a right to, and should, promote sustainable development. Policies and measures to protect the climate system against human-induced change should be appropriate for the specific conditions of each Party and should be integrated with national development programmes, taking into account that economic development is essential for adopting measures to address climate change.

In the UNFCCC, therefore, the promotion of sustainable development is framed as one of the "Principles" of the treaty, where it is described as a "right". This right to promote sustainable development appears to refer directly to the work of the parties to integrate environmental protection with development processes. It is also, however, framed as a hortatory commitment to "promote" ("should" rather than "shall" or "are bound to"). Further, once recognized, the parties immediately sought to further define this "principle" by noting in caveat that climate protection measures need to be appropriate for different parties and integrated into development programmes, and by the recognition that economic development is still "essential".

In sum, if sustainable development were a principle of international law (recognized in treaty and emerging as customary), it seems most likely that the norm would be mainly related to the integration of environment and socioeconomic development: that states shall take environmental protection into account in the development process and vice versa (as stated in the *Iron Rhine Railway* arbitration). A slightly more optimistic view would be that states are also building on this commitment to integration of environment, social and economic priorities in the development process, and beginning to recognize a right of states to promote sustainable development, implying a related duty not to interfere unduly with each others' efforts to do so (as implied in the *Uruguay River Pulp Mills* case). To support this contention, there is clearly a great deal of general state practice. And there appears to be *opinio juris* which supports the proposal that *certain* states including the EU members do this because they feel bound by a principle of sustainable development. However, there is a lingering lack of clarity as to whether *most* states undertake such a commitment due to a sense of legal obligation, or simply due to a common commitment to a noble political goal. It is not clear, essentially, that a principle of sustainable development has emerged in international customary law as yet.

Sustainable development as an object and purpose of international law

Whether or not sustainable development could be described as customary rule of international law, however, there are also other ways that the concept has legal relevance today. Indeed, a search for one agreed customary norm of sustainable development might actually be a search in the wrong direction. A second possibility is that sustainable development could be characterized as an objective of states, and even an internationally recognized policy objective of the world community as a whole. As a global objective, similar to other objectives such as "world peace", "respect for human rights" and "conservation of nature", sustainable development would therefore be first and foremost characterized as part of the object and purpose of many international treaties.

Policy objectives set out goals to be reached, generally improvements in some economic, political or social situation deemed desirable by the community.[35] Arguments of policy justify a political decision by showing that the decision advances or protects a collective goal of the community as a whole (Evans 2006). Policies may be persuasive but are not legally binding *as such* on judges though as Boyle argues, principles may very well be (Boyle 2006: 149).

Particular relevance is given to policy objectives when agreed among States. As argued by Martti Koskenniemi, to "say that international law is for 'peace', 'security' and 'justice' is to say that it is for peace, security and justice *as agreed and understood between the members of the system*" (Evans 2006). A policy objective is not irrelevant in international law. A great deal of international law is found in international treaties, which lay out the rules that govern a relationship between states that are parties to the accord. The customary rules governing treaties are laid out in the *Vienna Convention on the Law of Treaties*,[36] which "covers the most important areas and is the starting point for any description of the modern law and practice of treaties" (Aust 2000: 6). Article 31, as the general rule of interpretation, provides at 1 that: "A treaty shall be interpreted in good faith in accordance with the ordinary meaning to be given to the terms of the treaty in their context and in the light of its object and purpose." And at 2, the Convention further states that: "The context for the purpose of the interpretation of a treaty shall comprise, in addition to the text, including its preamble and annexes."[37] As such, although the clauses contained within Article 31 are not hierarchical, the starting point for interpretation is the ordinary meaning to be given to the terms, taking them in context, and in the light of the *object and purpose* of the treaty.

Sustainable development is part of the object and purpose for more than 30 treaties which explicitly commit to achieve it, including many trade and investment agreements.

It is also relevant in regimes to implement further treaties that are related to sustainable development, such as the several hundred agreements highlighted by states as delivery mechanisms for the priorities outlined in the Johannesburg Plan of Implementation of the World Summit on Sustainable Development 2002. As object and purpose of these treaties alone, the concept could be extremely important and influential in international law. It could affect interpretation of treaty obligations in a dispute related to environment or development issues, would guide the implementation of the agreements and would even shape the further evolution of the treaty regimes themselves. This is important because few international treaties today, particularly in the field of sustainable development, are simply contracts among states. As international relations theorists like Stephen Krasner (1999: 41–72) have suggested, to understand the norms found in international treaties and how they are implemented, it is important to analyse the broader institutions which form regimes around treaties.

References in the 1972 *Stockholm Declaration*, the UNGA Resolution on the *Brundtland Report*, the 1992 *Rio Declaration* and *Agenda 21*, and the 2002 *Johannesburg Declaration* and *Johannesburg Plan of Implementation* provide convincing evidence to justify finding sustainable development to be the object and purpose of international treaty law. This view is found, for instance, in Chapter 39 of Agenda 21, entitled International Legal Mechanisms and Instruments, at para 39.1, which refers to "the following vital aspects of the universal, multilateral and bilateral treaty-making process", focusing on "(a) The further development of international law on sustainable development, giving special attention to the delicate balance between environmental and developmental concerns; . . . (b) The need to clarify and strengthen the relationship between existing international instruments or agreements in the field of environment and relevant social and economic agreements or instruments, taking into account the special needs of developing countries", describing these accords as "treaty making in the field of international law on sustainable development". Agenda 21 also, at 39.10, refers to "disputes with other states in the field of sustainable development" and advocates "effective peaceful means of dispute settlement . . . and their inclusion in treaties relating to sustainable development". States are setting sustainable development as a goal or subject matter of international law, rather than as a principle of international law in itself.

In the 2002 Johannesburg World Summit on Sustainable Development, this characterization of "international law in the field of sustainable development" was not significantly modified. Rather, as noted above, the focus was on implementation. States agreed, in the Johannesburg Plan of Implementation at 148 (e) to mandate the UNCSD to "[t]ake into account significant legal developments in the field of sustainable development, with due regard to the role of relevant intergovernmental bodies in promoting the implementation of Agenda 21 relating to international legal instruments and mechanisms".

The grand majority of treaties which make specific reference to the concept do so in a way that further supports a characterization of sustainable development as "purpose" whether or not it is a "principle". For instance, and in contrast to certain elements of the *UN Framework Convention on Climate Change (UNFCCC)*, the Kyoto Protocol mentions sustainable development as an objective, providing a set of measures that states can take "in order to promote sustainable development" in the area of climate change. It states, at Article 2, that:

> Each Party included in Annex I, in achieving its quantified emission limitation and reduction commitments under Article 3, *in order to promote sustainable development*, shall: (a) Implement and/or further elaborate policies and measures in accordance with its national circumstances, such as . . .
>
> (emphasis added)

In the context of the UNFCCC, taking regime theory into account, it might even be suggested that while an uneasy agreement existed to permit recognition of the right to promote sustainable development as a Principle in the UNFCCC negotiations of 1990–1992, by the 1997 negotiations of the Kyoto Protocol, consensus had evolved sufficiently among the parties to recognize sustainable development as an "object and purpose" of the treaty.

As a second example, the 1994 UN Convention to Combat Desertification and Drought, especially in Africa (UNCCD) entered into force on 26 December 1996. In the UNCCD, states make over 40 references to "sustainable" development, use, management, exploitation, production and practices and/or unsustainable development and exploitation practices. While the sustainable use of land and water resources is, perhaps, set as a Principle in Article 3, states also clearly incorporated sustainable development as an "Objective" of the UNCCD.

In the treaty, states speak both to their intention that an integrated approach will "contribute to the achievement of sustainable development" in particular areas, and that the adoption of integrated strategies will focus on "sustainable management of land and water resources" leading to "improved living conditions". This resonates well with the concepts discussed above, in terms of integration of environmental, social and economic priorities in the development process, and the focus on human well-being.

In a third example, the 2001 FAO *International Treaty on Plant Genetic Resources for Food and Agriculture* (Seed Treaty), adopted by Conference Resolution 3/2001, seeks to secure conservation and sustainable use of plant genetic resources for food and agriculture and the fair and equitable sharing of benefits derived from their use, in harmony with the UNCBD, for sustainable agriculture and food security. The Seed Treaty contains 24 references to "sustainable" agricultural development, use and systems. Sustainable use of genetic resources is clearly recognized as an "Objective". In Part 1, which establishes Objectives at Article 1.1, states agree that the "objectives of this Treaty are the conservation and sustainable use of plant genetic resources for food and agriculture and the fair and equitable sharing of the benefits arising out of their use, in harmony with the Convention on Biological Diversity, *for sustainable agriculture and food security*". In Article 6, the parties actually define what is meant by sustainable use of plant genetic resources, including the development and maintenance of more than seven specific legal and policy measures. This is important as the Seed Treaty is a recent instrument, and therefore offers an insight into states' most current conception of the legal status of sustainable development. Also, in this Treaty, states focus on "sustainable use" in one particular context, that of plant genetic resources for food and agriculture. In this specific sector, it appears possible to pinpoint fairly precisely the meaning of sustainable use of the resource, and the type of measures that are required to ensure that it takes place.

Since the 1992 Rio Earth Summit, as noted earlier, international tribunals and courts have also begun to pronounce on sustainable development. While certain decisions, noted above, appear to support the contention that sustainable development is a customary principle of international law, others also support the policy objective approach. For instance, in the *Gabčíkovo-Nagymaros* Case,[38] the majority stated that:

> This need to reconcile economic development with protection of the environment is aptly expressed in *the concept of sustainable development*. For the purposes of the present case, this means that the Parties together should look afresh at the effects on the environment of the operation of the Gabčíkovo power plant. In particular they must find a satisfactory solution for the volume of water to be released into the old bed

of the Danube and into the side-arms on both sides of the river.

> (emphasis added)

To each achieve the objective, the Court ordered the parties to integrate environmental protection into their development project by requesting them to "look afresh at the effects on the environment" and "find a satisfactory solution". The majority could be requiring States to deliver on a commonly held sustainable development objective. The *Nuclear Tests* Case,[39] the *Kasikili/Sedudu* Case (esp. Judge Weeramantry's Dissent),[40] the findings in the Tribunal Award of the *Iron Rhine Arbitration*[41] and the Order on Provisional Measures in the *Pulp Mills on the River Uruguay* Case[42] of the International Court of Justice could also be interpreted in a way that supports this characterization.

Finally, while as discussed earlier, many national laws do refer to a principle of sustainable development when focusing on their intention to integrate environmental and social issues into development processes, many other national laws and policies adopted since the 1992 Rio Earth Summit appear to set sustainable development as an objective rather than principle.[43]

Sustainable development as an interstitial norm and its principles

In the context of many multilateral and bilateral treaties, states have committed themselves to a policy objective of sustainable development. Sustainable development was a once marginalized "second objective" of such environmental and economic treaties, but it is gaining prominence as these regimes develop and evolve. Several social and human rights treaties, inasmuch as they address development issues, are also incorporating a sustainable development objective. As the object and purpose of international treaty law, sustainable development will be taken into account and will shape the interpretation of the treaty rules and beyond.

Looking further, it is not certain that sustainable development has become a binding customary norm of international law, in itself, as yet. But neither is it accurate to describe sustainable development as simply a vague international policy goal, void of normative value outside the confines of treaties.

Outside specific treaty regimes, the concept may still serve as a type of norm in its own right, one that exerts a certain pull between conflicting international norms relating to environmental protection, social development and economic growth (Lowe 2000a: 214–15). Sustainable development, as presently applied in treaty negotiation or dispute settlement, might also be described as a "meta principle", one that acts "upon other legal rules and principles – a legal concept exercising a kind of interstitial normativity, pushing and pulling the boundaries of true primary norms when they threaten to overlap or conflict with each other" (Lowe 2000a). This characterization provides an alternative explanation to insert reasonings in the *Gabčíkovo-Nagymaros* case,[44] and could also be used to analyse other more recent relevant decisions in arbitrations and provisional measures cases.

From this viewpoint, the substantive aspect of the "interstitial norm" is the requirement that economic development decision making take social and environmental norms and concerns into account (and vice versa). All three sets of priorities need to be reflected in the substantive outcomes of a given dispute or conflict, even when this means extra costs for the proponent of a project (*Iron Rhine*), and also when states must and respect for a right to continue a development project once these issues have been taken into consideration (*Uruguay Pulp Mills*). While there are few bright lines, and no hard and fast rule, it is not "sustainable" to allow one or the other priority to completely "fall off the table" in situations where common international concerns are at stake. Viewed in this way, beyond treaty law, sustainable development can be invoked by judges and decision makers to curb the worst social and environmental excesses of nations in economic development activities, and exert persuasive pressure for the internalization of otherwise externalized or marginalized social, economic or environmental concerns.

While the question of sustainable development itself as a customary legal norm as well as an object/purpose of treaty law may not yet be resolved, it is clear that there exists a growing body of international law on sustainable development. As such, "international law on sustainable development" today can be used to describe a "group of congruent norms", a corpus of international legal principles and treaties which aim to promote sustainable development, often in the areas of intersection between international economic law, international environmental law and international human rights law (Cordonier Segger and Khalfan 2004). Certain procedural and substantive norms and instruments, which help to balance or integrate these fields, form part of this body of international law and play a role in its implementation. In its interstitial character, sustainable development may push or pull states to use and apply certain international mechanisms and practices, and guide the future development and implementation of international law.

Taking this interstitial character into account, evocation of the sustainable development "policy objective" might therefore imply further normative consequences. As states adopt sustainable development as a policy objective, this can bring further international legal norms into play to realize this interstitial purpose. Just as the prohibition on armed attack serves to maintain world peace, and a prohibition on trade in endangered species serves to conserve nature, so might a prohibition on exhaustion of a transboundary natural resource without good faith consultation with affected states serve to promote sustainable development.

Certain principles which aim to contribute to and achieve sustainable development *as an objective* may even come to be used so often, and to be accepted so generally, that they gain recognition as customary international rules themselves, binding on all States that have not persistently objected. The process of developing principles of international law related to sustainable development has been reasonably complex. The most important undertakings ran parallel to the global policy making events outlined earlier, and included the process of elaborating the 1972 *Stockholm Declaration*, the 1987 Brundtland Commission's Legal Experts Group on Principles of International Law for the Protection of the Environment and Sustainable Development, the 1992 Rio Declaration and other efforts.

In 2002, the International Law Association's Committee on the Legal Aspects of Sustainable Development released its New Delhi ILA *Declaration on Principles of International Law relating to Sustainable Development* as a Resolution of the 70th Conference of the International Law Association in New Delhi India, 2–6 April 2002 (New Delhi Declaration 2002). Adopting the approach discussed above, the ILA New Delhi Declaration notes that "sustainable development is now widely accepted as a global objective and that the concept has been amply recognized in various international and national legal instruments, including treaty law and jurisprudence at international and national levels . . ." The 2002 *New Delhi Declaration* provides the most current benchmark of the important principles in this field and outlines seven principles of international law on sustainable development (Cordonier Segger and Khalfan 2004). First, it recognizes a duty of states to ensure sustainable use of natural resources whereby States have sovereign rights over their natural resources, and a duty not to cause (or allow) undue damage to the environment of other States in the use of these resources. Second, it recognizes a principle of equity and the eradication of poverty. Third, it recognizes a principle of common but differentiated obligations. Fourth, it recognizes a principle of the

precautionary approach to human health, natural resources and ecosystems. Fifth, it underlines the principle of public participation and access to information and justice. Sixth, the ILA New Delhi Declaration posits a principle of good governance. Seventh, and perhaps most telling, the Declaration recognizes a principle of integration and interrelationship, in particular in relation to human rights and social, economic and environmental objectives. This last may indeed be simply another more accurate name for the norm discussed above as a "principle of sustainable development."

As such, several rather functional principles guide the main international treaties on sustainable development and are gaining recognition by states. This list is not exhaustive. And in the most part they are not yet recognized as binding rules of customary international law. In some cases, they might never be. However, they are increasingly made operational in binding international treaties, forming part of international law and policy in the field sustainable development.

Conclusions

This chapter has considered the normative status of sustainable development in international law. Is sustainable development a binding principle of international customary law? Is it a policy objective found as the purpose and subject matter of a growing number of international treaties? Is it something else as well?

In conclusion, it is not clear that sustainable development has yet been accepted as a binding customary norm in international law. However, as noted by Boyle and Freestone (1999: 17, citing Sands 1994): "[E]ven if there is no legal obligation to develop sustainably, there may nevertheless be, through incremental development, law 'in the field of sustainable development'." A growing body of international treaty law on sustainable development is being implemented by states, and when states commit to sustainable development in a treaty or international legal process, it is not legally meaningless. It involves an obligation to seek balance between sometimes conflicting economic, environmental and social priorities in the development process, in the interests of future generations. The balance can be achieved through procedures and substantive obligations which differ depending on the treaty instrument and the area of law and policy that it regulates. Furthermore, the normative consequences of a commitment to sustainable development may not be the same as a straightforward prohibition or prescription. However, if one adopts a more complex view of international law as part of a series of interactional regimes, a legal commitment to sustainable development has interstitial meaning and normative force both in international treaties, and in "soft law" cooperation arrangements. Its interstitial normative character may well encourage states to adopt and implement sustainable development related principles and measures, both inside existing treaty regimes, and even beyond.

A great deal of progress has been made in recent years, though more is needed. Turning to the future, states and others have increasingly begun to focus on implementation in different contexts, developing scientific and legal instruments to ensure more sustainable use or management of a particular resource, and to promote sustainable development by re-directing a specific type of economic activity. In this way, international law on sustainable development is defining new rights and duties among states. The challenge for future legal scholarship – and action – will be to implement this global commitment in the interest of a common future.

Notes

1 *Convention on International Trade in Endangered Species of Wild Fauna and Flora* (adopted March 3, 1973, entered into force July 1, 1975) 993 U.N.T.S. 243, 12 I.L.M. 1085.

2 In December 2000, the UN General Assembly (UNGA) decided to convene a 10-year review of progress since UNCED (A/RES/55/199). See United Nations 2000b.

3 Johannesburg Declaration (n. 75) [5].

4 The other significant commitments from the meeting include: using and producing chemicals in ways that do not harm human health and the environment; reducing biodiversity loss by 2010; restoring fisheries to their maximum sustainable yields by 2015; establishing a representative network of marine protected areas by 2012; improving developing countries' access to environmentally sound alternatives to ozone depleting chemicals by 2010; and undertaking initiatives by 2004 to implement the Global Programme of Action for the protection of the Marine Environment from Land Based Sources.

5 *Convention for Cooperation in the Protection and Sustainable Development of the Marine and Coastal Environment of the Northeast Pacific* (February 18, 2002).

6 Lowe 1999: 27; he references further, D'Amato 1990.

7 *North Sea Continental Shelf* (n. 120) [63].

8 For different views on this point, see Sands 1994.

9 *Case Concerning the Gabčíkovo-Nagymaros Project*: p. 85 (Separate Opinion of Vice-President Weeramantry).

10 *In the Arbitration Regarding the Iron Rhine* [58]–[59].

11 *In the Arbitration Regarding the Iron Rhine* [222].

12 *In the Arbitration Regarding the Iron Rhine* [223].

13 *Argentina vs. Uruguay, Case Concerning Pulp Mills on the River Uruguay* (2006) Request for the Indication of Provisional Measures: Order of July 13, 2006, General List No. 135, 45 ILM 1025 [67].

14 *Argentina vs. Uruguay, Case Concerning Pulp Mills* [67].

15 *Argentina vs. Uruguay, Case Concerning Pulp Mills* [80].

16 See also Inter-American Court of Human Rights *Case of the Sawhoyamaxa Community (Paraguay)* (2006) [137]–[141]; Inter-American Court of Human Rights *Case of the Saramaka Peoples (Suriname)* (2007) [93]–[95], 122, 129–32; African Commission on Human and Peoples' Rights *Case of the Social and Economic Rights Action Center and the Center for Economic and Social Rights vs. Nigeria* (2002) 96 AJIL 937, 47 J African L 126 [52].

17 *Portugal vs. Australia, Case concerning East Timor* (1995) Judgment, Dissenting Opinion of Judge Weeramantry, General List No. 84, [1995] ICJ 90, 34 ILM 1581, pp. 197–200; *United Kingdom of Great Britain and Northern Ireland vs. Iceland, Case concerning the Fisheries Jurisdiction* (1974) Merits, Dissenting Opinion of Judge Petrel, General List No. 55, [1974] ICJ 3 p. 161; *Belgium vs. Spain, Case Concerning the Barcelona Traction, Light and Power Company, Limited (New Application: 1962)* (1970) (Second Phase, Separate Opinion of Judge Jessup) General List No. 50, [1970] ICJ 3, pp. 165–167; United Nations 1972b: XXVII [1]; Weiss and Schrijver 2004.

18 *Nicaragua vs. USA, Case concerning Military and Paramilitary* [98].

19 *France vs. United States of America, Case Concerning Rights of Nationals of the United States of America in Morocco* (1952) Merits, General List No. 11, ICJ 176, p. 200; *Colombia vs. Peru, Asylum Case* (1950) Judgment, General List No. 7, ICJ 266, pp. 276–7.

20 Cheng 1965; *Federal Republic of Germany/Netherlands, North Sea Continental Shelf* (1968) Judgment of February 20, 1969, General List: Nos. 51 and 52, ICJ [43].

21 *Nuclear Tests Case (New Zealand vs. France)* (1995) Request for an Examination of Situation in Accordance with Paragraph 63 of Court's Judgment of December 20, 1974: Order, Dissenting opinion by Judge Weeramantry, General List No. 97, ICJ 288.

22 *Certain Phosphate Lands in Nauru (Nauru vs. Australia)* (1992) Preliminary Objections: Judgment, General List No. 80, ICJ 240, 32 ILM 1471.

23 *Case Concerning the Gabčíkovo-Nagymaros Project.*

24 *In the Arbitration Regarding the Iron Rhine (Ijzeren Rijn) Railway, Belgium vs. Netherlands* (2005) Arbitral Award of May 24, 2005. Available at http://www.pca-cpa.org/showfile.asp?fil_id=377.

25 *Argentina vs. Uruguay, Case Concerning Pulp Mills.*

26 *Case Concerning the Gabčíkovo-Nagymaros Project (Hungary/Slovakia)* (Memorial submitted by the Slovak Republic) 294. http://www.icj-cij.org/docket/files/92/10939.pdf.

27 *In the Arbitration Regarding the Iron Rhine (Ijzeren Rijn) Railway (Belgium vs. Netherlands),* (Memorial submitted by Belgium). http://www.pca-cpa.org/upload/files/BE%20Memorial.pdf.

28 *Case Concerning Pulp Mills on the River Uruguay (Argentina vs. Uruguay)* (Verbatim Record of the Public sitting held on Thursday June 8, 2006,

at 3 p.m., at the Peace Palace) 30-31.http://www.icj-cij.org/docket/files/135/13128.pdf.

29 For example, the Indian cases address environmental pollution as an issue affecting the human right to life: *Charan Lal Sahu vs. Union of India* AIR 1990 SC 1480; *Koolwal vs. Rajasthan* AIR 1998, Raj.2; other national cases include *Leatch v. National Parks and Wildlife Service and Shoalhaven City Council,* 81 LGERA 270 (1993) (NSW Land and Environment Court, Australia); *Vellore Citizens Welfare Forum vs. Union of India* [1996] 5 SCC 647 (Supreme Court, India); *Balankulama vs. The Secretary, Ministry of Industrial Development, SAER,* Vol 7(2) June 2000 (Supreme Court, Sri Lanka – Supreme Court of the Democratic Socialist Republic of Sri Lanka). See also *Minors Oposa vs. Secretary of the Department of Environment and Natural Resources (DENR),* 33 I.L.M. 173 (1994) (Philippines), although the case addressed mainly questions of standing in national law on behalf of future generations. And see *Rajendra Parajuli and Others vs. Shree Distillery Pvt. Ltd. and Others,* the Supreme Court of Nepal (Writ No. 3259, 1996) stated that sustainable development means "every industry has an obligation to run its development activities without creating environmental deterioration. The environment should not be viewed narrowly. It is imperative for any industry to be cautious towards the environment while it is in operation." The Court ordered the company to comply with a prior agreement to keep the environment free of pollution in the affected area.

30 Evans 2006: 123–129.

31 *Agenda 21*: Ch 11, 12, 18, 20, 21 and 22. See also Chinkin 1989.

32 *Case Concerning the Gabčíkovo-Nagymaros Project* [90].

33 *Basis for Relations between Finland and the Russian Federation* (signed January 20, 1992, entered into force July 11, 1992) 1691 UNTS 255.

34 Consolidated Versions of the Treaty on European Union (signed February 17, 1992) OJ C 321E of December 29, 2006. http://eur-lex.europa.eu/en/treaties/index.htm.

35 See also Koskenniemi (2006b: 64–6), where he argues: "We do not honour the law because of the sacred aura of its text or its origin but because it enables us to reach valuable human purposes . . ." However, as he argues later, "there never are simple, well-identified objectives behind formal rules. Rules are legislative compromises, open-ended

and bound in clusters expressing conflicting considerations."

36 Vienna Convention on the Law of Treaties (signed May 23, 1969, entered into force January 27, 1980) 1155 UNTS 331, 8 ILM 679. The provisions on interpretation of treaties contained in Articles 31 and 32 of the Vienna Convention reflect pre-existing customary international law, as referred to in Article 4 of the Convention, and thus may (unless there are particular indications to the contrary in the treaty itself) be applied even to treaties concluded before the entry into force of the *Vienna Convention on the Law of Treaties* in 1980 and also to non-parties.

37 The International Court of Justice has applied customary rules of interpretation, now reflected in Articles 31 and 32 of the Vienna Convention, to a treaty concluded in 1955: *Case Concerning the Territorial Dispute (Libyan Arab Jamahiriya vs. Chad)* (Judgment) General List No. 83 [1994] ICJ 6, (1994) 33 ILM 571 [41]; and to a treaty concluded in 1890, bearing on rights of states that even on the day of the judgment were still not parties to the Vienna Convention: *Kasikili/Sedudu Island (Botswana/Namibia)* (Judgement) General List No. 99 [1999] ICJ 1045, (2000) 39 ILM 310 [18]; In another case, the Court noted that Indonesia was not a party to the Vienna Convention, but nevertheless applied the rules as formulated in Articles 31 and 32 of that Convention to a treaty concluded in 1891, Indonesia did not dispute that the rules codified in these articles were applicable. See *Case Concerning Sovereignty over Pulau Ligitan and Pulau Sipadan (Indonesia vs. Malaysia)* (Judgment) General List No. 102 [2002] ICJ 625 [37]–[38].

38 *Case Concerning the Gabčíkovo-Nagymaros Project* [140].

39 *Nuclear Tests Case* [341]–[344].

40 *Kasikili/Sedudu Island* [87]–[88] (Dissenting Opinion by Judge Weeramantry).

41 *In the Arbitration Regarding the Iron Rhine* [58]–[59].

42 *Argentina vs. Uruguay, Case Concerning Pulp Mills* [80].

43 See Peru's State Policies on Sustainable Development and Environment. Available at http://www.conam.gob.pe/modulos/home/PolicitaDeEstado.asp; see also Colombia's 2007 Report on the National Development Plan. http://www.dnp.gov.co/paginas_detalle.aspx?idp=235. For a survey of advances in more than 60 countries of all regions of the world, see FAO, *Law and Sustainable Development Since Rio: Legal trends in agriculture and natural resource management* FAO Legislative Study 73 (FAO, Rome 2002).

44 *Case Concerning the Gabčíkovo-Nagymaros Project*.

26

WTO law and sustainable development

Markus W. Gehring

This chapter focuses on the interface between trade and sustainable development. It first gives an introduction and overview of WTO law then briefly examines the historical development of the WTO as a legal order explaining the most important legal principles, such as most favored nation and national treatment. After a short explanation of the dispute settlement system, the chapter illustrates some of the most important sustainable development challenges as defined in the World Summit on Sustainable Development. It proposes three fields of study of the trade – sustainable development interface: negotiation, trade disputes and innovative instruments. The chapter discusses how limited attempts have been made to introduce the concept of sustainable development into the international trading system. This hesitation, largely due to a "trade-only" ethos of the organization, was only overcome after certain seminal disputes had been decided. After the decision in U.S.–Shrimp that sustainable development figured prominently in the Doha Development Agenda. Two more recent disputes help to illustrate the nature of sustainable development arguments made in the WTO dispute settlement. The chapter then points to innovative mechanisms that have been used by WTO member states to integrate trade and environment or trade and sustainable development more broadly.

The chapter argues that the relationship between WTO law and sustainable development is not yet fully determined. To ensure that international trade law can deliver on sustainable development in the current context, a constructive, integrated approach is needed to address overlaps between social development, economic development and environmental protection. This approach must focus specifically on achieving solid results for developing countries and for development in general.

In recent years as international trade compacts have proliferated and the scope of World Trade Organization (WTO) activities has extended beyond purely economic parameters, there has been a growing awareness that trade has developmental, social, environmental, and health implications. Given these nexuses, it is crucial that trade law regulating transactions is informed by a holistic perspective that takes into account potential impacts from a sustainable development point of view. The infrastructure of sustainable development must reconcile three premises: the trade perspective is adamant that economic liberalization provides the most efficient means of environmental protection and societal betterment; the environmental viewpoint asserts that the status quo is fatally harming natural capital and must be modified; and the development schema prioritizes poverty eradication or at least reduction.

Trade law

The nature of the legal order of the World Trade Organization is an important starting point. Trade law is one of the oldest areas of international law. Most very early "international" treaties granted trade concessions and allowed products to be traded from one ancient city state to another. As such, there is no right to free trade in international law. This can be contrasted with, for instance, the freedom of the high seas, and means that it is every country's sovereign decision to allow trade with another country or not.

Early works by economists such as Adam Smith, David Ricardo, and John Stuart Mill suggested that countries could benefit economically from free trade between them, as it allows each to build on their respective comparative advantages. The advent of free trade treaties brought a moderate degree of liberalization, but by the 1860s many countries quickly returned to protectionist policies in response to fears of British economic dominance. After a period of relative stability based on the gold standard, countries began to exercise their sovereign right to determine trade relations, leading to a period of high protectionism after the depression of the late 1920s and 1930s. Several important countries sought to raise barriers and isolate themselves from the world economy, in order to protect their own industry. However, most countries returned to multilateralism in the late 1930s by developing reciprocity in their trading relationships, granting tariff concessions between countries on a mutual basis.

This multilateralism also formed the basis for the allied post-war economic discussions, which eventually led to the negotiation of the Charter for an International Trade Organization (the so-called Havana Charter), which included provisions mandating cooperation in many areas such as trade, labor, and competition. This comprehensive economic agenda failed, largely because the U.S. Senate did not approve the treaty. Nevertheless, one part of the Havana Charter, the General Agreement of Tariffs and Trade (GATT), was enacted provisionally in 1947 and formed the basis for almost 50 years of operation. The GATT focused specifically on trade in goods and did not include any other area of international trade or economic regulation. This narrow scope was part of its success in attracting many countries as contracting parties and achieving significant tariff reductions in seven rounds of trade negotiations. After significant tariff reductions, the GATT 1947 contracting parties recognized that other barriers – outside the purview of "trade in goods" – were becoming more important and impeded exports. Thus, during the late 1970s, in the Tokyo Round of trade negotiations, additional agreements were adopted, dealing with technical barriers to trade, food standards, dumping and subsidies. In 1994, after nearly a decade of deliberations and negotiations, the GATT was replaced by the WTO.

Today's world trade law is based on several levels of international trading regimes, and can be found in two major sets of agreements:

- law concerning the WTO
- international trade law stemming from bilateral or regional trade agreements.

The WTO, despite unsuccessful attempts to renegotiate some of its rules and a shift of focus within the international community towards regional trade agreements, is still at the heart of the international trade regime. At the time of publication, it has 152 extremely diverse member states, with some important international economic actors such as Russia involved in membership negotiations. Arguably, the exponential increase in trade in goods during recent decades was due to the stability and predictability of the international trading system. The Uruguay Round of negotiations leading to the creation of the WTO also saw the inclusion of new issues such as trade in services and trade-related intellectual property rights (IPRs), and aimed to bring agriculture and textiles back under GATT disciplines.

Fundamentally, the WTO is a member-driven organization with a comparatively small Secretariat. The WTO's mandate is to:

- administer the WTO agreements
- provide a forum for trade negotiations
- settle trade disputes
- monitor national trade policies
- facilitate technical assistance and training for developing countries and
- promote cooperation with other international organizations.

In addition to the development of the WTO regime, there has been rapid growth in regional trade agreements and bilateral agreements, which exist parallel to the ambit of the WTO but must conform to its principles. According to GATT rules, regional trade agreements should serve as "building blocks," not "stumbling blocks," to facilitate the functioning of the world trading system. This means that a multilayered analysis of agreements governing trade is crucial; it is not sufficient to only analyze the implications of WTO law, while ignoring preferential rules enshrined among trading partners in regional trade agreements or national rules which implement international trade law regimes.

WTO agreements

The WTO agreements and dispute settlement outcomes – the latter having at least strong persuasive power or *de facto* precedent character – largely determine international trade rules with relevance for both the private and public sector. These WTO agreements also contain guidelines governing international commercial conduct and guard against trade distorting behavior such as unlawful subsidizing

practices and "dumping" (i.e. product sale in a foreign country below the sales price in the country of origin or below cost plus distribution price).

The WTO agreements are broadly organized into three pillars – goods, services and intellectual property rights (see Table 26.1). The goods pillar is the largest, including agreements on many different aspects of international goods trade. There are also plurilateral agreements signed only by a subset of the WTO membership, and various cross-cutting accords.

Of course, such an overview of the WTO treaty framework provides only the beginnings of an accurate picture of WTO law. The main commitments of WTO members are contained in individual detailed country schedules attached to GATT (tariff schedules) and GATS (services schedules). These two documents are comprehensive listings of all the products for which the WTO member in question has accepted a commitment to a binding tariff at a particular level. For example, the tariff for microwave ovens for imports into the United States is bound at 4% according to value, and the United States has completely liberalized architectural services in cross-border supply.

Settlement of disputes in world trade law

Trade disputes were a common phenomenon in the later years of GATT 1947. Indeed, the animosity and absence of middle ground in some disputes between the United States and the European Union triggered a new approach to dispute settlement in the WTO. Instead of a positive vote to adopt a dispute settlement decision, as was required by the GATT, the WTO now operates in reverse, so that decisions under its dispute settlement mechanism can only be dismissed by the unanimous vote of all members. This negative consensus means that even the party who won the case must agree for a report

Table 26.1 Three pillars of WTO agreements

Pillar 1: Trade in goods General Agreement on Tariffs and Trade (GATT)	Agriculture Sanitary standards Textiles Technical standards Trade-related investment measures Antidumping measures Customs valuation methods Pre-shipment inspection Rules of origin Import licensing Subsidies and countermeasures Safeguards
Pillar 2: Trade in services General Agreement on Trade in Services (GATS)	Movement of natural persons annex Air transport annex Financial services annex Shipping annex Telecommunications annex
Pillar 3: Intellectual property rights Agreement on Trade-Related Aspects of Intellectual Property Rights (TRIPs)	
Cross-cutting agreements	Dispute settlement understanding Trade policy review mechanism
Plurilaterals	Agreement on trade in civil aircraft Agreement on government procurement

to be dismissed in the formal adoption meeting of the Dispute Settlement Body (which is identical to the General Council but acts under a different chairperson). This system makes the WTO's Dispute Settlement Understanding (DSU) highly effective and contributes to its objective of providing "a central element in providing security and predictability to the multilateral trading system" (Article 3.2 of the DSU). The requirement to settle disputes formally rests with the WTO members, which often devote significant time to the use of other pre-juridical techniques such as consultation and other arbitration-like elements of the dispute settlement mechanism. If these preliminary attempts to defuse a trade-related conflict fail to satisfy either party, the DSU process is set in motion and carried out first by a WTO panel (composed of three trade experts chosen ad hoc to hear the case and determine the facts) and, second, by the WTO Appellate Body

(a standing body of nine trade law experts, of whom three are called to hear legal appeals on the panel's determination).

Trade and sustainable development

On a theoretical level, trade is not automatically good or bad for the environment and social development (see, e.g. Nordström and Scott 1999). Rather, the specific contours of international trade rules and regimes and modes of implementation dictate the degree to which trade advances sustainable development goals. Public international law, the umbrella under which international trade law is situated, can and should adopt a principled approach to ensure that it can deliver on its global objective of sustainable development. A nuanced understanding of recent developments in world trade law, focusing on intersections between economic, social, and environmental fields of law and policy, can enhance the positive (and mitigate any negative) aspects of this complex relationship. In the context of ongoing trade law debates that encompass the negotiations in the 2003 Cancun Ministerial and the 2005 Hong Kong Ministerial, there has been anxiety that the WTO and other international trade institutions cannot adequately respond to the principal opportunities and threats that were identified by representatives of over 180 countries at the 2002 World Summit for Sustainable Development (WSSD):

> Globalization offers opportunities and challenges for sustainable development. We recognize that globalization and interdependence are offering new opportunities to trade, investment and capital flows and advances in technology, including information technology, for the growth of the world economy, development and the improvement of living standards around the world. At the same time, there remain serious challenges, including serious financial crises, insecurity, poverty, exclusion and inequality within and among societies.[1]

While any single international organization or process would be hard pressed to address this broad range of challenges alone, measures can certainly be taken to increase the likelihood that emerging international trade regimes will support sustainable development. Indeed, despite the negotiating gridlock that has characterized the latest round, there are even tentative signs of progress toward this goal.[2]

The next sections of this chapter explore emerging issues related to sustainable development that have gained prominence in the context of the recent "Doha Development Agenda" (DDA) of trade negotiations, taking into account the outcomes of the 2002 WSSD in Johannesburg, South Africa (Cordonier Segger and Khalfan 2004: 25–43). It aims to discuss the recent development of a constructive global trade and

sustainable development law agenda mainly through specific analysis of developing rules, procedural and substantive innovations, and emerging issues. World trade law is a multilayered system; it envelops supranational, regional, and bilateral components. In many of the last sort of agreement, innovative mechanisms are being tested to ensure mutual supportiveness[3] between trade, environment, and development law. Depending on the modalities chosen, intersections of these issue areas can create both an overlapping and crosscutting latticework of rules and stipulations. Not only do the linkages have a legal character, collaboration between IGOs (UNDP, UNEP), NGOs and multilateral environmental accords (i.e. UNCBD, UNFCCC) has resulted in institutional ties as well. The core negotiations and controversy surrounding the Doha Development Agenda along with relevant international economic law jurisprudence are particularly relevant, and in certain areas, closer adherence to principles and practices of sustainable development law might contribute to longer lasting and better world trade law.

Negotiating sustainable development in the WTO?

In the 1970s there emerged significant global concern for human rights and the environment, particularly in developed countries. This generated considerable controversy for developing countries (Hunter et al. 2001) as the latter planned to focus on the full exploitation of their natural resources in order to promote pressing priorities related to economic growth.[4] One study, "Limits to Growth," predicted a global disaster if international policies were not changed to balance economic development and the utilization of non-renewable natural resources (Meadows et al. 1972). In 1983, states established the World Commission on Environment and Development (WCED), an independent investigatory body composed

379

of international policy and scientific experts in accordance with U.N. General Assembly (UNGA) Resolution Res. 38/161. The outcome of the WCED process, the *Brundtland Report*, led to UNGA Resolution 42/187, which resolved that sustainable development "should become a central guiding principle of the United Nations, Governments and private institutions, organizations and enterprises."

Based on this foundation in the U.N. system, the concept of sustainable development became an overarching theme of the 1992 United Nations Conference on Environment and Development (UNCED) in Rio de Janeiro, which attracted over 140 heads of state – the largest global summit in history,[5] at that time. One of the conference outcomes, Agenda 21, highlighted that achieving enduring social and economic dimensions of development required that international trade and environment policies needed to be mutually supportive.[6] The outcomes of the 1992 UNCED influenced the drafting of the WTO preamble:

> *Recognizing* that their relations in the field of trade and economic endeavour should be conducted with a view to raising standards of living, ensuring full employment and a large and steadily growing volume of real income and effective demand, and expanding the production of and trade in goods and services, while allowing for the optimal use of the world's resources *in accordance with the objective of sustainable development*, seeking both to protect and preserve the environment and to enhance the means for doing so in a manner consistent with their respective needs and concerns at different levels of economic development.
>
> *Recognizing* further that there is need for positive efforts designed to ensure that developing countries, and especially the least developed among them, secure a share in the growth in international trade commensurate with the needs of their economic development.[7]
>
> (emphasis added)

While preambular statements are not legally binding in the same way that operational provisions can be,[8] they can play a role in interpretation of a treaty, particularly in identifying the treaty's object and purpose. Thus, it is important to understand the intended meaning of the Preamble to the WTO Agreement. In the Preamble, the concept of sustainable development is mentioned in connection with the optimal use of the world's resources. This may be partly because the Preamble was drafted as an expansion of the GATT 1947 Preamble, which referred conclusively to the need for "developing the full use of the resources of the world." It may also refer to the historical origins of the concept itself, in the "sustainable yield" management practices of an important agro-forestry industrial sector. It is important to note however, that the Preamble specifically recognizes the need to raise standards of living and income for people, to protect the environment, and to do so in a way that is consistent with the needs and concerns of developing countries, so that international trade can contribute to these countries' development needs.

Indeed, two years later in the 1996 Singapore Ministerial Declaration,[9] the Preamble of the WTO Agreement did not inspire new negotiations on binding rules. Instead, a short note appears in Paragraph 16, limited only to trade and environment issues, stating: "Full implementation of the WTO Agreements will make an important contribution to achieving the objectives of sustainable development."[10] In this reference, sustainable development objectives are clearly linked to the implementation of the international trade regime, rather than simply the optimal use of natural resources. It is an expanded recognition of the concept; nonetheless, the text manages to give the impression that sustainable development is a natural result of liberalized trade. In the 1998 Geneva Ministerial Conference, there was further movement towards establishing sustainable development as more than a reason for enhanced trade, or a way to constrain environmental measures. The preamble of the Ministerial Declaration states, at Para. 4: "We shall also continue to improve our efforts towards the objectives of sustained economic growth and sustainable development."[11]

As such, in 1998 the WTO and its member states formally recognized that sustainable development is not only related to natural resources or an inevitable result of the economic liberalization process, but is actually one of the goals of the WTO itself. The links between this concept and the concept of sustained economic growth are also put into relief. By 1998 several countries and regions had introduced the goal of sustainable development into their laws and policies,[12] and it is likely that they sought to reflect this commitment in one of the most important international economic law-making processes of the decade. Indeed, this position echoed developments in the other important forum in which WTO rules and regimes are clarified and interpreted: the dispute settlement system.

"Sustainable developments" in recent WTO disputes?

The WTO's view of the concept of sustainable development as it currently stands can be explained by examining: the U.S.–Shrimp Case,[13] the E.U.–Tariff Preferences Case,[14] and most recently the Brazil–Retreaded Tires Case.[15]

The U.S.–Shrimp Case concerned a regulation under the 1973 U.S. Endangered Species Act to protect five different species of endangered sea turtle. The U.S. requires that U.S. shrimp trawlers use "turtle excluder devices (TEDs)" in their nets. A different law then prohibited shrimp imports from regions where trawlers were not equipped with TEDs in the presence of sea turtles. India, Malaysia, Pakistan, and Thailand complained that the prohibition was inconsistent with U.S. GATT obligations. The panel and the Appellate

Body decided in favor of the complainants and asked the U.S. to bring its laws into compliance with GATT 1994 obligations.

In the case, the U.S. proposed that Art. XX GATT should be interpreted in the light of the preamble of the WTO Agreement; "[A]n environmental purpose is fundamental to the application of Article XX, and such a purpose cannot be ignored, especially since the preamble to the Marrakesh Agreement Establishing the World Trade Organization (the 'WTO Agreement') acknowledges that the rules of trade should be 'in accordance with the objective of sustainable development', and should seek to 'protect and preserve the environment'."[16] In its arguments, the U.S. omitted the reference to the world's resources and the statement concerning the "respective needs and concerns at different levels of economic development."

The Appellate Body decision considers the Preamble, but does not follow the U.S. argument:

> The words of Article XX(g), "exhaustible natural resources," were actually crafted more than 50 years ago. They must be read by a treaty interpreter in the light of contemporary concerns of the community of nations about the protection and conservation of the environment. While Article XX was not modified in the Uruguay Round, the preamble attached to the WTO Agreement shows that the signatories to that Agreement were, in 1994, fully aware of the importance and legitimacy of environmental protection as a goal of national and international policy. The preamble of the WTO Agreement – which informs not only the GATT 1994, but also the other covered agreements – explicitly acknowledges "the objective of sustainable development."[17]
> (emphasis added)

The enclosed legal note, as part of the Appellate Body's decision,[18] deserves particular attention. The Appellate Body refers to the objective of sustainable development and in a footnote, expands on its relevance to the case.

The Appellate Body explained that: "[T]his *concept* has been generally accepted as integrating economic *and* social development *and* environmental protection" (emphasis added). This is remarkable for two reasons. First, the WTO Appellate Body delineated its stance on the nature of sustainable development and agrees that it should be framed as a "concept" (as opposed to a principle, policy or rule), in world trade law. Second, a reading of the definition demonstrates the WTO's recognition of the need to integrate all three elements or "pillars" of sustainable development – social development, economic development and environmental protection. The recognition of the social dimension of the concept, effectively laid the groundwork for subsequent focus on this element in the 2002 WSSD.

The Appellate Body continued with their interpretation of the preamble in WTO law: "[W]e note once more that this language demonstrates recognition by WTO negotiators that optimal use of the world's resources should be made in accordance with the objective of sustainable development. As this preambular language reflects the intentions of negotiators of the *WTO Agreement*, we believe it must add colour, texture and shading to our interpretation of the agreements annexed to the *WTO Agreement*, in this case, the GATT 1994. We have already observed that Article XX(g) of the GATT 1994 is appropriately read with the perspective embodied in the above preamble."[19] This addition of "colour, texture and shading" seems to amplify the previous language: "interpretation based on the context of the agreement." It indicates that the Appellate Body understands that the concept of sustainable development informs members' intentions in all of the annexed agreements.

The Appellate Body insisted: "[W]e also note that since this preambular language was negotiated, certain other developments have occurred, which help to elucidate the objectives of WTO Members with respect to the relationship between trade and the environment. The most significant, in our view, was the Decision of Ministers at Marrakesh to establish a permanent Committee on Trade and Environment (the CTE). In their Decision on Trade and Environment, Ministers expressed their intentions, in part, as follows: . . . *Considering* that there should not be, nor need be, any policy contradiction between upholding and safeguarding an open, non-discriminatory and equitable multilateral trading system on the one hand, and acting for the protection of the environment, and the promotion of sustainable development on the other."[20] In this Decision, Ministers took "note" of the Rio Declaration on Environment and Development,[21] Agenda 21,[22] and its follow-up in the GATT, as reflected in the statement of the Council of Representatives to the 48th Session in 1992.[23]

Crucial explanatory comments are again found in the footnotes. The Appellate Body cites specific rules and provisions of the Rio Declaration and Agenda 21, which refer to balancing with regard to the needs of developing countries. As such, the Appellate Body presently interprets the preamble connection to 1992 UNCED and the 1992 Rio Conference outcomes.

This reasoning was adopted and applied in subsequent WTO Panel and Appellate Body reports related to the *U.S.–Shrimp Case*, when Malaysia took recourse to Article 21.5 of the WTO Dispute Settlement Understanding,[24] arguing that the measures taken by the U.S. did not comply with the recommendations and rulings of the DSB. In particular, the Panel stated that: "In that framework, assessing first the *object and purpose* of the WTO Agreement, we note that the WTO preamble refers to the notion of "sustainable development."[25] This means that in interpreting the terms of the chapeau, we must keep in mind that sustainable development is one of the objectives of the WTO Agreement.[26] On appeal, this interpretation was not overturned by the WTO Appellate Body.[27]

The *E.U.–Tariff Preferences Case*[28] concerned the scheme of generalized tariff preferences for developing countries. India complained that special preferences based on certain drug arrangements adopted by beneficiary countries were inconsistent with the most favored nation clause (Article 1.1 GATT 1994) and could not be justified under the *Decision on Differential and More Favourable Treatment, Reciprocity, and Fuller Participation of Developing Countries* (the "Enabling Clause").[29] Similar provisions exist for environmental and labor rights, but in the end these were not challenged. The panel found that the E.U.'s scheme was indeed inconsistent with Article 1.1 GATT and could not be justified under the enabling clause. This was because developed countries were compelled to grant identical tariff preferences under GSP schemes to all developing countries without differentiation and the panel found that it should apply to all developing countries. The Appellate Body reversed these last two findings but concluded that the drug criteria due to a closed list of beneficiary countries and unclear criteria for the selection of these countries were not covered by the exception.

The E.U. argued that because the Enabling Clause was designed to fulfill the objectives of the WTO, it should not be interpreted as an exception to Article 1.1 GATT but rather as an incentive for developed countries to confer preferences on their less developed counterparts.[30] The Appellate Body considered this argument and agreed with the initial observation. Indeed, it overturned one of the panel's findings – interpreting non-discrimination according to the objectives of the GATT and the WTO – and accepting that the differentiation between developing countries according to their needs was possible. The Appellate Body, citing its *U.S.–Shrimp* decision, found that the objectives of the WTO could be fulfilled through "General Exceptions." They noted in particular that "the optimal use of the world's resources in accordance with the objective of

sustainable development" could be achieved through application of the WTO exceptions, such as Article XX (g) GATT.

However, the Panel in the same case found that the E.U. could not justify its drug arrangements under Article XX (b) GATT, because it could not prove that its system was designed to protect human health in the European Union. Rather the panel agreed with India's argument that increased market access was intended to contribute to sustainable development of the beneficiary countries. As the fight against illicit drug production and exports were deemed to be part of a broader sustainable development objective (as confirmed by several multilateral instruments and the official justification to the Regulation setting up the E.U. System), these could not be justified as a measure which only sought to benefit the E.U. This decision demonstrates that both the "environmental" and the "development" aspects (including health) are part of the concept of sustainable development that the WTO dispute settlement body recognizes as a WTO objective.

The most recent decision in *Brazil–Retreaded Tires* is unique in that it was the first decision where a developing country invoked Art. XX GATT against a challenge by an industrialized country, in this case the European Union.[31] Brazil banned the import of retreated tires arguing that the large quantities of retreaded tires imported from the E.U. created environmental problems including dangers associated with mosquitoes that breed in tires and tires catching fire. The E.U. argued that Brazil had not shown that the ban on retreaded tires was necessary to protect human health. The panel cited the *U.S.–Shrimp* Appellate Body decision and the overall importance of the goal of sustainable development and interpreted Brazil's reference to environmental protection as meaning the protection of human, animal or plant life, or health (Art. XX (b) GATT).

The E.U. as one of the main exporters of used tires (they are very hard to sell in Europe) requested formal consultations in June

2005.[32] Shortly after the E.U. launched formal consultation Brazil raised the issue and justified its actions in the Committee on Trade and Environment: "Moreover, in order to achieve the cited objectives, and in harmony with the widely accepted *principle of sustainable development* – included in the preamble of the WTO Agreement – Brazil banned imports of used and retreaded tires"[33] (emphasis added). This submission can be considered an interesting choice of words, because previously only developed countries had sought to invoke a legally binding principle of sustainable development.

Among other legal issues the *Brazil–Retreaded Tires* case centered on a discussion of Art. XX GATT, particularly the exceptions that Brazil allowed for retreaded tires from Mercosur countries and due to court orders to the benefit of retreading companies. The panel found that the measure generally fulfilled Art. XX (b) GATT to protect animal, plant and human life, or health but constituted a disguised restriction on international trade and was thus not justified under Art. XX GATT.

It further emphasized the importance of the Preamble to the WTO Agreement: "The objective pursued is also the protection of *animal and plant life and health*. The risks at issue relate to: (i) the exposure of animals and plants to toxic emissions caused by tire fires; and (ii) the transmission of a mosquito-borne disease (dengue) to animals. The Panel acknowledges that the preservation of animal and plant life and health, which constitutes an essential part of the protection of the environment, is an important value, recognized in the WTO Agreement. The Panel recalls that in *U.S.–Shrimp*,[34] the Appellate Body underlined that the preamble of the Marrakesh Agreement establishing the WTO showed that the signatories to that Agreement were, in 1994, fully aware of the importance and legitimacy of environmental protection as a goal of national and international policy.[35] Therefore, the Panel finds that the objective of protection of animal and plant life and health

should also be considered important."[36] Interesting here is again the footnote which makes first reference to other WTO disputes and then to international documents related to sustainable development, even with specific relevance for the waste problem at hand, and then finally refers to the citation of the document by the opposing party, here the E.U. This use of the preamble is arguably further reaching than in other decisions and it suggests that the Doha negotiations might have influenced the importance that the panel attaches to the objective of sustainable development.

The Appellate Body upheld the panel's conclusion on the applicability of Art. XX (b) GATT. It added:

We recognize that certain complex public health or environmental problems may be tackled only with a comprehensive policy comprising a multiplicity of interacting measures. In the short-term, it may prove difficult to isolate the contribution to public health or environmental objectives of one specific measure from those attributable to the other measures that are part of the same comprehensive policy. Moreover, the results obtained from certain actions – for instance, measures adopted in order to attenuate global warming and climate change, or certain preventive actions to reduce the incidence of diseases that may manifest themselves only after a certain period of time – can only be evaluated with the benefit of time. In order to justify an import ban under Article XX(b), a panel must be satisfied that it brings about a material contribution to the achievement of its objective. Such a demonstration can of course be made by resorting to evidence or data, pertaining to the past or the present, that establish that the import ban at issue makes a material contribution to the protection of public health or environmental objectives pursued. This is not, however, the only type of demonstration that could establish such a contribution. Thus, a panel might conclude that an import ban is necessary on the basis of a demonstration that the import ban at issue is apt to produce a material contribution to the achievement of its objective. This demonstration could consist of quantitative projections in the future, or qualitative reasoning based on a set of hypotheses that are tested and supported by sufficient evidence.[37]

While Brazil was not ultimately successful, in this case the Appellate Body underscored the long-term sustainability of a measure adopted by the parties and vis à vis the *E.U.–Asbestos* decision further lowered the burden of proof in environmental cases.

The reasoning of the WTO dispute settlement body in these cases, taken together, demonstrates that the objective of sustainable development has become an integral part of the world trading system. Legal arguments encompassing an integrated developmental and environmental approach have been made by the parties and accepted by the relevant dispute settlement organs. On the one hand, it is clear that the panels and the Appellate Body will not accept sustainable development as a trump card. It cannot simply be invoked in order to justify non-compliance with established WTO disciplines. A solid legal understanding of the objective and its underlying principles, as well as the appropriate application of specific facts of each case embedded in a reasoned legal argument is required to make a successful sustainable development argument in world trade law.

New instruments in trade law for sustainable development

A highly practical example of the integration of economic, social, and environmental concerns is found in the increasing use of impact assessment tools in the international arena.[38] Impact assessments operate as a formalized consideration of the wider effects of particular policies (usually trade policies or development projects), and aim to ensure that trade and development decisions result from processes that promote sustainability and public participation. These tools come in various forms, ranging in scope from environmental impact assessments and human rights impact assessments to the broadest tool, sustainability impact assessments. Although it remains unusual for any national development decision or regional or bilateral trade agreement to require some form of impact assessment, the European Union, the United States and Canada have all adopted the tool to some degree to be used either before or after the decision or agreement has been concluded. Others such as New Zealand and Japan are considering similar steps.

At the international level, certain environmental treaties contain obligations to perform environmental impact assessments in situations where one country's activity may flow across a border or when areas of common concern, such as the high seas[39] or the Antarctic,[40] are involved. The application of such instruments to trade agreements is relatively new, but developing rapidly, and in some instances the assessments include a regulatory dimension.

In Canada, the Framework for Conducting Environmental Assessments of Trade Negotiations[41] has been used since 2001 to conduct environmental assessments of new bilateral and regional trade negotiations, and since 2005 this has also been applied to investment agreements. The assessments seek to assist Canadian negotiators in integrating environmental considerations into the negotiating process (as envisaged by the Doha Development Agenda), and to address public concerns. The framework includes provisions for actively seeking public input into assessments from non-governmental organizations, businesses, indigenous peoples and the general public. Similarly, the Office of the U.S. Trade Representative has conducted environmental reviews of all bilateral and regional trade agreements signed by the United States since 1999, in which regulatory impacts, public advice and potential impacts in the territory of the proposed new trading partner are taken seriously and addressed.[42] Developing countries have, in some cases, also found such assessments useful for economic policy making. For instance, as discussed by the International Institute for Sustainable Development, Senegal recently found that stocks of certain species of fish with high market values were being seriously depleted through the use of trade impact assessment.[43]

Sustainability impact assessments are more complex, innovative studies which take economic, environmental and social impacts into account to provide a complete picture of the expected effects of a trade policy or project. They include target-related indicators, which attempt to measure sustainability against a set of defined goals, and process-related indicators, which are based on the principle that the process itself by which policies and decisions are adopted plays a substantial role in achieving sustainable development goals. Indicators of sustainability used in the assessments fall into three categories:

- economic indicators, including average real income, fixed capital formation and employment rates
- social indicators, including poverty rates, health and education levels and equity
- environmental indicators, including air and water quality indicators, biological diversity and natural resources.[44]

Sustainability impact assessments are mostly in use within the European Union, which developed a framework for analysis in 1999. This framework has since been applied to the WTO Doha Round negotiations and EU bilateral and regional trade agreements with Chile, Mercosur, the African–Caribbean–Pacific nations and the Gulf Cooperation Council nations. EU sustainability impact assessments place significant emphasis on consultation both within EU member states and in the third country trade partners. The assessments themselves are conducted by independent experts commissioned by the

European Union, which then receives a response paper from the European Commission. All results are made public.

Sustainable development in the Doha development agenda

During the Seattle negotiations several countries made sustainable development related submissions and the public spotlight focused on the trade and environment and the trade and development debates. The successful conclusion of the Doha Ministerial Declaration resonated in some ways with these submissions and discussions. Ministers agreed in Para. 6 of the Ministerial Declaration:

> We strongly reaffirm our commitment to the objective of sustainable development, as stated in the Preamble to the Marrakesh Agreement. We are convinced that the aims of upholding and safeguarding an open and non-discriminatory multilateral trading system, and acting for the protection of the environment and the promotion of sustainable development can and must be mutually supportive. We take note of the efforts by Members to conduct national environmental assessments of trade policies on a voluntary basis. We recognize that under WTO rules, no country should be prevented from taking measures for the protection of human, animal or plant life or health, or of the environment at the levels it considers appropriate, subject to the requirement that they are not applied in a manner which would constitute a means of arbitrary or unjustifiable discrimination between countries where the same conditions prevail, or a disguised restriction on international trade, and are otherwise in accordance with the provisions of the WTO Agreements. We welcome the WTO's continued cooperation with UNEP and other inter-governmental environmental organizations. We encourage efforts to promote cooperation between the WTO and relevant international environmental and developmental organizations,

especially in the lead-up to the World Summit on Sustainable Development to be held in Johannesburg, South Africa, in September 2002.[45]

As is clear from this excerpt, the DDA was intended to be informed by sustainable development objectives. Ministers recognized sustainable development as a fundamental goal of the WTO, and placed it into a strengthened context, referring to practical measures such as the need for cooperation with other international environment *and development* organizations in the lead-up to the WSSD. From the macro perspective, the Doha Declaration provides an indication that sustainable development objectives are starting to be understood as involving both environmental and social development actors and organizations. There are indications that states may be prepared to move away from the traditional "trade-only" or "trade and environment only" approach. While expectations for a sustainable development infused WTO should be hedged because of recalcitrant powerful members, coherence between the preamble and the Appellate Body's balanced and integrated definition is legally compelling.[46] References to this objective in the Doha Ministerial Declaration clearly recognize environmental protection and social development aspects to be part of the mandate of a mainly economic organization.

Indeed, the ministers went further, and sought to operationalize the sustainable development goal for the WTO itself. At paragraph 51, a mechanism was created to ensure that this objective would be translated into concrete action.[47] In the organization and management of the work program section of the Declaration, WTO member governments agreed that: "[T]he Committee on Trade and Development and the Committee on Trade and Environment shall, within their respective mandates, each act as a forum to identify and debate developmental and environmental aspects of the negotiations, in order to help achieve the objective of hav-

ing sustainable development appropriately reflected."[48] The initial proposal by Canada, that the Committee on Trade and Environment should debate the environmental aspects of the expected Seattle negotiations, was broadened to include the Committee on Trade and Development.[49] It is unclear whether these two committees will be able to fulfill their mandates to identify and debate environmental and development aspects of the negotiations in addition to helping to ensure that sustainable development can be appropriately reflected in the trade negotiations.

The WTO clearly considers itself bound by its commitment to sustainable development as an objective, and arguably, may also be influenced by sustainable development in its role as an "interstitial norm" in public international law. As such, the outcomes of trade negotiations may present opportunities to modify certain trade rules in order to ensure that they can better support sustainable development. Many caveats remain and these have become doubly apparent in subsequent Doha Round negotiations in Cancun and Hong Kong. At first there were high initial expectations as it was widely understood that the agenda underpinning the DDA was intended to place development priorities at the very heart of the new negotiations. However, in spite of recent Appellate Body and WTO statements on the importance of delivering on the development promises of world trade, and of ensuring that trade law contributes to the objective of sustainable development, the process has been inconsistent and repeatedly obstructed. While developing countries have made great efforts to ensure that their voices and interests are heard and taken into account, there has been little tangible advancement on important development issues. Similarly, progress has been scant in constructively addressing overlaps between trade and human rights questions or trade and environment questions, in a way that seamlessly integrates development interests.

Conclusion

The norm development is not concluded – the content of the concept of sustainable development itself is still contested. Furthermore, while members of the WTO may now be bound by a particular reading of sustainable development objectives at the global level, this may not mean they feel obliged to develop "sustainable" trade laws or policies either internally, or in their further bilateral and regional trade treaties with other countries (see Gehring and Cordonier Segger 2005). According to the letter of international trade law, all countries are free to choose their own economic system and trade policies. However, where "discrimination" is alleged, clashes with principles of the WTO will ultimately result in binding dispute settlement procedures for its members. To ensure that international trade law can deliver on sustainable development in the current context, a constructive, integrated approach is needed to address overlaps between social development, economic development and environmental protection. This approach will be important to ensure more coherent – and lasting – world trade law.

[Author note: This chapter shares thoughts with the Introduction of *Sustainable Development in World Trade Law* edited by Markus Gehring, and Marie-Claire Cordonier Segger (2005) and with *World Trade Law in Practice* by Markus Gehring, Jarrod Hepburn, and Marie-Claire Cordonier Segger (2007).]

Notes

1 "Johannesburg Declaration on Sustainable Development and Johannesburg Plan of Implementation", in Report of the World Summit on Sustainable Development (September 4, 2002) U.N. Doc A/CONF.199/L20 [45].

2 See Marrakesh Agreement Establishing the World Trade Organization (signed April 15, 1994, entered into force January 1, 1995) 1867

UNTS 4, 33 ILM 1144, Preamble; which recognizes that among WTO members: "Relations in the field of trade and economic endeavour should be conducted with a view to raising standards of living, ensuring full employment and a large and steadily growing volume of real income and effective demand, and expanding the production of and trade in goods and services, while allowing for the optimal use of the world's resources in accordance with the objective of sustainable development, seeking both to protect and preserve the environment and to enhance the means for doing so in a manner consistent with their respective needs and concerns at different levels of economic development . . . *Recognizing* further that there is need for positive efforts designed to ensure that developing countries, and especially the least developed among them, secure a share in the growth in international trade commensurate with the needs of their economic development." See also WTO, *United States: Import Prohibition of Certain Shrimp and Shrimp Products Sector–Report of the Appellate Body* (September 20, 1999) WT/DS58/AB/R [129] n 107; where the WTO Appellate Body observes that the Preamble to the WTO Agreement specifically refers to "the objective of sustainable development" and characterizes it as a concept that has "been generally accepted as integrating economic and social development and environmental protection."

3 Integration as part of the concept of sustainable development has mainly been proposed in trade policy discussions by the demand to "[e]nsure that environment and trade policies are mutually supportive, with a view to achieving sustainable development." "Agenda 21 (Annex 2)" in Report of the U.N. Conference on Environment and Development Vol. I (June 13, 1992) U.N. Doc A/CONF.151/26 (Vol. I); 31 ILM 874 [2.10].

4 See "Permanent Sovereignty over Natural Resources" UNGA Res 1803 (XVII) (December 14, 1962) U.N. Doc A/Res/1803 (XVII).

5 Among the outcomes of the UNCED were three international treaties (on climate change, biological diversity, and, a little later, desertification and drought) which recognized both environmental and sustainable development objectives, as well as the non-binding 1992 Rio Declaration and Agenda 21, which were adopted by governments. See "Rio Declaration on Environment and Develop-

ment (Annex 2)", Report of the U.N. Conference on Environment and Development Vol. I (June 13, 1992) U.N. Doc A/CONF.151/26 (Vol. I), (1992) 31 ILM 874; Agenda 21 (n 3).

6 Agenda 21 (n 6) [2.19] stated that: "Environment and trade policies should be mutually supportive. An open, multilateral trading system makes possible a more efficient allocation and use of resources and thereby contributes to an increase in production and incomes and to lessening demands on the environment. It thus provides additional resources needed for economic growth and development and improved environmental protection. A sound environment, on the other hand, provides the ecological and other resources needed to sustain growth and underpin a continuing expansion of trade. An open, multilateral trading system, supported by the adoption of sound environmental policies, would have a positive impact on the environment and contribute to sustainable development."

7 Marrakesh Agreement (n 2) Preamble.

8 In general international law the preamble is part of the context in which the international treaty has to be interpreted; see Vienna Convention on the Law of Treaties (singed May 23, 1969, entered into force January 27, 1980) 1155 UNTS 331, 8 ILM 679, art 31; "General rule of interpretation at 1. A treaty shall be interpreted in good faith in accordance with the ordinary meaning to be given to the terms of the treaty in their context and in the light of its object and purpose. 2. The context for the purpose of the interpretation of a treaty shall comprise, in addition to the text, including its preamble and annexes." The preamble can contain important information about the object and purpose of the treaty.

9 Please note that the ministerial declarations are generally political statements and not legally binding on members. An exception is the decision to engage in trade negotiations. If negotiations are commissioned the ministerial declaration acquires quasi legal status, because each formulation constitutes a negotiation mandate and sets the limitations of these negotiations. Nonetheless, ministerial declarations are adopted unanimously and reflect the political opinion of the overall development of the organization.

10 Singapore Ministerial Declaration (December 18, 1996) WT/MIN(96)/DEC, 36 ILM 218. Available at http://www.wto.org/english/thewto_e/minist_e/min96_e/singapore_declaration96_e.pdf.

11 Geneva Ministerial Declaration (20 May 1998) WT/MIN(98)/DEC/1. Available at http://docsonline.wto.org.

12 For example, large trading countries such as Germany amended their Constitutions to include the goal of sustainable development, see Grundgesetz für die Bundesrepublik Deutschland (German Constitution) art 20; and trading regions such as the European Union had accepted sustainable development as an objective of their integration, see Treaty of Amsterdam Amending the Treaty on European Union (signed October 2, 1997, entered into force May 1, 1999) [1997] OJ C 340/1, art 2. Available at http://www.europarl.europa.eu/topics/treaty/pdf/amsten.pdf; see also the outcomes of the Summit of the Americas on Sustainable Development, Declaration of Santa Cruz de la Sierra (adopted December 7, 1996). Available at http://www.summit-americas.org/Boliviadec.htm; as discussed generally in Cordonier Segger and Leichner Reynal 2005.

13 See WTO, *United States: Import Prohibition of Certain Shrimp and Shrimp Products Sector–Panel Report* (15 May 1998) WT/DS58/R; see also *United States: Shrimp–Appellate Body Report* (n 2).

14 WTO, *European Communities: Conditions for the Granting of Tariff Preferences to Developing Countries–Appellate Body Report* (20 April 2004) WT/DS246/AB/R.

15 WTO, *Brazil: Measures affecting Imports of Retreaded Tires–Panel Report* (June 12, 2007) WT/DS332/R.

16 *United States: Shrimp–Appellate Body Report* (n 2) [12].

17 Ibid. n 107; in the Appellate Body Report, reads: "This concept has been generally accepted as integrating economic and social development and environmental protection. See, e.g. Handl 1995: 35.

18 *United States: Shrimp–Appellate Body Report* (n 2) [123].

19 *United States: Shrimp–Appellate Body Report* (n 2) [153].

20 Ministerial Decision on Trade and Environment (April 15, 1994) LT/UR/D-5/8, 33 ILM 1267, preamble http://docsonline.wto.org.

21 We note that Principle 3 of the Rio Declaration on Environment and Development states: "The right to development must be fulfilled so as to equitably meet developmental and environmental needs of present and future generations." Principle 4 of the Rio Declaration on Environment and Development states that: "In order to achieve sustain-

able development, environmental protection shall constitute an integral part of the development process and cannot be considered in isolation from it."

22 Agenda 21 is replete with references to the shared view that economic development and the preservation and protection should be mutually supportive. For example, paragraph 2.3(b) of Agenda 21 states: "The international economy should provide a supportive international climate for achieving environment and development goals by . . . [m]aking trade and environment mutually supportive." Similarly, paragraph 2.9(d) states that an "objective" of governments should be: "To promote and support policies, domestic and international, that make economic growth and environmental protection mutually supportive."

23 Ministerial Decision on Trade and Environment (n 20).

24 WTO, *United States: Import Prohibition of Certain Shrimp and Shrimp Products Sector– Recourse by Malaysia to Article 21.5 of the DSU* (October 13, 2000) WT/DS58/17.

25 In the Panel Report, this citation reads: "*See the final texts of the agreements negotiated by Governments at the United Nation Conference on Environment and Development (UNCED), Rio de Janeiro, Brazil, June 3–14, 1992, specifically the Rio Declaration on Environment and Development (hereafter the "Rio Declaration") and Agenda 21* at www.unep.org; the concept is elaborated in detailed action plans in Agenda 21 so as to put in place development that is sustainable – i.e. that "meets the needs of the present generation without compromising the ability of future generations to meet their own needs"; see World Commission on Environment and Development (n 13).

26 WTO, *United States: Import Prohibition of Certain Shrimp and Shrimp Products Sector, Recourse to Article 21.5 by Malaysia–Panel Report* (June 15, 2001) WT/DS58/RW.

27 WTO, *United States: Import Prohibition of Certain Shrimp and Shrimp Products Sector, Recourse to Article 21.5 by Malaysia–Report of the Appellate Body* (October 22, 2001) WT/DS58/AB/RW.

28 WTO, *European Communities: conditions for the Granting of Tariff Preferences to Developing Countries* – Appellate Body Report (20 April 2004) WT/DS246/AB/R.

29 Differential and More Favourable Treatment Reciprocity and Fuller Participation of Developing Countries (November 28, 1979) L/4903, BISD 26S/203.

30 Ibid. [93]; interestingly a similar argument was made by one dissenting panel member in the panel case.

31 WTO, *Brazil: Measures affecting Imports of Retreaded Tires–Panel Report* (June 12, 2007) WT/DS332/R.

32 On June 20, 2005, the European Communities requested consultations with Brazil under Article XXII:1 of the General Agreement on Tariffs and Trade 1994 (the "GATT 1994") and Article 4 of the Understanding on Rules and Procedures Governing the Settlement of Disputes (the "DSU") regarding Brazil's imposition of measures that adversely affect exports of retreated tires from the European Communities to the Brazilian market.

33 Committee on Trade and Environment, *Trade in Used and Retreaded Tires– Submission by Brazil* (July 12, 2005) WT/CTE/W/241; see also Committee on Trade and Environment, *Report of the Meeting held on 6 July 2005* (September 2, 2005) WT/CTE/M/40 [82].

34 *United States: Shrimp–Appellate Body Report* (n 2) [129].

35 The preamble of the Marrakech Agreement establishing the WTO reads in its relevant part: "Recognizing that their relations in the field of trade and economic endeavor should be conducted with a view to raising standards of living, ensuring full employment and a large and steadily growing volume of real income and effective demand, and expanding the production of and trade in goods and services, *while allowing for the optimal use of the world's resources in accordance with the objective of sustainable development, seeking both to protect and preserve the environment* and to enhance the means for doing so in a manner consistent with their respective needs and concerns at different levels of economic development" (emphasis added). Moreover, in the 1994 Ministerial Decision on Trade and Environment, Ministers took note, *inter alia*, of the Rio Declaration on Environment and Development and Agenda 21. Of particular relevance is paragraph 4.19 of Agenda 21, which states, in part: "Society needs to develop effective ways of dealing with the problem of disposing of mounting levels of waste products and materials. Governments, together with industry, households and the public, should make a concerted effort to reduce the generation of wastes and waste products." The European Communities referred to the Rio Declaration and Agenda 21 in its response to question 37 by the Panel and in paragraph 138 of its first written submission.

36 *Brazil: Tires–Panel Report* (n 31) [7.112].
37 WTO, *Brazil: Measures affecting Imports of Retreaded Tires–Report of the Appellate Body* (December 3, 2007) WT/DS332/AB/R [151].
38 For details, see Gehring 2007; Gehring et al. 2007: 131.
39 United Nations Convention on the Law of the Sea (signed December 10, 1982, entry into force November 16, 1994) 1833 UNTS 396, 21 ILM 1245.
40 Protocol on Environmental Protection to the Antarctic Treaty (opened for signature October 4, 1991, entry into force January 14, 1998) 30 ILM 1461.
41 Department of Foreign Affairs and International Trade Canada, "Framework for Conducting Environmental Assessments of Trade Negotiations" http://www.international.gc.ca/trade-agreements-accords-commerciaux/ds/Environment.aspx.
42 Office of the United States Trade Representative, "Environmental Reviews in FTAs" www.ustr.gov/Trade_Sectors/Environment/Environmental_Reviews/Section_Index.html.
43 International Institute for Sustainable Development, *Environment and Trade: A Handbook* (2nd edn, UNEP, Geneva 2005): 112. Available at http://www.iisd.org/pdf/2005/envirotrade_handbook_2005.pdf.
44 European Commission, *Sustainability Impact Assessment*. Available at http://ec.europa.eu/comm/trade/issues/global/sia/index_en.htm.
45 Doha Ministerial Declaration (November 14, 2001) WT/MIN(01)/DEC/1. http://www.wto.org/english/thewto_e/minist_e/min96_e/singapore_declaration96_e.pdf.
46 See Seattle Proposals (all made *after* the Appellate Body's *U.S.–Shrimp* decision discussed earlier).
47 Doha Ministerial Declaration (n 45) [51]; this section of the Ministerial Declaration is binding for the negotiations.
48 Ibid.
49 Ibid. 3.

391

27

Looking ahead: international law's main challenges

Andrea Bianchi

This concluding chapter identifies several major challenges – or opportunities – faced by international law in the near future. These are the fight for inclusion as subjects with international legal personality by non-state actors, the need for suitable processes of lawmaking, the shifting boundaries of normativity, and associated questions about whether interstitial norms or soft law fully qualify as legal norms, the continuing problems raised by the absence in international law of the same kinds of enforcement mechanisms as may be found in domestic law, developments in the area of accountability mechanisms, including those applying to individuals and transnational corporations, whether the increasing complexity, specialization, and judicial fragmentation of international law place the system under strain or may be seen as a sign of maturity, and, finally, the similar questions raised by the fragmentation of theoretical discourse in international law.

Introduction

Short of a crystal ball, officially approved by Hogwarts,[1] nobody is really in a position to credibly predict the future of international law. Speculations are all the more risky at a time of increasing perplexity about the utility of the discipline for the understanding of inter-

national relations (Goldsmith and Posner 2005). In contrast, other members of the same profession have recently celebrated the entry of international law into its "post-ontological era" (Franck 1995: 6). Such shifting perceptions should not divert attention from the significant changes undergone by international law of late. It would be simplistic, and even erroneous, to presuppose that such changes are primarily due to the contingencies of international politics.

In fact, it is rather the structure and the changing demands of the societal body that have dramatically affected our understanding of international law and how it functions. The very idea of the international community has changed. The transformation of the international community "in potency" into the international community "in actuality" (de Visscher 1970: 123), could well be an accurate representation of the many achievements of international law in the 1990s: the decade of the materialization of international criminal justice and the world trading system, among other things. The proliferation of actors on the scene is also worth noting, together with the difficulty of accommodating them into a still predominantly state-centered system.

If to predict what lies ahead for international law pertains to the art of clairvoyance, to highlight its main future challenges appears a more feasible, if less reassuring task. The problem with challenges is that one does not know in advance whether they will be met and, if so, how. And yet, to investigate such challenges and societal changes is also a way of directing the development of international law. If law and its underlying societal structure are closely intertwined, the way in which we think of the law, and what the law is, are indissolubly linked as the law has no tangible existence, distinct from our way of conceiving of it. This is why by highlighting the challenges awaiting international law, one inevitably unveils his own view of what international law is as well as his sense (or wish) of where international law is heading.

The fight for inclusion: non-state actors' claims

The traditional positivistic approach to international law provided a neat theory of the subjects of international law, whereby a limited number of entities, primarily states, would be the bearers of international rights and responsibilities. The concept of international legal personality was used to describe those entities that "the legal system has cast to appear on the stage of the law" (Cheng 1991: 24). As the etymology of the words suggests, only those *personae* that played a direct role in the legal system could appear on stage, regardless of the other entities which might participate in the production of the play. The latter would be of interest to sociologists and political scientists but were irrelevant to legal analysis. The question "Who is the subject?" found an obvious answer in a strongly state-centered system, where states had the monopoly of law-making, law adjudication and law enforcement processes (Weil 1992: 122). In a somewhat tautological fashion, "indices" of the legal personality of entities at international law were traced to the capacity of certain entities to perform such functions as to exchange diplomatic missions

or to conclude treaties, which were all typical states' prerogatives (Cheng 1991: 38). Anomalies could always be accommodated and their marginal character posed no systemic threat (Arangio-Ruiz 1996). Over time, legal personality reached out to international organizations, in many ways a direct emanation of states, and the International Court of Justice Advisory Opinion on the *Reparation for Injuries* case paved the way for relativizing the doctrine of subjects and adjusting it to the new demands of the international community.[2]

Although mainstream scholarship still tends to reason in terms of "subjects" and international legal personality, the term "actor" borrowed from the language of political science has made its way into the common parlance of international lawyers. From the standpoint of theory, however, non-state actors have drawn little attention. The reluctance of international lawyers to provide a theoretical systematization to the doctrine of actors is nonetheless understandable. In fact, this is an issue that lies at the interface of theory and practice, law and policy and the stance one takes in relation to it is likely to have repercussions on such other systemic issues as law making and law enforcement. To use Jan Klabbers' words "subjects doctrine forms the clearing house between sources and substance: it is through subjects doctrine that the international allocation of values takes place, and as any political scientist knows, the authoritative allocation of values is one of the main political functions" (Klabbers 2003: 369).

Conceptual thinking about non-state actors poses numerous challenges. As regards terminology, one may wonder whether the term has merely a descriptive connotation, which is used to encompass those actors that are not states, or, whether, it refers, in a prescriptive fashion, to a particular status, recognized by the international legal order, to which specific legal connotations are attached. In fact, despite the increasing use of "non-state actors" as a term of art, no systematization seems to have been made in the literature which could satisfactorily account for, from the theoretical perspective, the role played by non-state actors in contemporary international law.

Henceforth, the doctrine of subjects has resisted any attempt at revision and remains as a cornerstone of positivistic legal analysis. Most textbooks and treaties still contain a section on the subjects of international law and the unity of the system is preserved by denying the existence of new scientific paradigms and schools of thought that, in the meantime, have done away with traditional theory and have proposed frameworks of analysis based on entirely different tenets. The merit of sociological approaches to international law is to have highlighted that the social fabric and structure of the international legal system, on the one hand, and its subjects/actors, on the other, are "mutually constitutive". Constructivist theories, elaborated in the field of international relations, have shown that the interaction among different actors constitutes the structure of the system, and that the latter shapes the identity, interests and expectations of the actors in a mutual process of influence (Arend 1998: 129; Mertus 1999–2000).

When and how the terminology of actors and/or participants made its way into international law is subject to controversy. Certainly, Rosalyn Higgins' critique of the old theory of subjects, and its advocacy of the notion of participants in international decision-making processes has greatly contributed to giving legitimacy to this new terminology. The argument that by construing the reality of international law in terms of "subjects" and "objects," "[w]e have erected an intellectual prison of our own choosing and then declared it to be an unalterable constraint" (Higgins 1994: 49) carries much force, particularly because the distinction does not seem to serve any particular functional purpose. This, however, is unlikely to convince the positivist who would rebut, not without reason, that the doctrine of sovereign

equality and the doctrine of subjects are constitutive fictions that require "acceptance if the whole edifice of the international legal system is not to be called into question" (Dupuy 2003a: 179). The point is well taken, insofar as it highlights that the way in which one conceives of international law inevitably reflects on the way in which such fundamental questions as "who makes the law" and "who is the subject of the law" are answered. In fact, to conceive of international law as a body of rules in a community of states or as a legal process in a community where "there are a variety of participants, making claims across state lines, with the object of maximizing various values" (Higgins 1994: 50) is not the same thing, and the use of a different terminology hardly hides a fundamental difference in thinking of the international legal system. The state of disarray in which the doctrine of subjects/actors seems to be is further attested by the attempt to pull together such different visions with a view to reconciling them.

Many commentators have highlighted the unsuitability of the doctrine of subjects in providing an accurate representation of the current realities. Emphasis has been placed on the changing societal structures of the international community and the need to develop new conceptual tools that adequately account for them. The inadequacy of the doctrine of subjects has been underscored by numerous authors. Key to any such critique is the acknowledgment that the changing social structure of the international community must be adequately accounted for, and that new conceptual tools are required. The solipsistic vision of state sovereignty as the quintessential element of the international community of states must give way to a contemporary assessment of the social forces that structure a wider community whose members have "values, identities and roles distinct from the geographic limitations of states" (McCorquodale 2006: 149). "The logic of the liberal representative state and consent-based notions of international law"

(Cutler 2001: 150) do not allow for a reconsideration of the state as the only subject of the international legal system, thus causing a "disjunction between theory and practice which is conducive to a legitimacy crisis" (Cutler 2001: 147 ff.). As is well known, despite Franck's effort to introduce legitimacy into the vocabulary of international law (Franck 1990), the term makes positivist lawyers diffident by their incapacity to attach to it sufficiently precise legal connotations. In this context, however, its meaning is self-evident. If the participants in international legal processes fail to see their social practices reflected in the law, the latter's claim to authority will be undermined (Cutler 2001: 147).

Whether the solution lies in relativizing the subjects, or rather, in subjectivizing the actors, remains open to doubt (Bianchi 2009). The constant swing of the pendulum from the normative to the descriptive mesmerizes the observer and makes him wonder whether the observed reality can provide the answers he is looking for. In fact, the disjunction between theory and practice and the strain between the different ways of looking at the same reality is a symptom of a more general disease affecting international law. The "politics of forms" (Schlag 1991: 1742) has long exhausted its ordering function and has been supplanted by a panoply of narratives that tell different stories about the same reality. If one acknowledges that international law has changed dramatically in the past few decades, the need to reformulate some of its foundational tenets seems an obvious solution. The contemporary international community, which provides the terrain on which the game of international law is played, is no longer perceived as consisting solely of states and, inevitably, the inclusion/exclusion mode with which the traditional theory of subjects has been set and used in a restrictive fashion to preserve the integrity of the system, needs to be reconsidered. An alternative conceptual framework has not been created and the language of other disciplines has been borrowed to provide a temporary accommodation. That the participants need "legitimacy" and must be made "accountable" is an expression which would mean little to many positivist lawyers and yet seems to have become part and parcel of the fabric of international law.

International law has proved many times to be flexible enough to adjust to change. In many ways, it is and will most likely remain a "pragmatic project," which tends to accommodate societal and normative developments in a pragmatic fashion. It may very well be that the attempt to distinguish between subjects and actors hardly meets any functional purpose. It would be simplistic, however, to think that terminology is neutral and that its underlying conceptual categories may even handedly serve different purposes. In fact, as Alston rightly noted, the "negative and euphemistic term" of non-state actors may not "stem from any language inadequacies" but may have been adopted "to reinforce the assumption that the state is not only the central actor, but also the indispensable and pivotal one around which all other entities revolve" (Alston 2005: 3). The doctrinal debate on subjects/actors fails to conceal the power struggle for recognition as a legitimate participant in international law processes. Inevitably, time will tell us who has won the battle for inclusion.

Law making and the need for general law

The most compelling challenge in the area of law making seems to be the lack of suitable mechanisms of general law making. On the one hand, when a prompt normative response is required there does not appear to be an adequate general law-making mechanism (Bianchi 2004: 515–18). Multilateral treaty making is a lengthy and cumbersome procedure. Ultimately, its capacity to become general law depends on the number of states that will ratify the relevant treaty.

In a community of nearly 200 states, the efficacy of a multilateral treaty appears as a daunting task, let alone the lapse of time required to have states duly ratify the treaty according to their domestic constitutional arrangements. Along similar lines, customary law making – at least as traditionally understood – is incapable of producing rules of general applicability when prompt action is required. No matter which particular theory of custom one adheres to, some generality of practice and *opinio juris* needs to be established. This is the reason why whenever a particular situation demands urgent regulation alternative mechanisms are required. The U.N. Security Council has recently gone well beyond the express powers originally conferred to it by the Charter when it has acted in a quasi-legislative capacity, imposing general obligations on the member states under Chapter VII of the Charter, although responding to a demand of the societal body (Bianchi 2006a: 889). Rightly or wrongly, in terms of legality and conformity with the letter of the Charter, there was a widespread perception among states that international terrorism required a prompt normative response at the general level. In fact, the Security Council was the only body that could produce such a prompt response in legally binding terms, by providing a broad and expanded reading of its powers to act to maintain or restore international peace and security. It is of some significance that neither the General Assembly, nor states individually, voiced any strong objection at the time of enactment of resolution 1373. Subsequent attempts by the Council to act as lawmaker have met with some opposition and qualifications appended by several states to their approval of resolution 1540. Whatever hubris one reproaches the SC for, its attempt to produce general law is also a way of making up for a lacuna in general international law making.

Yet another challenge lies in the attempt to revisit the process of customary law making. The much debated issue of how customary law rules come into being ought to be inquired afresh, as recent developments attest to the increasing difficulty of adhering to the traditional dualist doctrine of custom, whereby customary rules should be ascertained on the basis of a generality of practice accompanied by *opinio juris*. In some areas of international law, the dualist doctrine has been seriously called into question. As regards international humanitarian law, for instance, it has been contended by some authors that the requirement of practice is no longer indispensable when the "laws of humanity and the dictates of public conscience" widely support the existence of a norm (Cassese 2005: 160 ff., 2000). Such primary reliance on *opinio* is not deprived of practical consequences. It has allowed for a certain expansion of international criminal norms, arguably to the detriment of the principle of *nullum crimen*. Evidence of this trend can be traced to the jurisprudence of the ICTY. It suffices to think of the *Galic* case to realize that even in the absence of a general practice, the prohibition of terrorism can be considered a customary rule.[3] This finding by the ICTY, which raised the firm opposition of some dissenting judges, bears witness to the fact that the ascertainment of custom in some areas and by some international jurisdictions may remarkably depart from the standards traditionally applied by the ICJ and widely accepted by mainstream doctrine.

Similar considerations apply to the international regulation of the use of force under customary international law. As is well known, recent practice has remarkably strained the law of the U.N. Charter and different claims have been put forward either to foster an expansive reading of the Charter provisions, or to rely on customary international law which would be coterminous with the law of the Charter. The two instances of recent practice which best illustrate the current strains on the international legal regulation of the use of force are the military intervention by NATO countries in Kosovo and the U.S.-led military invasion of Iraq. As will be recalled, the use of force in Kosovo was justified on grounds of humanitarian intervention, undoubtedly a justification which falls outside the Charter. As far as Iraq is concerned, several justifications have been used over a period of time by the U.S., among which anticipatory self-defense stood out. Other uses of force have stirred up quite a lot of controversy, ranging from the intervention against Afghanistan in 2001 and the Israeli attack against Lebanon in 2006 to minor occurrences such as the U.S. bombings against alleged al Qaeda affiliates in Somalia in January 2007. There are many issues that remain unsettled. Is the use of force against terrorist groups on the territory of other states permitted? Can one intervene in anticipatory self-defense? If so, what are the circumstances which may trigger such intervention? In fact, the problems that have arisen in this particular area are as much related to the content of the law as they are to the way in which the law is perceived to be legitimately made and its existence ascertained.

In fact, it is difficult to characterize such instances in terms of customary international law. Bin Cheng used the qualification "instant customary law" to give account of similar instances of state practice, in which general practice and time requirements were relegated to a secondary role (Cheng 1965). Customary law rules regulating the conduct of states in outer space would thus form "instantly" as states that had the technical capability of undertaking such activities express them favorably as regards any given standard of conduct. However, as Jennings aptly put it (Jennings 1998: 742), one should have taken the hint that perhaps Bin Cheng in inventing the paradox had called it "instant" simply because it was not custom! Be that as it may, the traditional mechanisms of general law making at international law need to be revisited against the background of the changing demands of the international legal system. The late Jonathan Charney rightly emphasized the need for devising new mechanisms to create universal standards and

underscored the need to take into account the new modalities by which states could freely express themselves in international fora (Charney 1993). It must be conceded that to leave the evaluation of the legality of any given conduct to the *ex post* reaction of the international community certainly presents a major risk of over-contextualization of legal claims. However, this approach has the merit of respecting the inherent characteristics of the dynamic of customary law making, namely the formation of law by evaluating the reaction vis à vis the unilateral claims put forward. The latter may be accepted, refused or acquiesced, thus giving rise to a confirmation of the existing law or to its modification. The fact that the claim of anticipatory self-defense, primarily if not exclusively, used by the United States to justify its military intervention in Iraq has been largely rejected is not without consequence for evaluating what the current state of the law on the use of force is. By the same token, the not negligible acquiescence in the military intervention in Kosovo leaves the door open to further developments, which may confirm the communal perception of the legality of certain practices of armed intervention in specific contexts, where massive violations of human rights need be brought to a halt. Furthermore, such methodology to reconstruct the content of the law is no less predictable than the current state of uncertainty where practically any argument can be put forward to justify the use of force.

The attempt to stretch the notion of self-defense to its outer boundaries at the detriment of the credibility of international law is evidence of the inadequacy of the current regulation, as well as the methods used to ascertain its content. To portray certain instances of the use of force such as the U.S. air raids against Afghanistan, Sudan, and Iraq in the 1990s as instances of self-defense rather than armed reprisals is to pay lip service to international law. If the law mystifies the realities of the societal body from which it emanates, it is doomed to lose both its credibility and its capacity to control the social processes it aims to regulate. To abandon a formalistic approach to the law and opt for a regulatory scheme, which takes into account recent practice is likely to increase respect for the law and avoid sanctioning the power politics that thrives on the current uncertainties. It is somewhat unfortunate that the ICJ, which wields a certain power in directing the development of international law, has been unable to take a firm stance on the issue of the use of force. Presumably divided within its ranks, the Court has clumsily addressed the most challenging issues and carefully avoided providing guidance to international actors.[4]

Shifting boundaries of normativity

As Sir Gerald Fitzmaurice acutely noted once, if in domestic legal systems there is often uncertainty about "what is the law," the additional difficulty at international law is that this uncertainty also relates to "what the law is" (Fitzmaurice 1973: 251). In fact, the difficulty in identifying norms is tantamount to placing an element of systemic uncertainty at the heart of international law (Higgins 1994: 17). By no means, however, is this a new phenomenon. Even at the time when positivism represented the predominant and almost exclusive theoretical framework, some among the most eminent members of the profession critically approached the issue of sources and acknowledged the difference with domestic legal systems. Unlike domestic legal systems, where the status of sources is predetermined by constitutional arrangements and easily discernable, the absence of any centralized and hierarchically structured system of sources makes the task a difficult one in international law.

Traditionally viewed as originating from the sources listed in Article 38 of the Statute of the International Court of Justice, international law norms have been categorized according to the dichotomy legally binding/non-legally

binding. In particular, whatever falls outside the categories of treaties, custom or general principles of law is considered to lie outside the realm of international legal normativity. The current approach to normativity is still based on the paradigms hard/soft law and legally binding/non-legally binding norms. Although such parameters still provide the main framework of reference, they no longer provide a satisfactory explanation of normative phenomena in international law. Suffice to cast a glance at international case law to realize that such distinctions are far from being straightforward and clear cut and that the way in which decisions are taken and judgments rendered by courts does not always entail rigorous adherence to such paradigms.

Attention to relative normativity was drawn by Prosper Weil in a pioneering article at the beginning of the 1980s, in which a clear warning was issued about relativizing normativity in international law (Weil 1983). Weil's work has shaped the subsequent debate and has caused international lawyers to approach the subject along similar lines. Most prominently the distinction between hard and soft law is made. As aptly noted by Abi-Saab (Abi-Saab 1987: 206f.), the expression soft law is not deprived of ambiguities as it may refer to the norm, the *negotium* (a soft legal norm). By way of example, a treaty norm worded in such a qualified and conditional manner as to suggest no real undertaking by the state will be difficult to enforce, regardless of the binding nature of the instrument in which it is contained. Or, soft law may be taken to point to the *instrumentum* (a soft legal instrument), that is the instrument containing the norm. For instance a norm of a General Assembly resolution may derive its legal strength from the importance of the instrument or the voting process, but remains legally non-binding.

This distinction can be used either to set aside as non-legal whatever normative prescription falls short of a binding effect, holding that the very essence of legal norms lies in their being binding (Klabbers 1998). Or it can be used to differentiate between the binding character and the legal effect of a prescriptive statement, the two elements being distinct. In so doing this approach divorces the question of what constitutes a norm from whether or not the norm is legally binding by arguing that although some norms are non-legally binding, they are nevertheless often more efficacious in practice than their legally binding equivalents, and that these instances of "soft law" are just as effective in addressing the needs of the international community as legally binding norms.

These distinctions are not as clear cut as one would like to think and soft law may become relevant in highly heterogeneous contexts. It may set the preparatory stage for the development of international hard law, be it a treaty or a custom, or provide a model for internal legislation. It may provide the normative standards to enforce treaty or customary due diligence obligations or be used interpretatively to give further strength arguments based on hard law. Overall, an effort must be made to better grasp the functioning of soft law. It has to be acknowledged that soft law fulfills important functional needs within the system, as an increasing recourse to it by states clearly attests. To look at soft law as a form of normative pathology has little connection with the realities of international relations. Soft law could be regarded instead as a sign of maturity that the system has attained, and as an important component of "post-tribal international law" (Allott 1998: 413). In fact, all developed societies are familiar with the "complexification of normative space" phenomenon. Rather than intervening by traditional command and control instruments, domestic decision makers often prefer to opt for recommendations and incentives. International law may be going through a similar process.

As the use of the binary code legal/illegal is what characterizes and distinguishes the law from other social practices at both the domestic and international level, one needs to inquire afresh if the connotations we traditionally attach to these terms are still accurate representations of the current reality. In particular, the parameters by which the binary code is made operational are shifting and need to be reassessed. Similarly, the traditional approach to the hierarchy of norms in international law demands a re-evaluation consistent with current practice. Whereas *jus cogens* norms are traditionally viewed as voiding the competing norm, practice suggests that they play a more nuanced role in reality and are perhaps better seen as reflecting the fundamental values of the international community and serve to influence *inter alia* the interpretation of rules. This may well be the way to bring *jus cogens* forward, as suggested by Judge Dugard in his concurrent opinion attached to the ICJ's judgment on the *Armed Activities on the Territory of the Congo* case, where the Court finally sanctioned the category of peremptory norms.[5] While agreeing with the Court that *jus cogens* may not sweep away everything that stands in its way, including the principle of the requirement of consent for the exercise of jurisdiction by the ICJ, Dugard highlights the peculiar nature of peremptory norms on the grounds of their alleged hierarchical superiority. Peremptory norms do not only express fundamental principles, they also give legal form to the fundamental policies of the international community, thus advancing both principle and policy.[6] By attributing to them a predominant interpretive role in the process of judicial choice, peremptory norms may eventually bring about the desired result of fostering their underlying values, while at the same time avoiding the rigidities of their mechanical application which pretends to trump any conflicting norm (Bionchi 2008).

An additional challenge to normativity is represented by what Lowe calls "interstitial norms", yet another by-product of the complexity of international law. By this expression, reference is made to normative concepts, which do not possess an autonomous normative charge of their own, but rather aim to "direct the manner in which competing or conflicting norms that do have their own normativity should interact in practice" (Lowe 2000b: 216). The examples are numerous. Such concepts as proportionality or reasonableness are often called to fulfill the function of mediating and reconciling opposite or conflicting normative claims on the basis of flexibility and ad hoc interest accommodation. These and other normative concepts emerge from the societal body and they tend both to express the policies that the community wants to pursue and to occupy normative space. By exercising a strong pull towards primary rules they influence their content and shape their interpretation. Other concepts such as sustainable development and the precautionary principle, on the one hand, or elementary considerations of humanity or the dictates of public conscience underlying the Martens clause, on the other, are apt illustrations (in such diverse areas as environmental law and international humanitarian law) of normative concepts that escape traditional categorizations (Bianchi 2006b). The function performed by interstitial norms is not simply that of ensuring a higher degree of systematic coherence in international law. Although they serve the purpose of directing law making, interpretation and adjudication with a view to conforming to the policies that the international community thinks desirable to pursue, they also have the capacity to provide the degree of generality and flexibility required to adjust the law to the changing demands of the societal body.

The capacity to accommodate such normative developments in the fabric of international law theory and practice will be crucial to enhance its credibility and, arguably, its future functioning.

Efficacy: international lawyer's inferiority complex

International lawyers have long suffered from an inferiority complex towards their fellow domestic lawyers. The complex has caused a great deal of negative effects, as the frustration of international lawyers has long been a reason for them to demonstrate that international law is like domestic law. Such an effort, inevitably doomed to failure, given the differences between the two legal orders, lies at the root of many theories developed by international lawyers in a vain attempt to appeal to their domestic law colleagues. As is well known, the disdain of domestic lawyers for international law is largely due to the absence of adequate enforcement mechanisms in the international legal system. The existence of rules would not suffice to confer the dignity of the "law" to standards that remain unenforceable. As to be expected, international law has not evolved in the direction of developing enforcement mechanisms similar to those in domestic legal systems. Although there has been a proliferation of international courts and tribunals, "enforcement," as traditionally understood in domestic legal orders, is not international law's main strength. This may well be evidence of a lost battle or of a lack of communication that has created a major misunderstanding.

It is noteworthy that in his famous book on how nations behave, Louis Henkin boldly asserted that "almost all nations observe almost all principles of international law and almost all of their obligations almost all of the time" (Henkin 1989: 69). What might have been the strenuous defense of the corporation by one of its members, has turned out to be a widely accepted proposition, the empirical value of which has been given support by a number of sectoral studies. The reason why nations obey international law has been thoroughly investigated and interesting theories have been put forward to explain why this may be so. Koh, for instance, argued against the background of his theory of transnational legal process that a transnational actor's moral obligation to obey international law is internalized in domestic legal systems to become a domestic legal obligation that shapes domestic law by international law, thus contributing to a mutually reinforcing process of interest and identity creation between the national and the international spheres (Koh 1991, 1996b).

Certainly, the overall efficacy of the system can be further enhanced. What can hardly be denied, however, is that there is a great deal of spontaneous observance of international law. When judging the overall efficacy of the system, regard should be had not only to enforcement mechanisms, properly so called, but to all those elements that can contribute to the effective implementation of international standards. Little matters whether the vocabulary used varies and reference is alternatively made to compliance, observance, obedience, or whatever else. The goal is no longer to show how close to domestic legal orders the international legal system is, but rather to appreciate its overall capacity to ensure respect for its normative standards.

The traditional obsession of international lawyers with efficacy has presumably made international legal scholarship fertile ground for the law and economics movement to thrive. Rational choice and game theories provide for many the ultimate explanation of why there is international law compliance, even if this disrupts the very idea of law, in particular the idea of the law that the real participants on the ground actually have of the game they are playing. The mantra that the "law is efficient" pervasively permeates recent scholarship and heralds new times for international law (Guzman 2008). The bundle of normative assumptions and presuppositions of the law and economics movement makes the boundary between the descriptive and prescriptive dimensions of the theory a tenuous one. Whether rational choice is the behavioral model that shapes the conduct of the actors in international law remains unsubstantiated against the background of empirical observation. To be sure, the new myth that the "law is efficient" is appeasing the conscience and scientific zeal of many an international lawyer but, whether actual social practices can be satisfactorily explained on the basis of such theory remains open to question.

Accountability mechanisms and their heterogeneous character

Admittedly, the notion of accountability is not strictly legal. Responsibility and liability would rather be the preferred terms for lawyers to describe the way in which an individual or an entity can be held accountable at law. And yet the term "accountability" seems better suited to encompass and describe the panoply of mechanisms that can be used to control the conduct of relevant international law actors. The standards against which such an evaluation must be performed are numerous and not all of them are amenable within the purview of the law, properly so called. That said, it would be misleading to think that accountability stands in contradistinction to legal responsibility, which continues to be the most relevant form of accountability for some of the actors, such as states, international organizations and individuals.

As far as states are concerned, the adoption by the International Law Commission in 2001 of the "Articles on State Responsibility" after more than 40 years since the inception of the codification process – admittedly the longest period of time it has ever taken for the ILC to accomplish codification of an area of international law – significantly contributed to systematizing one of the most controversial areas of international law (Crawford 2002a). The ICJ has sanctioned the Articles, endorsed the same year by the General Assembly,[7] on different occasions and held some of them as declaratory of customary law.[8] This process of mutual reinforcement and legitimization between the Court and the ILC is evidence that the formal status of the Articles, certainly an instrument of soft law at the outset, is largely irrelevant to their practical impact on international practice. This, in turn, may be an argument to advise against their being submitted to a treaty negotiation process with a view to the adoption of a convention on state responsibility. This option, so far put off

401

by the General Assembly, would have the obvious disadvantage of re-opening negotiation on the most sensitive issues of state responsibility and would make the overall efficacy of the would-be convention dependent on the number of states that eventually ratify it. It is to be hoped that the accomplishment of the ILC in bringing to completion such a difficult codification will not be disrupted by untimely diplomatic initiatives, particularly at a time when the articles appear to be steadily consolidating in state practice.

As is well known, the ILC has also undertaken the codification of the responsibility of international organizations.[9] Partly to be developed by analogy to the law of state responsibility, partly to be inferred from the rules of each organization's constitutive instrument, the codification is no easy task. Piercing the veil of the international organization, and holding individual member states accountable for their own conduct, are among the numerous difficulties. It must be conceded that the recent case law of international tribunals, often influenced by considerations of political expediency and opinable judicial policies,[10] are unlikely to help the task of the ILC special rapporteur in putting forth fair and socially acceptable solutions. Be that as it may, the success of the codification process, which could be sanctioned simply by its completion in a reasonable time frame, is likely to enhance the system of accountability mechanisms at international law with reference to entities the activities of which are more and more relevant to international law.

As far as individuals are concerned, mechanisms of legal accountability have steadily developed since Nuremberg. The principle of individual criminal liability for at least some core international law crimes is widely recognized as a matter of customary international law, and individual criminal liability is also attached to a number of conducts proscribed by specific treaties. If the principle of individual criminal liability is no longer seriously called into question, major flaws still hamper its effective implementation. International criminal jurisdictions have been scant until recently, and the International Criminal Court is still in its infancy. Domestic jurisdictions, which, according to the principle of complementarity,[11] will bear the main burden for adjudicating international crimes, have not been very active on the enforcement side (Ratner and Abrams 2001: 160 ff.), mostly due to the carelessness of national legislators in failing to provide domestic courts with the necessary enabling legislation to apply international criminal law standards.

Different considerations apply to the accountability of transnational corporations. International legal scholarship has extensively dealt with this subject. The most impressive account of a theory of the legal responsibility of corporations for human rights abuses is Steven Ratner's book-length *Yale Law Journal* article (2001–2002). Ratner develops an international law-based theory of corporate responsibility, whereby international obligations can be deemed to address corporate entities insofar as the latter cooperate with states and commit violations of human dignity "of those with whom they have special ties" (Ratner 2001–2002: 449). An array of tools for the implementation of the theory is also put forward, ranging from corporate-initiated codes of conduct, NGO scrutiny, and national legal regimes to soft international law and treaties. The merit of Ratner's theory lies in its comprehensive character and in its foundation on international law rather than the domestic law of any particular state. Given that a large part of domestic litigation involving the human rights abuses of corporate entities has taken place in the U.S. on the basis of the Alien Tort Claims Act, and that most of the literature relies on this strand of domestic case law to account for the responsibility of corporate entities (Joseph 2004), such a wider focus is indeed welcome. Furthermore, Ratner emphasizes the importance of other elements, not necessarily of a legal character, which may prompt the accountability of corporate entities (Ratner

2001–2002: 545). Corporate social responsibility as well as market incentives to comply with international standards in certain areas may well provide additional tools for a comprehensive system of corporate accountability.

A different approach to the same issue, based on an expansive reading and use of the law of state responsibility, has been recently advocated in international legal scholarship (McCorquodale and Simons 2007). By focusing on the applicability of human rights obligations incumbent on the home state to the extraterritorial acts of the national corporate entity, the application of the relevant rules of state responsibility to the conduct of home states with a view to holding them accountable for the acts of their corporate entities has been invoked.[12] This approach has the merit of fostering solutions that are clearly available within the system, the rules on state responsibility, and to provide states with an incentive to act diligently if they want to avoid international responsibility. To argue that states should be responsible for the acts of national corporate entities abroad makes sense, particularly as one realizes that home states attempt to impose their laws and regulations on foreign subsidiaries of corporate nationals in a number of areas, ranging from export controls to antitrust regulation. The argument that the same states should be accountable for the acts of the same entities, when these violate human rights standards could reasonably follow. Criteria of attribution for the purpose of state responsibility, such as the exercise of elements of governmental authority or the direction or control by the state of the relevant activities could well provide adequate tools for the implementation of such normative strategy.

Two considerations, however, might stand in the way. The first is the acknowledgment that states do not seem inclined to accept such an expansive reading of their obligations under international law and international practice does not seem to develop in that direction. The second remark stems from an assessment of the judicial policy of the International Court of Justice on matters of attribution. It will be recalled that in one of the few instances of conflicting jurisprudence among international jurisdictions the ICJ made use of the criterion of "effective control" to attribute the conduct of groups of individuals to a state,[13] whereas the Appeals Chamber of the International Tribunal on Former Yugoslavia (ICTY) later adopted a much softer criterion, that of "overall control."[14] In the recent *Genocide* case,[15] the ICJ has reiterated its previous jurisprudence and made clear, not without some institutional acrimony,[16] that general international law requires "effective control" for conduct by an individual or a group of individuals to be attributed to a state. Besides the institutional aspects of the dispute between the two tribunals, it is reasonable to speculate that the ICJ, whose self-perception as the guardian of the international legal system is traditionally strong, when opting for the much more stringent criterion of "effective control" must have had in mind not only the circumstances of the case, but also the potential application of the criterion to other areas, including state responsibility for terrorist acts and state responsibility for the extraterritorial acts of corporate entities. The discussion boils down to determining whether for the purpose of assuring the accountability of nonstate actors, to have recourse to traditional mechanisms of state responsibility is a good normative strategy to ensure greater effectiveness. At the very least, this can be doubted.

As regards the accountability of NGOs, reliance on traditional international law mechanisms of accountability is of no avail. In this area, the most engaging attempts to develop mechanisms of accountability rely on interdisciplinary approach (Bluemel 2005–2006), where an attempt is being made to move the debate of accountability from the actor to the function performed. In so doing, a composite theory of NGO accountability in international governance has been put forward, which does away with many of the traditional dividing lines peculiar to the field of law such as international/domestic and public/private. To speak in terms of international governance rather than in terms of international legal order may be more an issue of disciplinary allegiance than a real difference of conceptual categories. Furthermore, to dismiss as "non-law" social practices that constitute the fabric of day-to-day international life and are increasingly perceived by the relevant actors as demanding respect as a matter of law, may be an attitude that fosters certain vested professional interests, but it is unlikely to advance the cause of international law and to enhance its credibility (Krisch and Kingsbury 2006b). In this respect, interdisciplinary dialog may well produce interesting outcomes and, for once, may be instrumental in providing a better understanding of societal dynamics.

Complexity, specialization, and judicial fragmentation: the system under strain or a sign of maturity?

It may well be true that the ever-increasing expansion and complexity of international law is credited to its maturity (Franck 1995: 4ff.). However, the very same phenomenon is likely to produce deep anxieties among international lawyers and to cause some objective difficulties in ensuring the smooth functioning of the system. Inevitably, in a highly complex normative system without any centralized authority, issues of coordination and conflict among its different components are likely to arise and their solution may not be immanent.

One effect of the complexification of international law is the drifting of the discipline towards a higher degree of specialization. Indeed, the extent to which specialization may affect the way in which we look at the world is greatly affected by specialization (Kuhn 1996: 50–51). As Bernhardt once said, the fact that many of those working at the European Court of Human Rights

are more familiar with domestic law, in particular constitutional law, may be linked to the development of the evolutive interpretation doctrine by the Court and the characterization of the European Convention as a "living instrument" (Bernhardt 1999: 24). Indeed, a sociological analysis of interpretation can help us understand that a specialization in a particular domain of international law provides the "interpretive community" with a "correct" understanding of the law (Fish 1980: 167–73). The "correct" interpretation assured by the interpretive community has the effect of marginalizing alternative interpretations. As Foucault famously said, the culture of the discipline is an effective procedure to control and delimit the discourse in the discipline (Foucault 1981: 61). The actors of any given "interpretive community" not only speak the same language and share the same set of values, they may also have the same vested interests in preserving the monopoly of what is regarded as a legitimate interpretation and tend to support one another in the effort of maintaining their position of power within the discipline. That specialization has created a panoply of interpretive communities has produced a widespread perception of a patchy reality, composed of different normative regimes, each characterized by a certain degree of independence. However, the problem is the fragmentation into interpretive communities!

A fatal blow to the self-reassuring perception of the international legal order as a unitary system has been struck by the fragmentation of international jurisprudence. As the very essence of the judicial function implies an objective and independent assessment, the existence of conflicting assessments in a system where there is no judicial hierarchy risks jeopardizing the international legal order. The absence of a hierarchical structure is frequently recognized by international courts and tribunals, which tend to look at themselves as autonomous international judicial bodies.[17] The jurisprudential fragmentation of international law has thus created a certain anxiety, reinforced by the proliferation of international courts and tribunals. In fact, there is reason to be concerned, as international courts have the tendency to view legal problems through the looking glass of their particular expertise. As Mark Twain aptly said: "[T]o a man with a hammer, everything looks like a nail."

The illusion that "managerial skills" would limit such a risk by guaranteeing the sound management of conflict and coordination between different sets of rules has rapidly turned into disillusionment about the capacity of "legal techniques" to address and solve such problems. The International Law Commission, aware of the need to act promptly to address such compelling concerns, has recently produced a study,[18] which attests to the difficulty of bringing order, by way of interpretive techniques, in the intricacies of regimes and norms collision and/or coordination that characterize a highly incoherent reality.[19]

It is an irony of sorts that the debate on the expansion, complexity and fragmentation of international law has gone hand in hand with a parallel debate on the constitutionalization of the international legal order. Some strands of international legal scholarship have emphasized varying aspects of what can be roughly defined as the emergence of a constitutional order in international law. The obvious temptation for mainstream scholarship lies in looking at the U.N. Charter as an international constitution of sorts, either standing prominently as the only international document resembling a constitution (Dupuy 1997; Fassbender 1998b), or approaching such a status, despite falling short of some fundamental requirements usually associated with national constitutions.

By and large, however, the normative, as opposed to the institutional, dimension of international constitutionalism has been emphasized. Thriving on an ever increasing consolidation of the notion of international community and its foundational normative tenets, such as *jus cogens* and obligations *erga*

omnes, numerous scholars have identified fundamental norms with the distinguishing traits of the constitutionalization process (Mosler 1974; Simma 1994; Tomuschat 1993). Hierarchically ordered norms, even without the backing of adequate institutional mechanisms, could fulfill constitutional functions (Peters 2006). Although the issue of legitimacy is a cause for concern, the existence of universal values that can be enforced at international, regional and domestic law levels is tantamount to a constitutional structure in which different but complementary components may be looked at as a whole (de Wet 2006a, 2006b). Other eclectic versions have been proposed with a view to reconciling the institutional and normative elements (Frowein 1994). The interaction of different layers of normative authority and levels of governance, which already present varying degrees of constitutionalization, is advocated as the paradigm for the twenty-first-century constitutionalism (Cottier and Hertig 2003). Integration of such constitutional elements as human rights protection into existing allegedly self-contained regimes is also perceived as a way of constitutionalizing international law (Petersmann 2006). Imaginative models of would-be international orders continue to blossom and never has the debate on constitutionalism been so alive.

In fact, the contradiction between such dramatically distinct ways of looking at current developments is more apparent than real, and attests to the existence of those "postmodern anxieties" which characterize much of the contemporary literature (Koskenniemi and Leino 2002). On the one hand, attention is drawn to the difficulties of keeping the unity of the system and ensuring its coherence by interpretive techniques and institutional coordination. On the other, such unity is postulated and guaranteed by an alleged process of "constitutionalization" that makes international law look like domestic legal systems. It is a vision driven by despair or more simply an act of faith. Such divergent representations of the same reality pave the way for further remarks on the relevance of the theoretical discourse to the future of international law.

The fragmentation of the theoretical discourse and its practical consequences

By far the most compelling threat, however, seems to be the fragmentation of the doctrinal discourse and theory's difficulty to provide a satisfactory framing of the increasing complexity of international law. It is an irony of sorts that fertile grounds for new approaches and theories to develop have been provided by the inadequacy of formalism and the unsuitability of critical legal studies – admittedly among the most prominent approaches to international law – to supply a satisfactory framework of analysis.

Formalism, meant to refer to mainstream positivistic doctrine, is still in many ways the prevailing lingua franca of international law. This approach suggests that we look at practice as raw materials that need be rationalized and ordered in a systematic fashion. Inspired and shaped by some of the fundamental tenets of western philosophy, this approach tends to project into the practice the ideal of an absolute coherence, both diachronically and synchronically, at the price of distorting reality by discarding any variance, which is at odds with the preordained theoretical model. Contradictions are banned and the coherence of the international legal order not only presupposed but often times imposed. Rules are considered as still and immutable normative propositions to which reality is doomed to bend. The obsession with rules as they appear on paper goes well beyond reasonableness, when theory simply ignores the practice of international law in order to defend dogmatically what it thinks to be the applicable rules. When even states are ready to shift the legal paradigms of self-defense,

some commentators continue to think that this is a distortion of the extant rules, as if the latter were immutable.

Critical legal studies import into international law, by way of contrast, is mainly taken up with criticizing the presuppositions of the traditional international legal discourse, which, according to the critique, is a projection of political paradigms, namely those of international legal liberalism. The internal inconsistencies of the liberal paradigm would cause international law to swing constantly from apology to utopia, from concreteness to normativity (Koskenniemi 1990, 2006). The skeptical outlook of critical legal scholars does not provide a satisfactory account of international law either. Criticism takes place at quite a high level of abstraction and its intended objective is not to provide an alternative theory but rather to "trash" the various mythologies of liberal legalism. If it were not temerity, one would be tempted to trace similarities between such apparently distinct approaches. First of all, they both tend to neglect the social practice of international law, characterized by its own logic and by the perception of the "players." Furthermore, by underscoring the international legal system's inherent contradictions, critical legal studies ends up construing its arguments starting from the posture of formalism, namely the assumption of the coherence of law. Be that as it may, both formalism and its mortal enemy, the critical legal studies movement fails to provide guidance in understanding international law. The former by failing to adjust its frame of analysis to the changing demands of international law and by pretending to continue to use intellectual categories which no longer account for the current realities, and the latter by limiting itself, by its own vocation, to a critique and deconstruction of the traditional approach, without venturing into a *pars construens* or alternative normative project. Admittedly, this has left an empty space for new approaches to burgeon and prosper.

The "mushrooming of theory" (Carty 1991: 93) has thus spurred countless approaches and methods, among which even the skilled reader will have difficulty in orientating herself. The once "invisible college of scholars" (Schachter 1977) has turned into myriad highly visible professional circles. There is no universal language of international law anymore: there are as many dialects as there are observers and commentators. Most of the problems find their roots in the way in which we think of international law. It may well be true that in diversity lies richness. It would be simplistic, however, to believe that such a huge variety of approaches leading to an extreme doctrinal fragmentation has no bearing on the practice of international law and, consequently, on the functioning of the international legal system.

The reason lies in the very ontology of law, more particularly in its psychological nature. As Philip Allott has noted: "[S]ociety and law exist nowhere else than in the human mind" (Allott 2000: 70). Paul Amselek, too, is convinced that law has no separate existence in nature, nor can one bump into it in the actual world: it only inhabits "l'esprit des hommes" (Amselek 1989: 29–30). The acknowledgment of the psychological nature of the law brings with it important consequences. Unlike other instruments of physical measure, the legal rule is a relative instrument of measure: it may vary. One of the factors of such variations is the different manner in which it may be conceptualized, which is scholars' main task. The extreme fragmentation of the theoretical discourse of international law may well lead to normative relativism and eventually, to the demise of the system. By altering the relevant actors' perception of their activities, theory may alter the way in which the legal world is constructed (Fish 1989: 208). Scholars must be aware that theory matters. If nihilistic and excessively skeptical approaches dominate, there is a risk of significant change in practice. Among new theoretical approaches to international law there are movements that may have important practical effects on the functioning of the international legal system.

What is striking, however, is that most would concede that the ultimate object of thinking about international law is to improve mechanisms of global governance and the condition of humankind (Slaughter and Ratner 1999). Such a noble cause rejoins the sophisticated analysis of other authors who, at the (provisional) end of a stimulating, albeit winding, intellectual itinerary, look at international law as a kind of "secular faith," a "project of critical reason" geared to "re-establishing hope for the human species" (Koskenniemi 2007a: 30). It is both stimulating and disconcerting that the panoply of theories and opinions converge, after years of confrontation, at such fundamental a truth. Divergences persist, however, on how to achieve such an ambitious goal.

Conclusion

The problem with so many different theories is that they all have a certain degree of plausibility and explanatory force. Through the looking glass of each and every theory some bits and pieces of the system seem to become more readily comprehensible and easy to grasp. However, when such theories lay claim to providing an all encompassing and unitary vision of the larger whole, their capacity to explain the nooks and crannies of the international legal system subsides and gives way to a deep sense of dissatisfaction. Perhaps, one sensible way to move the debate forward is to realize that international law as a social practice remains a pragmatic project. The inconsistencies that according to some would undermine its credibility are perhaps what allow the system to be operational and to fulfill its regulatory function, by constantly evolving and adjusting to the changing demands of a heterogeneous societal body.

Whether a grand political project will emerge to shape and sustain such a diverse reality is premature to tell. Meanwhile, international law should continue to represent a driving force in assuring, in a flexible and pragmatic manner, the orderly interplay between the different social forces that shape contemporary international relations. But besides its pragmatic character, international law is also capable of materializing collective beliefs and coalescing consensus on them. In this respect, international law is an important part of any political project, whatever connotations the latter may take up.

It is against this background that the challenges expounded above ought to be evaluated. The fascinating character of any challenge lies in the uncertainty of the outcome. Ultimately, whether or not these challenges will be met depends on a number of variables, the most important of which are not within the purview of international law. Almost certainly, the way in which we have long understood international law is inadequate.

The old king is dead. Long live the new king or queen. Only time will tell us who he or she is.

Notes

1 The worldwide popularity of Harry Potter and his saga hardly warrants the specification that Hogwarts is the school of magic arts that our eponymous hero attends.
2 "The subjects of law in any legal system are not necessarily identical in their nature or in the extent of their rights, and their nature depends upon the needs of the community. Throughout its history, the development of international law has been influenced by the requirements of international life," ICJ Reports 1949, p. 178.
3 See *Prosecutor vs. Stanislav Galić*, Case No. IT-98-29-A, Judgment, Trial Chamber December 5, 2003, and Appeals Chamber, November 30, 2006.
4 See *Islamic Republic of Iran vs. United States of America* (Case Concerning Oil Platforms), Judgment of November 6, 2003, ICJ Reports 2003, p. 161; *Legal Consequences of the Constru-*

ction of a Wall in the Occupied Palestinian Territory, ICJ Advisory Opinion, July 9, 2004, ICJ Reports 2004, p. 136; *Congo vs. Uganda* (Case Concerning Armed Activities on the Territory of the Congo), Judgement of December 19, 2005, ICJ Reports 2005, p. 168.
5 See *Congo vs. Rwanda* (Case Concerning Armed Activities on the Territory of the Congo), Judgment of February 3, 2006, ICJ Reports 2006, paras. 64, 125, pp. 32, 52.
6 See *Congo vs. Rwanda, Separate Opinion of Judge ad hoc Dugard*, ICJ Reports 2006, para. 10, p. 89.
7 General Assembly, Resolution 56/83 of December 12, 2001.
8 *Legal Consequences of the Construction of a Wall in the Occupied Palestinian Territory*, ICJ Advisory Opinion, July 9, 2004, ICJ Reports 2004, paras. 147 ff.; *Bosnia and Herzegovina vs. Serbia and Montenegro* (Application of the Convention on the Prevention and Punishment of the Crime of Genocide), Judgment of February 26, 2007, paras. 385, 398, 407, 431.
9 Special Rapporteur G. Gaja has so far submitted six reports. See Sixth Report on Responsibility of International Organizations by G. Gaja Special Rapporteur, International Law Commission, 60th Session, A/CN.4/597.
10 For a recent example, see European Court of Human Rights, *Behrami vs. France* (application no. 71412/01) and *Saramati vs. France, Germany and Norway* (no. 78166/01), Grand Chamber, May 2, 2007; *Berić and Others vs. Bosnia and Herzegovina* (Application no. 36357/04), Admissibility decision, October 16, 2007).
11 Article 17 of the Rome Statute of the International Criminal Court provides for the inadmissibility of cases that are being investigated or prosecuted by a state that has jurisdiction over them, unless that state is unwilling or unable genuinely to carry out the investigation or the prosecution, thus creating a primacy of national jurisdictions over the ICC.
12 For an earlier approach along similar lines, see Fatouros 1983. More generally, on the applicability of the rules of state responsibility to the conduct of individuals or groups of individuals, see Roucounas 2005 and Wolfrum 2005.
13 *Nicaragua vs. United States of America* (Case Concerning Military and Paramilitary Activities in and against Nicaragua), ICJ Reports 1986, pp. 64–5, para. 115.
14 See *Prosecutor vs. Dusko Tadic*, ICTY, No. IT-94-1-A, Appeals Chamber, July 15, 1999, paras. 115–45.
15 See *Bosnia and Herzegovina vs. Serbia and Montenegro* (Case Concerning the Application

of the Convention on the Prevention and Punishment of the Crime of Genocide), ICJ Reports 2007, paras. 396–407.

16 Ibid., para. 403.

17 See the following cases: *Celebici*, IT-96-21-A, ICTY, Appeals Chamber, Judgment of February 20, 2001, para. 24; *The Right to Information on Consular Assistance in the Framework of the Guaranteed of the Due Process of Law*, ICtHR, Advisory Opinion, OC-

16/99 of October 1, 1999, Series A No. 16, para. 61.

18 "Fragmentation of International Law: Difficulties Arising from the Diversification and Expansion of International Law. Report of the Study Group of the International Law Commission", finalized by Martti Koskenniemi, A/CN.4/L.682, April 13, 2006.

19 For a critique of the kind of coherence the study focuses on, see Del Mar 2008.

Bibliography

Abbott, F. (ed.) (1999) *The Making of the International Intellectual Property System*, The Hague: Kluwer.

—— (2000) "NAFTA and the legalization of world politics: a case study", *IO*, 54: 519–47.

Abbott, K. W. (1989) "Modern international relations theory: a prospectus for international lawyers", *YJIL*, 14: 335–411.

—— (1992) "International law and international relations theory: building bridges – elements of a joint discipline", *PASIL*, 86: 167–72.

—— (1999) "International relations theory, international law, and the regime governing atrocities in internal conflicts", *AJIL*, 93: 361–79.

—— (2000) "Twenty-fifth anniversary commemoration: commentaries on Kenneth W. Abbott, modern international relations theory: a prospectus for international lawyers: a prospectus in retrospect and prospect", *YJIL*, 25: 273–6.

—— (2004) "Pathways to international cooperation", in E. Benvenisti and M. Hirsch (eds) *The Impact of International Law on International Cooperation: Theoretical Perspectives*, Cambridge: Cambridge University Press.

—— (2005) "The concept of legalization", in J. Goldstein, K. Miles, R. O. Keohane and A.-M. Slaughter (eds) *Legalization and World Politics*, Cambridge, MA: MIT Press.

—— (2007) "Commentary: privately generated soft law in international governance", in T. J. Biersteker, P. J. Spiro, C. L. Sriram, and V. Raffo (eds) *International Law and International Relations*, London: Routledge.

——, Keohane, R. O., Moravcsik, A., Slaughter, A. and Snidal, D. (2000) "The concept of legalization", *IO*, 54(3): 401–19.

—— and Snidal, D. (2000) "Hard and soft law in international governance", *IO*, 54: 421–456.

Abbot, K. W. and Snidal, D. (2004) "Pathways to International Cooperation" in E. Benvenisti and M. Hirsch (eds) *The Impact of International Law on International Cooperation*, Cambridge: Cambridge University Press.

Abi-Saab, G. (1987) "Cours général de droit international public", *RC*, 207(VII): 9–464.

—— (1998) "Whither the international community?", *EJIL*, 9: 248–65.

Abou-el-Wafa, A. (2005) "Contributions of Islam to the development of a global community based on rules of international law", in R. S. Macdonald and D. M. Johnston (eds) *Towards World Constitutionalism: Issues in the Legal Ordering of the World Community*, Leiden: Martinus Nijhoff Publishers.

Abrams, I. (1957) "The emergence of the international law societies", *RP*, 19(3): 361–80.

Abuya, E. O. (2007) "Past reflections, future insights: African asylum law and policy in historical perspective", *IJRL*, 19: 51–95.

Acheson, D. (1963a) "Remarks", *Proceedings of the American Society of International Law*, 57: 13–14.

—— (1963b) "Remarks by the Honorable Dean Acheson", *PASIL*, 57: 13–15.

Ackerman, B. (1997) "The rise of world constitutionalism", *VLR*, 83(4): 771–97.

Adamson, F. B. (2007) "International terrorism, nonstate actors, and transnational political mobilization: a perspective from international relations", in T. J. Biersteker, P. J. Spiro, C. L. Sriram and V. Raffo (eds) *International Law and International Relations*, London: Routledge.

Adcock, F. and Mosley, D. J. (1975) *Diplomacy in Ancient Greece*, London: Thames & Hudson.

Adewopo, A. (2002) "The global intellectual property system and sub-Saharan Africa: a prognostic reflection", *UTLR*, 33.

―― and Oguamanam, C. (1999) "The Nigerian trademark regime and the challenges of economic development", *IRIPCL*, 30: 632.

Adler, E. and Haas, P. (1992) "Conclusion: epistemic communities, world order, and the creation of a reflective research program", *IO*, 46: 367–90.

Afshari, R. (2007) "On historiography of human rights: reflections on Paul Gordon Lauren's *The Evolution of International Human Rights*: visions seen", *HRQ*, 29: 1–67.

Agbakwa, S. C. (2002) "Reclaiming humanity: economic, social, and cultural rights as the cornerstone of African human rights", *YHRDLJ*, 5: 177–216.

―― (2003) "A line in the sand: international (dis)order and the impunity of non-state corporate actors in the developing world", in A. Anghie, B. Chimni, K. Mickelson and O. Okafor (eds) *The Third World and International Order: Law, Politics, and Globalization*, New York: Kluwer Law International.

Ago, R. (1982) "The first international communities in the Mediterranean world", *BYIL*, 53: 213.

Ahdar, R. and Leigh, I. (2005) *Religious Freedom in the Liberal State*, New York: Oxford University Press.

Akashi, K. (1998) *Cornelius van Bynkershoek: His Role in the History of International Law*, The Hague: Kluwer Law International.

Akehurst, M. (1974–5) "The concept of custom in international law", *BYIL*, 47: 1–54.

―― (1975) "The hierarchy of the sources of international law", *BYIL*, 47: 273–85.

Akhavan, P. (2001) "Beyond impunity: can international criminal justice prevent future atrocities?", *AJIL*, 95(1): 7–31.

Alario Di Filippo, M. (1943) *La Doctrina Suárez en el Derecho Internacional Americano*, Bogotá: Pontificia Universidad Javeriana, Penitenciaría Central.

Albert, M. (2007) "Beyond legalization: reading the increase, variation and differentiation of legal and law-like arrangements in international relations through world society theory", in C. Brütsch and D. Lehmkuhl (eds) *Law and Legalization in Transnational Relations*, London: Routledge.

Alcorta, A. (1883) "La ciencia del derecho internacional. A propósito de la obra de Calvo", *Nueva Revista*, 7: 464–83.

Aldrich, G. H. (2002) "The Taliban, al Qaeda, and the determination of illegal combatants", *AJIL*, 96: 891.

Aleinikoff, T. A. (1992) "State-centered refugee law: from resettlement to containment", *Michiagan JIL*, 14: 120–39.

Alexandrowicz, C. H. (1965) "Kautilyan Principles and the Law of Nations", *BYIL*, 41: 301.

Alexandrowicz, C. (1967) *An Introduction to the History of the Law of Nations in the East Indies: Sixteenth, Seventeenth and Eighteenth Centuries*, Oxford: Clarendon Press.

―― (1973) *The European-African Confrontation: A Study in Treaty-Making*, Leiden: Martinus Nijhoff Publishers.

Ali, U. (2007) "The Islamic headscarf problem before secular legal systems: factual and legal developments in Turkish, French and European human rights law", *EJML*, 9(4): 419–33.

Allott, P. (1990) *Eunomia: New Order for a New World*, Oxford: Oxford University Press.

―― (1998) "The true function of law in the international community", *IJGLS*, 5: 391–413.

―― (2000) "The concept of international law", in M. Byers (ed.) *The Role of Law in International Politics*, Oxford: Oxford University Press.

―― (2001) *Eunomia*, Oxford: Oxford University Press.

―― (2002a) *The Health of Nations*, Cambridge: Cambridge University Press.

―― (2002b) "Intergovernmental societies and the idea of constitutionalism", in *The Health of Nations: Society and Law beyond the State*, Cambridge: Cambridge University Press.

―― (2003) "International law and the American mind", *ASILP*, 97: 129.

Alston, P. (1997) "The myopia of the handmaidens: international lawyers and globalization", *EJIL*, 8: 435–48.

―― (2005a) "The 'not-a-cat' syndrome: can the international human rights regime accommodate non-state actors?", *NSAHR, Collected Courses of the Academy of European Law* 13: 3–36.

―― (2005b) "Ships passing in the night: the current state of the human rights and development debate see through the lens of the millennium development goals", *HRQ*, 27: 755–829.

Alter, K. J. (2000) "The European Union's legal system and domestic policy: spillover or backlash?", *IO*, 54: 489–518.

Álvarez, A. (1905) "Origen y desarrollo del derecho internacional Americano", paper presented at Tercer Congreso Científico Latino Americano, Rio de Janeiro.

411

—— (1907a) *La Nationalité dans le Droit International Américain*, Paris: A. Pedone.

—— (1907b) "Le droit international américain, son origine et son évolution", *RGDIP*, 14: 393.

—— (1909a) *American Problems in International Law*, New York: Baker.

—— (1909b) "Latin America and international law", *AJIL*, 3: 269–353.

—— (1910) *Le Droit International Américain: Son Fondement, sa Nature: d' apres l'Histoire diplomatique des États du Nouveau Monde et leur Vie Politique et Économique*, Paris: A. Pedone.

—— (1911a) "La doctrine de Monroe à la quatrième conférence pan-américaine", *RGDIP*, 37.

—— (1911b) "The Monroe Doctrine at the fourth panamerican conference", *ANAAPSS*.

—— (1917) "The Monroe Doctrine from the Latin American point of view", *SLLR*, 2: 135–46.

—— (1923) *La Codificación de Derecho Internacional en America; Trabajos de la Tercera Comision de la Asamblea de Jurisconsultos Reunida en Santiago de Chile*, Santiago de Chile: Impresora Universitaria.

—— (1924) *The Monroe Doctrine: Its Importance in the International Life of the States of the New World*, New York: Oxford University Press.

Alvarez, J. E. (1996) "Judging the Security Council", *AJIL*, 90: 1.

—— (2001) "Constitutional interpretation in international organizations", in J.-M. Coicaud and V. Heiskanen (eds) *The Legitimacy of International Organizations*, New York: United Nations University Press.

—— (2003) "Hegemonic international law revisited", *AJIL*, 97: 873–88.

American Anthropological Association (1947) "Statement on human rights", *AA*, 49: 539–43.

American Institute of International Law, Pan American Union and Scott, J. B. (1925) *Codificación del Derecho Internacional Americano; Proyectos de Convenios Preparados por el Instituto Americano de Derecho Internacional, a Solicitud del Consejo Directivo de la Unisn Panamericano, de 2 de Enero de 1924, para ser Sometidos a la Comisisn Internacional de Jurisconsultos. Presentados al Consejo el 2 de Marzo de 1925*, Havana.

Amit, M. (1970) "Hostages in Ancient Greece", *RFIC*, 98: 129.

—— (1973) *Great and Small Poleis*, Brussels: Latomus.

Amselek, P. (1989) "Le droit dans les esprits" in P. Amselek and C. Grzegorczyk (eds) *Controverses autour de l'Ontologie du Droit*, Paris: Presses Universitaires de France, 27–49.

Anaya, J. (1990) "The capacity of international law to advance ethnic or nationality rights claims", *ILR*, 75: 837–44.

—— (1996) *Indigenous Peoples in International Law*, New York: Oxford University Press.

Anderson, K. (2005) "Squaring the circle? Reconciling sovereignty and global governance through global government networks", *HLR*, 118, 1255–312.

Anderson, M. S. (1993) *The Rise of Modern Diplomacy, 1450–1919*, London: Longman.

Andreas, P. and Nadelmann, E. (2006) *Policing the Globe: Criminalization and Crime Control in International Relations*, Oxford: Oxford University Press.

Anghie, A. (1996) "Francisco de Vitoria and the colonial origins of international law", *SLS*, 5: 321–36.

—— (2004) "International financial institutions", in C. Reus-Smit (ed.) *The Politics of International Law*, Cambridge: Cambridge University Press.

—— (2005) *Imperialism, Sovereignty and the Making of International Law*, Cambridge: Cambridge University Press.

Anker, D. E. (2002) "Refugee Law, Gender, and the Human Rights Paradigm", *HHRJ*, 15: 133–54.

——, Fitzpatrick, J. and Shacknove, A. (1998) "Crisis and cure: a reply to Hathaway/Neve and Schuck", *HHRJ*, 11: 295–310.

An-Na'im, A. A. (ed.) (1992) *Human Rights in Cross-Cultural Perspectives: A Quest for Consensus*, Philadelphia, PA: University of Pennsylvania Press.

—— and Deng, F. M. (eds) (1990) *Human Rights in Africa: Cross-Cultural Perspectives*, Washington, DC: The Brookings Institution.

Apodaca, C. (1998) "Measuring women's economic and social rights achievement", *HRQ*, 20: 139–72.

Arangio-Ruiz, G. (1996) "On the nature of the international personality of the Holy See", *RBDI*, 29: 354–69.

Arat, Z. F. K. (2006) "Forging a global culture of human rights: origins and prospects of the international bill of rights", *HRQ*, 28: 416–37.

Arend, A. C. (1996) "Toward an understanding of international rules", in R. J. Beck, A. C. Arend and R. Vander Lugt (eds) *International Rules: Approaches from International Law and International Relations*, Oxford: Oxford University Press.

—— (1998) "Do legal rules matter? International law and international politics", *VJIL*, 38: 107–53.

—— (1999) *Legal Rules and International Society*, Oxford: Oxford University Press.

—— and Beck, R. J. (1993) *International Law and the Use of Force: Beyond the U.N. Charter Paradigm*, London: Routledge.

Aristotle (1972) *Politics* (trans. H. Rackham), Cambridge, MA: Harvard University Press.

—— (1980) *Rhetorik*, Munich: Flink.

Armstrong, D., Farrell, T. and Lambert, H. (2007) *International Law and International Relations*, Cambridge: Cambridge University Press.

Arroyo Rivera, A. (1952) *La no Intervención en el Derecho Internacional Americano*, Mexico City: Talleres Graficos de la Penitenciaria.

Arts, B. and Kerwer, D. (2007) "Beyond legalization? How global standards work", in C. Brütsch and D. Lehmkuhl (eds) *Law and Legalization in Transnational Relations*, London: Routledge.

Ashby, W. R. (1960) *Design for a Brain*, London: Chapman & Hall.

Audinet, E. (1914) "Les traces du droit international et dans l'Iliade et dans l'Odyssée", *RGDIP*, 21: 29.

Aust, A. (1986) "The theory and practice of informal international instruments", *ICLQ*, 35: 787.

—— (2000) *Modern Treaty Law and Practice*, Cambridge: Cambridge University Press.

Austin, J. (1954) *The Province of Jurisprudence Determined and the Uses of the Study of Jurisprudence*, London: Weidenfeld & Nicolson.

—— (1954 [1832]) "The province of jurisprudence determined" (introduction by H. L. A. Hart (ed.)), *The Province of Jurisprudence Determined and the Uses of the Study of Jurisprudence*, Indianapolis, IN: Hackett.

Axelrod, R. (1981) "The emergence of cooperation among egoists", *APSR*, 75(2): 306–18.

Bach, C., Dimaranan, B., Hertel, T. W. and Martin, W. (2002) "Market growth, structural change and the gains from the Uruguay Round", *RIE*, 8: 295.

Baderin, M. A. (2001) "A macroscopic analysis of the practice of Muslim state parties to international human rights treaties: conflict or congruence?", *HRLR*, 1(2): 265–303.

—— (2007) "Islam and the realization of human rights in the Muslim world: a reflection on two essential approaches and two divergent perspectives", *MWJHR*, 4: 1.

—— (ed.) (2008) *International Law and Islamic Law*, Aldershot: Ashgate.

Baer, F. B. (1996) "International refugees as political weapons", *HILJ*, 37: 243–59.

Baez, C. (1936) *Derecho Internacional Público, Europeo y Americano*, Asuncion: Impresora Nacional.

Bailey, T. A. (1974) *A Diplomatic History of the American People*, 9th edn, Upper Saddle River, NJ: Prentice-Hall.

Bank, R. and Lehmkuhl, D. (2005) "Law and politics and migration research", in M. Bommes and E. T. Morawska (eds) *International Migration Research: Constructions, Omissions and the Promises of Interdisciplinarity*, Aldershot: Ashgate.

Bantekas, I. (2007) "Religion as a source of international law", in J. Rehman and S. C. Breau (eds) *Religion, Human Rights and International Law*, The Hague: Brill.

Barker, J. C. (2000) *International Law and International Relations*, London/New York: Continuum International Publishing Group Ltd.

Barnett, M. N. (2002) *Eyewitness to a Genocide: The United Nations and Rwanda*, Ithaca, NY: Cornell University Press.

—— and Finnemore, M. (1999) "The politics, power, and pathologies of international organizations", *IO*, 53: 699–732.

Barsh, R. (1996) *Forests, Indigenous Peoples and Biodiversity: Contribution of the Four Directions Council*, submission to the Secretariat for the Convention on Biological Diversity, Lethbridge, Canada: Four Directions Council.

Bartelson, J. (1995) *A Genealogy of Sovereignty*, Cambridge: Cambridge University Press.

Barton, J., Goldstein, J., Josling, T. and Steinberg, R. (2006) *The Evolution of the Trade Regime: Politics, Law and Economics of the GATT and the WTO*, Princeton, NJ: Princeton University Press.

Bass, G. J. (2000) *Stay the Hand of Vengeance: The Politics of War Crimes Tribunals*, Princeton, NJ: Princeton University Press.

Bassiouni, M. C. (2004) "The history of universal jurisdiction and its place in international law", in S. Macedo (ed.) *Universal Jurisdiction: National Courts and the Prosecution of Serious Crimes Under International Law*, Philadelphia, PA: University of Pennsylvania Press.

——, Paust, J. J., Williams, S. A., Scharf, M., Gurule, J. and Zargaris, B. (eds) (1999) *International Criminal Law: Cases and Materials*, Ardsley: Transnational Publishers.

Bauer, D. (2004) "The importance of medieval canon law and the scholastic tradition for the emergence of the early modern international legal order", in R. Lesaffer (ed.) *Peace Treaties and International Law in European History: From the Late Middle Ages to World War One*, Cambridge: Cambridge University Press.

Bauslaugh, R. A. (1991) *The Concept of Neutrality in Classical Greece*, Berkeley, CA: University of California Press.

413

Baxi, U. (2006) *The Future of Human Rights*, Delhi: Oxford University Press.

—— and Thomas, P. (1986) *Mass Disasters and Multinational Liability: The Bhopal Case*, Bombay: N. M. Tripathi.

Baxter, R. (1974) "A skeptical look at the concept of terrorism", *ALR*, 7: 380.

Beck, R. J. (1996) "International law and international relations: the prospects for interdisciplinary collaboration", in R. J. Beck, A. C. Arend and R. Vander Lugt (eds) *International Rules: Approaches from International Law and International Relations*, Oxford: Oxford University Press.

—— (1999) "Britain and the 1933 refugee convention: national or state sovereignty?", *IJRL*, 11: 597–624.

—— (2006) "Review of *International Relations – The Path Not Taken: Using International Law to Promote World Peace and Security*", *LPBR*, 16: 863–7.

——, Arend, A. C. and Vander Lugt, R. (eds) (1996) *International Rules: Approaches from International Law and International Relations*, Oxford: Oxford University Press.

Becker Lorca, A. (2005) "Mestizo international law", unpublished dissertation, Harvard Law School, Harvard University.

—— (2006) "International law in Latin America or Latin American international law? Rise, fall, and retrieval of a tradition of legal thinking and political imagination", *HILJ*, 47.

Beckman, R. C. (2005) "International responses to combat maritime terrorism", in V. V. Ramraj, M. Hor and K. Roach (eds) *Global Anti-Terrorism Law and Policy*, Cambridge: Cambridge University Press.

Bederman, D. J. (2000) "What's wrong with international law scholarship? I hate international law scholarship (sort of)", *CJIL*, 1: 75–84.

—— (2001a) "Constructivism, positivism, and empiricism in international law (reviewing *Legal Rules and International Society*)", *GLJ*, 89: 469–99.

—— (2001b) *International Law in Antiquity*, Cambridge: Cambridge University Press.

—— (2004) "Religion and the sources of international law in antiquity", in M. Janis and C. Evans (eds) *Religion and International Law*, 2nd edn, Leiden: Martinus Nijhoff Publishers.

Bedjaoui, M. (1978) "Poverty of the international order", in R. Falk, F. Kratochwil and S. Mendlovitz (eds) *International Law: A Contemporary Perspective*, Boulder, CO: Westview Press.

Beer, S. (1959) *Cybernetics and Management*, London: English Universitites Press.

Beier, F. K. (1980) "The significance of the patent system for technical, economic, and social progress", *IRIPCL*, 11.

Beitz, C. R. (1979) *Political Theory and International Relations*, Princeton, NJ: Princeton University Press.

Belch, S. (1965) *Paulus Vladimiri and his Doctrine Concerning International Law and Politics*, The Hague: Mouton.

Bélissa, M. (1998) *Fraternité Universelle et Intérêt National (1713–1795). Les Cosmopolitiques du Droit des Gens*, Paris: Kimé.

Bell, D. A. (1996) "The East Asian challenge to human rights: reflections on an east–west dialogue", *HRQ*, 18: 641–67.

Bellinger III, J. B. (2007) "The United States and international law", remarks at The Hague, Netherlands, 6 June. Available at http://www.state.gov/s/l/rls/86123.htm.

Bellomo, M. (1995) *The Common Legal Past of Europe, 1000–1800* (trans. L. G. Cochrane), Washington, DC: Catholic University of America Press.

Benjamin, W. (1973) "Theses on the philosophy of history", in J. O'Neill (ed.) *Modes of Individualism and Collectivism*, London: Heinemann.

Bentham, J. (1843) "Principles of international law", in J. Bowring (ed.) *The Works of Jeremy Bentham*, vol. 2, London/Edinburgh: W. Tait.

Benvenisti, E. (2000) "Domestic politics and international resources: what role for international law?", in M. Byers (ed.) *The Role of Law in International Politics*, Oxford: Oxford University Press.

—— (2004) "Customary international law as a judicial tool for promoting efficiency", in E. Benvenisti and M. Hirsch (eds) *The Impact of International Law on International Cooperation: Theoretical Perspectives*, Cambridge: Cambridge University Press.

—— (2006) " 'Coalitions of the willing' and the evolution of informal international law", Tel Aviv University Legal Working Paper Series, No. 31. Available at http://law.bepress.com/taulwps/fp/art31.

—— and Hirsch, M. (eds) (2004a) *The Impact of International Law on International Cooperation: Theoretical Perspectives*, Cambridge: Cambridge University Press.

—— (2004b) "Introduction", in E. Benvenisti and M. Hirsch (eds) *The Impact of International Law on International Cooperation: Theoretical Perspectives*, Cambridge: Cambridge University Press.

Beres, L. R. (1995) "The legal meaning of terrorism for the military commander", *CJIL*, 11: 1.

Bergen, P. L. (2002) "Excerpts from Holy War, Inc.", *PKPF*, 82: 26.

Berkowitz, R. (2005) *The Gift of Science: Leibniz and the Modern Legal Tradition*, Cambridge, MA: Harvard University Press.

Berman, F. D. (1994) "The international lawyer, inside and outside foreign ministries", in C. Hill and P. Beshoff (eds) *Two Worlds of International Relations*, London: Routledge.

Berman, H. (1983) *Law and Revolution: The Formation of the Western Legal Tradition*, Cambridge, MA: Harvard University Press.

Berman, N. (2007) "Les ambivalences impériales", in E. Jouannet and H. Ruiz-Fabri (eds) *Impérialisme et le Droit International en Europe et aux États-Unis*, Paris: Société de Législation Comparée.

Bernhardt, R. (1999) "Evolutive treaty interpretation, especially of the European Convention on Human Rights", *GYIL*, 42: 11–25.

Bertrand, P. (1993) "An operational approach to international refugee protection", *CILJ*, 26: 495–594.

Besson, S. (2007) "Institutionalizing global *demoi*-cracy", in L. Meyer (ed.) *International Law, Justice and Legitimacy*, Cambridge: Cambridge University Press.

Betts, A. (2005) "Convention plus: continuity or change in north–south responsibility-sharing?", paper presented at New Asylum Paradigm? workshop, COMPAS, Oxford, 14 June 2005.

—— (2006) "Towards a Mediterranean solution? Implications for the region of origin", *IJRL*, 18: 652–76.

—— and Durieux, J. F. (2007) "Convention plus as a norm-setting exercise", *JRS*, 20: 509–35.

Bianchi, A. (2004) "Enforcing international law norms against terrorism: achievements and prospects", in A. Bianchi (ed.) *Enforcing International Law Norms against Terrorism*, Oxford: Hart Publishing.

—— (2006a) "Assessing the effectiveness of the UN Security Council's anti-terrorism measures: the quest for legitimacy and cohesion", *EJIL*, 17: 880–919.

—— (2006b) "Principi di diritto, modularità funzionale e relatività normativa: il concetto di precauzione nel diritto internazionale", in A. Bianchi and M. Gestri (eds) *Il Principio Precauzionale nel Diritto Internazionale e Comunitario*, Milano: Giuffrè Editore.

—— (2008a) "Human rights and the magic of jus cogens", *EJIL*, 19: 491–508.

—— (2009) "Relativizing the subjects or subjectivizing the actors: is that the question?", in A. Bianchi (ed.) *International Law and Non-state Actors*, Aldershot: Ashgate.

Bickerman, E. J. (1952) "Hannibal's covenant", *AJP*, 73: 1.

Bickley, L. S. (2000) "U.S. resistance to the International Criminal Court: is the sword mightier than the law?", *EILR*, 14: 213–76.

Biersteker, T. J., Spiro, P. J., Sriram, C. L. and Raffo, V. (eds) (2007) *International Law and International Relations*, London: Routledge.

Black, C. E. and Falk, R. A. (eds) (1969–1972) *The Future of the International Legal Order*, Princeton, NJ: Princeton University Press.

Black, J. (2001) *British Diplomats and Diplomacy, 1688–1800*, Exeter: University of Exeter Press.

Blair, T. (1999) "Doctrine of the international community", speech given at Economic Club, Chicago. Available at http://www.number10.gov.uk/output/Page1297.asp.

—— (2004) Speech, given to Sedgefield Constituency, 5 March 2004. Available at http://www.pm.gov.uk/output/Page5087.asp.

Blakeney, M. (1996) *Trade Related Aspects of Intellectual Property Rights: A Concise Guide to the TRIPs Agreement*, London: Sweet & Maxwell.

Bloxham, D. (2006) "Beyond 'realism' and legalism: a historical perspective on the limits of international humanitarian law", *ER*, 14(4): 457–70.

Bluemel, E. B. (2005–2006) "Overcoming NGO accountability concerns in international governance", *BJIL*, 31: 139–206.

Bluntschli, J. C. (1872) *Das moderne Völkerrecht der civilisierten Staaten als Rechtsbuch dargestellt*, 2nd edn, Nördlingen: Beck.

Boak, A. E. R. (1921) "Greek interstate associations and the League of Nations", *AJIL*, 15: 375.

Bodansky, D. (2005) "Customary (and not so customary) international environmental law", *IJGLS*, 3: 105.

Bodin, J. (1962) *The Six Books of the Commonwealth Facsimile Reprint of the English Translation of 1606, Corrected and Supplemented in the Light of a New Comparison with the French and Latin Texts* (K. D. McRae ed.), Cambridge, MA: Harvard University Press.

Bokhari, F. and Fidler, S. (2007) "Rivalries rife in lair of leaders", *Financial Times*, p. 5, col. 8, 5 July. Available at http://search.ft.com/ftArticle?queryText=rivalries+rife+in+lair+of+leaders&aje=false&id=070705000356&ct=0&nclick_check=1.

Bolton, J. R. (2000) "The risks and the weaknesses of the International Criminal Court from America's perspective", *VJIL*, 41: 186–203.

Bonfil Batalla, G. (1981) *Utopía y Revolución: El Pensamiento Político Contemporáneo de los Indios en América Latina*, Mexico City: Editorial Nueva Imagen.

Bothe, M. (1980) "Legal and non-legal norms – a meaningful distinction in international relations", *NYIL*, 11: 76.

Bourdieu, P. (1987) "The force of law: toward a sociology of the juridical field", *HLJ*, 38: 805.

Bouwsma, W. J. (1973) "Lawyers and early modern culture", *AHR*, 78: 303–27.

Bowett, D. W. (1958) *Self-Defence in International Law*, Manchester: Manchester University Press.

Bowring, J. (ed.) (1843) *The Works of Jeremy Bentham*, vol. 2, Edinburgh: W. Tait.

Boyle, A. E. (1999) "Some reflections on the relationship of treaties and soft law", *ICLQ*, 48: 901.

—— (2006) "Soft law in international law-making", in M. Evans (ed.) *International Law*, 2nd edn, Oxford: Oxford University Press.

—— and Chinkin, C. (2007) *The Making of International Law*, Oxford: Oxford University Press.

—— and Freestone, D. (eds) (1999) *International Law and Sustainable Development: Past Achievements and Future Challenges*, Oxford: Oxford University Press.

Boyle, H. (2001) "The land problem: what does the future hold for South Africa's land reform program? A comparative analysis with Zimbabwe's land reform program: a lesson on what not to do", *IICLR*, 11: 665–96.

Bradley, C. A. (2003) "International delegations, the structural constitution, and non-self-execution", *SLR*, 55: 1557.

—— and Goldsmith, J. L. (1997) "Customary international law as federal common law: a critique of the modern position", *HLR*, 110: 816.

Brierly, J. L. (1958) *The Basis of Obligation in International Law and Other Papers*, Aalen: Scientia Verlag (1977 reprint).

—— (1963) *The Law of Nations: An Introduction to the International Law of Peace* (H. Waldock ed.), 6th edn, New York: Oxford University Press.

Brockliss, L. (1996) "Curricula", in H. de Ridder-Symoens (ed.) *A History of the University in Europe: Volume II, Universities in Early Modern Europe (1500–1800)*, Cambridge: Cambridge University Press.

Brown, B. S. (2004) "Intervention, Self-Determination, Democracy and the Residual Responsibilities of the Occupying Power in Iraq1", *U.C. Davis Journal of International Law and Policy*, 11: 23–73.

Brown, C. (1992) *International Relations Theory: New Normative Approaches*, New York: Columbia University Press.

Brownlie, C. and Lowe, G. (2000) "Memoranda on Kosovo to House of Commons Foreign Affairs Committee", *ICLQ*, 49: 876–943.

Brownlie, I. (1963) *International Law and the Use of Force by States*, Oxford: Clarendon Press.

—— (1974) "Humanitarian intervention", in J. N. Moore (ed.) *Law and Civil War in the Modern World*, Baltimore, MD: Johns Hopkins University Press.

Brown Weiss, E. (2004) "Rethinking compliance with international law", in E. Benvenisti and M. Hirsch (eds) *The Impact of International Law on International Cooperation: Theoretical Perspectives*, Cambridge: Cambridge University Press.

Brundage, J. (2004) *The Profession and Practice of Medieval Canon Law*, Aldershot: Ashgate.

Brunnée, J. and Toope, S. J. (2004) "The Use of Force: International Law after Iraq," *International & Comparative Law Quarterly*, 53: 785–806.

Brunnée, J. and Toope, S. J. (2004) "Sloughing towards new 'just' wars: the hegemon after September 11th", *International Relations*, 18(4): 405–423.

Brush, S. (ed.) (1996) *Is Common Heritage Outmoded?*, Washington, DC: Island Press.

Brütsch, C. and Lehmkuhl, D. (eds) (2007a) *Law and Legalization in Transnational Relations*, London: Routledge.

—— (2007b) "Complex legalization and the many moves to law", in C. Brütsch and D. Lehmkuhl (eds) *Law and Legalization in Transnational Relations*, London: Routledge.

Bryde, B.-O. (2003) "Konstitutionalisierung des Völkrechts und Internationalisierung des Verfassungsrechts", *DS*, 42: 61–76.

—— (2005) "International democratic constitutionalism", in R. S. Macdonald and D. M. Johnston (eds) *Towards World Constitutionalism: Issues in the Legal Ordering of the World Community*, Leiden: Brill.

Buchanan, A. (2004) *Justice, Legitimacy, and Self-Determination: Moral Foundations for International Law*, Oxford/New York: Oxford University Press.

—— and Keohane, R. (2006) "The legitimacy of global governance institutions", *EIA*, 20(4): 405–37.

—— and Powell, R. (2008) "Constitutional democracy and the rule of international law: are they compatible?", *Journal of Political Philosophy* 16(3): 326–49.

Buck, T. and Sevastopulo, D. (2007) "Brussels threatens Americans with reciprocal travel restrictions", *Financial Times*, p. 1, col. 3.

Buckley, W. (ed.) (1968) *Modern Systems Research for the Behavioral Scientist*, Chicago, IL: Aldine Publishing Co.

Buergenthal, T. (2006) "The evolving international human rights system", *AJIL*, 100: 783–807.

Bugbee, B. W. (1961) *The Early American Law of Intellectual Property: The Historical Foundations of the United States Patent and Copyright Systems*, Ann Arbor, MI: University of Michigan Press.

Bull, H. (1966) "The Grotian conception of international society", in H. Butterfield and M. Wight (eds) *Diplomatic Investigations: Essays in the Theory of World Politics*, London: Allen & Unwin.

—— (1977) *The Anarchical Society*, New York: Columbia University Press.

—— and Watson, A. (eds) (1984) *The Expansion of International Society*, Oxford: Oxford University Press.

Burger, J. (1987) *Report from the Frontier: The State of the World's Indigenous Peoples*, London: Zed Books.

Burke, E. (1774) "Speech to the electors of Bristol", 3 November 1774. Available at http://press-pubs.uchicago.edu/founders/documents/v1ch13s7.html.

—— (1790) "Reflections on the revolution in France". Available at http://www.constitution.org/eb/rev_fran.htm.

Burley, A. M. and Mattli, W. (1993) "Europe before the court: a political theory of legal integration", *IO*, 47: 41–76.

Busch, M. and Reinhardt, E. (2003) "Developing countries and GATT/WTO dispute settlement", *JWT*, 37(4): 719–35.

Bush, G. W. (2001) "Address to the nation by the president of the United States", 147 Congressional Record, H5737, 5859, 5861.

—— (2002a) "State of the union address by the president of the United States", 148 Congressional Record, H83, 98, 99.

—— (2002b) "West Point commencement address", speech at West Point, June 2002. Available at http://www.whitehouse.gov/news/releases/2002/06/20020601-3.html.

—— (2003) "State of the union address", 39 Weekly Compilation of Presidential Documents, 109.

—— "Transcript of President Bush's Remarks on the End of Major Combat in Iraq," (2003) *New York Times*, 2 May 2003, A16. Available at LexisNexis Academic (accessed 28 September 2007).

Butterfield, H. and Wight, M. (eds) (1966) *Diplomatic Investigations*, London: Allen & Unwin.

Buzzini, G. P. (2004) "La 'généralité' du droit international general: reflexions sur la polysémie d'un concept", *RGDIP*, 108(2): 381–406.

Byers, M. (1995) "Custom, power and the power of rules: an interdisciplinary perspective on customary international law", *MJIL*, 109–80.

—— (1997) "Taking the law out of international law: a critique of the iterative perspective", *HILJ*, 38: 201–5.

—— (1999) *Custom, Power, and the Power of Rules*, Cambridge: Cambridge University Press.

—— (ed.) (2000) *The Role of Law in International Politics*, Oxford: Oxford University Press.

—— (2003) "Introduction: the complexities of foundational change", in M. Byers and G. Nolte (eds) *United States Hegemony and the Foundations of International Law*, Cambridge: Cambridge University Press.

—— (2004) "Policing the high seas: the proliferation security initiative", *AJIL*, 98(3): 526–45.

—— and Nolte, G. (eds) (2003) *United States Hegemony and the Foundations of International Law*, Cambridge: Cambridge University Press.

Byford, G. (2002) "The wrong war", *FA*, 85.

Byrne, R., Noll, G. and Vedsted-Hansen, J. (2004) "Understanding refugee law in an enlarged European Union", *EJIL*, 15: 355–79.

Caicedo Castilla, J. J. (1970) *El Derecho Internacional en el Sistema Interamericano*, Madrid: Edic. Cultura Hispánica.

Caillaux, J. (1994) "Biological resources and the convention on biological resources", *JELPLAC*, 1: 9.

Caldani, C. and Ángel, M. (2004) "El derecho internacional ante una possible 'preconstitucionalidad' mundial", *ADCL*, 10(2): 859–75.

Calvo, C. (1862) *Colección Completa de los Tratados, Convenciones, Capitulaciones, Armisticios y Otros Actos Diplomáticos: De Todos los Estados de la América Latina: Comprendidos entre el Golfo de Mejico y el Cabo de Hornos: Desde el Año de 1493 hasta Nuestros Días Precedidos de una Memoria sobre el Estado Actual de la América, de Cuadros Estadísticos, de un Diccionario Diplomático y de una Noticia Histórica sobre Cada uno de los Tratados más Importantes*, Paris: A. Durand.

—— (1883) "Polèmica Calvo-Alcorta", *NRBA*, 8: 629–31.

Caral, J. (2004) "Lessons from ICANN: is self-regulation of the internet fundamentally flawed?", *International Journal of Law and Information Technology*, 12: 1–31.

Carcano, A. (2006) "End of Occupation in 2004? The Status of the Multinational Force in Iraq after the Transfer of Sovereignty to the Interim Iraqi Government," *Journal of Conflict and Security Law*, 11: 41–66.

Cardenas, S. (2000) "Crossing disciplinary boundaries: international relations meets international law", *ISR*, 2: 147–9.

Carr, E. H. (1946a) *The Twenty Years' Crisis, 1919–1939: An Introduction to the Study of*

International Relations, New York: Harper & Row.

—— (1946b) *The Twenty-Years' Crisis, 1919–1939*, 2nd edn, London: Macmillan.

Carty, A. (1986) *The Decay of International Law? Limits of Legal Imagination in International Relations*, Manchester: Manchester University Press.

—— (1990) "The UK, the compulsory jurisdiction of the ICJ and the peaceful settlement of disputes", in A. Carty and G. Danilenko (eds) *Perestroika and International Law*, Edinburgh: Edinburgh University Press.

—— (1991) "Critical international law: recent trends in the theory of international law", *EJIL*, 2: 66–96.

—— (2005) "Distance and contemporaneity in exploring the practice of states: the British archives in relation to the 1957 Oman and Muscat incident", *SYBIL*, 9: 75–85.

—— (2007a) *Philosophy of International Law*, Edinburgh: Edinburgh University Press.

—— (2007b) "The yearning for unity and the eternal return of the Tower of Babel", *EJLS*, 1.

—— and Smith, R. A. (2000) *Sir Gerald Fitzmaurice and the World Crisis, A Legal Adviser in the Foreign Office, 1932–1945*, The Hague: Kluwer Law International.

Cass, D. Z. (2005) *The Constitutionalization of the World Trade Organization: Legitimacy, Democracy, and Community in the International Trading System*, Oxford: Oxford University Press.

Cassel, D. (2004) "The globalization of human rights: consciousness, law and reality", *NUJIHR*, 2: 1–140.

Cassese A. (ed.) (1986) *The Current Legal Regulation of the Use of Force*, Dordrecht: Martinus Nijhoff Publishers.

—— (1988) "Sabra and Shatila", in *Violence and Law in the Modern Age*, Princeton, NJ: Princeton University Press.

—— (1999) "*Ex iniuria ius oritur*: are we moving towards international legitimation of forcible humanitarian countermeasures in the world community?", *EJIL*, 10: 23–30.

—— (2000) "The Martens clause: half a loaf or simply pie in the sky?", *EJIL*, 11: 187–216.

—— (2001) *International Law*, Oxford: Oxford University Press.

—— (2005) *International Law*, 2nd edn, Oxford: Oxford University Press.

Castro Ramirez, M. (1915) *Hay Problemas de Derecho Internacional, especialmente Americanos*, paper presented at the 2nd Congreso Scientifico Pan-Americano, San José, Costa Rica: Impresora Alsina.

Catellani, E. (1933) "Les maîtres de l'école italienne du droit international au XIXe siècle", *RC*, 46(IV): 705–826.

Charlesworth, H. (1998) "The mid-life crisis of the Universal Declaration of Human Rights", *WLLR*, 55: 781–96.

—— (1999) "Feminist methods in international law", *AJIL*, 93: 379–94.

——, Chinkin, C. and Wright, S. (1991) "Feminist approaches to international law", *AJIL*, 85: 613–45.

Charney, J. I. (1993) "Universal international law", *AJIL*, 87(4): 529–61.

Charnovitz, S. (2003) "The emergence of democratic participation in global governance (Paris 1919)", *IJGLS*, 10(1): 45–77.

Chayes, A. and Chayes, A. H. (1993) "On compliance", *IO*, 47: 175–205.

—— (1995) *The New Sovereignty: Compliance with International Regulatory Agreements*, Cambridge, MA: Harvard University Press.

Checa Drouet, B. (1936) *La Doctrina Americana del Uti Possidetis de 1810 (un Estudio de Derecho Internacional Público Americano)*, Lima: Gil.

Cheng, B. (1965) "United Nations resolutions on outer space: 'instant' international customary law?", *IJIL*, 5: 23–48.

—— (1991) "Introduction to subjects of international law", in M. Bedjaoui (ed.) *International Law: Achievements and Prospects*, Dordrecht: Martinus Nijhoff Publishers.

Cherrington, M. (2006) "United Nations General Assembly declines to vote on declaration on indigenous rights", *WIN* (8 December 2006). Available at http://www.cs.org/publications/win/win-article.cfm?id=2911.

Chertoff, M. (2006) "Secretary of homeland security", remarks to Federalist Society's Annual Lawyers Convention. Available at http://www.dhs.gov/xnews/speeches/sp_1163798467437.shtm.

Chesterman, S. (2001) *Just War or Just Peace?: Humanitarian Intervention and International Law*, Oxford: Oxford University Press.

Chetail, V. (2001) "Le principe de non-refoulement et le statut de réfugié en droit international", in V. Chetail (ed.) *La Convention de Genève du 28 Juillet 1951 relative au Statut des Réfugiés 50 Ans après: Bilan et Perspectives*, Brussels: Bruylant.

Chiappetta, V. (2000) "The desirability of agreeing to disagree: The WTO, TRIPS, international IPR exhaustion and a few other things", *Michigan JIL*, 21.

Chimni, B. S. (1998) "The geopolitics of refugee studies: a view from the south", *JRS*, 11: 350–74.

—— (2001) "Reforming the international refugee regime: a dialogic model", *JRS*, 14: 151–68.

—— (2004) "International institutions today: an imperial global state in the making", *EJIL*, 15: 1–37.

—— (2006) "Co-option and resistance: two faces of global administrative law", *NYUJILP*, 37: 799–827.

Chinen, M. A. (2001) "Game theory and international law: a response to Professors Goldsmith and Posner", *MJIL*, 23: 143–90.

Chinkin, C. (1989) "The challenge of soft law: development and change in international law", *ICLQ*, 38: 850.

—— (1999) "A critique of the public/private dimension", *European Journal of International Law*, 2: 387–95.

—— (2000) "Human rights and the politics of representation: is there a role for international law?", in M. Byers (ed.) *The Role of Law in International Politics*, Oxford: Oxford University Press.

Christian Solidarity Worldwide (2007) *North Korea: A Case to Answer – A Call to Act*, New Malden: Christian Solidarity Worldwide.

Christiano, T. (2006) "Democracy", Stanford Online Encyclopedia of Philosophy. Available at http://plato.stanford.edu/entries/democracy/.

Churchill, R. (1975) "The fisheries jurisdiction cases", *ICLQ*, 24: 82–105.

Cinotti, D. N. (2003) "Incoherence of neutrality: a case for eliminating neutrality from religion clause jurisprudence", *JCS*, 45: 499–533.

Clark, G. and Sohn, L. B. (1958) *World Peace through World Law*, Cambridge, MA: Harvard University Press.

Claude, I. L., Jr. (1966) "Collective legitimization as a political function of the United Nations", *IO*, 20: 367–79.

—— (1988) *States and the Global System: Politics, Law, and Organization*, London: Macmillan.

CNN (2001) "US Quits ABM Treaty". Available at: http://archives.cnn.com/2001/ALLPOLITICS/12/13/rec.bush.abm/

Cobban, A. B. (1975) *The Medieval Universities: Their Development and Organization*, London: Methuen.

Cobbett, P. (1922) *Leading Cases on International Law*, 4th edn, London: Sweet & Maxwell.

Cock Arango, A. (1948) *Derecho Internacional Americano*, Bogotá: Impresora Nacional.

Cohen, E. (2007) "The harmonization of private commercial law: the case of secured finance", in C. Brütsch and D. Lehmkuhl (eds) *Law and Legalization in Transnational Relations*, London: Routledge.

Coleman, W. D. and Reed, A. J. (2007) "Legalization, transnationalism and organic agriculture", in C. Brütsch and D. Lehmkuhl (eds) *Law and Legalization in Transnational Relations*, London: Routledge.

Commission on the Responsibilities of the Authors of the War on the Enforcement of Penalties (1920), "Report", *AJIL*, 14(1): 95–154.

Coombe, R. (1995) "The cultural life of things: anthropological approaches to law and society in conditions of globalization", *AUJILP*, 10.

Cordonier Segger, M. C. (2004) "Governing and reconciling economic, social and environmental regimes", in M. C. Cordonier Segger and C. G. Weeramantry (eds) *Sustainable Justice: Reconciling Economic, Social and Environmental Law*, Leiden: Martinus Nijhoff Publishers.

—— and Khalfan, A. (2004) *Sustainable Development Law: Principles, Practices and Prospects*, Oxford: Oxford University Press.

—— and Leichner Reynal, M. (eds) (2005) *Beyond the Barricades: An American Trade and Sustainability Agenda*, Aldershot: Ashgate.

Corntassel, J. (2007) "Partnership in action? Indigenous political mobilization and co-optation during the first UN indigenous decade (1995–2004)", *HRQ*, 29: 137–66.

Correa, C. (2002) *Intellectual Property Rights, the WTO and Developing Countries: The TRIPs Agreement and Policy Options*, New York: Zed Books.

Cosnard, M. (2003) "Sovereign equality: the Wimbledon sails on", in M. Byers and G. Nolte (eds) *United States Hegemony and the Foundations of International Law*, Cambridge: Cambridge University Press.

Cottier, M. (1999) "Die Anwendbarkeit von völkerrechtlichen Normen im innerstaatlichen Bereich als Ausprägung der Konstitutionalisierung des Völkerrechts", *SZIER*, 9(4/5): 403–40.

Cottier, T. and Hertig, M. (2003) "The prospects of 21st century constitutionalism", *MPYUNL*, 7: 261–322.

Coulter, M. (1991) *Property in Ideas: The Patent Question in Mid-Victorian Britain*, Kirksville, MO: Thomas Jefferson University Press.

Cox, R. W. (1981) "Social forces, states and world orders: beyond international relations theory", *M*, 10(2): 126–55.

Coyne, R. T. (2005) "Escaping victor's justice by the use of truth and reconciliation commissions", *OLR*, 58: 11–20.

Crawford, J. (2002a) "The ILC's articles on responsibility of states for internationally wrongful acts: a retrospect", *AJIL*, 96: 874–90.

—— (2002b) *International Law as an Open System: Selected Essays*, London: Cameron May.

Crawford, R. M. A. and Jarvis, D. (eds) (2001) *International Relations – Still an American Social Science: Toward Diversity in International Thought*, Albany, NY: State University of New York Press.

Curtis, M. (1995) *The Ambiguities of Power, British Foreign Policy since 1945*, London: Zed Books.

—— (1998) *The Great Deception, Anglo-American Power and World Order*, London: Pluto.

—— (2003) *Web of Deceit: Britain's Real Role in the World*, London: Vintage.

Cutler, A. C. (2001) "Critical reflections on the Westphalian assumptions of international law and organization: a crisis of legitimacy", *RIS*, 27: 133–50.

—— (2002) "Law in the global polity", in M. Ougaard and R. A. Higgott (eds) *Towards a Global Polity*, London: Routledge.

—— (2003) *Private Power and Global Authority: Transnational Merchant Law in the Global Political Economy*, Cambridge: Cambridge University Press.

Cutter, C. (1999) "The legal culture of Spanish America on the eve of independence", in E. Zimmerman (ed.) *Judicial Institutions in Nineteenth Century Latin America*, London: Institute of Latin American Studies, University of London.

D'Amato, A. (1971) *The Concept of Custom in International Law*, Ithaca, NY/London: Cornell University Press.

—— (1975) "Towards a reconciliation of positivism and naturalism: a cybernetic approach to a problem of jurisprudence", *WOLR*, 14: 171.

—— (1985) "The law-generating mechanisms of the law of the sea conferences and convention", in J. M. Van Dyke (ed.) *Consensus and Confrontation: The United States and the Law of the Sea Convention*, Honolulu: The Law of the Sea Institute, University of Hawaii.

—— (1990) "Agora: What Obligation Does Our Generation Owe to the Next? An Approach to Global Environmental Responsibility", *AJIL*, 84: 190.

—— (2004) *The Collected Papers: International Law Sources*, The Hague/London: Martinus Nijhoff Publishers.

Damrosch, L. and Scheffer, D. J. (eds) (1991) *Law and Force in the New World Order*, Boulder, CO/Oxford: Westview.

Danius, S., Jonsson, S. and Spivak, G. (1993) "An interview with Gayatri Chakravorty Spivak", *B*, 20(2): 24–50.

Danner, A. M. (2006) "When courts make law: how the International Criminal Tribunals recast the laws of war", *VLR*, 59(1): 1–66.

Darrow, M. (2003) *Between Light and Shadow: The World Bank, the International Monetary Fund and International Human Rights Law*, Oxford/Portland, OR: Hart Publishing.

David, P. (1993) "Intellectual property institutions and the panda's thumb: patents, copyrights, and trade secrets in economic theory and history", in M. B. Wallerstein, M. E. Mogee, and R. A. Schoen (eds) *Global Dimensions of Intellectual Property Rights in Science and Technology*, Washington, DC: National Academy Press.

Davis, G. B. (1908) *The Elements of International Law*, New York: Harper & Row.

Death Penalty Information (2005) "U.S. abandons optional protocol" speech to the Vienna Convention on Consular Relations, 10 March 2005. Available at http://www.deathpenaltyinfo.org/article.php?did=1375&scid=64.

de Búrca, G. and Gerstemberg, O. (2006) "The denationalization of constitutional law", *HILJ*, 47(1): 243–62.

Decleris, M. (no date) "The law of sustainable development: general principles, a report for the European Commission". Available at http://ec.europa.eu/environment/law/pdf/sustlaw.pdf.

Delbrück, J. (1993/4) "Globalization of law, politics, and markets – implications for domestic law – a European perspective", *IJGLS*, 1: 9–36.

Del Mar, M. (2008) "System values and understanding legal language", *LJIL*, 21: 29–61.

de Martens, F. (1883–87) *Traité de Droit International*, Paris: Chevalier-Marescq et cie.

de Montesquieu, B. (1949) *The Spirit of The Laws* (trans. T. Nugent, introduction by F. Neumann), New York: Hafner.

Deng, F. M. (1990) "A cultural approach to human rights among the Dinka", in A. A. An-Na'im and F. M. Deng (eds) *Human Rights in Africa: Cross-Cultural Perspectives*, Washington, DC: The Brookings Institution.

—— (2007) "The guiding principles on internal displacement and the development of international norms", in T. J. Biersteker, P. J. Spiro, C. L. Sriram and V. Raffo (eds) *International Law and International Relations*, London: Routledge.

Denza, E. (2006) "The relationship between international and national law", in M. D. Evans (ed.) *International Law*, 2nd edn, Oxford: Oxford University Press.

Department of the Army (2007 [2006]) *The U.S. Army/Marine Corps Counterinsurgency Field Manual*, U.S. Army Field Manual No. 3-24; Marine Corps Warfighting Publication No. 3-33.5 Chicago, IL: University of Chicago Press.

de Rayneval, G. (1803) *Institutions de la Nature et des Gens*, 2nd edn, Paris: Leblanc.

de Rohan, H. (1995 [1638]) "De l'intérêt des princes et des états de la chrétienté", in C. Lazzeri (ed.) *De l'Intérêt des Princes et des États de la Chrétienté*, Paris: Presses Universitaires de France.

de Valoir, T. (1995) "The obviousness of cloning", *IPJ*, 9: 349.

de Visscher, C. (1970) *Théories et Réalités en Droit International Public*, 4th edn, Paris, A. Pedone.

de Wet, E. (2006a) "The emergence of international and regional value systems as a manifestation of the emerging international constitutional order", *LJIL*, 19: 611–32.

—— (2006b) "The international constitutional order", *ICLQ*, 55: 51–76.

Diamond, A. S. (1971) *Primitive Law Past and Present*, London: Methuen.

Dias, C. J. (2007) "International relations and international law: from competition to complementarity", in T. J. Biersteker, P. J. Spiro, C. L. Sriram and V. Raffo (eds) *International Law and International Relations*, London: Routledge.

Dickinson, L. A. (2002) "Using legal process to fight terrorism: detentions, military commissions, international tribunals, and the rule of law", *SCLR*, 75: 1407–92.

Diehl, P. F., Ku, C. and Zamora, D. (2003) "The dynamics of international law: the interaction of normative and operating systems", *IO*, 57: 43–75.

Diez De Medina, E. (1946) "Pan-America: revista de derecho internacional Americano", *AJIL*, 39(4): 758–67.

Dinmore, G. (2006) "Pressure grows on US rendition policy", *Financial Times*, p. 3, col. 1, 21 November 2006. Available at http://search.ft.com/ftArticle?queryText=pressure+grows+of+US+rendition+policy&aje=false&id=061120008138&ct=0.

Dinstein, Y. (1985) "International law as a primitive legal system", *NYUJILP*, 19: 1.

—— (2001) *War, Aggression and Self-Defence*, 3rd edn, Cambridge: Cambridge University Press.

—— (2005) *War, Aggression and Self-Defence*, 4rd edn, Cambridge: Cambridge University Press.

Dinstein, Y. Y. (2005) "The Gulf War, 1990–2004," *Israel Yearbook on Human Rights*, 35: 1–14.

Distefano, G. (2004) "Le protocole de Londres du 17 janvier 1871: miroir du droit international", *RHDI*, 6: 79–142.

Donnelly, J. (1994) "Post-cold war reflections on the study of international human rights", *EIA*, 8: 97–117.

—— (1995) "Post-cold war reflections on the study of international human rights", in J. H. Rosenthal (ed.) *Ethics and International Affairs: A Reader*, Washington, DC: Georgetown University Press.

—— (2003) *Universal Human Rights in Theory and Practice*, Ithaca, NY: Cornell University Press.

—— (2007) "The relative universality of human rights", *HRQ*, 29: 281–306.

Dorril, S. (2000) *MI6: Fifty Years of Special Operations*, London: Fourth Estate.

Downs, G. W. and Jones, M. A. (2004) "Reputation, compliance and development", in E. Benvenisti and M. Hirsch (eds) *The Impact of International Law on International Cooperation: Theoretical Perspectives*, Cambridge: Cambridge University Press.

——, Rocke, D. M. and Barsoom, P. (1996) "Is the good news about compliance good news about cooperation?" *IO*, 50: 379–406.

Drahos, P. (1997) "Indigenous knowledge and the duties of the intellectual property owners", *IPJ*, 11: 179–201.

—— (1998) "The universality of intellectual property rights: origins and development", intellectual property and human rights, a panel discussion to commemorate the 50th anniversary of the Universal Declaration of Human Rights, Geneva, 9 November 1998, WIPO, Geneva (1999): 25–6.

Dumont, J. (1726) *Corps Universel Diplomatique du Droit des Gens*, Amsterdam: P. Brunel.

Dunne, T. (1998) *Inventing International Society: A history of the English School*, New York: St. Martin's Press.

Dunoff, J. L. (2006) "Constitutional conceits: the WTO's 'constitution' and the discipline of international law", *EJIL*, 17: 647–75.

—— and Trachtman, J. P. (1999) "The law and economics of humanitarian law violations in internal conflict", *AJIL*, 93: 395–409.

Du Plessis, M. (2003) "Historical injustice and international law: an exploratory discussion of reparation for slavery", *HRQ*, 25: 624–59.

Dupuy, P.-M. (1995) *Droit International Public*, 3rd edn, Paris: Dalloz.

—— (1997) "The constitutional dimension of the charter of the United Nations revisited", *MPYUNL*, 1: 1–33.

—— (2002) "L'unité de l'ordre juridique international", *RC*, 297: 9–490.

—— (2003a) "Comments", in M. Byers and G. Nolte (eds) *United States Hegemony and the Foundations of International Law*, Cambridge: Cambridge University Press.

—— (2003b) "L'unité de l'ordre juridique international: cours général de droit international public", *RC*, 207.

—— (2005) "Some reflections on contemporary international law and the appeal to universal values: a response to Martti Koskenniemi", *EJIL*, 16: 131–7.

Dupuy, R.-J. (1986) *La Communauté Internationale entre le Mythe et l'Histoire*, Paris: Economica/ UNESCO.

Durchhardt, H. (2004) "Peace treaties from Westphalia to the revolutionary era", in R. Lesaffer (ed.) *Peace Treaties and International Law in European History: From the Late Middle Ages to World War One*, Cambridge: Cambridge University Press.

Dutfield, G. (1999) "The public and private domains: intellectual property rights in traditional ecological knowledge", *OEJLPR*, WP 03/99.

Eckersley, R. (2004) "Soft law, hard politics, and the climate change treaty", in C. Reus-Smit (ed.) *The Politics of International Law*, Cambridge: Cambridge University Press.

Edwards, A. (2005) "Human rights, refugees, and the right 'to enjoy' asylum", *IJRL*, 17: 293–330.

Elberling, B. (2007) "The *ultra vires* character of legislative action by the Security Council", in *International Institutional Reform. 2005 Hague Joint Conference on Contemporary Issues of International Law*, 30 June–2 July 2005, The Hague: TMC Asser Press.

Elias, N. (1994) *The Civilizing Process: The History of Manners, State Formation and Civilization*, Oxford: Blackwell.

Endeshaw, A. (2002) "The paradox of intellectual property law-making in the new millennium: universal templates as terms of surrender for non-industrial nations; piracy as an offshoot", *CJICL*, 10(47): 44–77.

Esbeck, C. H. (1997) "A constitutional case for governmental co-operation with faith-based social service providers", *ELJ*, 46: 1.

Espiell, H. G. (2001) "La doctrine du droit international en amérique latine avant la première conférence panaméricaine (Washington 1898)", *JHIL*, 3: 1–17.

Esquirol, J. L. (2001) "Excessive Legalism, Lawlessness and Other Stories about Latin American Law", SJD Dissertation, Harvard Law School.

Evans, C. (2005) "The double-edged sword: religious influences on international humanitarian law", *Michigan JIL*, 6, 1.

Evans, M. (2005) *War and the Law of Nations. A General History*, Cambridge: Cambridge University Press.

—— (ed.) (2006) *International Law*, 2nd edn, Oxford: Oxford University Press.

Evans, T. (2005) "International human rights law as power/knowledge", *HRQ*, 27: 1046–68.

Evenett, S. (2007) "Five hypotheses concerning the fate of the Singapore issues", *OREP*, 23(3): 392–414.

Ewens, L. (2000) "Seeds wars: biotechnology, intellectual property and the quest for high yield seeds", *BCICLR*, 23.

Eyre, D. B. and Suchman, M. C. (1996) "Status, norms, and the proliferation of conventional weapons: an institutional theory approach", in P. Katzenstein (ed.) *The Culture of National Security: Norms and Identity in World Politics*, New York: Columbia University Press.

Falk, R. A. (1983) *The End of World Order: Essays on Normative International Relations*, New York: Holmes & Meier.

—— (1984) *Law, Morality, and War in the Contemporary World*, Westport, CT: Greenwood Press.

—— (1987) *The Promise Of World Order: Essays In Normative International Relations*, Philadelphia, PA: Temple University Press.

—— (2000) *Human Rights Horizons: The Pursuit of Justice in a Globalizing World*, New York: Routledge.

—— (2001) *Religion and Humane Global Governance*, New York: Palgrave Macmillan.

—— (2002) "Religion and global governance: harmony or clash?", *IJWP*, 19(1): 2–37.

Farley, C. (1997) "Protecting folklore of indigenous peoples: is intellectual property the answer?", *CLR*, 30: 1.

Fassbender, B. (1998a) *UN Security Council Reform and the Right to Veto: A Constitutional Perspective*, The Hague/Boston, MA: Kluwer Law International.

—— (1998b) "The United Nations Charter as constitution of the international community", *CJTL*, 36: 529–619.

—— (2005) "The meaning of international constitutional law", in R. S. Macdonald and D. M. Johnston (eds) *Towards World Constitutionalism: Issues in the Legal Ordering of the World Community*, Leiden: Brill.

—— (2007) "Grund und Grenzen der Konstitutionellen Idee im Völkerrecht", in O. Depenheuer, M. Jestaedt and P. Axer (eds) *Staat im Wort: Festschrift für Josef Isensee*, Heidelberg: C. F. Müller.

Fatouros, A. A. (1983) "Transnational enterprises in the law of state responsibility", in R. B. Lillich (ed.) *The International Law of State Responsibility for Injuries to Aliens*, Charlottesville, VA: University Press of Virginia, 361–91.

Febvre, L. P. V., Mauss, M., Tonnelat, É., Nicefore, A. and Weber, L. (1930) *Civilisation, le Mot et l'Idée*, Paris, Renaissance du Livre.

Fehl, C. (2004) "Explaining the International Criminal Court: a 'practice test' for rationalist and constructivist approaches", *EJIR*, 10(3): 357–94.

Feldman, N. (2002) "Choices of law, choices of war", *HJLPP*, 25: 457.

Felice, W. F. (2003) *The Global New Deal: Economic and Social Human Rights in World Politics*, Lanham, MD: Rowan & Littlefield.

Feller, E., Turk, V. and Nicholson, F. (eds) (2003) *Refugee Protection in International Law – UNHCR's Global Consultations on International Protection*, Cambridge: Cambridge University Press.

Fidler, S. (2007) "Radicalising wave crosses the Atlantic", *Financial Times*, p. A1, col. 1, 5 July 2007, London. Available at http://search.ft.com/ftArticle?queryText=Radicalising+wave+crosses+the+Atlantic&y=7&aje=false&x=6&id=070704008469&ct=0.

—— and Bokhari, F. (2007) "Rivalries rife in lair of leaders", *Financial Times*, p. 8, 5 July 2007, London. Available at http://search.ft.com/ftArticle?queryText=Rivalries+rife+in+lair+of+leaders&y=11&aje=true&x=5&id=070705000356&ct=0.

Finnemore, M. (1996) *National Interests in International Society*, Ithaca, NY: Cornell University Press.

—— (2000) "Are legal norms distinctive?" *NYUJILP*, 32: 699–705.

—— (2007) "New directions, new collaborations for international law and international relations", in T. J. Biersteker, P. J. Spiro, C. L. Sriram and V. Raffo (eds) *International Law and International Relations*, London: Routledge.

—— and Sikkink, K. (1998) "International norm dynamics and political change", *IO*, 52: 887–917.

—— and Toope, S. J. (2001a) "Alternatives to 'legalization': richer views of law and politics", *IO*, 55(3): 743–58.

—— (2001b) "Comment on 'legalization' and world politics", *IO*, 55(3): 743–58.

Fisch, J. (1984) *Die europäische Expansion und das Völkerrecht*, Stuttgart: Steiner.

Fischer-Lescano, A. (2003) "Die Emergenz der Globalverfassung", *ZAORV*, 63(3): 717–60.

—— and Teubner, G. (2004) "Regime-collisions: the vain search for legal unity in the fragmentation of global law", *Michigan JIL*, 25(4): 999–1045.

Fish, S. (1980) *Is There a Text in This Class? The Authority of Interpretive Communities*, Cambridge, MA: Harvard University Press.

—— (1989) *Doing What Comes Naturally. Change, Rhetoric, and the Practice of Theory*, Oxford: Clarendon Press.

Fisler Damrosch, L. and Oxman, B. H. (2003) "Agora: future implications of the Iraq conflict", *AJIL*, 97, 553–642.

Fitzmaurice, G. (1973) "The future of public international law and of the international legal system in the circumstances of today", Special Report, *Annuaire IDI*, Livre du Centenaire, 196–363.

Flauss, J. F. (2001) "Les droits de l'homme et la Convention de Genève du 28 juillet 1951 relative au statut des réfugiés", in V. Chetail (ed.) *La Convention de Genève du 28 Juillet 1951 relative au Statut des Réfugiés 50 ans après: Bilan et Perspectives*, Brussels: Bruylant.

Fonteyne, J. P. (1974) "The customary international law doctrine of humanitarian intervention: its current validity under the UN Charter", *CWILJ*, 4: 203.

Foot, R. (2007) "The United Nations, counter-terrorism, and human rights: institutional adaptation and embedded ideas", *HRQ*, 29: 489–514.

Forsythe, D. P. (1972) *United Nations Peacemaking: The Conciliation Commission for Palestine*, Baltimore, MD: Johns Hopkins University Press.

—— (2006) "United States policy toward enemy detainees in the 'war on terrorism'", *HRQ*, 28: 465–91.

Fortna, V. P. (2003) "Scraps of paper? Agreements and the durability of peace", *IO*, 57: 337–72.

Foucault, M. (1972) *The Archaeology of Knowledge* (trans. A. M. Sheridan Smith), New York: Pantheon Books.

—— (1981) "The order of discourse", in R. Young (ed.) *Untying the Text: A Post-Structuralist Reader*, London: Routledge & Kegan Paul.

Fox, G. H. (1992) "The Right to Political Participation in International Law," *Yale Journal of International Law*, 17: 539–607.

—— (2005) "The Occupation of Iraq," *Georgetown Journal of International Law*, 36: 195–297.

—— and Roth, B. R. (eds) (2000) *Democratic Governance and International Law*, Cambridge: Cambridge University Press.

Fox, J. (2001) "Religion as an overlooked element of international relations", *ISR*, 3(3): 53–73.

Franck, T. M. (1970) "Who killed Article 2(4)?: or changing norms governing the use of force by states", *AJIL*, 64: 809–37.

—— (1990) *The Power of Legitimacy among Nations*, New York: Oxford University Press.

—— (1992) "The emerging right to democratic governance", *AJIL*, 86(1): 46–91.

—— (1995) *Fairness in International Law and Institutions*, Oxford: Clarendon Press.

—— (2002) "Epistemology at a time of perplexity", *EJIL*, 13: 1025–30.

—— (2002) *Recourse to Force: State Action against Threats and Armed Attacks*, Cambrige: Cambridge University Press.

—— (2003) "Is the UN Charter a constitution?", in J. A. Frowein, K. Scharioth, I. Winkelmann and R. Wolfrum (eds) *Verhandeln für den Frieden – Negotiating for Peace: Liber Amicorum Tono Eitel*, Heidelberg: Springer.

French, D. (2005) *International Law and Policy of Sustainable Development*, Manchester: Manchester University Press.

Friedman, T. L. (2006) "Islam and the Pope", *N.Y. Times*, A23, Col. 5, 29 September 2006, New York.

Friedmann, W. G. (1964) *The Changing Structure of International Law*, New York: Columbia University Press.

Friends of the Earth (1995) *Intellectual Property Rights and the Biodiversity Convention: The Impact of GATT*, Bedford: Friends of the Earth.

Frowein, J. A. (1994) "Reactions by not directly affected states to breaches of public international law", *RC*, 248: 345–437.

—— (2000) "Konstitutionalisierung des Völkerrechts", in C. Dicke et al. (eds) *Völkerrecht und Internationales Privatrecht in einem sich globalisierenden internationalen System: Auswirkungen der Enstaatlichung transnationaler Rechtsbeziehungen*, Heidelberg: Müller.

Fuller, L. L. (1964) *The Morality of Law*, New Haven, CN: Yale University Press.

Gana, R. (1995) "Has creativity died in the third world? Some implications of the internationalization of intellectual property", *DJILP*, 24(1): 109–44.

Ganshof, F. L. (1971) *The Middle Ages: A History of International Relations* (trans. R. I. Hall), New York: Harper & Row.

García-Villegas, M. (2003) "Symbolic power without symbolic violence?", *FLR*, 55, 158–89.

García y García, A. (1992) "The faculties of law", in H. de Ridder-Symoens (ed.) *A History of the University in Europe*, vol. 1, Cambridge: Cambridge University Press.

Gardiner, R. (1994) "Language and the law of patents", *CLP*, 47: 255.

Garrett, G., Kelemen, R. D. and Schultz, H. (1998) "The European Court of Justice, national governments, and legal integration in the European Union", *IO*, 52: 149–76.

Gaubatz, K. T. (1996) "Democratic states and commitments in international relations", *IO*, 50: 109–39.

Gehring, M. (2007) *Nachhaltigkeit durch Verfahren im Welthandel*, Berlin: Duncker & Humblot.

——, Hepburn, J. and Cordonier Segger, M. C. (2007) *World Trade Law in Practice*, London: Globe Law and Business Publishing.

Gerald, G. F. (1990) "Bush hints US to seek war-crime trial of Iraq's leaders for actions in Kuwait", *Wall Street Journal*, 16 October 1990.

—— (1991) "Les Douze proposent que M. Saddam Hussein soit jugé pour 'tentative de génocide'", *Le Monde*, 17 April 1991.

Gerstenberg, O. (2005) "What international law should (not) become. A comment on Koskenniemi", *EJIL*, 16: 125–30.

Gervais, D. (2002) "The internationalization of intellectual property: new challenges from the very old and the very new", *FIPMELJ*, 12.

—— (2003) *The TRIPS Agreement: Drafting History and Analysis*, London: Sweet & Maxwell.

Gibney, M. J. (2004) *The Ethics and Politics of Asylum*, Cambridge: Cambridge University Press.

Gil-Bazo, M. T. (2006) "The practice of Mediterranean states in the context of the European Union's Justice and Home Affairs External Dimension. The safe third country concept revisited", *IJRL*, 18: 571–600.

Gilbert, G. (1998) *Transnational fugitive offenders in international law: extradition and other mechanisms*, The Hague/London: Martinus Nijhoff Publishers.

—— (2005) "Editorial", *IJRL*, 17: 1–6.

Gilligan, M. J. (2006) "Is enforcement necessary for effectiveness? A model of the international criminal regime", *IO*, 60(4): 935–67.

Gilpin, R. (1981) *War and Change in World Politics*, Cambridge: Cambridge University Press.

Glennon, M. J. (2001) *Limits of Law, Prerogatives of Power: Interventionism After Kosovo*, New York: Palgrave.

—— and Hayward, A. R. (1994) "Collective security and the constitution: can the commander-in-chief power be delegated to the United Nations?", *GLJ*, 82: 1573.

Glynn, P., Kobrin, S. J. and Naím, M. (1997) "The globalization of corruption", in K. A. Elliott (ed.) *Corruption and the Global Economy*, Washington, DC: Peterson Institute for International Economics.

Goberna Falque, J. R. (1999) *Civilización: Historia de una Idea*, Santiago de Compostela: Universidade de Santiago de Compostela.

Gold, J. (1996) *Interpretation: The IMF and International Law*, London/The Hague: Kluwer Law International.

Goldsmith, J. L. (2000a) "Should international human rights law trump US domestic law?", *CJIL*, 1, 327–39.

—— (2000b) "Book review: sovereignty, international relations theory, and international law", *SLR*, 52: 959–86.

—— (2003a) "Liberal democracy and cosmopolitan duty", *SLR*, 55: 1667–96.

—— (2003b) "The self-defeating International Criminal Court", *ChLR*, 70(1): 89–104.

—— (2007) "The global convergence on terror", *Financial Times*, 1 August 2007.

—— and Posner, E. A. (1999) "Theory of customary international law", *UCLR*, 66: 1113–77.

—— (2000) "Understanding the resemblance between modern and traditional customary international law", *VJIL*, 40: 639–72.

—— (2002) "Moral and legal rhetoric in international relations: a rational choice perspective", *JLS*, 31: S115–39.

—— (2003) "International agreements: a rational choice approach", *VJIL*, 44: 113–43.

—— (2005) *The Limits of International Law*, Oxford: Oxford University Press.

Goldsmith, Lord (2003) "Iraq: legality of armed force", 646 Parliamentary Debate, House of Lords (5th Ser), WA2–WA3.

Goldstein, J., Kahler, M., Keohane, R. O. and Slaughter, A.-M. (2000) "Introduction: legalization and world politics", *IO*, 54: 385–99.

—— (eds) (2005) *Legalization and World Politics*, Cambridge, MA: MIT Press.

Goldstein, J. and Martin, L. L. (2000) "Legalization, trade liberalization, and domestic politics: a cautionary note", *IO*, 54: 603–32.

—— (2005) "Legalization, trade liberalization, and domestic politics: a cautionary note", in J. Goldstein, M. Kahler, R. O. Keohane and A.-M. Slaughter (eds) *Legalization and World Politics*, Cambridge, MA: MIT Press.

Gollin, M. (1991) "Using intellectual property to improve environmental protection", *HJLT*, 4 (Spring): 193–235.

Golove, D. M. (2000) "Treaty-making and the nation: the historical foundations of the nationalist conception of the treaty power", *McLR*, 98(5): 1075–319.

—— (2002) "Human rights treaties and the U.S. Constitution", *DLR*, 52: 579.

Gong, G. W. (1984) *The Standard of "Civilization" in International Society*, Oxford: Clarendon Press.

Goodwin-Gill, G. S. (1999) "Refugee identity and protection's fading prospect", in F. Nicholson and P. Twomey (eds) *Refugee Rights and Realities: Evolving International Concepts and Regimes*, Cambridge: Cambridge University Press.

—— (2004) "Refugees and their human rights", Refugee Studies Centre Working Paper No. 17, Oxford: Refugee Studies Centre. Available at http://www.rsc.ox.ac.uk/PDFs/workingpaper17.pdf.

—— (2006) "International protection and assistance for refugees and the displaced: institutional challenges and United Nations reform", paper presented at the Refugee Studies Centre Workshop, Refugee Protection in International Law: Contemporary Challenges, Oxford, 24 April 2006.

—— and McAdam, J. (2007) *The Refugee in International Law*, 3rd edn, Oxford: Oxford University Press.

Gorpin, M. (2002) *Holy War, Holy Peace: How Religion Can Bring Peace to the Middle East*, New York: Oxford University Press.

Gowlland-Debbas, V. (ed.) (1996) *The Problem of Refugees in the Light of Contemporary International Law Issues*, The Hague: Martinus Nijhoff Publishers.

—— (2000) "The functions of the United Nations Security Council in the international legal system", in M. Byers (ed.) *The Role of Law in International Politics*, Oxford: Oxford University Press.

—— (2001) "La Charte des Nations Unies et la Convention de Genève du 28 juillet 1951 relative au statut des réfugiés", in V. Chetail (ed.) *La Convention de Genève du 28 Juillet 1951 relative au Statut des Réfugiés 50 ans après: Bilan et Perspectives*, Brussels: Bruylant.

Grahl-Madsen, A. (1966) *The Status of Refugees in International Law*, vol. 1, Leiden: Martinus Nijhoff Publishers.

Gratwick, S. (1972) "Having regard to what was known and used", *LQR*, 88: 341.

Graubart, J. (2001–02) "Giving meaning to new trade-linked 'soft law' agreements on social values: a law-in-action analysis of NAFTA's environmental side agreement", *UCLAJIFA*, 6: 425.

Gray, C. (2004) *International Law and the Use of Force*, 2nd edn, Oxford: Oxford University Press.

Greaves, T. (ed.) (1994) *Intellectual Property Rights for Indigenous Peoples: A Source Book*, Oklahoma City, OK: Society for Applied Anthropology.

Green, L. C. and Dickason, O. P. (1989) *The Law of Nations and the New World*, Edmonton: University of Alberta Press.

Greenberg, K. J. and Dratel, J. L. (eds) *The Torture Papers: The Road to Abu Ghraib*, Cambridge: Cambridge University Press, 405–556.

Greenstock, J. (2002) "Combating international terrorism: the contribution of the United Nations", an address at the Symposium by the chairman of the Counter-Terrorism Committee (CTC), Vienna. Available at http://www.un.org/sc/ctc/ViennaNotes.htm.

Greenwood, C. (1992) "New world order or old?", *MLR*, 55: 153–78.

—— (2002) "International law and the 'war against terrorism'", *IA*, 78: 301.

—— (2003) "International law and the pre-emptive use of force", *SDILJ*, 4: 7–37.

Grewe, W. (2000) *The Epochs of International Law* (trans. and rev. M. Byers), Berlin: Walter de Gruyter.

Grewlich, K. W. (2006) "Internet governance und 'völkerrechtliche Konstitutionalisierung' nach dem Weltinfomrationsgipfel 2005 in Tunis", *Kommunikation und Recht*, 4, 156–65.

Grieco, J. M. (1988) "Anarchy and the limits of cooperation: a realist critique of newest liberal institutionalism", *IO*, 42: 485–507.

Gros Espiell, H. (2001) "La doctrine du droit international en amérique latine avant la première conférence panaméricaine (Washington, 1889)", *JHIL*, 3: 1–17.

Gross, H. (1975) *Empire and Sovereignty*, Chicago, IL: Chicago University Press.

Gross, L. (1948) "The peace of Westphalia, 1648–1948", *AJIL*, 42(1): 20–41.

Grosz, E. and Spivak, G. (1985) "Criticism, feminism, and the institution: an interview with Gayatri Spivak", *Thesis Eleven*, 10/11: 175–89 [reprinted in S. Harasym (ed.) (1990) *The Post-Colonial Critic: Interviews, Strategies, Dialogues*, New York: Routledge].

Grotius, H. (1925) "Prolegomena", *De Jure Belli Ac Pacis*, in V. Scott (ed.) *Classics of International Law*, Washington, DC: Carnegie Institution.

—— (1925) *De Jure Belli ac Pacis Libri Tres* (trans. F. Kelsey), Oxford: Clarendon Press.

—— (1995) *De Jure Praedae Commentarius* (trans. G. Williams), Buffalo, NY: Hein.

Gruber, L. (2000) *Ruling the World: Power Politics and the Rise of Supranational Institutions*, Princeton, NJ: Princeton University Press.

Grundmann, H. (1976) "Foreign patent monopolies in developing countries: an empirical analysis", *JDS*, 12.

Guillemain, B. (1962) *La Cour pontificale d'Avignon (1309–1376): Étude d'une Société*, Paris: Boccard.

Guiraudon, V. (2000) "European court and foreigners' rights: a comparative study of norms diffusion", *IMR*, 34: 1088–125.

Gunn, T. J. (2003) "The complexity of religion and the definition of 'religion' in international law", *HHRJ*, 16: 189–215.

Gurowitz, A. (2004) "International law, politics, and migrant rights", in C. Reus-Smit (ed.) *The Politics of International Law*, Cambridge: Cambridge University Press.

Guynn, J. and Infield, T. (2003) "Few supporting nations offering troops for Iraq battle", *Knight Ridder Newspapers*, March 24.

Guzman, A. T. (2008) *How International Law Works: a Rational Choice Theory*, New York: Oxford University Press.

Gwam, C. U. (2002) "Adverse effects of the illicit movement and dumping of hazardous, toxic, and dangerous wastes and products on the enjoyment of human rights", *FJIL*, 14: 427–74.

Haas, E. B. (1975) "Is there a hole in the whole? Knowledge, technology, interdependence, and the construction of international regimes", *IO*, 29(3): 827–76.

Haas, P. (1992) "Introduction: epistemic communities and international policy coordination", *IO*, 46: 1–35.

Habermas, J. (1985) *Der philosophische Diskurs der Moderne*, Frankfurt am Main: Suhrkamp.

—— (1993) *Faktizität und Geltung: Beiträge zur Diskurstheorie des Rechts und des demokratischen Rechtsstaats*, Frankfurt am Main: Suhrkamp.

—— (1996) *Die Einbeziehung des Anderen*, Frankfurt am Main: Suhrkamp.

—— (2003) "Interpreting the fall of a monument", *GrLJ*, 4: 701–708.

—— (2005) "*Eine politische Verfassung für die pluralistische Weltgesellscheft?*", *KJ*, 38(3): 222–47.

Hackett, R. I. J. (2005) "Rethinking the role of religion in changing public spheres: some comparative perspectives", *BYULR*, 659.

Hafner, G. (2003) "The effect of soft law on international economic relations", in S. Grilled (ed.) *International Economic Governance and Non-Economic Concerns: New Challenges for the International Legal Order*, Vienna/New York: Springer.

Hall, R. B. and Biersteker, T. J. (eds) (2002) *The Emergence of Private Authority in Global Governance*, Oxford: Oxford University Press.

Hall, W. E. (1884) *Treatise on International Law*, 2nd edn, Oxford: Clarendon Press.

Hamidullah, M. (1977) *The Muslim Conduct of State*, rev. 7th edn, Lahore: Sh. Muhammad Ashraf.

Hamilton, C. and Whalley, J. (1996) *The Trading System after the Uruguay Round*, Washington, DC: Institute for International Economics.

Handl, G. (1995) "Sustainable development: general rules versus specific obligations", in W. Lang (ed.) *Sustainable Development and International Law*, London: Graham & Trotman.

Hanisch Espíndola, H. (1983) *Andrés Bello y su Obra en Derecho Romano*, Santiago: Ediciones del Consejo de Rectores de las Universidades Chilenas.

Hannig, M. (1996) "An examination of the possibility to secure intellectual property rights for plant genetic resources developed by indigenous peoples of the NAFTA states: domestic legislation under the international convention for new plant varieties", *AJICL*, 13: 175.

Harris, W. V. (1974) *War and Imperialism in Republican Rome, 327–70 BC*, Oxford: Clarendon Press.

Hart, H. L. A. (1994) *The Concept of Law*, Oxford: Oxford University Press.

—— (1998) *The Concept of Law*, 2nd edn, Oxford: Oxford University Press.

Hartigan, R. S. (1983) *Lieber's Code and the Law of War*, Chicago, IL: Precedent.

Harvey, C. J. (1998) "Reconstructing refugee law", *JCL*, 3: 159–90.

—— (1999) "Talking about refugee law", *JRS*, 12: 101–34.

Hathaway, J. C. (1991) "Reconceiving refugee law as human rights protection", *JRS*, 4: 113–31.

—— (2002) "Who should watch over refugee law?", paper presented at the IARLJ Conference in FMR, 14: 23–7.

—— (2003) "A forum for the transnational development of refugee law: the IARLJ's advanced refugee law workshop, *IJRL*, 15(3): 418–21.

—— (2005) *The Rights of Refugees under International Law*, Cambridge: Cambridge University Press.

—— (2007) "Why refugee law still matters", *Melbourne JIL*, 8: 89–103.

—— and Neve, R. A. (1997) "Making international refugee law relevant again: a proposal for collectivized and solution oriented protection", *HHRJ*, 10: 115–211.

Hathaway, O. A. (2006) *The Promise and Limits of International Law*, New York: Foundation Press. Available at http://www.law.columbia.edu/null/Hathaway,+Oona+A+-+Spring+06+WS+-+Background+Reading?exclusive=filemgr.download&file_id=961191&showthumb=0.

—— and Koh, H. H. (eds) (2005) *Foundations of International Law and Politics*, New York: Foundation Press.

Hautefeuille, L. B. (1868) *Des Droits et Devoirs des Nations neutres en Temps de Guerre maritime*, 3rd edn, Paris: Guillemain.

Haynes, J. (2005) "Religion and international relations after 9/11", *Dm*, 12(3): 398–413.

Heffter, A. W. (1881) *Das europäische Völkerrecht der Gegenwart*, in F. H. Geffcken (ed.) Berlin: E. H. Schroeder.

Heinze, E. (2001) "Sexual orientation and international law: a study in the manufacture of cross-cultural 'sensitivity'", *MJIL*, 22: 283–309.

Held, D. (1995) *Democracy and the Global Order*, Cambridge: Polity Press.

Helmholz, R. H. (ed.) (1992) *Canon Law in Protestant Lands*, Berlin: Duncker & Humblot.

—— (2001) *The Ius Commune in England: Four Studies*, Oxford: Oxford University Press.

Helton, A. C. (2002) *The Price of Indifference – Refugees and Humanitarian Action in the New Century*, Oxford: Oxford University Press.

Henkin, L. (1968) *How Nations Behave: Law and Foreign Policy*, New York: Praeger.

—— (1971) "The reports of the death of Article 2(4) are greatly exaggerated", *AJIL*, 65.

—— (1979) *How Nations Behave: Law and Foreign Policy*, 2nd edn, New York: Columbia University Press.

—— (1989) "International law: politics, values and functions", *RC*, 216(4): 9–416.

—— (1990) *The Age of Rights*, New York: Columbia University Press.

—— (1995a) *International Law: Politics and Values*, The Hague: Kluwer Law International.

—— (1995b) "US ratification of human rights conventions: the ghost of Senator Bricker", *AJIL*, 89: 341–50.

—— (1996) *Foreign Affairs and the United States Constitution*, 2nd edn, Oxford: Clarendon Press.

Henriquez, H. (1948) *Origen y Evolucion del Derecho Internacional Americano*, Ciudad Trujillo: R. D. Imprenta Arte y Cine.

Henriquez Vergez, H. (1966) *Manual de Derecho internacional Americano*, Homero: Arte y Cine.

Hepburn, J., Gehring, M., Goh, M. P. and Endicott, M. (2007) "Sustainable development in regional trade and investment agreements: policy innovations in Asia?", CISDL Working Paper. Available at http://www.cisdl.org/pdf/cisdl_studie_asia.pdf.

Hershey, A. S. (1912) *The Essentials of Public International Law*, New York: Macmillan.

Hessler, K. (2005) "Resolving interpretive conflicts in international human rights law", *JPP*, 13(4): 490.

Hevener, N. K. (1978) "The 1971 south–west African opinion: a new juridical philosophy", *ICLQ*, 24: 790.

Higgins, R. (1994 [1995]) *Problems & Process: International Law and How We Use It*, Oxford: Clarendon Press.

Hilf, M. and Oeter, S. (2005) *WTO-Recht – Rechtsordnung des Welthandels*, Baden-Baden: Nomos.

Hillgenberg, H. (1999) "A fresh look at soft law", *EJIL*, 10: 499.

Hinsley, F. H. (1963) *Power and the Pursuit of Peace. Theory and Practice in the History of Relations between States*, Cambridge: Cambridge University Press.

Hirsch, M. (2004) "Compliance with international norms in an age of globalization: two theoretical perspectives", in E. Benvenisti and M. Hirsch (eds) *The Impact of International Law on International Cooperation: Theoretical Perspectives*, Cambridge: Cambridge University Press.

Hirschman, A. O. (1997) *The Passions and the Interests. Political Arguments for Capitalism before its Triumph*, 20th anniversary edn, Princeton, NJ: Princeton University Press.

Ho, D. E. (2002) "Compliance and international soft law: why do countries implement the Basle Accord?", *JIEL*, 5: 647–88.

Hobbes, T. (1968) *Leviathan*, in C. B. Macpherson (ed.), Baltimore, MD: Penguin.

Hochberg, M. (ed.) (1996) *Aspects of the Genesis and Maintenance of Biological Diversity*, Oxford: Oxford University Press.

Hoebel, E. A. (1954) *The Law of Primitive Man*, Cambridge, MA: Harvard University Press.

Hoekman, B. and Kostecki, M. (2001) *The Political Economy of the World Trading System: The WTO and Beyond*, Oxford: Oxford University Press.

Hoffmann, S. (1977) "An American social science: international relations", *D*, 106: 41–60.

Hohfeld, W. (2001) *Fundamental Legal Conceptions as Applied in Judicial Reasoning*, Sudbury, MA: Dartmouth Publishing Company.

Hollis, M. and Smith, S. (1990) *Explaining and Understanding International Relations*, New York: Oxford University Press.

Holloday, A. J. and Goodman, M. D. (1986) "Religious scruples in ancient warfare", *CQ*, 36: 150.

Holmes, J. (2001) "Jurisdiction and admissibility", in R. S. Lee (ed.) *The International Criminal Court: Elements of Crimes and Rules of Procedure and Evidence*, Ardsley, NY: Transnational Publishers.

Hooker, J. T. (1976) *Mycenaean Greece*, London: Routledge.

Hoopes, T. (2006) "The Leyla Sahin v Turkey case before the European Court of Human Rights", *ChJIL*: 719–22.

Hopf, T. (1998) "The promise of constructivism in international relations theory", *IS*, 23: 171–200.

Horn, D. B. (1961) *The British Diplomatic Service, 1689–1789*, Oxford: Clarendon Press.

Hountondji, P. J. (1986) "The master's voice – remarks on the problem of human rights in Africa", in UNESCO (ed.) *Philosophical foundations of human rights*, Paris: UNESCO.

Howard, R. (1993) "Cultural absolutism and the nostalgia for community", *HRQ*, 15: 315–38.

Howard-Hassmann, R. E. (2005) "The second great transformation: human rights leapfrogging in the era of globalization", *HRQ*, 27: 1–40.

Howse, R. (2004) "Back to the court after *Shrimp–Turtle*: India's challenge to labor and environmental linkages in the EC generalized system of preferences", in E. Benvenisti and M. Hirsch (eds) *The Impact of International Law on International Cooperation: Theoretical Perspectives*, Cambridge: Cambridge University Press.

—— and Nicolaïdis, K. (2003) "Enhancing WTO legitimacy", *G*, 16(1): 73–94.

Huban, M. (2004) "Interpol urges more sharing of terror intelligence", *Financial Times*, 8 June 2004.

Hume, D. (1948) "Treatise of human nature", in H. Aiken (ed.) *Hume's moral and political philosophy*, New York: Hafner.

Hunter, D., Salzman, J. and Zaelke, D. (2001) *International Environmental Law and Policy*, 2nd edn, New York: Foundation Press.

Huntington, S. (1996) *The Clash of Civilizations and the Remaking of World Order*, New York: Simon & Schuster.

Hurd, E. S. (2004) "The political authority of secularism in international relations", *EJIR*, 10: 235–62.

Hurd, I. (1999) "Legitimacy and authority in international politics", *IO*, 53: 379–408.

Hurrell, A. (1993) "International society and the study of regimes: a reflective approach", in V. Rittberger (ed.) *Regime Theory and International Relations*, Oxford: Oxford University Press.

—— (2000) "Conclusion: international law and the changing constitution of international society", in M. Byers (ed.) *The Role of Law in International Politics*, Oxford: Oxford University Press.

—— (2005) "Legitimacy and the use of force: can the circle be squared?", *RIS*, 31: 15–32.

Ibhawoh, B. (2000) "Between culture and constitution: evaluating the cultural legitimacy of human rights in the African state", *HRQ*, 22: 838–60.

Idike, C. E. (2006) "Deflectionist institutions or beacons of hope? A study of national human rights commissions in anglophone Africa", PhD thesis, York University.

Ignatieff, M. (2001) *Human Rights as Politics and Idolatry*, Princeton, NJ: Princeton University Press.

Ikenberry, G. J. (2001) *After Victory: Institutions, Strategic Restraint, and the Rebuilding of Order after Major Wars*, Princeton, NJ: Princeton University Press.

Institut de Droit International (1885) *Annuaire de l'Institut de droit international (1885–1886)* 8, Berlin: Institut de Droit International.

International Institute for Sustainable Development (2005) *Environment and Trade: A Handbook*, 2nd edn, Geneva: UNEP. Available at http://www.iisd.org/pdf/2005/envirotrade_handbook_2005.pdf.

Isaac, E. (1970) *Geography of Domestication*, Englewood Cliffs, NJ: Prentice-Hall.

Ittersum, M. J. von (2006) *Profit and Principle: Hugo Grotius, Natural Rights Theories and the Rise of Dutch Power in the East Indies, 1595–1615*, Leiden: Brill.

Jackson, J. H. (1997) *The World Trading System – Law and Policy of International Economic Relations*, 2nd edn, Cambridge, MA: MIT Press.

Jackson, R. H. (1987) "Quasi-states, dual regimes and neoclassical theory: international jurisprudence and the third world", *IO*, 41: 519–49.

—— (1999) *Race, Caste, and Status: Indians in Colonial Spanish America*, Albuquerque: University of New Mexico Press.

Jacobini, H. B. (1954) *A Study of the Philosophy of International Law as Seen in the Works of Latin American Writers*, The Hague: Martinus Nijhoff Publishers .

Jain, M. (1999) "Global trade and the new millennium: defining the scope of intellectual property protection of plant genetic resources and traditional knowledge in India", *HICLR*, 22: 777.

Jain, S. C. (2003) "Jainism, war and international law", *IJIL*, 43(4): 748–57.

Jamar, S. D. (2001) "Religion and international law", *JLR*, 16(2): 609–12.

Janis, M. W. (1993) "Religion and international law", *ASILP*, 87.

—— (2004) "Religion and the literature of international law: some standard tests", in M. Janis and C. Evans (eds) *Religion and International Law*, 2nd edn, Leiden: Martinus Nijhoff Publishers.

—— (2005) *The American Tradition in International Law. Great Expectations 1789–1914*, Oxford: Oxford University Press.

—— and Evans, C. (eds) (2004) *Religion and International Law*, 2nd edn, Leiden: Martinus Nijhoff Publishers.

Jaquemet, S. (2001) "The cross-fertilization of international humanitarian law and international refugee law", *IRRC*, 83: 651–74.

Jawara, F. and Kwa, A. (2003) *Behind the Scenes at the WTO: The Real World of International Trade Negotiations*, London: Zed Books.

Jaye, T. (2003) *Issues of Sovereignty, Strategy, and Security in the Economic Community of West African States' Intervention in the Liberian Civil War*, Lewiston, NY: Edwin Mellen Press.

Jefferson, T. (1802) "Jefferson's letter to the Danbury Baptists" (01/01/1802) US Library of Congress. Available at http://www.loc.gov/loc/lcib/9806/danpost.html.

Jehl, D. and Schmitt, E. (2004) "In abuse: a portrait of ill-prepared overwhelmed GIs", *New York Times*, May 9.

—— (2004a) "Officer Says Army Tried to Curb Red Cross Visits to Prison in Iraq," *New York Times*, 19 May 2004, A1.

Jellinek, G. (1880) *Die rechtliche Natur der Staatenverträge*, Vienna: Hölder.

—— (1882) *Die Lehre von den Staatsverbindungen*, Vienna: Hölder.

Jenkins, B. M. and Rubin, A. P. (1978) "New vulnerabilities and the acquisition of new weapons by nongovernmental groups", in A. E. Evans and J. F. Murphy (eds) *Legal Aspects of International Terrorism*, Lexington, MA/Toronto: D. C. Heath.

Jenks, D. T. (1995) "The convention on biological diversity: an efficient framework for the preservation of life on earth?", *NJILB*, 15(3): 636.

Jennings, R. Y. (1938) "The Caroline and McLeod cases", *AJIL*, 32: 82.

—— (1980) "What is international law and how do we tell it when we see it?", in *The Cambridge-Tilburg Law Lectures*, Deventer: Kluwer.

Jochnick, C. (2004) "Cleavages in the human rights movement" in *Proceedings of the 20th Anniversary Celebrations of the Harvard Law School Human Rights Program: Speeches, Panels, and Roundtable Held at Harvard Law School*, October 2004, Harvard Law School Human Rights Program.

Johnson, M. (1992) "Research on traditional environmental knowledge: its development and its role", in M. Johnson (ed.) *Lore: Capturing Traditional Environmental Knowledge*, Ottawa: IDRC.

Johnston, D. M. (1997) *Consent and Commitment in the World Community*, Irvington-on-Hudson, NY: Transnational Publishers.

—— (2005) "World constitutionalism in the theory of international law", in R. S. Macdonald and D. M. Johnston (eds) *Towards World Constitutionalism: Issues in the Legal Ordering of the World Community*, Leiden: Brill.

Jones, D. V. (1982) *License for Empire: Colonialism by Treaty in Early America*, Chicago, IL: University of Chicago Press.

Joseph, S. (2004) *Corporations and Transnational Human Rights Litigation*, Oxford: Hart Publishing.

Jovanovic, M. A. (2005) "Recognizing minority identities through collective rights", *HRQ*, 27: 625–51.

429

Joyner, C. C. (1984) "Reflections on the lawfulness of invasion", *AJIL*, 78: 131–44.

Juss, S. (1998) "Toward a morally legitimate reform of refugee law: the uses of cultural jurisprudence", *HHRJ*, 11: 311–54.

—— (2004) "Free movement and the world order", *IJRL*, 16: 289–335.

Justinian (1985) *Digest*, Latin text edited by T. Mommsen and P. Kruger, translation edited by A. Watson, Philadelphia: University of Pennsylvania Press.

Kacowicz, A. M. (2001) "Studying international norms", in A. S. Klieman, D. Vital and A. Ben-Zvi (eds) *Global Politics: Essays in Honour of David Vital*, London: Frank Cass.

—— (2004) "Compliance and non-compliance with international norms in territorial disputes: the Latin American record of arbitrations", in E. Benvenisti and M. Hirsch (eds) *The Impact of International Law on International Cooperation: Theoretical Perspectives*, Cambridge: Cambridge University Press.

Kadelbach, S. and Kleinlein, T. (2006) "Überstaatliches Verfassungsrecht", *AV*, 44(3): 235–66.

Kagan, R. (2002) "Power and weakness", *PR*, 113. Available at http://www.hoover.org/publications/policyreview/3460246.html.

—— (2003) *Of Paradise and Power: America and Europe in the New World Order*, New York: Alfred A. Knopf.

—— (2004) "America's crisis of legitimacy", *FA*, 83: 65–87.

Kahler, M. (2000a) "Legalization as strategy: the Asia-Pacific case" *IO*, 54: 549–71.

—— (2000b) "Conclusion: the causes and consequences of legalization", *IO*, 54: 661–83.

Kahn, P. W. (2000) "Speaking law to power: popular sovereignty, human rights, and the new international order", *CJIL*, 1(1): 1–18.

Kant, I. (1991) "The idea for a universal history with a cosmopolitan purpose", in H. Reiss (ed.) *Political Writings*, 2nd edn, Cambridge: Cambridge University Press.

Karavites, P. (1982) *Capitulations and Greek Inter-State Relations*, Göttingen: Vandenhoeck & Ruprecht.

—— (1987) "Diplomatic envoys in the Homeric world", *RIDA*, 34(3): 41.

—— with T. Wren (1992) *Promise-Giving and Treaty-Making: Homer and the Near East*, Leiden: Brill.

Karmis, D. and Norman, W. (eds) (2005) *Theories of Federalism: a Reader*, New York: Palgrave Macmillan.

Karpik, L. (1999) *French Lawyers: A Study in Collective Action, 1274 to 1994* (trans. N. Scott), Oxford: Clarendon Press.

Karsh, E. (2006) *Islamic Imperialism: A History*, New Haven, CN: Yale University Press.

Kastemont, G. (1974) *Diplomatique en Droit International en Asie Occidentale (1600–1220 av. J.C.)*, Louvain-la-Neuve: Université Catholique de Louvain.

Kastrup, J. (1997) "The internationalization of indigenous rights from the environmental and human rights perspective", *TJIL*, 32: 97–122.

Kaufer, E. (1989) *The Economics of the Patent System*, Chur: Harwood Academic Publishers.

Kaufman, L. and Mallory, K. (eds) (1993) *The Last Extinction*, Cambridge, MA: MIT Press.

Keck, M. E. and Sikkink, K. (1998) *Activists Beyond Borders*, Ithaca, NY: Cornell University Press.

Keen, M. (1965) *The Laws of War in the Late Middle Ages*, London: Routledge & Kegan Paul.

Keene, E. (2002) *Beyond the Anarchical Society: Grotius, Colonialism and Order in World Politics*, Cambridge: Cambridge University Press.

—— (2007) "A case study of the construction of international hierarchy: British treaty-making against the slave trade in the early nineteenth century", *IO*, 61(2): 311–39.

Keens-Soper, H. M. A. (1972) "The French political Academy", *ESR*, 2.

Kelley, D. R. (1970) *Foundations of Modern Historical Scholarship: Language, Law and History in the French Renaissance*, New York: Columbia University Press.

Kelley, J. G. (2007) "Who keeps international commitments and why? The International Criminal Court and bilateral nonsurrender agreements", *APSR*, 101(3): 573–89.

Kellow, A. (2006) "A new process for negotiating environmental agreements? The Asia–Pacific climate partnership beyond Kyoto", *AJIA*, 60: 287–303.

Kelly, J. M. (1992) *A Short History of Western Legal Theory*, Oxford: Clarendon Press.

Kelsen, H. (1928) *Das Problem der Souveränität und die Theorie des Völkerrechts*, 2nd edn, Tübingen: Mohr.

—— (1942) "Lecture two: the nature of international law", in *Law and Peace in International Relations*, Cambridge, MA: Harvard University Press.

—— (1960) *Reine Rechtslehre*, 2nd edn, Vienna: F. Deuticke.

—— (1966) *Principles of International Law*, in R. W. Tucker (ed.) 2nd edn, New York: Holt, Rinehart & Winston.

Kennan, G. F. (1984) "Diplomacy in the modern world", in *American Diplomacy*, expanded edn, Chicago, IL: University of Chicago Press.

Kennedy, D. (1980) "Toward a historical understanding of legal consciousness: the case of classical legal thought in America 1850–1940", *RLS*, 3: 3–24.

—— (1987) "The move to institutions", *CLR*, 8(5): 841–988.

—— (1988) "A new stream of international law scholarship: lectures 1 and 3", *WILJ*, 7: 1–39.

—— (1994a) "The international style in postwar law and policy", *ULR*, 1: 7–104.

—— (1994b) "A semiotics of legal argument", reprinted with "European introduction: four objections" and bibliographies in *Collected Courses of the Academy of European Law, Book 2*, Netherlands: Kluwer Academic Publishers.

—— (1996) "International law and the nineteenth century: history of an illusion", *NJIL*, 65: 385–420.

—— (1998 [1975]) *The Rise and Fall of Classical Legal Thought*, Cambridge: AFAR.

—— (1999) "The disciplines of international law and policy", *LJIL*, 12: 9–133.

—— (2000) "When renewal repeats: thinking against the box", *NYUJILP*, 32: 335–500.

—— (2003) "Two globalizations of law and legal thought: 1850–1968", *SULR*, 36.

—— (2004) "Images of religion in international legal theory" in M. Janis and C. Evans (eds) *Religion and International Law*, 2nd edn, Leiden: Martinus Nijhoff Publishers.

—— (2005) *The Dark Side of Virtue*, Princeton, NJ: Princeton University Press.

—— (2006) *Law and War*, Princeton, NJ: Princeton University Press.

Kent, A. (2007) *Beyond Compliance. China, IOs, and Global Security*, Stanford, CA: Stanford University Press.

Keohane, R. O. (1982) "The demand for international regimes", *IO*, 36: 325–55.

—— (1984) *After Hegemony: Cooperation and Discord in the World Political Economy*, Princeton, NJ: Princeton University Press.

—— (1988) "International institutions: two approaches", *ISQ*, 32: 379–96.

—— (1997) "International relations and international law: two optics", *HILJ*, 38: 487–502.

——, Macedo, S. and Moravscic, A. (unpublished paper) "Democracy-enhancing multilateralism", Robert Keohane Working Papers, 5 June 2007. Available at http://www.princeton.edu/~rkeohane/workingpapers/DemocracyEnhancingMultilateralism.pdf.

——, Moravcsik, A. and Slaughter, A. (2000) "Legalized dispute resolution: interstate and transnational", *IO*, 54: 457–88.

Kern, H. (2004) "Strategies of legal change: Great Britain, international law and the abolition of the transatlantic slave trade", *JHIL*, 6: 233–58.

Kersch, K. I. (2005) "The new legal transnationalism, the globalized judiciary, and the rule of law", *WGSLR*, 4: 345.

Khadduri, M. (1966) *The Islamic Law on Nations. Shaybani's Siyar*, Baltimore, MD: Johns Hopkins University Press.

Khalaf, R. and Fidler, S. (2007) "From frontline attack to terror by franchise", *Financial Times*, col. 1, 5 July 2007, London. Available at http://search.ft.com/search?queryText=From+frontline+attack+to+terror+by+franchise&aje=false&dse=&dsz=&x=9&y=6.

Khan, I. (2004) *Proceedings of the 20th Anniversary Celebrations of the Harvard Law School Human Rights Program: Speeches, Panels, and Roundtable Held at Harvard Law School, October 2004*, Harvard Law School Human Rights Program.

Kibre, P. (1948) *The Nations in the Medieval Universities*, Cambridge, MA: Medieval Academy of America.

Kingsbury, B. (2000) "Reconstructing self-determination: a rational approach", in P. Aikio and M. Scheinin (eds) *Operationalizing the Right of Indigenous Peoples to Self-Determination*, Åbo, Finland: Institute for Human Rights, Åbo Akademi University.

——, Krisch, N. and Stewart, R. B. (2005) "The emergence of global adminsitrative law", *LCP*, 68: 15–61.

Kirsch, P. and Robinson, D. (2002) "Reaching agreement at the Rome Conference", in A. Cassese, P. Gaeta and J. R. W. D. Jones (ed.) *The Rome Statute of the International Criminal Court: A Commentary*, Oxford: Oxford University Press.

Kirton, J. J. and Trebilcock, M. J. (2004) *Hard Choices, Soft Law*, Burlington, VT: Ashgate.

Kiss, A. C. and Shelton, D. (1986) "Systems analysis of international law: a methodological inquiry", *NYIL*, 17.

—— (1994) *International Environmental Law*, 2nd edn, New York: Transnational Publishers.

Kiss, E. (2000) "Moral ambition within and beyond political constraints: reflections on restorative justice", in R. I. Rotberg and D. Thompson (ed.) *Truth v. Justice: The Morality of Truth Commissions*, Princeton, NJ: Princeton University Press.

Klabbers, J. (1998) "The undesirability of soft law", *NJIL*, 67: 381–91.

—— (1999) "Review of M. Byers, *Custom, Power and the Power of Rules: International Relations and Customary International Law*", *FYIL*, 10: 451–9.

—— (2003) "(I can't get no) recognition: subjects doctrine and the emergence of non-state actors", in J. Petman and J. Klabbers (eds) *Nordic Cosmopolitism. Essays in International Law for Martti Koskenniemi*, Leiden/Boston, MA: Martinus Nijhoff Publishers.

—— (2004) "Constitutionalism lite", *IOLR*, 1(1): 31–58.

—— (2005) "The relative autonomy of international law or the forgotten politics of inter-disciplinarity", *JILIR*, 1: 35–48.

—— (2006) "The right to be taken seriously: self-determination in international law", *HRQ*, 28: 186–206.

Klein, P. (2000) "Les problèmes soulevés par la référence à la 'communauté internationale' comme facteur de légitimité", in O. Corten and B. Delcourt (eds) *Droit, Légitimation et Politique Extérieure: l'Europe et la Guerre du Kosovo*, Brussels: Bruylant.

—— (2003) "The effects of US predominance on the elaboration of treaty regimes and on the evolution of the law of treaties", in M. Byers and G. Nolte (eds) *United States Hegemony and the Foundations of International Law*, Cambridge: Cambridge University Press.

Klippel, D. (1976) *Politische Freiheit und Freiheitsrechte im deutschen Naturrecht des 18 Jahrhunderts*, Paderborn: Schöninghaus.

Klir, G. (1969) *An Approach to General Systems Theory*, New York: Van Nostrand Reinhold.

Knop, K. (2002) *Diversity and Self-Determination in International Law*, Cambridge/New York: Cambridge University Press.

Koh, H. H. (1991) "Transnational public law litigation", *YLJ*, 100: 2347–402.

—— (1994) "The 'Haiti paradigm' in United States human rights policy", *YLJ*, 103: 2391–435.

—— (1996a) "Transnational legal process", *NLR*, 75(1): 181–208.

—— (1996b) "Why do nations obey international law", *YLJ*, 106: 2599–659.

—— (1997a) "Review essay: why do nations obey international law?" *YLJ*, 106: 2599–659.

—— (1997b) "The 1998 Frankel lecture: bringing international law home", *HLR*, 35: 623–81.

—— (1999) "How is international human rights law enforced?", *ILJ*, 74: 1397–417.

—— (2002) "Agora: military commissions", *AJIL*, 96(2): 320–58.

—— (2007) "Commentary: a world drowning in guns", in T. J. Biersteker, P. J. Spiro, C. L. Sriram and V. Raffo (eds) *International Law and International Relations*, London: Routledge.

Kohen, M. (2003) "The use of force by the United States after the end of the cold war and its impact on international law", in M. Byers and G. Nolte (eds) *United States Hegemony and the Foundations of International Law*, Cambridge: Cambridge University Press.

Kolb, R. (2001) "La structure constitutionnelle du droit international public", *CYIL*, 39: 69–115.

Kongolo, T. (1999) "Trademarks and geographic indications within the frameworks of the African Intellectual Property Organization agreement and the TRIPS agreement", *JWIP*, 2: 832.

Koremenos, B. (2001) "Loosening the ties that bind: a learning model of agreement flexibility", *IO*, 55: 289–325.

Koskenniemi, M. (1989) *From Apology to Utopia: The Structure of International Legal Argument*, Helsinki: Finnish Lawyers' Publishing Company.

—— (1990) "The politics of international law", *EJIL*, 1: 4–32.

—— (1991) "The future of statehood", *HILJ*, 32(2): 397.

—— (1999) "Letter to the editors of the symposium", *AJIL*, 93: 351–61.

—— (2000) "Carl Schmitt, Hans Morgenthau, and the image of law in international relations", in M. Byers (ed.) *The Role of Law in International Politics*, Oxford: Oxford University Press.

—— (2001) *The Gentle Civilizer of Nations. The Rise and Fall of International Law 1870–1960*, Cambridge: Cambridge University Press.

—— (2002) "Iraq and the 'Bush doctrine' of pre-emptive self-defence", *Crimes of War Project*. Available at http://www.crimesofwar.org/expert/bush-koskenniemi.html.

—— (2005a) *From Apology to Utopia. The Structure of International Legal Argument. Reissue with a New Epilogue*, Cambridge: Cambridge University Press.

—— (2005b) "International law in Europe: between tradition and renewal", *EJIL*, 16: 113–24.

—— (2006a) *From Apology to Utopia. The Structure of International Legal Argument* (reissue with a new epilogue), Cambridge: Cambridge University Press.

—— (2006b) "What is international law for?", in M. Evans (ed.) *International Law*, 2nd edn, Oxford: Oxford University Press.

—— (2007a) "The fate of international law: between technique and politics", *MLR*, 70: 1–32.

—— (2007b) "Not excepting the Iroquois themselves", in *Machiavelli, Pufendorf, and the Prehistory of International Law*, Florence: EUI, Max Weber Lecture Series.

—— (2008) "Into positivism: Georg Friedrich von Martens (1756–1821) and modern international law", *CIJCDT*, 15.

—— and Leino, P. (2002) "Fragmentation of international law. Postmodern anxieties?", *LJIL*, 15: 553–79.

Krasner, S. D. (1982) "Structural causes and regime consequences: regime as intervening variables", *IO*, 36: 185–205 [reprinted in S. Krasner (ed.) (1983) *International Regimes*, Ithaca, NY: Cornell University Press].

—— (ed.) (1983a) *International Regimes*, Ithaca, NY: Cornell University Press.

—— (1993) "Westphalia and all that", in J. Goldstein and R. Keohane (eds) *Ideas and Foreign Policy*, Ithaca, NY: Cornell University Press.

—— (1999) *Sovereignty: Organized Hypocrisy*, Princeton, NJ: Princeton University Press.

Kratochwil, F. (1989) *Rules, Norms and Decisions: On the Conditions of Legal and Practical Reasoning in International Relations and Domestic Affairs*, Cambridge: Cambridge University Press.

—— (1998) "Politics, norms, and peaceful change", in T. Dunne, R. W. Cox and K. Booth (eds) *The Eighty Years Crisis*, Cambridge: Cambridge University Press.

—— (2000) "How do norms matter?", in M. Byers (ed.) *The Role of Law in International Politics*, Oxford: Oxford University Press.

—— (2006) "The genealogy of multilateralism", in E. Newman, R. Thakur and J. Tirman (eds) *Multilateralism under challenge?*, Tokyo: United Nations University Press.

Krisch, N. (2003) "More equal than the rest? Hierarchy, equality and US predominance in international law", in M. Byers and G. Nolte (eds) *United States Hegemony and the Foundations of International Law*, Cambridge: Cambridge University Press.

—— (2005) "International law in times of hegemony: unequal power and the shaping of the international legal order", *EJIL*, 16: 369.

—— (2006) "The pluralism of global administrative law", *EJIL*, 17: 247–78.

—— and Kingsbury, B. (2006a) "Global governance and global administrative law in the international legal order", *EJIL*, 17: 1–13.

—— (2006b) "Introduction: global governance and global administrative law in the international legal order", *EJIL*, 17: 13–45.

Kritsiotis, D. (2004) "When states use armed force", in C. Reus-Smit (ed.) *The Politics of International Law*, Cambridge: Cambridge University Press.

Kritsiotis, D. (2004) "Arguments of Mass Confusion," *European Journal of International Law*, 15: 233–78.

Ku, C. (2005) "Forging a multilayered system of global governance", in R. S. Macdonald and D. M. Johnston (eds) *Towards World Constitutionalism: Issues in the Legal Ordering of the World Community*, Leiden: Brill.

—— and Diehl, P. F. (2006) "Filling in the gaps: extra-systemic mechanisms for addressing imbalances between the international legal operating and normative systems", *GG*, 12: 161–83.

——, Diehl, P. F., Simmons, B. A., Dallmeyer, D. G. and Jacobson, H. K. (2001) "Exploring international law: opportunities and challenges for political science research: a roundtable", *ISR*, 3: 3–23.

Ku, J. G. (2000) "The delegation of federal power to international organizations: new problems with old solutions", *MnLR*, 85: 71.

—— and Nzelibe, J. (2006) "Do international criminal tribunals deter or exacerbate humanitarian atrocities?", *WULQ*, 84(4): 777–833.

Kuhn, A. (1996) *The Structure of Scientific Revolution*, 3rd edn, Chicago. IL: University of Chicago Press.

Kumar, C. R. (2006) "National human rights institutions and economic, social, and cultural rights: toward the institutionalization and developmentalization of human rights", *HRQ*, 28: 755–79.

Kumm, M. (2004) "The legitimacy of international law: a constitutionalist framework of analysis", *EJIL*, 15(5): 907–31.

Kurlantzick, J. (2007) *Charm Offensive: How China's Soft Power is Transforming the World*, New Haven, CN: Yale University Press.

Kuruk, P. (1999) "Protecting folklore under modern intellectual property regimes: a reappraisal of the tensions between individual and communal rights in Africa and the United States", *AULR*, 48: 769.

Kwakwa, E. (2000) "Regulating the international economy: what role for the state?", in M. Byers (ed.) *The Role of Law in International Politics*, Oxford: Oxford University Press.

—— (2003) "The international community, international law and the United States: three in one, two against one or one and the same?", in M. Byers and G. Nolte (eds) *United States Hegemony and the Foundations of International Law*, Cambridge: Cambridge University Press.

Kymlicka, W. (1989) *Liberalism, Community, and Culture*, Oxford: Clarendon Press.

Labra, R. M. D. (1912) *España y América, 1812–1912; Estudios Políticos, Históricos y de*

Derecho Internacional, Madrid: Tipografia del Sindicato de Publicidad.

Laghmani, S. (2003) *Histoire de Droit des Gens. Du Jus Gentium au Jus Publicum Europaeum*, Paris: A. Pedone.

Lambert, H. (1999) "Protection against *refoulement* from Europe: human rights law comes to the rescue", *ICLQ*, 48: 515–44.

—— (2005) "The European Convention on Human Rights and the protection of refugees: limits and opportunities", *RSQ*, 24: 39–55.

—— (2006) "The EU Asylum Qualification Directive, its impact on the jurisprudence of the United Kingdom and international law", *ICLQ*, 55: 161–92.

Langdon, S. and Gardiner, A. H. (1920) "The treaty of alliance between Hatusili, King of the Hittites, and the Pharaoh Rameses II of Egypt", *JEA*, 6: 179.

Larsen, J. A. O. (1968) *Greek Federal States: Their Institutions and History*, Oxford: Clarendon Press.

Lasswell, H. D. and McDougal, M. S. (1943) "Legal education and public policy: professional training in the public interest", *YLJ*, 52: 203–95.

Laszlo, E. (ed.) (1972) *The Relevance of General Systems Theory*, New York: George Braziller.

—— (ed.) (1973) *The World System: Models, Norms, Variations*, New York: George Braziller.

Lauren, P. G. (2003) *The Evolution of International Human Rights: Visions Seen*, Philadelphia, PA: University of Pennsylvania Press.

—— (2007) "'To preserve and build on its achievements and to redress its shortcomings': the journey from the Commission on Human Rights to the Human Rights Council", *HRQ*, 29: 307–45.

Lauterpacht, E. and Bethlehem, D. (2003) "The scope and content of the principle of *non-refoulement*: opinion", in E. Feller, V. Turk and F. Nicholson (eds) *Refugee Protection in International Law – UNHCR's Global Consultations on International Protection*, Cambridge: Cambridge University Press.

Lauterpacht, H. (1927 [1923]) *Private Law Sources and Analogies of International Law*, London: Longman.

—— (1931) "The so-called Anglo-American and continental schools of thought in international law", *BYIL*, 12: 31–62.

—— (1933) *The Function of Law in the International Community*, Oxford: Clarendon Press.

Lavalle, B. (1993) *Las Promesas Ambiguas: Ensayos sobre el Criollismo Colonial en los Andes*, Lima: Pontificia Universidad Católica.

Lawrence, T. J. (1885) *Essays on Some Disputed Questions in Modern International Law*, Cambridge: Deighton & Bell.

Laycock, D. (1990) "Formal, substantive and dis-aggregated neutrality toward religion", *DLR*, 39: 993–1018.

LeBlanc, L. J. (1977) *OAS and the Promotion and Protection of Human Rights*, The Hague: Martinus Nijhoff Publishers.

—— (1984) "The intent to destroy groups in the genocide convention: the proposed U.S. understanding, *AJIL*, 78: 369–85.

Lee, R. S. (1999) "Introduction: the Rome Conference and its contribution to international law", in R. S. Lee (ed.) *The International Criminal Court: the Making of the Rome Statute – Issues, Negotiations, and Results*, The Hague: Kluwer Law International.

Legro, J. W. (1997) "Which norms matter? Revisiting the 'failure' of internationalism", *IO*, 51: 31–63.

Leon De Ellias, A. (1946) *El Principio de la no Intervención y su Influencia en el Desarrollo del Derecho Internacional Americano*, Mexico City: D. F. Tipografica Ortega.

Lesaffer, R. (2000) "The medieval canon law of contract and early modern treaty law", *JHIL*, 2: 178–98.

—— (2004) "Peace treaties from Lodi to Westphalia", in R. Lesaffer (ed.) *Peace Treaties and International Law in European History: From the Late Middle Ages to World War One*, Cambridge: Cambridge University Press.

Levack, B. P. (1981) "The English civilians, 1500–1750", in W. Prest, (ed.) *Lawyers in Early Modern Europe and America*, New York: Holmes & Meier.

Lewis, C. (2005) "UNHCR's contribution to the development of international refugee law: its foundations and evolution", *IJRL*, 17: 67–90.

Lichtenstein, C. (2001) "Hard law v. soft law: unnecessary dichotomy?", *IL*, 35: 1433.

Lieber, F. (1868) *Nationalism and Inter-nationalism*, New York: Scribner.

Limbach, J. (2001) "The concept of the supremacy of the constitution", *MLR*, 64: 1.

Lincoln, A. (1838) "The perpetuation of our political institutions", in address to the Young Men's Lyceum of Springfield, Illinois, 27 January 1838. Available at http://teachingamericanhistory.org/library/index.asp?document=157.

Lindley, M. F. (1969 [1926]) *The Acquisition and Government of Backward Territory in International Law*, London: Longman, Green & Co.

Linklater, A. and Suganami, H. (2006) *The English School of International Relations*, Cambridge: Cambridge University Press.

Lippert, O. (1999) "One trip to the dentist is enough – reasons to strengthen intellectual property rights through the free trade area of the Americas now", in O. Lippert (ed.) *Competitive Strategies for the Protection of Intellectual Properties*, Vancouver: The Fraser Institute.

Lipson, C. (1991) "Why are some international agreements informal?", *IO*, 45: 495–538.

Livy (1929 [1982]) *History of Rome* (trans. B. O. Foster), Cambridge, MA: Loeb Classical Library.

Lochore, R. A. (1935) *History of the Idea of Civilization in France (1830–1870)*, Bonn: L. Röhrscheid.

Locke, J. (1689) *The Two Treatises of Civil Government*, London: A. Millar.

López Medina, D. E. (2004) *Teoría impura del derecho: la transformación de la cultura jurídica latinoamericana*, Bogotá: Ediciones Universidad de los Andes/Universidad Nacional.

Lorimer, M. J. (1884) "'La Doctrine de la Reconnaissance', Fondement du Droit International", *RDILC*, 16: 333–59.

Low, P. (2007) *Interstate Relations in Classical Greece*, Cambridge: Cambridge University Press.

Lowe, V. (1999) "Sustainable Development and Unsustainable Arguments", in A. Boyle and D. Freestone (eds) *International Law and Sustainable Development: Past Achievements and Future Challenges*, Oxford: Oxford University Press.

—— (2000a) "The politics of law-making: are the method and character of norm creation changing?", in M. Byers (ed.) *The Role of Law in International Politics*, Oxford: Oxford University Press, 207–26.

Lowenstein, J. (2002) *The Author's Due: Printing and the Pre-History of Copyright*, Chicago, IL: University of Chicago Press.

Lubbers, R. (2003) "Foreword", in E. Feller, V. Turk and F. Nicholson (eds) *Refugee Protection in International Law*, Cambridge: Cambridge University Press.

Luhmann, N. (1983) *Rechtssoziologie*, Opladen: Westdeutscher Verlag.

—— (1995a) *Das Recht der Gesellschaft*, Frankfurt am Main: Suhrkamp.

—— (1995b) *Social Systems*, Stanford, CA: Stanford University Press.

—— (1997) *Die Gesellschaft der Gesellschaft*, Frankfurt am Main, Suhrkamp.

Luig, K. (1972) "The institutes of national law in the seventeenth and eighteenth centuries", *JR*, 17: 193–226.

Lund, J. (2001) "Barbarian theorizing and the limits of Latin American exceptionalism", *CC*, 47: 54–90.

Lutz, E. L. (2007a) "Adoption of U.N. Declaration a matter of course", *Indian Country Today*, 1 June 2007. Available at http://www.indiancountry.com/content.cfm?id=1096415122.

—— (2007b) "Commentary: international criminal accountability at the intersection of law and politics", in T. J. Biersteker, P. J. Spiro, C. L. Sriram and V. Raffo (eds) *International Law and International Relations*, London: Routledge.

—— and Sikkink, K. (2000) "International human rights law and practice in Latin America", *IO*, 54: 633–59.

Mably, A. de (Gabriel Bonnot) (1758) *The Principles of Negotiation, or An Introduction to the Public Law of Europe Founded on Treaties*, London: James Rivington & James Fletcher.

Macalister-Smith, P. and Schwietzke, J. (2001) "Bibliography of the textbooks and comprehensive treatises on positive international law of the 19th century", *JHIL*, 3: 75–142.

McCarthy, C. (2005) "The Paradox of the International Law of Military Occupation: Sovereignty and the Reformation of Iraq," *Journal of Conflict and Security Law*, 10: 43–74.

McCarthy, D. J. (1963) *Treaty and Covenant*, Rome: Pontifical Biblical Institute.

McCorquodale, R. (2006) "Beyond state sovereignty: the international legal system and non-state participants", *RCDI*, 8: 103–59.

—— and Simons, P. (2007) "Responsibility beyond borders: state responsibility for extraterritorial violations by corporations of international human rights law", *MLR*, 70: 598–625.

McCulloch, W. (1965) *Embodiments of Mind*, Cambridge, MA: MIT Press.

McDonald, L. (1998) "Can collective and individuals rights coexist?", *MULR*, 22: 310.

McDonald, M. (1991) "Should communities have rights? Reflections on liberal individualism", *CJLJ*, 4: 217–38.

McDougal, M. S. (1955) "The hydrogen bomb tests and the international law of the sea", *AJIL*, 49(3): 356–61.

—— (1960) "Some basic concepts about international law: a policy orientated approach", *JCR*, 4: 337–54.

—— and Feliciano, F. P. (1961) *Law and Minimum World Public Order: The Legal Regulation of International Coercion*, New Haven, CN/London: Yale University Press.

—— and Lasswell, H. D. (1959) "The identification and appraisal of diverse systems of public order", *AJIL*, 53: 1–29.

435

McGinnis, J. O. (2006) "The comparative disadvantage of customary international law", *HJLPP*, 30(1): 7–14.

Machlup, F. (1958) *An Economic Review of the Patent System, Study of the Subcommittee on Patents, Trademarks, and Copyrights of the Committee on the Judiciary*, Washington, DC: US Printing Printing Office.

Mackenzie, M. (1955) *Los Ideales de Bolívar en el Derecho Internacional Americano*, Bogotá: Impresora Nacional.

Macleod, C. (1988) *Inventing the Industrial Revolution: The English Patent System, 1660–1800*, Cambridge: Cambridge University Press.

Macmillan, L. and Olsson, L. (2001) "Rights and accountability", *FM*, 10: 38–42.

McNair, A. (1956) *International Law Opinions*, London: Cambridge University Pres.

McNamara, D. (1998) "The law and the protection of refugees: the way ahead", paper presented at The Realities of Refugee Determination on the Eve of a New Millenium: The Role of the Judiciary, 3rd Conference, October 1998, Ottawa, Canada.

Mahmassani, S. (1966) "The principles of international law in the light of Islamic doctrine", *RC*, Collected Course, 117(1): 201–328.

Maine, H. S. (1887) *International Law. The Whewell Lectures 1887*, London: Murray.

Mainville, R. (2001) *An Overview of Aboriginal and Treaty Rights and Compensation for their Breach*, Saskatoon: Purich.

Mallet, R. (1999) "Sub-Saharan Africa in the global economy", *LPIB*, 30.

March, J. G. and Olsen, J. P. (1999) "The institutional dynamics of international political orders", in P. J. Katzenstein, R. O. Keohane and S. D. Krasner (eds) *Exploration and Contestation in the Study of World Politics*, Cambridge, MA: MIT Press.

Marshall, M. G. and Gurr, T. R. *Peace and Conflict 2005: A Global Survey of Armed Conflicts, Self Determination Movements and Democracy*. University of Maryland: CIDCM.

Marston, G. (1986) "United Kingdom materials on international law", *BYIL*, 57.

—— (1990) "The evidences of British state practice in the field of international law", in A. Carty and G. Danilenko (eds) *Perestroika and International Law, Current Anglo-Soviet Approaches to International Law*, Edinburgh: Edinburgh University Press.

Martens, G. F. von (1795) *Summary of the Law of Nations, Founded on the Treaties and Customs of the Modern Nations of Europe* (trans. W. Cobbett), Philadelphia, PA: Thomas Bradford.

Martin, V. (1940) *La Vie Internationale dans la Grèce des Cités*, Paris: Recueil Sirey.

Martin, W. and Winters, A. (eds) (1996) *The Uruguay Round and Developing Countries*, Cambridge: Cambridge University Press.

Martines, L. (1968) *Lawyers and Statecraft in Renaissance Florence*, Princeton, NJ: Princeton University Press.

Martinez Cobo, J. (1984) "Study of the problem of discrimination against indigenous populations", Geneva: United Nations Commission on Human Rights, Sub-Commission on Prevention of Discrimination and Protection of Minorities.

Matthaei, L. E. (1907) "On the classification of Roman allies", *CQ*, 1: 182.

Mattingley, G. (1955) *Renaissance Diplomacy*, London: Jonathan Cape.

Maturana, H. R. and Varela, F. J. (1980) *Autopoiesis and Cognition: The Realization of the Living*, Dordrecht: Reidel.

Maury, L.-F.-A. (1859) *Histoire des Religions de la Grèce Antique*, Paris: Librairie Philosophique de Ladrange.

Mavroidis, P. C. (2004) "Human rights, developing countries, and the WTO constraint: the very thing that makes you rich makes me poor?", in E. Benvenisti and M. Hirsch (eds) *The Impact of International Law on International Cooperation: Theoretical Perspectives*, Cambridge: Cambridge University Press.

Mayer, F. (2004) "Völkerrecht und Cyberspace: Entgrenztes Recht und entgrenzte Medien", in U. Thiedeke (ed.) *Soziologie des Cyberspace: Medien, Strukturen und Semantiken*, Wiesbaden: VS Verlag für Sozialwissenschaften.

Mazzetti, M. (2007) "Joint chiefs nominee blames Iraqis for lack of progress", *N.Y. Times*, A11, col. 1, 1 August 2007, New York.

—— and Sanger, D. E. (2007) "Bush advisers see a failed strategy against al Qaeda", *N.Y. Times*, pg. A1, col. 1, 18 July 2007, New York.

Mazzotti, J. A. (ed.) (2000) *Agencias Criollas: La Ambigüedad "colonial" en las Letras Jispanoamericanas*, Pittsburgh, PA: Instituto Internacional de Literatura Iberoamericana.

Meadows, D. H., Meadows, D. L., Randers, J. and Behrens, W. W., III (1972) *Limits to Growth*, Cambridge, MA: MIT Press.

Meidinger, E. (2007) "Beyond Westphalia: competitive legalization in emerging transnational regulatory systems", in C. Brütsch and D. Lehmkuhl (eds) *Law and Legalization in Transnational Relations*, London: Routledge.

Meier, C. (1990) *The Greek Discovery of Politics* (trans. D. McLintock), Cambridge, MA: Harvard University Press.

"Memorandum for Alberto R. Gonzales, Counsel to the President, and Willaim J. Haynes II, General Counsel of the Department of Defense, Re: Application of Treaties and Law to al Qaeda and Taliban Detainees" (25 January 2002). Available at http://lawofwar.org/Torture_Memos_analysis.htm.

"Memorandum for Alberto R. Gonzales, Counsel to the President, Re; Standards of Conduct of Interrogation under 18 U.S.C. Sections 2340-2340A" (30 December 2004). Available at http://www.usdoj.gov/olc/18usc23402340a2.htm.

Mendelson, A. (1995) "The subjective element in customary international law", BYIL: 66–277.

Mendenhall, G. (1955) Law and Covenant in Israel and the Ancient Near East, Pittsburgh, PA: Presbyterian Board of Colportage of Western Pennsylvania.

Méndez, J. E. (2001) "National reconciliation, transnational justice, and the International Criminal Court", EIA, 15(1): 25–44.

Merges, R. (1988) "Intellectual property in higher life forms: the patent system and controversial technologies", MLR, 47: 1051.

Meron, T. (2000) "The humanization of humanitarian law", AJIL, 94: 239.

Mertus, J. (1999–2000) "Considering non-state actors in the new millennium: toward expanded participation in norm generation and norm application", NYUJILP, 32: 537–66.

Meyer, L. (2006) "Soft Law for Solid Contracts? A Comparative Analysis of the Value of the UNIDROIT Principles of International Commercial Contracts and the Principles of European Contract Law to the Process of Contract Law Harmonization", DJILP, 34: 119.

Mgbeoji, I. (2003) "The Juridical Origins of the International Patent System: Towards a Historiography of the Role of Patents in Industrialization", JHIL, 5: 403.

—— (2004) "Review: issues of sovereignty, strategy, and security in the economic community of West African states' intervention in the Liberian Civil War", EJIL, 15(1): 218–25.

—— (2005) "The juridical origins of the international patent system: towards a historiography of the role of patents in industrialization", JHIL, 5.

—— (2006) Global Biopiracy: Patents, Plants, and Indigenous Knowledge, Ithaca, NY: Cornell University Press.

—— (2007) "TRIPS and TRIPS plus impacts in Africa", in D. Gervais (ed.) Strategies to Optimize Economic Development in a TRIPS Plus Era, Oxford: Oxford University Press.

Michelman, F. I. (2003) "Constitutional legitimation for political acts", MLR, 66(1): 1–15.

Mickelson, K. (1998) "Rhetoric and rage: third world voices in international legal discourse", WILJ, 16(2): 353–419.

Mill, J. (1825) "The law of nations", in The Supplement to the Encyclopaedia Britannica, London: Innes.

Miller, R. A. and Bratspies, R. M. (eds) (2008) Progress in International Law and Institutions, The Hague, Martinus Nijhoff Publishers.

Miller, R. H. (1971) "The convention on the non-applicability of statutory limitations to war crimes and crimes against humanity", AJIL, 65: 476

Milner, H. V., Rosendorff, B. P. and Mansfield, E. D. (2004) "International trade and domestic politics: the domestic sources of international trade agreements and institutions", in E. Benvenisti and M. Hirsch (eds) The Impact of International Law on International Cooperation: Theoretical Perspectives, Cambridge: Cambridge University Press.

Mirow, M. C. (2001) "Latin American legal history: some essential Spanish terms", LRLJ, 12: 43–86.

Mitchell, R. B. (1994) "Regime design matters: international oil pollution and treaty compliance", IO, 48: 425–58.

Mommsen, T. and Kruger, P. (eds) (1985) Justinian's Digest (trans. A. Watson), Philadelphia, PA: University of Pennsylvania Press.

Monson, R. A. (1982) "The West German statute of limitations on murder: a political, legal and historical exposition", AJCL, 30: 605.

Moore, J. N. (ed.) (2004) Civil Litigation against Terrorism, Durham, NC: Carolina Academic Press.

Moravcsik, A. (2000) "The origins of human rights regimes: democratic delegation in postwar Europe", IO, 54: 217–52.

Morgan, E. S. (1972) "Slavery and freedom: the American paradox", JAH, 59(1): 5–29.

Morgan, W. (2000) "Queering international human rights law", in C. Stychin and D. Herman (eds) Sexuality in the Legal Arena, Athlone: Continuum International Publishing Group Ltd.

Morgenthau, H. J. (1929) Die internationale Rechtspflege: ihr Wesen und ihre Grenzen, Leipzig: R. Noske.

—— (1946) Politics among Nations, Chicago, IL: Chicago University Press.

Morris, M. (2007) "International humanitarian law: state collusion and the conundrum of jurisdiction", in T. J. Biersteker, P. J. Spiro, C. L. Sriram and V. Raffo (eds) *International Law and International Relations*, London: Routledge.

Morsink, J. (1999) *The Universal Declaration of Human Rights: Origins, Drafting & Intent*, Philadelphia, PA: University of Pennsylvania Press.

Mosler, H. (1974) "The international society as a legal community", *RC*, 140: 1–320.

Mosley, D. (1973) *Envoys and Diplomacy in Ancient Greece*, Wiesbaden: Steiner.

Moyo, S. (2004) "The politics of land distribution and race relations in Southern Africa", *Identities, Conflict and Cohesion Programme Paper*, No. 10, December 2004, United Nations Research Institute for Social Development.

Muggah, R. (2007) "Moving forward? Assessing normative and legal process in dealing with small arms", in T. J. Biersteker, P. J. Spiro, C. L. Sriram and V. Raffo (eds) *International Law and International Relations*, London: Routledge.

Muldoon, J. (1972) *Popes, Lawyers and Infidels: The Church and the Non-Christian World, 1250–1550*, Philadelphia, PA: University of Pennsylvania Press.

Murphy, J. F. (1990) "Defining international terrorism: a way out of the quagmire", *IYHR*, 19: 13.

—— (2002) "Computer network attacks by terrorists: some legal dimensions", in M. H. Schmitt and B. T. O'Donnell (eds) *Computer Network Attack and International Law*, New Port, RI: Naval War College Press.

Murphy, J. (1992) "De Jure War in the Gulf: Lex Specialis of Chapter VII Actions Prior to, During, and in the Aftermath of the United Nations War against Iraq", *NYILR*, 5: 71–88.

—— (2004) *The United States and the Rule of Law in International Affairs*, Cambridge: Cambridge University Press.

—— (2005) "The control of international terrorism", in J. N. Moore and R. F. Turner (eds) *Casebook on National Security Law*, 2nd edn, Durham, NC: Carolina Academic Press.

Murphy, S. (ed.) (2001) "Contemporary practice of the United States relating to international law", *AJIL*, 95(4): 873–903.

Murphy, S. D. (2004) "Assessing the Legality of Invading Iraq," *Georgetown Law Journal*, 92: 173–257.

Murray, R. and Viljoen, F. (2007) "Towards non-discrimination on the basis of sexual orientation: the normative basis and procedural possibilities before the African Commission on Human and Peoples' Rights and the African Union", *HRQ*, 29: 86–111.

Mutua, M. W. (1995) "Why redraw the map of Africa: a legal and moral inquiry", *Michigan JIL*, 16: 1113–76.

—— (2000) "Politics and human rights: an essential symbiosis", in M. Byers (ed.) *The Role of Law in International Politics*, Oxford: Oxford University Press.

—— (2001) "Savages, victims, and saviors: the metaphor of human rights", *HILJ*, 42: 201–45.

—— (2002) *Human Rights: A Political and Cultural Critique*, Philadelphia, PA: University of Pennsylvania Press.

Myjer E. and White, N. (2002) "The Twin Towers attack: an unlimited right to self-defence", *JCSL*, 7: 5.

Nadelmann, E. (1990) "Global prohibition regimes: the evolution of norms in international society", *IO*, 44: 470–526.

Nanda, V. P. "International law in ancient Hindu India", in M. Janis and C. Evans (eds) *Religion and International Law*, 2nd edn, Leiden: Martinus Nijhoff Publishers.

—— (1991) "International Law in Ancient Hindu India", in M. W. Janis (ed.) *The Influence of Religion on the Development of International Law*, 51.

Nardin, T. (1983) *Law, Morality, and the Relations of States*, Princeton, NJ: Princeton University Press.

Narlikar, A. (2003) *International Trade and Developing Countries: Bargaining Coalitions in the GATT and WTO*, London: Routledge.

—— (2005) *The World Trade Organization: A Very Short Introduction*, Oxford: Oxford University Press.

—— and Odell, J. (2006) "The strict distributive strategy for a bargaining coalition: the like minded group in the World Trade Organization", in J. Odell (ed.) *Negotiating Trade: Developing Countries in the WTO and NAFTA*, Cambridge: Cambridge University Press.

Nathwani, N. (2000) "The purpose of asylum", *IJRL*, 12: 354–79.

Neff, S. C. (2005) *War and the Law of Nations. A General History*, Cambridge, Cambridge University Press.

—— (2006) "A short history of international law", in M. Evans (ed.) *International Law*, 2nd edn, Oxford: Oxford University Press.

Nesiah, V. (1993) "Toward a feminist internationality: a critique of U.S. feminist legal scholarship", *HWLJ*, 16: 189–210.

Neuman, G. L. (2006) "International law as a resource in constitutional interpretation", *HJLPP*, 30(1): 177–90.

Newman, D. G. (2007) "Collective rights", *PB*, 48: 221–32.

Nicolaidis, K. and Tong, J. L. (2004) "Diversity or cacophony? New sources of norms in international law", *Michigan JIL*, 25(4): 329.

438

Nicolis, G. and Prigogine, I. (1989) *Exploring Complexity*, New York: W. H. Freeman & Co. Ltd.

Nielsen Reyes, F. (1934) "Aspectos del derecho internacional Americano", paper presented at VII Conferencia Panamericana de Montevideo, Jena, Leipzig, W. Gronau.

Nieuwkoop, M. and Uquillas, J. E. (2000) "Defining Ethnodevelopment in Operational Terms: Lessons from the Ecuador Indigenous and Afro-Ecuadorian Peoples Development Project: Latin America and Caribbean Region Sustainable Development", Working Paper No. 6, Ecuador: The World Bank.

Niezen, R. (2005) "The indigenous claim for recognition in the international public sphere", *FJIL*, 17: 583–601.

Nijar, G. S. (1994) "Towards a legal framework for protecting biological diversity and community intellectual rights – a third world perspective", in *Third World Network Discussion Paper*, Penang, Malaysia: Third World Network.

—— (1996) *TRIPS and Biodiversity: The Threat and Responses – A Third World View*, Penang, Malaysia: Third World Network.

Nolte, G. (1999) *Eingreifen auf Einladung*, Berlin: Springer.

—— (2000) "The limits of the Security Council's powers and its functions in the international legal system: some reflections", in M. Byers (ed.) *The Role of Law in International Politics*, Oxford: Oxford University Press.

Nordström, H. and Scott, V. (1999) "Trade and Environment", WTO's Special Studies series #4. Available at http://www.wto.org/english/tratop_e/envir_e/environment.pdf.

North, T. (Justice) (2005) "A proposal for the establishment of an international judicial commission on refugees", paper presented at Moving On: Forced Migration and Human Rights Conference, New South Wales Parliament House, 22 November 2005.

Numelin, R. (1950) *The Beginnings of Diplomacy*, New York: Philosophical Library.

Nussbaum, A. (1947) *A Concise History of the Law of Nations*, New York: Macmillan.

—— (1954) *A Concise History of International Law*, New York: Macmillan.

Nyamu, C. I. (2000) "How should human rights and development respond to cultural legitimization of gender hierarchy in developing countries?", *HILJ*, 41: 381–418.

Nye, J. S., Jr. (2002) *The Paradox of American Power: Why the World's Only Superpower Can't Go It Alone*, New York: Oxford University Press.

Obregón, L. (2002) *Completing Civilization: Nineteenth Century Creole Interventions in International Law*, Cambridge, MA: Harvard Law School.

—— (2006) "Completing civilization: creole consciousness and international law in nineteenth-century Latin America", in A. Orford (ed.) *International Law and its Others*, Cambridge: Cambridge University Press.

O'Connell, M. E. (1999) "New international legal process", *AJIL*, 93(2): 334–51.

—— (2007) "Crying war", in T. J. Biersteker, P. J. Spiro, C. L. Sriram and V. Raffo (eds) *International Law and International Relations*, London: Routledge.

Oddi, S. (1989) "Beyond obviousness: invention protection in the twenty-first century", *AULR*, 38: 1097.

—— (1996) "TRIPS – natural rights and a 'polite' form of economic imperialism", *VJTL*, 29: 415.

Odell, J. (ed.) (2006) *Negotiating Trade: Developing Countries in the WTO and NAFTA*, Cambridge: Cambridge University Press.

Oestreich, G. (1982) "Neostoicism and the early modern state", in B. Oestreich and H. G. Koenigsberger (ed.) (trans. D. McLintock), *Neostoicism and the Early Modern State*, Cambridge: Cambridge University Press.

O'Hanlon, M. E. and Pollack, K. M. (2007) "A war we just might win", *N.Y. Times*, A17, col. 2, 30 July 2007, New York.

Okafor, O. C. and Agbakwa, S. C. (2001) "Re-Imagining International Human Rights Education in Our Time: Beyond Three Constitutive Orthodoxies", *LJIL*, 14: 563–90.

Okafor, O. C. (2002) "Entitlement, process, and legitimacy in the emergent international law of secession", *IJMGR*, 9: 41–70.

—— (2006) *Legitimizing Human Rights NGOs: Lessons from Nigeria*, Trenton, NJ: Africa World Press.

—— (2007) *The African Human Rights System: Activist Forces and International Institutions*, New York: Cambridge University Press.

—— and Agbakwa, S. C. (2001) "Re-imagining international human rights education in our time: beyond three constitutive orthodoxies", *LJIL*, 14: 563–90.

—— (2002) "On legalism, popular agency and voices of suffering: the Nigerian National Human Rights Commission in context", *HRQ*, 24: 662–720.

Olivier, M. (2002) "The relevance of 'soft law' as a source of international human rights", *CILSA*, 35: 290–307.

Oloka-Onyango, J. (1995) "Beyond the rhetoric: reinvigorating the struggle for economic and social rights in Africa", *CWILJ*, 26: 1–73.

—— (1999) "Heretical reflections on the right to self-determination: prospects and problems for a democratic global future in new millennium", *AUILR*, 15: 151–208.

—— and Tamale, S. (1995) " 'The personal is political,' or why women's rights are indeed human rights: an African perspective on international feminism", *HRQ*, 17(4): 691–731.

Olowu, D. (2006) "The United Nations' special rapporteur on the adverse effects of the illicit movement and dumping of toxic and dangerous wastes on the enjoyment of human rights: a critical evaluation of the first ten years", *ELR*, 8: 199–217.

Onuf, N. G. (1985) "Do rules say what they do? From ordinary language to international law", *HILJ*, 26: 385–410.

—— (1989) *World of Our Making: Rules and Rule in Social Theory and International Relations*, Columbia, SC: University of South Carolina Press.

—— (1998) *The Republican Legacy in International Thought*, Cambridge: Cambridge University Press.

Oppenheim, L. (1948) *International Law*, in H. Lauterpacht, 7th edn, London: Longman.

Opsahl, T. (1961) "An 'international constitutional law'?", *ICLQ*, 10: 760–84.

Orentlicher, D. F. (2007) "Whose justice? Reconciling universal jurisdiction with democratic principles", in T. J. Biersteker, P. J. Spiro, C. L. Sriram and V. Raffo (eds) *International Law and International Relations*, London: Routledge.

Oro Maini, A. D. (1951) *La Conquista de América y el Descubrimiento del Moderno Derecho Internacional: Estudios sobre las Ideas de Francisco de Vitoria*, Buenos Aires: G. Kraft.

Orrico Esteves, N. (1956) *Soluciones Pacíficas en el Derecho Internacional Americano*, Mexico City: Talleres Graficos de la Penitenciaria.

Osiander, A. (1994) *The States System of Europe, 1640–1990: Peacemaking and the Conditions of International Stability*, Oxford: Oxford University Press.

—— (2000) *Die internationale Gemeinschaft im Völkerrecht*, Munich: C. H. Beck.

—— (2001) "Sovereignty, international relations, and the Westphalian myth", *IO*, 55(2): 251–87.

Ostry, S. (2001) "Global integration: currents and countertrends", Walter Gordon Lecture, Massey College, University of Toronto, 23 May 2001. Available at http://www.utoronto.ca/cis/ostry/docs_pdf/GlobalIntegration.pdf.

—— (2002) "The Uruguay Round north–south grand bargain: implications for future negotiations", in D. L. M. Kennedy and J. D.

Southwick, *The Political Economy of International Trade Law*, Cambridge: Cambridge University Press.

Oxman, B. (2002) "Complementary agreements and compulsory jurisdiction", *AJIL*, 95: 277.

Packer, G. (2005) "Name calling", *The New Yorker*. Available at http://www.newyorker.com/archive/2005/08/08/050808ta_talk_packer.

Pagden, A. (ed.) (1989) *The Languages of Political Theory in Early Modern Europe*, Cambridge: Cambridge University Press.

—— (1995) *Lords of All the World: Ideologies of Empire in Spain, Britain and France, ca. 1500–1800*, New Haven: Yale University Press.

Pallis, M. (2006) "The operation of UNHCR's accountability mechanisms", *NYUJILP*, 37: 869–918.

Panjabi, R. (1993) "International law and the preservation of species: an analysis of the Convention on Biological Diversity signed at the Rio Earth Summit", *DJIL*, 11: 187.

Papastavridis, E. (2007) "Interpretation of Security Council resolutions under Chapter VII in the aftermath of the Iraqi crisis", *ICLQ*, 56(1): 83–118.

Paradisi, B. (1951) "L'amitié internationale: les phases critiques de son ancienne histoire", *RC*, 78(1): 325–78.

Paredes, J. F. (1924) *Derecho Internacional Americano. Arbitraje Amplio y Obligatorio*, San Salvador, República de El Salvador: Impresorsa Nacional.

Partner, P. (1990) *The Pope's Men: The Papal Civil Service in the Renaissance*, Oxford: Clarendon Press.

Paulus, A. (2001a) "International law after postmodernism. Towards renewal or decline of international law", *LJIL*, 14: 727–55.

—— (2001b) *Die internationale Gemeinschaft im Völkerrecht*, Munich: C. H. Beck.

—— (2003) "The influence of the United States on the concept of the 'international community'", in M. Byers and G. Nolte (eds) *United States Hegemony and the Foundations of International Law*, Cambridge: Cambridge University Press.

—— (2004a) "From territoriality to functionality? Towards a legal methodology of globalization", in I. F. Dekker and W. G. Werner (eds) *Governance and International Legal Theory*, Leiden/Boston, MA: Martinus Nijhoff Publishers.

—— (2004b) "The war against Iraq and the future of international law: hegemony or pluralism?", *Michigan JIL*, 25: 691–733.

—— (2005) "Jus cogens in a time of hegemony and fragmentation", *NJIL*, 74: 297–334.

—— (2008a) "Between incapacity and indispensability: the United Nations and international order in the 21st century", in R. A. Miller and R. M. Bratspies (eds) *Progress in International Law and Institutions*, The Hague, Martinus Nijhoff Publishers.

—— (2008b) "Subsidiarity, fragmentation and democracy: towards the demise of general international law?", in T. Broude and Y. Shany (eds), in *The Allocation of Authority in International Law, Melanges in Honour of Ruth Lapidoth*, Oxford: Hart Publishing.

Pauwelyn, J. (2001) "The role of public international law in the WTO: how far can we go?", *AJIL*, 95: 535.

Pennington, K. (1993) *The Prince and the Law, 1200–1600: Sovereignty and Rights in the Western Legal Tradition*, Berkeley, CA: University of California Press.

Penrose, E. T. (1951) *The Economics of the International Patent System*, Baltimore, MD: Johns Hopkins University Press.

Perez-Rivas, M. (2001) "US quits ABM treaty", Washington, CNN, 14 December 2001. Available at http://archives.cnn.com/2001/ALLPOLITICS/12/13/rec.bush.abm.

Pernice, I. (1999) "Multilateral constitutionalism and the Treaty of Amsterdam: European constitution-making revisited", *CMLR*, 36: 703–50.

—— (2002) "Multilevel constitutionalism in the European Union", *ELR*, 27: 511–29.

Peters, A. (2005) "Global constitutionalism in a nutshell", in K. Dicke, S. Hobe, K.-U. Meyn et al. (eds) *Weltinnenrecht – Liber amicorum Jost Delbruck, Veröffentlichungen des Walther-Schücking-Instituts für Internationales Recht an der Universität Kiel*, Band 155, Berlin: Duncker & Humblot.

—— (2006) "Compensatory constitutionalism: the function and potential of fundamental international norms and structures", *LJIL*, 19(3): 579–610.

Petersen, K. (1992) "Recent intellectual property trends in developing countries", *HILJ*, 33: 277.

Petersmann, E.-U. (1996/7) "Constitutionalism and international organizations", *Northwestern Journal of International Law and Politics*, 17: 398–469.

—— (1997) "How to Reform the UN system? Constitutionalism, international law, and international organizations", *LJIL*, 10: 421–74.

—— (2002) "Time for a United Nations' 'global impact' for integrating human rights into the law of worldwide organizations", *EJIL*, 13(3): 621–50.

—— (2006) "Human rights, constitutionalism and the World Trade Organization: challenges for World Trade Organization jurisprudence and civil society", *LJIL*, 19: 633–67.

Petito, F. and Hatzopoulos, P. (eds) (2003) *Religion in International Relations: The Return from Exile*, New York: Palgrave.

Phillimore, R. (1879) *Commentaries on International Law*, 3nd edn, vol. 1, Philadelphia, PA: T. & J. W. Johnson.

Phillipson, C. (1911) *The International Law and Custom of Ancient Greece and Rome*, London: Macmillan.

Pieth, M. (2007) "Multi-stakeholder initiatives to combat money laundering and bribery", in C. Brütsch and D. Lehmkuhl (eds) *Law and Legalization in Transnational Relations*, London: Routledge.

Planas Suarez, S. B. (1924) *La Doctrina de Monroe y la Doctrina de Bolivar: los Grandes Principios de la Política Internacional Americana*, Habana, El Siglo XX.

Pocock, J. G. A. (1973) *Politics, Language and Time: Essays on Political Thought and History*, New York: Athanaeum Press.

—— (1987) *The Ancient Constitution and the Feudal Law: A Study of English Historical Thought in the Seventeenth Century*, Cambridge: Cambridge University Press.

Pogge, T. W. (1989) *Realizing Rawls*, Ithaca, NY/London: Cornell University Press.

Pollock, F. (1916) "Cosmopolitan custom and international law", *HLR*, 29: 565–81.

Polybius (1922) *The Histories* (trans. W. R. Paton), Cambridge, MA: Loeb Classical Library.

Polzer, T. (2007) "Adapting to changing legal frameworks: Mozambican refugees in South Africa", *IJRL*, 19: 22–50.

Popper, K. R. (1968) *The Logic of Scientific Discovery*, New York: Harper & Row.

Posner, E. A. (2003) "Do states have a moral obligation to comply with international law?", *SLR*, 55: 1901–19.

—— and Yoo, J. (2006) "International law and the rise of China", *CJIL*, 7: 1–15.

Post, G. (1964) *Studies in Medieval Legal Thought: Public Law and the State, 1100–1322*, Princeton, NJ: Princeton University Press.

Povinella, E. (2002) *The Cunning of Recognition: Indigenous Alterities and the Making of Australian Multiculturalism*, Durham, NC: Duke University Press.

Power, S. (2007) "Our war on terror", *New York Times Book Review*, p. 1, 29 July 2007, New York.

Preiser, W. (1954) "Zum Völkerrecht der vorklassischen Antike", *AV*, 4: 257.

—— (1984) "History of the law of nations: basic questions and principles", in R. Bernhardt (ed.) *Encyclopedia of Public International Law*, Heidelberg: Max Planck Institute.

Prest, W. (ed.) (1981) *Lawyers in Early Modern Europe and America*, New York: Holmes & Meier.

—— (1986) *The Rise of the Barristers: A Social History of the English Bar, 1590–1640*, Oxford: Clarendon Press.

Preu, P. (1980) *Polizeibegriff und Staatszwecklehre. Die Entwicklung des Polizeibegriffs durch die Rechts- und Staatswissenschaften des 18 Jahrhunderts*, Göttingen: Schwarz.

Price, R. (2004) "Emerging customary norms and anti-personnel landmines", in C. Reus-Smit (ed.) *The Politics of International Law*, Cambridge: Cambridge University Press.

—— and Reus-Smit, C. (1998) "Dangerous liaisons? Critical international theory and constructivism", *EJIR*, 4: 259–94.

Proudhon, P.-J. (1927 [1861]) *La Guerre et la Paix, Recherches sur la Constitution du Droit des Gens, Oevres Complètes*, rev. edn, Paris: Rivière.

Pufendorf, S. (1934 [1688]) *The Law of Nature and of Nations. Eight Books* (trans. C. H. Oldfather and W. A. Oldfather), Oxford: Clarendon Press.

Puig, J. C. (1952) *Principios de Derecho Internacional Público Americano*, Buenos Aires: Abeledo.

—— (1984) *América Latina: Políticas Exteriores Comparadas*, Buenos Aires: Grupo Editor Latinoamericano.

Quane, H. (2005) "The rights of indigenous peoples and the development process", *HRQ*, 27: 652–82.

Quashigah, E. K. (1999) "Legitimate governance: the pre-colonial African perspective", in E. K. Quashigah and O. C. Okafor (eds) *Legitimate Governance in Africa: International and Domestic Legal Perspectives*, The Hague: Kluwer Law International.

Queller, D. E. (1967) *The Office of Ambassador in the Middle Ages*, Princeton, NJ: Princeton University Press.

Quesada, E. (1916) *El Nuevo Panamericanismo y el Congreso Científico de Washington*, Buenos Aires: Tall. Gráf. del Ministerio de Agricultura de la Nación.

Rabkin, J. A. (1998) *Why Sovereignty Matters*, 2nd edn, Washington DC: AEI Press.

—— (1999) "International law vs. the American Constitution – something's got to give", *NI*, 55: 30–41.

—— (2004) *The Case for Sovereignty: Why the World Should Welcome American Independence*, Washington DC: AEI Press.

—— (2005) *Law without Nations: Why Constitutional Government Requires Sovereign States*, Princeton, NJ: Princeton University Press.

Raffo, V., Sriram, C. L., Spiro, P. J. and Biersteker, T. J. (2007) "Introduction: international law and international politics – old divides, new developments", in T. J. Biersteker, P. J. Spiro, C. L. Sriram and V. Raffo (eds) *International Law and International Relations*, London: Routledge.

Rajagopal, B. (1998–1999) "Locating the third world in cultural geography", *TWLS*, 1: 1–20.

—— (2003) *International Law from Below: Development, Social Movements, and Third World Resistance*, Cambridge/New York: Cambridge University Press.

—— (2006) "Martti Koskenniemi's *From Apology to Utopia*: a reflection", *GrLJ*, 7: 1089–94.

Rama, Á. (1996) *The Lettered City*, Durham, NC: Duke University Press.

Ratner, S. R. (2001–2002) "Corporations and human rights: a theory of legal responsibility", *YLJ*, 111: 443–545.

—— and Abrams, J. S. (ed.) (2001) *Accountability for Human Rights Atrocities in International Law: Beyond the Nuremberg Legacy*, Oxford/New York: Oxford University Press.

—— and Slaughter, A. (1999) "Appraising the methods of international law: a prospectus for readers", *AJIL*, 93: 291–302.

Raustiala, K. (2002) "The architecture of international cooperation: transgovernmental networks and the future of international law", *VJIL*, 43: 1–92.

—— (2005) "Form and substance in international agreements", *AJIL*, 99: 581.

—— and Victor, D. G. (2004) "The regime complex for plant genetic resources", *IO*, 58: 277–309.

Ravitch, F. (2004) "A funny thing happened on the way to neutrality: broad principles, formalism, and the establishment clause", *GLR*, 38: 489–573.

Rawls, J. (1971) *A Theory of Justice*, Cambridge, MA: Harvard University Press.

—— (1996) *Political Liberalism*, New York: Columbia University Press.

—— (1999) *The Law of Peoples*, Cambridge, MA/London: Harvard University Press.

Redgwell, C. (2003) "US reservations to human rights treaties: all for one and none for all?" in M. Byers and G. Nolte (eds) *United States Hegemony and the Foundations of International Law*, Cambridge, Cambridge University Press.

Reichman, J. H. (1995) "Universal minimum standards of intellectual property protection under the TRIPS component of the WTO Agreement", *IL*, 29: 345.

Reif, L. C. (2004) *The Ombudsman, Good Governance, and the International Human Rights System*,

Leiden/Boston, MA: Martinus Nijhoff Publishers.

Reimann, M. (2003) "Introduction: the Yahoo! case and conflict of laws in the cyberage", *MJIL*, 24, 663–65.

Reisman, W. M. (1990) "Sovereignty and human rights in contemporary international law", *AJIL*, 89: 866C–76.

—— (2000a) "Eritrea-Yemen arbitration (award, phase II: maritime delimitation)", *AJIL*, 94(4): 721–29.

—— (2000b) "Unilateral action and the transformations of the world constitutive process", *EJIL*, 11(1): 3–18.

—— and Armstrong, A. (2006) "The past and future of the claim of preemptive self-defense", *AJIL*, 100: 525–48.

Renault, L. (1932 [1879]) *Introduction à l'Étude de Droit International*, Paris: L'Ouvre Internationale de Louis Renault.

Reno, W. (2007) "Small arms, violence, and the course of conflicts", in T. J. Biersteker, P. J. Spiro, C. L. Sriram and V. Raffo (eds) *International Law and International Relations*, London: Routledge.

Rensmann, T. (2006) "The constitution as a normative order of values: the influence of international human rights law on the evolution of modern constitutionalism", in P.-M. Dupuy, B. Fassbender, M. N. Shaw and K.-P. Sommermann (eds) *Common Values in International Law: Essays in Honour of Christian Tomuschat*, Kehl: Engel.

Restelli, E. (1912) *Exposición de la Doctrina de Drago; su Importancia en el Derecho Internacional Americano*, London: Wertheimer.

Reus-Smit, C. (1999) *The Moral Purpose of the State: Culture, Social Identity, and Institutional Rationality in International Relations*, Princeton, NJ: Princeton University Press.

—— (2001) "The strange death of liberal international theory", *EJIL*, 2: 573–93.

—— (2002) "Imagining society: constructivism and the English school", *BJPIR*, 4: 487–509.

—— (2003) "Politics and international legal obligation", *EJIR*, 9: 591–625.

—— (ed.) (2004a) *The Politics of International Law*, Cambridge: Cambridge University Press.

—— (2004b) "Introduction", in C. Reus-Smit (ed.) *The Politics of International Law*, Cambridge: Cambridge University Press.

—— (2004c) "Society, power, and ethics", in C. Reus-Smit (ed.) *The Politics of International Law*, Cambridge: Cambridge University Press.

Rice, C. (2000) "Promoting the national interest", *FA*, 79: 45–62.

Rich, J.W. (1976) *Declaring War in the Roman Empire in the Period of Transmarine Expansion*, Brussels: Latomus.

Ridder-Symoens, H. de. (1996) "Mobility", in H. de Ridder-Symoens (ed.) *A History of the University in Europe*, vol. II, Cambridge: Cambridge University Press.

Rivkin, D. B., Jr. and L. A. Casey (2000/2001) "The rocky shoals of international law", *NI*, 62: 35–45.

Röben, B. (2003) *Johann Caspar Bluntschli, Francis Lieber und das moderne Völkerrecht 1861–1881*, Baden-Baden: Nomos.

Roberts, A. E. (2001) "Traditional and modern approaches to customary international law: a reconciliation", *AJIL*, 95: 757.

Robilant, A. di (2006) "Genealogies of soft law", *AJCL*, 54: 499.

Robinson, M. (1993) "Human rights at the dawn of the 21st century", *HRQ*, 15: 629–39.

—— (2003) "Making human rights matter: Eleanor Roosevelt's time has come", *HHRJ*, 16: 1–11.

Robinson, R. and Gallagher, J. (1981) *Africa and the Victorians: The Official Mind of Imperialism*, 2nd edn, London: Macmillan.

Rodin, D. (2002) *War and Self-Defence*, Oxford: Oxford University Press.

Roelofsen, C. G. (1989) "Grotius and state practice of his day", *GNS*, 10.

Roht-Arrioza, N. (1996) "Of seeds and shamans: the appropriateness of the scientific and technical knowledge of indigenous and local communities", *Michigan JIL*, 17: 940.

Rojas, C. (2001) *Civilization and Violence: Regimes of Representation in Nineteenth-Century Colombia*, Minneapolis, MN: University of Minnesota Press.

Rolin-Jaequemyns, G. (1869) "De l'étude de la législation comparée et de droit international", *RDILC*, 1.

Rosand, E. (2005) "The Security Council as 'global legislator': ultra vires or ultra innovative?", *FILJ*, 28: 542.

Rosenberg, J. (1994) *The Empire of Civil Society*, London: Verso.

Rosenne, S. (1958) "The influence of Judaism on the development of international law", *NILR*, 5: 119.

—— (2004) "The influence of Judaism on the development of international law: an assessment", in M. Janis and C. Evans (eds.) *Religion and International Law*, 2nd edn, Leiden: Martinus Nijhoff Publishers.

Rostovtseff, M. (1922) "International relations in the ancient world", in E. Walsh (ed.) *The History and Nature of International Relations*, New York: Macmillan.

Roth, B. R. (1999) *Governmental Illegitimacy in International Law*, Oxford, Clarendon Press.

—— (2003) "Bending the law, breaking it, or developing it? The United States and the humanitarian use of force in the post-cold war era", in M. Byers and G. Nolte (eds) *United States Hegemony and the Foundations of International Law*, Cambridge: Cambridge University Press.

Roth, K. (2000) "The charade of US ratification of international human rights treaties", *CJIL*, 1(2): 347–53.

—— (2004) "The law of war in the war on terror", *FA*, 83(1): 2–7.

Roucounas, E. (2005) "Non-state actors: areas of international responsibility in need of further exploration", in M. Ragazzi (ed.) *International Responsibility Today: Essays in Memory of Oscar Schachter*, Leiden: Brill.

Rousseau, J.-J. (1761 [1756]) Extrait du projet de paix perpétuelle de m. L'abbé de saint-pierre. Available at ftp://ftp.ac-toulouse.fr/pub/philosophie/rousseauextraitduprojetdepaixperpetuelledemlabbedesaintpierre.rtf.

—— (1967) *The Social Contract and Discourse on the Origin and Foundation of Inequality Among Mankind* (L. G. Crocker ed.), New York: Washington Square Press.

Rudolph, C. (2001) "Constructing an atrocities regime: the politics of war crimes tribunals", *IO*, 55: 655–91.

Rueda Villareal, I. A. (1948) *La No Intervención en el Derecho Internacional Americano*, Mexico City: Universidad Nacional Autónoma de México, School of Law.

Ruggie, J. G. (1998) "What makes the world hang together? Neo-utilitarianism and the social constructivist challenge", *IO*, 52: 855–85.

—— and Kratochwil, F. (1986) "International organization: a state of the art on an art of the state", *IO*, 40(4): 753–75.

Ruiz-Fabri, H. and Grewe, C. (2004) "La constitutionalisation à l'épreuve du droit international et du droit européen", in A. Pedone (ed.) *Les Dynamiques du Droit Européen en Début de Siècle: Études en l'Honneur de Jean Claude Gautron*, Paris: A. Pedone.

Sá Vianna, M. Á. de S. (1912) *De la non existence d'un droit international americain*; dissertation presentée au Congres scientifique Latino-Américain (Premier Pan-Américain), 11 (Rio de Janeiro, L. Figueredo).

Sadat, L. N. (2006) "Ghost Prisoners and Black Sites: Extraordinary Rendition under Internaitonal Law," *Case Western Reserve Journal of International Law*, 37: 309–42.

Sadat, L. (2007) "The International Criminal Court and universal international jurisdiction: a return to first principles", in T. J. Biersteker, P. J. Spiro, C. L. Sriram and V. Raffo (eds) *International Law and International Relations*, London: Routledge.

Safadi, R. and Laird, S. (1996) "The Uruguay Round agreements: impact on developing countries", *WD*, 24: 1223.

Safran, D. (1983) "Protection of inventions in the multinational marketplace: problems and pitfalls in obtaining and using patents", *NCJILCR*, 9: 117.

Sagoe, T. E. (1992) "Industrial property law in Nigeria", *CLYIB*, 14.

Sanchez I Sanchez, C. A. (1941) *Los Problemas de la Seguridad Continental en el Derecho Internacional de America*, Trujillo: Impresora Montalvo.

—— (1958) *Instituciones de Derecho Internacional Americano*, Trujillo: Impresora Dominicana.

Sanders, D. (1983) "The re-emergence of indigenous questions in international law", *CHRY*, 1(3): 3–31.

—— (1996) "Getting lesbian and gay issues on the international human rights agenda", *HRQ*, 18: 67–106.

Sandholtz, W. and Sweet, A. S. (2004) "Law, politics, and international governance", in C. Reus-Smit (ed.) *The Politics of International Law*, Cambridge: Cambridge University Press.

Sands, P. (1994) "International law in the field of sustainable development", *BYIL*, 65.

—— (2003) *Principles of International Environmental Law*, 2nd edn, Cambridge: Cambridge University Press.

—— (2006) *Lawless World*, London: Penguin.

Santos, B. S. (1995) *Toward a New Common Sense: Law, Science and Politics in the Paradigmatic Transition*, New York: Routledge.

Sastry, K. R. (1966) "Hinduism and international law", *RC*, 117(I): 503–614.

Saufert, S. A. (2007) "Closing the Door to Refugees: The Denial of Due Process for Refugee Claimants in Canada", *SsLR*, 70: 27–51.

Saulnier, C. (1980) "Le rôle des prêtres fétiaux et l'application du 'ius fétiale' à Rome", *RHDFE*, 58: 171.

Savigny, F. C. von (1880) *A Treatise on the Conflict of Laws and The Limits of Their Operation in Respect of Place and Time*, 2nd edn (trans. W. Guthrie), London: Stevens & Sons.

Scalise, D. and Nugent, D. (1995) "International intellectual protection for living matter: biotechnology, multinational conventions and the exception for agriculture", *CWRJIL*, 27: 83.

Scelle, G. (1932–1934) *Précis de Droit des Gens: Principes et Systématique*, Paris: Librairie du Recueil Sirey.

Schabas, W. A. (2000) *Genocide in International Law*, Cambridge: Cambridge University Press.

Schachter, O. (1977) "The invisible college of international lawyers", *NULR*, 72: 217–26.

—— (1985) *International Law in Theory and Practice: General Course in Public International Law*, Dordrecht: Martinus Nijhoff Publishers.

—— (1997) "The decline of the nation state", *CJTL*, 36(7): 8–15.

Schäfer, A. (2006) "Resolving deadlock: why international organizations introduce soft law", *EuLJ*, 12(2): 194–208.

Schanze, E. (2007) "International standards: functions and links to law", in C. Brütsch and D. Lehmkuhl (eds) *Law and Legalization in Transnational Relations*, London: Routledge.

Scharpf, F. (1999) *Governing Europe: Effective and Democratic?*, Oxford: Oxford University Press.

Scheffer, D. J. (2002) "Staying the course with the International Criminal Court", *CILJ*, 35: 47–100.

Scheinin, M. (2000a) "The rght to self-determination under the covenant on civil and political rights", in P. Aikio and M. Scheinin (eds) *Operationalizing the Right of Indigenous Peoples to Self-Determination*, Åbo, Finland: Institute for Human Rights, Åbo Akademi University.

—— (2000b) "The right to enjoy a distinct culture: indigenous and competing uses of land", in T. Orlin, A. Rosas and M. Scheinin (eds) *The Jurisprudence of Human Rights Law*, Åbo, Finland: Åbo Akademi University.

Scherer, A. G. and Baumann, D. (2007) "The role of the transnational corporation in the process of legalization: insights from economics and corporate social responsibility", in C. Brütsch and D. Lehmkuhl (eds) *Law and Legalization in Transnational Relations*, London: Routledge.

Scheve, K. and Slaughter, M. (2007) "A new deal for globalization?", *FA*, 86(4): 34–47.

Scheyli, M. (2002) "Der Schutz des Klimas als Pruefstein voelkerrechtlicher Konstitutionalisierung", *AV*, 40(3): 273–330.

Schlag, P. (1991) "The problem of the subject", *TLR*, 69: 1627–743.

Schmelzing, J. (1818) *Systematische Grundrisse des positiven europäischen Völkerrechts*, Rudolfstadt: Hof-, Buch- und Kunsthandlung.

Schmitt, C. (1988) *Der Nomos der Erde im Völkerrecht des Jus Publicum Europaeum*, 3rd edn, Berlin: Duncker & Humblot.

—— (1996) *The Concept of the Political* (trans. G. Schwab), Chicago, IL: University of Chicago Press.

Schoenbaum, T. J. (2006) *International Relations: The Path Not Taken: Using International Law to Promote World Peace and Security*, Cambridge: Cambridge University Press.

Schou, A. (1963) *Histoire de l'Internationalisme*, vol. III, Oslo: Aschehoug.

Schou, N. (2000) "Instances of human rights regimes", in T. M. Franck (ed.) *Delegating State Powers: The Effect of Treaty Regimes on Democracy and Sovereignty*, Ardsley, NY: Transnational Publishers.

Schröder, J. (2000) "Die Entstehung des modernen Völkerrechtsbegriffs im Naturrecht der frühen Neuzeit", *JRE*, 8: 59–67.

Schulz, W. F. (2003) *Tainted Legacy: 9/11 and the Ruin of Human Rights*, New York: Thunder's Mouth Press/Nation Books.

Schwab, G. (1987) "Enemy or friend?: a conflict of modern politics, *T*, 72: 194.

Scott, H. S. (2007) *International Finance: Transactions, Policy and Regulation*, 14th edition. Eagen, MS: Foundation Press.

Scott, J. B. (1930) *El Descubrimiento de America y su Influjo en el Derecho Internacional*, Madrid: Tipografia de Archivos.

—— (1934) *The Spanish Origin of International Law: Francisco de Vitoria and his Law of Nations*, Oxford: Clarendon Press.

Scott, S. V. (2003) "The impact on international law of US non-compliance", in M. Byers and G. Nolte (eds) *United States Hegemony and the Foundations of International Law*, Cambridge: Cambridge University Press.

—— (2004a) *International Law in World Politics: An Introduction*, Boulder, CO: Lynne Rienner.

—— (2004b) "Is there room for international law in *Realpolitik*?: accounting for the US 'attitude' towards international law", *RIS*, 30: 71–88.

—— (2004c) *The Political Interpretation of Multilateral Treaties*, Leiden: Martinus Nijhoff Publishers.

Scupin, H.-U. (1984) "History of the law of nations: ancient times to 1648", in R. Bernhardt (ed.) *Encyclopedia of Public International Law*, Heidelberg: Max Planck Institute.

Searle, J. R. (1995) *The Construction of Social Reality*, London: Penguin.

—— (2003) *Rationality in Action*, Cambridge, MA: MIT Press.

Seay, N. (1988–9) "Protecting the seeds of innovation: patents plants", *AIPLAQJ*, 3/4: 419.

Seed, P. (1982) "The social dimensions of race: Mexico City, 1753", *HAHR*, 62: 569–606.

—— (1999) *Development as Freedom*, Oxford: Oxford University Press.

Sen, A. (2004) "Elements of a theory of human rights", *PPA*, 32: 315–56.

Sepúlveda, C. (1960) *Curso de Derecho Internacional Público*, Mexico: Editorial Porrúa.

Setear, J. K. (1996) "An iterative perspective on treaties: a synthesis of international relations theory and international law", *HILJ*, 37: 139–229.

—— (1997) "Responses to breach of a treaty and rationalist international relations theory: the rules of release and remediation in the law of treaties and the law of astate responsibility", *VLR*, 83: 1–126.

Sewall, S. (2006) "Introduction to 'a radical field manual'", in *The U.S. Army/Marine Corps Counterinsurgency Field Manual*, U.S. Army Field Manual No. 3–24, Marine Corps Warfighting Publication No. 3–33.5, Chicago, IL: University of Chicago Press.

Shacknove, A. E. (1985) "Who is a refugee?", *E*, 95: 274–84.

Shane, S., et al. (2007) "Secret U.S. Endorsement of Severe Interrogations," *New York Times*, 4 October 2007, A1.

Shaw, M. N. (1986) *International Law*, 2nd edn, Cambridge: Grotius Publishers.

—— (2003) *International Law*, 5th edn, Cambridge: Cambridge University Press.

Shelton, D. (ed.) (2000) *Commitment and Compliance: The Role of Non-Binding Norms in the International Legal System*, Oxford: Oxford University Press.

Shihata, I. (1962) "Islamic law and the world community", *HICJ*, 4: 101–13.

Shirley, J. (2004) "The role of international human rights and the law of diplomatic protection in resolving Zimbabwe's land crisis", *BCICLR*, 27(1): 161–72.

Shiva, V. (1988) *Staying Alive: Women, Ecology and Development*, London: Zed Books.

—— (2000) *The Violence of the Green Revolution*, 4th edn, Penang, Malaysia: Zed Books.

Silbey, S. S. (2005) "After legal consciousness", *ARLSS*, 1: 323–68.

Silverburg, S. R. (2005) "Review of the limits of international law", *LPBR*, 15: 336–9.

—— (2006) "Review of the impact of international law on international cooperation: theoretical perspectives", *LPBR*, 16: 50–2.

Simma, B. (1994) "From bilateralism to community interest in international law", *RC*, 250: 217–384.

—— and Paulus, A. L. (1998) "The 'international community': facing the challenge of globalization", *EJIL*, 9: 266–77.

—— (1999) "The responsibility of individuals for human rights abuses in internal conflicts: a positivist view", *AJIL*, 93: 302–16.

Simma, B. and Pulkowski, D. (2006) "Of planets and the universe: self-contained regimes in international law", *EJIL*, 17(3): 483–529.

Simmons, B. A. (2000) "The legalization of international monetary affairs", *IO*, 54: 573–602.

—— and Danner, A. M. (2007) "Credible commitments and the International Criminal Court", *IntLR*, 13: 1–7.

—— and Steinberg, R. A. (eds) (2006) *International Law and International Relations*, Cambridge: Cambridge University Press. Available at http://ilreports.blogspot.com/2007/09/danner-simmons-credible-commitments-and.html.

Simon, J. D. (2002) "The global terrorist threat", *PKPF*, 82: 10.

Simpson, G. (2004) *Great Powers and Outlaw States*, Cambridge: Cambridge University Press.

—— (2005) "Dueling agendas: international relations and international law (again)", *JILIR*, 1: 61–74.

—— and Wheeler, N. J. (2007) "Preemption and exemption: international law and revolutionary Power", in T. J. Biersteker, P. J. Spiro, C. L. Sriram and V. Raffo (eds) *International Law and International Relations*, London: Routledge.

Sinclair, I. (1982) "The practice of international law: the Foreign and Commonwealth Office", in B. Cheng (ed.) *International Law Teaching and Practice*, London: Sweet & Maxwell.

Skinner, Q. (2002) *Visions of Politics*, vol. 1, Cambridge: Cambridge University Press.

Sklan, M. (1978) "African patent statutes and technology transfer", *CWRJIL*, 10.

Skordas, A. (2003) "Hegemonic custom", in M. Byers and G. Nolte (eds) *United States Hegemony and the Foundations of International Law*, Cambridge: Cambridge University Press.

Slaughter, A. M. (1994) "A typology of transnational communication", *URLR*, 29: 99–137.

—— (1995) "International law in a world of liberal states", *EJIL*, 6: 503–38.

—— (2000a) "Governing the global economy through government networks", in M. Byers (ed.) *The Role of Law in International Politics*, Oxford: Oxford University Press.

—— (2000b) "A liberal theory of international law", *ASILP*, 94: 240–8.

—— (2000c) "Judicial globalization", *VJIL*, 40: 1103–24.

—— (2003) "A global community of courts", *HILJ*, 44: 191–219.

—— (2004a) "International law and international relations theory: a prospectus", in E.

446

Benvenisti and M. Hirsch (eds) *The Impact of International Law on International Cooperation: Theoretical Perspectives*, Cambridge: Cambridge University Press.

—— (2004b) *A New World Order*, Princeton, NJ: Princeton University Press.

—— and Burke-White, W. (2006) "The future of international law is domestic (or, the European way of law)", *HILJ*, 47: 327–52.

—— and Ratner, S. R. (1999) "The method is the message", *AJIL*, 93: 410–23.

——, Tulumello, A. S. and Wood, S. (1998) "International law and international relations theory: a new generation of interdisciplinary scholarship", *AJIL*, 92: 367–97.

Slaughter Burley, A. (1993) "International law and international relations theory: a dual agenda", *AJIL*, 87: 205–39.

—— and Mattli, W. (1993) "Europe before the court: a political theory of legal integration", *IO*, 47: 41–76.

Smith, H. A. (1932) "Preface", in *Great Britain and the Law of Nations*, vol. 1, London: P. S. King & Son Ltd.

Smith, J. M. (2000) "The politics of dispute settlement design: explaining legalism in regional trade pacts", *IO*, 54: 137–80.

Smith, S. (2000) "The discipline of international relations: still an American social science?", *BJPIR*, 2: 374–402.

Snyder, F. (1994) "Soft law and institutional practice in the European Community", in S. Martin (ed.) *The Construction of Europe*, The Hague: Kluwer.

Snyder, J. L. and Vinjamuri L. (2003–04) "Trials and errors: principle and pragmatism in strategies of international justice", *IS*, 28(3): 5–44.

Soefer, A. (2003) "On the necessity of preemption", *EJIL*, 14(2): 209–26.

Sommer, D. (1999) *Proceed with Caution, when Engaged by Minority Writing in the Americas*, Cambridge, MA: Harvard University Press.

Sorensen, M. (1946) *Les Sources du Droit International: Étude sur la Jurisprudence de la Cour Permanente de Justice Internationale*, Copenhagen: Einar Munksgaard.

Spiro, P. J. (2000a) "Globalization, international law and the Academy", *NYUJILP*, 32: 567–90.

—— (2000b) "The new sovereigntists – American exceptionalism and its false prophets", *FA*, 79: 6–15.

—— (2007) "Disaggregating US interests in international law: sketching a theory of liberal transnationalism", in T. J. Biersteker, P. J. Spiro,

C. L. Sriram and V. Raffo (eds) *International Law and International Relations*, London: Routledge.

Sripati, V. (2000) "India's National Human Rights Commission: a shackled commission?", *BUILJ*, 18: 1–46.

—— (2005) "National human rights institutions: the ombudsman and its hybrid versions – the emerging actors on the constitutionalism scene", *HRQ*, 27: 1137–42.

Sriram, C. L. (2005) "Book review: *The Limits of International Law* and *The Politics of International Law*", *APSR*, 3: 686–8.

—— (2006) "International law, international relations theory and post-atrocity justice: towards a genuine dialogue", *IA*, 82: 467–78.

—— and Mahmoud, Y. (2007) "Bringing security back in: international relations theory and moving beyond the 'justice versus peace' dilemma in transitional societies", in T. J. Biersteker, P. J. Spiro, C. L. Sriram and V. Raffo (eds) *International Law and International Relations*, London: Routledge.

Stahnke, T. and Blitt, R. C. (2005) "The religion–state relationship and the right to freedom of religion or belief: a comparative textual analysis of the constitutions of predominantly Muslim countries", *GJIL*, 36(4): 88–105.

Starobinski, J. (1993) "The word civilization", in *Blessings in Disguise, or, the Morality of Evil*, Cambridge, MA: Harvard University Press.

"Statement of Brigitte Mabandia South Africa's Minister for Justice and Constitutional Development" (2007), on July 5, 2007, reported in AllAfrica, Inc., Africa News.

Steiger, H. (2001) "From the international law of Christianity to the international law of the world citizen – reflections on the formation of the epochs of the history of international law", *JHIL*, 3: 180–93.

Steinberg, R. H. (2002) "In the shadow of law or power? Consensus–based bargaining and outcomes in the GATT/WTO", *IO*, 56: 339–74.

Steiner, H. J. and Alston P. (2000) *International Human Rights in Context: Law, Politics, Morals*, Oxford/New York: Oxford University Press.

Stern, B. (2000) "How to regulate globalization", in M. Byers (ed.) *The Role of Law in International Politics*, Oxford: Oxford University Press.

Stevenson, R. W. (2005) "President makes it clear: phrase is 'war on terror'", *New York Times*, 4 August 2005.

Stoll, P. (2003) "Compliance: multilateral achievements and predominant powers", in M. Byers and G. Nolte (eds) *United States Hegemony and the Foundations of International Law*, Cambridge: Cambridge University Press.

Stoltenberg, T. (1991) "Human rights and refugees", in A. Eide and J. Helgesen (eds) *The Future of Human Rights Protection in a Changing World*, Oslo: Norwegian University Press.

Stone, J. (1958) *Aggression and World Order: A Critique of United Nations Theories of Aggression*, Berkeley, CA: University of California Press.

Storey, H. (2003) "The Advanced Refugee Law Workshop Experience: An IARLJ Perspective", *IJRL*, 15: 422–9.

Stumpf, C. A. (2005) "Christian and Islamic traditions of public international law", *JHIL*, 7: 69–80.

Suchman, M. C. (1995) "Managing legitimacy: strategic and institutional approaches", *AMR*, 20: 571–610.

Suganami, H. (1989) *The Domestic Analogy and World Order Proposals*, Cambridge: Cambridge University Press.

Sutherland, J. (1973) *A General Systems Philosophy for the Social and Behavioral Sciences*, New York: George Braziller.

Sylvest, C. (2005) "International law in nineteenth-century Britain", *BYIL*, 75: 12–18.

Szasz, P. and the Crucible Group (2002) "The Security Council starts legislating", *AJIL*, 96(4): 901–5.

Taft, W. H., IV (2006) "A view from the top: American perspectives on international law after the cold war", *YJIL*, 31: 503–12.

—— and Buchwald, T. F. (2003) "Preemption, Iraq, and international law", *AJIL*, 97: 557–63.

Ténékidès, G. M. (1956) "Droit international et communautés fédérales dans la Grèce des cités", *RCADIH*, 90: II.

Tennant, C. (1994) "Indigenous peoples, international institutions and the international legal literature 1945–1993", *HRQ*, 16: 1–57.

Tesón, F. R. (1992) "The Kantian theory of international law", *CLR*, 92(1): 53–102.

—— (2005) *Humanitarian Intervention: An Inquiry into Law and Morality*, New York: Transnational Publishers.

Teubner, G. (1989) *Recht als autopoietisches System*, Frankfurt am Main: Suhrkamp.

—— (1997) *Global Law without a State*, Dartmouth. NH: Aldershot.

—— and Fischer-Lescano, A. (2004) "Regime-collisions: the vain search for legal unity in the fragmentation of global law", *Michigan JIL*, 25: 999–1046.

Théodoridès, A. (1975) "Les relations de l'Egypte pharaonique avec ses voisins", *RIDA*, 3(23): 87.

Thirlway, H. (2003) "The sources of international law", in M. Evans (ed.) *International Law*, Oxford: Oxford University Press.

Thomas, S. M. (2000) "Taking religious and cultural pluralism seriously: the global resurgence of religion and the transformation of international society", *M*, 29(3): 815–41.

—— (2005) *The Global Resurgence of Religion and the Transformation of International Relations*, New York: Palgrave Macmillan.

Thornberry, P. (2000) "Self-determination and indigenous peoples: objections and responses", in P. Aikio and M. Scheinin (eds) *Operationalizing the Right of Indigenous Peoples to Self-Determination*, Åbo, Finland: Institute for Human Rights, Åbo Akademi University.

—— (2002) *Indigenous Peoples and Human Rights*, Manchester: Manchester University Press.

Thucydides (1919) *History of the Peloponnesian War* (trans. C. F. Smith), Cambridge, MA: Loeb Classical Library.

Tiefenbrun, S. (2003) "A semiotic approach to a legal definition of terrorism", *ILSAJICL*, 9: 357.

Tierney, B. (1997) *The Idea of Natural Rights: Studies on Natural Rights, Natural Law and Church Law, 1150–1625*, Atlanta, GA: Scholars' Press.

Tietje, C. (1999) "The changing legal structure of international treaties as an aspect of an emerging global governance architecture", *GYIL*, 42: 26–55.

Tolley, H. (2004) "William Schulz, tainted legacy: 9/11 and the ruin of human rights", *HRQ*, 26: 539–42.

Tomasevski, K. (2005) "Unasked questions about economic, social, and cultural rights from the experience of the special rapporteur on the right to education (1998–2004): a response to Kenneth Roth, Leonard S. Rubenstein, and Mary Robinson", *HRQ*, 27: 709–20.

Tomuschat, C. (1993) "Obligations arising for states without or against their will", *RC*, IV(241): 195–374.

—— (1997) "International law as the constitution of mankind", in United Nations (ed.) *International Law on the Eve of the Twenty-First Century: Views from the International Law Commission*, New York: United Nations.

—— (1999) "International law: ensuring the survival of mankind on the eve of a new century", *RC*, 281: 9–438.

—— (2003) *Human Rights: Between Idealism and Realism*, Oxford: Oxford University Press.

—— and Thouvenin, J.-M. (eds) (2006) *The Fundamental Rules of the International Legal Order: Jus Cogens and Obligations Erga Omnes*, Boston, MA: Martinus Nijhoff Publishers.

Tönnies, F. (1935) *Gemeinschaft und Gesellschaft: Grundbegriffe der reinen Soziologie*, Leipzig: Buske.

Toope, S. (2000) "Emerging patterns of governance and international law", in M. Byers, (ed.) *The Role of Law in International Politics: Essays in International Relations and International Law*, Oxford: Oxford University Press.

—— (2003) "Powerful but unpersuasive? The role of the USA in the evolution of customary international law", in M. Byers and G. Nolte (eds) *United States Hegemony and the Foundations of International Law*, Cambridge: Cambridge University Press.

Townsend, J. (1977) *Oman: The Making of a Modern State*, New York: St. Martin's Press.

Trachtman, J. P. (2006) "The constitutions of the WTO", *EJIL*, 17, 623–46.

Trubek, D. M. and Trubek, L. G. (2005) "Hard and soft law in the construction of social Europe: the role of the open method of co-ordination", *EuLJ*, 11(3): 343–64.

—— and Santos, A. (2006) *The New Law and Economic Development. A Critical Appraisal*, Cambridge: Cambridge University Press.

Tuck, R. (1979) *Natural Rights Theories: Their Origin and Development*, Cambridge: Cambridge University Press.

—— (1987) "The 'modern' theory of natural law", in A. Pagden (ed.) *The Languages of Political Theory in Early Modern Europe*, Cambridge: Cambridge University Press.

—— (1993) *Philosophy and Government, 1572–1651*, Cambridge: Cambridge University Press.

—— (1999) *The Rights of War and Peace: Political Thought and the International Order from Grotius to Kant*, Oxford: Oxford University Press.

Tucker, J. B. (2002) "A farewell to germs. The US renunciation of biological and toxin warfare, 1969–70", *IS*, 27(1): 107–48.

Tully, J. (1992) *An Approach to Political Philosophy: Locke in Contexts*, Cambridge: Cambridge University Press.

Uerpmann, R. (2003) *International Law as an Element of European Constitutional Law: International Supplementary Constitutions*, Jean Monnet Working Paper 9/03, Heidelberg: Max Planck Institute.

Upadhye, S. (2000) "The international watercourse: an exploitable resource for the developing nation under international law?", *CJICL*, 8: 61.

Uriarte, G. (1915) *Problemas de Política Internacional Americana, a Proposito de las Doctrinas Controvertidas por los Doctores Alejandro Alvarez y sá Vianna, sobre Derecho Internacional Americano; Opiniones Autorizadas acerca de ese Concepto del Derecho, Expresadas con Motivo de la Fundación del Instituto Americano de Derecho Internacional*, Buenos Aires: Tall. Graf. J. Perrotti.

Uribe Urán, V. M. (2000) *Honorable Lives: Lawyers, Family, and Politics in Colombia 1789–1850*, Pittsburgh, PA: University of Pittsburgh Press.

Vagts, D. F. (2001) "Hegemonic international law", *AJIL*, 97, 843–8.

Vakulenko, A. (2007) "Islamic headscarves and the European Convention on Human Rights: an intersectional perspective", *SLS*, 16(2): 183–99.

van Nieuwkoop, M. and Uquillas, J. E. (2003) "Social capital as a factor in indigenous peoples' development in Ecuador", The World Bank Latin America and Caribbean Region. Sustainable Development Working Paper No. 15, New York: World Bank.

Van Schaack, B. and Slye, R. C. (2007) *International Criminal Law and its Enforcement*, New York: Foundation Press.

Vaver, D. (1997) *Intellectual Property*, Concord, Ontario: Irwin Law.

Vazquez, C. (2008) "Treaties as law of the land: the supremacy clause and presumption of self-execution", *HLR*, 19.

Vec, M. (2006) *Recht und Normierung in der industriellen Revolution. Neue Strukuren der Normierung in Völkerrecht, staatlicher Gesetzgebung und gesellschaftlicher Selbstnormierung*, Frankfurt am Main: Klostermann.

Verdross, A. (1926) *Die Verfassung der Völkerrechtsgemeinschaft*, Berlin/Vienna: Duncker & Humblot.

—— and Simma, B. (1984) *Universelles Völkerrecht: Theorie und Praxis*, 3rd edn, Berlin: Duncker & Humblot.

Vereshchet, V. S. (1996) "New constitutions and the old problem of the relationship between international law and national law", *EJIL*, 7(1): 29–41.

Vergé, C. (1864) "Le droit des gens avant et depuis 1789", in G. F. V. Martens (ed.) *Précis de Droit des Gens Moderne de l'Europe*, 2nd edn, vol. 1, Paris: Guillemain.

Vernon, R. (1995) 'The World Trade Organization: a new stage in international trade and development", *HILJ*, 36: 329.

Vicuña, F. O. (2004) *International Dispute Settlement in an Evolving Global Society: Constitutionalization, Accessibility, Privatization*, Cambridge: Cambridge University Press.

Viljoen, F. and Louw, L. (2007) "State compliance with the recommendations of the African Commission on Human and Peoples' Rights, 1994–2004", *AJIL*, 101: 1–34.

Vinogradoff, P. (1920) *Outlines of Historical Jurisprudence*, London: Oxford University Press.

449

Vitoria, F. de (1917) *De Indis et de Iure Belli Relectiones* (trans. and ed. F. Nys), Washington, DC: Carnegie Institute.

Vizard, P. (2005) *The Contributions of Professor Amartya Sen in the Field of Human Rights*, London: Centre for Analysis of Social Exclusion.

von Bertalanffy, L. (1962) "General systems theory – a critical review", in *General Systems*, 7: 1–20.

—— (1968) *General Systems Theory: Foundations, Development, Applications*, New York: George Braziller.

—— and Rapaport, A. (eds) (1956) *General Systems: Yearbook of the Society for General Systems Research*, New York: George Braziller.

von Bogdandy, A. (2006) "Constitutionalism in international law: comment on a proposal from Germany", *HILJ*, 47(1): 223–42.

von der Pfordten, D. (2001) *Rechtsethik*, Munich: C. H. Beck.

von Martens, G. F. (1796) *Einleitung in das positive europäische Völkerrecht*, Göttingen: Vorbericht.

von Mohl, R. (1860) *Staatsrecht, Völkerrecht und Politik*, vol. 1, Tübingen: Laun.

von Stachau, K. K. (1847) *Kritik des Völkerrechts*, Leipzig: Meyer.

Wade, P. (1997) *Race and Ethnicity in Latin America*, London: Pluto Press.

Wade, R. (2006) "The Doha talks must fail for the sake of the world's poor", *Guardian*, Monday, 3 July.

Walker, T. A. (1899) *A History of the Law of Nations*, Cambridge: Cambridge University Press.

Waluchow, W. (2001) "Savages, victims and saviors: the metaphor of human rights", *HILJ*, 42: 201.

—— (2007) "Constitutionalism". Available at http://setis.library.usyd.edu.au/stanford/entries/constitutionalism.

Wa Mutua, M. (2000) "What is TWAIL?", *ASILP*, 94.

—— (2001) "Savages, Victims and Saviors: The Metaphor Of Human Rights", *Harvard International Law Journal*, 42: 201.

Warbrick, C. (2004) "The European response to terrorism in an age of human rights", *EJIL*, 15: 989.

Ward, C. A. (2007) "Commentary: convergence of international law and international relations in combating international terrorism – the role of the United Nations", in T. J. Biersteker, P. J. Spiro, C. L. Sriram and V. Raffo (eds) *International Law and International Relations*, London: Routledge.

Ward, R. (1795) *An Enquiry into the Foundation and History of the Law of Nations in Europe since the time of the Greeks and Romans to the Age of Grotius*, London: J. Butterworth.

Warioba, J. S. (2001) "Monitoring compliance with and enforcement of binding decisions of international courts", in J. A. Frowein and W. Rüdiger (eds) *MPYUNL*, vol. 5, The Hague: Kluwer.

Watson, A. (1993) *International Law in Archaic Rome: War and Religion*, Baltimore, MD: Johns Hopkins University Press.

Watts, A. (2000) "The importance of international law", in M. Byers (ed.) *The Role of Law in International Politics*, Oxford: Oxford University Press.

—— (2001) "Enhancing the effectiveness of procedures of international dispute settlement", in J. A. Frowein and R. Wolfrum (eds) *MPYUNL*, vol. 5, The Hague: Kluwer.

Wedgwood, R. and Roth, K. (2004) "Combatants or criminals? How Washington should handle terrorists", *FA*, 83(3): 199–322.

Weeramantry, C. G. (2004) *Universalising International Law*, Leiden: Martinus Nijhoff Publishers.

Weil, P. (1983) "Towards relative normativity in international law?", *AJIL*, 77: 413–42.

—— (1992) "Le droit international en quête de son identité: cours général de droit international public", *RC*, 237: 9–370.

Weis, P. (1953) "Legal aspects of the Convention of 28 July 1951 relating to the status of refugees", *BYIL*, 30: 478–89.

—— (ed.) (1995) *The Refugee Convention 1951 – Travaux Préparatoires Analysed, with a Commentary by the Late Dr Paul Weis*, New York: Cambridge University Press.

Weiss, E. B. and Jacobson, H. (eds) (1998) *Engaging Countries: Strengthening Compliance with International Environmental Accords*, Cambridge, MA: MIT Press.

Weiss, J. F. and Schrijver, N. (eds) (2004) *International Law and Sustainable Development: Principles and Practice*, Leiden: Martinus Nijhoff Publishers.

Weissbrodt, D. and Bergquist, A. (2006) "Extraordinary Rendition: A Human Rights Analysis," *Harvard Human Rights Journal*, 19: 123–60.

Weller, M. (1990) "When Saddam is brought to court . . .", *The Times*, 3 September 1990.

—— (1997) "The reality of the emerging universal constitutional order: putting the pieces of the puzzle together", *CRIA*, 10: 40–63.

Wendt, A. (1999) *Social Theory of International Politics*, Cambridge: Cambridge University Press.

—— (2001) "Driving with the rearview mirror: on the rational science of institutional design", *IO*, 55: 1019–49.

Westlake, J. (1910) *International Law*, 2nd edn, vol. II, Cambridge: Cambridge University Press.

Wheatley, S. (2006) "The Security Council, democratic legitimacy and regime change in Iraq", *EJIL*, 17(3): 531–51.

Wheaton, H. (1845) *History of the Law of Nations in Europe and America; From the Earliest Times to the Treaty of Washington, 1842*, New York: Gould, Banks & Co.

—— (1853) *Histoire de Progrés de Droit des Gens en Europe depuis la Paix de Westphalie jusqu'à nos Jours*, 3rd edn, vol. 2, Leipzig: Brockhaus.

Wheeler, E. L. (1984) "Sophistic interpretations and Greek treaties", *GRBS*, 25: 253.

Wheeler, N. J. (2000) *Saving Strangers: Humanitarian Intervention in International Society*, Oxford: Oxford University Press.

—— (2004) "The Kosovo bombing campaign", in C. Reus-Smit (ed.) *The Politics of International Law*, Cambridge: Cambridge University Press, pp.

White House (2008) "President Bush meets with President Kufuor of Ghana". Available at http://www.whitehouse.gov/news.

White, L., Jr. (1967) "Jacopo Acontio as an engineer", *AHR*, 72.

Wickremasinghe, C. (ed.) (2000) *The International Lawyer as Practitioner*, London: British Institute of International and Comparative Law.

Wiedemann, T. (1987) "The fetials: a reconsideration", *CQ*, 36: 480.

Wiener, N. (1948) *Cybernetics: Or the Control and Communications in the Animal and the Machine*, Cambridge, MA: MIT Press.

Wiessner, S. and Willard, A. R. (1999) "Policy-oriented jurisprudence and human rights abuses in internal conflict: toward a world public order of human dignity", *AJIL*, 93: 316–34.

Wight, M. (1977) *Systems of States* (H. Bull ed.), Leicester: Leicester University Press.

—— (1978) *Power Politics* (H. Bull and C. Holbraad eds), Leicester: Leicester University Press.

Wijffels, A. (2004) "Martinus Garatus Laudensis on treaties", in R. Lesaffer (ed.) *Peace Treaties and International Law in European History: From the Late Middle Ages to World War One*, Cambridge: Cambridge University Press.

Wilde, R. (2001) "The refugee convention at 50: forced migration policy at the turn of the century", *JRS*, 14: 135–50.

Williams, C. A. (2004) "Civil society initiatives and 'soft law' in the oil and gas industry", *NYU-JILP*, 36: 457.

Williams, R. A. (1990) "Encounters on the frontiers of international human rights law: redefining the terms of indigenous peoples' survival in the world", *DLJ*, 4: 660–704.

Williams, S. A. (1999) "Article 12: preconditions to the exercise of jurisdiction", in O. Triffterer (ed.) *Commentary on the Rome Statute of the International Criminal Court*, Baden-Baden: Nomos.

Wilson, W. (1969) "Notes for a classroom lecture", in A. S. Link (ed.) *The Papers of Woodrow Wilson*, Princeton, NJ: Princeton University Press.

Winkel, L. (2004) "The peace treaties of Westphalia as an instance of the reception of Roman law", in R. Lesaffer (ed.) *Peace Treaties and International Law in European History: From the Late Middle Ages to World War One*, Cambridge: Cambridge University Press.

Wippman, D. (2004) "The International Criminal Court", in C. Reus-Smit (ed.) *The Politics of International Law*, Cambridge: Cambridge University Press.

Wiredu, K. (1990) "An Akan perspective on human rights", in A. A. An-Na'im and F. M. Deng (eds) *Human Rights in Africa: Cross-Cultural Perspectives*, Washington, DC: The Brookings Institution.

Wisborg, P. and Rohde, R. (2005) "Contested land tenure reform in South Africa: experiences from Namaqualand", *DSA*, 22: 400–27.

Witte, J., Jr. (2002) *Law and Protestantism: The Legal Teachings of the Lutheran Reformation*, Cambridge: Cambridge University Press.

Wolfrum, R. (2005) "State responsibility for private actors: an old problem of renewed relevance", in M. Ragazzi (ed.) *International Responsibility Today: Essays in Memory of Oscar Schachter*, Leiden: Brill.

Woods, J. M. (2005) "Emerging paradigms of protection for 'second-generation' of human rights", *LJPIL*, 6: 103–28.

—— and Donovan, J. M. (2005) "'Anticipatory self-defense' and other stories", *KJLPP*, 14: 487–523.

Woodward, B. (2007) *State of Denial: Bush at War, Part III*, New York: Simon & Schuster.

Woofson, C. (2006) "Working environment and 'soft law' in the post-communist new member state", *JCMS*, 44: 195–215.

Woolsey, T. (1879) *Introduction to the Study of International Law*, 5th edn, London: Sampson.

WorldPublicOpinion.org (2007) "World thinks that China will catch up with the US – and that's OK". Available at http://www.worldpublicopinion.org/pipa/articles/home_page/366.php?nid=&id=&pnt=366&lb=hmpg1.

Wright, L. (2004) "The terror web", *The New Yorker*, 2 August.

Wu, D. (2006) "Can international human rights laws change the state of minority education in the United States?", *RRLR*, 8: 139–66.

Wüstemann, J. and Kierzek, S. (2007) "Transnational legalization of accounting: the case of international financial reporting standards", in C. Brütsch and D. Lehmkuhl (eds) *Law and Legalization in Transnational Relations*, London: Routledge.

Xue, H. (2007) "Chinese observations on international law", *CJIL*, 6(1): 83–93.

Yamin, A. E. (2005) "The future in the mirror: incorporating strategies for the defense and promotion of economic, social, and cultural rights into the mainstream human rights agenda", *HRQ*, 27: 1200–44.

Yepes, J. M. (1930) *El Panamericanismo y el Derecho Internacional*, Bogotá: Impresora Nacional.

—— (1938) *Alejandro Alvarez, Créateur du Droit International Américain. La Notion de l'Universalité du Droit des Gens en Rapport avec les Conceptions Internationales Américaines*, Paris: Les Éditions Internationales.

—— (1952) "Introduction à l'étude du droit enternational américain", *RGDIP*, XXIII: 687.

—— and Colombia: Ministerio De Relaciones Exteriores (1927) *La Codificación del Derecho Internacional Americano y la Conferencia de Rio de Janeiro*, Bogotá: Impresora Nacional.

Yoo, J. C. (1998) "New sovereignty and the old constitution: the chemical weapons convention and the appointments clause", *CC*, 15(87): 1–15.

—— (2000) "Kosovo, war powers, and the multilateral future", *UPLR*, 148: 1673–715.

—— (2003) "International law and the war in Iraq", *AJIL*, 97: 563–75.

—— (2004) "War, responsibility, and the age of terrorism", *SLR*, 57: 10–14.

Yoo, J. (2004) "Iraqi Reconstruction and the Law of Occupation," *U.C. Davis Journal of International Law and Policy*, 11: 7–22.

Young, J. (1990) *Sustaining the Earth*, Cambridge, MA: Harvard University Press.

Young, O. (1972) "International law and social science: the contributions of Myres S. McDougal", *AJIL*, 66: 60–76.

—— (1986–7) "International regimes: toward a new theory of institutions", *WP*, 39: 104–22.

Young, R. (2006) "Defining terrorism: the evolution of terrorism in international law and its influence on definitions in domestic legislation", *BCICLR*, 29.

Zacher, M. (2001) "The territorial integrity norm: international boundaries and the use of force", *IO*, 55: 215–50.

Zagaris, B. (2006) "Inquiry shows Canadian, U.S. officials violated Arar's human rights", *IELR*, 22: 435.

Zárate, L. C. (1957) *El Asilo en el Derecho Internacional Americano; con un Apéndice de la Corte Internacional de Justicia y de Anexos de la Cancillería de Colombia*, Bogotá: Universidad Nacional de Colombia, Department of Law.

Zeleza, P. T. (2004) "The struggle for human rights in Africa", in P. T. Zeleza and P. J. McConnaughay (eds) *Human Rights, the Rule of Law, and Development in Africa*, Philadelphia, PA: University of Pennsylvania Press.

Zetter, R. (2000) "Refugees and refugee studies: a valedictory editorial", *JRS*, 13: 349–55.

Ziegler, K.-H. (2004) "The influence of medieval Roman law on peace treaties", in R. Lesaffer (ed.) *Peace Treaties and International Law in European History: From the Late Middle Ages to World War One*, Cambridge: Cambridge University Press.

Zion, J. (1992) "North American Indian perspectives on human rights", in A. An-Na'im (ed.) *Human Rights in Cross Cultural Perspectives*, Philadelphia, PA: University of Pennsylvania Press.

Zoller, E. (1977) *La Bonne Foi en Droit International Public*, Paris: A. Pedone.

Zumbansen, P. (2001) "Die vergangene Zukunft des Völkerrechts", *KJ*, 34: 46–68.

Index

Abbott, Kenneth 13, 17, 19, 23, 25
Abi-Saab, George 47, 398
Abu Ghraib prison 233–5, 237
accountability 52, 255–7, 258, 395, 401–4
accretion 259–60
Acheson, Dean 91, 201–2
Advisory Opinion on Namibia 83
Afghanistan 202–3, 286–7, 397
Africa: bio-cultural knowledge 320–3; colonial
    IPR heritage 327–9; colonization of 317–18;
    human rights system 306; imposition of
    Eurocentric IPR on 316–18; indigenous
    peoples 334; and the inventive process 323–5;
    and IPRs 7, 316–29; marginalization 318;
    patent offices 327; patent system 320; public
    domain 325; traditional knowledge 322–3
African Charter on Human and Peoples' Rights 306,
    309
African Intellectual Property Organization
    (OAPI) 327
African Regional Industrial Property
    Organization (ARIPO) 327
African Union 335
Agenda 21 357, 365, 368, 389n6, 390n22
Aid for Trade agenda 296
Akehurst, M. 85
Akhavan, Payam 243
Alcorta, Amancio 159, 163n24
Alexandrowicz, Charles 132
Alfaro, Ricardo 270

Algeria 327
alienage 346
Allott, Philip 181, 184, 407
al-Qaeda 46, 167, 234, 283–4, 285, 286, 287,
    290, 397
Alston, P. 305, 395
"Alternatives to 'legalization': richer views of
    law and politics" (Finnemore and Toope)
    31n42
Álvarez, Alejandro 145, 159–61, 161, 164n28
Ambiguities of Power, The (Curtis) 93–4
American Anthropological Association 335–6
American Institute of International Law 160
American Journal of International Law 16–17, 26
Amselek, Paul 407
Anarchical Society, The (Bull) 117
anarchy 60, 61
Anaya, James 336, 339
ancient international law 4
ancient world 115–16, 124–5; diplomacy
    118–20; religion 123–4; state systems
    116–18, 121, 125; treaty practices 120–3;
    war in 123–4
Anghie, Antony 23, 132
Angola 94
Anker, D. E. 349
Annan, Kofi 207
Antarctica 77
Anti-Ballistic Missile Treaty 219
Arar, Maher 289